Summary of Contents

Build Your Own ASP.NET Website Using C# & VB.NET

by Zak Ruvalcaba

Build Your Own ASP.NET Website Using C# & VB.NET

by Zak Ruvalcaba

Copyright © 2004 SitePoint Pty. Ltd.

Editor: Georgina Laidlaw   **Expert Reviewer**: Kevin Yank
Managing Editor: Simon Mackie   **Technical Editor**: Rich Deeson
Cover Design: Julian Carroll   **Index Editor**: Bill Johncocks
Printing History:
   First Edition: April 2004
Latest Update: May 2005

Notice of Rights

Notice of Liability

Trademark Notice

Published by SitePoint Pty. Ltd.

424 Smith Street Collingwood
VIC Australia 3066.
Web: www.sitepoint.com
Email: business@sitepoint.com

ISBN 0–9579218–6–1
Printed and bound in the United States of America

About The Author

Zak Ruvalcaba has been designing, developing and researching for the Web since 1995. He holds a Bachelor's Degree from San Diego State University and a Master of Science in Instructional Technology from National University in San Diego.

In the course of his career, Zak has developed Web applications for such companies as Gateway, HP, Toshiba, and IBM. More recently, he's worked as a wireless software engineer developing .NET solutions for Goldman Sachs, TV Guide, The Gartner Group, Microsoft and Qualcomm. Currently, Zak holds a programming position with ADCS Inc. in San Diego supporting internal .NET applications.

Previous books by Zak Ruvalcaba include *The 10 Minute Guide to Dreamweaver 4* (Que Publishing) and *Dreamweaver MX Unleashed* (Sams Publishing). He also lectures on various technologies and tools including Dreamweaver and ASP.NET for the San Diego Community College District.

About The Expert Reviewer

As Technical Director for SitePoint, Kevin Yank oversees all of its technical publications—books, articles, newsletters and blogs. He has written over 50 articles for SitePoint on technologies including PHP, XML, ASP.NET, Java, JavaScript and CSS, but is perhaps best known for his book, *Build Your Own Database Driven Website Using PHP & MySQL*, also from SitePoint.

Having graduated from McGill University in Montreal with a Bachelor of Computer Engineering, Kevin now lives in Melbourne, Australia. In his spare time he enjoys flying light aircraft and learning the fine art of improvised acting. Go you big red fire engine!

About The Technical Editor

Rich Deeson wrote his first programs at the age of 10 on his father's work machine, a 380Z with 256k RAM. Since then, his career has taken him around Europe, and has taught him the ins and outs of many languages, from C++ to Java, from QuickBasic (the precursor to Visual Basic) to VB.NET, from Perl and CGI to JSP and ASP.NET. Currently, he is lead JSP developer at ICTI in the UK, and most of his free time is taken up at University, having returned to study last year.

About SitePoint

SitePoint specializes in publishing fun, practical and easy-to-understand content for Web Professionals. Visit http://www.sitepoint.com/ to access our books, newsletters, articles and community forums.

For my wife Jessica.

Table of Contents

Preface

Here I am, seven years after the inception of ASP, still using a technology that I initially only glanced over as I searched for a server-side alternative to ColdFusion.

It was 1997, a big year for me. I graduated college, landed a job as a creative director, and decided it was time to build on my experience with HTML and JavaScript. I didn't consider myself a programmer—my true passions lay in design—but within months of starting my new job, I was developing the firm's Website, Intranet, and company portal. The dynamic portions of these projects were developed using CGI written in Perl. As you might expect, I was lost! After looking around, I decided ColdFusion was my best bet—the language seemed to parallel closely the constructs of HTML, and I found it easy to pick up. However, I soon discovered that ColdFusion's limitations in terms of accessing a server's file system, and error handling, posed problems.

ASP and VBScript seemed like the best alternative. I'd taken basic programming classes in college, and I guess they helped, because these two technologies came easily to me. Shortly thereafter, I went back to school and got into Visual Basic, COM, DCOM, and more. A whole new world was opening up to me through simplicity offered by ASP.

Seven years, and countless Windows, Web, and wireless applications later, I still swear by the next generation of a technology that I've always considered superior to the major alternatives. ASP.NET represents a new and efficient way of creating Web applications using the programming language with which you feel most comfortable. Though it can take some time to learn, ASP.NET is simple to use. Whether you want to create Web Forms complete with Web and validation controls, or you aim to build a feature-rich shopping cart using `DataTables`, all the tools you'll need to get up and running are immediately available, easy to install, and require very little initial configuration.

My guess is that if you're reading this book, you're in the same boat I was: a longtime designer dabbling with HTML. Or maybe you're an advanced HTML and JavaScript developer looking to take the next step. Perhaps you're a seasoned PHP, JSP, or ColdFusion veteran who wants to know what all the fuss is about. Whatever the case, I'm sure you'll find this book helpful in showing you how simple and feature-rich ASP.NET really is.

Who Should Read This Book?

This book is aimed at beginner, intermediate, and advanced Web designers looking to make the leap into server-side programming with ASP.NET. You'll be expected to feel comfortable with HTML, as very little explanation is provided here.

By the end of this book, you should have a firm grasp on what it takes to download and install ASP.NET and the .NET Framework, configure and start your Web server, create and work with basic ASP.NET pages, install and run either Access or MSDE, create database tables, work with advanced, dynamic ASP.NET pages that query, insert, update, and delete information within a database.

All examples provided in the book are written in both Visual Basic .NET and C#, the two most popular languages for writing ASP.NET Websites. They start at beginners' level and work up. As such, no prior knowledge of the two languages is required in order to read, learn from, and apply the knowledge provided in this book. Experience with other programming or scripting languages (such as JavaScript) will certainly grease the wheels, however, and will enable you to grasp the fundamental programming concepts more quickly.

What's Covered In This Book?

This book is comprised of the following seventeen chapters. Read them from beginning to end to gain a complete understanding of the subject, or skip around if you feel you need a refresher on a particular topic.

Chapter 1: *Introduction to .NET and ASP.NET*
Before you can start building your database-driven Web presence, you must ensure you have the right tools for the job. In this first chapter, I'll tell you how to find, download, and configure the .NET Framework. I'll explain where the Web server is located and how to install and configure it. Next, we'll walk through the installation of two Microsoft database solutions: Access and MSDE. Finally, we'll create a simple ASP.NET page to make sure that everything's running and properly configured.

Chapter 2: *ASP.NET Basics*
In this chapter, you'll create your first useful ASP.NET page. We'll cover all of the parts that make up a typical ASP.NET page, including directives, controls, and code. We'll then walk through the process of deployment, fo-

cusing specifically on allowing the user to view the processing of a simple ASP.NET page through the Web browser.

Chapter 3: *VB.NET and C# Programming Basics*

In this chapter, we'll look at two of the programming languages used to create ASP.NET pages: VB.NET and C#. You'll learn about the syntax of the two languages as we explore the concepts of variables, data types, conditionals, loops, arrays, functions, and more. Finally, we'll see how the two languages accommodate Object Oriented Programming principles by allowing you to work with classes, methods, properties, inheritance, and more.

Chapter 4: *Web Forms and Web Controls*

ASP.NET is bundled with hundreds of controls that you can use within your applications, including HTML controls, Web controls, and more. This chapter will introduce you to the wonderful world of Web controls and how Microsoft basically reinvented HTML forms.

Chapter 5: *Validation Controls*

This chapter introduces validation controls. With validation controls, Microsoft basically eliminated the heartache of fumbling through and configuring tired, reused client-side validation scripts.

Chapter 6: *Database Design and Development*

Undoubtedly one of the most important chapters in the book, Chapter 6 will help you prepare to work with databases in ASP.NET. We'll cover the essentials you'll need in order to create a database using either Access or MSDE. In this chapter, we'll begin to build the database for our project.

Chapter 7: *Structured Query Language*

This chapter introduces the language we'll use to facilitate communications between the database and the Web application: Structured Query Language, or SQL. After a gentle introduction to the basic concepts of SQL, we'll move on to more advanced topics such as expressions, conditions, and joins.

Chapter 8: *ADO.NET*

The next logical step in database driven Web applications involves ADO.NET. This chapter explores the essentials of the technology, and will have you reading data in a database directly from your Web applications in just a few short steps. We'll then help you begin the transition from working with static applications to database-driven ones.

Chapter 9: *The DataGrid and DataList Controls*

Taking ADO.NET further, this chapter shows you how to utilize the DataGrid and DataList controls provided within the .NET Framework. DataGrid and DataList play a crucial role in the simplicity of presenting information with ASP.NET. In learning how to present database data within your applications in a cleaner and more legible format, you'll gain an understanding of the concept of data binding at a much higher level.

Chapter 10: *DataSets*

One of the most challenging concepts to grasp when transitioning from ASP to ASP.NET is that of disconnected data. In this chapter, you'll learn how to use DataSets to create virtual database tables within your Web applications. You'll also learn how to work with DataTables, and how to filter and sort information within DataSets and DataTables using DataViews.

Chapter 11: *Web Applications*

Chapter 11 explores the features of a Web application. We'll discuss the many parts of the Web.config file in depth, and understand how to work with the Global.asax file, application state, and session state. Finally, we'll look at the ways in which caching can improve the performance of your Web applications.

Chapter 12: *Building an ASP.NET Shopping Cart*

In this chapter, we'll create an ASP.NET shopping cart. Using the topics we've explored in previous chapters, including DataTables and session state, we'll walk through the process of building a purely memory-resident shopping cart for our project.

Chapter 13: *Error Handling*

Learning to handle gracefully unforeseen errors within your Web applications is the topic of this chapter. Initially, we'll discuss basic page and code techniques you can use to handle errors. We'll then talk about the debugger that's included with the .NET Framework SDK and understand how to leverage it by setting breakpoints, reading the autos and locals window, and setting watches. Finally, we'll discuss how you can take advantage of the Event Viewer to write errors as they occur within your applications.

Chapter 14: *Security and User Authentication*

This chapter will introduce you to securing your Web applications with ASP.NET. Here, we'll discuss the various security models available, including IIS, Forms, Windows, and Passport, and discusses the roles the Web.config and XML files can play.

Chapter 15: *Working with Files and Email*

In this chapter, we'll look at accessing your server's file system, including drives, files, and the network. The chapter will then show you how to work with file streams to create text files, write to text files, and read from text files on your Web server. Finally, you'll learn how to send emails using ASP.NET.

Chapter 16: *Rich Controls and User Controls*

Chapter 16 explores ASP.NET's rich controls. You'll learn how to create an interactive meeting scheduler using the `Calendar` control, sessions, and serialization. You'll also learn how to format XML with XSLT utilizing the `Xml` control. Lastly, we'll look at randomizing banner advertisements on your site using the `AdRotator` control.

Chapter 17: *XML Web Services*

The newest buzzword in the development community is "Web Services," and this chapter hopes to shed some light on the topic. We first define Web Services before moving on to explain how they're used, where they can be found, and what WSDL and UDDI are. In this chapter, you'll create a couple of different Web Services from scratch, including one that queries your database to present information within a Web application. You'll also learn how to build a search application using the Google Search Web Service.

The Book's Website

Located at http://www.sitepoint.com/books/aspnet1/, the Website that supports this book will give you access to the following facilities:

The Code Archive

As you progress through this book, you'll note a number of references to the code archive. This is a downloadable ZIP archive that contains complete code for all the examples presented in the book.

The archive contains one folder for each chapter of the book. Each of these folders in turn contains **CS** and **VB** subfolders, which contain the C# and VB.NET versions of all the examples for that chapter, respectively. In later chapters, these files are further divided into two more subfolders: **Lessons** for standalone examples presented for a single chapter, and **Project** for files associated with the Dorknozzle Intranet Application, a larger-scale project that we'll work on throughout the book, which I'll introduce in Chapter 4.

Updates and Errata

No book is perfect, and we expect that watchful readers will be able to spot at least one or two mistakes before the end of this one. The Errata page on the book's Website will always have the latest information about known typographical and code errors, and necessary updates for new releases of ASP.NET and the various Web standards that apply.

The SitePoint Forums

If you'd like to communicate with me or anyone else on the SitePoint publishing team about this book, you should join SitePoint's online community[2]. The .NET forum[3] in particular can offer an abundance of information above and beyond the solutions in this book.

In fact, you should join that community even if you *don't* want to talk to us, because there are a lot of fun and experienced Web designers and developers hanging out there. It's a good way to learn new stuff, get questions answered in a hurry, and just have fun.

The SitePoint Newsletters

In addition to books like this one, SitePoint publishes free email newsletters including *The SitePoint Tribune* and *The SitePoint Tech Times*. In them, you'll read about the latest news, product releases, trends, tips, and techniques for all aspects of Web development. If nothing else, you'll get useful ASP.NET articles and tips, but if you're interested in learning other technologies, you'll find them especially valuable. Sign up to one or more SitePoint newsletters at http://www.sitepoint.com/newsletter/.

Your Feedback

If you can't find your answer through the forums, or if you wish to contact us for any other reason, the best place to write is books@sitepoint.com. We have a well-manned email support system set up to track your inquiries, and if our support staff members are unable to answer your question, they will send it

---

[2] http://www.sitepoint.com/forums/
[3] http://www.sitepoint.com/forums/forumdisplay.php?f=141

straight to me. Suggestions for improvements as well as notices of any mistakes you may find are especially welcome.

Acknowledgements

First and foremost, I'd like to thank the SitePoint team for doing such a great job in making this book possible, for being understanding as deadlines inevitably slipped past, and for the team's personal touch, which made it a pleasure to work on this project.

Particular thanks go to Simon Mackie, whose valuable insight and close cooperation throughout the process has tied up many loose ends and helped make this book both readable and accessible. Thanks again Simon for allowing me to write this book—I appreciate the patience and dedication that you've shown.

Finally, returning home, I'd like to thank my wife Jessica, whose patience, love and understanding throughout continue to amaze me.

1

Introduction to .NET and ASP.NET

It's being touted as the "next big thing." Microsoft has invested millions in marketing, advertising, and development to produce what it feels is the foundation of the future Internet. It's a corporate initiative, the strategy of which was deemed so important, that Bill Gates himself, Microsoft Chairman and CEO, decided to oversee personally its development. It is a technology that Microsoft claims will reinvent the way companies carry out business globally for years to come. In his opening speech at the Professional Developers' Conference (PDC) held in Orlando Florida in July of 2000, Gates stated that a transition of this magnitude only comes around once every five to six years. What is this show-stopping technology? It's .NET.

What is .NET?

.NET is the result of a complete make-over of Microsoft's software development products, and forms part of the company's new strategy for delivering software as a service. The key features that .NET offers include:

❑ **.NET Platform:** The .NET platform includes the .NET Framework and tools to build and operate services, clients, and so on. ASP.NET, the focus of this book, is a part of the .NET Framework.

❑ **.NET Products:** .NET products currently include MSN.NET, Office.NET, Visual Studio.NET, and Windows Server 2003, originally known as Windows .NET Server. This suite of extensively revised systems provides developers with a friendly, usable environment in which they may create applications with a range of programming languages including C++. NET, Visual Basic.NET, ASP.NET, and C#. Because all these products are built on top of .NET, they all share key components, and underneath their basic syntaxes you'll find they have much in common.

❑ **.NET My Services:** An initiative formerly known as "Hailstorm", .NET My Services is a set of XML Web Services[1] currently being provided by a host of partners, developers, and organizations that are hoping to build corporate services and applications for devices and applications, as well as the Internet. The collection of My Services currently extends to passport, messenger, contacts, email, calendars, profiles, lists, wallets, location, document stores, application settings, favorite Websites, devices owned, and preferences for receiving alerts.

The book focuses on one of the core components within the .NET Framework: **ASP.NET**.

What is ASP.NET?

For years now, Active Server Pages (ASP) has been arguably the leading choice for Web developers building dynamic Websites on Windows Web servers. ASP has gained popularity by offering the simplicity of flexible scripting via several languages. That, combined with the fact that it's built into every Microsoft Windows-based Web server, has made ASP a difficult act to follow.

Early in 2002, Microsoft released its new technology for Internet development. Originally called ASP+, it was finally released as ASP.NET, and represents a leap forward from ASP both in sophistication and productivity for the developer. It continues to offer flexibility in terms of the languages it supports, but instead of a range of simple scripting languages, developers can now choose between several fully-fledged programming languages. Development in ASP.NET requires not only an understanding of HTML and Web design, but also a firm grasp of the concepts of object-oriented programming and development.

In the next few sections, I'll introduce you to the basics of ASP.NET. I'll walk you through installing it on your Web server, and take you through a simple

---

[1] Don't worry if you don't yet know what a Web Service is. I'll explain all about them in Chapter 17.

dynamic example that demonstrates how ASP.NET pages are constructed. First, let's define what ASP.NET actually is.

ASP.NET is a server-side technology for developing Web applications based on the Microsoft .NET Framework. Let's break that jargon-filled sentence down.

ASP.NET is server-side; that is, it runs on the Web server. Most Web designers start by learning client-side technologies like HTML, JavaScript, and Cascading Style Sheets (CSS). When a Web browser requests a Web page created with client-side technologies, the Web server simply grabs the files that the browser (the **client**) requests and sends them down the line. The client is entirely responsible for reading the code in the files and interpreting it to display the page on the screen. Server-side technologies, like ASP.NET, are different. Instead of being interpreted by the client, server-side code (for example, the code in an ASP.NET page) is interpreted by the Web server. In the case of ASP.NET, the code in the page is read by the server and used dynamically to generate standard HTML/JavaScript/CSS that is then sent to the browser. As all processing of ASP.NET code occurs on the server, it's called a server-side technology. As Figure 1.1 shows, the user (client) only sees the HTML, JavaScript, and CSS within the browser. The server (and server-side technology) is entirely responsible for processing the dynamic portions of the page.

Figure 1.1. The Web server is responsible for processing the server-side code and presenting the output to the user (client).

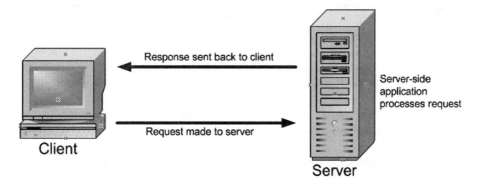

ASP.NET is a technology for developing Web applications. A Web application is just a fancy name for a dynamic Website. Web applications usually (but not always) store information in a database on the Web server, and allow visitors to the site to access and change that information. Many different programming technologies and supported languages have been developed to create Web applications; PHP, JSP (using Java), CGI (using Perl), and ColdFusion (using CFML) are just a few of the more popular ones. Rather than tying you to a specific technology and language, however, ASP.NET lets you write Web applications using a variety of familiar programming languages.

Finally, **ASP.NET is based on the Microsoft .NET Framework.** The .NET Framework collects all the technologies needed for building Windows applications, Web applications, and Web Services into a single package with a set of more than twenty programming languages. To develop Websites with ASP.NET, you'll need to download the .NET Framework Software Development Kit, which I'll guide you through in the next few sections.

Even with all the jargon demystified, you're probably still wondering: what makes ASP.NET so good? Compared with other options for building Web applications, ASP.NET has the following advantages:

❑ ASP.NET lets you use your favorite programming language, or at least one that's really close to it. The .NET Framework currently supports over twenty languages, four of which may be used to build ASP.NET Websites.

❑ ASP.NET pages are **compiled**, not interpreted. Instead of reading and interpreting your code every time a dynamic page is requested, ASP.NET compiles dynamic pages into efficient binary files that the server can execute very quickly. This represents a big jump in performance when compared with the technology's interpreted predecessor, ASP.

❑ ASP.NET has full access to the functionality of the .NET Framework. Support for XML, Web Services, database interaction, email, regular expressions, and many other technologies are built right into .NET, which saves you from having to reinvent the wheel.

❑ ASP.NET allows you to separate the server-side code in your pages from the HTML layout. When you're working with a team composed of programmers and design specialists, this separation is a great help, as it lets programmers modify the server-side code without stepping on the designers' carefully crafted HTML—and vice versa.

With all these advantages, ASP.NET has relatively few downsides. In fact, only two come to mind:

❑ ASP.NET is a Microsoft technology. While this isn't a problem in itself, it does mean that, at least for now, you need to use a Windows server to run an ASP.NET Website. If your organization uses Linux or some other operating system for its Web servers, you're out of luck.

❑ Serious ASP.NET development requires an understanding of object-oriented programming, which we'll cover over the next few chapters.

Still with me? Great! It's time to gather the tools and start building!

What Do I Need?

For the moment, if you're going to learn ASP.NET, you'll need a Windows-based Web server. Open source initiatives are underway to produce versions of ASP.NET that will run on other operating systems, such as Linux; however, these are not expected to be available in stable form for a while.

While developers had the option of getting their feet wet with ASP on Windows 95, 98, or ME, using a scaled-down version of IIS called a Personal Web Server (PWS), ASP.NET requires the real deal. As a bare minimum, you'll need a computer equipped with Windows 2000 Professional before you can get started. Windows XP Professional will work fine too, as will any of the Windows 2000 Server packages and Windows 2003 Server.

Other than that, all you need is enough disk space to install the Web server **Internet Information Services** (18 MB), the .NET Framework SDK (which includes ASP.NET; 108 MB), and a text editor. Notepad or Web Matrix[1] will be fine for getting started, and are certainly all you'll need for this book. However, if you get serious about ASP.NET, you'll probably want to invest in a development environment like Visual Studio .NET[2].

Installing the Required Software

This section tackles the necessary installation and configuration of software that you'll need for this book, including:

❑ **Internet Information Services (IIS):** IIS is the Web server we will use. You'll need your copy of the Windows CD for the installation and configuration.

---

[1] http://www.asp.net/webmatrix/
[2] http://msdn.microsoft.com/vstudio/

❑ **A Modern Web Browser:** You can use any modern, standards-compliant browser to test your work. Throughout this book, we'll be using Internet Explorer 6.

❑ **The .NET Framework Redistributable:** As you've already learned in this chapter, the .NET Framework is what drives ASP.NET. Installing the .NET Framework installs the necessary files to run ASP.NET.

❑ **The .NET Framework SDK:** The .NET Framework Software Development Kit (SDK) contains necessary Web application development tools, a debugger for error correcting, a development database engine in MSDE, and a suite of samples and documentation.

We're also going to need a database. In this book, we'll use:

❑ **Microsoft Access:** Access is a cheap and easy-to-use alternative to its more robust big brother, SQL Server, and can be purchased separately, or installed from a Microsoft Office CD.

Or alternatively, you might use:

❑ **Microsoft SQL Server Desktop Engine (MSDE):** SQL Server is the enterprise alternative to smaller databases such as Access. If you're working within a corporation where your company's data is its lifeblood, then SQL Server is the perfect choice. MSDE is a free, cut down version of SQL Server that you can use for development purposes.

❑ **Web Data Administrator:** If you're going to use MSDE, then you'll need a tool for modifying the data within the database. Web Data Administrator is Microsoft's free Web-based database management tool.

Installing Internet Information Services (IIS)

Do you need to install IIS locally even if the final site will not be hosted locally? The answer is: yes. Even if you're uploading your Web applications via FTP to your Web host, installing IIS allows you to view, debug, and configure your applications locally before deployment.

IIS comes with most versions of server-capable Windows operating systems, including Windows 2000 Professional, Server, and Advanced Server, Windows XP Professional, and Windows Server 2003, but it's not installed automatically in all versions, which is why it may not be present on your computer. To see whether you have IIS installed and running, simply navigate to your Administrative Tools menu and check to see if Internet Information Services is an option. Users of Windows 2000 Professional will find the Administrative Tools in their Control Panels, while XP and Server family users also have shortcuts in their start menus.

If the shortcut is not visible, then you don't have it installed. To install IIS, simply follow these steps:

1. In the Control Panel, select Add or Remove Programs.

2. Choose Add/Remove Windows Components. The list of components will become visible within a few seconds.

3. In the list of components, check Internet Information Services (IIS).

4. Click Next. Windows prompts you to insert the Windows CD and installs IIS.

Once IIS is installed, close the Add or Remove Programs dialog. You can check that IIS has installed correctly by seeing if you can find it within the Administrative Tools menu. If you can, it's installed.

You are now ready to begin hosting Web applications. Although we won't cover the configuration of IIS for external use, I will show you how to configure IIS to support local development of ASP.NET applications in order that they may be uploaded to your external Web hosting provider later.

Installing Internet Explorer

As a Windows user, you have Internet Explorer installed by default, but I recommend you run at least version 5.5. You can check your version by selecting About Internet Explorer from the Help menu.

If your version of Internet Explorer is earlier than 5.5, you can download the latest version (version 6 SP1 as of this writing) for free from the Internet Explorer Website[3]. Remember, although ASP.NET will work with older versions of IE, certain ASP.NET functionality works best with the latest version.

The Internet Explorer Website does not allow you to install a version of your choice; it permits you to download only the most recent version that's available.

---

[3] http://www.microsoft.com/windows/ie/

Because the newest versions of Internet Explorer will include the latest patches, it's a good idea to stick with what they give you.

Installing the .NET Framework and SDK

To begin creating ASP.NET applications, you'll need to install the .NET Framework and SDK. The .NET Framework includes the necessary files to run and view ASP.NET pages, while the .NET Framework SDK includes samples, documentation, and a variety of free tools.

The .NET Framework SDK also provides you with the ability to install MSDE, the free database server that you can use with this book. Once the .NET Framework and SDK are installed, little else needs to be done for you to begin working with ASP.NET. The .NET Framework is installed as part of the operating system if you're lucky enough to be running Windows .NET Server 2003, in which case you can skip directly to installing the SDK. If not, you will need to download the .NET redistributable package, which is approximately 21 MB, and includes the files necessary for running ASP.NET applications.

To develop .NET applications, you also need to install the software development kit, which includes necessary tools along with samples and documentation. Be aware that the .NET Framework SDK is 108 MB in size—be prepared to wait!

 Installing the .NET Framework before you install IIS will prevent your applications from working correctly.

Download and Install the Redistributable

The best method of acquiring the .NET Framework is to download and install it directly from the Web. To accomplish this, simply follow the steps outlined below:

1. Go to the ASP.NET support site at http://www.asp.net/ and click the Download link.

2. Click the Download .NET Framework Redist Now link. Remember, we will install the redistributable first, then we will install the SDK. The link will advance you to a download page.

3. Choose the language version of the install you want, and click Download.

4. When prompted, save the file to a local directory by choosing Save.

5. After the download is complete, double-click the executable to begin the installation.

6. Follow the steps presented by the .NET Setup Wizard until installation completes.

Download and Install the SDK

Now that you've installed the redistributable, you need to install the software development kit (SDK):

1. Go to the ASP.NET support site at http://www.asp.net/ and click the Download link.

2. Click the Download .NET Framework SDK Now link. The link will advance you to a download page.

3. Choose the language version of the install you want to use and click Download, as you did to download the redistributable.

4. When prompted to do so, save the file to a local directory by choosing Save.

5. After the download is complete, double-click the executable to begin the installation. Before you do, I strongly recommend closing all other programs to ensure the install proceeds smoothly.

6. Follow the steps outlined by the .NET Setup Wizard until installation completes.

The SDK will take slightly longer to install than the redistributable. Once it's finished, check to see if it exists in your programs menu; navigate to Start > Programs > Microsoft .NET Framework SDK.

Configuring IIS

Although little configuration needs to be done before you begin working with IIS, I'll use this section to introduce some basic features and functionality within IIS:

❑ Determining whether ASP.NET installed correctly

❑ Determining where files are located on the Web server

❑ Using localhost

❑ How to start and stop the Web server

❑ How to create a new virtual directory and modify its properties

Determining whether ASP.NET Installed Correctly

Once IIS is installed on your computer, you can open it by selecting Internet Information Services from the Administrative Tools menu. The first task is to make sure that ASP.NET was integrated into IIS when you installed the .NET Framework. Although, logically, ASP.NET should install automatically because it's a component of the .NET Framework, sometimes it doesn't. Don't let this alarm you—it's a common occurrence and is addressed in the Microsoft Knowledge Base. You can determine whether IIS was installed correctly by following these steps:

1. Open IIS, if you haven't already done so, and click on the + symbol next to your computer's name.

2. Right-click Default Web Site and select Properties.

3. Navigate to the Documents tab. If `default.aspx` appears within the list, ASP.NET was installed correctly.

Another way to check whether ASP.NET installed correctly is by following these steps:

1. Navigate to the Application Mappings menu by right-clicking the root Website node (your computer's name) and choosing Properties.

2. Select the Home Directory tab, and choose Configuration.

3. The Application Mappings menu displays all of the extensions and their associated ISAPI Extension DLLs, as we see in Figure 1.2.

Figure 1.2. If the `.aspx` ISAPI Extension DLL appears within the Application Mappings menu, then ASP.NET was installed correctly.

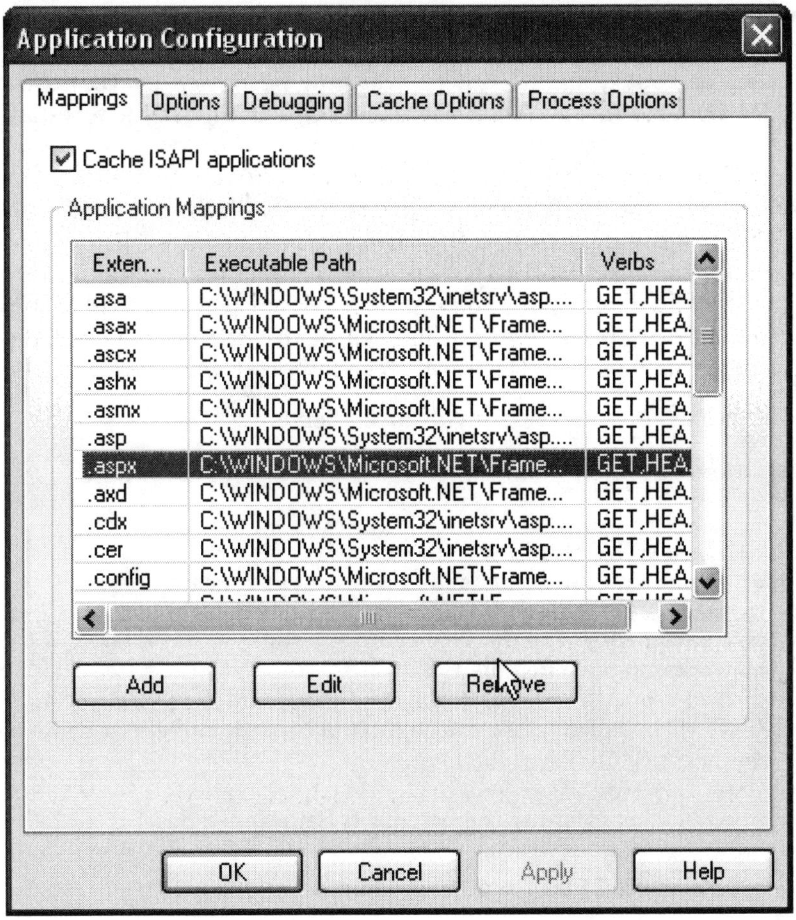

Since I can imagine you're dying to know what an ISAPI Extension DLL is, let me explain. You may know that a DLL is a **Dynamically Linked Library**, which is essentially a self-contained code module that any number of applications can draw on. When a Web server hosts a dynamic Website, page requests must be processed by program code running on the server before the resultant HTML can be sent back to the requesting browser (the **client**). Now, as was the case with traditional ASP, ASP.NET performs this processing with the help of its **Internet Server Application Programming Interface (ISAPI)** extension DLL. ISAPI allows Web requests to be processed through the Web server by a DLL, rather than an EXE, as is the case with **Common Gateway Interface (CGI)** pages. This approach is advantageous because DLLs are much more efficient, and require far less resources and memory than executables. IIS uses the file extension of a requested page to determine which DLL should process the request according to the mappings shown in the screenshot above. So, we can see that pages ending in .aspx, .asmx, or .ascx, among others, will now be passed by IIS to the ASP.NET DLL (aspnet_isapi.dll) for processing. OK, enough of the tech-talk. Let's get back to it!

If you've come to the conclusion that ASP.NET was not installed on your computer, you'll have to install it manually from the command prompt:

1. Open the command prompt by selecting Start > Run, type CMD, and select OK.

2. Type the following command (all on one line) to install ASP.NET on Windows 2000 Professional, Server, or Advanced Server:

    ```
    C:\WINNT\Microsoft.NET\Framework\ver\aspnet_regiis.exe -i
    ```

    Or on Windows XP Professional:

    ```
    C:\WINDOWS\Microsoft.NET\Framework\ver\aspnet_regiis.exe -i
    ```

    In these commands, *ver* is the directory corresponding to the version of the .NET Framework you have installed.

3. Once ASP.NET is installed, close the command prompt and check again to confirm whether ASP.NET installed correctly.

If it still hasn't installed, try visiting the Microsoft Knowledge Base[6] for help.

Where Do I Put My Files?

Now that you have ASP.NET up and running, let's take a look at where the files for your Web applications are kept on the computer. You can readily set IIS to look for Web applications within any folder of your choice, including the My Documents folder or even a network share. By default, IIS maps the wwwroot subfolder of C:\Inetpub on the server to your Website's root directory, and it is generally considered a good repository for storing and managing your Web applications.

---

[6] http://support.microsoft.com/

If you open this wwwroot folder in Windows Explorer, and compare it with the folder tree that appears on the left of the IIS console, you'll notice that the folders in Explorer also appear under your Default Web Site node. Note that, while several of these folders have the regular Explorer folder icon in the IIS view, others have a special Web application icon, indicating that these folders contain the pages and other items for a particular Web application. These special folders are what IIS calls **Virtual Directories**, and, in fact, they do not have to share the name of the physical folder to which they map. We'll see more on this shortly.

Using Localhost

By putting your files within C:\Inetpub\wwwroot, you've given your Web server access to them. If you've been developing Web pages for a long time, habit may drive you to open files directly in your browser by double-clicking on the HTML files. Because ASP.NET is a server-side language, your Web server needs to have a crack at the file before it's sent to your browser for display. If the server doesn't get this opportunity, the ASP.NET code is not converted into HTML that your browser can understand. For this reason, ASP.NET files can't be opened directly from Windows Explorer.

Instead, you need to open them in your browser using the special Web address that indicates the current computer, http://localhost/. If you try this now, IIS will open up some HTML help documentation, because we've not yet set up a default Website. This localhost name is, in fact, equivalent to the so-called **loopback IP address**, 127.0.0.1, IP which you can check out by entering http://127.0.0.1/ in your browser; you should see the same page you saw using localhost. If you know them, you can also use the name of your server or the real IP address of your machine to the same effect.

Note that if you do try any of these equivalents, a dialog will appear before the page is opened, asking for your network credentials, because you're no longer using your local authentication implicit with localhost.

Stopping and Starting IIS

Now that we have IIS up and running, and ASP.NET installed, let's look at how you can start, stop, and restart IIS if the need arises. For the most part, you'll always want to have IIS running, except when you're using certain programs locally that open ports and allow intruders to compromise the security of your computer. Some programs, like Kazaa, automatically stop IIS upon launch, because of potential security vulnerabilities. If you want to stop IIS when it's not being used, simply follow the steps outlined below:

1. With IIS open, select Default Web Site. The Play, Stop, and Pause icons will become visible.

2. Select Stop, as shown in Figure 1.3.

Figure 1.3. Select the Stop icon to stop IIS.

3. To start IIS again, all you need to do is click the Play icon.

Virtual Directories

I've already briefly introduced the concept of **virtual directories**, which are a key mechanism in IIS; now I'd like to define a virtual directory a little more clearly.

A virtual directory is simply a name (or **alias**) that points to a local folder or network share on the server. This alias is then used to access the Web application held in that physical location. For instance, imagine your company has a Web server that serves documents from `C:\Inetpub\wwwroot\mySiteA`. Your users can access these documents through this URL:

http://www.mycompany.com/mySiteA/

You could also set up another physical location as a different virtual directory in IIS. If, for instance, you were developing another Web application, you could store the files for it in `C:\dev\newSiteB`. You could then create in IIS a new virtual directory called, say, `CoolPages`, which maps to this location. This new site would then be accessible through this URL:

http://www.mycompany.com/CoolPages/

As this application is in development, you would probably want to set IIS to hide this virtual directory from the public until the project is complete. Your existing Website would still be visible.

Let's create a virtual directory on your server now:

1. Right-click on Default Web Site and select Virtual Directory from the New submenu. The Virtual Directory Creation Wizard will appear. Click Next.

2. Type in an alias for your virtual directory. I'll type in **WebDocs**. Click Next.

3. Browse for the directory in which your application is located. For this example, I'm going to choose the My Pictures folder located within the My Documents directory. Click Next.

4. Set Access Permissions for your directory. Typically, you'll want to check Read, Run scripts, and Browse. You will not need to select Write until we get into accessing the file system, discussed in Chapter 15. Click Next.

5. Click Finish.

Once your new virtual directory has been created, it will appear within the Website list as shown in Figure 1.4.

Figure 1.4. Once the virtual directory has been created, it will appear within the list of sites.

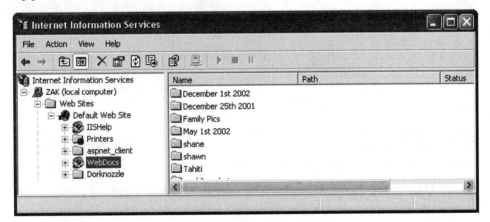

Now, if you type http://localhost/WebDocs/ in your browser, IIS will recognize that you're looking for a Website held in the My Pictures directory. By default, when we request a virtual directory in this way, IIS looks for an index HTML page such as index.html or default.htm. If there is no index page—in this case there isn't—IIS assumes we want to see the contents of the requested location.

However, viewing the entire content of a location like this is not usually something we want our users to do; they could then freely see and access all the files and directories that make up our Web page. Not only is this a little messy and unprofessional, but it also can provide information to hackers that could let them attack our site. So, by default, IIS won't allow this—we'll receive a message reading, "Directory Listing Denied" in our browser.

Bearing that in mind, there are, however, circumstances in which we *do* want to allow directory listings, so let's see how we can enable this in IIS. First, we have to right click the virtual directory in the IIS console, and choose Properties. Then, we select the Virtual Directory tab, and check the Directory browsing box. When we click OK and open (or refresh) the same URL in our browser, we'll see a list of all the files within the `My Pictures` folder.

The Properties dialog that we've just used lets us configure various other useful properties, including:

Virtual Directory	Allows you to configure directory-level properties including path information, virtual directory name, access permissions, etc. Everything that was set up through the wizard is modifiable through this tab.
Document	Allows you to configure a default page that displays when the user types in a full URL. For instance, because `default.aspx` is listed as a default page, the user needs only to type in http://www.mysite.com/ into the browser's address bar, rather than http://www.mysite.com/default.aspx. You can easily change and remove these by selecting the appropriate button to the right of the menu.
Directory Security	Provides you with security configuration settings for the virtual directory.
HTTP Headers	Gives you the ability to forcefully control page caching on the server, add custom HTTP Headers, Edit Ratings (helps identify the content your site provides to users), and create MIME types. Don't worry about this for now.
Custom Errors	Allows you to define your own custom error pages. Rather than the standard error messages that appear within Internet Explorer, you can customize error

messages with your company's logo and an error message of your choice.

One thing to note at this point is that we can set properties for the Default Web Site node, and choose to have them 'propagate' down to all the virtual directories we've created. So, let's now go ahead and enable directory browsing as the default for our Web applications. Please do remember what I've said about the dangers of allowing directory browsing on a production Web application, and keep in mind that you should never normally allow it in a publicly accessible environment (even on an intranet). However, during development, this facility can be very handy, as it allows us to navigate and run all our virtual directories by clicking on the listing in our browser, rather than having to type in long URLs each time.

To enable directory browsing:

1. Right-click Default Web Site and select Properties. The Default Web Site Properties dialog will appear.

2. First, we need to remove the default setting which opens up the IIS help documentation for our root directory, so choose the Documents tab.

3. Select `iisstart.asp`, and click Remove.

4. Now choose the Home Directory tab.

5. Check the Directory Browsing check box and select OK.

6. When the Inheritance Overrides dialog appears, click Select All and then OK.

To try it out, open your browser and type http://localhost/ in the address bar. The directory listing will appear within the browser as shown in Figure 1.5.

Figure 1.5. Enabling directory browsing for the Web server provides you with the ability to view directories in a way that's similar to the view you'd see within Windows Explorer.

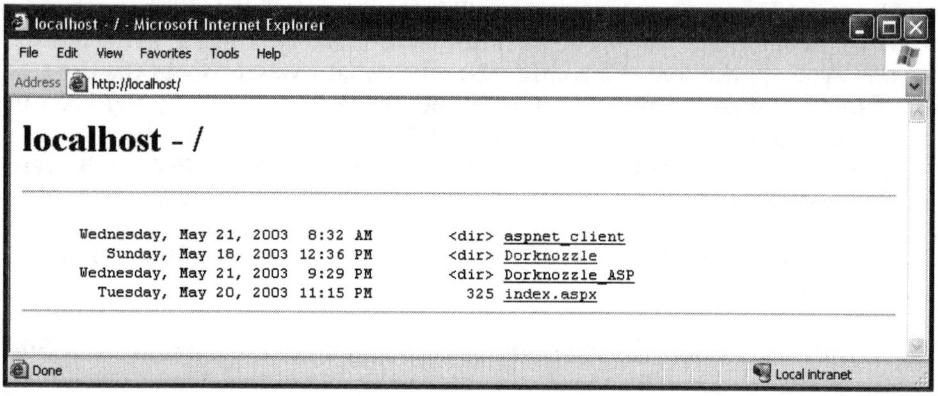

As you create Web applications, you'll only need to select the directory that the Web application resides in to launch your work, but do remember to disable directory browsing should you later make your IIS Web server publicly visible.

Installing Microsoft Access

Access is Microsoft's database solution for both developers and small companies who need to house data within a small yet reliable store. Because Microsoft Access is widely available, it's usually the perfect choice for discussion and use within books such as this. Although we won't be covering data access until Chapter 5, you may want to start thinking about the scope of your or your company's needs and choose a database accordingly. If you're a small company looking for something cheap, reliable, and easy to use, then Access is for you. This book will cover examples using both Access and MSDE. Even if you plan on using MSDE, you may still want to read this section, as Access provides some good data modeling tools that aren't available to you through Web Data Administrator.

You can find more information on Access from the Access Website[15]. Here, you can find the latest updates, news, and purchase information for Microsoft Access.

---

[15] http://www.microsoft.com/office/access/

Access is bundled with Professional editions of the Microsoft Office suite, so you may already have it installed. If you've already installed Microsoft Office on your computer, but didn't install Access at the same time, you'll need to add it to your installation. The following assumes that you have either Microsoft Office 2000 or XP Professional handy, and that you'll be installing from that CD:

1. Navigate to the Add or Remove Programs menu located within the Control Panel.

2. Select your Microsoft Office installation from the Programs menu and select Change.

3. When the Microsoft Office Setup dialog appears, select Add/Remove Features and click Next.

4. Select Run from My Computer from the Access program menu.

5. Click Update. You will be prompted to insert your Microsoft Office CD, so make sure you have it handy. Access will now install.

If you plan to purchase Access, you might like to consider purchasing the Microsoft Office bundle, as you receive Access, Word, Outlook, PowerPoint, and Excel for much less than the total cost of each of the components. Installing Access from either the Microsoft Access or Microsoft Office CDs is easy—just insert the CD, follow the onscreen prompts, and accept the default installation.

That's all there is to it. You are now ready to begin working with database-driven Web applications.

Installing SQL Server Desktop Engine (MSDE)

SQL Server 2000 is Microsoft's database solution for medium to large companies and enterprises. It is quite a bit more expensive than Access, generally requires its own dedicated "database server", and, at times, requires the hiring of a certified database administrator (DBA) to maintain; yet it offers a robust and scalable solution for larger Web applications.

I'll assume that if you're reading this book, you probably don't want to invest in something as massive as SQL Server, and that your needs are better suited to something free that's nearly as powerful for testing and development purposes. If this is the case, then Microsoft's SQL Server Desktop Engine, or MSDE, is perfect for you. MSDE is Microsoft's free database alternative to SQL Server. It functions and stores data exactly as SQL Server does, but is licensed for development purposes only.

Once the .NET Framework SDK is installed, installing MSDE is a snap and can be completed as follows:

1. Select Start > Programs > Microsoft Framework SDK, and choose Samples and QuickStart Tutorials.

2. Choose the Download and Install the Microsoft SQL Server 2000 Desktop Engine link. You will be redirected to a download page on Microsoft's Website.

3. Select Step 1: Download the Microsoft SQL Server 2000 Desktop Engine (68.4 MB).

4. Save the file onto your hard drive. At nearly 70 MB, this may take some time, so you may want to move onto the section called "Your First ASP.NET Page" later in this chapter while the download continues, as our first example doesn't use a database. Once the download is done, come back and continue the installation process.

5. Double-click the downloaded file and follow the instructions to unpack the MSDE setup files.

6. Open the Command Prompt by selecting Start > Run; type **cmd**, and select OK.

7. Change to the directory to which you extracted the files using cd on the command line. MSDE extracts to `C:\sql2ksp3\MSDE` by default.

8. Type the following command (all on one line) in the MSDE directory to set up MSDE:

```
Setup.exe /qb+ INSTANCENAME=NetSDK DISABLENETWORKPROTOCOLS=1
SAPWD=PASSWORD
```

The complete set of commands is shown in Figure 1.6.

Figure 1.6. Install MSDE by running the command line executable and setting necessary parameters.

It's a good idea to set a suitable system administrator password using the SAPWD parameter as shown above, although you can apply the traditional blank password by using the **BLANKSAPWD=1** parameter instead.

9.   MSDE will now install.

10. Restart your computer for changes to take effect.

If all goes well, when the computer restarts, you'll notice in the task bar tray a small icon that looks like a cylinder with a play icon on top, as shown in Figure 1.7.

Figure 1.7. MSDE runs out of sight within the task bar tray.

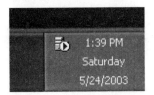

That icon represents the database Service Manager. It lets you start and stop the database engine; all you have to do is double-click that icon within the task bar tray. Double-click the icon now to open the Service Manager Dialog, where you can select the Play icon to start the service, or the Stop icon to stop the service.

In some cases, you may not see either a green triangle or a red square; instead, you see an empty white circle. When you open Service Manager, you'll see the message "Not Connected" appear in the status bar at the bottom. You'll need to type *YourComputer***netsdk** in the Server drop-down (where *YourComputer* is the name of your computer), and click Refresh services. MSDE should then connect, and the green triangle should appear.

Installing and Configuring Web Data Administrator

In order to use MSDE effectively, you'll need some sort of administration tool to work with your databases. Web Data Administrator is another free tool provided by Microsoft that allows you to manage your instance of MSDE locally and remotely using a Web-based interface. You can download this program from Microsoft's ASP.NET Tools & Utilities page[16].

Once you've downloaded it, simply double-click the .msi file to install. Once installed, Web Data Administrator can be accessed through your browser at the URL http://localhost/SqlWebAdmin, but before it can be used, you'll need to enable what is known as **SQL Mixed Mode authentication**.

This involves making a small change to the registry, but don't be put off. If you follow these instructions exactly, you won't do any harm. Let's do it! Click Start, then Run.... In the dialog, type **regedit** and press Enter to open the registry editor. Now expand the HKEY_LOCAL_MACHINE node in the left hand pane, then expand the SOFTWARE node. Next, find and open the Microsoft node, and, inside that, open one labeled Microsoft SQL Server. In there, you should find a node called NETSDK, which contains another, called MSSQLServer. Select that node, and find the key (in the right hand pane) called LoginMode. Double-click that, and change its Value data from 1 to 2, then click OK. Now, close regedit, and restart your computer. Phew! That was a bit of a trek, but I hope you found it easier in practice than it appears on paper!

Now, open the Web Data Administrator URL given above. You'll be asked for the login, password, and server name for your instance of MSDE. Type **sa** in the user name box, and the password that you supplied during the installation of MSDE. If you're unsure what the name of your server is, double-click the database engine icon within the task bar tray. The name of your server is located within the server drop-down menu.

Once you've done this and clicked Login, you will see a list of the databases that are currently available from MSDE, as shown in Figure 1.8.

---

[16] http://msdn.microsoft.com/asp.net/downloads/tools/

Figure 1.8. Web Data Administrator allows you to work with your databases within MSDE.

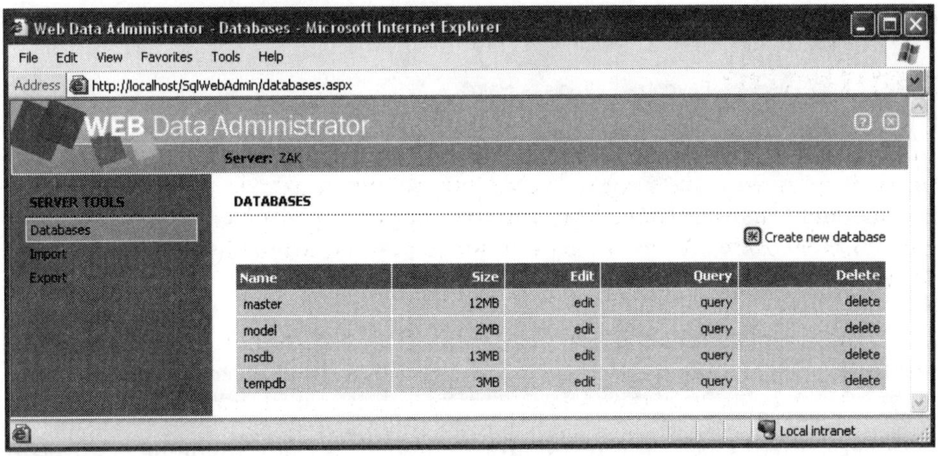

More information on Web Data Administrator, MSDE, and databases will be covered in Chapter 6.

Your First ASP.NET Page

For your first run at ASP.NET, we'll create the simple example shown in Figure 1.9.

Figure 1.9. We'll create a simple ASP.NET page that says "Hello there" and displays the time.

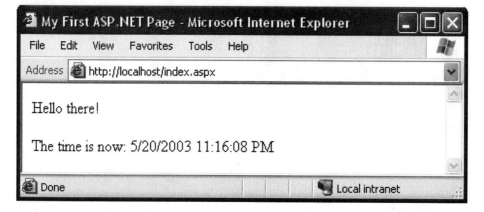

Let's get started! Open your text editor (Notepad[2] is fine). If you have software that creates ASP.NET pages automatically, such as Visual Studio .NET, please do not use it yet. These programs provide lots of powerful tools for building complex ASP.NET pages in a hurry, but for simple examples like this one, they tend to get in the way, rather than provide assistance.

Open your text editor, and start by entering the plain HTML for our page:

```
<html>
<head>
<title>My First ASP.NET Page</title>
</head>
<body>
<p>Hello there!</p>
<p>The time is now: </p>
</body>
</html>
```

So far, so good, right? Now, we'll add some ASP.NET code that will create the dynamic elements of the page, starting with the time.

```
<html>
<head>
```

---

[2]If you do use Notepad, be aware that you need to put quotes around any filename that doesn't end with .txt in the Save As dialog. Most ASP.NET file names end with .aspx; if you forget to put quotes around them when saving, you'll end up with files called *filename*.aspx.txt!

```
<title>My First ASP.NET Page</title>
</head>
<body>
<p>Hello there!</p>
<p>The time is now: <asp:Label runat="server" id="lblTime" /></p>
</body>
</html>
```

We've added an `<asp:Label>` tag to the document. This is a special tag that lets us insert dynamic content into the page. The `asp:` part of the tag name identifies it as a built-in ASP.NET tag. ASP.NET comes with numerous built-in tags; `<asp:Label>` is arguably the simplest.

The `runat="server"` attribute identifies the tag as something that needs to be handled on the server. In other words, the Web browser will never see the `<asp:Label>` tag; ASP.NET sees it and converts it to regular HTML tags before the page is sent to the browser. It's up to us to write the code that will tell ASP.NET to replace this particular tag with the current time.

To do this, we must add some script to our page. Like ASP before it, ASP.NET gives you the choice of a number of different languages to use in your scripts. The two most common languages are Visual Basic.NET (VB.NET) and C# (pronounced "C sharp"). Let's take a look at examples using both. Here's a version of the page in VB.NET:

VB.NET   File: **FirstPage.aspx**

```
<html>
<head>
<title>My First ASP.NET Page</title>
<script runat="server" language="VB">
Sub Page_Load(s As Object, e As EventArgs)
  lblTime.Text = DateTime.Now.ToString()
End Sub
</script>
</head>

<body>
<p>Hello there!</p>
<p>The time is now: <asp:Label runat="server" id="lblTime" /></p>
</body>
</html>
```

Here's the same page written in C#:

C#   File: **FirstPage.aspx**

```
<html>
<head>
<title>My First ASP.NET Page</title>
<script runat="server" language="C#">
protected void Page_Load(Object s, EventArgs e)
{
   lblTime.Text = DateTime.Now.ToString();
}
</script>
</head>

<body>
<p>Hello there!</p>
<p>The time is now: <asp:Label runat="server" id="lblTime" /></p>
</body>
</html>
```

Both versions of the page achieve exactly the same thing. If you've never done any server-side programming before, this may be starting to look a little scary. Let's break down the new elements of this page:

File: **FirstPage.aspx (excerpt)**

```
<script runat="server">
```

This tag, otherwise known as a **code declaration block**, marks the start of server-side code. Like the `<asp:Label>` tag, this `<script>` tag uses the `runat="server"` attribute to let ASP.NET know that the tag should be processed before sending the page to the browser.

VB.NET   File: **FirstPage.aspx (excerpt)**

```
Sub Page_Load(s As Object, e As EventArgs)
```

C#   File: **FirstPage.aspx (excerpt)**

```
protected void Page_Load(Object s, EventArgs s) {
```

I won't go into too much detail here. For now, all you need to know is that you can write script fragments that are run in response to different events, such as a button being clicked or an item being selected from a drop-down list. What the first line basically says is "execute the following script whenever the page is loaded." Note that C# groups code into blocks with curly braces, while Visual Basic tends to use statements such as `End Sub` to mark the end of a particular sequence. So, the curly brace in the C# code above ({) marks the start of the script that will be executed when the page loads for the first time. For the technically minded, the code we've just seen is a method definition for a page load event handler, which is essentially the code that the server runs when the page is requested for the first time.

Finally, here's the line that actually displays the time on the page:

VB.NET   File: **FirstPage.aspx (excerpt)**

```
lblTime.Text = DateTime.Now.ToString()
```

C#   File: **FirstPage.aspx (excerpt)**

```
lblTime.Text = DateTime.Now.ToString();
```

You can see that these two .NET languages have much in common, because they are both built on the .NET Framework. In fact, the only difference with the above line is that C# ends code lines with a semicolon (;). In plain English, here's what this line says:

> Set the `Text` property of `lblTime` to the current date/time, expressed as a string of text.

Note that `lblTime` is the value we gave for the `id` attribute of the `<asp:Label>` tag where we want to show the time. So, `lblTime.Text`, the `Text` property of `lblTime`, refers to the text that will be displayed by the tag. `DateTime` is a **class** that's built into the .NET Framework, and which lets you perform all sorts of useful functions with dates and times. There are thousands of these **classes** that do all sorts of useful things within the .NET Framework. These classes are also known as the **.NET Framework Class Library**.

The `DateTime` class has a **property** called `Now` that always contains the current date and time. This `Now` property has a **method** called `ToString()` that expresses that date and/or time as text (a segment of text is commonly called a **string** in programming circles). Classes, properties, and methods: these are all important words in the vocabulary of any programmer, and we'll discuss them later on in the book. For now, all you need to take away from this discussion is that `DateTime.Now.ToString()` will give you the current date and time as a text string, which you can then tell your `<asp:Label>` tag to display. The rest of the script block simply ties up loose ends:

VB.NET   File: **FirstPage.aspx (excerpt)**

```
End Sub
</script>
```

```
C#                                          File: FirstPage.aspx (excerpt)
}
</script>
```

The closing (End Sub) and (}) mark the end of the script to be run when the page is loaded, and the </script> tag marks the end of the script block.

Create a new subdirectory of C:\Inetpub\wwwroot on your Web server, and save your file there under the name FirstPage.aspx. Now, open your browser and point type this URL in the address bar:

http://localhost/test/FirstPage.aspx

Replace *test* with the name that you gave to the directory in which you saved the file. You should see a page similar to the one we saw in Figure 1.9.

If the time isn't displayed, chances are that you opened the file directly in your browser instead of loading it through your Web server. Because ASP.NET is a server-side language, your Web server needs to access the file before it's sent to your browser for display. If it doesn't get access to the file, the ASP.NET code is never converted into HTML that your browser can understand, so make sure you load the page by typing an actual URL (e.g. http://localhost/test/index.aspx), not just a path and filename.

With the page displayed in your browser, use the View Source feature (View, Source in Internet Explorer) to view the HTML code for the page. Here's what you'll see:

```
<html>
<head>
<title>My First ASP.NET Page</title>
</head>
<body>
<p>Hello there!</p>
<p>The time is now: <span id="lblTime">10/13/2003 1:55:09
PM</span></p>
</body>
</html>
```

Notice that all the ASP.NET code has gone! Even the script block has been completely removed, and the <asp:Label> tag has been replaced by a <span> tag (with the same id attribute as the <asp:Label> tag that we used) containing the date and time string.

That's how ASP.NET works. From the Web browser's point of view, there is nothing special about an ASP.NET page; it's just plain HTML like any other. All the ASP.NET code is run by your Web server and converted to plain HTML that's sent to the browser. So far, so good: the example above was fairly simple. The next chapter will get a bit more challenging as we begin to introduce you to some valuable programming concepts.

The ASP.NET Support Site

The official Microsoft ASP.NET support Website can be found at http://www.asp.net/. As you develop ASP.NET Web applications, you will undoubtedly have questions and problems that need to be answered. The ASP.NET support Website was developed by Microsoft as a portal for the ASP.NET community to answer the questions and solve the problems that developers have while using ASP.NET. The support Website provides useful information, such as news, downloads, articles, and discussion forums. You can also ask questions of the experienced community members in the SitePoint Forums[20].

Summary

In this chapter, you learned about .NET. You also learned of the benefits of ASP.NET and that it's a part of the .NET Framework. First, you learned about the constructs of ASP.NET and how to locate and install the .NET Framework. Then, we explored the software that's required not only for this book, but also in order for you or your company to progress with ASP.NET.

You've gained a solid foundation in the world of ASP.NET! The next chapter will build on this knowledge and begin to introduce you to ASP.NET in more detail, including page structure, languages to use, programming concepts, and form processing.

---

[20] http://www.sitepoint.com/forums/

ASP.NET Basics

So far, you've learned what ASP.NET is, and what it can do—you even know how to create a simple ASP.NET page. Don't worry if it seems a little bewildering right now, because, as this book progresses, you'll learn how to use ASP.NET at more advanced levels. So far, you've installed the necessary software to get going and have been introduced to some very simple form processing techniques.

As the next few chapters unfold, we'll introduce more advanced topics, including controls, programming techniques, and more. Before we can begin developing applications with ASP.NET, however, you'll need to understand the inner workings of a typical ASP.NET page. This will help you identify the various parts of the ASP.NET page referenced by the many examples within the book. In this chapter, we'll talk about some key mechanisms of an ASP.NET page, specifically:

❑ Page structure

❑ View state

❑ Namespaces

❑ Directives

We'll also cover two of the "built-in" languages supported by the .NET Framework: VB.NET and C#. As this section begins to unfold, we'll explore the differences, similarities, and power that the two languages provide in terms of creating ASP.NET applications.

So, what exactly makes up an ASP.NET page? The next few sections will give you an in-depth understanding of the constructs of a typical ASP.NET page.

ASP.NET Page Structure

ASP.NET pages are simply text files with the `.aspx` file name extension that can be placed on an IIS server equipped with ASP.NET. When a browser requests an ASP.NET page, the ASP.NET runtime (as a component of the .NET Framework's Common Language Runtime, or CLR) parses and compiles the target file into a .NET Framework class. The application logic now contained within the new class is used in conjunction with the presentational HTML elements of the ASP.NET page to display dynamic content to the user. Sounds simple, right?

An ASP.NET page consists of the following elements:

- Directives

- Code declaration blocks

- Code render blocks

- ASP.NET server controls

- Server-side comments

- Server-side include directives

- Literal text and HTML tags

It's important to remember that ASP.NET pages are just text files with an `.aspx` extension that are processed by the runtime to create standard HTML, based on their contents. Presentational elements within the page are contained within the `<body>` tag, while application logic or code can be placed inside `<script>` tags. Remember this pattern from the sample at the end of the previous chapter? Figure 2.1 illustrates the various parts of that page.

Figure 2.1. All the elements of an ASP.NET page are highlighted. Everything else is literal text and HTML tags.

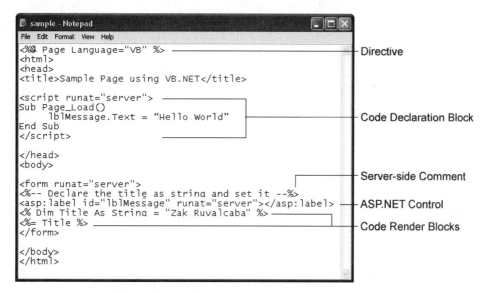

As you can see, this ASP.NET page contains examples of all the above components (except server-side includes) that make up an ASP.NET page. You won't often use every single element in a given page, but you should become familiar with these elements, the purpose that each serves, and how and when it's appropriate to use them.

Directives

The directives section is one of the most important parts of an ASP.NET page. **Directives** control how a page is compiled, specify settings when navigating between pages, aid in debugging (error-fixing), and allow you to import classes to use within your page's code. Directives start with the sequence <%@, followed by the directive name, plus any attributes and their corresponding values, then end with %>. Although there are many directives that you can use within your pages, the two most important are the Import and Page directives. We will discuss directives in greater detail later, but, for now, know that the Import and Page directives are the most useful for ASP.NET development. Looking at the sample ASP.NET page in Figure 2.1, you can see that a Page directive was used at the top of the page as shown:

VB.NET
```
<%@ Page Language="VB" %>
```

C#
```
<%@ Page Language="C#" %>
```

The Page directive, in this case, specifies the language that's to be used for the application logic by setting the Language attribute appropriately. The value provided for this attribute, in quotes, specifies that we're using either VB.NET or C#. There's a whole range of different directives; we'll see a few more later in this chapter.

Unlike ASP, in ASP.NET, directives can appear anywhere on a page, but are most commonly written as the very first lines.

Code Declaration Blocks

In Chapter 3 we'll talk about code-behind pages and how they let us separate our application logic from an ASP.NET page's HTML presentation code. If you're not working with code-behind pages, however, **code declaration blocks** must be used to contain all the application logic of your ASP.NET page. This application logic defines variables, subroutines, functions, and more. In our page, we place the code inside <script> tags, like so:

VB.NET
```
<script runat="server">
Sub mySub()
  ' Code here
End Sub
</script>
```

Here, the tags enclose some VB.NET code, but it could just as easily be C# if our page language were set thus:

C#
```
<script runat="server">
void mySub() {
  // Code here
}
</script>
```

Comments in VB.NET and C# Code

Both of these code snippets contain **comments**—explanatory text that will be ignored by ASP.NET, but which serves to describe how the code works.

In VB.NET code, a single quote or apostrophe (') indicates that the remainder of the line is to be ignored as a comment.

In C# code, two slashes (/ /) does the same. C# code also lets you span a comment over multiple lines by beginning it with / * and ending it with * /.

Before .NET emerged, ASP also supported such script tags using a `runat="server"` attribute, although they could only ever contain VBScript, and, for a variety of reasons, they failed to find favor among developers. Code declaration blocks are generally placed inside the `<head>` tag of your ASP.NET page. The sample ASP.NET page shown in Figure 2.1, for instance, contained the following code declaration block:

VB.NET

```
<script runat="server">
Sub Page_Load()
  lblMessage.Text = "Hello World"
End Sub
</script>
```

Perhaps you can work out what the equivalent C# code would be:

C#

```
<script runat="server">
void Page_Load() {
  lblMessage.Text = "Hello World";
}
</script>
```

The `<script runat="server">` tag accepts two other attributes, as well. You can set the language used in the block with the `language` attribute:

VB.NET

```
<script runat="server" language="VB">
```

C#

```
<script runat="server" language="C#">
```

If you don't specify a language within the code declaration block, the ASP.NET page will use the language provided by the `language` attribute of the `Page` directive. Each page may only contain code in a single language; for instance, it is not possible to mix VB.NET and C# in the same page.

The second attribute available is src, which lets you specify an external code file to use within your ASP.NET page:

VB.NET
```
<script runat="server" language="VB" src="mycodefile.vb">
```

C#
```
<script runat="server" language="C#" src="mycodefile.cs">
```

Code Render Blocks

You can use **code render blocks** to define inline code or inline expressions that execute when a page is rendered, and you may recognize these blocks from traditional ASP. Code within a code render block is executed immediately as it is encountered, usually when the page is loaded or rendered for the first time, and every time the page is loaded subsequently. Code within a code declaration block, on the other hand, occurring within script tags, is only executed when it is called or triggered by user or page interactions. There are two types of code render blocks: **inline code** and **inline expressions**, both of which are typically written within the body of the ASP.NET page.

Inline code render blocks execute one or more statements and are placed directly inside a page's HTML within <% and %> characters.

Inline expression render blocks can be compared to Response.Write() in classic ASP. They start with <%= and end with %>, and are used to display values of the variables and methods on a page.

Looking back at Figure 2.1, you can see both types of code render blocks:

VB.NET
```
<% Dim Title As String = "Zak Ruvalcaba" %>
<%= Title %>
```

This equates to the following C#:

C#
```
<% String Title = "Zak Ruvalcaba"; %>
<%= Title %>
```

The first line represents an inline code render block and must contain complete statements in the appropriate language. Here, we're setting the value of the `Title` variable to the string `Zak Ruvalcaba`. The last line is an example of an inline expression render block used to write out the value of the `Title` variable, `Zak Ruvalcaba`, onto the page.

ASP.NET Server Controls

At the heart of ASP.NET pages lies the **server controls**, which represent dynamic elements that your users can interact with. There are four basic types of server control: ASP.NET controls, HTML controls, validation controls, and user controls.

All ASP.NET controls must reside within a `<form runat="server">` tag in order to function correctly. The only two exceptions to this rule are the `HtmlGenericControl` and the `Label` Web control.

Server controls offer the following advantages to ASP.NET developers:

❑ We can access HTML elements easily from within our code: we can change their characteristics, check their values, or even dynamically update them straight from our server-side programming language of choice.

❑ ASP.NET controls retain their properties even after the page has been processed. This process is known as **view state**. We'll be covering view state later in this chapter. For now, just know that view state prevents the user from losing data that has already been entered into a form once it's been sent to the server for processing. When the response comes back to the client's browser, text box values, drop-down list selections, etc., are all retained through view state.

❑ With ASP.NET controls, developers are able to separate the presentational elements (everything the user sees) and application logic (dynamic portions of the ASP.NET page) of a page so that each can be considered separately.

Because ASP.NET is all about controls, we'll be discussing them in greater detail as we move through this book. For instance, in the next few chapters, we'll discuss HTML controls and Web controls (Chapter 4), Validation controls (Chapter 5), Data controls (Chapter 9), and so on.

Server-Side Comments

Server-side comments allow you to include, within the page, comments or notes that will not be processed by ASP.NET. Traditional HTML uses the `<!--` and `-->` character sequences to delimit comments; anything found within these will not be displayed to the user by the browser. ASP.NET comments look very similar, but use the sequences `<%--` and `--%>`.

Our ASP.NET example contains the following server-side comment block:

VB.NET

```
<%-- Declare the title as string and set it --%>
```

The difference between ASP.NET comments and HTML comments is that ASP.NET comments are not sent to the client at all. Don't use HTML comments to try and comment out ASP.NET code. Consider the following example:

VB.NET

```
<!--
<button runat="server" id="myButton" onServerClick="Click">Click
Me</button>
<% Title = "New Title" %>
-->
```

Here, it looks as if a developer has attempted to use an HTML comment to hide not only an HTML button control, but a code render block as well. Unfortunately, HTML comments will only hide things from the browser, not the ASP.NET runtime. So, in this case, while we won't see anything in the browser that represents these two lines, they will, in fact, have been processed by ASP.NET, and the value of the variable `Title` will be changed to `New Title`. The code could be modified to use server-side comments very simply:

VB.NET

```
<%--
<button runat="server" id="myButton" onServerClick="Click">Click
Me</button>
<% Title = "New Title" %>
--%>
```

Now, the ASP.NET runtime will ignore the contents of this comment, and the value of the `Title` variable will not be changed.

Server-Side Include Directives

Server-side include directives enable developers to insert the contents of an external file anywhere within an ASP.NET page. In the past, developers used server-side includes when inserting connection strings, constants, and other code that was generally repeated throughout the entire site.

There are two ways your server-side includes can indicate the external file to include: using either the `file` or the `virtual` attribute. If we use `file`, we specify its filename as the physical path on the server, either as an absolute path starting from a drive letter, or as a path relative to the current file. Below, we see a `file` server-side include with a relative path:

```
<!-- #INCLUDE file="myinclude.aspx" -->
```

`virtual` server-side includes, on the other hand, specify the file's location on the Website, either with an absolute path from the root of the site, or with a path relative to the current page. The example below uses an absolute virtual path:

```
<!-- #INCLUDE virtual="/directory1/myinclude.aspx" -->
```

Note that although server-side includes are still supported by ASP.NET, they have been replaced by a more robust and flexible model known as **user controls**. Discussed in Chapter 16, user controls allow for developers to create a separate page or module that can be inserted into any page within an ASP.NET application.

Literal Text and HTML Tags

The final element of an ASP.NET page is plain old text and HTML . Generally, you cannot do without these elements, and HTML is the means for displaying the information from your ASP.NET controls and code in a way that's suitable for the user. Returning to the example in Figure 2.1 one more time, let's focus on the literal text and HTML tags:

```
VB.NET
<%@ Page Language="VB" %>
<html>
<head>
<title>Sample Page</title>

<script runat="server">
Sub ShowMessage(s As Object, e As EventArgs)
  lblMessage.Text = "Hello World"
```

```
End Sub
</script>

</head>
<body>

<form runat="server">
<%-- Declare the title as string and set it --%>
<asp:Label id="lblMessage" runat="server" />
<% Dim Title As String = "Zak Ruvalcaba's Book List" %>
<%= Title %>
</form>

</body>
</html>
```

As you can see in the bold code, literal text and HTML tags provide the structure for presenting our dynamic data. Without them, there would be no format to the page, and the browser would be unable to understand it.

Now you should understand what the structure of an ASP.NET page looks like. As you work through the examples in this book, you'll begin to realize that in many cases you won't need to use all these elements. For the most part, all of your development will be modularized within code declaration blocks. All of the dynamic portions of your pages will be contained within code render blocks or controls located inside a <form runat="server"> tag.

In the following sections, we'll outline the various languages used within ASP.NET, talk a little about view state, and look at working with directives in more detail.

View State

As I mentioned briefly in the previous section, ASP.NET controls automatically retain their data when a page is sent to the server by a user clicking a submit button. Microsoft calls this persistence of data **view state**. In the past, developers would have to hack a way to remember the item selected in a drop-down menu or keep the contents of a text box, typically using a hidden form field. This is no longer the case; ASP.NET pages, once submitted to the server for processing, automatically retain all information contained within text boxes, items selected within drop-down menus, radio buttons, and check boxes. Even better, they keep dynamically generated tags, controls, and text. Consider the following ASP page, called sample.asp:

```
<html>
<head>
  <title>Sample Page using VBScript</title>
</head>
<body>
<form method="post" action="sample.asp">
  <input type="text" name="txtName"/>
  <input type="Submit" name="btnSubmit" text="Click Me"/>
<%
If Request.Form("txtName") <> "" Then
  Response.Write(Request.Form("txtName"))
End If
%>

</form>
</body>
</html>
```

If you save this example in the WebDocs subdirectory of wwwroot that you created in Chapter 1, you can open it in your browser by typing http://localhost/WebDocs/sample.asp, to see that view state is not automatically preserved. When the user submits the form, the information that was previously typed into the text box is cleared, although it is still available in Request.Form("txtName"). The equivalent page in ASP.NET, ViewState.aspx, demonstrates data persistence using view state:

VB.NET   File: **ViewState.aspx**

```
<html>
<head>
<title>Sample Page using VB.NET</title>
<script runat="server" language="VB">
Sub Click(s As Object, e As EventArgs)
  lblMessage.Text = txtName.Text
End Sub
</script>
</head>

<body>
<form runat="server">
  <asp:TextBox id="txtName" runat="server" />
  <asp:Button id="btnSubmit" Text="Click Me" OnClick="Click"
      runat="server" />
  <asp:Label id="lblMessage" runat="server" />
</form>
```

```
</body>
</html>
```

C#   File: **ViewState.aspx**

```
<html>
<head>
<title>Sample Page using C#</title>
<script runat="server" language="C#">
void Click(Object s, EventArgs e) {
  lblMessage.Text = txtName.Text;
}
</script>
</head>

<body>
<form runat="server">
  <asp:TextBox id="txtName" runat="server" />
  <asp:Button id="btnSubmit" Text="Click Me" OnClick="Click"
      runat="server" />
  <asp:Label id="lblMessage" runat="server" />
</form>
</body>
</html>
```

In this case, the code uses ASP.NET controls with the `runat="server"` attribute. As you can see in Figure 2.2, the text from the box appears on the page when the button is clicked, but also notice that the data remains in the text box! The data in this example is preserved because of view state:

Figure 2.2. ASP.NET supports view state. When a page is submitted, the information within the controls is preserved.

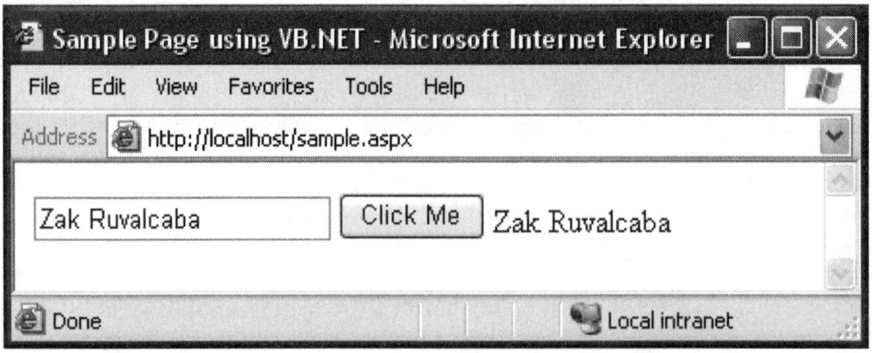

You can see the benefits of view state already. But where is all that information stored? ASP.NET pages maintain view state by encrypting the data within a hidden form field. View the source of the page after you've submitted the form, and look for the following code:

```
<input type="hidden" name="__VIEWSTATE" value="dDwtMTcyOTAyO
DAwNztOPDtsPGk8Mj47PjtsPHQ8O2w8aTwzPjs+O2w8dDxwPGw8aW5uZXJJodG
1sOz47bDxIZWxsbyBXb3JsZDs+Pjs7Pjs+Pjs+d2w17GlhgweO9L1UihS
FaGxk6t4=" />
```

This is a standard HTML hidden form field with the value set to the encrypted data from the form element. As soon as you submit the form for processing, all information relevant to the view state of the page is stored within this hidden form field.

View state is enabled for every page by default. If you do not intend to use view state, you can turn it off, which will result in a slight performance gain in your pages. To do this, set the `EnableViewState` property of the `Page` directive to `false`:

```
<%@ Page EnableViewState="False" %>
```

Speaking of directives, it's time we took a closer look at these curious beasts!

Working With Directives

For the most part, ASP.NET pages resemble traditional HTML pages, with a few additions. In essence, just using an extension like `.aspx` on an HTML file will make the .NET Framework process the page. However, before you can work with certain, more advanced features, you will need to know how to use directives.

We've already talked a little about directives and what they can do earlier in this chapter. You learned that directives control how a page is created, specify settings when navigating between pages, aid in finding errors, and allow you to import advanced functionality to use within your code. Three of the most commonly used directives are:

Page	Defines page-specific attributes for the ASP.NET page, such as the language used.
Import	Makes functionality defined elsewhere available in a page through the use of namespaces. You will become very familiar with this directive as you progress through this book.

Register   As you will see in Chapter 16, you would use this directive to link a user control to the ASP.NET page.

You will become very familiar with these three directives, as they're the ones that we'll be using the most in this book. You've already seen the `Page` directive in use. The `Import` directive imports extra functionality for use within your application logic. The following example, for instance, imports the `Mail` class, which you could use to send email from a page:

```
<%@ Import Namespace="System.Web.Mail" %>
```

The `Register` directive allows you to register a **user control** for use on your page. We'll cover these in Chapter 16, but the directive looks something like this:

```
<%@ Register TagPrefix="uc" TagName="footer" Src="footer.ascx" %>
```

ASP.NET Languages

As we saw in the previous chapter, .NET currently supports many different languages and there is no limit to the number of languages that could be made available. If you're used to writing ASP, you may think the choice of VBScript would be obvious. With ASP.NET however, Microsoft has done away with VBScript and replaced it with a more robust and feature-rich alternative: VB.NET. ASP.NET's support for C# is likely to find favor with developers from other backgrounds. This section will introduce you to both these new languages, which are used throughout the remainder of the book. By the end of this section, you will, I hope, agree that the similarities between the two are astonishing—any differences are minor and, in most cases, easy to figure out.

Traditional server technologies are much more constrained in the choice of development language they offer. For instance, old-style CGI scripts were typically written with Perl or C/C++, JSP uses Java, Coldfusion uses CFML, and PHP is a language in and of itself. .NET's support for many different languages lets developers choose based on what they're familiar with, and start from there. To keep things simple, in this book we'll consider the two most popular, VB.NET and C#, giving you a chance to choose which feels more comfortable to you, or stick with your current favorite if you have one.

VB.NET

Visual Basic.NET or VB.NET is the result of a dramatic overhaul of Microsoft's hugely popular Visual Basic language. With the inception of **Rapid Application**

Development (RAD) in the nineties, Visual Basic became extremely popular, allowing in-house teams and software development shops to bang out applications two-to-the-dozen. VB.NET has many new features over older versions of VB, most notably that it has now become a fully object-oriented language. At last, it can call itself a true programming language on a par with the likes of Java and C++. Despite the changes, VB.NET generally stays close to the structured, legible syntax that has always made it so easy to read, use, and maintain.

C#

The official line is that Microsoft created C# in an attempt to produce a programming language that coupled the simplicity of Visual Basic with the power and flexibility of C++. However, there's little doubt that its development was at least hurried along. Following legal disputes with Sun about Microsoft's treatment (some would say abuse) of Java, Microsoft was forced to stop developing its own version of Java, and instead developed C# and another language, which it calls J#. We're not going to worry about J# here, as C# is preferable. It's easy to read, use, and maintain, because it does away with much of the confusing syntax for which C++ became infamous.

Summary

In this chapter, we started out by introducing key aspects of an ASP.NET page including directives, code declaration blocks, code render blocks, includes, comments, and controls. As the chapter progressed, you were introduced to the two most popular languages that ASP.NET supports, which we'll use throughout the book.

In the next chapter, we'll create more ASP.NET pages to demonstrate some form processing techniques and programming basics, before we finally dive in and look at object oriented programming for the Web.

VB.NET and C# Programming Basics

As you learned at the end of the last chapter, one of the great things about ASP.NET is that we can pick and choose which of the various .NET languages we like. In this chapter, we'll look at some key programming principles using our two chosen languages, VB.NET and C#. We'll start off with a run-down of some basic programming concepts as they relate to ASP.NET using both languages. We'll introduce programming fundamentals such as control and page events, variables, arrays, functions, operators, conditionals, and loops. Next, we'll dive into namespaces and address the topic of classes—how they're exposed through namespaces, and which you'll use most often.

The final sections of the chapter cover some of the ideas underlying modern, effective ASP.NET design, starting with that of code-behind and the value it provides by helping us separate code from presentation. We finish with an examination of how object-oriented programming techniques impact the ASP.NET developer.

Programming Basics

One of the building blocks of an ASP.NET page is the application logic: the actual programming code that allows the page to function. To get anywhere with this, you need to grasp the concept of **events**. All ASP.NET pages will contain controls, such as text boxes, check boxes, lists, and more, each of these controls allowing the user to interact with it in some way. Check boxes can be checked, lists can be scrolled, items on them selected, and so on. Now, whenever one of these actions is performed, the control will raise an event. It is by handling these events with code that we get our ASP.NET pages to do what we want.

For instance, say a user clicks a button on an ASP.NET page. That button (or, strictly, the ASP.NET `Button` control) raises an event (in this case it will be the `Click` event). When the ASP.NET runtime registers this event, it calls any code we have written to handle it. We would use this code to perform whatever action that button was supposed to perform, for instance, to save form data to a file, or retrieve requested information from a database. Events really are key to ASP.NET programming, which is why we'll start by taking a closer look at them. Then, there's the messy business of writing the actual handler code, which means we need to check out some common programming techniques in the next sections. Specifically, we're going to cover the following areas:

❏ Control events and handlers

❏ Page events

❏ Variables and variable declaration

❏ Arrays

❏ Functions

❏ Operators

❏ Conditionals

❏ Loops

It wouldn't be practical, or even necessary, to cover all aspects of VB.NET and C# in this book, so we're going to cover enough to get you started, completing the projects and samples using both languages. Moreover, I'd say that the programming concepts you'll learn here will be more than adequate to complete the great majority of day-to-day Web development tasks using ASP.NET.

Control Events and Subroutines

As I just mentioned, an event (sometimes more than one) is raised, and handler code is called, in response to a specific action on a particular control. For instance, the code below creates a server-side button and label. Note the use of the `OnClick` attribute on the Button control:

File: **ClickEvent.aspx (excerpt)**

```
<form runat="server">
  <asp:Button id="btn1" runat="server" OnClick="btn1_Click"
      Text="Click Me" />
  <asp:Label id="lblMessage" runat="server" />
</form>
```

When the button is clicked, it raises the `Click` event, and ASP.NET checks the `OnClick` attribute to find the name of the handler subroutine for that event. Here, we tell ASP.NET to call the `btn1_Click()` routine. So now we have to write this **subroutine**, which we would normally place within a code declaration block inside the <head> tag, like this:

VB.NET   File: **ClickEvent.aspx (excerpt)**

```
<head>
<script runat="server" language="VB">
  Public Sub btn1_Click(s As Object, e As EventArgs)
    lblMessage.Text = "Hello World"
  End Sub
</script>
</head>
```

C#   File: **ClickEvent.aspx (excerpt)**

```
<head>
<script runat="server" language="C#">
  public void btn1_Click(Object s, EventArgs e) {
    lblMessage.Text = "Hello World";
  }
</script>
</head>
```

This code simply sets a message to display on the label that we also declared with the button. So, when this page is run and users click the button, they'll see the message "Hello World" appear next to it.

I hope you can now start to come to grips with the idea of control events and how they're used to call particular subroutines. In fact, there are many events that your controls can use, some of which are only found on certain controls—not others. Here's the complete set of attributes the Button control supports for handling events:

OnClick   As we've seen, the subroutine indicated by this attribute is called for the `Click` event, which occurs when the user clicks the button.

OnCommand   As with `OnClick`, the subroutine indicated by this attribute is called when the button is clicked.

OnLoad   The subroutine indicated by this attribute is called when the button is loaded for the first time—generally when the page first loads.

OnInit   When the button is initialized, any subroutine given in this attribute will be called.

OnPreRender   We can run code just before the button is rendered, using this attribute.

OnUnload   This subroutine will run when the control is unloaded from memory—basically, when the user goes to a different page or closes the browser entirely.

OnDisposed   This occurs when the button is released from memory.

OnDataBinding   This fires when the button is bound to a data source.

Don't worry too much about the intricacies of all these events and when they happen; I just want you to understand that a single control can produce a number of different events. In the case of the `Button` control, you'll almost always be interested in the `Click` event, as the others are only useful in rather obscure circumstances.

When a control raises an event, the specified subroutine (if there is one) is executed. Let's now take a look at the structure of a typical subroutine that interacts with a Web control:

VB.NET

```
Public Sub mySubName(s As Object, e As EventArgs)
  ' Write your code here
End Sub
```

C#

```
public void mySubName(Object s, EventArgs e) {
  // Write your code here
}
```

Let's break down all the components that make up a typical subroutine:

Public
public

Defines the **scope** of the subroutine. There are a few different options to choose from, the most frequently used being `Public` (for a global subroutine that can be used anywhere within the entire page) and `Private` (for subroutines that are available for the specific class only). If you don't yet understand the difference, your best bet is to stick with `Public` for now.

Sub
void

Defines the chunk of code as a subroutine. A subroutine is a named block of code that doesn't return a result; thus, in C#, we use the `void` keyword, which means exactly that. We don't need this in VB.NET, because the `Sub` keyword already implies that no value is returned.

mySubName **(...)**

This part gives the name we've chosen for the subroutine.

s As Object
Object s

When we write a subroutine that will function as an event handler, it must accept two **parameters**. The first is the control that generated the event, which is an `Object`. Here, we are putting that `Object` in a **variable** named s (more on variables later in this chapter). We can then access features and settings of the specific control from our subroutine using the variable.

e As EventArgs
EventArgs e

The second parameter contains certain information specific to the event that was raised. Note that, in many cases, you won't need to use either of these two parameters, so you don't need to worry about them too much at this stage.

As this chapter progresses, you'll see how subroutines associated with particular events by the appropriate attributes on controls can revolutionize the way your user interacts with your application.

Page Events

Until now, we've considered only events that are raised by controls. However, there is another type of event—the **page event**. The idea is the same as for control events[1], except that here, it is the page as a whole that generates the events. You've already used one of these events: the `Page_Load` event. This event is fired when the page loads for the first time. Note that we don't need to associate handlers for page events the way we did for control events; instead, we just place our handler code inside a subroutine with a preset name. The following list outlines the page event subroutines that are available:

Page_Init	Called when the page is about to be initialized with its basic settings
Page_Load	Called once the browser request has been processed, and all of the controls in the page have their updated values.
Page_PreRender	Called once all objects have reacted to the browser request and any resulting events, but before any response has been sent to the browser.
Page_UnLoad	Called when the page is no longer needed by the server, and is ready to be discarded.

The order in which the events are listed above is also the order in which they're executed. In other words, the `Page_Init` event is the first event raised by the page, followed by `Page_Load`, `Page_PreRender`, and finally `Page_UnLoad`.

The best way to illustrate the `Page_Load` event is through an example:

VB.NET   File: **PageEvents.aspx (excerpt)**
```
<html>
<head>
<script runat="server" language="VB">
Sub Page_Load(s As Object, e As EventArgs)
  lblMessage.Text = "Hello World"
End Sub
```

---

[1] Strictly speaking, a page is simply another type of control, and so page events *are* actually control events. When you're first coming to grips with ASP.NET, however, it can help to think of them differently, especially since you don't usually use On*EventName* attributes to assign subroutines to handle them.

```
</script>
</head>

<body>
<form runat="server">
<asp:Label id="lblMessage" runat="server" />
</form>
</body>
</html>
```

C#   File: **PageEvents.aspx (excerpt)**

```
<html>
<head>
<script runat="server" language="C#">
void Page_Load(Object s, EventArgs e) {
  lblMessage.Text = "Hello World";
}
</script>
</head>

<body>
<form runat="server">
<asp:Label id="lblMessage" runat="server" />
</form>
</body>
</html>
```

You can see that the control on the page does not specify any event handlers. There's no need, because we're using the special Page_Load subroutine, which will be called when the page loads. As the page loads, it will call the Page_Load routine, to display "Hello World" in the Label control, as shown in Figure 3.1.

Figure 3.1. The Page_Load event is raised, the subroutine is called, and the code within the subroutine is executed.

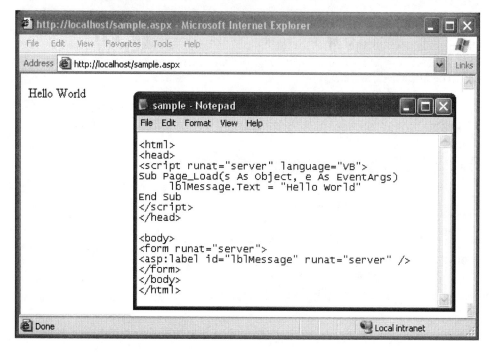

Variables and Variable Declaration

Variables are fundamental to programming, and you've almost certainly come across the term before. Basically, they let you give a name, or **identifier**, to a piece of data; we can then use that identifier to store, modify, and retrieve the data.

However, there are, of course, many different kinds of data, such as strings, integers (whole numbers), and floating point numbers (fractions or decimals). Before you can use a variable in VB.NET or C#, you must specify what type of data it can contain, using keywords such as `String`, `Integer`, `Decimal`, and so on, like this:

VB.NET

```
Dim strName As String
Dim intAge As Integer
```

```
C#
string strName;
int intAge;
```

These lines declare what type of data we want our variables to store, and are therefore known as **variable declarations**. In VB.NET, we use the keyword Dim, which stands for "dimension", while in C#, we simply precede the variable name with the appropriate data type.

Sometimes, we want to set an initial value for variables that we declare; we can do this using a process known as **initialization**:

```
VB.NET
Dim strCarType As String = "BMW"
```

```
C#
string strCarType = "BMW";
```

We can also declare and/or initialize a group of variables of the same type all at once:

```
VB.NET
Dim strCarType As String, strCarColor As String = "blue"
```

```
C#
string strCarType, strCarColor = "blue";
```

Table 3.1 below lists the most useful data types available in VB.NET and C#.

Table 3.1. A List of the Commonly Used Data Types

VB.NET	C#	Description
Integer	int	Whole numbers in the range -2,147,483,648 to 2,147,483,647.
Decimal	decimal	Up to 28 decimal places. You'll use decimal most often when dealing with costs of items.
String	string	Any text value.
Char	char	A single character (letter, number, or symbol).
Boolean	bool	True or false.
Object	Object	In .NET, all types are ultimately a type of object, and so variables of this type can hold just about any kind of data.

There are many more data types that you may encounter as you progress, but this list provides an idea of the ones you'll use most often.

So, to sum up, once you've declared a variable as a given type, it can only hold data of that type. You can't put a string into an integer variable, for instance. However, there are frequently times when you'll need to convert one data type to another. Have a look at this code:

VB.NET
```
Dim intX As Integer
Dim strY As String = "35"
intX = strY + 6
```

C#
```
int intX;
String strY = "35";
intX = strY + 6;
```

Now, while you or I might think that this could make sense—after all, the string strY *does* contain a number, so we may well wish to add it to another number—the computer will not be happy, and we'll get an error. What we have to do is explicitly convert, or **cast**, the string into an integer first:

VB.NET
```
Dim intX As Integer
Dim strY As String = "35"
intX = Int32.Parse(strY) + 6
```

```
C#
int intX;
String strY = "35";
intX = Convert.ToInt32(strY) + 6;
```

Now, the computer will be happy, as we've told it that we want to turn the string into an integer before it's used as one. This same principle holds true when mixing other types in a single expression.

Arrays

Arrays are a special variety of variable tailored for storing related items of the same data type. Any one item in an array can be accessed using the array's name, followed by that item's position in the array (its **offset**). Let's create a sample page to show what I mean:

VB.NET   File: **Arrays.aspx**

```
<html>
<head>
<script runat="server" language="VB">
Sub Page_Load()

  ' Declare an array
  Dim drinkList(4) As String

  ' Place some items in it
  drinkList(0) = "Water"
  drinkList(1) = "Juice"
  drinkList(2) = "Soda"
  drinkList(3) = "Milk"

  ' The line below accesses an item in the array by its position
  lblArrayList.Text = drinkList(1)
End Sub
</script>
</head>

<body>
<form runat="server">
<asp:Label id="lblArrayList" runat="server"/>
</form>
</body>
</html>
```

```
C#                                                          File: Arrays.aspx
<html>
<head>
<script runat="server" language="C#">
void Page_Load() {

    // Declare an array
    String[] drinkList = new String[4];

    // Place some items in it
    drinkList[0] = "Water";
    drinkList[1] = "Juice";
    drinkList[2] = "Soda";
    drinkList[3] = "Milk";

    // The line below accesses an item in the array by its position
    lblArrayList.Text = drinkList[1];
}
</script>
</head>

<body>
<form runat="server">
<asp:Label id="lblArrayList" runat="server"/>
</form>
</body>
</html>
```

There are some important points to pick up from this code. First, notice how we declare an array. In VB.NET, it looks like a regular declaration for a string, except that the number of items we want the array to contain is given in brackets after the name:

```
VB.NET                                             File: Arrays.aspx (excerpt)
    Dim drinkList(4) As String
```

In C#, it's a little different. First, we declare that drinkList is an array by following the datatype with two empty square brackets. We must then specify that this is an array of four items, using the new keyword:

```
C#                                                 File: Arrays.aspx (excerpt)
    String[] drinkList = new String[4];
```

A crucial point to realize here is that the arrays in both C# and VB.NET are what are known as **zero-based** arrays. This means that the first item actually has position 0, the second has position 1, and so on, through to the last item, which will have a position that's one less than the size of the array (3, in this case). So, we specify each item in our array like this:

VB.NET   File: **Arrays.aspx (excerpt)**
```
drinkList(0) = "Water"
drinkList(1) = "Juice"
drinkList(2) = "Soda"
drinkList(3) = "Milk"
```

C#   File: **Arrays.aspx (excerpt)**
```
drinkList[0] = "Water";
drinkList[1] = "Juice";
drinkList[2] = "Soda";
drinkList[3] = "Milk";
```

Notice that C# uses square brackets for arrays, while VB.NET uses standard parentheses. We have to remember that arrays are zero-based when we set the label text to the second item, as shown here:

VB.NET   File: **Arrays.aspx (excerpt)**
```
lblArrayList.Text = drinkList(1)
```

C#   File: **Arrays.aspx (excerpt)**
```
lblArrayList.Text = drinkList[1];
```

To help this sink in, you might like to try changing this code to show the third item in the list instead of the second. Can you work out what change you'd need to make?

That's right—you only need to change the number given in the brackets to match the position of the new item (don't forget to start at zero). In fact, it's this ability to select one item from a list using only its numerical location that makes arrays so useful in programming, as we'll see as we get further into the book.

Functions

Functions are exactly the same as subroutines, but for one key difference: they return a value. In VB.NET, we declare a function using the Function keyword in place of Sub, while, in C#, we simply have to specify the return type in place of using void. The following code shows a simple example:

VB.NET   File: **Functions.aspx**

```
<html>
<head>
<script runat="server" language="VB">

' Here's our function
Function getName() as String
  Return "Zak Ruvalcaba"
End Function

' And now we'll use it in the Page_Load handler
Sub Page_Load(s As Object, e As EventArgs)
  lblMessage.Text = getName()
End Sub
</script>
</head>

<body>
<form runat="server">
<asp:Label id="lblMessage" runat="server" />
</form>
</body>
</html>
```

C#   File: **Functions.aspx**

```
<html>
<head>
<script runat="server" language="C#">

// Here's our function
string getName() {
  return "Zak Ruvalcaba";
}

// And now we'll use it in the Page_Load handler
void Page_Load() {
  lblMessage.Text = getName();
}
</script>
</head>

<body>
<form runat="server">
<asp:Label id="lblMessage" runat="server" />
</form>
```

```
</body>
</html>
```

Figure 3.2 shows the result in the browser.

Figure 3.2. The Page_Load event is raised, the function is called, and the code within the function is executed.

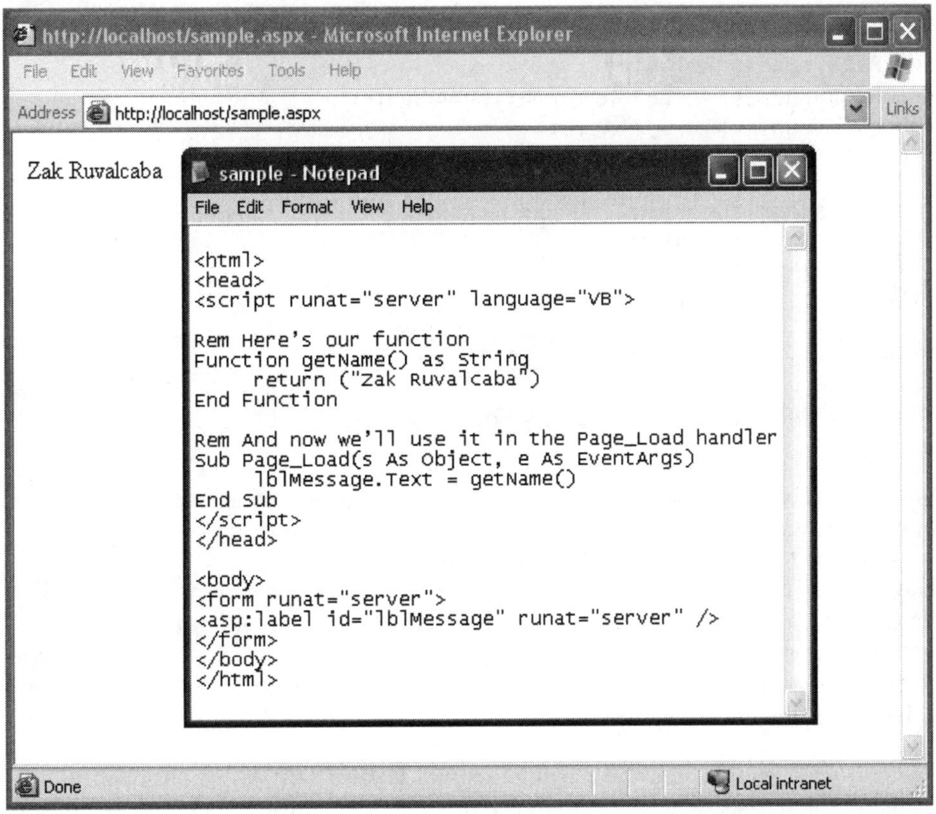

Here's what's happening: the line in our Page_Load subroutine calls our function, which returns a simple string that we can then assign to our label. I hope this illustrates what functions are about and how you can use them. In this simple example, we're merely returning a fixed string (my name), but the function could just as well retrieve the name from a database—or somewhere else. The point is that, regardless of how the function gets its data, we use it (that is, call it) in just the same way.

When we're declaring our function, we must remember to specify the correct **return type**. Take a look at the following code:

VB.NET

```
' Here's our function
Function addUp(x As Integer, y As Integer) As Integer
  Return x + y
End Function

' And now we use it in Page_Load
Sub Page_Load(s As Object, e As EventArgs)
  lblMessage.Text = addUp(5, 5).ToString()
End Sub
```

C#

```
// Here's our function
int addUp(int x, int y) {
  return x + y;
}

// And now we use it in Page_Load
void Page_Load() {
  lblMessage.Text = Convert.ToString(addUp(5, 5));
}
```

You can easily adapt the previous example to use this new code and see the results in your browser.

Have a look at this code, and see if you can spot what's different and why. The first thing you might notice is that our function now accepts **parameters**. Any function or subroutine can take any number of parameters, each of any type (there's no need for parameter types to match the return type—that's just coincidental in this example).

We can then readily use the parameters inside the function or subroutine just by using the names we gave them in the function declaration (here, we've chosen x and y, but we could have chosen different names).

The other difference between this and the function declaration we had before is that we now declare our function with a return type of Integer or int, rather than String, because we want it to return a whole number.

When we now call the new function, we simply have to specify the required number of parameters, and remember that the function will return a value with the type we specified. In this case, that means we have to convert the integer value it returns to a string, so we can assign it to the label.

In VB.NET, we tack `.ToString()` onto the end of the function call, while in C# we use the `Convert.ToString(...)`. Note the differences in how these two methods are used—converting numbers to strings is a very common task in ASP.NET, so it's good to get a handle on it early. Don't be too concerned if you're a little confused by how these conversions work, though—the syntax will become clear once we discuss the object oriented concepts involved later in this chapter.

Again, a complete discussion of functions could take up an entire chapter, but I hope the brief examples here are enough to prepare you for what we're going to cover in future chapters. Don't worry too much if you're still a bit unsure what functions and subroutines are all about right now—they'll become second nature very quickly.

Operators

Throwing around values with variables and functions isn't much use unless you can use them in some meaningful way, and to do this we use **operators**. An operator is a symbol that has a certain meaning when applied to values. Don't worry—they're nowhere near as scary as they sound! In fact, in the last example, when our function added two numbers, we were using an operator—the **addition operator**, +. Most of the other available operators are just as well known, although there are one or two that will probably be new to you. Table 3.2 outlines the operators that you'll use most often.

Table 3.2. ASP.NET Operators

VB.NET	C#	Description
>	>	greater than
>=	>=	greater than or equal to
<	<	less than
<=	<=	less than or equal to
<>	!=	not equal to
=	==	equals
=	=	assigns a value to a variable
Or	||	or
And	&&	and
&	+	concatenate strings
New	New	create object or array
*	*	multiply
/	/	divide
+	+	add
-	-	subtract

The following code uses some of these operators:

VB.NET
```
If (user = "Zak" And itemsBought <> 0) Then
  lblMessage.Text = "Hello Zak! Do you want to proceed to " & _
    "checkout?"
End If
```

C#
```
if (user == "Zak" && itemsBought != 0) {
  lblMessage.Text = "Hello Zak! Do you want to proceed to " +
    "checkout?";
}
```

Here, we use the equality, inequality (not equals to) and logical 'and' operators in an If statement to print a message only for a given user, and only when he or she has bought something. Of particular note is C#'s equality operator, ==, which is used when comparing two values to see if they are equal. Don't use a single equals sign in C# unless you are assigning a value to a variable, or your code will have a very different meaning than you expect!

Breaking Long Lines of Code

Since the message string in the above example was too long to fit on one line in this book, I also used the string concatenation operator to combine two shorter strings on separate lines to form the complete message. In VB.NET, I also had to break one line of code into two using the line continuation symbol (_, an underscore at the end of the line to be continued). Since C# marks the end of each command with a semicolon (;), I can split a single command over two lines without having to do anything special.

I'll use these techniques throughout this book to show long lines of code within a limited page width. Feel free to recombine the lines in your own code if you like—there is no actual length limit on lines of code in VB.NET and C#.

Conditional Logic

As you develop ASP.NET applications, there will be many instances in which you'll need to perform an action only if a certain condition is met, for instance, if the user has checked a certain checkbox, selected a certain item from a `DropDownList` control, or typed a certain string into a `TextBox` control.

We check for such things using **conditionals**, the simplest of which is probably the `If` statement. This statement is often used in conjunction with an `Else` statement, which specifies what should happen if the condition is not met. So, for instance, we may wish to check *if* the name entered in a text box is "Zak," redirecting to one page if it is, or *else* redirecting to an error page:

VB.NET
```
If (txtUsername.Text = "Zak") Then
  Response.Redirect("ZaksPage.aspx")
Else
  Response.Redirect("errorPage.aspx")
End If
```

C#
```
if (txtUsername.Text == "Zak") {
  Response.Redirect("ZaksPage.aspx");
} else {
  Response.Redirect("errorPage.aspx");
}
```

Often, we want to check for one of many possibilities, and perform a particular action in each case. In that event, we can use the `Select Case` (VB.NET) or `switch` (C#) construct:

VB.NET
```
Dim strName As String = txtUsername.Text
Select Case strName
  Case "Zak"
    Response.Redirect("ZaksPage.aspx")
  Case "Mark"
    Response.Redirect("MarksPage.aspx")
  Case "Fred"
    Response.Redirect("FredsPage.aspx")
  Case Else
    Response.Redirect("errorPage.aspx")
End Select
```

C#
```
string strName = txtUsername.Text;
switch (strName) {
  case "Zak":
    Response.Redirect("ZaksPage.aspx");
    break;
  case "Mark":
    Response.Redirect("MarksPage.aspx");
    break;
  case "Fred":
    Response.Redirect("FredsPage.aspx");
    break;
  default:
    Response.Redirect("errorPage.aspx");
    break;
}
```

Loops

As you've just seen, an `If` statement causes a code block to execute once if the value of its test expression is true. Loops, on the other hand, cause a code block to execute repeatedly for as long as the test expression remains true. There are two basic kinds of loop:

❑ `While` loops, also called `Do` loops, which sounds like something Betty Boop might say!

❑ For loops, including For Next and For Each

A While loop is the simplest form of loop; it makes a block of code repeat for as long as a particular condition is true. Here's an example:

```vbnet
VB.NET
Dim Counter As Integer = 0

Do While Counter <= 10

  ' Convert out Integer to a String
  lblMessage.Text = Counter.ToString()

  ' Below we use the += operator to increase our variable by 1
  Counter += 1
Loop
```

```csharp
C#
int counter = 0;

while (counter <= 10) {

  // Below we use a sneaky way to convert our int to a string
  lblMessage.Text = counter + "";

  // C# has the operator ++ to increase a variable by 1
  counter++;
}
```

You can try out this code—enter it inside a Page_Load subroutine of one of the pages you've already created. The page illustrating Page_Load at the start of this chapter would be ideal. Make sure you remove any other code in the subroutine, and that there is an ASP.NET Label control in the HTML of the page with the ID lblMessage. When you open the page, the label will be set to show the number 0, then 1, then 2, all the way to 10. Of course, since all this happens in Page_Load (i.e. before any output is sent to the browser), you'll only see the last value assigned, 10.

This demonstrates that the loop repeats until the condition is no longer met. Try changing the code so that the counter variable is initialized to 20 instead of 0. When you open the page now, you won't see *anything* on screen, because the loop condition was never met.

There is another form of the While loop, called a Do While loop, which checks if the condition has been met at the *end* of the code block, rather than at the beginning:

VB.NET

```
Dim Counter As Integer = 0

Do

    ' Convert our Integer to a String
    lblMessage.Text = Counter.toString()

    ' Below we use the += operator to increase our variable by 1
    Counter += 1
Loop While Counter <= 10
```

C#

```
int counter = 0;

do {

    // Below we use a sneaky way to convert our int to a string
    lblMessage.Text = counter + "";

    // C# has the operator ++ to increase a variable by 1
    counter++;
} while (counter <= 10);
```

If you run this code, you'll see it provides the exact same output we saw when we tested the condition before the code block. However, we can see the crucial difference if we again change it so the counter variable is initialized to 20. In this case, we will, in fact, see 20 on screen, because the loop code is executed once before the condition is even checked! There are some instances when this is just what we want, so being able to place the condition at the end of the loop can be very handy.

A For loop is similar to a While loop, but is typically used when the number of times we need it to execute is known beforehand. The following example displays the count of items within a DropDownList control called ddlProducts:

VB.NET

```
Dim i As Integer
For i = 1 To ddlProducts.Items.Count
    lblMessage.Text = i.toString()
Next
```

```
C#
int i;
for (i = 1; i <= ddlProducts.Items.Count; i++) {
  lblMessage.Text = Convert.ToString(i);
}
```

In VB.NET, the loop syntax specifies the starting and ending values for our counter variable in the For statement itself. In C#, we assign a starting value (i = 1), a condition to be tested each time through the loop, just like a While loop (i <= ddlProducts.Items.Count), and how the counter variable should be incremented after each loop (i++). While this allows for some powerful variations on the theme in C#, it can be confusing at first. In VB.NET, the syntax is considerably simpler, but can be a bit limiting in exceptional cases.

The other type of For loop is For Each, which loops through every item within a collection. The following example loops through an array called arrayName:

```
VB.NET
For Each item In arrayName
  lblMessage.Text = item
Next
```

```
C#
foreach (string item in arrayName) {
  lblMessage.Text = item;
}
```

You may also come across instances in which you need to exit a loop prematurely. In this case, you would use Exit (VB.NET) or break (C#) to terminate the loop:

```
VB.NET
Dim i As Integer
For i = 0 To 10
  If (i = 5) Then
    Response.Write("Oh no! Not the number 5!!")
    Exit For
  End If
Next
```

```
C#
int i;
for (i = 0; i <= 10; i++) {
  if (i == 5) {
    Response.Write("Oh no! Not the number 5!!");
    break;
```

```
    }
}
```

In this case, as soon as our `For` loop hits 5, it displays a warning message, using the `Response.Write()` method that will be familiar to those with past ASP experience, and exits the loop so that no further passes through the loop will be made.

Although we have only scratched the surface, VB.NET and C# provide a great deal of power and flexibility to the Web developer, and time spent learning the basics now will more than pay off in the future.

Understanding Namespaces

Because ASP.NET is part of the .NET Framework, we have access to all the goodies that are built into it in the form of the **.NET Framework Class Library**. This library represents a huge resource of tools and features in the form of **classes**, all organized in a hierarchy of **namespaces**. When we want to use certain features that .NET provides, we have only to find the namespace that contains that functionality, and **import** that namespace into our ASP.NET page. Once we've done that, we can make use of the .NET classes in that namespace to achieve our own ends.

For instance, if we wanted to access a database from a page, we would import the namespace that contains classes for this purpose, which happens to be the `System.Data.OleDb` namespace. The dots (`.`) here indicate different levels of the hierarchy I mentioned—in other words, the `System.Data.OleDb` namespace is grouped within the `System.Data` namespace, which in turn is contained in the `System` namespace.

To import a particular namespace into an ASP.NET page, we use the `Import` directive. Consider the following excerpt from an ASP.NET page; it imports the `System.Data.OleDb` namespace, which contains classes called `OleDbConnection`, `OleDbCommand`, and `OleDbDataReader`. Importing the namespace lets us use these classes in a subroutine to display records from an Access database:

VB.NET
```
<%@ Import Namespace="System.Data.OleDb" %>
<html>
<head>
<script runat="server" language="VB">
Sub ReadDatabase(s As Object, e As EventArgs)
  Dim objConn As New OleDbConnection( _
```

```
      "Provider=Microsoft.Jet.OLEDB.4.0;" & _
      "Data Source=C:\Database\books.mdb")
   Dim objCmd As New OleDbCommand("SELECT * FROM BookList", _
      objConn)
   Dim drBooks As OleDbDataReader

   objConn.Open()
   drBooks = objCmd.ExecuteReader()
   While drBooks.Read()
      Response.Write("<li>")
      Response.Write(drBooks("Title"))
   End While
   objConn.Close()
End Sub
</script>
</head>
```

C#

```
<%@ Import Namespace="System.Data.OleDb" %>
<html>
<head>
<script runat="server" language="C#">
void ReadDatabase(Object s, EventArgs e) {
   OleDbConnection objConn = new OleDbConnection(
      "Provider=Microsoft.Jet.OLEDB.4.0;" +
      "Data Source=C:\\Database\\books.mdb");
   OleDbCommand objCmd = new OleDbCommand("SELECT * FROM BookList",
      objConn);
   OleDbDataReader drBooks;
   objConn.Open();
   drBooks = objCmd.ExecuteReader();
   while (drBooks.Read()) {
      Response.Write("<li>");
      Response.Write(drBooks["Title"]);
   }
   objConn.Close();
}
</script>
</head>
```

Don't worry too much about the code right now (we cover this in detail in Chapter 6). Suffice it to say that, as we've imported that namespace, we have access to all the classes that it contains, and we can use them to get information from an Access database for display on our page.

Specifically, the classes from `System.Data.OleDb` that are used in the above code are:

`OleDbConnection`	Used for connecting to the database
`OleDbCommand`	Used for creating a statement of contents to read from the database.
`OleDbDataReader`	Used for actually reading contents from database

Object Oriented Programming Concepts

VB.NET and C# are great programming languages because they offer a structured way of programming. By structured, I mean that code is separated into modules, where each module defines classes that can be imported and used in other modules. Both languages are relatively simple to get started with, yet offer features sophisticated enough for complex, large-scale enterprise applications.

The languages' ability to support more complex applications—their scalability—stems from the fact that both are **object oriented programming (OOP)** languages. But ask a seasoned developer what OOP really *is*, and they'll start throwing out buzzwords and catch phrases that are sure to confuse you—terms like **polymorphism**, **inheritance**, and **encapsulation**. In this section, I aim to explain the fundamentals of OOP and how good OOP style can help you develop better, more versatile Web applications down the road. This section will provide a basic OOP foundation angled towards the Web developer. In particular, we'll cover the following concepts:

❑ Objects

❑ Properties

❑ Methods

❑ Classes

❑ Scope

❑ Events

❑ Inheritance

Objects

In OOP, one thinks of programming problems in terms of objects, properties, and methods. The best way to get a handle on these terms is to consider a real world object and show how it might be represented in an OOP program. Many books use the example of a car to introduce OOP. I'll try to avoid that analogy and use something friendlier: my dog, an Australian Shepherd named Rayne.

Rayne is your average great, big, friendly, loving, playful mutt. You might describe him in terms of his physical properties: he's gray, white, brown, and black, stands roughly one and a half feet high, and is about three feet long. You might also describe some methods to make him do things: he sits when he hears the command "Sit", lies down when he hears the command "Lie down", and comes when his name is called.

So, if we were to represent Rayne in an OOP program, we'd probably start by creating a class called `Dog`. A **class** describes how certain types of objects look from a programming point of view. When we define a class, we must define the following two things:

Properties   Properties hold specific information relevant to that class of object. You can think of properties as characteristics of the objects that they represent. Our `Dog` class might have properties such as `Color`, `Height`, and `Length`.

Methods   Methods are actions that objects of the class can be told to perform. Methods are subroutines (if they don't return a value) or functions (if they do) that are specific to a given class. So the `Dog` class could have methods such as `sit()`, and `lie_down()`.

Once we've defined a class, we can write code that creates **objects** of that class, using the class a little like a template. This means that objects of a particular class expose (or make available) the methods and properties defined by that class. So, we might create an **instance** of our `Dog` class called Rayne, set its properties accordingly, and use the methods defined by the class to interact with Rayne, as shown in Figure 3.3.

Figure 3.3. The methods defined by the class interact with the object.

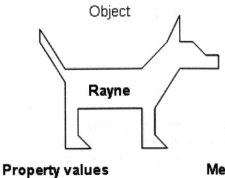

Object

Rayne

Property values
Color: Gray, White, and Black
Eye Color: Blue and Brown
Height: 18 Inches
Length: 36 Inches
Weight: 30 Pounds

Methods
Sit
Lay Down
Shake
Come

This is just a simple example to help you visualize what OOP is all about. In the next few sections, we'll cover properties and methods in greater detail, talk about classes and class instances, scope, events, and even inheritance.

Properties

As we've seen, properties are characteristics shared by all objects of a particular class. In the case of our example, the following properties might be used to describe any given dog:

☐ `Color`

☐ `Height`

☐ `Length`

In the same way, the more useful ASP.NET `Button` class exposes properties including:

❑ Width

❑ Height

❑ ID

❑ Text

❑ ForeColor

❑ BackColor

Unfortunately for me, if I get sick of Rayne's color, I can't change it. ASP.NET objects, on the other hand, let us change their properties very easily in the same way that we set variables. For instance, we've already used properties when setting text for the `Label` control, which is actually an object of class `Label` in the namespace `System.Web.UI.WebControls`:

VB.NET
```
lblMyText.Text = "Hello World"
```

C#
```
lblMyText.Text = "Hello World";
```

In this example, we're using a `Label` control called `lblMyText`. Remember, ASP.NET is all about controls, and, as it's built on OOP, all control types are represented as classes. In fact, as you'll learn in Chapter 4, all interaction with ASP.NET pages is handled via controls. When we place a control on a page, we give it a name through its `id` attribute, and this ID then serves as the name of the control. Rayne is an object. His name, or ID, is Rayne. Rayne has a height of eighteen inches. The same holds true for the `Label` control. The `Label` control's name or ID in the previous example is `lblMyText`. Next, we use the **dot operator** (`.`) to access the property `Text` that the object exposes and set it to the string "Hello World."

Methods

With our dog example, we can make a particular dog do things by calling commands. If I want Rayne to sit, I tell him to sit. If I want Rayne to lie down, I tell him to lie down. In object oriented terms, I tell him what I want him to do by calling a predefined command or **method**, and a resulting action is performed. In VB.NET or C#, we would write this as `rayne.Sit()`, or `rayne.LieDown()`.

As Web developers, we frequently call methods when a given event occurs. For instance, the example earlier in this chapter that took information from an Access database created an object called `objConn` to represent the connection to the database. We then opened the connection by calling the `Open()` method on that object as follows:

```
VB.NET
Dim objConn As As New OleDbConnection(
   "Provider=Microsoft.Jet.OLEDB.4.0;" & _
   "Data Source=C:\Database\books.mdb")
...
objConn.Open()
```

We say that the `Open()` method is **exposed** by the connection object, and that we're calling the `Open()` method on the `OleDbConnection` object stored in `objConn`. We don't need to know what dark secrets the method uses to do its magic; all we need to know is its name and what we use it for.

Classes

You can think of a class as a template for building as many objects as you like of a particular type. When you create an instance of a class, you are creating an object of that class, and the new object has all the characteristics and behaviors (properties and methods) defined by the class.

In our dog example, Rayne was an instance of the `Dog` class as shown in Figure 3.4.

Figure 3.4. A class serves as the blueprint for an object.

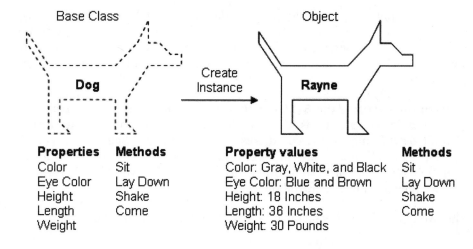

Properties	Methods	Property values	Methods
Color	Sit	Color: Gray, White, and Black	Sit
Eye Color	Lay Down	Eye Color: Blue and Brown	Lay Down
Height	Shake	Height: 18 Inches	Shake
Length	Come	Length: 36 Inches	Come
Weight		Weight: 30 Pounds	

We see that Rayne is an object of class `Dog`. In our code, we could create a new instance of the `Dog` class, call it `rayne`, and use all the properties and methods exposed by the object.

In OOP, when we create new instances of a class, we say we're **instantiating** that class. For instance (no pun intended!), if we need to programmatically create a new instance of the `Button` control class, we could write the following code:

VB.NET
```
Dim myButton As New Button()
```

C#
```
Button myButton = new Button();
```

As you can see, we've essentially created a new object called `myButton` from the `Button` class. We can then access the properties and methods that the `Button` exposes through our new instance:

VB.NET
```
myButton.Text = "Click Me!"
```

C#
```
myButton.Text = "Click Me!";
```

Scope

You should now have a concept of programming objects as entities that exist in a program and are manipulated through the methods and properties they expose. However, in some cases, we want to create methods to use inside our class, which are not available when that class is used in code. Let's return to the Dog class to illustrate.

Imagine we're writing the Sit() method inside this class, and we realize that before the dog can sit, it has to shuffle its back paws forward a little (Just bear with me on this one...)! We could create a method called ShufflePaws(), then call that method from inside the Sit() method. However, we don't want code in an ASP.NET page or in some other class to call this method—it'd just be silly. We can prevent this by controlling the **scope** of that method.

The two types of scope available in VB.NET and C# that you should know about are:

Public   Defining a property or method of a class as public allows that property or method to be called from outside the class itself. In other words, if an instance of this class is created inside another object (remember, too, that ASP.NET pages themselves are objects), public methods and properties are freely available to the code that created it. This is the default scope in VB.NET and C# classes.

Private   If a property or method of a class is private, it cannot be used from outside the class itself. If an instance of this class is created inside an object of a different class, the creating object has no access to private methods or properties of the created object.

Events

We've covered **events** fairly well already. To sum up, events occur when a control object sends a message in response to some change that has happened to it. Generally, these changes occur as the result of user interaction with the control in the browser. For instance, when a button is clicked, a Click event is raised, and we can handle that event to perform some action. The object that **triggers** the event is referred to as the **event sender**, while the object that receives the event is referred to as the **event receiver**. You'll learn more about these terms in Chapter 4.

Understanding Inheritance

The term **inheritance** refers to the ability for one class to use properties and methods exposed by another class.

In our dog example, we first created a class called `Dog`, then created instances of that class to represent individual dogs such as Rayne. However, dogs are types of animals, and many characteristics of dogs are shared by all (or most) animals. For instance, Rayne has four legs, two ears, one nose, two eyes, etc. It might be better, then, for us to create a **base class** called `Animal`. When we then define the `Dog` class, it would **inherit** from the `Animal` class, and all public properties and methods of `Animal` would be available to instances of the `Dog` class.

Similarly, we could create a new class based on the `Dog` class. In programming circles, this is called **deriving a subclass** from `Dog`. For instance, we might create a class for Australian Shepherd and one for my other dog Amigo, called Chihuahua, both of which would **inherit** the properties and methods of the `Dog` base class, and define new ones specific to each breed.

Don't worry too much if this is still a little unclear. The best way to appreciate inheritance is to see it used in a real program. The most obvious use of inheritance in ASP.NET comes with the technique of code-behind.

Separating Code From Content With Code-Behind

Most companies that employ development teams usually split projects into two groups, visual design and functional development, because software engineers are usually poor designers, and designers are often poor engineers. Until now, our ASP.NET pages have contained code render blocks that place VB.NET or C# code directly within the ASP.NET page. The problem with this approach is that there is no separation between the presentational elements of the page and the application logic. Traditional ASP was infamous for creating "spaghetti" code, which was scattered and intertwined throughout the presentation elements. This made it very tricky to manage the code between development teams, as you'll know if you've ever tried to pick apart someone else's ASP code. In response to these problems, ASP.NET introduces a new way of developing pages that allows code developers to work separately from the presentational designers who lay out individual pages.

This new method, called **code-behind**, keeps all of your presentational elements (controls) inside the `.aspx` file, but moves all your code to a separate class in a `.vb` or `.cs` code-behind file. Consider the following ASP.NET page, which displays a simple button and label:

VB.NET

```
<html>
<head>
  <title>Sample Page using VB.NET</title>
  <script runat="server" language="VB">
    Sub Click(s As Object, e As EventArgs)
      lblMessage.Text = "Hello World"
    End Sub
  </script>
</head>

<body>
  <form runat="server">
    <asp:Button id="btnSubmit" Text="Click Me" runat="server"
      OnClick="Click" />
    <br /><br /><asp:Label id="lblMessage" runat="server" />
  </form>
</body>
</html>
```

C#

```
<html>
<head>
  <title>Sample Page using C#</title>
  <script runat="server" language="C#">
    void Click(Object s, EventArgs e) {
      lblMessage.Text = "Hello World";
    }
  </script>
</head>

<body>
  <form runat="server">
    <asp:Button id="btnSubmit" Text="Click Me" runat="server"
      OnClick="Click" />
    <br /><br /><asp:Label id="lblMessage" runat="server" />
  </form>
</body>
</html>
```

Let's see how this example could be separated into the following two distinct files:

sample.aspx   layout, presentation, and static content

sample.vb
sample.cs   code-behind files containing a custom page class

First, we take all the code and place it in the code-behind file (sample.vb or sample.cs). This file is a pure code file, and contains no HTML or other markup tags. What it *does* contain is a class definition. Nevertheless, we can still access presentation elements from this file, using their IDs, such as lblMessage:

VB.NET   File: **sample.vb**

```
' First off we import some useful namespaces
Imports System
Imports System.Web.UI
Imports System.Web.UI.WebControls

' All code-behind classes generally inherit from Page
Public Class Sample
  Inherits Page

  ' Declare the presentation elements on the ASPX page
  Protected WithEvents lblMessage As Label
  Protected WithEvents btnSubmit As Button

  ' Here's the Click handler just as it appeared before
  Sub Click(s As Object, e As EventArgs)
    lblMessage.Text = "Hello World"
  End Sub
End Class
```

C#   File: **sample.cs**

```
// First off we import some useful namespaces
using System;
using System.Web.UI;
using System.Web.UI.WebControls;

// All code-behind classes generally inherit from Page
public class Sample : Page
{
  // Declare the presentation elements on the ASPX page
  protected Label lblMessage;
  protected Button btnSubmit;
```

```
// Here's the Click handler just as it appeared before
public void Click(Object s, EventArgs e) {
  lblMessage.Text = "Hello World";
}
}
```

Without code, the main ASP.NET page becomes much simpler:

VB.NET   File: **sample.aspx**

```
<%@ Page Inherits="Sample" Src="Sample.vb" %>
<html>
<head>
  <title>Sample Page using VB.NET</title>
</head>

<body>
  <form runat="server">
    <asp:Button id="btnSubmit" Text="Click Me" runat="server"
      OnClick="Click" />
    <br /><br /><asp:Label id="lblMessage" runat="server" />
  </form>
</body>
</html>
```

C#   File: **sample.aspx**

```
<%@ Page Inherits="Sample" Src="Sample.cs" %>
<html>
<head>
  <title>Sample Page using C#</title>
</head>

<body>
  <form runat="server">
  <asp:Button id="btnSubmit" Text="Click Me" runat="server"
    OnClick="Click" />
  <br /><br /><asp:Label id="lblMessage" runat="server" />
  </form>
</body>
</html>
```

As you can see, the only line that's different between the .aspx pages is the Page directive:

VB.NET   File: **sample.aspx (excerpt)**

```
<%@ Page Inherits="Sample" Src="Sample.vb" %>
```

C#   File: **sample.aspx (excerpt)**

```
<%@ Page Inherits="Sample" Src="Sample.cs" %>
```

The only real change between the VB.NET and C# versions of the page is the source filename extension. In both cases, the page **inherits** from the class `Sample`.

The code-behind file is written differently from what you're used to seeing so far. While we no longer need `<script>` tags, we find a class definition in its place. Looking at the VB.NET example, we start with three lines that import namespaces to be used in the code:

VB.NET   File: **sample.vb (excerpt)**

```
Imports System
Imports System.Web.UI
Imports System.Web.UI.WebControls
```

The next lines create a new class, named `Sample`. Because our code-behind page contains code for an ASP.NET page, our class inherits from the `Page` class:

VB.NET   File: **sample.vb (excerpt)**

```
Public Class Sample
  Inherits Page
```

This is the practical application of inheritance that I mentioned above. Instead of using the built-in `Page` class, the code-behind method has you derive a subclass of `Page` for each page in your site. Next, we have to declare the controls that we want to use from the `.aspx` page—if we forget this step, we won't be able to access them from our code:

VB.NET   File: **sample.vb (excerpt)**

```
  Protected WithEvents lblMessage As Label
  Protected WithEvents btnSubmit As Button
```

Finally, we create the `Click` subroutine just as before, and terminate the class:

VB.NET   File: **sample.vb (excerpt)**

```
  Sub Click(s As Object, e As EventArgs)
     lblMessage.Text = "Hello World"
  End Sub
End Class
```

As I hope you can see, code-behind files are reasonably easy to work with, and they can make managing and using our pages much more straightforward. On a typical project, I tend to use code-behind files quite frequently, but for simplicity's sake, we'll stick with code declaration blocks for at least the next few chapters.

Summary

Phew! That's quite a few concepts to understand over the course of a single chapter. Don't worry—with a little practice, these concepts will become second nature. I hope you leave this chapter with a basic understanding of programming concepts as they relate to the Web developer. The next chapter will begin to put all the concepts that we've covered so far into practice, beginning by covering HTML Controls, Web Forms, and Web Controls, before launching into our first hands-on project.

4

Web Forms and Web Controls

At the heart of ASP.NET is its ability to create dynamic form content. Whether you're creating a complex shopping cart application, or a simple page to collect user information and send the results out via email, Web Forms have a solution. They allow you to use HTML controls and Web controls to create dynamic pages with which users can interact. In this chapter, you will learn how Web Forms, HTML controls, and Web controls, in conjunction with VB.NET and C# code, should change the way you look at, and develop for, the Web. In this chapter I'll introduce you to the following concepts:

❑ HTML controls

❑ Web Forms

❑ Web controls

❑ Handling page navigation

❑ Formatting controls with CSS

Toward the end of the chapter, you'll put all of these concepts to work into a real world application! I'll introduce the Dorknozzle Intranet Application that you'll be building throughout this book, and see how what you learned in this chapter can be applied to some of the pages for the project.

Working with HTML Controls

HTML controls are outwardly identical to plain old HTML 4.0 tags, but employ the `runat="server"` attribute. For each of HTML's most common tags, a corresponding server-side HTML control exists, although Microsoft has added a few tags and some extra properties for each. Creating HTML controls is easy—we simply stick a `runat="server"` attribute on the end of a normal HTML tag to create the HTML control version of that tag. The complete list of current HTML control classes and their associated tags is given in Table 4.1.

These HTML control classes are all contained within the `System.Web.UI.HtmlControls` namespace.

Because HTML controls are processed on the server side by the ASP.NET runtime, we can easily access their properties through code elsewhere in the page. If you're familiar with JavaScript, HTML, and CSS, then you'll know that manipulating text within HTML tags, or even manipulating inline styles within an HTML tag, can be cumbersome and error-prone. HTML controls aim to solve this by allowing you to manipulate the page easily with your choice of .NET language, for instance, using VB.NET or C#. We'll start by looking at the HTML controls library, then we'll explore in more detail the properties exposed by the controls when we process a simple form containing HTML controls and code.

Table 4.1. HTML Control Classes

Class	Associated Tags
HtmlAnchor	`<a href="…" runat="server">`
HtmlButton	`<button runat="server">`
HtmlForm	`<form runat="server">`
HtmlImage	`<img runat="server">`

HtmlInputButton	`<input type="submit" runat="server">`
	`<input type="reset" runat="server">`
	`<input type="button" runat="server">`

HtmlInputCheckBox	`<input type="checkbox" runat="server">`
HtmlInputFile	`<input type="file" runat="server">`
HtmlInputHidden	`<input type="hidden" runat="server">`
HtmlInputImage	`<input type="image" runat="server">`
HtmlInputRadioButton	`<input type="radio" runat="server">`
HtmlInputText	`<input type="text" runat="server">`
HtmlSelect	`<select runat="server">`
HtmlTable	`<table runat="server">`
HtmlTableRow	`<tr runat="server">`
HtmlTableCell	`<td runat="server">` `<th runat="server">`
HtmlTextArea	`<textarea runat="server">`

HtmlGenericControl	All other HTML tags, including
	
	`<span runat="server">`
	`<div runat="server">`
	`<body runat="server">`
	`<font runat="server">`

HtmlAnchor

The HtmlAnchor control creates a server-side HTML `<a href="…">` tag.

```
<a href="somepage.aspx" runat="server">Click Here</a>
```

This line would create a new hyperlink with the text "Click Here." Once the link is clicked, the user would be redirected to `somepage.aspx` as given by the `href` attribute.

HtmlButton

The `HtmlButton` control creates a server-side HTML `<button>` tag.

```
<button id="myButton" OnServerClick="Click" runat="server">Click
Here</button>
```

Notice that we're using events here. On HTML controls, we need to use `OnServer-Click` to specify the ASP.NET handler for clicks on the button, because `onclick` is reserved for handling clicks with JavaScript on the client side. In this example, the handler subroutine is called `Click`, and would be declared in a script block with the same form as the `Click` handlers we looked at for `<asp:Button>` tags previously:

VB.NET
```
<script runat="server" language="VB">
Sub Click(s As Object, e As EventArgs)
  Response.Write(myButton.ID)
End Sub
</script>
```

C#
```
<script runat="server" language="C#">
void Click(Object s, EventArgs e) {
  Response.Write(myButton.ID);
}
</script>
```

In this case, when the user clicks the button, the `ServerClick` event is raised, the `Click()` subroutine is called to handle it, and the ID of the `HtmlButton` control is written onto the screen with `Response.Write()` (the `Write()` method of the `Response` object).

HtmlForm

The `HtmlForm` control creates a server-side `<form>` tag. Most HTML controls, Web controls, etc., must be placed inside an `HtmlForm` control.

```
<form runat="server">
<!-- ASP.NET controls in here -->
</form>
```

HtmlImage

The `HtmlImage` control creates a server-side `<img>` tag. The following code shows how we might place an `HtmlImage` control on a page, along with an `HtmlButton`:

```
<img id="myimage" src="arrow.gif" runat="server" />
<button id="myButton" runat="server" OnServerClick="Click">Click
Here</button>
```

The user could change this image dynamically by pressing the button if we add code as follows:

VB.NET

```
<script runat="server" language="VB">
Sub Click(s As Object, e As EventArgs)
  myimage.Src = "welcome.gif"
End Sub
</script>
```

C#

```
<script runat="server" language="C#">
void Click(Object s, EventArgs e) {
  myimage.Src = "welcome.gif";
}
</script>
```

What will happen if these controls are placed on a page along with the script block? First of all, the image `arrow.gif` will appear. When the `HtmlButton` control is clicked, it changes to `welcome.gif`. Behind the scenes, the `ServerClick` event is raised when the button is clicked, thus the `Click()` subroutine is called, and the `Src` property of the `HtmlImage` control is changed from `arrow.gif` to `welcome.gif`.

HtmlGenericControl

The `HtmlGenericControl` creates a server-side control for HTML tags that do not have an HTML control associated with them. Perfect examples of this are the `<span>` and `<div>` tags. The following example illustrates how you can modify text within a <span> tag to change the content from I like ASP.NET to Why would anyone need PHP? dynamically.

```
<span id="myGenericControl" runat="server">I like ASP.NET</span>
<br />
<button id="myButton" runat="server" OnServerClick="Click">Click
Here</button>
```

We simply add the following code to respond to the ServerClick event and change the text:

VB.NET

```
<script runat="server" language="VB">
Sub Click(s As Object, e As EventArgs)
  myGenericControl.InnerText = "Why would anyone need PHP?"
End Sub
</script>
```

C#

```
<script runat="server" language="C#">
void Click(Object s, EventArgs e) {
  myGenericControl.InnerText = "Why would anyone need PHP?";
}
</script>
```

HtmlInputButton

The HtmlInputButton control creates a server-side <input type="submit">, <input type="reset">, or <input type="button"> HTML tag.

```
<input type="submit" value="Click Here" runat="server" />
```

```
<input type="reset" value="Click Here" runat="server" />
```

```
<input type="button" value="Click Here" runat="server" />
```

As with HtmlButton, you can assign a server-side event handler to controls of this type with the OnServerClick attribute.

HtmlInputCheckBox

The HtmlInputCheckBox control creates a server-side <input type="checkbox"> HTML tag.

```
<input type="checkbox" id="cb1" value="ASP.NET" runat="server"
  />ASP.NET<br />
<input type="checkbox" id="cb2" value="PHP" runat="server"
  />PHP<br />
<input type="checkbox" id="cb3" value="JSP" runat="server"
  />JSP<br />
<input type="checkbox" id="cb4" value="CGI" runat="server"
  />CGI<br />
<input type="checkbox" id="cb5" value="Coldfusion" runat="server"
  />Coldfusion<br>
```

The `HtmlInputCheckBox` control is the perfect choice when you want to allow your users to select multiple items from a list.

HtmlInputFile

The `HtmlInputFile` control creates a server-side `<input type="file">` tag in the HTML. This displays a text box and Browse button to allow users to upload files from ASP.NET pages. There is no Web control equivalent for this tag, so it's typically required when working with file uploads—even with Web Forms (which we'll discuss shortly).

```
<input type="file" id="fileUpload" runat="server" />
```

HtmlInputHidden

The `HtmlInputHidden` control creates a server-side `<input type="hidden">` tag.

```
<input type="hidden" id="hiddenField" runat="server" />
```

Try viewing the source of any one of your ASP.NET pages from your browser, and you're likely to find this tag being used to store view state information.

HtmlInputImage

The `HtmlInputImage` control creates a server-side `<input type="image">` tag.

```
<input type="image" id="imgMap" runat="server"
  src="ButtonImage.jpg" />
```

This tag provides an alternative to the `HtmlInputButton` control. They both function in the same way; the difference is that the `HtmlInputImage` control uses a custom image rather than the beveled gray Windows-style button. The mouse coordinates are also sent along with the form submission when the user clicks a control of this type.

HtmlInputRadioButton

The `HtmlInputRadioButton` control creates a server-side radio button. The following code, for instance, offers a choice of Male or Female:

```
Gender?<br />
<input type="radio" id="radio1" runat="server" />Male<br />
<input type="radio" id="radio2" runat="server" />Female
```

Similar to the `HtmlInputCheckBox` control, the `HtmlInputRadioButton` control creates a list of items for users to choose from. The difference, however, is that the user is only able to select one item at a time.

HtmlInputText

The `HtmlInputText` control creates a server-side `<input type="text">` or `<input type="password">` tag.

```
Please Login<br />
Username:<br />
<input type="text" id="username" runat="server" /><br />
Password:<br />
<input type="password" id="password" runat="server" />
```

The preceding code creates a typical login screen layout.

HtmlSelect

The `HtmlSelect` control creates a server-side version of the `<select>` tag for creating drop-down lists or list boxes. The following code creates a drop-down menu:

```
Select your favorite movie:<br />
<select id="selectMovie" runat="server">
<option>Star Wars</option>
<option>Spider Man</option>
<option>The Godfather</option>
<option>Lord of the Rings</option>
</select>
```

The following code creates a multiple-selection list box:

```
Which of these movies do you like?<br />
<select id="selectMovie" runat="server" multiple="true" size="4">
<option>Star Wars</option>
<option>Spider Man</option>
<option>The Godfather</option>
<option>Lord of the Rings</option>
</select>
```

You'll notice the `<option>` tag within the main `<select>` tag; this is used to denote each item to appear in the list box or drop-down menu.

HtmlTable, HtmlTableRow and HtmlTableCell

The `HtmlTable`, `HtmlTableRow`, and `HtmlTableCell` controls create server-side versions of the `<table>`, `<tr>`, `<td>`, and `<th>` tags. The following code creates a server-side table:

```
<table id="myTable" border="1" cellspacing="0" cellpadding="0"
runat="server">
<tr runat="server" id="row1">
<td runat="server" id="cell1">Table Data 1</td>
<td runat="server" id="cell2">Table Data 2</td>
</tr>
<tr runat="server" id="row2">
<td runat="server" id="cell3">Table Data 3</td>
<td runat="server" id="cell4">Table Data 4</td>
</tr>
</table>
<button id="myButton" OnServerClick="Click" runat="server">Click
Here</button>
```

You could add the following code to respond to the `Click` event raised by the `HtmlButton` control and change the content of the first cell to read "Hello World."

VB.NET
```
<script runat="server" language="VB">
Sub Click(s As Object, e As EventArgs)
  cell1.InnerText = "Hello World"
End Sub
</script>
```

C#

```
<script runat="server" language="C#">
void Click(Object s, EventArgs e) {
  cell1.InnerText = "Hello World";
}
</script>
```

HtmlTextArea

The `HtmlTextArea` control creates a server-side version of the `<textarea>` tag.

```
<textarea cols="60" rows="10" runat="server"></textarea>
```

We've glanced only briefly over the HTML controls, as they should all be fairly familiar from your experience with HTML. But if you'd like more information on the HTML controls including the properties, methods, and events for each, see Appendix A.

Processing a Simple Form

Now that you have a basic understanding of ASP.NET page structure, the languages VB.NET and C#, and HTML controls, let's put everything together and create a simple ASP.NET application. The application that we will create, in VB.NET and C#, will be a simple survey form that uses the following HTML controls:

- ❏ HtmlForm
- ❏ HtmlButton
- ❏ HtmlInputText
- ❏ HtmlSelect

Let's begin by creating a new file within your favorite code editor. The following code creates the visual interface for the survey:

File: **SimpleForm.aspx (excerpt)**

```
<html>
<head>
...
</head>
```

```
<body>
<form runat="server">
  <h2>Take the Survey!</h2>
  <p>Name:<br />
  <input type="text" id="txtName" runat="server" /></p>
  <p>Email:<br />
  <input type="text" id="txtEmail" runat="server" /></p>
  <p>Which server technologies do you use?<br />
  <select id="servermodel" runat="server" multiple="true">
    <option>ASP.NET</option>
    <option>PHP</option>
    <option>JSP</option>
    <option>CGI</option>
    <option>Coldfusion</option>
  </select></p>
  <p>Do you like .NET so far?<br />
  <select id="likedotnet" runat="server">
    <option selected>Yes</option>
    <option>No</option>
  </select></p>
  <p><button id="myButton" OnServerClick="Click" runat="server">
  Confirm</button></p>
</form>
</body>
</html>
```

From what we've already covered on HTML controls, you should have a good idea of what this page will look like. All we've done is place some `HtmlInputText` controls, an `HtmlButton` control, and an `HtmlSelect` control inside the obligatory `HtmlForm` control. Remember, HTML controls are essentially just HTML tags with the `runat="server"` attribute. When it's complete, the interface will resemble Figure 4.1.

Figure 4.1. Create the interface of the ASP.NET page using HTML controls.

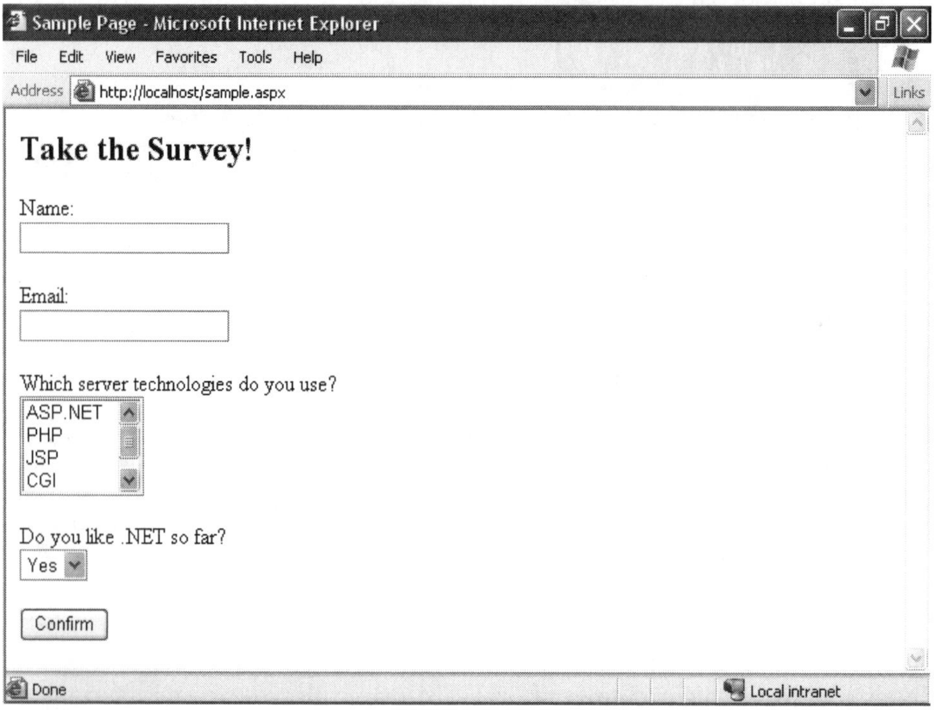

When users click the button, we'll simply display their responses in their browsers. In a real application, we'd probably be more likely to save this to a database and perhaps show the results as a chart. Whatever the case, we'd access the properties of the HTML controls as shown in the following code:

VB.NET   File: **SimpleForm.aspx (excerpt)**

```
<script runat="server" language="VB">
Sub Click(s As Object, e As EventArgs)
  Dim i As Integer
  Response.Write("Your name is: " & txtName.Value & "<br />")
  Response.Write("Your email is: " & txtEmail.Value & "<br />")
  Response.Write("You like to work with:<br />")
  For i = 0 To servermodel.Items.Count - 1
    If servermodel.Items(i).Selected Then
      Response.Write(" - " & servermodel.Items(i).Text & "<br />")
    End If
  Next i
```

```
      Response.Write("You like .NET: " & likedotnet.Value)
End Sub
</script>
```

C#   File: **SimpleForm.aspx (excerpt)**

```
<script runat="server" language="C#">
void Click(Object s, EventArgs e) {
  Response.Write("Your name is: " + txtName.Value + "<br />");
  Response.Write("Your email is: " + txtEmail.Value + "<br />");
  Response.Write("You like to work with:<br />");
  for (int i = 0; i <= servermodel.Items.Count - 1; i++) {
    if (servermodel.Items[i].Selected) {
      Response.Write(" - " + servermodel.Items[i].Text + "<br />");
    }
  }
  Response.Write("You like .NET: " + likedotnet.Value);
}
</script>
```

Just as you've seen with examples from previous chapters, we place our VB.NET and C# code inside a server-side script block within the <head> part of the page. Next, we create a new Click event handler which takes the two usual parameters. Finally, we use the Response object's Write() method to print out the user's responses within the page.

Once you've written the code, you can save your work and test the results from your browser. Enter some information and click the button. What you type in should appear at the top of the page when the button is clicked.

Introduction to Web Forms

With the inception of new technologies, there's always new terminology to master. ASP.NET is no different. With ASP.NET, even the simplest terms that were previously used to describe a Web page have changed to reflect the processes that occur within them. Before we begin to describe the process followed by Web Forms, let's discuss the foundation concept of Web pages.

On the most basic level, a **Web page** is a text file that contains markup. Web pages are meant to be viewed from a browser window, which parses the file containing markup to present the information to the user in the layout envisaged by the developer. Web pages can include text, video, sound, animations, graphics, and even chunks of "code" from a variety of technologies.

An **HTML form**, as you learned in the previous sections, is a page that contains one or more form elements grouped together within an HTML <form> tag. Users interact with the various form elements to make certain choices, or provide certain information; this information is then sent to the server for processing upon the click of a submit button. This is useful to us as ASP.NET developers because regular HTML forms have a built-in mechanism that allows forms to be submitted to the server. Once the form has been submitted, some kind of extra technology—in this case, ASP.NET—needs to be present on the server to perform the actual form processing.

In ASP.NET, we call Web pages **Web Forms**; they contain presentational elements (ASP.NET Web controls) in an HTML form, as well as any code (the processing logic) we've added for the page's dynamic features.

A typical Web Form is shown in Figure 4.2:

Figure 4.2. A Web Form contains code for processing logic and Web controls for presentational purposes.

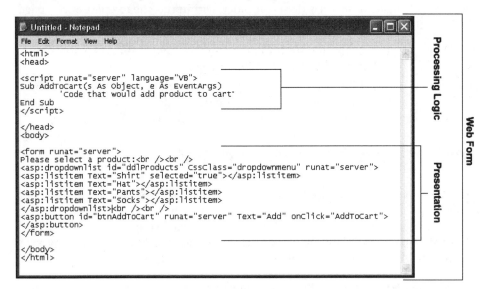

The next section looks at the various Web controls and how they may be used within your Web Forms. They're very similar in appearance to HTML, so you shouldn't have any trouble coming to grips with them.

Introduction to Web Controls

As we've just seen, Web Forms allow users to interact with our site using **Web controls**. With Web controls, Microsoft basically reinvented HTML from scratch. For example, it created two different Web controls that correspond to the two different versions of the HTML `<select>` tag: a `DropDownList` control and a `ListBox` control. This means there isn't a direct one-to-one correspondence between the Web controls and standard HTML tags, as there is with HTML controls. Web controls follow the same basic pattern as HTML tags, but the tag name is preceded by `asp:` and the name is capitalized using "CamelCasing." Consider the HTML `<input>` tag, which creates an input text box on screen:

```
<input type="text" name="username" size="30" />
```

The equivalent Web control is the `TextBox` control, and it would look like this:

```
<asp:TextBox id="username" Columns="30" runat="server">
</asp:TextBox>
```

Note that, unlike many HTML tags, Web controls always require a closing tag (the `</asp:TextBox>` part above). We can also use the shorthand `/>` syntax if our Web control tag doesn't contain anything between its opening and closing tags. So, we could also write this `TextBox` like so:

```
<asp:TextBox id="username" Columns="30" runat="server" />
```

To sum up, the key points to remember when working with Web controls are:

❑ All Web controls must be placed within a `<form runat="server">` tag to function properly.

❑ All Web controls require `id` and `runat="server"` properties to function properly.

❑ All Web controls follow the same pattern, but different properties (attributes) are available to different controls.

❑ They all start with the `asp` prefix, followed by a colon.

There are more Web controls than HTML controls, and some offer advanced features that simply aren't available in HTML alone. Controls that we'll discuss in this and future chapters are as follows:

❏ basic Web controls (Chapter 4)

❏ validation Web controls (Chapter 5)

❏ data controls (Chapter 9)

❏ user controls (Chapter 16)

❏ rich controls (Chapter 16)

Basic Web Controls

The basic Web controls perform the on-screen layout of a Web page, and mirror in many ways the HTML controls that are based on regular HTML. However, they offer some new refinements and enhancements, and should be used in place of HTML whenever possible. In this section, we'll look at the controls in this group, namely:

❏ `Label`

❏ `TextBox`

❏ `Button`

❏ `Image`

❏ `ImageButton`

❏ `LinkButton`

❏ `HyperLink`

❏ `RadioButton`

❏ `RadioButtonList`

❏ `CheckBox`

❏ `CheckBoxList`

❏ `DropDownList`

❏ `ListBox`

☐ Panel

☐ PlaceHolder

Label

The easiest way to display static text on your page is simply to add the text to the body of the page without enclosing it in any tag. However, if you want to modify the text displayed on a page from ASP.NET code, you can display your text within a **Label** control. Here's a typical example:

```
<asp:Label id="lblMessage" Text="" runat="server" />
```

The following code sets the **Text** property of the **Label** control to display the text "Hello World":

```
VB.NET
Public Sub Page_Load()
  lblMessage.Text = "Hello World"
End Sub
```

```
C#
public void Page_Load() {
  lblMessage.Text = "Hello World";
}
```

Reading this **Page_Load()** handler code, we can see that when the page first loads, the **Text** property of the **Label** control with the ID of **lblMessage** will be set to "Hello World."

TextBox

The **TextBox** control is used to create on screen a box in which the user can type or read standard text. This Web control can be set to display a standard HTML text input field, an HTML password field, or an HTML text area, using the **TextMode** property. The following code shows how we might use it in a simple login page:

```
<p>Username:
<asp:TextBox id="txtUser" TextMode="SingleLine" Columns="30"
    runat="server" /></p>

<p>Password:
<asp:TextBox id="txtPassword" TextMode="Password" Columns="30"
```

```
    runat="server" /></p>

<p>Comments:
<asp:TextBox id="txtComments" TextMode="MultiLine" Columns="30"
    Rows="10" runat="server" /></p>
```

In each of the three instances above, the attribute `TextMode` dictates the kind of text box to render.

Button

By default, the `Button` control renders the same form submit button that's rendered by the HTML `<input type="Submit">` tag. When a button is clicked, the form containing the button is submitted to the server for processing, and both click and command events are raised. The following code displays a `Button` control and a `Label`:

```
<asp:Button id="btnSubmit" Text="Submit" runat="server"
    OnClick="WriteText" />
<asp:Label id="lblMessage" runat="server" />
```

Notice the `OnClick` attribute on the control. Unlike the `HtmlButton` HTML control, `OnClick` assigns a *server-side* event handler—there is no need to remember to use `OnServerClick`. When the button is clicked, the `Click` event is raised and the `WriteText()` subroutine is called. The `WriteText()` subroutine will contain the code that performs the intended function for this button, such as displaying a message for the user:

VB.NET
```
Public Sub WriteText(s As Object, e As EventArgs)
    lblMessage.Text = "Hello World"
End Sub
```

C#
```
public void WriteText(Object s, EventArgs e) {
    lblMessage.Text = "Hello World";
}
```

It's important to realize that most Web controls have events associated with them, and the basic idea and techniques are the same as for the `Click` event of the `Button` control.

Image

An Image control places on the page an image that can be accessed dynamically from code; it equates to the `<img>` tag in HTML. Here's an example:

```
<asp:Image id="myImage" ImageUrl="mygif.gif" runat="server"
    AlternateText="description" />
```

ImageButton

An ImageButton control is similar to a Button control, but it uses an image you supply in place of the typical gray Windows-style button. For example:

```
<asp:ImageButton id="myImgButton" ImageUrl="myButton.gif"
    runat="server" />
```

LinkButton

A LinkButton control renders a hyperlink on your page. From the point of view of ASP.NET code, LinkButtons can be treated in much the same way as buttons, hence the name.

```
<asp:LinkButton id="myLinkButton" Text="Click Here" runat="server"
    />
```

HyperLink

The HyperLink control, which is similar to the LinkButton control, creates a hyperlink on your page. It's simpler and faster to process than LinkButton, but, unlike the LinkButton control, which offers features such as Click events and validation, HyperLink can be used only to click and navigate from one page to the next.

```
<asp:HyperLink id="myLink" NavigateUrl="http://www.example.com/"
    ImageUrl="myButton.gif" runat="server">My Link</asp:HyperLink>
```

The ImageUrl attribute, if specified, causes the control to display a linked image instead of the text provided.

RadioButton

You can add individual radio buttons to your page one by one, using the RadioButton control. Radio buttons are grouped together using the GroupName property. Only one RadioButton control from each group can be selected at a time.

```
<asp:RadioButton id="radSanDiego" GroupName="City"
    Text="San Diego" runat="server" />
<asp:RadioButton id="radBoston" GroupName="City" Text="Boston"
    runat="server" />
<asp:RadioButton id="radPhoenix" GroupName="City" Text="Phoenix"
    runat="server" />
<asp:RadioButton id="radSeattle" GroupName="City" Text="Seattle"
    runat="Server" />
```

The main event associated with RadioButtons is the CheckChanged event; which can be handled with the OnCheckChanged attribute.

RadioButtonList

Like the RadioButton control, the RadioButtonList control represents radio buttons. However, the RadioButtonList control represents a list of radio buttons and uses more compact syntax. Here's an example:

```
<asp:RadioButtonList id="radlFavColor" runat="server">
  <asp:ListItem Text="Red" Value="red" />
  <asp:ListItem Text="Blue" Value="blue" />
  <asp:ListItem Text="Green" Value="green" />
</asp:RadioButtonList>
```

One of the great features of the RadioButtonList is its ability to **bind** to a data source. For instance, imagine you have a list of employees in a database. You could create a page that binds a selection from that database to the RadioButtonList control, to list dynamically certain employees within the control. The user would then be able to select one (and only one) employee from that list, and our code could determine the choice.

The most useful event produced by RadioButtonList is the SelectedIndexChanged event, to which you can assign a handler with the OnSe-lectedIndexChanged attribute

CheckBox

You can use a CheckBox control to represent a choice that can be only a yes (checked) or no (unchecked) value.

```
<asp:CheckBox id="chkQuestion" Text="I like .NET!" runat="server"
  />
```

As with the RadioButton control, the main event associated with a CheckBox is the CheckChanged event; which can be handled with the OnCheckChanged attribute.

CheckBoxList

As you may have guessed, the CheckBoxList control represents a group of check boxes; it's equivalent to using several CheckBox controls in row:

```
<asp:CheckBoxList id="chklFavDrinks" runat="server">
  <asp:ListItem Text="Pizza" Value="pizza" />
  <asp:ListItem Text="Tacos" Value="tacos" />
  <asp:ListItem Text="Pasta" Value="pasta" />
</asp:CheckBoxList>
```

Like the RadioButtonList control, the CheckBoxList control has the capability to bind to a data source, and produces a SelectedIndexChanged event that you can handle with OnSelectedIndexChanged.

DropDownList

A DropDownList control is similar to the HTML <select> tag. The DropDownList control allows you to select one item from a list using a drop-down menu.

```
<asp:DropDownList id="ddlFavColor" runat="server">
  <asp:ListItem Text="Red" value="red" />
  <asp:ListItem Text="Blue" value="blue" />
  <asp:ListItem Text="Green" value="green" />
</asp:DropDownList>
```

As is the case with other collection-based controls, such as the CheckBoxList and RadioButtonList controls, the DropDownList control can be bound to a database, thus allowing you to extract dynamic content into a drop-down menu. The main event produced by this control, as you might expect, is SelectedIndexChanged, handled with OnSelectedIndexChanged.

ListBox

A ListBox control equates to the HTML <select> tag with the size attribute set to 2 or more. The ListBox control allows you to select items from a multiline menu. If you set the `SelectionMode` attribute to `Multiple`, the user will be able to select more than one item from the list, as in this example:

```
<asp:ListBox id="listTechnologies" runat="server"
    SelectionMode="Multiple">
  <asp:ListItem Text="ASP.NET" Value="aspnet" />
  <asp:ListItem Text="JSP" Value="jsp" />
  <asp:ListItem Text="PHP" Value="php" />
  <asp:ListItem Text="CGI" Value="cgi" />
  <asp:ListItem Text="Coldfusion" Value="cf" />
</asp:ListBox>
```

Again, because the `ListBox` control is a collection-based control, it can be dynamically bound to a data source. The most useful event that this control provides is—you guessed it—`SelectedIndexChanged`, with the corresponding `OnSelectedIndexChanged` attribute.

Panel

The `Panel` control functions similarly to the `<div>` tag in HTML, in that the set of items that resides within the tag can be manipulated as a group. For instance, the `Panel` could be made visible or hidden by a `Button`'s `Click` event:

```
<asp:Panel id="pnlMyPanel" runat="server">
  <p>Username:
    <asp:TextBox id="txtUsername" Columns="30" runat="server" />
  </p>
  <p>Password:
    <asp:TextBox id="txtPassword" TextMode="Password"
        Columns="30" runat="server" /></p>
</asp:Panel>

<asp:Button id="btnHide" Text="Hide Panel" OnClick="HidePanel"
    runat="server" />
```

The code above creates two `TextBox` controls within a `Panel` control. The `Button` control is outside of the panel. The `HidePanel()` subroutine would then control the `Panel`'s visibility by setting its `Visible` property to `False`:

VB.NET

```
Public Sub HidePanel(s As Object, e As EventArgs)
  pnlMyPanel.Visible = False
End Sub
```

```
C#
public void HidePanel(Object s, EventArgs e) {
  pnlMyPanel.Visible = false;
}
```

In this case, when the user clicks the button, the `Click` event is raised and the `HidePanel()` subroutine is called, which sets the `Visible` property of the `Panel` control to `False`.

PlaceHolder

The `PlaceHolder` control lets us add elements at a particular place on a page at any time, dynamically, through code.

```
<asp:PlaceHolder id="phMyPlaceHolder" runat="server" />
```

The following code dynamically adds a new `HtmlButton` control within the place holder.

```
VB.NET
Public Sub Page_Load()
  Dim btnButton As HtmlButton = New HtmlButton()
  btnButton.InnerText = "My New Button"
  phMyPlaceHolder.Controls.Add(btnButton)
End Sub
```

```
C#
public void Page_Load() {
  HtmlButton btnButton = new HtmlButton();
  btnButton.InnerText = "My New Button";
  phMyPlaceHolder.Controls.Add(btnButton);
}
```

That's it for our quick tour of the basic Web controls. For more information on Web controls, including the properties, methods, and events for each, have a look at Appendix B.

Handling Page Navigation

Links from page to page are what drives the Web. Without linking, the Web would be little more than a simple page-based information source. Links enable us to move effortlessly from page to page with a single click; they bridge the gaps between related ideas, regardless of the boundaries imposed by geography and politics. This section focuses on page navigability using:

❏ the `HyperLink` control

❏ navigation objects and their methods

Suppose for a minute that you have created a Website that allows your users to choose from a selection of items on one page. You could call this page `viewcatalog.aspx`. Imagine that you have a second page, called `viewcart.aspx`. Once users select an item from `viewcatalog.aspx`, you'd probably want to link them directly to `viewcart.aspx` so that they can keep track of their orders. To achieve this, we clearly must pass the information from the `viewcatalog.aspx` page over to the `viewcart.aspx` page.

Using The `HyperLink` Control

The `HyperLink` control creates a simple HTML hyperlink on a page. Once it's clicked, the user is redirected to the page specified by the `NavigateUrl` property. For instance:

```
<asp:HyperLink id="hlAddToCart" NavigateUrl="viewcart.aspx"
    runat="server" Text="View Cart" />
```

Here, the `NavigateUrl` property specifies that this link leads to the page called `viewcart.aspx`. Figure 4.3 shows how the `HyperLink` control is rendered in the browser.

Figure 4.3. The `HyperLink` control renders similar to the anchor tag in the browser.

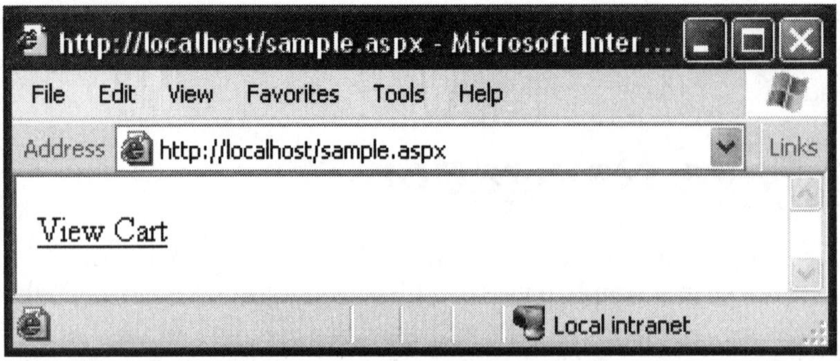

However, once we've arrived at the new page, it has no way of accessing the information from the first page. If we need to provide the user some continuity of information, we need something else.

Navigation Objects And Their Methods

The previous example rendered a simple control similar to the HTML anchor tag. Once the link is followed, however, we have no record of the previous page or any data it contained (the Web is a **stateless** technology).

If we wish to pass information from one page to the next, we can use one of the three methods listed below to create the link between the pages:

Response.Redirect()   Navigates to a second page from code. This is equivalent to using the HyperLink control, but allows us to set parameters on the query string dynamically.

Server.Transfer()   Ends the current Web Form and begins executing a new Web Form. This method only works when the user is navigating to a new Web Form page (.aspx).

Server.Execute()   Begins executing a new Web Form while displaying the current Web Form. The contents of both forms are combined in the response sent to the browser. Again, this method only works when the user is navigating to a Web Forms page (.aspx).

The easiest and quickest way to redirect your users from the viewcatalog.aspx page to the viewcart.aspx page would be using Reponse.Redirect():

```
VB.NET
Sub linkClk(s As Object, e As EventArgs)
  Response.Redirect("viewcart.aspx")
End Sub
```

```
C#
void linkClk(Object s, EventArgs e) {
  Response.Redirect("viewcart.aspx");
}
```

You could then use the LinkButton control to call this subroutine as follows:

```
<asp:LinkButton id="lbAddToCart" Text="Add To Cart"
    OnClick="linkClk" runat="server"/>
```

This time, when you click the `LinkButton` control, the `Click` event is raised, the subroutine is called, and `Response.Redirect()` is called with the name of the page we want to link to as a parameter. In this way, we're redirecting to the new page directly from the code, rather than by using a particular tag. This enables us to pass information to the new page in the **query string**.

The query string is a list of variables and their respective values that we can append to a page's URL, allowing us to retrieve those variables and values from that page's code.

As an illustration, imagine you have a drop-down list that contains the following product information:

```
<p><asp:DropDownList id="ddlProducts" runat="server">
  <asp:ListItem Text="Pants" />
  <asp:ListItem Text="Shirt" />
  <asp:ListItem Text="Hat" />
  <asp:ListItem Text="Socks" />
</asp:DropDownList></p>

<p><asp:LinkButton id="lbAddToCart" Text="Add To Cart"
    OnClick="linkClk" runat="server" /></p>
```

The code you use to handle link clicks will need to find the item selected in the drop-down list and append it to the query string of the URL to which the user is to be redirected, as follows:

```
VB.NET
Sub linkClk(s As Object, e As EventArgs)
  Dim strQueryStr As String = "?Product=" & _
    Server.UrlEncode(ddlProducts.SelectedItem.Text)
  Response.Redirect("viewcart.aspx" & strQueryStr)
End Sub
```

```
C#
void linkClk(Object s, EventArgs e) {
  string strQueryStr = "?Product=" +
    Server.UrlEncode(ddlProducts.SelectedItem.Text);
  Response.Redirect("viewcart.aspx" + strQueryStr);
}
```

Note the use of the `Server.UrlEncode()` method, which converts characters not allowed in query string values (e.g. &) to URL-safe character codes (e.g. %26) that the browser will understand. You should always use this method when adding arbitrary values to query strings.

When a user selects an item from the drop-down list and clicks the LinkButton control, the viewcart.aspx page is opened with the selected product appended as a parameter of the query string. This is illustrated in Figure 4.4.

Figure 4.4. Append the selected item to the query string.

Address http://localhost/viewcart.aspx?Product=Shirt

Now that you've passed the product to the viewcart.aspx page, you have to grab it from the query string in the new page. We get hold of variables from the query string by accessing the Request.QueryString collection, like so:

```
VB.NET
Sub Page_Load()
  lblResult.Text = Request.QueryString("Product")
End Sub
```

```
C#
void Page_Load() {
  lblResult.Text = Request.QueryString["Product"];
}
```

Here, we simply display the value of the Product query string parameter, as we see in Figure 4.5.

Figure 4.5. Set the text property of the label control within a Page_Load event handler to accept the new parameter value.

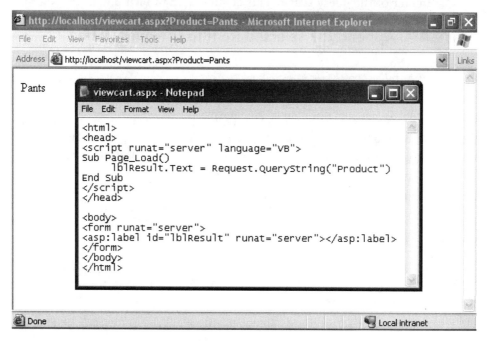

Now, when you select a product and add it to the cart, the result is displayed in the redirected page on a label with an `id` of `lblResult`. Now sure, a real product catalog and shopping cart has a lot more to it, but in this section we've uncovered an important building block.

Postback

Postback can be confusing to newcomers because, while most ASP.NET developers know what it is, they can't seem to explain it clearly. The topics we've covered so far, like subroutines, functions, and events, are not new to most Web developers. HTML, in combination with client-side JavaScript, has been doing all that for years. ASP.NET is different to this model, though, because it is a server-side, not client-side, technology—events that occur on a page are handled by code running on the server. For this to work, ASP.NET uses the mechanism of postback.

When an event is triggered, for instance, a button is clicked, or an item in a grid is selected, the page is submitted back to the server for processing, along with information about the event and any preexisting data on the page (via view state). We say the page "posts back" to the server. This is a powerful concept to grasp because it is postback that lets us run code on the server rather than on the client's browser, and it is postback that lets our server code know which items within a drop-down list were selected, or what information a user typed into a text box.

But what would happen if you had multiple DropDownList controls that were populated with database data? Users could interact with those DropDownList controls and, in turn, we could set certain options within the page based on what they selected from the drop-down menus. Although this seems like a common task, with traditional ASP it incurred considerable overhead. The problem is that while the data that's bound to the drop-down menu from the database never changes, every time the user selects an item from the drop-down menu and a postback has to be done, the database must be accessed again to rebuild the contents of each drop-down list on the page. However, this is not a problem in ASP.NET.

In ASP.NET we can check for postback with the IsPostBack property, and thus avoid performing any time consuming tasks unnecessarily. IsPostBack is a page-level property—meaning that it's a property of the page itself—and we'd most commonly use it in the Page_Load() event handler to execute code only when the page is first loaded. Consider the following example:

VB.NET   File: **PostBack.aspx**

```
<html>
<head>
<script runat="server" language="VB">
Sub Page_Load(s As Object, e As EventArgs)
  lblMessage1.Text = Now()
  If Not IsPostBack Then
    lblMessage2.Text = Now()
  End If
End Sub
</script>
</head>

<body>
<form runat="server">
  <p>Not Checking for postback:<br />
    <asp:Label id="lblMessage1" runat="server" /></p>
  <p>Checking for postback:<br />
    <asp:Label id="lblMessage2" runat="server" /></p>
```

```
  <p><asp:Button id="btnClick" Text="Click Me" runat="server" />
  </p>
</form>
</body>
</html>
```

C#   File: **PostBack.aspx**

```
<html>
<head>
<script runat="server" language="C#">
void Page_Load(Object s, EventArgs e) {
  lblMessage1.Text = Convert.ToString(DateTime.Now);
  if (!IsPostBack) {
    lblMessage2.Text = Convert.ToString(DateTime.Now);
  }
}
</script>
</head>

<body>
<form runat="server">
  <p>Not Checking for postback:<br />
    <asp:Label id="lblMessage1" runat="server" /></p>
  <p>Checking for postback:<br />
    <asp:Label id="lblMessage2" runat="server" /></p>
  <p><asp:Button id="btnClick" Text="Click Me" runat="server" />
  </p>
</form>
</body>
</html>
```

The result will look similar to Figure 4.6.

Figure 4.6. The IsPostBack property checks to make sure the user isn't resubmitting the page.

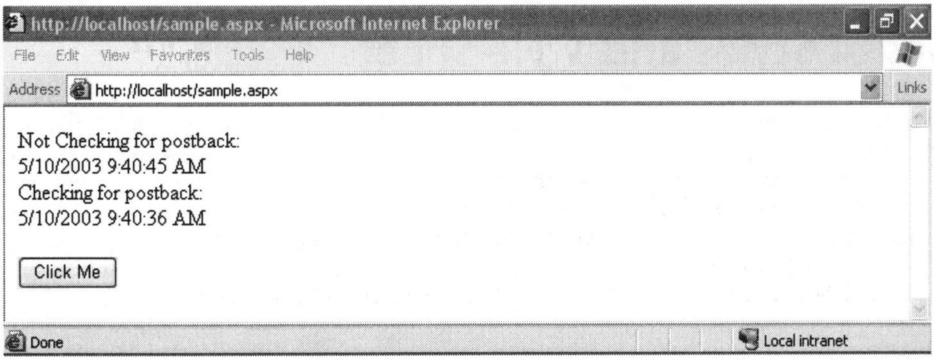

In this example, the IsPostBack check means that the second label doesn't refresh when the Button control is clicked. Similarly, we could use IsPostBack within the Page_Load() subroutine to set up database-driven drop-down menus just once within each user's session, making the online experience smoother, and making our application more scalable. Don't worry if postback seems a bit confusing now—we'll use it more in upcoming chapters, so if it doesn't yet, it should make sense after a few more practical examples.

Formatting Controls with CSS

HTML was deliberately designed to pay little attention to the specifics of how particular items on a page were rendered. It is left up to the individual browser to work out these intricacies, and tailor the output to the limitations and strengths of the user's machine. While we can change font styles, sizes, colors, and so on using HTML tags, this is a practice that can lead to verbose code and pages that are very hard to restyle at a later date.

The **Cascading Style Sheets (CSS)** language aims to provide the degree of control, flexibility, and pizzazz that modern Web designers seek. It's a standard that's widely supported by all the popular browsers, in its oldest version (CSS1) at the very least.

CSS is a powerful tool for Web developers because it gives us the power to create one set of styles in a single sheet, and apply those styles to all the pages in our Website. All the pages then use the same fonts, colors, and sizes for the same sections, giving the site a consistent feel throughout. Regardless of whether our site contains three pages or three hundred, when we alter the styles in the style sheet, those changes are immediately applied to all pages based on that style sheet.

Types of Styles and Style Sheets

There are three different ways of associating styles to elements of a particular Web page. I've already mentioned the first, and usually the best, which is an external file:

External File   By placing your **style rules** in an external style sheet, you can link this one file to any Web pages where you want those styles to be used. This makes updating a Website's overall look a cakewalk.

Document Wide   Rather than having an external sheet, you can place style rules for a page within a `<style>` tag inside that page's head element. The problem is that we can't then use those styles in another page without typing them in again, which makes global changes to the entire site difficult to manage.

Inline   Inline styles allow us to set styles for a single tag using the `style` attribute. For instance, we might create a text box in regular HTML with a `style` attribute that draws a border around the text box like so:

```
<input type="text"
    style="border-style:groove" />
```

CSS style rules create styles that are applied to elements of a page in one of two ways[1]:

Classes   Arguably the most popular way to use styles within your pages, classes allow you to set up a custom style that will be applied to any tag or control that has a `class` attribute that matches the name of your custom style.

---

[1]This is, to some extent, a simplified view of how CSS works. For the complete story, refer to *HTML Utopia: Designing Without Tables Using CSS* (SitePoint, ISBN 0-9579218-2-9).

Tag Redefinition   Redefining a tag affects the appearance of certain standard HTML tags. For instance, the `<hr>` tag is generally given a width of 100% by default, but you could redefine the tag in CSS to have a width of 50%.

Whether you're building external, document-wide, or inline style sheets, properties for classes and tag redefinitions use the same syntax. To create a class within an external style sheet file, you'd use the following syntax:

```
.myClass {
  font-family: arial;
  font-size: 10pt;
  color: red;
}
```

This would then be saved in a file with a `.css` extension, such as `styles.css`, and linked into the Web Form with the following line in the `<head>` tag of your document:

```
<link href="styles.css" rel="stylesheet" />
```

Similarly, to define a class within a document-wide style sheet, you would use the following syntax:

```
<head>
<style type="text/css">
  .myClass {
    font-family: arial;
    font-size: 10pt;
    color: red;
  }
</style>
</head>
```

When you're using inline styles, use the following syntax:

```
<span style="font-family: arial; font-size: 10pt; color: red;">My
Stylized Text</span>
```

For inline styles, simply add all properties to the tag in question with the `style` attribute. Above, we've used the `<span>` tag, but the principle remains the same for the other tags.

Now that you have a basic understanding of some of the fundamental concepts behind CSS, let's look at the different types of styles that can be used within our ASP.NET applications.

Style Properties

There are many different types of properties that you can modify using style sheets. Below is a list of the common types:

Font	This category provides you with the ability to format text level elements, including their font face, size, decoration, weight, color, etc.
Background	This category allows you to customize backgrounds for objects and text. Modifying these values gives you control over the color, image, and whether or not you want to repeat an image.
Block	This category allows you to modify the spacing between paragraphs, lines of text, and spaces between text and words.
Box	The box category provides changes and customizations for tables. If you need to modify borders, padding, spacing, and colors on a table, row, or cell, you can modify elements within this category.
Border	This category lets you draw boxes of different colors, styles and thicknesses around page elements.
List	This category allows you to customize the way ordered and unordered lists are created.
Positioning	Modifying positioning allows you to move and position tags and controls freely.

These categories provide a list of what can generally be modified using CSS. As we progress through the book, the many types of properties will become evident.

The `CssClass` Property

Once you have defined a class in a style sheet (be it external or internal), you'll want to begin associating that class with elements in your Web Forms. You can associate classes with ASP.NET Web controls using the `CssClass` property. The following example uses classes defined within a document-wide style sheet:

```
<html>
<head>
<style type="text/css">
  .dropdownmenu {
    font-family: Arial;
    background-color: #0099FF;
  }
  .textbox {
    font-family: Arial;
    background-color: #0099FF;
    border: 1px solid;
  }
  .button {
    font-family: Arial;
    background-color: #0099FF;
    border: 1px solid;
  }
  .text {
    font-family: Arial, Helvetica, sans-serif;
    font-size: 10px;
  }
</style>
</head>

<body>
<form runat="server">
<p class="text">Please select a product:</p>
<p><asp:DropDownList id="ddlProducts" CssClass="dropdownmenu"
    runat="server">
  <asp:ListItem Text="Shirt" selected="true" />
  <asp:ListItem Text="Hat" />
  <asp:Listitem Text="Pants" />
  <asp:ListItem Text="Socks" />
</asp:DropDownList></p>
<p><asp:TextBox id="txtQuantity" CssClass="textbox" runat="server"
    /></p>
<p><asp:Button id="btnAddToCart" CssClass="button" runat="server"
    Text="Add To Cart" /></p>
```

```
</form>
</body>
</html>
```

A Navigation Menu and Web Form for the Intranet Application

Now that you have a solid foundation in HTML controls, Web Forms, Web controls, Page Interaction, Navigation, and Style Sheets, you're ready to begin working on the project that we'll build on throughout the remainder of this book. With the **Dorknozzle Intranet Application**, I hope to introduce you to real world development in simple stages, as we work through the following chapters together.

Introducing the Dorknozzle Intranet Application

While most books give you a series of simple, isolated examples to illustrate particular techniques, this book is a little different. Many of the examples provided in these pages will involve work on a single project—an intranet application for the fictional Dorknozzle company. We'll build on this application as we go along, illustrating the many different concepts that are important to developers of any type of Web application. The intranet application we'll develop will offer the following functionality:

Welcome   Displays company event information to the user of the Web application.

Helpdesk   Allows any Dorknozzle employees to submit a problem as a helpdesk ticket to an IT administrator regarding issues they experience with software, hardware, or their computer.

Employee Store   Employee stores boost company morale. By building an online store, we'll allow Dorknozzle employees to buy life-enriching items such as mugs, shirts, and mouse pads. All will proudly bear the Dorknozzle logo, of course!

Newsletter Archive   Another way to improve morale is to keep employees informed of company events and news. Each month, the Dorknozzle HR Manager will send out a company newsletter to all employees.

Employee Directory
Employees will likely want to call each other to discuss important, company-related affairs... such as last night's television viewing! The employee directory should let employees find other staff members' details.

Address Book
While the employee directory houses handy information for use by staff, the purpose of the address book is to provide more detailed information about all of the employees within the company

Admin Tools
Administrators will need a way to modify closed helpdesk tickets, delete the records of fired employees, create newly hired employees' profiles, modify information on current employees, and more. The admin tools section will provide the interface for this.

Before we can begin creating all these smaller applications, we must build the framework that will act as a template across the site. In this section, we'll accomplish the following introductory tasks for the development of our intranet application:

❏ Build the navigation menu.

❏ Create the style sheet.

❏ Design the template and Web Form for the helpdesk application.

Building the Navigation Menu

Once it's complete, our fictitious intranet application will have modules for an IT helpdesk, employee store, newsletter archive, employee directory, address book, and admin console. Obviously, we're going to need some kind of navigation menu to make those sub-applications simple to find. Throughout this chapter, we've studied numerous ways of navigating from page to page, and we could use any of these methods here. We've discussed controls such as the `Button` control, `HyperLink` control, and `LinkButton` control, and we've explored various objects and methods for navigating from code. Although all these would work to a certain degree, in this case, only one makes the most sense in terms of performance and practicality.

Before we begin, you'll want to obtain the necessary files from the code archive for this book. The files for this chapter include a starting template that you can use for this project, as well as the complete version in case you run into problems.

Because we're not submitting any data for processing, we can eliminate the `Button` and `LinkButton` controls; each involves extra work from the server in order to process the `Click` event it raises. As we only want to link from one page to the next, and don't care about performing any tasks programmatically, we can use the simpler `HyperLink` control instead. Remember, we add a `HyperLink` control to the page by inserting the following code inside the form:

```
<asp:HyperLink NavigateUrl="index.aspx" runat="server"
    Text="Home" />
```

This would add a link that showed the text "Home."

Open up your text editor and create a new file with the standard HTML tags required by ASP.NET pages, including an empty form with a `runat="server"` attribute. Inside this form, add the `HyperLink` controls for helpdesk, employee store, newsletter archive, employee directory, address book, and admin tools, like so:

File: **index.aspx (excerpt)**

```
<!-- HyperLink controls for navigation -->
<img src="Images/book_closed.gif" width="16" height="16" alt="+"
    />
<asp:HyperLink NavigateUrl="index.aspx" runat="server" Text="Home"
    />
<br />
<img src="Images/book_closed.gif" width="16" height="16" alt="+"
    />
<asp:HyperLink NavigateUrl="helpdesk.aspx" runat="server"
    Text="HelpDesk" />
<br />
<img src="Images/book_closed.gif" width="16" height="16" alt="+"
    />
<asp:HyperLink NavigateUrl="employeestore.aspx" runat="server"
    Text="Employee Store" />
<br />
<img src="Images/book_closed.gif" width="16" height="16" alt="+"
    />
<asp:HyperLink NavigateUrl="newsletterarchive.aspx" runat="server"
    Text="Newsletter Archive" />
<br />
<img src="Images/book_closed.gif" width="16" height="16" alt="+"
```

```
    />
<asp:HyperLink NavigateUrl="employeedirectory.aspx" runat="server"
    Text="Employee Directory" />
<br />
<img src="Images/book_closed.gif" width="16" height="16" alt="+"
    />
<asp:HyperLink NavigateUrl="addressbook.aspx" runat="server"
    Text="Address Book" />
<br /><br />
<img src="Images/book_closed.gif" width="16" height="16" alt="+"
    />
<asp:HyperLink NavigateUrl="admintools.aspx" runat="server"
    Text="Admin Tools" />
<!-- End HyperLink controls -->
```

Once the links have been added to the page and you've placed the
book_closed.gif file in a subdirectory called Images, you could save your work
(as index.aspx) and view the results in your browser. At this stage, however, it
would look fairly bland. What we need is a few pretty graphics to provide visual
appeal! Although modern Web design practices would have us use CSS for our
page layout and visual design, we'll resort to HTML tables here in order to stay
focused on the server-side aspects of our application.

Open index.aspx and create the following two regular (i.e. not server-side)
HTML tables at the very start of the page body:

File: **index.aspx (excerpt)**

```
<body>
<form runat="server">

<table width="100%" border="0" cellspacing="0" cellpadding="0"
    background="Images/header_bg.gif">
  <tr>
    <td><img src="Images/header_top.gif" width="450" height="142"
        alt="the official dorknozzle company intranet"
        /></td>
  </tr>
</table>

<table width="100%" border="0" cellspacing="0" cellpadding="0">
  <tr>
    <td width="157"><img src="Images/header_bottom.gif"
        width="157" height="37" alt="" /></td>
    <td></td>
```

```
  </tr>
</table>
```

We'll want to place our links in a table too. While we're there, we'll add some news items to the main index page. Open up `index.aspx` once more, and place the following HTML table around the links we've already added:

File: **index.aspx (excerpt)**

```
<table width="100%" border="0" cellspacing="0" cellpadding="10">
  <tr>
    <td valign="top" width="160">
      <!-- HyperLink controls for navigation -->
      ...
      <!-- End HyperLink controls -->
    </td>
    <td valign="top">
      <h1>Company News:</h1>
      <p>We'll add some news later.</p>
      <h1>Company Events:</h1>
      <p>We'll add company events later.</p>
    </td>
  </tr>
</table>

</form>
</body>
</html>
```

The result will look similar to Figure 4.7.

Figure 4.7. Add `HyperLink` controls for the Intranet navigation menu.

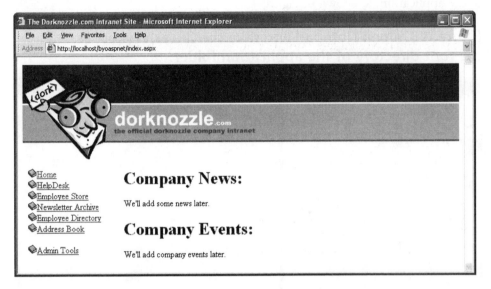

Isn't it amazing the difference some well-chosen graphics can make? Don't forget to place the pictures from the download in the `Images` subdirectory. You can, of course, find the completed source in the code archive, although I do recommend you type the code in yourself as we progress, for practice value.

Create the Corporate Style Sheet

If you don't mind the ordinary look of standard Web pages, then you can skip this section. If, however, you don't like standard blue hyperlinks, black, Times New Roman text, and beveled form controls, this section is for you.

As you've already read, style sheets provide developers with flexibility and control over the "look" of Web applications. In this section, we'll explore the addition of a customizable style sheet to our fictitious intranet application. We will define styles for the following elements within our application:

❑ Hyperlinks

❑ Text (including body text and headings)

❑ Boxed controls (including text boxes and drop-down menus)

You can start by creating the CSS file that the styles will reside in. I've opened Notepad and immediately saved the file as `styles.css` within the root directory of the application, as shown in Figure 4.8.

Figure 4.8. Open Notepad and save the file as `styles.css` within the root directory of the application folder.

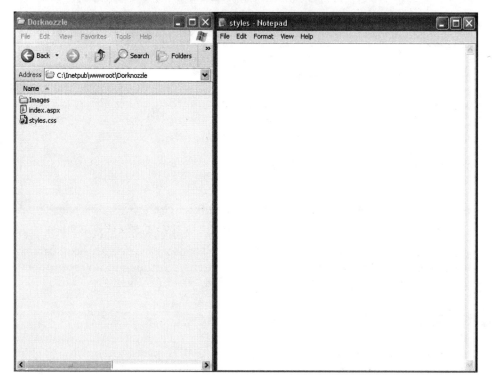

Now, let's apply some style properties to the following tags:

☐ `body`

☐ `p`

☐ `h1`

☐ `a:link`

☐ `a:hover`

You'll notice the `a:link` and `a:hover` items in this list, which are not strictly-speaking tags. In the world of CSS, these are known as a **pseudo-elements**. `a:link` narrows the selection to `<a>` tags that are links (as opposed to `<a name="…">` tags, which are targets). Assigning properties to `a:hover` will apply those properties only to links over which the user is hovering the mouse.

We'll also define a few classes for certain Web controls that don't map directly to a particular HTML tag:

.textbox	For `<asp:TextBox>` controls, which become `<input type="text">` and `<textarea>` tags when sent to the browser.
.button	For `<asp:Button>` controls, which become `<input type="button">`, `<input type="submit">`, and `<input type="reset">` tags.
.dropdownmenu	For `<asp:DropDownList>` controls, which become `<select>` tags.

Below is the code for the CSS rules that will apply the desired basic formatting to our site. Type the following just as it appears into your `styles.css` file:

```css
body {
  background: #FFFFFF;
  color: #000000;
  margin: 0;
  padding: 0;
}
p {
  font-family: Arial;
  font-size: 12px;
}
h1 {
  font-family: Arial;
  font-size: 14px;
  color: #000000;
}
a:link {
  font-family: Arial;
  font-size: 12px;
  color: #000000;
}
a:hover {
  font-family: Arial;
```

```
  font-size: 12px;
  color: #FF0000;
}
.textbox {
  font-family: Arial;
  font-size: 12px;
  border: 1px solid black;
}
.button {
  font-family: Arial;
  border: 1px solid black;
  background-color: #CCCCCC;
}
.dropdownmenu {
  font-family: Arial;
  font-size: 12px;
  background-color: #CCCCCC;
}
```

Now that the style sheet file has been created, we can link the style sheet file to index.aspx by inserting the following line into the <head> tag of the document:

```
<link href="styles.css" rel="stylesheet" />
```

We'll need to assign the CSS classes we have defined (textbox, button, and dropdownmenu) to relevant controls as we create them, but for now our simple HTML template will automatically benefit from the tags we have redefined.

Remember, we're not limited to these styles. If, throughout the development of our application, we decide to add more styles, we'll simply need to open the styles.css file and add them as necessary.

You can save your work at this point, and view it in the browser.

Design the Web Form for the Helpdesk Application

The last part of the project is to add the employee Helpdesk request Web Form. This will be a Web page that allows our fictitious employees to report hardware, software, and workstation problems. The Web Form will be arranged as a series of simple steps that users can follow to report their problems:

❑ Pick from a predefined category of potential problem areas. (`DropDownList` control)

❑ Pick from predefined subjects within the categories. (`DropDownList` control)

❑ Type a description of the problem. (Multiline `TextBox` control)

❑ Submit the request. (`Button` control)

Rather than creating a new, blank page and retyping all the code, you can simply copy `index.aspx` and rename it `helpdesk.aspx` (or save a copy with the new name if it's already open in your editor). The only portion of the code that will change to accommodate the HelpDesk interface is the last table in the body—the one that contains the news items on `index.aspx`. Everything else stays the same, because we want to have a single look for all our pages[2]. Change the final column in the table to create two drop-down lists, a multiline text box, and a button, as shown:

```
    <!-- End HyperLink controls -->
  </td>
  <td valign="top">
    <h1>Employee HelpDesk Request</h1>
    <p>Problem Category:<br />
      <asp:DropDownList id="ddlCategory" CssClass="dropdownmenu"
          runat="server" /></p>
    <p>Problem Subject:<br />
      <asp:DropDownList id="ddlSubject" CssClass="dropdownmenu"
          runat="server" /></p>
    <p>Problem Description:<br />
      <asp:TextBox id="txtDescription" CssClass="textbox"
          Columns="40" Rows="4" TextMode="MultiLine"
          runat="server" /></p>
    <p><asp:Button id="btnSubmit" CssClass="button"
          Text="Submit Request" runat="server" /></p>
  </td>
```

Notice how we've applied our CSS classes to the appropriate controls here.

Don't worry that the `DropDownList` controls don't have items associated with them—the categories and subjects will be predefined within database tables. Later, we'll bind these database tables to their respective controls.

When you're finished, save your work and view it in a browser.

---

[2]We'll see better ways to do this in later chapters...

Summary

In this chapter, we discussed HTML controls, Web Forms, and Web controls. We also explored how to link between pages, and how to add style to controls. You even built your first project, putting together the information you've learned in this and previous chapters.

Your Web application efforts will focus predominantly on Web controls. In the next chapter, we'll learn how to check user input on those Web controls through the use of the ASP.NET validation controls.

Validation Controls

Ever needed to ensure that a user typed an email address into a text box? How about making sure that a user typed numbers only into a phone number or social security number field? **Validation** involves checking that the data your application's users have entered is correct. This has historically been achieved with some sort of client-side script, such as JavaScript, and has often been problematic for Web developers.

Fortunately for you, ASP.NET provides a set of **validation controls** that ease the problems that have beset Web developers in the past! This chapter will teach you how to use them.

Client-Side vs. Server-Side Validation

Traditional ASP form validation would be accomplished in one of two ways. You could write JavaScript code (client-side) that risked becoming lengthy and unmanageable, or you could use ASP (server-side) code, and validate the user input when the form was processed on the server.

Client-side validation has its benefits—it provides instant feedback to your users. If users fail to enter their names into a text box, the page provides them with an error message immediately, without making a trip to the server. It's quick and efficient, and good for the overall user experience. However, the problems with client-side validation are twofold. First, users must have JavaScript enabled on their browsers, or validation will simply not occur. Second, the developer almost always has to write code that supports multiple versions of browsers: what works in Netscape does not necessarily work in Internet Explorer. And the headaches increase when you're developing for small form factor devices such as PDAs and phones. For this reason, developers have traditionally chosen server-side validation methods. Because server-side validation functions equally in all browsers, it is considered a safer alternative. The downside to server-side validation is the fact that the application has to make a trip to the server before the user can be alerted to any errors.

Fortunately, validation controls in ASP.NET provide client-side validation while virtually eliminating the need for developers to know JavaScript. Additionally, they do not require complex server-side scripting. To use ASP.NET validation controls you just add an object to the page, and configure some simple properties.

For example, let's take a look at a basic ASP.NET login page:

File: **RequiredFieldValidator.aspx**

```
<html>
<head>
  <title>Validation Controls Sample</title>
</head>
<body>
<form runat="server">
  <p>User name:<br />
    <asp:TextBox id="username" runat="server" /><br />
    <asp:RequiredFieldValidator id="rfvUsername"
      ControlToValidate="username"
      ErrorMessage="User name is required!" runat="server" /></p>
  <p>Password:<br />
    <asp:TextBox id="password" TextMode="Password" runat="server"
      /><br />
    <asp:RequiredFieldValidator id="rfvPassword"
      ControlToValidate="password"
      ErrorMessage="Password is required!" runat="server" /></p>
  <p><asp:Button id="btnSubmit" Text="Submit" runat="server"
      /></p>
</form>
</body>
</html>
```

Using validation controls makes the code cleaner, easier to read, and much more manageable. Figure 5.1 shows the functionality within the browser. When we click the Submit button, we receive instantly an error message that tells us we forgot to type in a user name or password.

Figure 5.1. Validation Controls streamline the way Web Controls are validated for the user.

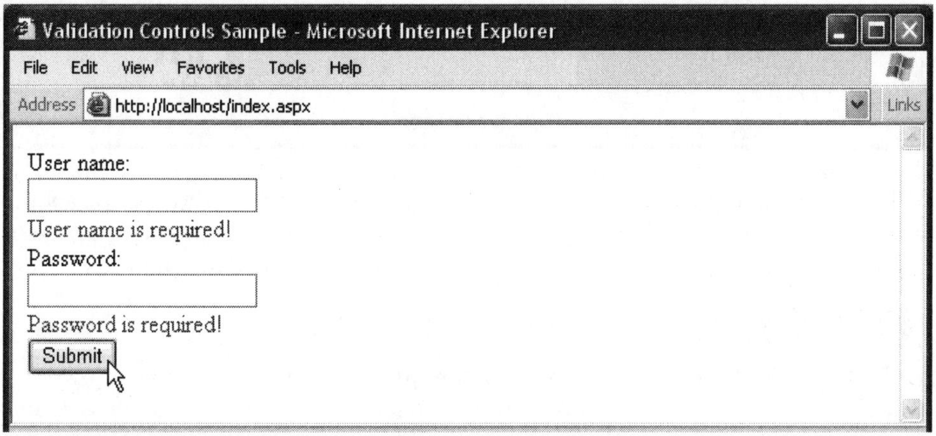

The beauty of ASP.NET validation controls is that they determine whether or not the browser is capable of supporting client-side validation[1]. If it is, ASP.NET automatically creates the necessary client-side JavaScript; if not, the form is validated on the server.

Configuring Client-Side Validation

Before we get into the actual validation controls, let's take a look at how the .NET Framework processes them. Validation controls make use of a JavaScript library that is installed automatically with the .NET Framework. The library is located in a file named WebUIValidation.js within the aspnet_client folder of your Web server's root directory. If you change the root directory of your Web server, you'll need to copy the aspnet_client folder to the new root; otherwise, you'll receive an error like that shown in Figure 5.2.

---

[1]At least in the initial versions, ASP.NET has a demonstrated tendency to assume that non-Microsoft browsers do not support client-side validation. While this is unfortunate, the backup server-side validation means that it still works on those browsers—if more slowly.

Figure 5.2. Changing the root directory of your Web server and failing to copy the `aspnet_client` folder over results in an error.

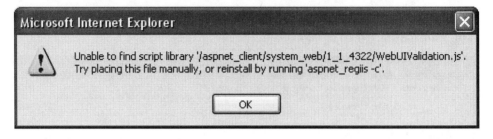

When you request a page that contains a validation control, JavaScript code is automatically sent to the browser. If you wish to disable client-side validation for some reason, simply add the following attribute to the `Page` directive:

```
<%@ Page ClientTarget="downlevel" %>
```

ASP.NET is very clever. When a page is requested from a particular browser, it will check the type and version of the browser, and what functionality it does and does not support; it then adjusts the HTML generated by the requested ASP.NET page accordingly. The above directive indicates that we should always generate HTML that's suitable for older ('downlevel') browsers, regardless of the actual browser in use. As older browsers typically offer very limited support for JavaScript, this means that client-side validation will be disabled. Unfortunately, it also means that all ASP.NET controls will be rendered using HTML 3.2, so we lose the ability to use certain features of HTML 4.0, such as style sheets and advanced JavaScript.

Thus, you may prefer to disable client-side validation for individual controls, rather than for the whole page, by setting the `EnableClientScript` property of the specific control to `False`. Similarly, we can force ASP.NET to implement our validation controls in JavaScript by setting the `ClientTarget` attribute of the `Page` directive to `uplevel`, or by setting the `EnableClientScript` property of specific controls to `True`. It's also worth noting that, even when validation is performed on the client, ASP.NET nevertheless performs server-side validation upon submission of the page. This is done to prevent hackers causing ASP.NET to accept bogus data by tricking it into thinking a form has already been validated on the client side.

Using Validation Controls

Now that you have an understanding of what validation controls can do, let's have a look at the different controls available in ASP.NET:

☐ RequiredFieldValidator

☐ CompareValidator

☐ RangeValidator

☐ ValidationSummary

☐ RegularExpressionValidator

☐ CustomValidator

Validation controls are similar to Web controls in that they are inserted as tags with the `asp:` prefix. Once a validation control is inserted, it validates an existing control elsewhere on the page, and presents an error message to the user if necessary. Can you see the benefit? All you'll ever have to do is insert a control—no JavaScript or clumsy server-side code to write by hand!

The `RequiredFieldValidator`, for example, could look something like this:

```
<asp:RequiredFieldValidator id="rfv1" ControlToValidate="txtEmail"
  ErrorMessage="You need to insert an email address!"
  runat="server" />
```

Notice two important properties of the `RequiredFieldValidator` control above. First of all, the `ControlToValidate` property specifies which Web control this validation control will validate—in this case, a control with an ID of `txtEmail`. The second property is `ErrorMessage`. This property contains the customized error message that appears in red if the user does not enter a value into the Web control with which the `RequiredFieldValidator` is associated.

Let's take a look at the ASP.NET validation controls in detail.

RequiredFieldValidator

The `RequiredFieldValidator` control is the simplest of the validation controls. It does exactly what its name says: it makes sure that a user enters a value into a Web control. Although this is the control's sole function, `RequiredFieldValidator` plays a vital role in form validation. Before you validate specifics within a control, you will, at the very least, want to check whether a user actually typed something in.

We used the `RequiredFieldValidator` control in the login page example presented earlier:

File: **RequiredFieldValidator.aspx**

```
<html>
<head>
  <title>Validation Controls Sample</title>
</head>
<body>
<form runat="server">
  <p>User name:<br />
    <asp:TextBox id="username" runat="server" /><br />
    <asp:RequiredFieldValidator id="rfvUsername"
      ControlToValidate="username"
      ErrorMessage="User name is required!" runat="server" /></p>
  <p>Password:<br />
    <asp:TextBox id="password" TextMode="Password" runat="server"
      /><br />
    <asp:RequiredFieldValidator id="rfvPassword"
      ControlToValidate="password"
      ErrorMessage="Password is required!" runat="server" /></p>
  <p><asp:Button id="btnSubmit" Text="Submit" runat="server"
      /></p>
</form>
</body>
</html>
```

As you can see, two `RequiredFieldValidator` controls are used on this page. One validates the `username` TextBox control, while the second validates the `password` TextBox control. These assignments are made using the `ControlToValidate` property of the `RequiredFieldValidator` controls. The `ErrorMessage` property contains the error message that will be displayed when the user fails to enter a value into each control.

Now, let's apply the `RequiredFieldValidator` control to the Dorknozzle Intranet helpdesk request page. We can start by identifying the controls that will require values from the user:

txtStationNum   This will be a new `TextBox` control that we'll add, al-
                          lowing the users to enter their station numbers so that
                          the IT personnel will know which computers need
                          their attention.

txtDescription   In an ideal world, users always explain their IT prob-
                          lems accurately and thoroughly, making helpdesk life
                          much easier. ASP.NET isn't yet advanced enough to
                          check for the "perfect description." However, we can
                          at least ensure the user has bothered to enter *something*
                          before we tear our beleaguered support technician
                          away from his donuts.

The `RequiredFieldValidator` control to validate the station number `TextBox`
should look like this:

File: **helpdesk.aspx (excerpt)**

```
<asp:RequiredFieldValidator id="rfvStationNum"
  ControlToValidate="txtStationNum"
  ErrorMessage="You must enter a station number!" runat="server"
  />
```

You also need a second `RequiredFieldValidator` control to validate the description `TextBox`:

File: **helpdesk.aspx (excerpt)**

```
<asp:RequiredFieldValidator id="rfvDescription"
  ControlToValidate="txtDescription"
  ErrorMessage="You must enter a description of the problem!"
  runat="server" />
```

The important properties here are the `ControlToValidate` property, which associates the `RequiredFieldValidator` control with the appropriate Web control,
and `ErrorMessage`, which displays the actual error message within the Web page.
Also, keep in mind that the error message for a validation control is displayed
where the control is placed. For this reason, you'll want to place each validation
control either beside or just below the Web control it is validating.

Once you've made these additions, the helpdesk form should resemble the following:

File: **helpdesk.aspx (excerpt)**

```
<h1>Employee HelpDesk Request</h1>
<p>Station Number:<br />
  <asp:TextBox id="txtStationNum" CssClass="textbox"
      runat="server" /><br />
  <asp:RequiredFieldValidator id="rfvStationNum"
      ControlToValidate="txtStationNum"
      ErrorMessage="You must enter a station number!"
      runat="server" /></p>
<p>Problem Category:<br />
  <asp:DropDownList id="ddlCategory" CssClass="dropdownmenu"
      runat="server" /></p>
<p>Problem Subject:<br />
  <asp:DropDownList id="ddlSubject" CssClass="dropdownmenu"
      runat="server" /></p>
<p>Problem Description:<br />
  <asp:TextBox id="txtDescription" CssClass="textbox"
      Columns="40" Rows="4" TextMode="MultiLine"
      runat="server" /><br />
  <asp:RequiredFieldValidator id="rfvDescription"
      ControlToValidate="txtDescription"
  ErrorMessage="You must enter a description of the problem!"
      runat="server" /></p>
<p><asp:Button id="btnSubmit" CssClass="button"
      Text="Submit Request" runat="server"/></p>
```

Figure 5.3 displays the result when the Submit button is clicked before the user has entered values into the station number and description text boxes.

Figure 5.3. Failing to enter required values results in an error.

CompareValidator

One of the most useful validation controls is the CompareValidator control, which performs a comparison between data entered into a TextBox control and another value. The other value can be a fixed value such as a number, a value entered into another control, or even a data type.

Let's look at an example, which builds on the login example from the previous section:

File: **CompareValidator1.aspx**

```
<html>
<head>
  <title>CompareValidator Control Sample</title>
</head>
<body>
```

```
<form runat="server">
  <p>User name:<br />
    <asp:TextBox id="username" runat="server" /></p>
  <p>Password:<br />
    <asp:TextBox id="password" TextMode="Password" runat="server"
        /><br />
    <asp:RequiredFieldValidator id="rfvPassword"
        ControlToValidate="password"
        ErrorMessage="Password is required!" runat="server" /></p>
  <p>Confirm Password:<br />
    <asp:TextBox id="confirmpassword" TextMode="Password"
        runat="server" /><br />
    <asp:RequiredFieldValidator id="rfvConfirmPassword"
        ControlToValidate="confirmpassword"
        ErrorMessage="Please confirm your password!"
        runat="server" /><br />
    <asp:CompareValidator id="cvConfirmPassword"
        ControlToCompare="password"
        ControlToValidate="confirmpassword"
        ErrorMessage="Your passwords do not match up!"
        runat="server" /></p>
  <p><asp:Button id="btnSubmit" Text="Submit" runat="server"
        /></p>
</form>
</body>
</html>
```

In this case, we added a TextBox control to allow users to confirm their password entry. By adding the CompareValidator control to the form, we're able to compare the value of the password text box with that of the confirmpassword text box, to make sure that the user has entered the same password into both. If the values do not match up, an error message similar to Figure 5.4 is presented to the user.

Figure 5.4. An error message is displayed if the values of the password and confirm password text boxes do not match up.

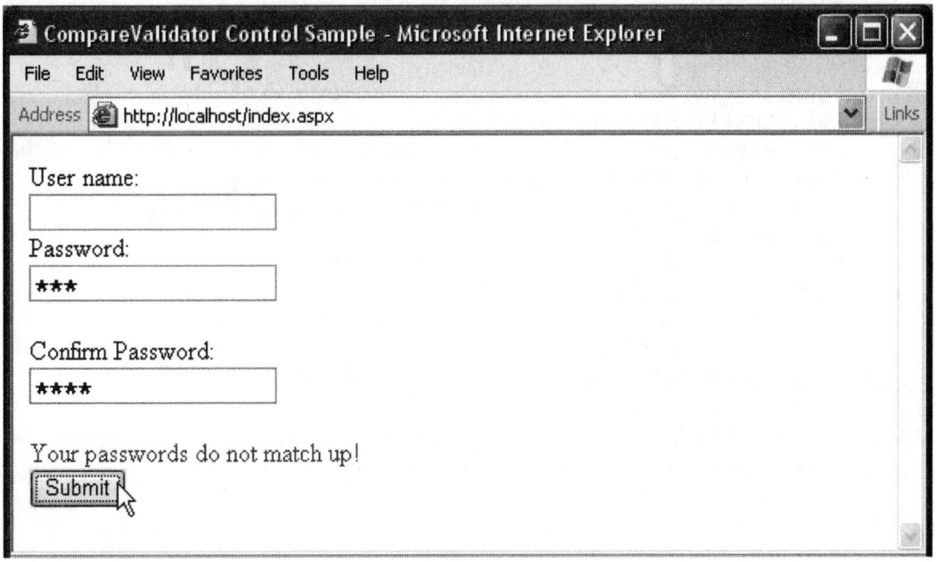

As you've probably noticed, the CompareValidator control differs very little from the RequiredFieldValidator control:

File: **CompareValidator1.aspx (excerpt)**

```
<asp:CompareValidator id="cvConfirmPassword"
    ControlToCompare="password"
    ControlToValidate="confirmpassword"
    ErrorMessage="Your passwords do not match up!"
    runat="server" /></p>
```

The only difference is that it has a ControlToCompare property, which we set to the ID of the control to which we want to compare. The ControlToValidate property is set to the confirmpassword text box, and the ControlToCompare property is set to the password text box.

We can also perform data type checks using the CompareValidator control. In the next example, the CompareValidator control is used to make sure a user types a date into the text box:

File: **CompareValidator2.aspx**

```
<html>
<head>
  <title>CompareValidator Control Sample</title>
</head>
<body>
<form runat="server">
  <p>What is your date of birth?<br />
    <asp:TextBox id="dob" runat="server" /><br />
    <asp:CompareValidator id="cvAge" Operator="DataTypeCheck"
        Type="Date" ControlToValidate="dob" runat="server"
    ErrorMessage="You must enter a date in the format mm/dd/yyyy!"
        /><br />
    <asp:Button id="btnSubmit" Text="Submit" runat="server" /></p>
</form>
</body>
</html>
```

As you can see, the `Operator` property of the control is set to perform a `DataTypeCheck`. Next, we set the `Type` property to `Date`. The result is shown in Figure 5.5.

Figure 5.5. Use the Operator and Type properties to make data type checks.

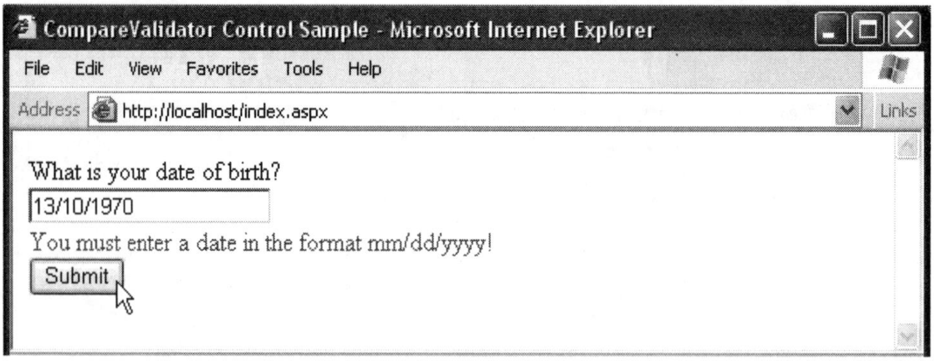

Let's try another example:

File: **CompareValidator3.aspx (excerpt)**

```
<html>
<head>
  <title>CompareValidator Control Sample</title>
```

```
</head>
<body>
<form runat="server">
  <p>What is your bid?<br />
    <asp:TextBox id="bidamount" runat="server" /><br />
    <asp:CompareValidator id="cvBid" Operator="GreaterThan"
        Type="Currency" ControlToValidate="bidamount"
        ValueToCompare="2000.00"
        ErrorMessage="You must enter a number above 2000!"
        runat="server" /><br />
    <asp:Button id="btnSubmit" Text="Submit Bid" runat="server"
        /></p>
</form>
</body>
</html>
```

In this case, the `CompareValidator` control is used to perform a currency check on a potential bid for a fictitious auction board. Here, the example sets the `Operator` property of the `CompareValidator` to `GreaterThan`. Next, we set the `Type` property to check for a `Currency`. Finally, we use the `ValueToCompare` property to make sure that the value the user enters into the text box is greater than the hard-coded value of $2,000.00.

Now, let's see how the `CompareValidator` can be used within our project. Take the `txtStationNum` Web control, for example. Because station numbers can only be whole numbers (integers), a data type check is called for.

The `CompareValidator` control used to validate the data type of the station number text box would look like this:

File: **helpdesk.aspx (excerpt)**

```
<asp:CompareValidator id="cvStationNum"
    ControlToValidate="txtStationNum"
    Operator="DataTypeCheck"
    ErrorMessage="Station number must be a number!"
    Type="Integer" runat="server" />
```

The important properties are `ControlToValidate`, which tells the `CompareValidator` control which Web control to validate; `Operator`, which indicates that the type of validation to be performed will be a data type check; `Type`, which indicates the actual data type required; and `ErrorMessage`, which provides the error message to show the user of the Web page.

The complete code at this stage looks like this:

File: **helpdesk.aspx (excerpt)**

```
<h1>Employee HelpDesk Request</h1>
<p>Station Number:<br />
  <asp:TextBox id="txtStationNum" CssClass="textbox"
      runat="server" /><br />
  <asp:RequiredFieldValidator id="rfvStationNum"
      ControlToValidate="txtStationNum"
      ErrorMessage="You must enter a station number!"
      runat="server" /><br />
  <asp:CompareValidator id="cvStationNum"
      ControlToValidate="txtStationNum"
      Operator="DataTypeCheck" Type="Integer"
      ErrorMessage="Station number must be a number!"
      runat="server" /></p>
<p>Problem Category:<br />
  <asp:DropDownList id="ddlCategory" CssClass="dropdownmenu"
      runat="server" /></p>
<p>Problem Subject:<br />
  <asp:DropDownList id="ddlSubject" CssClass="dropdownmenu"
      runat="server" /></p>
<p>Problem Description:<br />
  <asp:TextBox id="txtDescription" CssClass="textbox"
      Columns="40" Rows="4" TextMode="MultiLine"
      runat="server" /><br/>
  <asp:RequiredFieldValidator id="rfvDescription"
      ControlToValidate="txtDescription"
  ErrorMessage="You must enter a description of the problem!"
      runat="server" /></p>
<p><asp:Button id="btnSubmit" CssClass="button"
      Text="Submit Request" runat="server" /></p>
```

This time, when we enter the text "twenty five" for my station number and click the Submit button, an error message is displayed, similar to Figure 5.6.

Figure 5.6. Failing to enter the appropriate data type into a text box results in an error.

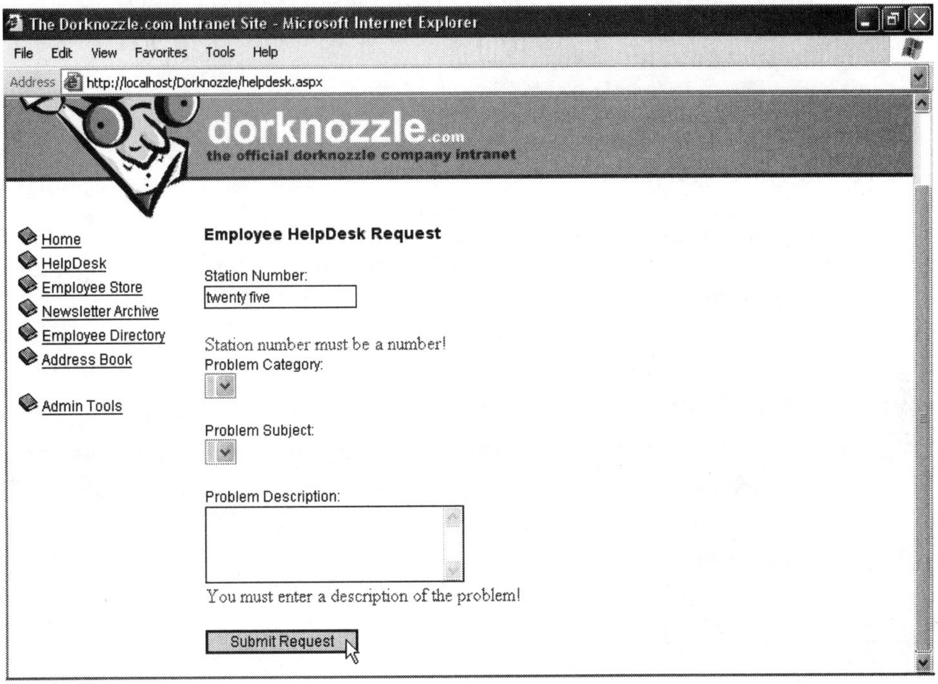

RangeValidator

The RangeValidator control checks whether the value of a form field falls between minimum and maximum values. For instance, we could make sure that users visiting our Website are within a certain age range. If they are, we will let them in; if they aren't, we could present them with an error message.

Let's take a look at an example:

File: **RangeValidator.aspx**

```
<html>
<head>
  <title>RangeValidator Control Sample</title>
</head>
<body>
<form runat="server">
  <p>What date would you like to book your space flight?<br />
```

```
    <asp:TextBox id="booking" runat="server" /><br />
    <asp:RangeValidator id="rvbooking" Type="Date"
        ControlToValidate="booking"
        MaximumValue="12/31/2008" MinimumValue="1/1/2005"
        ErrorMessage="Please enter a date between 2005 and 2008!"
        runat="server" /><br />
    <asp:Button id="btnSubmit" Text="Submit" runat="server" /></p>
</form>
</body>
</html>
```

Here, we validate a `TextBox` control with ID `booking`. Our `RangeValidator` control checks whether the value entered falls within the permitted range, and shows an error message similar to Figure 5.7 if it doesn't.

Figure 5.7. Use the `RangeValidator` control to display an error message if a value does not fall within a certain range.

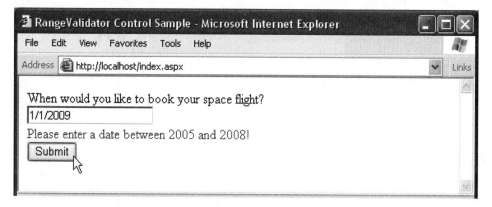

Note that the `Type` property of the `RangeValidator` control specifies the data type that's expected in the associated control.

Let's now apply the `RangeValidator` control to our helpdesk page. There's one obvious control that would be a suitable candidate for range validation: `txtStationNum`. At the moment, the user can enter any number into this box, but we want to limit it. Let's say our company only has fifty computers. Therefore, users should be able to enter only a station number that falls between one and fifty.

The following `RangeValidator` control would perform the check we need:

File: **helpdesk.aspx (excerpt)**

```
<asp:RangeValidator id="rvStationNum"
    ControlToValidate="txtStationNum"
    MinimumValue="1" MaximumValue="50"
    ErrorMessage="Number must be between 1 and 50"
    Type="Integer" runat="server" />
```

As was the case with the CompareValidator control, the RangeValidator contains four important properties. The ControlToValidate property, as you should now know, tells the RangeValidator which Web control to validate, while the ErrorMessage property contains the error message to show the user. The MinimumValue and MaximumValue properties specify the range permitted for that control. Once you've added the RangeValidator control to the page, the code should resemble the following:

File: **helpdesk.aspx (excerpt)**

```
<h1>Employee HelpDesk Request</h1>
<p>Station Number:<br />
  <asp:TextBox id="txtStationNum" CssClass="textbox"
      runat="server" /><br />
  <asp:RequiredFieldValidator id="rfvStationNum"
      ControlToValidate="txtStationNum"
      ErrorMessage="You must enter a station number!"
      runat="server" /><br />
  <asp:CompareValidator id="cvStationNum"
      ControlToValidate="txtStationNum"
      Operator="DataTypeCheck" Type="Integer"
    ErrorMessage="Station number must be a numerical value!"
      runat="server" /><br />
  <asp:RangeValidator id="rvStationNum"
      ControlToValidate="txtStationNum"
      MinimumValue="1" MaximumValue="50"
      ErrorMessage="Number must be between 1 and 50"
      Type="Integer" runat="server" /></p>
<p>Problem Category:<br />
  <asp:DropDownList id="ddlCategory" CssClass="dropdownmenu"
      runat="server" /></p>
<p>Problem Subject:<br />
  <asp:DropDownList id="ddlSubject" CssClass="dropdownmenu"
      runat="server" /></p>
<p>Problem Description:<br />
  <asp:TextBox id="txtDescription" CssClass="textbox"
      Columns="40" Rows="4" TextMode="MultiLine"
      runat="server" /><br/>
  <asp:RequiredFieldValidator id="rfvDescription"
```

```
      ControlToValidate="txtDescription"
  ErrorMessage="You must enter a description of the problem!"
      runat="server" /></p>
<p><asp:Button id="btnSubmit" CssClass="button"
      Text="Submit Request" runat="server" /></p>
```

Try viewing the new page in the browser. If you enter a value outside our range into the station number text box and move the focus away from that text box, the error is immediately reported.

You're probably beginning to notice the growing amount of space between the station number and problem category. The problem is that validation controls take up space on the page. We can remedy this situation by setting the `Display` property within the validation control to `Dynamic`, which assures us that the validation control will take up space only when the error message is being displayed. Let's do the same for all existing validation controls on our helpdesk page:

File: **helpdesk.aspx (excerpt)**

```
<h1>Employee HelpDesk Request</h1>
<p>Station Number:<br />
  <asp:TextBox id="txtStationNum" CssClass="textbox"
      runat="server" /><br />
  <asp:RequiredFieldValidator id="rfvStationNum"
      ControlToValidate="txtStationNum"
      ErrorMessage="You must enter a station number!"
      Display="Dynamic" runat="server" />
  <asp:CompareValidator id="cvStationNum"
      ControlToValidate="txtStationNum"
      Operator="DataTypeCheck" Type="Integer"
    ErrorMessage="Station number must be a numerical value!"
      Display="Dynamic" runat="server" />
  <asp:RangeValidator id="rvStationNum"
      ControlToValidate="txtStationNum"
      MinimumValue="1" MaximumValue="50"
      ErrorMessage="Number must be between 1 and 50"
      Type="Integer" Display="Dynamic" runat="server" /></p>
<p>Problem Category:<br />
  <asp:DropDownList id="ddlCategory" CssClass="dropdownmenu"
      runat="server" /></p>
<p>Problem Subject:<br />
  <asp:DropDownList id="ddlSubject" CssClass="dropdownmenu"
      runat="server" /></p>
<p>Problem Description:<br />
  <asp:TextBox id="txtDescription" CssClass="textbox"
      Columns="40" Rows="4" TextMode="MultiLine"
```

```
         runat="server" /><br/>
    <asp:RequiredFieldValidator id="rfvDescription"
        ControlToValidate="txtDescription"
   ErrorMessage="You must enter a description of the problem!"
        Display="Dynamic" runat="server" /></p>
   <p><asp:Button id="btnSubmit" CssClass="button"
        Text="Submit Request" runat="server" /></p>
```

We have also deleted the extra `<br />` tags between validation controls. When you view the page in the browser this time, you'll see that the controls do not take up space until their respective error message is shown to the user.

ValidationSummary

We'd use the `ValidationSummary` control if we wanted to present all the errors on a page in a single location. Imagine we have a form that contained 100 different form fields; if the page contains errors, it could be difficult for a user to figure out which control caused a given error, simply because the page is so big. The `ValidationSummary` control can alleviate this problem by presenting the user with a list of form fields that caused errors at one place on the page. We can even set the `ValidationSummary` control to present the user with a message box error that displays a list of form fields that caused errors.

Let's have a look at the `ValidationSummary` control in use:

File: **ValidationSummary.aspx**

```
<html>
<head>
  <title>ValidationSummary Control Sample</title>
</head>

<body>
<form runat="server">

  <p>User name:<br />
    <asp:TextBox id="username" runat="server" /><br />
    <asp:RequiredFieldValidator id="rfvUsername"
        ControlToValidate="username" Display="Dynamic"
        ErrorMessage="User name is required!" runat="server"
        /></p>

  <p>Password:<br />
    <asp:TextBox id="password" runat="server" /><br />
    <asp:RequiredFieldValidator id="rfvPassword"
```

```
            ControlToValidate="password" Display="Dynamic"
            ErrorMessage="Password is required!" runat="server" /></p>

  <p>Age:<br />
    <asp:TextBox id="age" runat="server" /><br />
    <asp:RequiredFieldValidator id="rfvage"
        ControlToValidate="age" ErrorMessage="Age is required!"
        Display="Dynamic" runat="server" />
    <asp:RangeValidator id="cvAge" MinimumValue="18"
        MaximumValue="110" Type="Integer" ControlToValidate="age"
        ErrorMessage="You are not old enough!" Display="Dynamic"
        runat="server" /></p>

  <p><asp:Button id="btnSubmit" Text="Submit" runat="server"
        /><br />
    <asp:ValidationSummary id="vsForm" runat="server" /></p>
</form>
</body>
</html>
```

When the user clicks the Submit button, the ValidationSummary presents a list of all the errors on the page as you can see in Figure 5.8.

Figure 5.8. Use the `ValidationSummary` control to display a list of errors to the user.

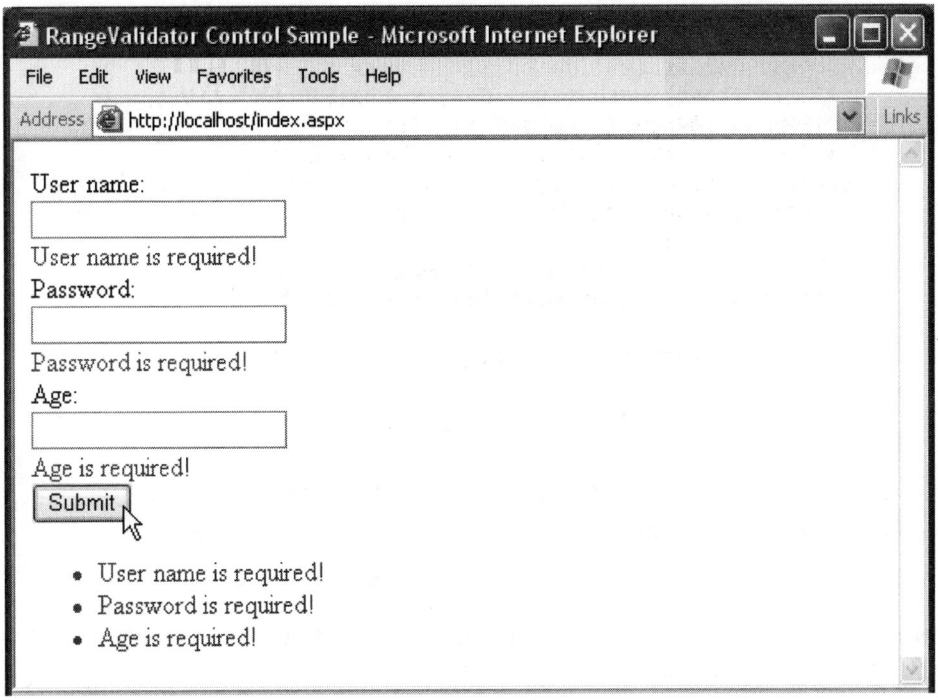

If you set the `Display` property of all the other validation controls on the page to `None`, you can use a `ValidationSummary` in this way to show all the errors in one place.

Alternatively, if you set the `ShowMessageBox` property of the `ValidationSummary` control to `True`, you'll create a message box describing the errors similar to Figure 5.9. In this case, I've also set the `ShowSummary` property to `False` to hide the in-page list of errors.

Figure 5.9. You can set the `ShowMessageBox` property to display a message box of errors to the user.

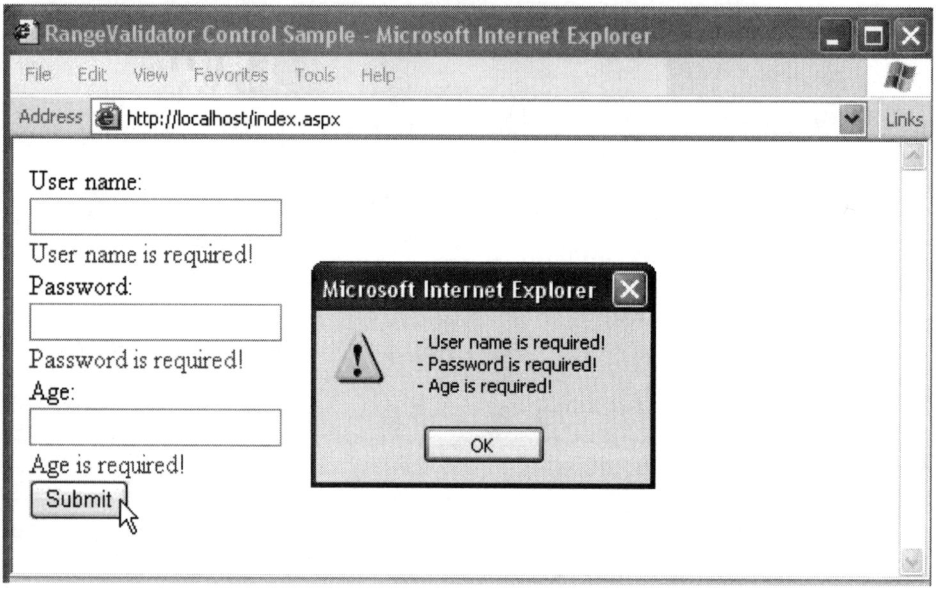

Now that you have an idea as to how the `ValidationSummary` control works, let's add it to our helpdesk form just below the Submit button :

```
<asp:validationsummary id="vsSummary" ShowMessageBox="true"
  ShowSummary="false" runat="server" />
```

When it's finished, the code should look like this:

File: **helpdesk.aspx (excerpt)**

```
<h1>Employee HelpDesk Request</h1>
<p>Station Number:<br />
  <asp:TextBox id="txtStationNum" CssClass="textbox"
      runat="server" /><br />
  <asp:RequiredFieldValidator id="rfvStationNum"
      ControlToValidate="txtStationNum"
      ErrorMessage="You must enter a station number!"
      Display="Dynamic" runat="server" />
  <asp:CompareValidator id="cvStationNum"
      ControlToValidate="txtStationNum"
      Operator="DataTypeCheck" Type="Integer"
    ErrorMessage="Station number must be a numerical value!"
```

```
            Display="Dynamic" runat="server" />
    <asp:RangeValidator id="rvStationNum"
        ControlToValidate="txtStationNum"
        MinimumValue="1" MaximumValue="50"
        ErrorMessage="Number must be between 1 and 50"
        Type="Integer" Display="Dynamic" runat="server" /></p>
<p>Problem Category:<br />
    <asp:DropDownList id="ddlCategory" CssClass="dropdownmenu"
        runat="server" /></p>
<p>Problem Subject:<br />
    <asp:DropDownList id="ddlSubject" CssClass="dropdownmenu"
        runat="server" /></p>
<p>Problem Description:<br />
    <asp:TextBox id="txtDescription" CssClass="textbox"
        Columns="40" Rows="4" TextMode="MultiLine"
        runat="server" /><br/>
    <asp:RequiredFieldValidator id="rfvDescription"
        ControlToValidate="txtDescription"
 ErrorMessage="You must enter a description of the problem!"
        Display="Dynamic" runat="server" /></p>
<p><asp:Button id="btnSubmit" CssClass="button"
        Text="Submit Request" runat="server" /></p>
<asp:ValidationSummary id="vsSummary" ShowMessageBox="true"
    ShowSummary="false" runat="server" />
```

This time, when the users enter incorrect values and try to submit the form, they are presented with a list of errors in a message box.

RegularExpressionValidator

Suppose for a moment that you wanted to be able to validate an email address. The problem with validating an email address is that there are so many different possibilities that a user may enter. The RegularExpressionValidator lets you specify a **regular expression** that describes all the allowable values for a field. Regular expressions are powerful tools for manipulating strings, and are supported by many programming languages. Regular expressions are commonly used to check for patterns inside strings. Consider, for instance, the following regular expression:

```
^\S+@\S+\.\S+$
```

Translating this to plain English, this expression will **match** any string that begins with one or more non-whitespace characters followed by a @ character, then one or more non-whitespace characters, then a dot (.), then one or more non-whitespace characters, followed by the end of the string.

This describes any one of these three email addresses:

zak@modulemedia.com
zak@host.modulemedia.com
zak_ruvalcaba@modulemedia.za

However, that regular expression would fail if the user typed in one of these entries:

zak@modulemedia
zak ruvalcaba@modulemedia

Although regular expressions cannot check to see if the email address itself is valid, they can, at the very least, provide a way of determining whether or not the user entered a string of characters that had all the key components required for a valid email address.

Here's a full example that makes use of the above regular expression:

File: **RegularExpressionValidator.aspx (excerpt)**

```
<html>
<head>
  <title>RegularExpressionValidator Control Sample</title>
</head>
<body>
<form runat="server">
  <p>Email:<br />
    <asp:TextBox id="email" runat="server" /><br />
    <asp:RegularExpressionValidator id="revEmail"
      ControlToValidate="email"
      ValidationExpression="^\S+@\S+\.\S+$"
      ErrorMessage="You must enter a valid email!"
      runat="server" /></p>
  <p><asp:Button id="btnSubmit" Text="Submit" runat="server"
    /></p>
</form>
</body>
</html>
```

The important property within this control is ValidationExpression, to which we assign the appropriate regular expression to handle our custom validation functionality. Figure 5.10 shows the error message that appears when a user enters an incorrect email address.

Figure 5.10. An error message is displayed to users when they enter an incorrect email address.

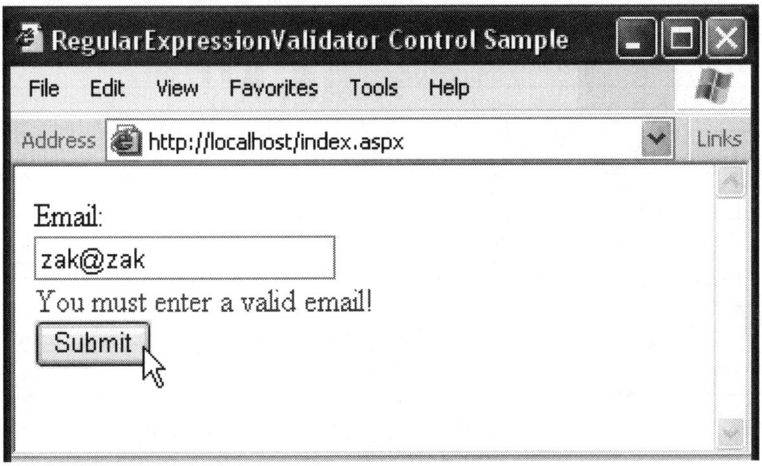

Some Useful Regular Expressions

Writing regular expressions can be tricky, and a comprehensive discussion is outside the scope of this book. Instead, Table 5.1 lists the most common special characters that you may use in regular expressions. It should help you when putting together your own expressions.

Table 5.1. Common RegExp Characters and their Descriptions

Character	Description
^	Beginning of string
$	End of string
\d	Numeric digit
\s	Whitespace character
\S	Non-whitespace character
(...)	A group of characters
?	Preceding character or group is optional
+	One or more of the preceding character or group
*	Zero or more of the preceding character or group
{5}	Exactly five of the preceding character or group
{2,7}	Two to seven of the preceding character or group
(a|b)	Either a or b

There are quite a few more codes that can be used in regular expressions. You'll find a complete guide and reference in the .NET Framework SDK Documentation. Now, let's take a look at some common expressions and their usages.

US phone numbers, (555) 555-5555 or 555-555-5555:

```
^\(?\d{3}\)?(\s|-)\d{3}-\d{4}$
```

International phone number (begins with a digit, followed by from 7 to 20 digits and/or dashes):

```
^\d(\d|-){7,20}$
```

Email address[2]:

```
^\S+@\S+\.\S+{2,4}$
```

Five-digit ZIP code:

```
^\d{5}$
```

---

[2]This and many of the other regular expressions presented here are nowhere near as rigorous as they could be, but are still quite useful. The book *Mastering Regular Expressions* (O'Reilly, ISBN 1-56592-257-3) contains a single expression for checking email addresses that tops out at over 6,000 characters!

Nine-digit ZIP code:

```
^\d{5}-\d{4}$
```

Either five-digit or nine-digit ZIP code:

```
^(\d{5})|(\d{5}\-\d{4})$
```

US Social Security Number:

```
^\d{3}-\d{2}-\d{4}$
```

Web URL:

```
^https?://\S+\.\S+$
```

You should be able to look up the components of these regular expressions in the table provided and begin to see how they work. If you would like more help with regular expressions, try the following resources:

☐ RegExLib.com[1]: a searchable library of regular expressions

☐ *Using Regular Expressions in PHP*[2]: a great article on the use of regular expressions and PHP

☐ *Regular Expressions in JavaScript*[3]: another great article, this time on the use of regular expressions with JavaScript

CustomValidator

The validation controls included with ASP.NET allow you to handle nearly all kinds of validation. However, certain types of validation cannot be performed with the built-in controls. For instance, say you needed to validate a user's email address by checking against a database table. Although this task doesn't seem all that common, there are instances when you will log into a Website and, while logging in, you'll be asked to provide a user name and a unique email address. The CustomValidator control can be helpful in this situation and others like it. Let's see how:

---

[1] http://www.regexlib.com/
[2] http://www.sitepoint.com/article/974
[3] http://www.sitepoint.com/article/286

VB.NET   File: **CustomValidator.aspx**

```
<html>
<head>
<title>CustomValidator Control Sample</title>
<script runat="server" language="VB">
Sub ValidateEmail(s As Object, e As ServerValidateEventArgs)
  ' In a real app, this would check against a database
  If (e.Value <> "zak@modulemedia.com") Then
    ' Note how we indicate failure for our validator control
    e.IsValid = False
  Else
    Response.Redirect("goodpage.aspx")
  End If
End Sub
</script>
</head>

<body>
<form runat="server">
  <p>Email:<br />
    <asp:TextBox id="email" runat="server" /><br />
    <asp:CustomValidator id="cvEmail" ControlToValidate="email"
        OnServerValidate="ValidateEmail"
        ErrorMessage="You have entered the wrong credentials!"
        runat="server" /></p>
  <p><asp:Button id="btnSubmit" Text="Submit" runat="server"
        /></p>
</form>
</body>
</html>
```

C#   File: **CustomValidator.aspx**

```
<html>
<head>
<title>CustomValidator Control Sample</title>
<script runat="server" language="C#">
void ValidateEmail(Object s, ServerValidateEventArgs e) {
  // In a real app, this would check against a database
  if (e.Value != "zak@modulemedia.com") {
    // Note how we indicate failure for our validator control
    e.IsValid = false;
  } else {
    Response.Redirect("goodpage.aspx");
  }
}
</script>
```

```
</head>

<body>
<form runat="server">
  <p>Email:<br />
    <asp:TextBox id="email" runat="server" /><br />
    <asp:CustomValidator id="cvEmail" ControlToValidate="email"
        OnServerValidate="ValidateEmail"
        ErrorMessage="You have entered the wrong credentials!"
        runat="server" /></p>
  <p><asp:Button id="btnSubmit" Text="Submit" runat="server"
      /></p>
</form>
</body>
</html>
```

In this example, when the form is submitted, the `CustomValidator` control raises the `ServerValidate` event. The `ValidateEmail` subroutine/method is called as a result, and the email address is checked. If the address doesn't exist, the `IsValid` property of the `ServerValidateEventArgs` object for the event is set to `False`, and the error message is displayed. If the email address is valid, the user is simply redirected to `goodpage.aspx`. Although this example shows a simple `CustomValidator`, you can certainly imagine the possibilities.

Although we won't explore it in this book, you can also provide a client-side validation function for your `CustomValidator` controls by means of the `ClientValidationFunction` property. For details, refer to the .NET Framework SDK Documentation for the `CustomValidator` control.

Summary

As you have seen, the validation controls available through ASP.NET are powerful. This chapter taught you how to validate required form fields with the `RequiredFieldValidator`, compare form fields with the `CompareValidator`, check for a numeric range within form fields with the `RangeValidator`, provide a user with a summary of errors using the `ValidationSummary` control, check for email addresses with the `RegularExpressionValidator`, and perform your own custom validation with the `CustomValidator`. The next chapter will begin to introduce you to application development and prepare you for future chapters.

6

Database Design and Development

As you begin to build dynamic Web applications, it will become increasingly obvious that you need to store data and allow users access to it through your application. Whether you are building a company-wide intranet with access limited to employees, or a feature-rich ecommerce site that millions will visit, you'll need a system for storing information. Enter: the database.

An Introduction to Databases

In 1970, E.F. Codd, an employee of IBM, proposed his idea for what would become the first relational database design model. His model, which offered new methods for storing and retrieving data in large applications, far surpassed any idea or system that was in place at the time. The concept of "relational data" stemmed from the fact that data, and the relationships between data elements, were organized in "relations," or what we know today as tables.

Before we become mired in techno-speak, let's take a step back and consider the project at hand—the Dorknozzle Intranet—and how it can benefit from a relational database. By the end of this book, our site will be able to do all sorts of things, but it's a bit of a no-brainer that our company intranet will, at least on some level, need to keep track of the employees in our company. The employee directory we plan to build would be a sorry sight indeed without a list of employees!

So, how do we go about building that information into our site? Experience with static Web design might lead you to create a Web page entitled "Employee Directory" with a table or list of some kind, and to type in the details of each of the employees in the company. But, unless Dorknozzle is a really small company, a single page containing all the details of all the employees is going to grow prohibitively large. Instead, you might only list the employees' names, and link each to an individual profile page. Okay, so this will be a bit of a hassle to type up, but it's the kind of job you can assign to the boss's son on his summer internship.

But imagine that, a month or two down the track, Dorknozzle undergoes a corporate re-branding (a bright idea no doubt proposed by the boss's son one night at the dinner table!), and the entire Website needs to be updated to match the "new look" of the company. By now, Dorknozzle Jr. is back at school and the mind-numbing job of manually updating each of the employee profile pages falls right in your lap. Lucky you!

Life would be a lot more pleasant if a database were added to the mix. A **database** (for our purposes, MS Access, MSDE, or SQL Server) is a program that can store large amounts of information in an organized format that's easily accessible by programs such as ASP.NET Websites written in VB.NET or C#. For example, you could make the Dorknozzle Intranet site look in a database for a list of employees that you'd like to appear on the employee directory page.

In this example, the employee records would be stored entirely in the database. The advantages of this approach would be twofold. First, instead of having to write an HTML file for each employee profile page, you could write a single ASP.NET Web form that was designed to fetch any employee's details from the database and display them as a profile. This single form could be updated quite easily in the event of corporate re-branding or some other disaster. Second, adding an employee to the directory would be a simple matter of inserting a new record into the database. The Web form would take care of the rest, automatically displaying the new employee profile along with the others when it fetched the list from the database.

And, because this slick, ultra-manageable system reduces the burden of data entry and maintenance, you can assign the boss's son to clean the coffee machine in his spare time!

Let's run with this example as we look at how data is stored in a database. A database is composed of one or more **tables**, each of which contains a list of *things*. For our employee database, we'd probably start with a table called `Employees` that would contain a list of employees. Each table in a database has one or more **columns**, or **fields**. Each column holds a certain piece of information about each item in the table. In our example, the `Employees` table might have columns for the employee's name, network user name, and phone extension. Each employee that we stored in this table would then be said to be a **row** in the table. These rows and columns form a table that looks like Figure 6.1.

Figure 6.1. Structure of a typical database table

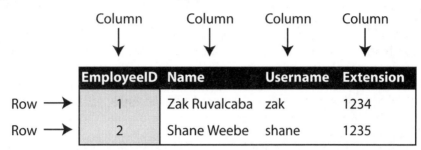

Notice that, in addition to columns for the employee's name (`Name`), user name (`Username`), and extension (`Extension`), I included a column named `EmployeeID`. As a matter of good design, a database table should always provide a way to identify uniquely each of its rows. In this particular case, it's unlikely that two employees would share the same network user name, but that's something for our network administrator to worry about. Just in case, the function of the `EmployeeID` column is to assign a unique number to each employee in the database, so we have an easy way to refer to each, and to keep track of which employee is which. We'll discuss such database design issues in greater depth shortly.

So, to review, the above is a four-column table with two rows, or entries. Each row in the table contains four fields, one for each column in the table: the employee's ID, name, user name, and telephone extension. With this basic terminology under your belt, you're ready to dig in and build your first database!

The Database Management System

The **Database Management System (DBMS)** is the application that allows you to design, store, and manage all the databases that you need.

SQL Server Enterprise Manager is a perfect example of a database management system. If you plan to use MSDE, **Web Data Administrator** will just about do in its place. Although SQL Server Enterprise Manager would be the perfect choice for the DBMS examples within this book, it only comes with SQL Server, which is expensive. For that reason, we'll stick with Web Data Administrator, which is, of course, free!

Smaller databases, such as Access, do not have what is traditionally known as a DBMS, as these packages allow you to manage only a single database file at any time. However, this is the only real difference between a DMBS and Access's database manager.

Creating the Database for the Intranet Application

Inside your DBMS are individual databases that contain data related to particular projects. Although most projects only need one database, at some point in the future you may realize that your project has grown beyond the scope of a single database, or perhaps security and maintenance requirements mean that you need more. Figure 6.2 shows the Web Data Administrator with a list of the various databases that are housed within its framework.

Figure 6.2. Web Data Administrator and a list of the databases.

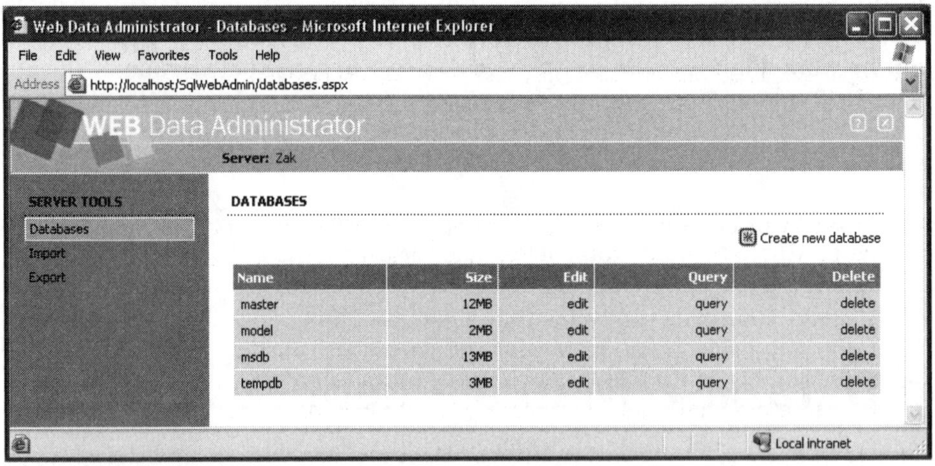

Access, on the other hand, functions a little differently. Rather than providing you with a list of all of your databases, Access allows you only to open and manage a single database file (an .mdb file) at any time. Once open, Access provides a visual means—that is, the standard Windows drag-and-drop function-ality—for creating and working with your databases.

Are you ready to create the intranet database? By now, I'm sure you're getting anxious to begin working with dynamic data in your Web projects, and creating the database is the first step! Let's get started.

Creating the Database in Access

To create the new database within Access, proceed as follows:

1. Open Access, select File, New..., then choose Blank database... from the New File menu on the right.

2. Give your database the name Dorknozzle and choose the location in which you plan to save your file. I generally like to save my databases within the root directory of my projects during development (though it's important to note that, upon moving our application to a production server, we wouldn't do this for security reasons).

3. Click Create.

That's it! The database has now been created for the application. Don't forget that you can simply grab this complete solution, including databases, from this book's code archive.

Creating the Database in Web Data Administrator

To create the Dorknozzle database within Web Data Administrator, simply follow the steps outlined here:

1. Open Web Data Administrator from your browser by navigating to the address http://localhost/SqlWebAdmin. You may want to bookmark this URL for easy access.

2. Supply the user details and server information, and click Login.

3. Create a new database by selecting Create new database, located at the top right of the Web Data Administrator.

4. Type the name of the new database as **Dorknozzle**. Click Create.

5. To view the database within the database list, select Databases from the navigation menu on the left. The Dorknozzle database will appear within the list.

Designing Tables for the Intranet Application

Let's start creating the tables for our intranet application. Tables can be thought of as the drawers in a filing cabinet. Just as we could separate different information into different drawers, we can break information about employees, departments, helpdesk requests, and newsletters into different tables. You can organize the tables within your database using either Web Data Administrator for MSDE, or within Access for your database file, depending on which solution you prefer.

In just a minute, we'll dive in and create our first table. But before we do, it's worth giving some thought to how many tables our application will need and exactly what they'll contain. At the start of this chapter, I described tables as lists of *things*. Though that may seem a bit obvious, it can be more subtle than you might expect. Allow me to illustrate.

Say that in addition to a name, user name, and telephone extension, you wanted to keep track of the department in which each employee works at Dorknozzle. Simply adding a column to the `Employees` table we discussed above, as shown in Figure 6.3, would seem like the logical choice.

Figure 6.3. Department names are stored in the table of employees.

EmployeeID	Name	Username	Extension	Department
1	Zak Ruvalcaba	zak	1234	Executive
2	Shane Weebe	shane	1235	Engineering

Looks good, right? Unfortunately, this leads to a couple of potential problems:

☐ Every time you insert a new employee record, you'll have to provide the name of the department in which that employee works. Make even the slightest spelling error, and, as far as the database is concerned, you have a new department. Now, I don't know about you, but I'd be pretty upset if my employee record showed me as the only person working in a department called "Enineering." And what if Dorknozzle Sr. decides to rename one of the departments? You might try to update all the affected employee records with the new department name, but, even if you only miss one, your database will again contain inconsistent information. Database design experts refer to this sort of problem as an **update anomaly**.

❑ It would be natural for you to rely on your database to provide a list of all the departments in the company, so you could then choose to view the employees in a particular department. But if for some reason you deleted the records of all the employees in that department (don't ask me why—your human resource issues aren't *my* problem!), you'd remove any record that the department had ever existed (although, if you really *did* have to fire everyone, that might be a good thing…). Database design experts call this a **delete anomaly**.

These problems—and more—can be dealt with very quickly. Instead of storing the information for the departments in the Employees table, let's create an entirely new table for our list of departments. Similarly to the Employees table, this new Departments table will include a column called DepartmentID to identify each of our departments with a unique number. We can then use those department IDs in our Employees table to associate departments with their employees. This new database layout is shown in Figure 6.4.

Figure 6.4. The DepartmentID field associates each row in Employees with a row in Departments.

Employees				
EmployeeID	**Name**	**Username**	**Extension**	**DepartmentID**
1	Zak Ruvalcaba	zak	1234	5
2	Shane Weebe	shane	1235	6
3	Ted Lindsey	ted	1236	6

Departments	
DepartmentID	**Department**
5	Executive
6	Engineering

What these tables show are three employees and two departments. The DepartmentID column of the Employees table provides a **relationship** between the two tables, indicating that Zak Ruvalcaba works in department 5, while Shane Weebe and Ted Lindsey work in department 6. Notice also that, as each department now only appears once in the database, and appears independently of the employees who work in it, we've avoided all the problems outlined above.

The most important characteristic of this database design, however, is that, since we're storing information about two types of *things* (employees and departments), it's most appropriate to have two tables. This is a rule of thumb that you should always keep in mind when designing a database:

> *Each type of entity (or "thing") that you want to be able to store inform-*
> *ation about should be given its own table.*

With this rule in mind, we can sit back and think about the application we want to build, as we described it back in Chapter 4, in terms of the **entities** (or things) that we'll need to keep track of, and come up with a preliminary list of tables. This is something you'll grow more comfortable with as you gain experience, but it's worth giving it a try on your own at this stage. When you're done, compare your list to mine and see how you did!

Employees	The employees in our company, each of which has an associated department
Departments	The departments in our company
CompanyEvents	The events planned for our company
Newsletters	The issues of the company newsletter, each of which will feature an employee, an event, and an item from the employee store
EmployeeStore	The items for sale in our employee store
HelpDesk	The problem reports that have been filed at our employee helpdesk, each of which will have an associated category, subject, and status
HelpDeskCategories	The categories that are available for helpdesk items ("Hardware", "Software", etc.)
HelpDeskSubjects	The subjects that are available for helpdesk items ("Computer crashes", "My chair is broken", etc.)

HelpDeskStatus	The states in which a helpdesk item can be ("open" or "closed")

Don't worry if your analysis missed the last few—helpdesk item categories, subjects, and states aren't obvious entities in our application. But remember that whenever you predict you'll have a field in your database that should only accept values from a specific list, it makes sense to create a table to hold that list. This approach makes it easy to execute changes to the list in future; it also reduces the amount of disk space required by your database, by storing only a single copy of strings like "My chair is broken."

This process of planning out the entities, tables, and relationships between the tables to eliminate maintenance problems and redundant data is called database **normalization**. Although I'll speak a bit more about normalization before the end of this chapter, I'll only ever discuss it in an informal, hands-on (i.e. non-rigorous) way. As any computer science major will tell you, database design is a serious area of research, with tested and mathematically provable principles that, while useful, are beyond the scope of this text. If you want more information, stop by http://www.datamodel.org/ for a list of good books, as well as several useful resources on the subject. In particular, check out the *5 Rules of Normalization* in the Data Modelling section of the site.

So, we've got our list of tables. In the next section, we'll discuss the columns within those tables, and how to choose their characteristics. Although we won't go over the creation of all the tables for the `Dorknozzle` database, we will create one: our `Employees` table. Once you understand how to create a new table, you can create the rest in your own time based on the descriptions I'll provide. Or, if you prefer, you can simply grab the finished database from the code archive.

Columns and Data Types

Once you've outlined all your tables, as we did in the previous section, the next step is to decide what information will be included within those tables. For instance, you may want to include first name, last name, phone number, address, city, state, zip code, and so on, for all employees within the `Employees` table. Similarly, you would need to include product names, descriptions, and inventory counts within your `EmployeeStore` table. Let's see how you can define these columns as you create the `Employees` table for the `Dorknozzle` database.

Creating a Table in Access

You can begin creating the Employees table and associated columns for the Dorknozzle database on your own within Access by following the steps outlined below:

1. Open the Dorknozzle database.

2. Select Create table in Design view.

When the design view opens, you can begin to enter all the column names that will be used within that table. You also have to select a **data type** that corresponds with the type of information those fields will contain. Data types restrict the type of information the column will accept, which helps ensure that all records (or rows) contain consistent information. The Access data types that we'll be using most are listed below:

Text
Text is the most commonly used data type, and can contain up to 255 characters and/or numbers.

Memo
Similar to the text data type, the memo data type supports up to 65,535 characters. You'd basically only use this data type if you were going to be dealing with large amounts of text.

Number
Use the number data type when you expect to perform calculations, for example, if you need to calculate the total number of items that a user has bought.

Currency
Similar to the number data type, currency should be used when money is involved. You should use the currency data type when defining your cost column within the EmployeeStore table.

AutoNumber
AutoNumber is used for columns whose value you want to increment automatically as more rows are added to the table. Generally, AutoNumber is reserved for the column that we define as our Primary Key, because it ensures that all data items within that column are unique. We'll talk about Primary Keys later in this chapter.

Date/Time
The date/time data type is most useful when you want to sort items in your fields chronologically.

Yes/No   The yes/no data type is useful when something is either selected, or it is not. It returns either a true or a false value and generally simulates a checkmark effect.

Hyperlink   When you want the field to jump to a Web address, use the hyperlink data type.

Add your columns to the table simply by writing the required names and types into the grid on the screen. Access also lets you add a description for each column (or field), but if you choose the column names appropriately, their purpose should be clear enough. The Employees table should contain the columns listed in Table 6.1.

Table 6.1. Create the Employees Table with Column Names and Data Types

Column Name	Data Type
EmployeeID	AutoNumber
DepartmentID	Number
Name	Text
Username	Text
Password	Text
Address	Text
City	Text
State	Text
Zip	Text
HomePhone	Text
Extension	Text
MobilePhone	Text

Once complete, save your work by selecting Save As from the File menu, type **Employees**, make sure it will be saved as a table, and click OK. Access will pop up a dialog about primary keys—just click No for now; we'll come back to this issue later. The new Employees table will resemble Figure 6.5.

Figure 6.5. Access shows the Employees table in design view along with all of the columns and data types that are associated with it.

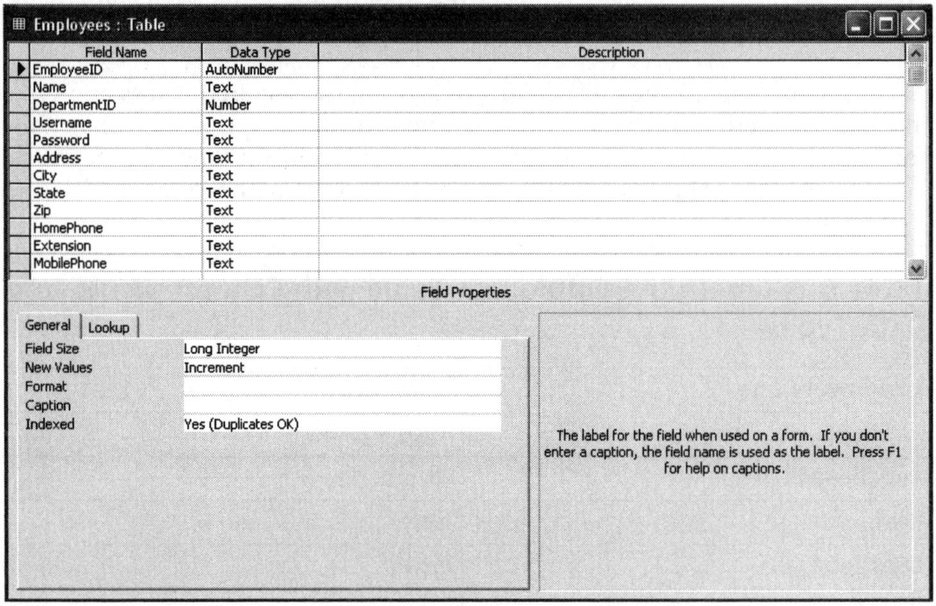

We'll create the rest of the tables a little later in the chapter.

If you don't feel like creating all of these tables from scratch, again, the complete Access database can be found in the code archive.

Creating a Table in Web Data Administrator

You can create tables and columns within Web Data Administrator for MSDE by following the steps outlined below:

1. Open Web Data Administrator and click the Dorknozzle database in the database list.

2. Select Create new table.

3. Enter a name of **Employees** for the new table.

4. Click Create.

Data types for SQL Server are treated differently from those in Access. Below is a list of the common data types that we'll be using within this book:

Int   Use the Int data type when you expect to perform calculations. The equivalent in Access would be Number.

Bit   Use the Bit data type when something is either true or false. The equivalent in Access would be Yes/No.

Decimal   Use the Decimal data type when working with decimals, as you might with mathematical equations.

SmallMoney   The SmallMoney data type should be used when money is involved. The equivalent in Access would be Currency.

DateTime   The DateTime data type is most useful when you want to sort items in your fields chronologically. The equivalent in Access would be Date/Time.

Nvarchar   The Nvarchar data type is the most commonly used data type, and can contain up to 8000 Unicode characters and/or numbers.

With the column editor open, enter the necessary information, including column name and data type. Note, however, that MSDE works a bit differently than Access. Rather than having a separate data type called AutoNumber, MSDE columns have unique identities. If you want a column to have a unique identity, check Identity, and that column will automatically increment. You'll also notice an option called Allow Null. If you want records in this table to require a value for this column, uncheck this box.

The Employees table should be created in Web Data Administrator according to the information listed in Table 6.2. Don't worry about the other options that Web Data Administrator provides for each column.

Table 6.2. Create the Employees table with column names and data types within Web Data Administrator.

Column Name	Data Type	Identity (Checked)	Allow Null
EmployeeID	Int	Yes	No
DepartmentID	Int	No	Yes
Name	Nvarchar	No	Yes
Username	Nvarchar	No	Yes
Password	Nvarchar	No	Yes
Address	Nvarchar	No	Yes
City	Nvarchar	No	Yes
State	Nvarchar	No	Yes
Zip	Nvarchar	No	Yes
HomePhone	Nvarchar	No	Yes
Extension	Nvarchar	No	Yes
MobilePhone	Nvarchar	No	Yes

When complete, your table will resemble Figure 6.6.

Figure 6.6. The Web Data Administrator shows the `Employees` table along with all the columns and data types that are associated with it.

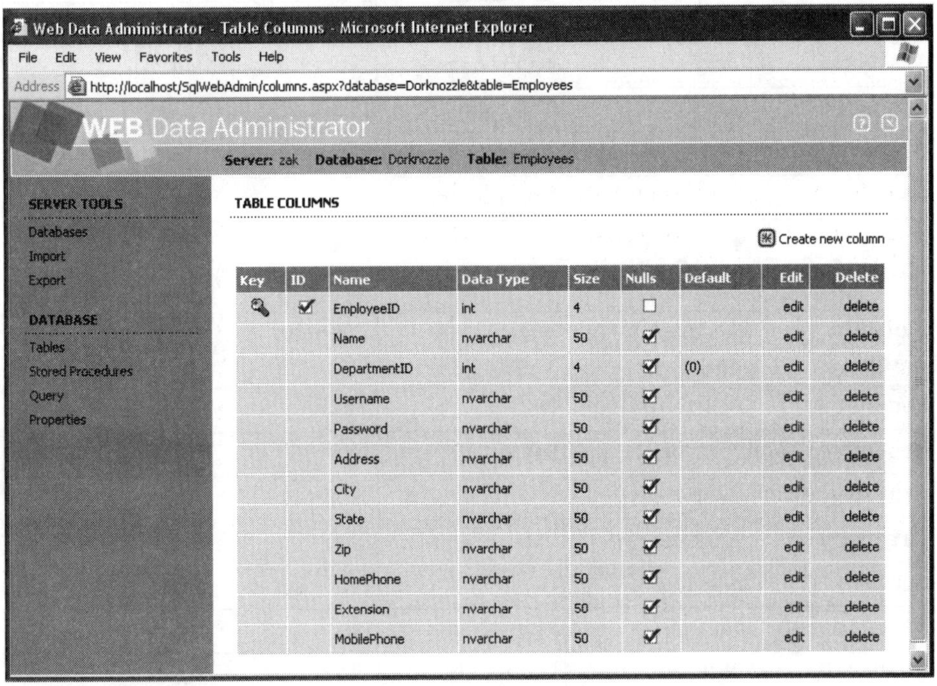

Creating the Remaining Tables

Let's create the rest of the database tables. Table 6.3 to Table 6.10 outline all of the tables that we'll need in our database. If you're using Access, you only need the Column Name and Access Data Type columns, whereas if you're using MSDE, you'll need to look at the Column Name, SQL Data Type, Identity, and Allow Null columns.

Table 6.3. The `Departments` Table

Column Name	Access Data Type	SQL Data Type	Identity	Allow Null
DepartmentID	AutoNumber	Int	Yes	No
Department	Text	Nvarchar	No	Yes

Table 6.4. The `EmployeeStore` Table

Column Name	Access Data Type	SQL Data Type	Identity	Allow Null
ItemID	AutoNumber	Int	Yes	No
ItemName	Text	Nvarchar	No	Yes
ImageURL	Text	Nvarchar	No	Yes
Quantity	Number	Int	No	Yes
Cost	Currency	SmallMoney	No	Yes

Table 6.5. The `HelpDesk` Table

Column Name	Access Data Type	SQL Data Type	Identity	Allow Null
RequestID	AutoNumber	Int	Yes	No
EmployeeID	Number	Int	No	Yes
StationNumber	Text	Nvarchar	No	Yes
CategoryID	Number	Int	No	Yes
SubjectID	Number	Int	No	Yes
Description	Memo	Nvarchar	No	Yes
StatusID	Number	Int	No	Yes

Table 6.6. The `CompanyEvents` Table

Column Name	Access Data Type	SQL Data Type	Identity	Allow Null
EventID	AutoNumber	Int	Yes	No
Event	Memo	Nvarchar	No	Yes
Date	Date/Time	DateTime	No	Yes
Location	Memo	Nvarchar	No	Yes

Table 6.7. The `Newsletters` Table

Column Name	Access Data Type	SQL Data Type	Identity	Allow Null
NewsletterID	AutoNumber	Int	Yes	No
Introduction	Memo	Nvarchar	No	Yes
ItemID	Number	Int	No	Yes
EventID	Number	Int	No	Yes
EmployeeID	Number	Int	No	Yes

Table 6.8. The `HelpDeskCategories` Table

Column Name	Access Data Type	SQL Data Type	Identity	Allow Null
CategoryID	AutoNumber	Int	Yes	No
Category	Text	Nvarchar	No	Yes

Table 6.9. The `HelpDeskSubjects` Table.

Column Name	Access Data Type	SQL Data Type	Identity	Allow Null
SubjectID	AutoNumber	Int	Yes	No
Subject	Text	Nvarchar	No	Yes

Table 6.10. The `HelpDeskStatus` Table

Column Name	Access Data Type	SQL Data Type	Identity	Allow Null
StatusID	AutoNumber	Int	Yes	No
Status	Text	Nvarchar	No	Yes

Wow, that was a ton of information! If you don't feel like creating all those tables from scratch, you can grab the complete Access database, or a script to create the tables in Web Data Administrator, from the code archive.

Importing a Database into MSDE

Unlike Access, which uses a single database file, Web Data Administrator manages databases within the SQL Server Engine. For this reason, if you're not up for creating all the tables manually, you must import a `.sql` script to recreate the table structure I've already built and exported. Import the `Dorknozzle.sql` file from the code archive by following the steps outlined below:

1. Select Import from the navigation menu on the left.

2. Browse for the `Dorknozzle.sql` file and click Open.

3. Select Import. Wait a few moments for the database to be recreated within Web Data Administrator. You will receive a green success message when the file finishes importing.

4. Switch to Databases from the navigation menu on the left to view the newly imported database.

You now have the basic structure for your database. The next section will teach you about the actual data contained within the tables.

IMPORTANT

Edits required for MSDE

The `Dorknozzle.sql` file supplied in the code archive will work without modification on SQL Server, but for MSDE configurations a couple of edits are required.

Open the file in any text editor (such as Notepad) and look for the two file names in the `CREATE DATABASE` query near the top of the file. They should look something like this:

```
C:\Program Files\Microsoft SQL Server\MSSQL\data\Dorknozzle.mdf
C:\Program Files\Microsoft SQL Server\MSSQL\data\Dorknozzle.ldf
```

Check the contents of the `Microsoft SQL Server` directory on your computer. If you are running MSDE, chances are it will contain a folder called `MSSQL$NETSDK` instead of `MSSQL`. Alter the two file names in `Dorknozzle.sql` accordingly, and you should then be able to import the file as described above without difficulty.

Inserting Rows

If tables represent drawers in a filing cabinet, rows represent individual paper records in those drawers. Suppose that the intranet Web application was a real application. As people begin registering and interacting with the application, the rows within the various tables would begin to fill up with information about those people.

Access provides two views for editing columns and rows. You can use the Design View, which we used earlier, to edit columns and their data types, or the Datasheet View to add and edit rows in your table. Figure 6.7 shows the `Employees` table in Datasheet View with some fictitious employees.

Figure 6.7. Access displays rows of information within a Datasheet View.

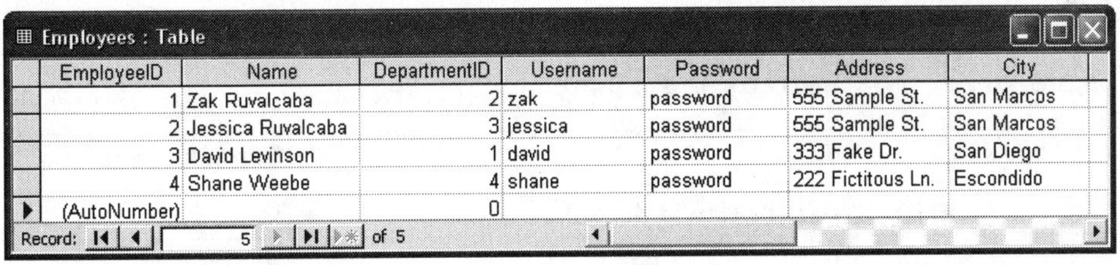

EmployeeID	Name	DepartmentID	Username	Password	Address	City
1	Zak Ruvalcaba	2	zak	password	555 Sample St.	San Marcos
2	Jessica Ruvalcaba	3	jessica	password	555 Sample St.	San Marcos
3	David Levinson	1	david	password	333 Fake Dr.	San Diego
4	Shane Weebe	4	shane	password	222 Fictitous Ln.	Escondido
(AutoNumber)		0				

Record: 5 of 5

Adding rows of information is as easy as typing information into the cells within the Datasheet View. In fact, let's begin by adding data to some of the tables so that we can use the database in later chapters. Table 6.11 to Table 6.23 represent the tables and data you should add.

Table 6.11. The `CompanyEvents` Table

EventID	Event	Date	Location
1	4th of July Fireworks Party	7/4/2003	Coronado Yacht Club
2	Company Bowling Night	7/14/2003	San Diego Bowl
3	Padres Baseball Night	7/21/2003	Qualcomm Stadium Gate F
4	Night at the Races	7/28/2003	Del Mar Racetrack

Table 6.12. The Departments Table

DepartmentID	Department
1	Accounting
2	Administration
3	Business Development
4	Customer Support
5	Engineering
6	Executive
7	Facilities
8	IT
9	Marketing
10	Operations

Table 6.13. The Employees Table

EmployeeID	Name	DepartmentID
1	Zak Ruvalcaba	6
2	Jessica Ruvalcaba	9
3	David Levinson	9
4	Shane Weebe	5
5	Ted Lindsey	5
6	Geoff Kim	1

The Employees table contains many more columns than the three outlined here, but, because of size constraints, I've left them out. Feel free to add your own data to the rest of the cells, or grab the complete version of this database from the code archive.

Table 6.14. The `EmployeeStore` Table

ItemID	ItemName	ImageURL	Quantity	Cost
1	Dorknozzle Shirt	Images/store/tshirt.gif	150	$12.99
2	Dorknozzle Hooded Sweat Shirt	Images/store/hoodie.gif	40	$32.99
3	Dorknozzle Longsleeve Shirt	Images/store/longsleeve.gif	60	$19.99
4	Dorknozzle Polo Shirt	Images/store/polo.gif	35	$29.99
5	Dorknozzle Sticker	Images/store/sticker.gif	1500	$1.99
6	Dorknozzle Mousepad	Images/store/mousepad.gif	1000	$5.99
7	Dorknozzle Mug	Images/store/coffeemug.gif	500	$5.99
8	Dorknozzle Water Bottle	Images/store/waterbottle.gif	300	$5.99
9	Dorknozzle Golf Balls	Images/store/golfballs.gif	100	$2.99
10	Dorknozzle Pen	Images/store/pen.gif	1500	$1.99
11	Dorknozzle Carry Bag	Images/store/carrybag.gif	80	$9.00

Table 6.15. The `HelpDeskCategories` Table

CategoryID	Category
1	Hardware
2	Software
3	Workstation

Table 6.16. The `HelpDeskStatus` Table

StatusID	Status
1	Open
2	Closed

Table 6.17. The `HelpDeskSubjects` Table

SubjectID	Subject
1	Computer not starting
2	Monitor won't turn on
3	Chair is broken
4	Office won't work
5	Windows won't work
6	Computer crashes

If you used one of the database tables from the code archive, and you see a table called `NavigationMenu`, don't worry about it for now. We'll add rows to that one in Chapter 9, during our discussion of `DataLists`.

Unfortunately, if you're using MSDE, Web Data Administrator doesn't provide an easy way for you to add data to your tables. For this reason, all the data is included in the SQL script that you can import from the code archive.

Beyond the Basics

Now that the basic structure of our database is out of the way, let's begin looking at what really drives the database.

Keys

Tables in your databases could contain hundreds or even thousands of rows of similar data. You could have several hundred employees in your `Employees` table, so, clearly, we need some way to identify any one record uniquely. As you'll recall, we created a column called `EmployeeID` for just this purpose. Such columns are called unique **keys**.

Why is uniqueness so important? Imagine that your program needs to update or delete the record for John Smith, and there are several people with that name in your organization. The database would not be certain to match the particular John Smith that you were trying to work with—it may even end up deleting the wrong record. We need to choose a column that will be unique for any given employee. In the case of our `Employee` table, the `EmployeeID` will always be unique, so that would be a suitable key.

There are two types of keys that we'll discuss here: **primary keys** and **foreign keys**.

Primary Keys

A primary key can be one or several columns; the main requirement is that the set values in those columns are unique for any given record. Databases usually let us create columns with an automatically incrementing number (like the `EmployeeID` column within the `Employees` table), so that as more records are added to the table, that field will increment by one for each new record, guaranteeing a completely unique value. Table 6.18 shows a simple table within a hypothetical database that might contain employees. The `EmployeeID` column in this table can be a primary key, as its value is unique for each row in the table.

Table 6.18. Example of the Use of a Primary Key

EmployeeID (Primary Key)	Employee
1	Zak Ruvalcaba
2	Jessica Ruvalcaba
3	John Smith
4	David Levinson
5	Shane Weebe
6	John Smith

Foreign Keys

A foreign key is a column of one table that refers to the primary key of another table. A foreign key may be null and, almost always, is not unique. Consider the following examples:

Table 6.19. The `Departments` Table has a Primary Key

DepartmentID (Primary Key)	Department
1	Accounting
2	Engineering
3	Executive
4	Marketing

Table 6.20. The `Employees` Table has a Primary Key and a Foreign Key

EmployeeID (Primary Key)	Employee	DepartmentID
1	Zak Ruvalcaba	3
2	Jessica Ruvalcaba	4
3	David Levinson	4
4	Shane Weebe	2
5	Jeff Martyn	1
6	Ted Lindsey	2
7	Geoff Kim	2

The `DepartmentID` column in the `Employees` table is a foreign key to the `DepartmentID` primary key in the `Departments` table. Notice that the `DepartmentID` primary key within the `Departments` table is unique, but the `DepartmentID` foreign key within the `Employees` table may repeat.

Defining Keys

For the most part, you can't explicitly create foreign keys—they're usually set up when relationships are defined (we'll be discussing relationships next). Primary keys, on the other hand, can be defined directly within Access's table manager or Web Data Administrator. To define the primary key for the `Employees` table within Access, simply follow the steps outlined below:

1. With the `Dorknozzle` database open, select the `Employees` table and click Design from the toolbar, or right-click and choose Design View.

2. Right click the `EmployeeID` column and select Primary Key.

Although we have essentially created the column as unique by specifying its data type as AutoNumber, making it a primary key will allow us to maintain relationships with foreign keys in other tables.

You can create a primary key for a column within Web Data Administrator by following these steps:

1. With the `Dorknozzle` database open within Web Data Administrator, select Edit from the `Employees` row.

2. Select Edit from the `EmployeeID` row.

3. Select the check box for Primary Key.

That's all there is to it. Table 6.21 outlines the complete set of primary keys for all tables. Set them up!

Table 6.21. Define a Primary Key for All Tables

Table	Primary Key Column
Employees	EmployeeID
Departments	DepartmentID
EmployeeStore	ItemID
HelpDesk	RequestID
HelpDeskCategories	CategoryID
HelpDeskSubjects	SubjectID
HelpDeskStatus	StatusID
Newsletters	NewsletterID
CompanyEvents	EventID

Relationship Management

When using tables in a database, relationships become an important consideration. Relationships describe how data in one table is linked to data in other tables. In fact, it is because relationships are so crucial that these types of databases are given the name "relational databases." Relationships exist for the sole purpose of associating one table with one or more tables using keys—primary keys and foreign keys. We've already looked at a couple of relationships between databases through our work in previous sections. A good example, once again, is that of the Employees and Departments tables. We'd expect to have multiple employees in each department of our company. While we could add the department that any employee works in to his or her employee record, as in Table 6.16, this would take up extra space in the database, and would be a maintenance nightmare if we ever wanted to change the name of a department!

Table 6.22. Adding the Department to the Employees table is restrictive and redundant.

EmployeeID	Department
1	Marketing
2	Marketing
3	Marketing
4	Marketing

Instead, we create a separate Department table, create a DepartmentID column to act as the unique identifier, and define that column as the primary key. We then create a relationship between that primary key and a foreign key in the Employees table (DepartmentID). Figure 6.8 displays a relationship between the Employees table and the Departments table as it would be displayed by Access.

Figure 6.8. Relationships are added to avoid data duplication within tables.

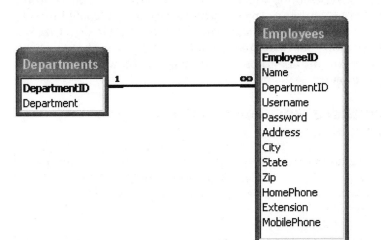

Now, instead of storing the actual *name* of the department in which an employee works, we simply store the unique ID of that department in the Employees table. That's much cleaner! See how relationships work?

Web Data Administrator does not currently provide a relationship editor, so if you use MSDE, we won't explicitly define the relationships in the database. But, just because a foreign key isn't explicitly defined doesn't mean it can't contain numbers that represent primary key values in another table. If you happen to be fortunate enough to have the full-blown SQL Server, you can read up on how to create relationships with Enterprise Manager in the accompanying documentation.

There are three types of relationships that can occur in databases:

❏ One-to-one relationships

❏ One-to-many relationships

❏ Many-to-many relationships

One-to-One Relationships

A one-to-one relationship means that for each record in one table, only one other related record can exist in some other table.

One-to-one relationships are rarely used, since it's usually more efficient just to combine the two records and store them together as columns in a single table. For example, every employee in our database will have a phone number stored in the HomePhone column of the Employees table. In theory, we could store the phone numbers in our database in a separate table and link to them with a foreign key in the Employees table, but this would be of no benefit to our particular application, so we can leave this one-to-one relationship (along with most others) out of our database design.

One-to-Many Relationships

A one-to-many relationship is by far the most common relationship type. A one-to-many relationship means that each record in one table can have multiple records associated with it in a second table. These records are usually related based on a unique primary key in the first table. In the employees/departments example, a one-to-many relationship exists between one department and the many possible employees that could belong to that department.

One-to-many relationships are usually signified in database diagrams by a line between two tables with a "1" next to the table that would have the one related item in it, and an infinity sign ( ) next to the table that could have many items related to that one record. Access actually shows these symbols, as we see in Figure 6.9, which illustrates a zoomed-in view of those icons next to their respective tables.

Figure 6.9. One-to-many relationships are easy to spot. Just look for the icons next to the tables.

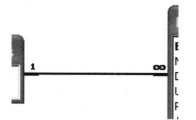

You can create a one-to-many relationship in Access as follows:

1. Select Tools, Relationships....

2. If Access doesn't immediately prompt you for the tables to display, select Show Table from the Relationships menu.

3. Add the Employees table and Departments table and click Close. The two tables will appear within the Relationships window as in Figure 6.10.

Figure 6.10. Add the Departments table and Employees table to the Relationship Editor.

4. Select the primary key column (DepartmentID) from within the Departments table and drag it over onto the foreign key (DepartmentID) within the Employees table. The Edit Relationship dialog will appear. You'll notice the relationship type toward the bottom of the dialog as one-to-many. The dialog allows you to check off a few boxes. The first, Enforce Referential Integrity, prevents users or applications from entering inconsistent data into our database (by, say, inserting in the Employees table a DepartmentID value that doesn't have a matching entry in the Departments table). In our application, every user must be associated with a valid department, so check this box. The next two, Cascade Update Related Fields and Cascade Delete Related Records, refer to the ability of the database to determine automatically whether a change that has been made to the first table should affect the related table. If for some reason we changed the ID of a department in the Departments table, would we want matching foreign key entries in the Employees table to be updated with the new ID? Absolutely, so check the first box. If, however, we *deleted* a department, would we want to delete all the

employees in that department too? I don't think so—let's leave that second checkbox blank. The result of the dialog will resemble Figure 6.11.

Figure 6.11. Check off Enforce Referential Integrity for your table relationship.

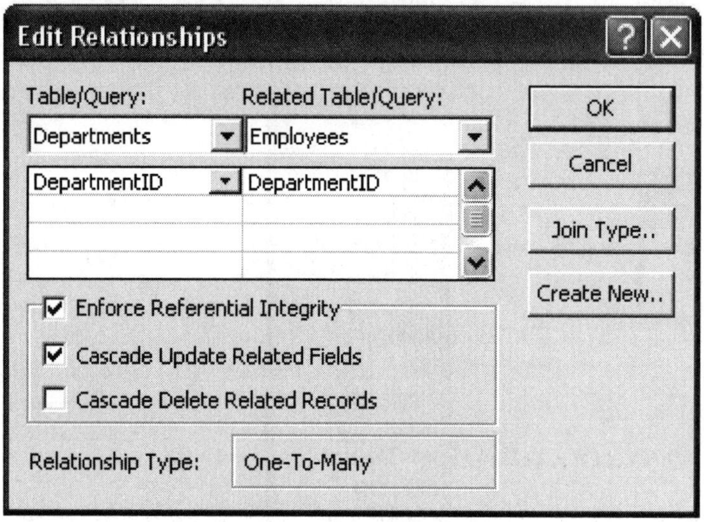

5. Select OK. The relationship will be created similar to that shown in Figure 6.12.

Figure 6.12. The relationship between the `Departments` table and `Employees` table is defined.

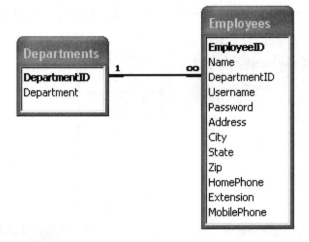

Many-to-Many Relationships

Many-to-many relationships are the most complicated relationship type you're likely to encounter in designing databases for Web applications. In order to keep things simple, the `Dorknozzle` database contains only one-to-many relationships. For the sake of completeness, however, let's consider a hypothetical enhancement to our database that would call for a many-to-many relationship.

Say you wanted a single employee to be able to belong to more than one department. Someone who works in "Engineering" could also be an "Executive," for example. A single employee might belong to many departments, and each department will contain many employees. This is a many-to-many relationship. But how do we represent it in our database?

Faced with this problem, many inexperienced developers begin to think of ways to store several values in a single column, because the obvious solution is to change the `DepartmentID` column in the `Employees` table so that it contains a *list* of the IDs of those departments to which each employee belongs. A second rule of thumb would be useful here:

> *If you need to store multiple values in a single column, your design is probably flawed.*

The correct way to represent a many-to-many relationship is to use a **look-up table**. This is a table that contains no actual data, but which defines pairs of entries that are related. Figure 6.13 shows what the database design would look like for our employees and departments.

Figure 6.13. The `DeptLookup` table associates pairs of rows from the `Employees` and `Departments` tables.

Employees			
EmployeeID	**Name**	**Username**	**Extension**
1	Zak Ruvalcaba	zak	1234
2	Shane Weebe	shane	1235
3	Ted Lindsey	ted	1236

DeptLookup	
EmployeeID	**DepartmentID**
1	5
1	6
2	6
3	6

Departments	
DepartmentID	**Department**
5	Executive
6	Engineering

The `DeptLookup` table associates employee IDs (`EmployeeID`) with department IDs (`DepartmentID`). In this example, we can see that Zak Ruvalcaba belongs to both the "Executive" and "Engineering" departments.

A look-up table is created in much the same way as is any other table. The difference lies in the choice of the primary key. Every table we've created so far has had a column named *something*ID that was designed to be the primary key for the table. Designating a column as a primary key tells the database not to allow two entries to have the same value in that column. It also speeds up database searches based on that column.

In the case of a look-up table, there is no single column that we want to force to have unique values. Each employee ID may appear more than once, as an employee may belong to more than one department, and each department ID may appear more than once, as a department may contain many employees. What we *don't* want to allow is the same *pair* of values to appear in the table twice. For this reason, we usually create look-up tables with a multi-column primary key.

In this example, the primary key for the `DeptLookup` table would consist of the `EmployeeID` and `DepartmentID` columns. This enforces the uniqueness that is appropriate to a look-up table, preventing a particular employee from being assigned to a particular department more than once.

If you'd like to learn more about many-to-many relationships, have a browse through your database's documentation, or check out some of the reading material at http://www.datamodel.org/.

Relationships in the `Dorknozzle` Database

Just about every table within the `Dorknozzle` database has a relationship with another table. The good news is that they are all one-to-many relationships. The bad news is that it's your turn to create the relationships, unless, of course, you've used the `.mdb` file from the code archive, in which case they've all been created for you!

Table 6.23 outlines the table the relationship starts from (Initial Table) along with its primary key (Primary Key) and the table the relationship goes to (Related Table). The foreign key, in this case, always has the same name as the corresponding primary key. It also indicates whether to enable cascading updates and cascading deletes (referential integrity should always be enabled).

Table 6.23. Define the Relationships for all your Tables

Initial Table	Primary Key	Related Table	Cascade Updates	Cascade Deletes
Departments	DepartmentID	Employees	Yes	No
Employees	EmployeeID	HelpDesk	Yes	Yes
HelpDeskCategories	CategoryID	HelpDesk	Yes	No
HelpDeskSubjects	SubjectID	HelpDesk	Yes	No
HelpDeskStatus	StatusID	HelpDesk	Yes	No
EmployeeStore	ItemID	Newsletters	Yes	No
CompanyEvents	EventID	Newsletters	Yes	No
Employees	EmployeeID	Newsletters	Yes	No

When it's complete, your relationship diagram should resemble Figure 6.14.

Figure 6.14. A complete relationship diagram for the Dorknozzle database.

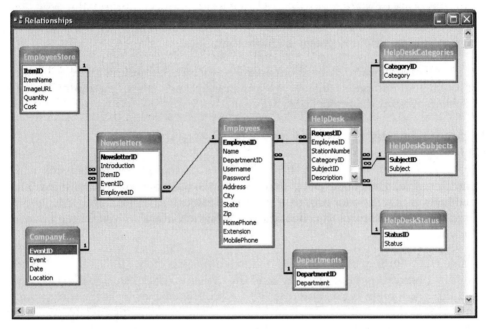

Stored Procedures

Stored procedures are a way of storing within a database code that is repeatedly used on that database. There are a few advantages to using stored procedures. First, you move some tasks from your Web server to the database server, resulting in less work for the Web server (assuming these are separate machines). Second, stored procedures are a means of modularizing repetitive code so that you never have to write the same line of code more than once within your applications. You simply create a stored procedure within your database and call it through your application, passing in parameters as necessary. In return, the stored procedure executes complex tasks and can return data back to the application that calls it. We'll get into programming simple stored procedures in Chapter 8.

Unfortunately, stored procedures are only available in MSDE, not Access.

Queries

Extracting information from your database is generally accomplished through the use of **queries**. Covered in greater detail in the next chapter, queries allow you to construct statements that, when executed, extract information from the database into a virtual table (called a **view**) for use within your applications.

Although "querying" is a generic term used for the extraction of data from a database, Access also has a category called "Queries" that allows you to manually construct statements for use within your applications. You can save those queries and use them within code, or reference them later by simply opening and viewing the constructed query. We'll cover these in greater detail in the next chapter.

Security

Ensuring that your database is secure and accessible only by certain individuals or departments is crucial. Many database management systems provide a means for setting security options for users and groups of users.

Security in Access

Access enables you to modify security settings by selecting Tools, Security. To set a password for a database, you have to make sure no other users are accessing it at the time; you do this by opening it exclusively. Follow the steps outlined below:

1. First, close the `Dorknozzle` database, then choose File, Open... to begin re-opening the database.

2. From the Open menu in the bottom right corner of the Open dialog, select Open Exclusive.

3. With the database now open exclusively to you, select Set Database Password from the Tools, Security menu.

4. Give the database a password and click OK.

That's it! Your database will only be available to those who know the password. Close Access and reopen the database to find out if it works.

Security in MSDE

MSDE, on the other hand, is meant for development purposes only. It relies on Windows Authentication by default. What this means is that MSDE checks credentials against your Windows login information.

Remember, though, that back in Chapter 1, we customized a few of MSDE's installation parameters. The first parameter, `DISABLENETWORKPROTOCOLS=1`, effectively changed the authentication mechanism from Windows Authentication to Mixed Mode Authentication. This meant that we were able to specify a login directly into MSDE, and allow MSDE to handle the authentication, rather than Windows. The second parameter, `SAPWD=PASSWORD`, effectively set the user name for the authentication within MSDE to your own customized user name with no password.

Summary

This chapter has introduced you to some simple yet important concepts relating to data storage. You learned about the underlying structure of a modern relational database, which is composed of tables, columns, and rows, and about crucial concepts that can aid in performance, maintenance, and efficiency. Chapter 7 goes beyond data storage and introduces you to the language used in data access—Structured Query Language.

7

Structured Query Language

So your database has been created, you've defined all of the tables you'll need, all of the columns for your tables, and even relationships between tables. The question now is, "How do you get to that data?" Sure, you can open the database, look at the data the tables contain and manually insert and delete records, but that does little to help your Web users to interact with that data. Mary in Accounting isn't going to want to open your database to retrieve another employee's phone extension—this functionality has to be provided by you, so staff members can access the data intuitively within your application. All of this can be done using Web Forms, Web Controls, some code, and a useful database programming language known as **Structured Query Language** or **SQL**.

SQL has its origins in a language developed by IBM in the 1970s called SEQUEL (for Structured English QUEry Language), and is still often referred to today as "sequel." It represents a very powerful way of interacting with current database technologies and the tables that make them up. SQL has roughly thirty keywords and is the language of choice for simple and complex database operations alike. The **queries** you will construct with these keywords range from the simple to complex strings of subqueries and table joins. This chapter cannot begin to cover all there is to know on the subject, but I hope it will provide you with an introduction to beginning and advanced SQL concepts.

Basic SQL

Information contained within a database is useless unless you have a means of extracting it. SQL is the language that does just that; it allows for quick but sophisticated access to the database data through the use of queries. Queries pose questions and return the results to your application. But don't think of SQL as simply a way of extracting information. The SQL language can accomplish a variety of tasks, allowing us to not only extract information from a database, but also to add, modify, and delete information as well.

For example, imagine that you're trying to extract information from the `EmployeeStore` table of the `Dorknozzle` database, which contains a list of company branded items that we added in the last chapter:

Table 7.1. Sample Contents of the `EmployeeStore` Table

ItemID	ItemName	Quantity	Cost
1	Dorknozzle Shirt	150	$12.99
2	Dorknozzle Hooded Sweat Shirt	40	$32.99
3	Dorknozzle Longsleeve Shirt	60	$19.99
4	Dorknozzle Polo Shirt	35	$29.99
5	Dorknozzle Sticker	1500	$1.99
6	Dorknozzle Mousep-ad	1000	$5.99
7	Dorknozzle Mug	500	$5.99
8	Dorknozzle Water Bottle	300	$5.99
9	Dorknozzle Golf Balls	100	$2.99
10	Dorknozzle Pen	1500	$1.99
11	Dorknozzle Carry Bag	80	$9.00

The `EmployeeStore` table contains four columns:

1. an `ItemID` with an AutoNumber (Access) or Int (Identity) (MSDE) that increments a value whenever an item is added

2. an `ItemName` that contains a Text (Access) or Nvarchar (MSDE) data type for the product title

3. an Integer (Access) or Int (MSDE) column for `Quantity` that allows us to store how many of a certain type of item we have left in stock

4. a `Cost` column, which allows us to store the cost of each item

In the following sections, you'll learn how to generate queries to view existing data, insert new data, modify data, and delete data from the `EmployeeStore` table.

The queries that we create here are for the demonstration of SQL only. Once you learn the fundamentals of SQL, the next step is to put everything together and begin building and coding the Web Forms that your users will interact with. Let's get started! Now is a great time to open Access or Web Data Administrator.

Working with the Query Editor in Access

You can generate your own queries in Access easily, using the Query Editor. We'll start with some queries that demonstrate particular principles. In the coming chapters, we'll take the SQL statements generated by the query editor and use them within our application. You can begin the process by following the steps outlined below:

1. With the `Dorknozzle` database open in the Access file manager, select Queries from the left-hand category menu.

2. Double-click Create query in Design view.

3. Add the `Employees` table and the `Departments` table from the Show Table dialog box, as shown in Figure 7.1, then click Close.

Figure 7.1. Add the `Employees` table and `Departments` table to the designer.

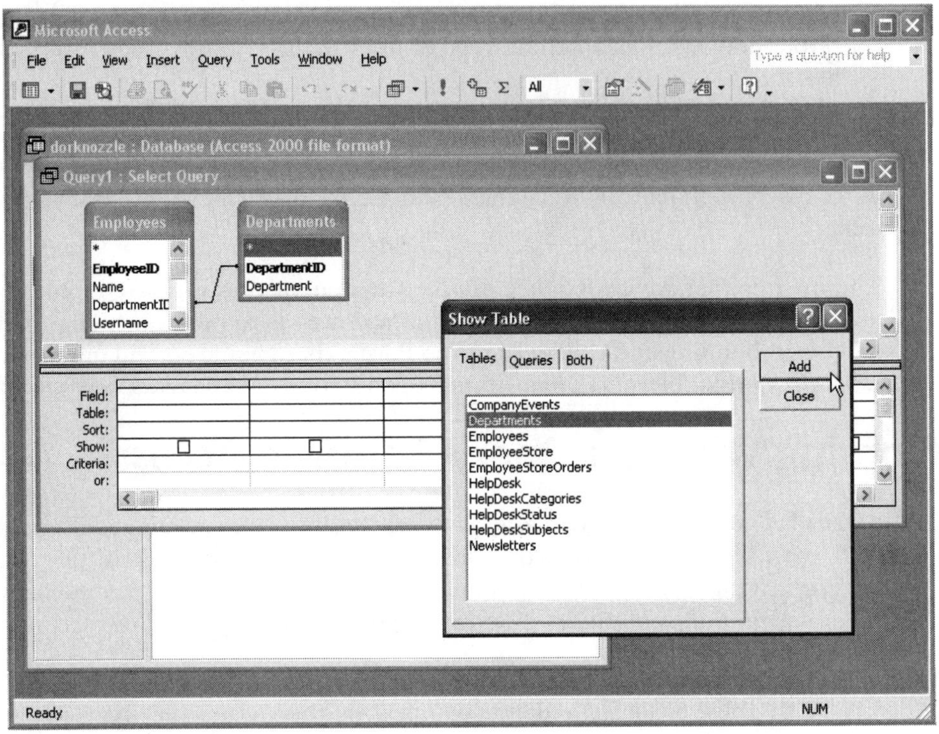

4. From the first Field drop-down in the lower half of the Query window, select `Employees.Name`—the `Name` column of the `Employees` table. From the second Field drop-down, select `Departments.Department` as shown in Figure 7.2. We've now selected the columns that we want to include in our query.

Figure 7.2. Select the fields to use within the query from both the Employees table and the Departments table.

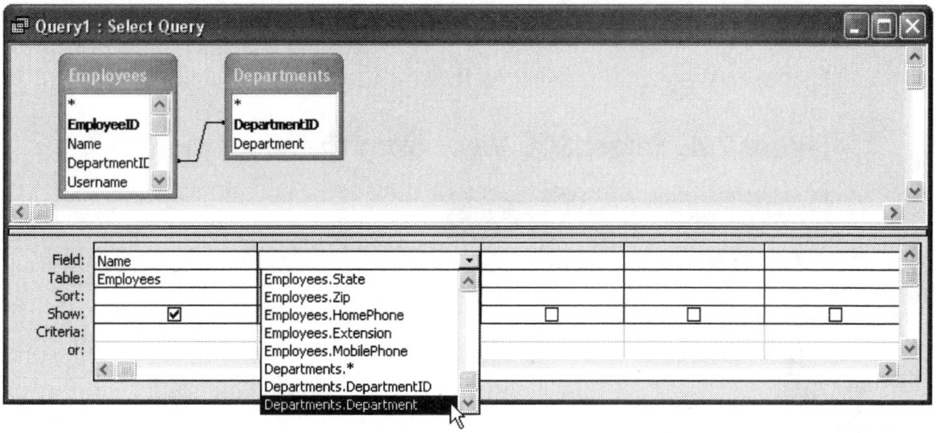

5. Click the red exclamation mark on the main Access toolbar—this runs the query. The result, similar to Figure 7.3, shows all the employees and their respective departments within one virtual table view.

Figure 7.3. All employees and their respective departments are shown within one virtual table view.

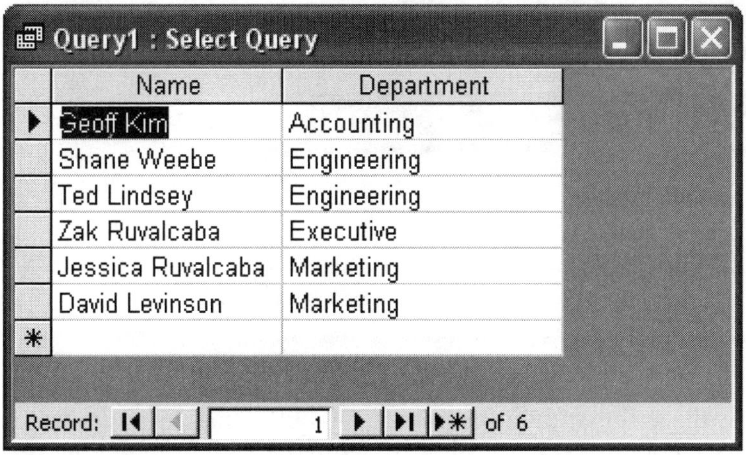

What you ultimately do with the query is entirely up to you. You can save the query for later use by selecting Save As from the File menu, or you can copy the generated SQL query using the SQL View feature of Access. To do this, follow the steps outlined below:

1. From the View menu, select SQL View as shown in Figure 7.4.

Figure 7.4. Select SQL View from the View menu.

2. The SQL View will appear similar to Figure 7.5.

Figure 7.5. The SQL View allows you manually to generate queries using SQL.

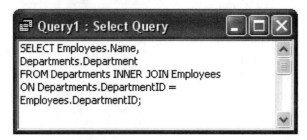

All that text is the automatically generated SQL query that corresponds to your query. In a few sections, you'll learn how to write these kinds of queries on your own.

Working with the Query Editor in Web Data Administrator

You can also generate your own queries in Web Data Administrator, using its Query Editor. Unfortunately, Web Data Administrator's Query Editor isn't as friendly as the Access Query Editor. Let's take a look:

1. Log into your instance of MSDE from the usual http://localhost/SqlWebAdmin page in a browser window.

2. Once you're inside the Web Data Administrator's DBMS, select Query for the `Dorknozzle` database.

3. You will be redirected to the Query Editor for the `Dorknozzle` database.

4. Now type the following simple SQL statement:

```
SELECT Employees.Name FROM Employees
```

5. Click Execute. The result will appear similar to Figure 7.6.

Figure 7.6. Web Data Administrator's Query Editor allows you to create and save queries using SQL.

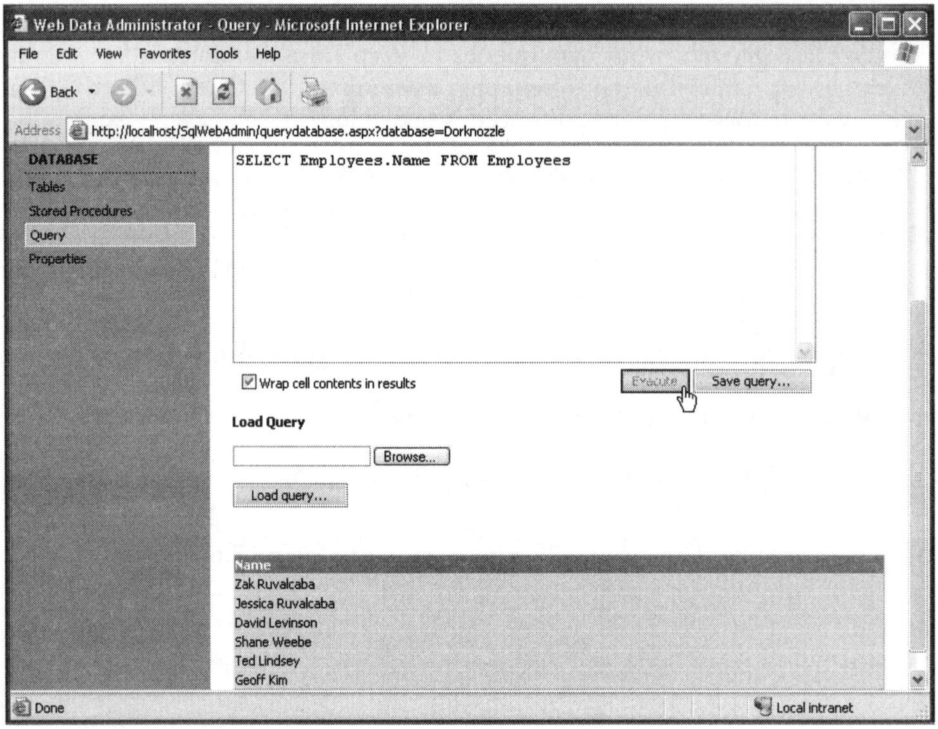

Now that you've got a feel for SQL, let's talk more about the clauses and keywords that make up SQL statements.

The SELECT Query

The foundation of all SQL queries is the SELECT query. This query is generally constructed using SELECT and FROM **clauses**. To understand this more clearly, take a look at the following statement, which will select all the records from the EmployeeStore table:

```
SELECT *
FROM EmployeeStore
```

In this case, the SELECT clause is SELECT *, which means you're selecting all columns—* means 'everything'. The FROM clause is FROM EmployeeStore, which means you want to pull records from the EmployeeStore table. Together, these two clauses create an SQL statement that extracts all columns from the Employ-eeStore table.

You've probably noticed that the two clauses appear on separate lines. If you wanted to keep the entire statement on one line, that's fine, but separating out the statements like this helps keeps the SQL readable. Also, SQL is not actually a case-sensitive language, but, as you can see, I've capitalized the SELECT and FROM keywords according to the popular convention.

To sum up then, here is the normal syntax for a SELECT query:

SELECT	This keyword indicates we want to retrieve data, rather than modify (which uses the UPDATE keyword), add (which uses INSERT), or delete (which uses DELETE) data.
column(s)	The names of the column(s) in the database table you want to retrieve. List more than one column by separating them with commas. You can also use * to select all columns.
FROM	The FROM clause identifies the table(s) from which the data will be extracted. This clause is required with all SELECT statements.
table(s)	The name(s) of the table(s) from which you want to extract data. List multiple tables by separating their names with commas.

Thus, the preceding example statement would retrieve all records from the Em-ployeeStore table, producing a set of results like that shown in Table 7.2.

Table 7.2. All Items within the `EmployeeStore` Table

ItemID	ItemName	Quantity	Cost
1	Dorknozzle Shirt	150	$12.99
2	Dorknozzle Hooded Sweat Shirt	40	$32.99
3	Dorknozzle Longsleeve Shirt	60	$19.99
4	Dorknozzle Polo Shirt	35	$29.99
5	Dorknozzle Sticker	1500	$1.99
6	Dorknozzle Mousepad	1000	$5.99
7	Dorknozzle Mug	500	$5.99
8	Dorknozzle Water Bottle	300	$5.99
9	Dorknozzle Golf Balls	100	$2.99
10	Dorknozzle Pen	1500	$1.99
11	Dorknozzle Carry Bag	80	$9.00

Now, you try it. If you're using Access, type this SQL query into the Access SQL View. When you're done, select the Run (red exclamation mark) icon as before to return the results shown in Figure 7.7.

Figure 7.7. Select all of the records from the `EmployeeStore` table in Access.

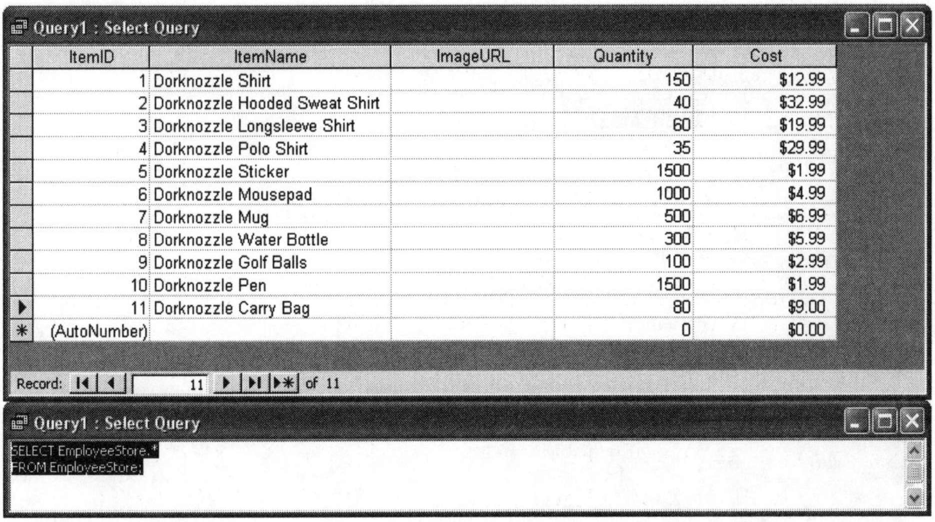

The results are presented to you within a datasheet. You can switch back and forth between the Datasheet View and SQL View using the View menu mentioned earlier.

If you're using Web Data Administrator, you can perform the same task. Type the SQL query into the Query Editor and click Execute. The results are presented in a tabular view at the bottom of the page similar to Figure 7.8.

Figure 7.8. Select all the records from the `EmployeeStore` table in Web Data Administrator.

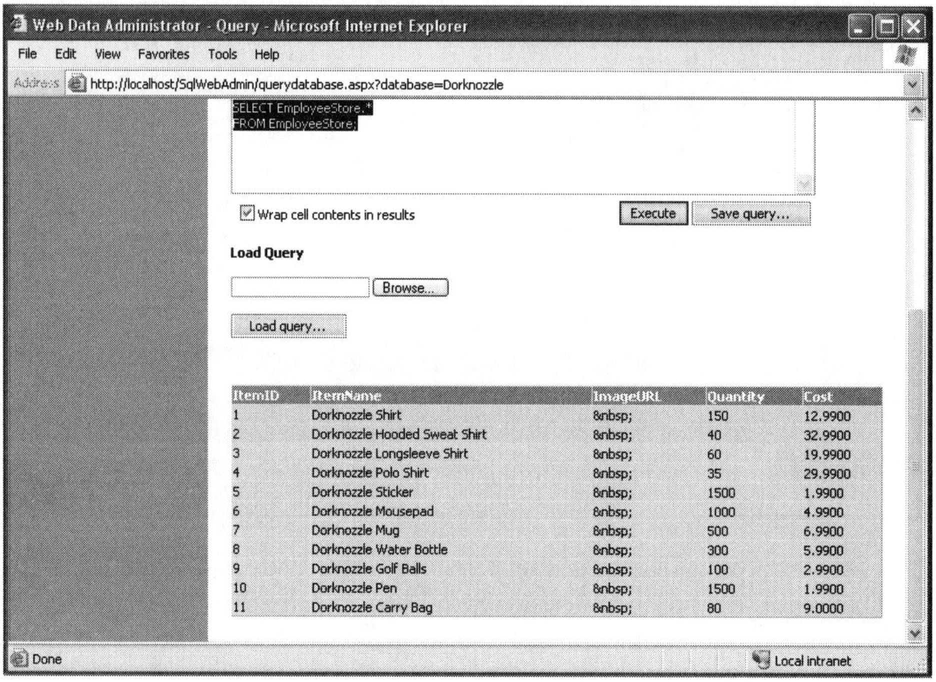

See how easy that is? The `SELECT` query is probably the one that you'll use the most. Now, let's move on and take a look at some variations of the `SELECT` query. Then we'll see how you can insert, modify, and delete items from the database using other keywords.

Selecting Certain Fields

If you did not want to select all the fields from the database table, you would include only the fields that you wanted in place of the *:

```
SELECT ItemName, Cost
FROM EmployeeStore
```

The preceding statement would retrieve the data from the `ItemName` and the `Cost` fields only. Rather than specifying the *, which would return all the fields within the database table, we specify only the fields that we need.

Note that the order of the fields determines the order in which the data will be retrieved. For example, switching the fields' names by placing Cost in front of ItemName would give the result set in Table 7.3:

Table 7.3. Selecting Specific Fields Rather than an Entire Table

Cost	ItemName
$12.99	Dorknozzle Shirt
$32.99	Dorknozzle Hooded Sweat Shirt
$19.99	Dorknozzle Longsleeve Shirt
$29.99	Dorknozzle Polo Shirt
$1.99	Dorknozzle Sticker
$5.99	Dorknozzle Mousepad
$5.99	Dorknozzle Mug
$5.99	Dorknozzle Water Bottle
$2.99	Dorknozzle Golf Balls
$1.99	Dorknozzle Pen
$9.00	Dorknozzle Carry Bag

Try it for yourself in Access or Web Data Administrator.

Selecting Unique Data with DISTINCT

The information within the EmployeeStore table contains duplicate values: some of the items share the same cost. If you constructed a query to retrieve all the item costs from the EmployeeStore table, some results would be replicated, because the mouse pad, mug, and water bottle all have a price of $5.99, and both the sticker and pen cost $1.99. Adding the DISTINCT keyword just before the table name extracts only unique instances of data contained within the table column. Take a look at the following SQL statement:

```
SELECT DISTINCT Cost
FROM EmployeeStore
```

This will produce the result in Table 7.4.

Table 7.4. Selecting Distinct Costs

Cost
$12.99
$32.99
$19.99
$29.99
$1.99
$5.99
$2.99
$9.00

In this case, because only the Cost column was included within the SQL state-ment, unique instances within the Cost column were returned.

You would probably never want to perform a query like this on this particular table in reality. Let's think of another, more realistic, example. Imagine you've stored the details of department managers and the IDs of the departments they manage in a table named Managers, as shown in Table 7.5.

Table 7.5. Managers and their Departments

Manager	DepartmentID
Zak Ruvalcaba	1
Zak Ruvalcaba	2
Jessica Ruvalcaba	4
Shane Weebe	3
David Levinson	3

In this case, Zak Ruvalcaba appears twice within the table. The reason for this is simple—I manage two departments. To simply get a list of managers in the company, we could use the DISTINCT keyword as follows:

```
SELECT DISTINCT Manager
FROM Managers
```

The result would be as follows:

Table 7.6. A Simple List of Managers

Manager
Zak Ruvalcaba
Jessica Ruvalcaba
Shane Weebe
David Levinson

OK, this is a fairly simplistic example. The point I'm trying to make is that DIS-TINCT can be a very useful keyword, and, in fact, can save us a lot of messing around when we make certain queries from code.

Row Filtering with WHERE

The WHERE clause is used in conjunction with SQL queries, including the SELECT query, to deliver more refined search results based on individual field criteria. The following example could be used to extract all items in the database that have a cost of $1.99:

```
SELECT *
FROM EmployeeStore
WHERE Cost=1.99
```

It returns the results shown in Table 7.7.

Table 7.7. Filtering Using the WHERE Clause

ItemID	ItemName	Quantity	Cost
5	Dorknozzle Sticker	1500	$1.99
10	Dorknozzle Pen	1500	$1.99

Notice that the SELECT only pulls rows where the criteria specified by the WHERE clause are true. If a record with a Cost of $1.99 did not exist, it wouldn't return anything. You could refine your search even further using the AND operator as follows:

```
SELECT *
FROM EmployeeStore
WHERE Cost=1.99 AND ItemName='Dorknozzle Sticker'
```

This SQL statement returns the result in Table 7.8.

Table 7.8. Using the WHERE Clause with the AND Operator

ItemID	ItemName	Quantity	Cost
5	Dorknozzle Sticker	1500	$1.99

Notice how the word AND has been placed in between the two conditions, Cost=1.99 and ItemName='Dorknozzle Sticker'. The word AND is known here as an **operator**. Operators are used in SQL, just as they are in C# and VB.NET, to evaluate expressions and, more specifically, to filter results returned by a query. Another example might occur if your company had thousands of employees and you needed to perform a query based on the name "John Smith." There could easily be two or three names that matched that criterion. Instead of creating the query to extract just John Smith, you could use the AND operator to extract records with the name John Smith and the desired location, for example.

Matching Patterns with LIKE

As you've just seen, the WHERE clause allows you to filter results based on criteria that you specify. There may be times, however, when you do not immediately know what those criteria are. For example, if you wanted to search your company's Employees table for all employees named Zak Ruvalcaba, you would use the following SQL statement:

```
SELECT *
FROM Employees
WHERE Name='Zak Ruvalcaba'
```

That's easy to do. We could also use the LIKE keyword to extract the same information from the Employees table as follows:

```
SELECT *
FROM Employees
WHERE Name LIKE 'Zak Ruvalcaba'
```

The benefit to using the LIKE keyword is that you can extract data based on partially complete information with the help of a **wildcard character**. In standard SQL, as supported by MSDE, the wildcard is the % symbol, while in Access it is *. This wildcard will match any sequence of zero or more characters. For instance, if we wanted to find all names within our Employees table with the last name of Ruvalcaba, we could modify the SQL query using a wildcard, as follows:

```
SELECT *
FROM Employees
WHERE Name LIKE '%Ruvalcaba'
```

Or, in Access, like so:

```
SELECT *
FROM Employees
WHERE Name LIKE '*Ruvalcaba'
```

Here, all records where the `Name` column ends with Ruvalcaba are returned as shown in Table 7.9.

Table 7.9. All Employees with a Last Name of Ruvalcaba are Returned

Name
Zak Ruvalcaba
Jessica Ruvalcaba

Because we knew the last name was Ruvalcaba, we only needed to place a wildcard before the last name. But what if you didn't know how to spell the entire last name? My name is pretty difficult to spell! You could modify your SQL statement to use two wildcards as follows:

```
SELECT *
FROM Employees
WHERE Name LIKE '%Ruv%'
```

In Access, this would be:

```
SELECT *
FROM Employees
WHERE Name LIKE '*Ruv*'
```

In this case, the wildcard is placed before and after the string `Ruv`. Although this statement would still return the same values as the table above, it would also return any employees whose names (first or last) contain the sequence Ruv. As SQL is case-insensitive, this would include the names Sarah Ruvdada, Jonny Noruvitch, Truvor MacDonald, etc.

Selecting Ranges of Values with BETWEEN

There may be times when you'll want to search within a database table for rows that fall within a certain range of values. For instance, if you wanted to retrieve all items in a certain price range from the EmployeeStore table, you could use the BETWEEN keyword, as follows:

```
SELECT *
FROM EmployeeStore
WHERE Cost BETWEEN 9 AND 20
```

In this case, all items that cost between $9 and $20 are returned. Note that this range is inclusive, so any items that are exactly $9 or exactly $20 will also be retrieved. You could also use the NOT keyword before the BETWEEN keyword to specify all items that fall outside this range, as follows:

```
SELECT *
FROM EmployeeStore
WHERE Cost NOT BETWEEN 9 AND 20
```

In this example, all rows are returned where the price is less than $9 or greater than $20, not including any items which are exactly $9 or $20.

The INSERT Statement

In the coming chapters, we'll build an application that will allow administrators to access the EmployeeStore table in order to add new items as they become available for employees to purchase. We can add data to the database using the INSERT INTO and VALUES clauses. Let's say we want to add a Dorknozzle License Plate Frame to our EmployeeStore table, with a quantity of 500 and a cost of $9.99. We don't have a URL for the image yet. We could generate a new record using the following statement:

```
INSERT INTO EmployeeStore (ItemName, ImageURL, Quantity, Cost)
VALUES ('Dorknozzle License Plate Frame', '', 500, 9.99)
```

The INSERT statement generally consists of:

INSERT INTO	These keywords indicate that this statement will add a new record to the database.
table	This is the name of the table in which you want to insert the values.

(columns)	This is the list of columns for which you'll be supplying data in this statement, separated by commas and enclosed in parentheses.
VALUES	This keyword comes between the list of columns and their values.
(values)	This is the list of values that you wish to supply for the columns listed above, respectively.

Try the above SQL statement. In Access:

1. Type the SQL statement above into SQL View.

2. Click Run. You will be presented with a message alerting you that the action cannot be undone. Click Yes.

3. To view the results of the insertion, use the SELECT statement as follows:

```
SELECT *
FROM EmployeeStore
```

4. Click Run.

5. The new addition will appear in Datasheet View as shown in Figure 7.9:

Figure 7.9. Add the License Plate Frame to the EmployeeStore table using Access.

ItemID	ItemName	ImageURL	Quantity	Cost
1	Dorknozzle Shirt		150	$12.99
2	Dorknozzle Hooded Sweat Shirt		40	$32.99
3	Dorknozzle Longsleeve Shirt		60	$19.99
4	Dorknozzle Polo Shirt		35	$29.99
5	Dorknozzle Sticker		1500	$1.99
6	Dorknozzle Mousepad		1000	$5.99
7	Dorknozzle Mug		500	$5.99
8	Dorknozzle Water Bottle		300	$5.99
9	Dorknozzle Golf Balls		100	$2.99
10	Dorknozzle Pen		1500	$1.99
11	Dorknozzle Carry Bag		80	$9.00
12	Dorknozzle License Plate Frame		500	$9.99
(AutoNumber)			0	$0.00

Record: 13 of 13

In Web Data Administrator:

1. Type the `INSERT` statement above into the Query Editor for the `Dorknozzle` database.

2. Click Execute.

3. To view the results of the insertion, use the `SELECT` statement as follows:

```
SELECT *
FROM EmployeeStore
```

4. The new addition will appear at the bottom of the page, as shown in Figure 7.10:

Figure 7.10. Add the License Plate Frame to the `EmployeeStore` table using Web Data Administrator's Query Editor.

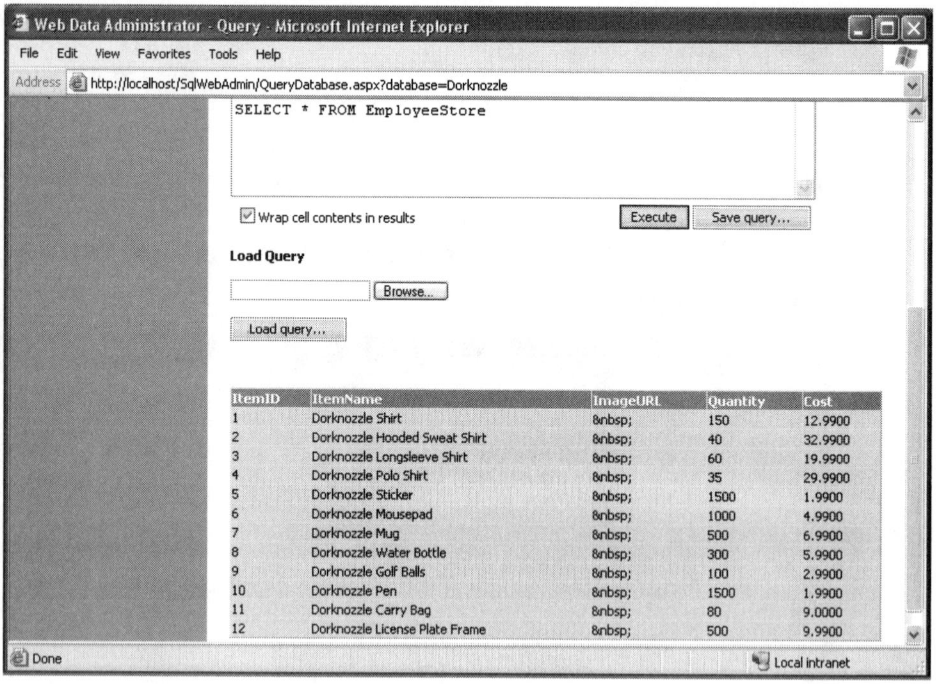

The UPDATE Statement

The UPDATE statement is used to make changes to existing records within your database tables. The UPDATE statement requires certain keywords, and usually a WHERE clause to modify particular records. For instance:

```
UPDATE Employees
SET Name='Zak Christian Ruvalcaba'
WHERE EmployeeID=1
```

This statement would change the name of the employee whose EmployeeID is 1. Let's take a look at the breakdown of the UPDATE statement syntax:

UPDATE *table*	This clause identifies this statement as one that modifies the named table in the database.
SET *column=value,* *column=value,* ...	The SET clause specifies the columns you want to modify and their new values.
WHERE *conditions*	The filter to use to select the row(s) from the table that are to be updated. Though this clause is optional, you probably wouldn't want to set *all* rows to have the name Zak Christian Ruvalcaba (although it is a very nice name)! So, you must filter the query using a WHERE clause.

Now, let's use an UPDATE statement on the EmployeeStore table to update the quantity of license plate frames in stock. In Access, follow the steps outlined below:

1. Switch to SQL View and type the following query:

```
UPDATE EmployeeStore
SET Quantity=200
WHERE ItemName='Dorknozzle License Plate Frame'
```

2. Select the exclamation icon to run the query. The result of the UPDATE statement within Access is similar to Figure 7.11.

Figure 7.11. Update the number of license plate frames within Access from 500 to 200.

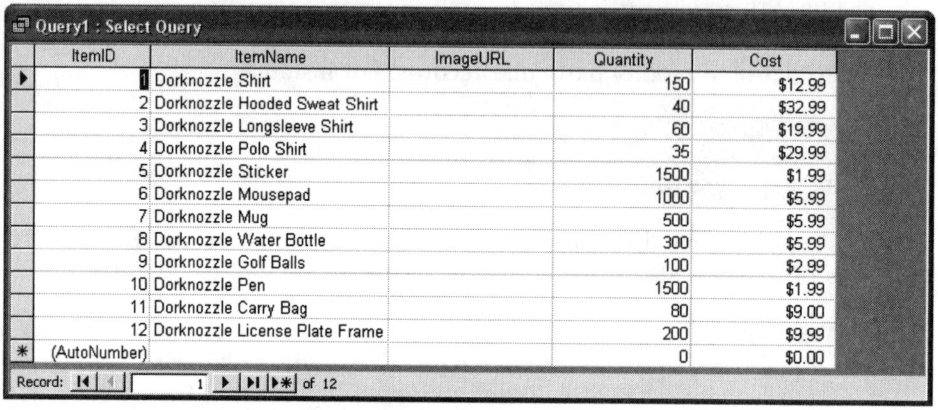

ItemID	ItemName	ImageURL	Quantity	Cost
1	Dorknozzle Shirt		150	$12.99
2	Dorknozzle Hooded Sweat Shirt		40	$32.99
3	Dorknozzle Longsleeve Shirt		60	$19.99
4	Dorknozzle Polo Shirt		35	$29.99
5	Dorknozzle Sticker		1500	$1.99
6	Dorknozzle Mousepad		1000	$5.99
7	Dorknozzle Mug		500	$5.99
8	Dorknozzle Water Bottle		300	$5.99
9	Dorknozzle Golf Balls		100	$2.99
10	Dorknozzle Pen		1500	$1.99
11	Dorknozzle Carry Bag		80	$9.00
12	Dorknozzle License Plate Frame		200	$9.99
(AutoNumber)			0	$0.00

In Web Data Administrator:

1. Type the same UPDATE statement we used for Access into the Query Editor for the Dorknozzle database.

2. Click Execute.

3. To view the results of the insertion, use the SELECT statement as follows:

```
SELECT *
FROM EmployeeStore
```

4. The result of the UPDATE statement within Web Data Administrator is shown in Figure 7.12.

Figure 7.12. Update the number of license plate frames within Web Data Administrator from 500 to 200.

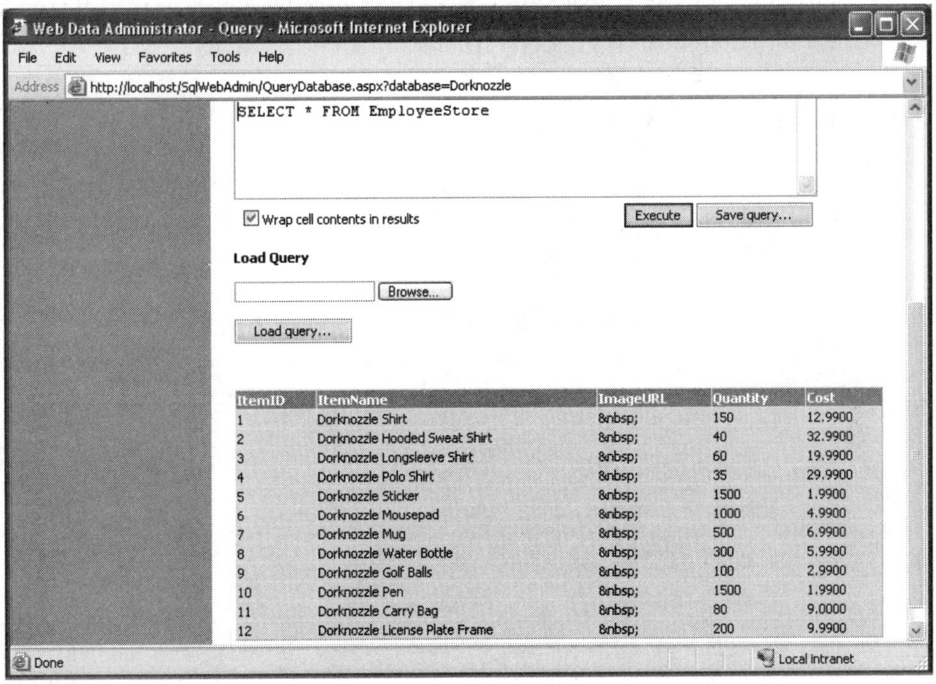

The DELETE Statement

The DELETE statement removes unwanted records from the database. You could (but please don't!) use it to delete all records from the EmployeeStore table, like so:

```
DELETE FROM EmployeeStore
```

Usually, we only want to remove records that meet certain criteria:

```
DELETE FROM EmployeeStore
WHERE ItemName='Dorknozzle License Plate Frame'
```

This statement would remove the license plate frame item from the EmployeeStore table. Be aware that you can't recover data once you've deleted it like this, so please be very careful when using this query.

Other Clauses

There are several other very useful clauses available within SQL, which allow the further refinement of SQL queries. Let's run through them.

The ORDER BY Clause

The ORDER BY clause provides you with a quick way of sorting the results of your query in either ascending or descending order. Consider the Employees table, shown in Table 7.10.

Table 7.10. A List of Employees

EmployeeID	Name	Username	Password
1	Zak Ruvalcaba	Zak	Zak
2	Jessica Ruvalcaba	Jessica	Jessica
3	David Levinson	David	David
4	Shane Weebe	Shane	Shane
5	Ted Lindsey	Ted	Ted
6	Geoff Kim	Geoff	Geoff

If you selected all the records using a simple SELECT statement, the results would be selected in the order in which the data was originally added to the database. Using the SELECT statement with an ORDER BY clause would allow you to sort the records on the basis of one of the columns, such as Name:

```
SELECT *
FROM Employees ORDER BY Name
```

The preceding statement would return results in alphabetical order based on Name, as shown in Table 7.11.

Table 7.11. Employees Ordered by Name in Ascending Order

EmployeeID	Name	Username	Password
3	David Levinson	David	David
6	Geoff Kim	Geoff	Geoff
2	Jessica Ruvalcaba	Jessica	Jessica
4	Shane Weebe	Shane	Shane
5	Ted Lindsey	Ted	Ted
1	Zak Ruvalcaba	Zak	Zak

Note that the default ordering here is ascending (i.e. running from A through Z). You could add the DESC designation (for descending) to the end of the statement, to order backwards:

```
SELECT *
FROM Employees ORDER BY Name DESC
```

Now, the results would be returned in descending order, as in Table 7.12.

Table 7.12. Employees Ordered by Name in Descending Order

EmployeeID	Name	Username	Password
1	Zak Ruvalcaba	Zak	Zak
5	Ted Lindsey	Ted	Ted
4	Shane Weebe	Shane	Shane
2	Jessica Ruvalcaba	Jessica	Jessica
6	Geoff Kim	Geoff	Geoff
3	David Levinson	David	David

You could also order by multiple columns by adding a comma after the field name and entering a second field name, as follows:

```
SELECT *
FROM Employees ORDER BY Name, Extension
```

In this case, the results are returned in alphabetical order by name, and any tying records (i.e. with the same name) will appear in order of phone number extension.

The GROUP BY and HAVING Clauses

These are two very useful clauses, but their use will not become clear until we've discussed SQL functions later in the chapter, so I'll leave explaining them until then.

Expressions

In programming, expressions are anything that, when calculated, result in a value. 1 + 1 is a very simple example of an expression. Expressions in SQL work in much the same way, but they don't necessarily have to be mathematical. Consider the example of table data in Table 7.13, which is merely a modification of the original Employees table.

Table 7.13. A List of Employees

EmployeeID	FirstName	LastName
1	Zak	Ruvalcaba
2	Jessica	Ruvalcaba
3	David	Levinson
4	Shane	Weebe

So far, you know how to create a SELECT statement to retrieve the first names or the last names of employees, but what if you want to get the complete name as a single string? The following SQL statement uses an expression that concatenates the FirstName and LastName fields:

```
SELECT EmployeeID, FirstName & LastName AS Name
FROM Employees
```

The & operator is used to concatenate, or join together, two fields into one virtual field that then takes the name given by the AS keyword. The results would be as in Table 7.14.

Table 7.14. A List of Employees Concatenated into One Field

EmployeeID	Name
1	ZakRuvalcaba
2	JessicaRuvalcaba
3	DavidLevinson
4	ShaneWeebe

Notice that there is no space between the first and last names. To add a space, you'll need to change the code as follows:

```
SELECT EmployeeID, FirstName & ' ' & LastName AS Name
FROM Employees
```

This provides the results shown below:

Table 7.15. A List of Employees Concatenated into One Field with Spaces

EmployeeID	Name
1	Zak Ruvalcaba
2	Jessica Ruvalcaba
3	David Levinson
4	Shane Weebe

Operators

Over the course of the previous sections, you've been introduced to the &, AND, NOT, and = operators. Operators are used in programming languages to evaluate expressions. Table 7.16 lists operators that you'll need to know to use SQL effectively.

Table 7.16. SQL Operators

Operator	Description
+	The addition operator adds two numerical fields or values together.
–	The minus operator is used when subtracting fields or values.
*	The multiplication operator is used when multiplying fields or values.
/	The divide operator is used when dividing fields or values.
>	The greater than operator is used in WHERE clauses to determine whether a first value is greater than the second, such as SELECT * FROM Employees WHERE EmployeeID > 10. The result would return all the records from the table whose EmployeeID is greater than ten (i.e. eleven and up).
<	The less-than operator is used in WHERE clauses to determine whether a first value is less than the second, such as SELECT * FROM Employees WHERE EmployeeID < 10. The result would return all the records from the table whose EmployeeID is less than ten (i.e. nine and lower).
>=	The greater than or equal to operator is used in WHERE clauses to determine whether a first value is greater than or equal to the second, such as SELECT * FROM Employees WHERE EmployeeID >= 10. The result would return the record with EmployeeID of ten, and every one after that.
<=	The less than or equal to operator is used in WHERE clauses to determine whether a first value is less than or equal to the second, such as SELECT * FROM Employees WHERE EmployeeID <= 10. The result would return the record with EmployeeID of ten, and every one before that.
<>	This operator is used to check whether a value is not equal to a second. You can also use != for this operator in MSDE (but not in Access).
OR	This operator is used with the WHERE clause in the SELECT statement. The OR operator can be used when a certain condition needs to be met, or when you can settle for a second, such as SELECT * FROM Employees WHERE EmployeeID=1 OR EmployeeID=2. The result would return the employee(s) with ID 1 or 2.

Operator	Description
AND	This operator works just like OR, except that it requires *all* of the conditions to be satisfied, not just *any* of them.
NOT	Typically used in conjunction with the LIKE operator, the NOT operator is used when a value is not going to be like the value of a second, such as SELECT * FROM Employees WHERE Name NOT LIKE 'Jess%'. This would return all employees whose name does not begin with 'Jess.'
_ or ?	The underscore operator is used in MSDE in WHERE clauses and matches any single character in a string. The equivalent in Access is ?. For instance, if you weren't sure of the first letter of Geoff Kim's surname, you could use SELECT * FROM Employees WHERE Name LIKE 'Geoff _im', which would return Geoff Kim's record, as well as Geoff Sim's, Geoff Vim's, etc., were there such employees in the database. Note that it has to match a single character, so Geoff Im would not be returned. To match zero or more you would use the % or * operator.
% or *	The multiple character operator is similar to the underscore operator, except that it matches multiple or zero characters, whereas the underscore operator only ever matches one. Use % in MSDE and other SQL-compliant databases. Use * in Access. You've already seen this operator in use.

Functions

Aside from using operators to manually construct expressions, SQL also provides some functions that you can use in queries. For the most part, SQL should have enough functions to accomplish any task that may arise. Be aware, however, that many databases support their own functions in addition to those provided by SQL. Some databases, including SQL Server and MSDE, support *many* more.

To use a function, we call it and pass as parameters the values we want the function to operate on. Unlike functions in VB.NET or C#, however, we can't create our own functions, and must use those that exist already. It's also important to note that although functions are very powerful, the functions available to you vary depending on the database you're using. For instance, Access doesn't support as many functions as does its big brother SQL Server. Other databases, such as Oracle or MySQL, for example, might support a function that performs the same action as one in Access or SQL Server, though it might be named or used slightly differently. If you are not using Access or MSDE, then some of the functions that we'll go over next may be different from those your database supports. Check with your database documentation for more information.

It's also important to note that SQL Server and Access each support hundreds of functions—too many in fact to list within this book. The next few sections outline those that you will probably use most.

Date and Time Functions

Date and time functions allow for the manipulation of dates and times that are stored within your database. Consider the `CompanyEvents` table shown in Table 7.17, and the data that you added in the previous chapter.

Table 7.17. Returning All Company Events by Date

EventID	Event	Date	Location
1	4th of July Fireworks Party	7/4/2003	Coronado Yacht Club
2	Company Bowling Night	7/14/2003	San Diego Bowl
3	Padres Baseball Night	7/21/2003	Qualcomm Stadium Gate F
4	Night at the Races	8/28/2003	Del Mar Racetrack

We could create a query like this:

```
SELECT *
FROM CompanyEvents
WHERE Date=#7/4/2003#
```

Note that we surround our literal date value with # characters instead of quotes to differentiate it from a text string. The result would look like Table 7.18.

Table 7.18. The Result of our Date Query

EventID	Event	Date	Location
1	4th of July Fireworks Party	7/4/2003	Coronado Yacht Club

Using the simple DATE() function, you could write a similar SQL query as follows:

```
SELECT *
FROM CompanyEvents
WHERE Date = DATE()
```

The DATE() function returns the current system date as a value. Assuming that today's date is July 4th 2003, the table listed above would be returned. Let's try another, more advanced example. If you wanted to find all the events occurring in the next month, you could use the DATEADD() function:

```
SELECT *
FROM CompanyEvents
WHERE Date BETWEEN DATE() AND DATEADD('m', 1, DATE())
```

Assuming that the current date was July 5th 2003, the results would match Table 7.19.

Table 7.19. Returning All Company Events for the Next Month

EventID	Event	Date	Location
2	Company Bowling Night	7/14/2003	San Diego Bowl
3	Padres Baseball Night	7/21/2003	Qualcomm Stadium Gate F

The DATEADD() function accepts three parameters. These parameters are:

❏ The units of date or time you wish to add or subtract. Typically, you would want to use one of three values: 'm' for month, 'w' for week, and 'd' for day. Here, we've used 'm'.

❏ How many of the specified units to add or subtract. In our example, one month is added, which would give us a date one month from today.

❏ The base date that you want to add to (or subtract from). In this case, we're calling the DATE() function to use today's date.

With July 5th 2003 as today's date, our query would thus return all events occurring between today and August 5th 2003.

Tip

List supported functions in Access

An easy way to see a list of all the supported functions in Access is to follow the steps outlined below:

1. Begin to build a query within Access by selecting Queries from the category selection menu.

2. Select Create query in Design view.

3. Add a table and click Close.

4. Select a field from the field drop-down menu selector.

5. Right-click the field name within the drop-down menu and select Build from the menu; the Expression Builder will appear. The Expression Builder allows you to construct expressions using operators, functions, etc., simply by selecting the various items from the menu.

6. Select Functions.

7. Select Built-In Functions. All Access's supported functions appear in the window on the right.

If you're concerned about the functions that MSDE supports, don't worry. MSDE supports the list that we covered before, plus a few more that, at this level, you probably don't need to worry about.

Aggregate Functions

This group of functions, which includes COUNT(), SUM(), AVG(), MIN() and MAX(), operates on the entire set of selected rows together, instead of individually.

The COUNT() Function

The COUNT() function returns the number of records selected by a query. Let's take the CompanyEvents table, shown in Table 7.20, as an example again.

Table 7.20. A List of Events in the `CompanyEvents` Table

EventID	Event	Date	Location
1	4th of July Fireworks Party	7/4/2003	Coronado Yacht Club
2	Company Bowling Night	7/14/2003	San Diego Bowl
3	Padres Baseball Night	7/21/2003	Qualcomm Stadium Gate F
4	Night at the Races	8/28/2003	Del Mar Racetrack

If you wanted to retrieve the total count of events that are listed in this table, you could run the following query:

```
SELECT COUNT(*) AS NumberOfEvents
FROM CompanyEvents
```

The result would be as shown in Table 7.21.

Table 7.21. The Number of Events

NumberOfEvents
4

In this case, a total of four events are listed in our `CompanyEvents` database table.

The `COUNT()` function is even more useful when combined with a `GROUP BY` clause, which I mentioned earlier.

The `GROUP BY` Clause

This tricky clause instructs the database to examine a particular column of a SE-LECT query's results and group together rows with matching values. Aggregate functions like `COUNT()` then operate on those groups of rows, instead of the entire result set.

Thinking back to our company events example, what if we wanted to know the number of events for each month? You could use a `GROUP BY` clause in this instance to group the orders by the month and year. We'll use another of SQL's date functions, `DATEPART()`, to extract the month and year of each event date:

```
SELECT DATEPART('m', Date) & '/' & DATEPART('yyyy', Date)
   AS Month, COUNT(*) AS NumberOfEvents
FROM CompanyEvents
GROUP BY DATEPART('m', Date) & '/' & DATEPART('yyyy', Date)
```

The result would be:

Table 7.22. Using the COUNT() Function on Grouped Events

Month	NumberOfEvents
7/2003	3
8/2003	1

This reflects the fact that there are three events in July and one in August.

The HAVING Clause

The HAVING clause works similarly to the WHERE clause, except that you use the HAVING clause immediately after the GROUP BY clause. Like the WHERE clause, the HAVING clause filters results based on criteria that you specify. The following query builds on the CompanyEvents example, seeking out months that contain more than two events (after all, we don't want our employees having *too* much fun!):

```
SELECT DATEPART('m', Date) & '/' & DATEPART('yyyy', Date)
   AS Month, COUNT(*) AS NumberOfEvents
FROM CompanyEvents
GROUP BY DATEPART('m', Date) & '/' & DATEPART('yyyy', Date)
HAVING NumberOfEvents > 2
```

This returns a result that's similar to the one we saw before, except that this query only returns the months that satisfy the condition(s) specified in the HAVING clause.

Table 7.23. Using the HAVING Clause

Month	NumberOfEvents
7/2003	3

What is the difference between the WHERE clause and the HAVING clause, you ask? The WHERE clause filters the result set *before* the GROUP BY clause does its thing, while the HAVING clause comes after. So in this example, you couldn't specify a condition involving the NumberOfEvents column in the WHERE because that column's values are calculated for each group generated by the GROUP BY clause. You must therefore use the HAVING clause for such conditions.

The SUM Function

Unlike the COUNT function, which returns a value reflecting the number of rows returned by a query, the SUM function performs a calculation on the data within those returned rows. If, for some reason, you needed to know the total number of all items in stock, you could query EmployeeStore with the following SQL:

```
SELECT SUM(Quantity) AS Total
FROM EmployeeStore
```

The statement would produce results something like Table 7.24:

Table 7.24. The Sum of the Quantities in the EmployeeStore Table

Total
5265

Rather than simply doing a count of the records, the sum is calculated based on the values contained within the specified column. As with COUNT, however, you can use GROUP BY to divide the results into groups and then calculate the SUM for each group.

The AVG Function

The AVG function returns the average of the values contained within specific fields. Let's query the EmployeeStore table:

```
SELECT AVG(Cost) AS Average
FROM EmployeeStore
```

This query would produce the result shown in Table 7.25.

Table 7.25. The Average of the Costs in the EmployeeStore Table

Average
11.8090

This tells us that the average price of the items in our employee shop is $11.81.

The `MIN` and `MAX` Functions

The `MIN` and `MAX` functions enable you to find the smallest and largest values of a specific column, respectively. To get the minimum price of items in the shop, you could write a query like this:

```
SELECT MIN(Cost) AS Minimum
FROM EmployeeStore
```

This query would produce the results shown in Table 7.26:

Table 7.26. The Minimum Order Within the `EmployeeStore` Table

Minimum
1.9900

To retrieve the maximum value of this column, try this query:

```
SELECT MAX(Cost) AS Maximum
FROM EmployeeStore
```

This would produce:

Table 7.27. The Maximum Order Within the `EmployeeStore` Table

Maximum
32.9900

Like the other functions we've seen, the `MIN` and `MAX` functions are great for the statistical analysis of records within the database. Using them, it wouldn't be difficult to put together a Web-based accounting application for monitoring sales per day that included totals, averages, and the minimum and maximum values for certain products sold.

Arithmetic Functions

Aside from the `SUM`, `MIN`, `MAX`, and `AVG` functions, a few other arithmetic functions can help you analyze fields within your database, including:

ABS   Returns the absolute value.

CEILING	Returns the smallest integer greater than the value passed in. In other words, this rounds up the value passed in. Not available in Access.
FLOOR	Returns the largest integer less than the value passed in. In other words, this rounds down the value passed in. Not available in Access
COS	Returns the cosine of the value where the value is the radians.
COSH	Returns the hyperbolic cosine of the value where the value is the radians.
SIN	Returns the sine of the value where the value is the radians.
SINH	Returns the hyperbolic sine of the value where the value is the radian.
TAN	Returns the tangent of the value where the value is the radians.
TANH	Returns the hyperbolic tangent of the value where the value is the radian.
EXP	Returns the mathematical constant e to the power specified.
MOD	Returns the remainder of one value divided by another.
SIGN	Returns the sign of the argument as -1, 0, or 1, depending on whether the value is negative, zero, or positive.
SQRT	Returns the non-negative square root of a value.
POWER	Returns the result of one value raised to the power of another.
LN	Returns the natural (base e) logarithm of a value.
LOG	Returns the logarithm of one value in the base of a another.

We can combine more than one function in a single query. For instance, say we wish to find the average price of items in our store, and round it up to the nearest dollar. We'd use a query something like this (note that the CEILING function is not available in Access):

```
SELECT CEILING(AVG(Cost)) AS Average
FROM EmployeeStore
```

The result we'd get would be as in Table 7.28.

Table 7.28. Returning Positive Numbers Using the ABS Function

Average
12.0000

String Functions

String functions are similar to other functions, except that they work with literal text values rather than numerical values.

UPPER	Returns the value passed in as all uppercase.
LOWER	Returns the value passed in as all lowercase.
LTRIM	Returns the value with the specified number of leftmost characters omitted.
RTRIM	Returns the value with the specified number of rightmost characters omitted.
REPLACE	Use the REPLACE function to change a portion of a string to a new sequence of characters that you specify. Takes three parameters: the source value (e.g. a field name), the search string, and a replacement string.
SUBSTRING	Returns the sequence of characters within a given value beginning at a specified start position and spanning a specified number of characters. Takes three parameters: the source value (e.g. a field name), the start position (where 1 is the start of the string), and the number of characters to return. Note that in Access, this function is called MID.
LEN	Returns length of a string in characters.

Let's try an example. The following SQL statement would return only the first ten letters of the ItemName field within the EmployeeStore table:

```
SELECT SUBSTRING(ItemName, 1, 10)
FROM EmployeeStore
```

The equivalent in Access would be:

```
SELECT MID(ItemName, 1, 10)
FROM EmployeeStore
```

Remember, the function accepts three parameters. First, the field name is passed in; second, we tell it the position within the string at which it must start; finally, we tell it how many characters to scan over.

Joins

Up to this point, we've primarily focused on extracting data from a single table. In many real world applications, you'll need to extract data from multiple tables at once. To do that, you'll need to use **joins**. Although there are several types of joins, the two most common types will be covered here: **inner joins** and **outer joins**.

INNER JOIN

An inner join is by far the most popular and simple type of join. An inner join allows you to see all the records of two tables between which a relationship is established. In our example database, the `Employees` table and the `Departments` table have a relationship established. A shortened version of the `Employees` table could resemble Table 7.29.

Table 7.29. A Shortened Version of the Employees Table

EmployeeID	Name	DepartmentID	Username
1	Zak Ruvalcaba	5	Zak
2	Jessica Ruvalcaba	1	Jessica
3	David Levinson	4	David
4	Shane Weebe	5	Shane

The `Departments` table would resemble Table 7.30.

Table 7.30. The `Departments` table

DepartmentID	Department
1	Accounting
2	Administration
3	Business Development
4	Customer Support
5	Engineering
6	Executive

Assume that you wanted to select all employees who worked within the Engineering department. If not for an inner join, you would have to perform two separate SELECT statements to get the data from the table. The first would obtain the ID of the Engineering department:

```
SELECT *
FROM Departments
WHERE Department='Engineering'
```

The results of this query would tell us that the Engineering department has ID 5. With this information, we could then make a second query to get the list of employees:

```
SELECT *
FROM Employees
WHERE DepartmentID=5
```

You can begin to see how tedious this could become—not to mention that it is completely inefficient. To solve this problem, an inner join could be performed as follows:

```
SELECT Employees.*, Departments.*
FROM Departments INNER JOIN Employees
ON Departments.DepartmentID = Employees.DepartmentID
WHERE Departments.Department='Engineering'
```

The first thing to notice here is that we're qualifying our column names by preceding them with the name of the table they belong to, and a period character (.). We have Employees.* instead of just *, and Departments.DepartmentID instead of simply DepartmentID, for instance. We need to do this because both tables have columns called by the same names, so we need a way to specify which table's column we're talking about at any one time.

As an analogy, imagine that you have two colleagues at work named John. If you needed to call John over the intercom, you might call for John Smith, otherwise both John Smith and John Thomas might answer. You need to use the first name qualified by the surname in this case. In fact, you could always use his full name, but it would be a bit tiresome, so you'd normally just use John. In exactly the same way, you could always refer to a column in a database using the `Table-Name.ColumnName` form, but it's only necessary when there's potential for ambiguity.

As for the join itself, the query pretty much speaks for itself. We are joining the `Departments` table and the `Employees` table (`Departments INNER JOIN Employees`) into a single, virtual table by matching the `DepartmentID` column in `Departments` with the `DepartmentID` column in `Employees` (`ON Departments.DepartmentID = Employees.DepartmentID`).

The join would effectively produce one virtual table of results as shown in Table 7.31.

Table 7.31. The `Employees` and `Departments` Tables Joined in a Single Result Set

EmployeeID	Name	DepartmentID	DepartmentID	Department
1	Zak Ruvalcaba	5	5	Engineering
4	Shane Weebe	5	5	Engineering

You will notice that the table above gives us exactly the information we needed by combining information from two different tables!

OUTER JOIN

Sometimes when you join two tables, you want to see every row in the first table, even when it has no related rows in the second table. At times like these, you need an outer join. Suppose you had an `Employees` table that resembled Table 7.32.

Table 7.32. A Version of the Employees Table

EmployeeID	Name	AddressID
1	Zak Ruvalcaba	45634
2	Jessica Ruvalcaba	34754
3	David Levinson	
4	Shane Weebe	97895

Imagine you also had an Addresses table that resembled Table 7.33.

Table 7.33. A Fictitious Addresses Table

AddressID	Address
45634	555 Sample St., San Diego
34754	343 Chestnut Rd., San Diego
97895	523 Main St., San Diego

To obtain a list of employees and their addresses, you might think to use an inner join on the preceding tables, like this:

```
SELECT Employees.Name, Employees.AddressID, Addresses.Address
FROM Employees INNER JOIN Addresses
ON Employees.AddressID = Addresses.AddressID
```

This would return the results shown in Table 7.34.

Table 7.34. The Employees and Address Tables Joined Together Using an Inner Join

Name	AddressID	Address
Zak Ruvalcaba	45634	555 Sample St., San Diego
Jessica Ruvalcaba	34754	343 Chestnut Rd., San Diego
Shane Weebe	97895	523 Main St., San Diego

Notice that because David Levinson didn't have an address associated with his employee record, his name was excluded from this list—probably not what we wanted! The solution is to use an outer join instead:

```
SELECT Employees.Name, Employees.AddressID, Addresses.Address
FROM Employees OUTER JOIN Addresses
ON Employees.AddressID = Addresses.AddressID
```

Because the outer join forces every entry in the first table (`Employees`) to appear at least once in the result set, we achieve our desired result as shown in Table 7.35.

Table 7.35. The `Employees` and `Address` Table Joined Together Using an Outer Join

Name	AddressID	Address
Zak Ruvalcaba	45634	555 Sample St., San Diego
Jessica Ruvalcaba	34754	343 Chestnut Rd., San Diego
David Levinson		
Shane Weebe	97895	523 Main St., San Diego

Subqueries

Sometimes, even with joins at your disposal, it may not be possible to retrieve the results that you need from a single `SELECT` query. On these occasions, you might need to create a `SELECT` query and compare the results to that of another query. For this, you'd want to use subqueries. A subquery is a query that's nested inside another query. Before you can nest one query inside another, you must first learn to use the `IN` operator.

The `IN` Operator

The `IN` operator is used in a `SELECT` query primarily to specify a list of values to match. A classic example involves finding all the employees who live in California, Indiana, and Maryland. You could write the following SQL statement to accomplish this task:

```
SELECT Name, State
FROM Employees
WHERE State = 'CA' OR State = 'IN' OR State = 'MD'
```

A better way to write this statement uses the `IN` operator as follows:

```
SELECT Name, State
FROM Employees
WHERE State IN ('CA', 'IN', 'MD')
```

The Embedded SELECT Statement

An embedded SELECT statement is used when you want to perform a second query within the WHERE clause of a primary query. Suppose you wanted to see a list of employees who have submitted help desk tickets. If that were the case, you could write the following statement:

```
SELECT *
FROM Employees
WHERE EmployeeID IN (SELECT DISTINCT EmployeeID FROM HelpDesk)
```

In this example, we use the IN operator to perform a second query, using an embedded SELECT statement within the WHERE clause of a primary query. Again, this statement effectively returns all employees first, then performs the second query to return all employees who have actual help desk tickets within the HelpDesk table.

There are a number of other ways to embed one SELECT statement inside another (all of which are types of subquery). For full details, consult the documentation for your database. For the purposes of this book, the above example is all you need to understand.

Summary

Data access is a crucial component to any application, and SQL provides the bridge to communicate with that data. As you have seen, SQL not only returns simple results from individual tables, but can produce complex data queries complete with filtering, sorting, expressions, and even nested statements. In Chapter 8, you'll begin to use the knowledge you've gained about databases and the language that connects to those databases together, to create a real, working application.

8

ADO.NET

I am fortunate to live in a beautiful city—San Diego, California—which offers its residents and visitors lots of things to do. I can drive about two hours northeast and go snowboarding in Big Bear Lake, drive about one hour east and go camping in the desert, or drive about twenty minutes west and go surfing in the ocean.

One place I recently visited was a small island named Coronado. There's a lot to do in Coronado, including visiting the Hotel Del Coronado, walking through downtown and window shopping, going to the marina, or just enjoying the beach community while strolling along the boardwalk. In order to get to Coronado, I had to cross a huge bridge called, you guessed it, the Coronado Bridge.

In order for tourists and commuters to get from Coronado to downtown San Diego, and vice versa, people must cross that bridge. The bridge comprises many parts that allow it to sustain the amount of traffic that passes over it on a daily basis. It has an actual road, barriers, a toll booth, pillars, etc., all of which work together to help people get from point A to point B. Without the Coronado Bridge, the island and all its beauty would be difficult to appreciate.

Like the Coronado Bridge, ADO.NET (ActiveX Data Objects .NET) provides a bridge between your data and your applications. It has many parts, all of which work together to help you move data from your database to your application smoothly.

Through the preceding chapters, you've made major strides in dynamic Web development using ASP.NET. You've learned about interface development using Web Forms and Web controls, you've learned about modeling and structuring your data within the framework of a database—you've even learned about the SQL language that is used to access the data stored within your database. What you have not yet learned is how to access data through your applications. This chapter will introduce you to ADO.NET, the data access "bridge" between your applications and the data store.

An Introduction to ADO.NET

The Coronado Bridge contains many parts: fifty-four inch diameter piles driven to depths of 100 feet in the bottom of San Diego Bay support thirty mission-arch shaped concrete piers. Braces and stiffeners for the bridge reside within the box girder superstructure through which cars pass. The thirty-four inch high barrier railing is designed to redirect out-of-control vehicles back onto the roadway with minimal damage. At the end of the bridge (on the Coronado side) lies a toll booth, where drivers must pay before they can pass into the laid-back beach community.

Likewise, ADO.NET is made up of many parts, all of which help you access data from within your applications. Like the toll booth at the end of the bridge, ADO.NET contains a `Connection` class that allows you to specify the database and any necessary credentials; a `Command` class, which, like the roadway overhead, provides passage for traffic between the mainland of your application and the island of your database; and a `DataReader` class, which, like the piers, piles, braces, and stiffeners, provides the intricate grid-like mesh that supports the ADO.NET superstructure. Every ADO.NET class contributes something to a successful link between your data and applications, just as every part of the Coronado Bridge helps allow cars to pass safely between the mainland and island.

In order to use the classes that ADO.NET exposes, you first have to decide which kind of database you'll use. If you plan to use Access, you'd simply need to import the `System.Data.OleDb` namespace. If you plan to use MSDE, you'll need to import the `System.Data.SqlClient` namespace.

Importing these namespaces gives your application code access to classes that expose the properties and methods you'll need for your particular type of database. Table 8.1 provides a list and a description of the most important classes contained within the `System.Data.OleDb` namespace.

Table 8.1. Classes Within the `System.Data.OleDb` Namespace

Class	Description
OleDbConnection	This class exposes properties and methods for establishing a direct connection to your OLE DB database (such as Access).
OleDbCommand	This class is used to hold the SQL queries and stored procedure names that are to be run on the database.
OleDbDataReader	Data is returned from the database into a DataReader. This class contains properties and methods that let you iterate through the data returned by your queries. Traditional ASP developers can think of the DataReader as being similar to a forward-only RecordSet, where data can only be read forward, one record at a time, and where you cannot move back to the beginning of the data stream.

Table 8.2 provides a list and a description of the most important classes contained within the `System.Data.SqlClient` namespace.

Table 8.2. Classes Within the `System.Data.SqlClient` Namespace

Class	Description
SqlConnection	This class exposes properties and methods for connecting to an SQL Server database (such as MSDE).
SqlCommand	This class holds the SQL queries and stored procedures that you intend to run on your SQL Server database.
SqlDataReader	Data is returned from the database into a DataReader. This class comes complete with properties and methods that let you iterate through the data it contains. Traditional ASP developers can think of the DataReader as being similar to a forward-only RecordSet, where data can only be read forward, one record at a time, and where you cannot move back to the beginning of the data stream.

As you can see, the only difference between the classes exposed by the two namespaces is that the `System.Data.OleDb` class names are prefixed by `Ole` and the `System.Data.SqlClient` class names are prefixed by `Sql`.

The most important classes here are `OleDbDataReader` and `SqlDataReader`—the two database-specific forms of `DataReader`. Once a connection is made to the database, the other classes populate a `DataReader` with the data returned by your queries. Discussed later in the chapter, the `DataReader` acts as if it were a database table in memory. It doesn't provide any built-in means to view the data it holds, but you could search through its contents from your application to find specific data, which can then be displayed using other ASP.NET controls within your application.

It's important to be aware that the namespaces `System.Data`, `System.Data.OleDb`, and `System.Data.SqlClient` expose more than the few classes listed in the tables above. We'll discuss some of the more advanced classes in the next chapter.

Once you're ready for coding, the process of establishing a link between the database and your application is a straightforward, six-step process:

1. Import the necessary namespaces into your ASP.NET page.

2. Create a code declaration block within the `<head>` tag of your ASP.NET page, complete with a suitable event handler (`Page_Load()` for instance).

3. Define a connection to your database with a `Connection` object inside that handler.

4. When you're ready to manipulate your database, set up the appropriate SQL statement(s) in a `Command` object.

5. Open the connection, execute the SQL statement(s) to return the results into a `DataReader` object.

6. Extract relevant database data from the `DataReader` object for display on your Web page.

Let's walk through each step, discuss the process, and provide an example of common usage.

First, we import the necessary namespace into the ASP.NET page. For Access, we would use:

```
<%@ Import Namespace="System.Data.OleDb" %>
```

If you're using MSDE, you would use the following line of code:

```
<%@ Import Namespace="System.Data.SqlClient" %>
```

Second, we define a code declaration block as we've seen in earlier chapters, with runat="server" and language attributes, like so:

VB.NET

```
<script runat="server" language="VB">
Sub Page_Load()

End Sub
</script>
```

C#

```
<script runat="server" language="C#">
void Page_Load() {

}
</script>
```

Next, we define the connection to our database by creating a new instance of the OleDbConnection class. To create this object, we must provide a **connection string**, as shown here:

VB.NET

```
<script runat="server" language="VB">
Sub Page_Load()
  Dim objConn As New OleDbConnection( _
    "Provider=Microsoft.Jet.OleDb.4.0;" & _
    "Data Source=C:\path\to\database.mdb")
End Sub
</script>
```

Though it is split in half to fit within this book, the connection string here is shown in bold, and specifies two things: the OLE DB provider and version (Microsoft Jet 4.0 is the provider for Access databases), and the filename on the server of the Access file that contains the database.

To connect to MSDE, we instantiate SqlConnection instead. In this case, the connection string must specify the name of the computer on which the database is located (if you're not sure of the name of your machine, right-click My Computer on your desktop, choose Properties, and the name will appear on the Network Identification tab) and the name assigned to the database server instance (NETSDK is the default for MSDE). Also required are the name of the database (such as DORKNOZZLE), the user ID (use sa in this case), and the password for that user account (which you specified when installing MSDE). Here's how we do it in VB.NET:

VB.NET

```
<script runat="server" language="VB">
Sub Page_Load()
  Dim objConn As New SqlConnection( _
    "Server=COMPUTERNAME\NETSDK;" & _
    "Database=DATABASENAME;" & _
    "User ID=USERNAME;Password=PASSWORD")
End Sub
</script>
```

If you get sick of typing quotes, ampersands, and underscores, you can of course combine the three bold strings in the above code (or the two in the Access code) into a single string. I'll continue to present connection strings as above in this book, as they are not only more readable, but they fit on the page too!

In C#, you connect to Access like this:

C#

```
<script runat="server" language="C#">
void Page_Load() {
  OleDbConnection objConn = new OleDbConnection(
    "Provider=Microsoft.Jet.OleDb.4.0;" +
    "Data Source=C:\\path\\to\\database.mdb");
}
</script>
```

Be aware that in C#, the backslash (\) character has a special meaning when it appears inside a string, so, when we wish to use one, we have to use a double backslash as shown above. To connect to MSDE in C#, your code would look something like this:

C#

```
<script runat="server" language="C#">
void Page_Load() {
  SqlConnection objConn = new SqlConnection(
    "Server=COMPUTERNAME\\NETSDK;" +
    "Database=DATABASENAME;" +
    "User ID=USERNAME;Password=PASSWORD");
}
</script>
```

Now we're at step four, in which we create a Command object and pass in our SQL statement. The Command object accepts two parameters: the first is the SQL statement, while the second is the connection object that we created in the previous step. The following code sample is written under the assumption that you're using an Access database. If you're using MSDE, simply switch the relevant class names from `OleDb` to `Sql` and use the appropriate connection string.

VB.NET

```
<script runat="server" language="VB">
Sub Page_Load()
  Dim objConn As New OleDbConnection( _
    "Provider=Microsoft.Jet.OleDb.4.0;" & _
    "Data Source=C:\Inetpub\wwwroot\Dorknozzle\Database\" & _
    "Dorknozzle.mdb")
  Dim objCmd As New OleDbCommand("SELECT * FROM Employees", _
    objConn)
End Sub
</script>
```

C#

```
<script runat="server" language="C#">
void Page_Load() {
  OleDbConnection objConn = new OleDbConnection(
    "Provider=Microsoft.Jet.OleDb.4.0;" +
    "Data Source=C:\\Inetpub\\wwwroot\\Dorknozzle\\Database\\" +
    "Dorknozzle.mdb");
  OleDbCommand objCmd =
    new OleDbCommand("SELECT * FROM Employees", objConn);
}
</script>
```

When we're ready to run the query, we open the connection, return the results of the command into a new `DataReader` by calling the `ExecuteReader()` method of the command object, and, finally, close the `DataReader` and `Connection` objects as follows:

VB.NET

```
<script runat="server" language="VB">
Sub Page_Load()
  Dim objConn As New OleDbConnection( _
    "Provider=Microsoft.Jet.OleDb.4.0;" & _
    "Data Source=C:\Inetpub\wwwroot\Dorknozzle\Database\" & _
    "Dorknozzle.mdb")
  Dim objCmd As New OleDbCommand("SELECT * FROM Employees", _
    objConn)
  objConn.Open()
  Dim objRdr As OleDbDataReader = objCmd.ExecuteReader()
  objRdr.Close()
  objConn.Close()
```

```
End Sub
</script>
```

C#

```
<script runat="server" language="C#">
void Page_Load() {
  OleDbConnection objConn = new OleDbConnection(
    "Provider=Microsoft.Jet.OleDb.4.0;" +
    "Data Source=C:\\Inetpub\\wwwroot\\Dorknozzle\\Database\\" +
    "Dorknozzle.mdb");
  OleDbCommand objCmd =
    new OleDbCommand("SELECT * FROM Employees", objConn);
  objConn.Open();
  OleDbDataReader objRdr = objCmd.ExecuteReader();
  objRdr.Close();
  objConn.Close();
}
</script>
```

Before we move on, let's take a look at a few methods that are being introduced here. Remember, all objects have properties and methods that are defined by their class. In this case, the connection object has two methods, called `Open()` and `Close()`. Before we can call the `ExecuteReader()` method of the command object, the connection must be opened; we close it again immediately afterwards. We don't have to do it like this—we could open the connection as soon as we create it, and leave it open until our program is done. However, this would be wasteful of database resources, which can be an issue in real-world applications where hundreds or more users might be accessing the same database at once. As such, it's best practice to keep the connection open for the minimum time.

A similar rule applies for the `DataReader`. When populated with data, the `DataReader` uses a certain amount of memory on our server, which, again, can be an issue when our application has many users. So, when you're done using the `DataReader`, call its `Close()` method, which effectively flushes its contents from memory, and frees up valuable server resources.

Now, let's display the data stored in the `DataReader` object on our page. For illustration, I'll simply use a `while` loop to show the data using `Response.Write()`. The `Response.Write()` method appends information directly to the response stream without any formatting. It's quick and dirty, and shouldn't really be used, except, occasionally, in debugging, for which it can be very handy. Also notice that we use the `DataReader`'s `Read()` method to loop through the data it contains, and its `Item()` method to retrieve the value for a specified column:

VB.NET

```
<script runat="server" language="VB">
Sub Page_Load()
  Dim objConn As New OleDbConnection( _
    "Provider=Microsoft.Jet.OleDb.4.0;" & _
    "Data Source=C:\Inetpub\wwwroot\Dorknozzle\Database\" & _
    "Dorknozzle.mdb")
  Dim objCmd As New OleDbCommand("SELECT * FROM Employees", _
    objConn)
  objConn.Open()
  Dim objRdr As OleDbDataReader = objCmd.ExecuteReader()
  While objRdr.Read()
    Response.Write(objRdr.Item("Name") & "<br />")
  End While
  objRdr.Close()
  objConn.Close()
End Sub
</script>
```

In C#, we don't need to use the `Item()` method as we did in VB.NET. Instead, we can simply place the column name we're after inside square brackets, as if the `DataReader` were an array, like so:

C#

```
<script runat="server" language="C#">
void Page_Load() {
  OleDbConnection objConn = new OleDbConnection(
    "Provider=Microsoft.Jet.OleDb.4.0;" +
    "Data Source=C:\\Inetpub\\wwwroot\\Dorknozzle\\Database\\" +
    "Dorknozzle.mdb");
  OleDbCommand objCmd =
    new OleDbCommand("SELECT * FROM Employees", objConn);
  objConn.Open();
  OleDbDataReader objRdr = objCmd.ExecuteReader();
  while (objRdr.Read()) {
    Response.Write(objRdr["Name"] + "<br />");
  }
  objRdr.Close()
  objConn.Close()
}
</script>
```

Once it's finished, with a bit of code shuffling to move all the variable declarations to the top, the completed page will look like this:

VB.NET   File: **simpleDataReader.aspx**

```vb
<%@ Import Namespace="System.Data.OleDb" %>

<html>
<head>
<title>Connecting to a Database using VB</title>
<script runat="server" language="VB">
Sub Page_Load()
  Dim objConn As OleDbConnection
  Dim objCmd As OleDbCommand
  Dim objRdr As OleDbDataReader

  objConn = New OleDbConnection( _
    "Provider=Microsoft.Jet.OleDb.4.0;" & _
    "Data Source=C:\Inetpub\wwwroot\Dorknozzle\Database\" & _
    "Dorknozzle.mdb")
  objCmd = New OleDbCommand("SELECT * FROM Employees", objConn)
  objConn.Open()
  objRdr = objCmd.ExecuteReader()
  While objRdr.Read()
    Response.Write(objRdr.Item("Name") & "<br />")
  End While
  objRdr.Close()
  objConn.Close()
End Sub
</script>
</head>
<body>

</body>
</html>
```

C#   File: **simpleDataReader.aspx**

```csharp
<%@ Import Namespace="System.Data.OleDb" %>

<html>
<head>
<title>Connecting to a Database using C#</title>
<script runat="server" language="C#">
void Page_Load() {
  OleDbConnection objConn;
  OleDbCommand objCmd;
  OleDbDataReader objRdr;

  objConn = new OleDbConnection(
    "Provider=Microsoft.Jet.OLEDB.4.0;" +
```

```
    "Data Source=C:\\Inetpub\\wwwroot\\Dorknozzle\\Database\\" +
    "Dorknozzle.mdb");
  objCmd = new OleDbCommand("SELECT * FROM Employees", objConn);
  objConn.Open();
  objRdr = objCmd.ExecuteReader();
  while (objRdr.Read()) {
    Response.Write(objRdr["Name"] + "<br />");
  }
  objRdr.Close();
  objConn.Close();
}
</script>
</head>
<body>

</body>
</html>
```

Viewing this page in the browser will produce something like Figure 8.1.

Figure 8.1. The completed code prints out the list of employees within the browser window.

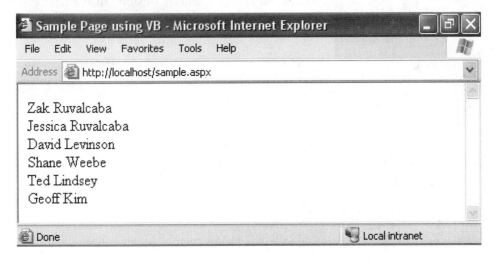

Performing Common Database Queries

Now that you have a basic idea as to how data is accessed with ADO.NET, let's create some useful applications. The previous example worked as a quick illustration, but it's based on the use of `Response.Write()`, which, as I said, is not something you'd normally do. In fact, it produces invalid HTML, as you can see if you view the source from your browser.

Instead, we can display our data by setting the `Text` property of ASP.NET `Label` controls, but there are other, more sophisticated, ASP.NET controls that are well suited to the display of database data—we'll cover these later in this chapter, and in future chapters.

The following sections build on what you've learned so far. Rather than simply displaying database data when the page loads, we'll display it when users interact with Web controls on the page. Then, we'll build on that to allow our users to search the database based on keywords that they specify within Web controls. Finally, we'll learn about data binding with Web controls and the `Repeater` control.

Responding to User Interaction

The previous example showed you how to create an ASP.NET page that displayed database data when the page loaded. Unfortunately, as we saw, this serves little purpose in real world applications, nor is it particularly flexible. Instead, we can display the database data when the user wishes, by adding a few controls onto the page that respond to user interaction:

VB.NET   File: **respondingToUserInteraction.aspx**

```
<%@ Import Namespace="System.Data.OleDb" %>

<html>
<head>
<title>Sample Page using VB</title>
<script runat="server" language="VB">
Sub getData(s As Object, e As EventArgs)
  Dim objConn As OleDbConnection
  Dim objCmd As OleDbCommand
  Dim objRdr As OleDbDataReader

  objConn = New OleDbConnection( _
    "Provider=Microsoft.Jet.OleDb.4.0;" & _
    "Data Source=C:\Inetpub\wwwroot\Dorknozzle\Database\" & _
    "Dorknozzle.mdb")
  objCmd = New OleDbCommand("SELECT * FROM Employees", objConn)
  objConn.Open()
  objRdr = objCmd.ExecuteReader()
```

```
  While objRdr.Read()
    Response.Write(objRdr.Item("Name") & "<br />")
  End While
  objRdr.Close()
  objConn.Close()
End Sub
</script>
</head>
<body>
<form runat="server">
  <asp:Button id="btnSubmit" OnClick="getData" Text="Get Data"
    runat="server" />
</form>
</body>
</html>
```

C#   File: **respondingToUserInteraction.aspx**

```
<%@ Import Namespace="System.Data.OleDb" %>

<html>
<head>
<title>Sample Page using C#</title>
<script runat="server" language="C#">
void getData(Object s, EventArgs e) {
  OleDbConnection objConn;
  OleDbCommand objCmd;
  OleDbDataReader objRdr;

  objConn = new OleDbConnection(
    "Provider=Microsoft.Jet.OLEDB.4.0;" +
    "Data Source=C:\\Inetpub\\wwwroot\\Dorknozzle\\Database\\" +
    "Dorknozzle.mdb");
  objCmd = new OleDbCommand("SELECT * FROM Employees", objConn);
  objConn.Open();
  objRdr = objCmd.ExecuteReader();
  while (objRdr.Read()) {
    Response.Write(objRdr["Name"] + "<br />");
  }
  objRdr.Close();
  objConn.Close();
}
</script>
</head>
<body>
<form runat="server">
  <asp:Button id="btnSubmit" OnClick="getData" Text="Get Data"
```

```
    runat="server" />
</form>
</body>
</html>
```

The changes to the code we had before are shown in bold. This time when the users are presented with the page, they have the option of selecting a button. When they click the Button control, the Click event is raised, the getData() method is called, and the data is written to the page as shown in Figure 8.2.

Figure 8.2. The user clicks the button, the Click event is raised, the method is called, and the data from the database is shown in the browser window.

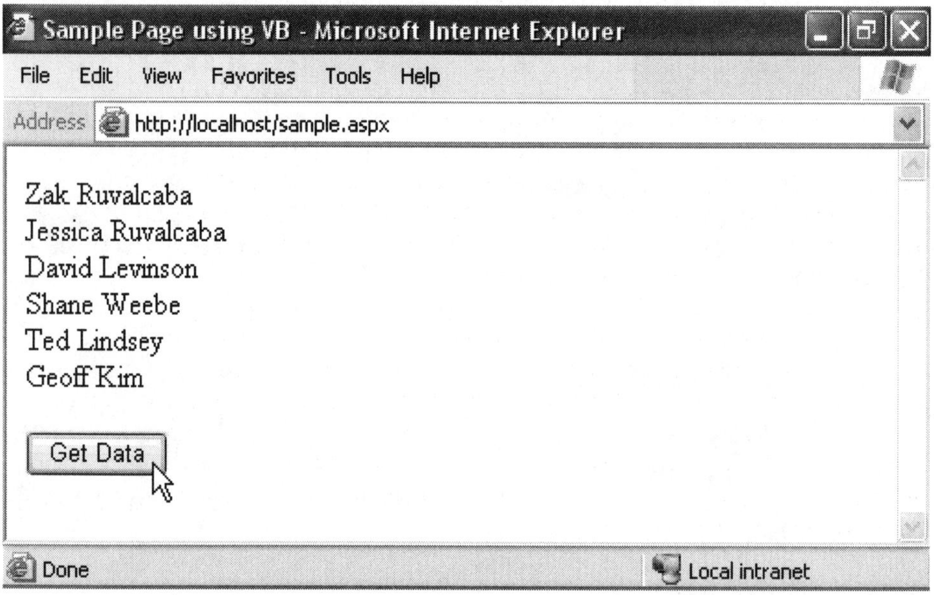

Even though we've provided some interaction for users, the functionality is still relatively bland and static. The users never get to see what they want; instead they are presented with data based on a hard coded SQL query. Let's see how we can change that...

Using Parameters with Queries

What if the user doesn't want to view information for all employees, but, instead, wants to see details for one specific employee alone? Let's add a `Textbox` control and allow users manually to type in the name of the employee whose information they want to see. Using parameters within your queries, you could allow your users to pass the text box value as a **parameter** from the control into the SQL statement, to set the filter within the `WHERE` clause.

Parameters are created within VB.NET code as follows:

```
VB.NET                                    File: queriesUsingParameters.aspx (excerpt)
objCmd = New OleDbCommand( _
  "SELECT * FROM Employees WHERE Name=@Name", objConn)
objCmd.Parameters.Add("@Name", txtSearch.Text)
```

C# is almost identical. You'll notice the only part of the SQL statement that's new here is `@Name`. By simply adding the `@` symbol, followed by a string of text, in this case, `Name`, we tell the SQL statement to accept a parameter. Next, we call the `Add()` method of the `Parameters` property of the `Command` object. We pass in the name of the parameter that was specified when the command object was created, `@Name`, and the value we want to set for that parameter, which will be the `Text` property of the `TextBox` control.

The `Parameters` property of the `Command` is what's called a **collection**. Very briefly, a collection in programming is, as the name suggests, simply a set of related items stored together for convenience. For each item, we store its name and value—this is what is frequently known as a name-value pair, or key-value pair. The key can then be used to access a particular value at a later time. To add a new item to a collection, we call the `Add()` method on the collection, passing in the name of the item (the key) and its new value.

Let's put this into action on our page:

```
VB.NET                                        File: queriesUsingParameters.aspx
<%@ Import Namespace="System.Data.OleDb" %>

<html>
<head>
<title>Sample Page using VB</title>
<script runat="server" language="VB">
Sub getData(s As Object, e As EventArgs)
  Dim objConn As OleDbConnection
```

```
    Dim objCmd As OleDbCommand
    Dim objRdr As OleDbDataReader

    objConn = New OleDbConnection( _
      "Provider=Microsoft.Jet.OleDb.4.0;" & _
      "Data Source=C:\Inetpub\wwwroot\Dorknozzle\Database\" & _
      "Dorknozzle.mdb")
    objCmd = New OleDbCommand( _
      "SELECT * FROM Employees WHERE Name=@Name", objConn)
    objCmd.Parameters.Add("@Name", txtSearch.Text)
    objConn.Open()
    objRdr = objCmd.ExecuteReader()
    While objRdr.Read()
      Response.Write("Employee ID: " & objRdr.Item("EmployeeID") & _
        "<br />")
      Response.Write("Name: " & objRdr.Item("Name") & "<br />")
      Response.Write("Username: " & objRdr.Item("Username") & _
        "<br />")
      Response.Write("Password: " & objRdr.Item("Password") & _
        "<br />")
    End While
    objRdr.Close()
    objConn.Close()
End Sub
</script>
</head>
<body>
<form runat="server">
  <asp:TextBox id="txtSearch" runat="server" />
  <asp:Button id="btnSubmit" OnClick="getData" Text="Get Data"
    runat="server" />
</form>
</body>
</html>
```

C#   File: **queriesUsingParameters.aspx**

```
<%@ Import Namespace="System.Data.OleDb" %>

<html>
<head>
<title>Sample Page using C#</title>
<script runat="server" language="C#">
void getData(Object s, EventArgs e) {
  OleDbConnection objConn;
  OleDbCommand objCmd;
  OleDbDataReader objRdr;
```

```
objConn = new OleDbConnection(
  "Provider=Microsoft.Jet.OLEDB.4.0;" +
  "Data Source=C:\\Inetpub\\wwwroot\\Dorknozzle\\Database\\" +
  "Dorknozzle.mdb");
objCmd = new OleDbCommand(
  "SELECT * FROM Employees WHERE Name=@Name", objConn);
objCmd.Parameters.Add("@Name", txtSearch.Text);
objConn.Open();
objRdr = objCmd.ExecuteReader();
while (objRdr.Read()) {
  Response.Write("Employee ID: " + objRdr["EmployeeID"] +
    "<br />");
  Response.Write("Name: " + objRdr["Name"] + "<br />");
  Response.Write("Username: " + objRdr["Username"] + "<br />");
  Response.Write("Password: " + objRdr["Password"] + "<br />");
}
objRdr.Close();
objConn.Close();
}
</script>
</head>
<body>
<form runat="server">
  <asp:TextBox id="txtSearch" runat="server" />
  <asp:Button id="btnSubmit" OnClick="getData" Text="Get Data"
    runat="server" />
</form>
</body>
</html>
```

This time, when the user clicks the button, the Click event is raised, the getData() method is called, the parameter is grabbed from the Text property of the TextBox control, the @Name parameter is passed into the SQL statement, and, finally, the filtered data is displayed to the user, as shown in Figure 8.3.

Figure 8.3. The user can filter the database results!

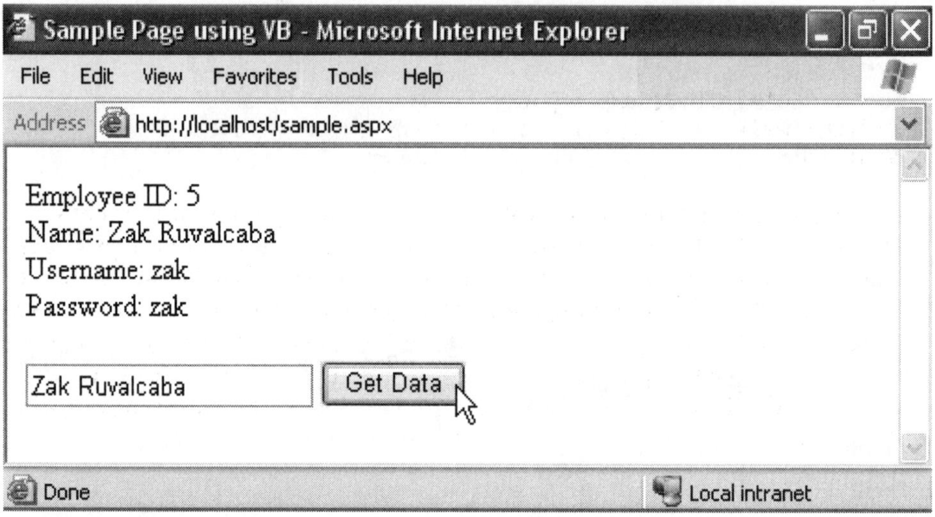

The application is starting to take shape. We've added some user interaction, including allowing users to filter results based on their own criteria. However, we're still using the far from satisfactory `Response.Write()` method to display our data. The next section will introduce a better way to display data: the `Repeater` control.

Using the Repeater Control

Great work! You're presenting data within the browser window based on user interaction, and you've even allowed your users to filter that data in accordance with their own search parameters. Unfortunately, the data that's being presented isn't very flexible. We're still using `Response.Write()` to display this data, which means that we can't control where it's placed. Fortunately, the .NET Framework comes bundled with the `DataGrid`, `DataList`, and `Repeater` controls, which allow us easily to format database data within our ASP.NET page. Before we discuss the `DataGrid` and `DataList`, let's start simply, and talk about the `Repeater` control.

The `Repeater` control is part of the .NET Framework's solution for the easier deployment and presentation of data directly from a data source. Usually involving only a handful of lines of code, the `Repeater` control is a quick way of presenting formatted data wherever you like within the page. Let's look at a quick example of how a `Repeater` control can be added to a page:

```
<asp:Repeater id="myRepeater" runat="server">
  <ItemTemplate>
    <%# Container.DataItem("Name") %>
  </ItemTemplate>
</asp:Repeater>
```

As you can see, the `Repeater` control looks like any other Web control that we've used thus far. The difference with this control is that it has an `<ItemTemplate>` **subtag**, otherwise known as a child tag, located within the main `<asp:Repeater>` tag, or parent tag. This child tag contains a code render block that specifies the particular data item we want to appear in the `Repeater`. Before this can happen, we have to join the `DataReader` that contains the results of an SQL query to the `Repeater` control dynamically, using the process known as **data binding**. This is done from a code block elsewhere on the page, like so:

VB.NET
```
myRepeater.DataSource = objRdr
myRepeater.DataBind()
```

It's that easy! In a moment, we'll display the code within the framework of our example. For now, let's discuss what's happening in more detail.

True to its name, the `Repeater` control lets you *repeat* some pattern of output for each record in a `DataReader`, substituting in values from those records wherever you like. You do this by providing **templates** for the `Repeater` to use. For example, if you wanted to display the results of a database query in an HTML table, then you could use a `Repeater` to generate an HTML table row (`<tr>` and its contents) for each record in that results set. To do this, you would provide a template containing a `<tr>` tag containing a number of `<td>` tags, and you would indicate where in that template you would want values taken from the result set to appear.

For more flexible output, the `Repeater` control actually lets you provide a number of templates, which it will use under various circumstances. Each of these must be given as a subtag of the `<asp:Repeater>` tag. The template tags supported by the `Repeater` control are listed with their effects below:

`<HeaderTemplate>`   This template provides a header for the resulting output. If you're generating an HTML table, for example, you could use this template to open the `<table>` tag, provide a row of header cells (`<th>`), and even provide a `<caption>` for the table.

`<ItemTemplate>` The only template that is actually required, this specifies the markup that should be output for each item in the data source. When generating an HTML table with one row per entry in the result set, this template would contain a `<tr>` tag and its contents.

`<AlternatingItemTemplate>` This template, if provided, will be applied for every second record in the data source instead of `ItemTemplate`, making it easy to produce effects such as alternating table row colors.

`<SeparatorTemplate>` This template provides markup that will appear *between* the items in the data source. It will not appear before the first item or after the last item.

`<FooterTemplate>` This template provides a footer for the resulting output, which will appear after all the items in the data source. If you're generating an HTML table, for example, you could use this template to close the `<table>` tag.

Now, let's actually write some working code using the `Repeater` control and its templates. As the available templates naturally lend themselves to generating an HTML table, let's start with that. First, we'll want a header that creates the table and a row of header cells:

File: **repeaterControl.aspx (excerpt)**

```
<asp:Repeater id="myRepeater" runat="server">
  <HeaderTemplate>
    <table width="400" border="1">
      <tr>
        <th>Employee ID</th>
        <th>Name</th>
        <th>User Name</th>
        <th>Password</th>
      </tr>
  </HeaderTemplate>
```

Now, we'll provide a template for each item in the result set. We want to output a table row with code render blocks that output the values taken from each record in the result set. Without getting into too much detail, you can access any field of the current result set entry as `Container.DataItem(fieldName)` in VB.NET, or `DataBinder.Eval(Container.DataItem, fieldName)` in C#. Here's the `ItemTemplate` we'll use for this example:

VB.NET   File: **repeaterControl.aspx (excerpt)**

```
<ItemTemplate>
  <tr>
    <td>
      <%# Container.DataItem("EmployeeID") %>
    </td>
    <td>
      <%# Container.DataItem("Name") %>
    </td>
    <td>
      <%# Container.DataItem("Username") %>
    </td>
    <td>
      <%# Container.DataItem("Password") %>
    </td>
  </tr>
</ItemTemplate>
```

C#   File: **repeaterControl.aspx (excerpt)**

```
<ItemTemplate>
  <tr>
    <td>
      <%# DataBinder.Eval(Container.DataItem, "EmployeeID") %>
    </td>
    <td>
      <%# DataBinder.Eval(Container.DataItem, "Name") %>
    </td>
    <td>
      <%# DataBinder.Eval(Container.DataItem, "Username") %>
    </td>
    <td>
      <%# DataBinder.Eval(Container.DataItem, "Password") %>
    </td>
  </tr>
</ItemTemplate>
```

In both languages, we refer to `Container.DataItem` to retrieve database values. `Container` basically means "the containing control." For our templates, the containing control is the `Repeater` control, to which we have bound our `DataReader` as a data source. In VB.NET, we can then simply call the `Repeater`'s

`DataItem()` method passing it the column name we wish to retrieve from its data source. The C# syntax is a bit different, but the basic idea is the same.

Finally, here's the `FooterTemplate` that closes the table.

File: **repeaterControl.aspx (excerpt)**

```
<FooterTemplate></table></FooterTemplate>
</asp:Repeater>
```

Here's the complete code:

VB.NET   File: **repeaterControl.aspx**

```
<%@ Import Namespace="System.Data.OleDb" %>

<html>
<head>
<title>Sample Page using VB</title>
<script runat="server" language="VB">
Sub getData(s As Object, e As EventArgs)
  Dim objConn As OleDbConnection
  Dim objCmd As OleDbCommand
  Dim objRdr As OleDbDataReader

  objConn = New OleDbConnection( _
    "Provider=Microsoft.Jet.OleDb.4.0;" & _
    "Data Source=C:\Inetpub\wwwroot\Dorknozzle\Database\" & _
    "Dorknozzle.mdb")
  objCmd = New OleDbCommand(
    "SELECT * FROM Employees WHERE Name=@Name", objConn)
  objCmd.Parameters.Add("@Name", txtSearch.Text)
  objConn.Open()
  objRdr = objCmd.ExecuteReader()
  myRepeater.DataSource = objRdr
  myRepeater.DataBind()
  objRdr.Close()
  objConn.Close()
End Sub
</script>
</head>
<body>
<form runat="server">
  <p><asp:TextBox id="txtSearch" runat="server"/>
  <asp:Button id="btnSubmit" OnClick="getData" Text="Get Data"
    runat="server" /></p>
  <p><asp:Repeater id="myRepeater" runat="server">
    <HeaderTemplate>
```

```
        <table width="400" border="1">
          <tr>
            <th>Employee ID</th>
            <th>Name</th>
            <th>User Name</th>
            <th>Password</th>
          </tr>
      </HeaderTemplate>
      <ItemTemplate>
        <tr>
          <td>
            <%# Container.DataItem("EmployeeID") %>
          </td>
          <td>
            <%# Container.DataItem("Name") %>
          </td>
          <td>
            <%# Container.DataItem("Username") %>
          </td>
          <td>
            <%# Container.DataItem("Password") %>
          </td>
        </tr>
      </ItemTemplate>
      <FooterTemplate></table></FooterTemplate>
    </asp:Repeater></p>
</form>
</body>
</html>
```

C#   File: `repeaterControl.aspx`

```
<%@ Import Namespace="System.Data.OleDb" %>

<html>
<head>
<title>Sample Page using C#</title>
<script runat="server" language="C#">
void getData(Object s, EventArgs e) {
  OleDbConnection objConn;
  OleDbCommand objCmd;
  OleDbDataReader objRdr;

  objConn = new OleDbConnection(
    "Provider=Microsoft.Jet.OLEDB.4.0;" +
    "Data Source=C:\\Inetpub\\wwwroot\\Dorknozzle\\Database\\ +
    "Dorknozzle.mdb");
```

```
  objCmd = new OleDbCommand(
    "SELECT * FROM Employees WHERE Name=@Name", objConn);
  objCmd.Parameters.Add("@Name", txtSearch.Text);
  objConn.Open();
  objRdr = objCmd.ExecuteReader();
  myRepeater.DataSource = objRdr;
  myRepeater.DataBind();
  objRdr.Close();
  objConn.Close();
}
</script>
</head>
<body>
<form runat="server">
  <p><asp:TextBox id="txtSearch" runat="server"/>
  <asp:Button id="btnSubmit" OnClick="getData" Text="Get Data"
    runat="server" /></p>
  <p><asp:Repeater id="myRepeater" runat="server">
    <HeaderTemplate>
      <table width="400" border="1">
      <tr>
        <th>Employee ID</th>
        <th>Name</th>
        <th>User Name</th>
        <th>Password</th>
      </tr>
    </HeaderTemplate>
    <ItemTemplate>
      <tr>
        <td>
          <%# DataBinder.Eval(Container.DataItem, "EmployeeID") %>
        </td>
        <td>
          <%# DataBinder.Eval(Container.DataItem, "Name") %>
        </td>
        <td>
          <%# DataBinder.Eval(Container.DataItem, "Username") %>
        </td>
        <td>
          <%# DataBinder.Eval(Container.DataItem, "Password") %>
        </td>
      </tr>
    </ItemTemplate>
    <FooterTemplate></table></FooterTemplate>
  </asp:Repeater></p>
</form>
```

```
</body>
</html>
```

Thanks to the Repeater control, we can now display the data wherever we like, such as under the Button and TextBox controls in this case. The results are shown in Figure 8.4.

Figure 8.4. The Repeater control allows us to display the database data quickly anywhere within the page.

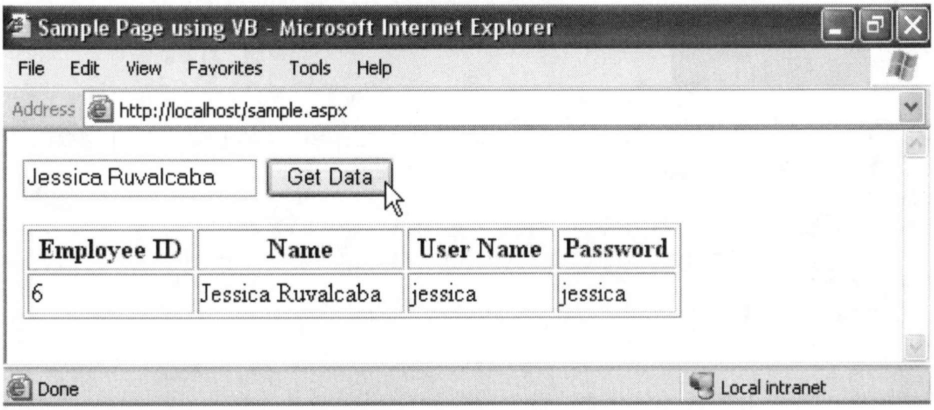

Let's now build the employee directory for our intranet Web application. Save a copy of the template.aspx file (located within the Template folder of the code download) under the name employeedirectory.aspx, and add to it the code shown in bold:

VB.NET   File: **employeedirectory.aspx**

```
<%@ Import Namespace="System.Data.OleDb" %>

<html>
<head>
<title>The Dorknozzle.com Intranet Site</title>
<script runat="server" language="VB">
Sub Page_Load()
  Dim objConn As OleDbConnection
  Dim objCmd As OleDbCommand
  Dim objRdr As OleDbDataReader

  objConn = New OleDbConnection( _
    "Provider=Microsoft.Jet.OleDb.4.0;" & _
    "Data Source=C:\Inetpub\wwwroot\Dorknozzle\Database\" & _
```

```
        "Dorknozzle.mdb")
    objCmd = New OleDbCommand("SELECT * FROM Employees", objConn)
    objConn.Open()
    objRdr = objCmd.ExecuteReader()
    rpcEmpDirectory.DataSource = objRdr
    rpcEmpDirectory.DataBind()
    objRdr.Close()
    objConn.Close()
End Sub
</script>
<link href="styles.css" rel="stylesheet" />
</head>
<body>
<form runat="server">

<table width="100%" border="0" cellspacing="0" cellpadding="0"
    background="Images/header_bg.gif">
  <tr>
    <td><img src="Images/header_top.gif" width="450" height="142"
          alt="the official dorknozzle company intranet" /></td>
  </tr>
</table>

<table width="100%" border="0" cellspacing="0" cellpadding="0">
  <tr>
    <td width="157"><img src="Images/header_bottom.gif"
        width="157" height="37" alt="" /></td>
    <td></td>
  </tr>
</table>

<table width="100%" border="0" cellspacing="0" cellpadding="10">
  <tr>
    <td valign="top" width="160">
      <!-- HyperLink Controls for navigation -->
      ...
      <!-- End HyperLink Controls -->
    </td>
    <td valign="top">
      <h1>Employee Directory</h1>
      <asp:Repeater id="rpcEmpDirectory" runat="server">
        <ItemTemplate>
          <p>Employee ID: <strong>
            <%# Container.DataItem("EmployeeID") %></strong><br />
            Name: <strong>
            <%# Container.DataItem("Name") %></strong><br />
```

```
        Extension: <strong>
        <%# Container.DataItem("Extension") %></strong></p>
    </ItemTemplate>
    <SeparatorTemplate><hr noshade="noshade" size="1" />
    </SeparatorTemplate>
  </asp:Repeater>
 </td>
</tr>
</table>

</form>
</body>
</html>
```

C#   File: **employeedirectory.aspx**

```
<%@ Import Namespace="System.Data.OleDb" %>

<html>
<head>
<title>The Dorknozzle.com Intranet Site</title>
<script runat="server" language="C#">
void Page_Load() {
  OleDbConnection objConn;
  OleDbCommand objCmd;
  OleDbDataReader objRdr;

  objConn = new OleDbConnection(
    "Provider=Microsoft.Jet.OLEDB.4.0;" +
    "Data Source=C:\\Inetpub\\wwwroot\\Dorknozzle\\Database\\" +
    "Dorknozzle.mdb");
  objCmd = new OleDbCommand("SELECT * FROM Employees", objConn);
  objConn.Open();
  objRdr = objCmd.ExecuteReader();
  rpcEmpDirectory.DataSource = objRdr;
  rpcEmpDirectory.DataBind();
  objRdr.Close();
  objConn.Close();
}
</script>
<link href="styles.css" rel="stylesheet" />
</head>
<body>
<form runat="server">

<table width="100%" border="0" cellspacing="0" cellpadding="0"
    background="Images/header_bg.gif">
```

```
    <tr>
      <td><img src="Images/header_top.gif" width="450" height="142"
            alt="the official dorknozzle company intranet" /></td>
    </tr>
</table>

<table width="100%" border="0" cellspacing="0" cellpadding="0">
  <tr>
    <td width="157"><img src="Images/header_bottom.gif"
        width="157" height="37" alt="" /></td>
    <td></td>
  </tr>
</table>

<table width="100%" border="0" cellspacing="0" cellpadding="10">
  <tr>
    <td valign="top" width="160">
      <!-- HyperLink Controls for navigation -->
      ...
      <!-- End HyperLink Controls -->
    </td>
    <td valign="top">
      <h1>Employee Directory</h1>
      <asp:Repeater id="rpcEmpDirectory" runat="server">
        <ItemTemplate>
          <p>Employee ID: <strong>
          <%# DataBinder.Eval(Container.DataItem, "EmployeeID") %>
            </strong><br />
            Name: <strong>
          <%# DataBinder.Eval(Container.DataItem, "Name") %>
            </strong><br />
            Extension: <strong>
          <%# DataBinder.Eval(Container.DataItem, "Extension") %>
            </strong></p>
        </ItemTemplate>
        <SeparatorTemplate><hr noshade="noshade" size="1" />
        </SeparatorTemplate>
      </asp:Repeater>
    </td>
  </tr>
</table>
</form>
</body>
</html>
```

As you can see from the code, we've added the following elements:

❏ A code declaration block, complete with Page_Load() event handler, database Connection object, Command object, and DataReader object. Once the reader has been filled with the database data, it is bound to the Repeater control's DataSource property.

❏ A Repeater control, complete with item and separator templates. The <ItemTemplate> tag contains code render blocks that display the correct DataItem from the DataReader.

Save your work and test it within the browser. The result will look similar to Figure 8.5.

Figure 8.5. All of the employees in the Employees table appear within the Employee Directory page through a Repeater control.

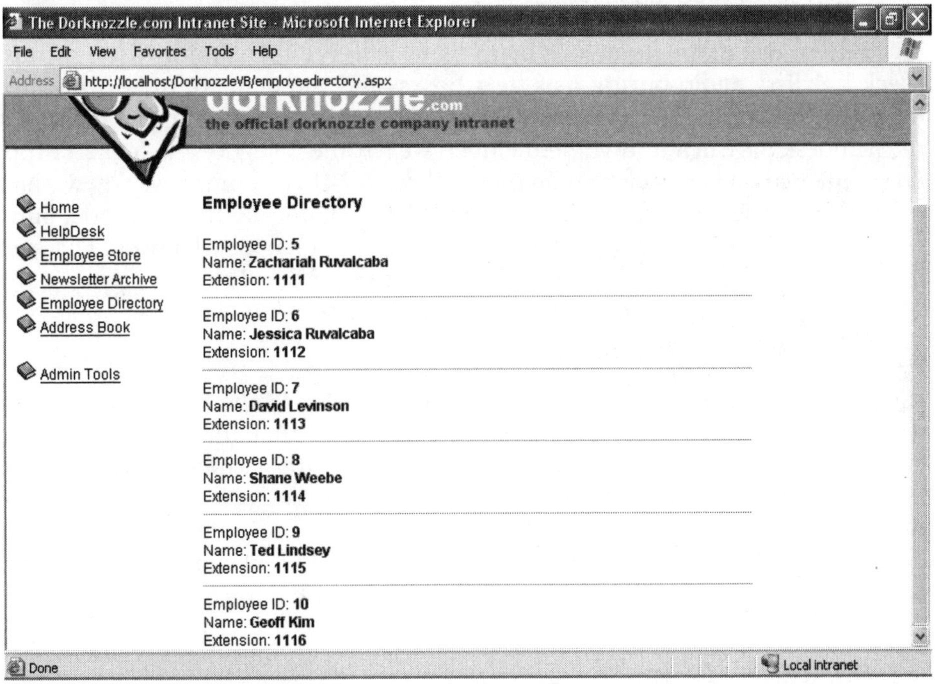

You may still be a bit confused as to how the DataReader's items are displayed within the Repeater control. As I've already pointed out, the DataReader is **bound** to the DataSource property of the Repeater control within the code. Let's discuss this process of data binding.

Data Binding

The term binding describes the act of associating a filled `DataReader` with a control using the `DataSource` property and the `DataBind()` method of that control. As you saw in the previous section, the `DataReader` was bound to the `Repeater` control as follows:

VB.NET   File: **employeedirectory.aspx (excerpt)**

```
rpcEmpDirectory.DataSource = objRdr
```

Once the `DataReader` is bound to the `DataSource` property, we call the `DataBind()` method to apply the binding as follows:

VB.NET   File: **employeedirectory.aspx (excerpt)**

```
rpcEmpDirectory.DataBind()
```

You can bind data to numerous controls in ASP.NET, including lists, menus, check box lists, radio button lists, text boxes, and the data controls (which we have yet to explore). To explore the process of control binding further, let's open the helpdesk page again. If you remember, we left the Category and Subject drop-down menus empty back in Chapter 4. We did this because we knew that, eventually, those items would have to be added dynamically through code. Sure, we could have hard-coded the values in ourselves, but imagine what would happen if additions or deletions needed to be made to that list. In order to make the necessary changes to the controls, we would have to open every page that contained lists of categories and subjects.

It's preferable, therefore, to bind the database tables to the drop-down menus within the helpdesk page—and any other page, for that matter. Whenever a change needs to be made, we can make it once within the database; all the `DropDownList` controls that are bound to that database table will change automatically. Let's go ahead and add the necessary code to a `Page_Load()` event handler within a script declaration block. Place the following script declaration block within the `<head>` tag at the top of the helpdesk page:

VB.NET   File: **helpdesk.aspx (excerpt)**

```
<script runat="server" language="VB">
Dim objConn As New OleDbConnection( _
  "Provider=Microsoft.Jet.OleDb.4.0;" & _
  "Data Source=C:\Inetpub\wwwroot\Dorknozzle\Database\" & _
  "Dorknozzle.mdb")
Dim objCmd As OleDbCommand
```

```
Dim objRdr As OleDbDataReader

Sub Page_Load()
  If Not IsPostBack Then
    objConn.Open()

    objCmd = New OleDbCommand("SELECT * FROM HelpDeskCategories",
      objConn)
    objRdr = objCmd.ExecuteReader()
    ddlCategory.DataSource = objRdr
    ddlCategory.DataValueField = "CategoryID"
    ddlCategory.DataTextField = "Category"
    ddlCategory.DataBind()
    objRdr.Close()

    objCmd = New OleDbCommand("SELECT * FROM HelpDeskSubjects",
      objConn)
    objRdr = objCmd.ExecuteReader()
    ddlSubject.DataSource = objRdr
    ddlSubject.DataValueField = "SubjectID"
    ddlSubject.DataTextField = "Subject"
    ddlSubject.DataBind()
    objRdr.Close()

    objConn.Close()
  End If
End Sub
</script>
```

C#   File: **helpdesk.aspx (excerpt)**

```
<script runat="server" language="C#">
OleDbConnection objConn = new OleDbConnection(
  "Provider=Microsoft.Jet.OleDb.4.0;" +
  "Data Source=C:\\Inetpub\\wwwroot\\Dorknozzle\\Database\\" +
  "Dorknozzle.mdb");
OleDbCommand objCmd;
OleDbDataReader objRdr;

void Page_Load() {
  if (!IsPostBack) {
    objConn.Open();

    objCmd = new OleDbCommand("SELECT * FROM HelpDeskCategories",
      objConn);
    objRdr = objCmd.ExecuteReader();
    ddlCategory.DataSource = objRdr;
```

```
    ddlCategory.DataValueField = "CategoryID";
    ddlCategory.DataTextField = "Category";
    ddlCategory.DataBind();
    objRdr.Close();

    objCmd = new OleDbCommand("SELECT * FROM HelpDeskSubjects",
        objConn);
    objRdr = objCmd.ExecuteReader();
    ddlSubject.DataSource = objRdr;
    ddlSubject.DataValueField = "SubjectID";
    ddlSubject.DataTextField = "Subject";
    ddlSubject.DataBind();
    objRdr.Close();

    objConn.Close();
  }
}
</script>
```

The only other change we need to make to this page is to add the line at the top that imports the OLE DB namespace:

File: **helpdesk.aspx (excerpt)**

```
<%@ Import Namespace="System.Data.OleDb" %>
```

The above code is then all we need in order to bind the data in our `DataReader` to the existing controls. Note that controls that can be bound each handle their bindings differently. In this case, the `DropDownList` control needs to be told which fields of the data source it should use for the values and text labels in the list. We do this by setting the DataValueField™ and `DataTextField` properties as follows:

VB.NET   File: **helpdesk.aspx (excerpt)**

```
ddlCategory.DataValueField = "CategoryID"
ddlCategory.DataTextField = "Category"
```

And:

VB.NET   File: **helpdesk.aspx (excerpt)**

```
ddlSubject.DataValueField = "SubjectID"
ddlSubject.DataTextField = "Subject"
```

This allows us to pass the ID of the category or subject along to any part of the application when a user makes a selection from the drop-down list.

When the page loads, all the categories and subjects will be bound to their respective DropDownList controls, as shown in Figure 8.6.

Figure 8.6. When the page loads, all categories and subjects are bound to their respective DropDownList controls.

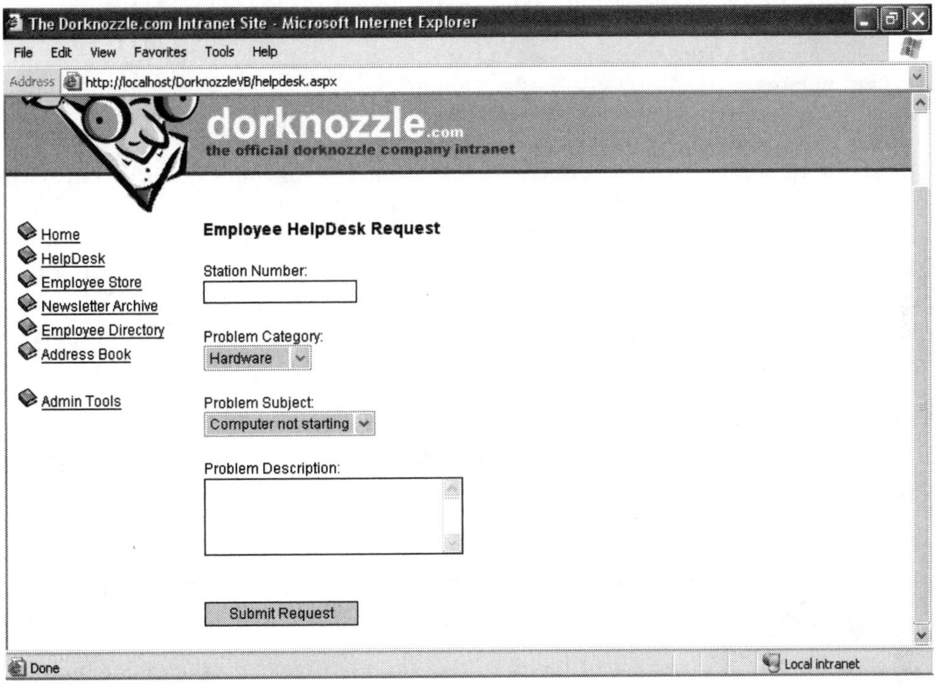

As usual, if you have any trouble reproducing this yourself, you can grab the finished code from this book's code archive.

Inserting Records

Inserting records into a database from your applications is virtually no different than performing simple queries with parameters. The difference between querying the database and inserting records into it is that, typically, a user enters information into a series of Web controls, clicks a button, and the data goes in thanks to an SQL INSERT statement.

A typical INSERT statement is coded as follows:

VB.NET

```
objCmd = New OleDbCommand( _
  "INSERT INTO HelpDesk (Field1, Field2, …) " & _
  "VALUES (@Value1, @Value2, …)", objConn)
```

Once the INSERT statement has been written, we simply pass in the necessary parameters similar to the way we have done previously for SELECT queries:

```
objCmd.Parameters.Add("@Value1", value1)
objCmd.Parameters.Add("@Value2", value2)
…
```

The more values we have to insert, the more parameters we need to create. To demonstrate the process of inserting records into the database, let's finish the helpdesk page. When employees visit the helpdesk page, it's because they're having some sort of problem. They'll fill out the necessary information, click Submit, and the information will be saved within the HelpDesk table. The HelpDesk table acts as a queue for IT personnel to review and respond to reported issues accordingly.

The only task left to complete for the HelpDesk page is to add an event handler for the Submit button. Begin by adding the OnClick attribute of the Button control as follows:

File: **helpdesk.aspx (excerpt)**

```
<asp:Button id="btnSubmit" CssClass="button" Text="Submit Request"
    OnClick="SubmitHelpDesk" runat="server" />
```

Next, inside the existing script block in the <head> tag, write the event handler for the control as follows, so that it performs the database insertion we want:

VB.NET   File: **helpdesk.aspx (excerpt)**

```
Sub SubmitHelpDesk(s As Object, e As EventArgs)
  objCmd = New OleDbCommand( _
    "INSERT INTO HelpDesk (EmployeeID, StationNumber, " & _
    "CategoryID, SubjectID, Description, StatusID) " & _
    "VALUES (@EmployeeID, @StationNumber, @CategoryID, " & _
    "@SubjectID, @Description, @StatusID)", objConn)
  objCmd.Parameters.Add("@EmployeeID", 5)
  objCmd.Parameters.Add("@StationNumber", txtStationNum.Text)
  objCmd.Parameters.Add("@CategoryID", _
    ddlCategory.SelectedItem.Value)
  objCmd.Parameters.Add("@SubjectID", _
    ddlSubject.SelectedItem.Value)
```

```
    objCmd.Parameters.Add("@Description", txtDescription.Text)
    objCmd.Parameters.Add("@StatusID", 1)
    objConn.Open()
    objCmd.ExecuteNonQuery()
    objConn.Close()
    Response.Redirect("helpdesk.aspx")
End Sub
```

C#   File: **helpdesk.aspx (excerpt)**

```csharp
void SubmitHelpDesk(Object s, EventArgs e) {
    objCmd = new OleDbCommand(
        "INSERT INTO HelpDesk (EmployeeID, StationNumber, " +
        "CategoryID, SubjectID, Description, StatusID) " +
        "VALUES (@EmployeeID, @StationNumber, @CategoryID, " +
        "@SubjectID, @Description, @StatusID)", objConn);
    objCmd.Parameters.Add("@EmployeeID", 5);
    objCmd.Parameters.Add("@StationNumber", txtStationNum.Text);
    objCmd.Parameters.Add("@CategoryID",
        ddlCategory.SelectedItem.Value);
    objCmd.Parameters.Add("@SubjectID",
        ddlSubject.SelectedItem.Value);
    objCmd.Parameters.Add("@Description", txtDescription.Text);
    objCmd.Parameters.Add("@StatusID", 1);
    objConn.Open();
    objCmd.ExecuteNonQuery();
    objConn.Close();
    Response.Redirect("helpdesk.aspx");
}
```

You'll notice the use of the `ExecuteNonQuery()` method. We use this method when executing any SQL statement that does not return a set of results, such as `INSERT`, `UPDATE`, and `DELETE`. You must remember that a query is a request made to the database, typically a `SELECT`. In this case, we're not requesting any data from the database; rather, we're telling it to insert records, so the `ExecuteNonQuery()` method is used instead of `ExecuteReader()`.

The other potentially unfamiliar tweak to this code is the final line, which uses `Response.Redirect()` to send the browser back to the blank form page. If we didn't end our event handler this way, the same page would be displayed in the browser, but ASP.NET would preserve all of the values that the user typed into the form fields. The user might not realize the form had even been submitted, and might submit the form repeatedly in the confusion. Redirecting in this way gets the browser to reload the page from scratch, clearing the form fields to clearly indicate the completed submission.

Save your work and run it in the browser. Now, we can enter our helpdesk information and click Submit as shown in Figure 8.7.

Figure 8.7. Enter the necessary information within the HelpDesk request form and click Submit.

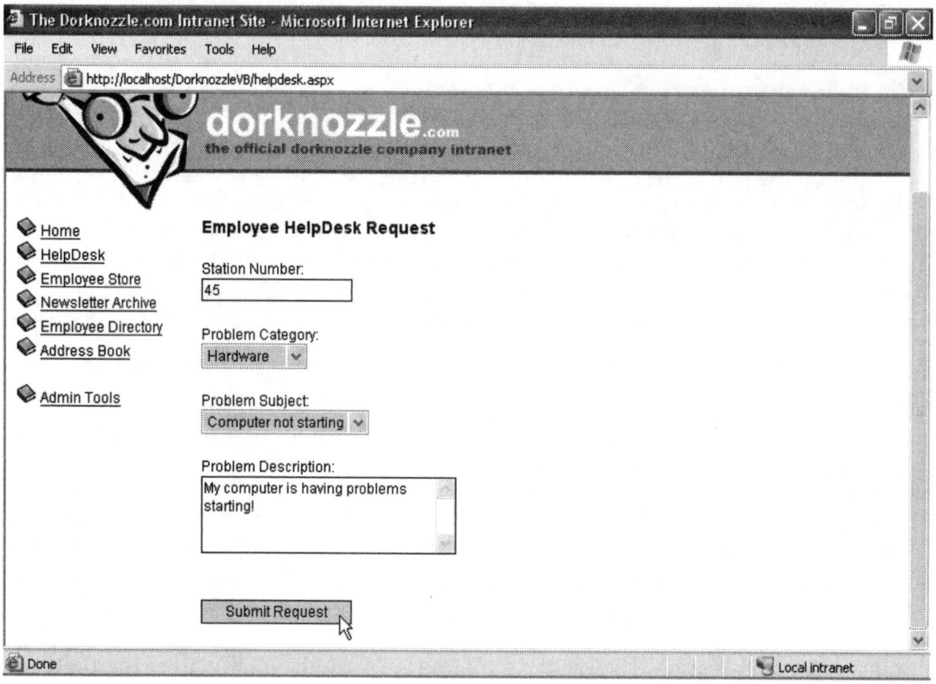

Once we click Submit, the `Click` event is raised, the `SubmitHelpDesk()` method is called, all the parameters from the form are passed into the SQL statement, and the data is inserted into the `HelpDesk` table. We can see this if we open the table in Access, as in Figure 8.8.

Figure 8.8. All of the helpdesk information for the user is inserted into the `HelpDesk` table within the database.

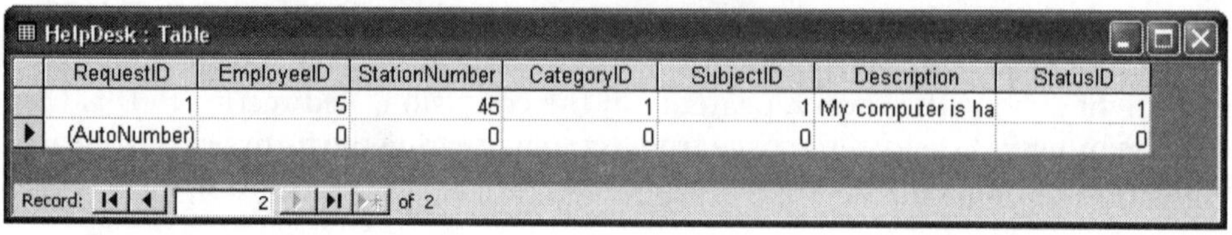

Access database errors due to file permissions

This example marks the first time in this book that an ASP.NET script has modified a database. On some server configurations, attempting to do this with an Access database can produce one of these database errors:

```
Operation must use an updateable query.
```

```
Could not delete from specified tables.
```

In the vast majority of cases, these errors occur because ASP.NET does not have permission to write to the database file or to the directory that contains it. To correct this, you need to edit the permissions on the directory containing the database file, and grant Full Control to the special ASPNET user on the server (not the IUSR_*machinename* account, as many online sources indicate). Before you can do this in Windows XP, you must disable the Use simple file sharing option on the View tab of Folder Options in the Windows Control Panel.

There are a couple of simplifications in this code that would probably not hold up in a practical application. You may wish to return to these items once you're finished this book and attempt to address them as an exercise:

1. How can we enter a user's EmployeeID if there isn't a spot for it within the form? Remember, there's a relationship between the Employees table and the HelpDesk table. Eventually, we'll know the users' EmployeeIDs when they log in, and we'll be able to pass it in from there. We'll be covering authentication in Chapter 14. For now, we've simply hard-coded a temporary value there.

2. Why isn't there a form element for the issue status? If you look closely at the database structure we have defined, you'll see that the StatusID field in the HelpDesk table refers to entries in the Status table. Since all newly-submitted helpdesk issues will be "Open", we have simply hard-coded the corresponding StatusID value. Strictly speaking, database IDs should not be hard-coded into ASP.NET code, since the database is responsible for managing them. Instead, the page should perform a database query to fetch the ID for "Open" from the Status table.

Updating Records

Updating records in the database is fairly similar to inserting records. The major difference with updating existing database records and inserting new ones is that you'll usually want to present the current information that exists within the database table to the user first. This gives the user a chance to review it, make the necessary changes, and, finally, submit the updated values. Before we get ahead of ourselves, however, let's take a look at the command we'll use to update records within the database table:

VB.NET
```
objCmd = New OleDbCommand( _
  "UPDATE Employees SET Field1=@Value1, Field2=@Value2, … " & _
  "WHERE UniqueField=@UniqueFieldValue", objConn)
```

Once a Command object has been created using this UPDATE statement, we simply pass in the necessary parameters as with the INSERT statement:

VB.NET
```
objCmd.Parametes.Add("@Value1", value1)
objCmd.Parametes.Add("@Value2", value2)
…
objCmd.Parametes.Add("@UniqueFieldValue", uniqueValue)
```

The important thing to remember when updating records is that you must make sure that you're performing the UPDATE on the correct record. To do this, you must include a WHERE clause that specifies the correct record using a value from a suitable unique column (such as an ID), as shown above.

Let's put all this into practice by building the "Admin Tools" page. There's no table within the database dedicated to this page, however, we *will* use the admin tools page as a centralized location for a number of tables associated with other pages, including the Employees and Departments tables. For instance, in this section's example, we'll allow an administrator to change information for a specific employee.

Save a copy of the template.aspx file as admintools.aspx, and begin creating the admin tools page by adding the following controls to the content area of the main table in the document:

File: **admintools.aspx (excerpt)**
```
  <h1>Admin Tools</h1>
  <p>Select an employee to update:<br />
    <asp:DropDownList id="ddlEmployees"
      CssClass="dropdownmenu" runat="server" />
    <asp:Button id="btnSelect" CssClass="Button" Text="Select"
      OnClick="SelectEmployee" runat="server" /></p>
  <p>Name: <asp:TextBox id="txtName" CssClass="textbox"
```

```
      runat="server" /><br />
User name: <asp:TextBox id="txtUsername"
  CssClass="textbox" runat="server" /><br />
Address: <asp:TextBox id="txtAddress" CssClass="textbox"
  runat="server" /><br />
City: <asp:TextBox id="txtCity" CssClass="textbox"
  runat="server" /><br />
State: <asp:TextBox id="txtState" CssClass="textbox"
  runat="server" /><br />
Zip: <asp:TextBox id="txtZip" CssClass="textbox"
  runat="server" /><br />
Home Phone: <asp:TextBox id="txtHomePhone"
  CssClass="textbox" runat="server" /><br />
Extension: <asp:TextBox id="txtExtension"
  CssClass="textbox" runat="server" /><br />
Mobile Phone: <asp:TextBox id="txtMobilePhone"
  CssClass="textbox" runat="server" /><br />
<asp:Button id="btnUpdate" CssClass="Button"
  Text="Update Employee" Enabled="False" runat="server"
  /></p>
```

We've added the following controls here:

DropDownList (ddlEmployees)

In order for administrators to select the employee whose details they want to update, we'll first have to bind the Employees table to this DropDownList control.

Button (btnSelect)

Once the users select the employee whose details they want to update, they'll click this Button control. When the button's clicked, the Click event will be raised, and the method named SelectEmployee() will be called. The value (EmployeeID) from the DropDownList control will be passed into the SQL statement.

TextBox (txtName etc.)

Within the SelectEmployee() method, we'll add some code that binds user information to this group of TextBox controls.

Button (btnUpdate)

When the users make the desired changes within the TextBox controls, they'll click this button to update the database.

To handle the control interaction, add the following code inside the <head> element:

VB.NET   File: **admintools.aspx (excerpt)**

```
<script runat="server" language="VB">
Dim objConn As New OleDbConnection( _
  "Provider=Microsoft.Jet.OleDb.4.0;" & _
  "Data Source=C:\Inetpub\wwwroot\Dorknozzle\Database\" & _
  "Dorknozzle.mdb")
Dim objCmd As OleDbCommand
Dim objRdr As OleDbDataReader

Sub Page_Load()
  If Not IsPostBack Then
    objCmd = New OleDbCommand("SELECT * FROM Employees", objConn)
    objConn.Open()
    objRdr = objCmd.ExecuteReader()
    ddlEmployees.DataSource = objRdr
    ddlEmployees.DataValueField = "EmployeeID"
    ddlEmployees.DataTextField = "Name"
    ddlEmployees.DataBind()
    objRdr.Close()
    objConn.Close()
  End If
End Sub

Sub SelectEmployee(s As Object, e As EventArgs)
  objCmd = New OleDbCommand( _
    "SELECT * FROM Employees WHERE EmployeeID=@EmployeeID", _
    objConn)
  objCmd.Parameters.Add("@EmployeeID", _
    ddlEmployees.SelectedItem.Value)
  objConn.Open()
  objRdr = objCmd.ExecuteReader()
  While objRdr.Read()
    txtName.Text = objRdr.Item("Name")
    txtUsername.Text = objRdr.Item("Username")
    txtAddress.Text = objRdr.Item("Address")
    txtCity.Text = objRdr.Item("City")
    txtState.Text = objRdr.Item("State")
    txtZip.Text = objRdr.Item("Zip")
    txtHomePhone.Text = objRdr.Item("HomePhone")
    txtExtension.Text = objRdr.Item("Extension")
    txtMobilePhone.Text = objRdr.Item("MobilePhone")
  End While
  objRdr.Close()
  objConn.Close()
  btnUpdate.Enabled = True
```

```
End Sub
</script>
```

```csharp
<script runat="server" language="C#">
OleDbConnection objConn = new OleDbConnection(
  "Provider=Microsoft.Jet.OleDb.4.0;" +
  "Data Source=C:\\Inetpub\\wwwroot\\Dorknozzle\\Database\\" +
  "Dorknozzle.mdb");
OleDbCommand objCmd;
OleDbDataReader objRdr;

void Page_Load(Object s, EventArgs e) {
  if (!IsPostBack) {
    objCmd = new OleDbCommand("SELECT * FROM Employees", objConn);
    objConn.Open();
    objRdr = objCmd.ExecuteReader();
    ddlEmployees.DataSource = objRdr;
    ddlEmployees.DataValueField = "EmployeeID";
    ddlEmployees.DataTextField = "Name";
    ddlEmployees.DataBind();
    objRdr.Close();
    objConn.Close();
  }
}

void SelectEmployee(Object s, EventArgs e) {
  objCmd = new OleDbCommand(
    "SELECT * FROM Employees WHERE EmployeeID=@EmployeeID",
    objConn);
  objCmd.Parameters.Add("@EmployeeID",
    ddlEmployees.SelectedItem.Value);
  objConn.Open();
  objRdr = objCmd.ExecuteReader();
  while (objRdr.Read()) {
    txtName.Text = (string) objRdr["Name"];
    txtUsername.Text = (string) objRdr["Username"];
    txtAddress.Text = (string) objRdr["Address"];
    txtCity.Text = (string) objRdr["City"];
    txtState.Text = (string) objRdr["State"];
    txtZip.Text = (string) objRdr["Zip"];
    txtHomePhone.Text = (string) objRdr["HomePhone"];
    txtExtension.Text = (string) objRdr["Extension"];
    txtMobilePhone.Text = (string) objRdr["MobilePhone"];
  }
  objRdr.Close();
```

```
    objConn.Close();
    btnUpdate.Enabled = true;
}
</script>
```

Once you've added these controls and code, you'll also need to import the OLE DB namespace as before:

File: **admintools.aspx (excerpt)**

```
<%@ Import Namespace="System.Data.OleDb" %>
```

The page should then load within the browser as shown in Figure 8.9.

Figure 8.9. The page loads with all employees within the drop-down menu.

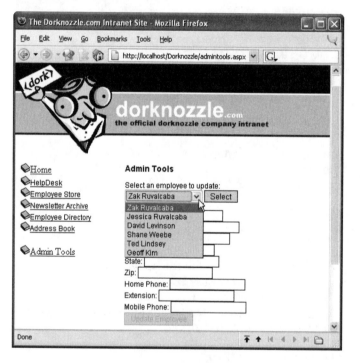

As you can see, all the employees are listed within the employee drop-down menu. Again, the employees' names are shown because the Name field is bound to the DataTextField property of the DropDownList control. Similarly, the EmployeeID field is bound to the DataValueField property of the DropDownList control, ensuring that the selected employee's ID will be submitted as the value of the field. You'll also notice the `TextBox` controls within the page. If I select an employee and click the Select button, the selected employee's information is bound to all the `TextBox` controls within the page, as shown in Figure 8.10.

Figure 8.10. All of the `TextBox` controls are bound with the employee's information.

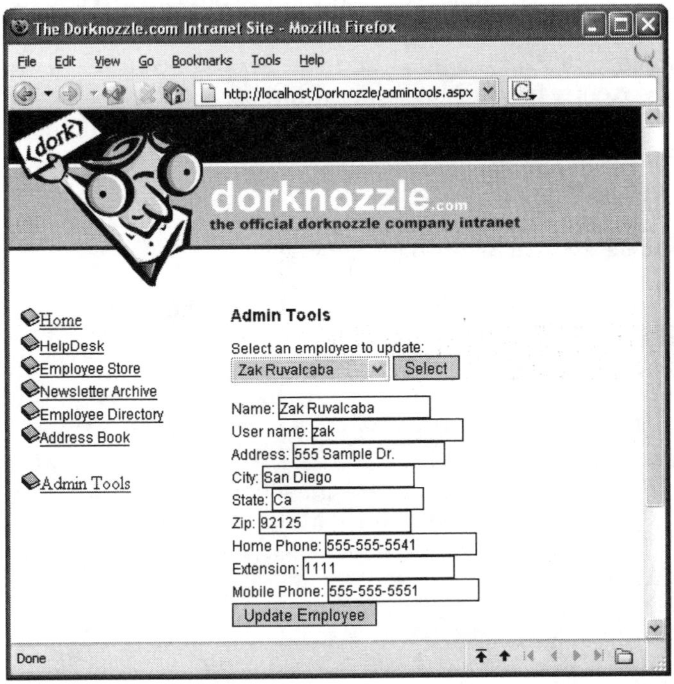

The last thing we need to do is add code to handle the update interaction. First, we must define a new method within the script block as follows:

VB.NET   File: **admintools.aspx (excerpt)**

```
Sub UpdateEmployee(s As Object, e As EventArgs)

End Sub
```

C#   File: **admintools.aspx (excerpt)**

```
void UpdateEmployee(Object s, EventArgs e) {

}
```

Next, we'll add the `OnClick` attribute to the `btnUpdate` tag, like so:

File: **admintools.aspx (excerpt)**

```
<asp:Button id="btnUpdate" CssClass="Button"
    Text="Update Employee" Enabled="False"
    OnClick="UpdateEmployee" runat="server" />
```

You may have noticed that the `Button` control has an `Enabled` property, which is set to `False`. The reason for this is simple: you don't want your users to update blank information. Rather, you want them to use the Update button only when data for an existing employee has been loaded into the `TextBox` controls. This prevents users from inadvertently clearing all fields within the database table for a selected employee. If you look at the bottom of the `SelectEmployee()` method, you'll notice that we enable this button after binding the user data to the fields:

VB.NET   File: **admintools.aspx (excerpt)**

```
btnUpdate.Enabled = True
```

Finally, let's add the necessary code to handle the update inside our `UpdateEmployee()` method as follows:

VB.NET   File: **admintools.aspx (excerpt)**

```
Sub UpdateEmployee(s As Object, e As EventArgs)
  objCmd = New OleDbCommand( _
    "UPDATE Employees SET Name=@Name, Username=@Username, " & _
    "Address=@Address, City=@City, State=@State, Zip=@Zip, " & _
    "HomePhone=@HomePhone, Extension=@Extension, " & _
    "MobilePhone=@MobilePhone " & _
    "WHERE EmployeeID=@EmployeeID", objConn)
  objCmd.Parameters.Add("@Name", txtName.Text)
  objCmd.Parameters.Add("@Username", txtUsername.Text)
  objCmd.Parameters.Add("@Address", txtAddress.Text)
  objCmd.Parameters.Add("@City", txtCity.Text)
  objCmd.Parameters.Add("@State", txtState.Text)
  objCmd.Parameters.Add("@Zip", txtZip.Text)
  objCmd.Parameters.Add("@HomePhone", txtHomePhone.Text)
  objCmd.Parameters.Add("@Extension", txtExtension.Text)
  objCmd.Parameters.Add("@MobilePhone", txtMobilePhone.Text)
  objCmd.Parameters.Add("@EmployeeID", _
    ddlEmployees.SelectedItem.Value)
  objConn.Open()
  objCmd.ExecuteNonQuery()
  objConn.Close()
End Sub
```

C#   File: **admintools.aspx (excerpt)**

```
void UpdateEmployee(Object s, EventArgs e) {
  objCmd = new OleDbCommand(
    "UPDATE Employees SET Name=@Name, Username=@Username, " +
    "Address=@Address, City=@City, State=@State, Zip=@Zip, " +
    "HomePhone=@HomePhone, Extension=@Extension, " +
    "MobilePhone=@MobilePhone " +
    "WHERE EmployeeID=@EmployeeID", objConn);
  objCmd.Parameters.Add("@Name", txtName.Text);
  objCmd.Parameters.Add("@Username", txtUsername.Text);
  objCmd.Parameters.Add("@Address", txtAddress.Text);
  objCmd.Parameters.Add("@City", txtCity.Text);
  objCmd.Parameters.Add("@State", txtState.Text);
  objCmd.Parameters.Add("@Zip", txtZip.Text);
  objCmd.Parameters.Add("@HomePhone", txtHomePhone.Text);
  objCmd.Parameters.Add("@Extension", txtExtension.Text);
  objCmd.Parameters.Add("@MobilePhone", txtMobilePhone.Text);
  objCmd.Parameters.Add("@EmployeeID",
    ddlEmployees.SelectedItem.Value);
  objConn.Open();
  objCmd.ExecuteNonQuery();
  objConn.Close();
}
```

As you can see, the only real difference between this and the INSERT query we saw in the helpdesk page is that have had to let the user pick out an entry in the database to update. We use that selection not only to populate the form fields with the existing database values, but to restrict our UPDATE query so that it only affects that one record.

By selecting my own employee record as in Figure 8.10, I can change my name from "Zak" to "Zachariah." Clicking the Update button updates the necessary field within the database table, as shown in Figure 8.11.

Figure 8.11. Clicking the `Update` `Button` control updates the necessary fields within the `Employees` table.

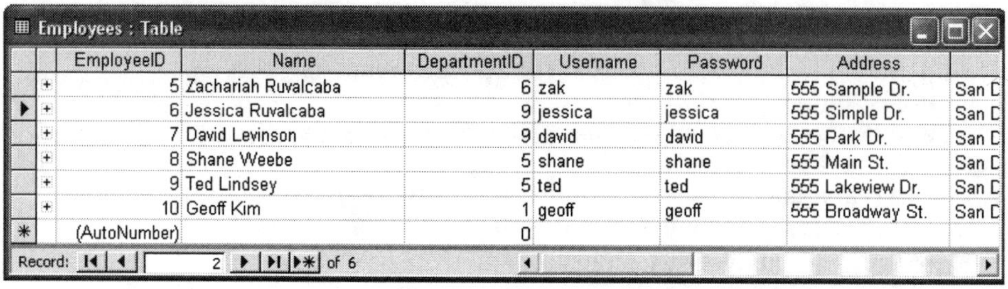

Employees : Table

EmployeeID	Name	DepartmentID	Username	Password	Address	
5	Zachariah Ruvalcaba	6	zak	zak	555 Sample Dr.	San D
6	Jessica Ruvalcaba	9	jessica	jessica	555 Simple Dr.	San D
7	David Levinson	9	david	david	555 Park Dr.	San D
8	Shane Weebe	5	shane	shane	555 Main St.	San D
9	Ted Lindsey	5	ted	ted	555 Lakeview Dr.	San D
10	Geoff Kim	1	geoff	geoff	555 Broadway St.	San D
(AutoNumber)		0				

Record: 2 of 6

As is the case with all examples in this book, you can get the completed code from the code archive.

Deleting Records

Just as you inserted and updated records within the database, you can also delete them. Again, most of the code for deleting records resembles what we have already seen. The only major part that changes is the SQL statement within the command:

VB.NET

```
objCmd = New OleDbCommand("DELETE FROM TableName " & _
    "WHERE UniqueField=@UniqueFieldValue", objConn)
```

Once you've created the `DELETE` command object, you simply pass in the necessary parameter:

```
objCmd.Parameters.Add("@UniqueFieldValue", uniqueValue)
```

To demonstrate the process of deleting an item from a database table, we'll simply expand on the admin tools page. Since we're allowing administrators to update information within the `Employees` table, let's also give them the ability to delete an employee from the database. To do this, we'll add a new `ListBox` control below the update interface as follows:

File: **admintools.aspx (excerpt)**

```
    <p>Select an employee to delete:<br />
      <asp:ListBox id="lbEmployees" CssClass="dropdownmenu"
        runat="server" /><br />
```

Next we'll modify the `Page_Load()` event handler to bind the same employees that are being bound to the `DropDownList` control within the `ListBox` control, as follows:

```
VB.NET                                          File: admintools.aspx (excerpt)

Sub Page_Load()
  If Not IsPostBack Then
    objCmd = New OleDbCommand("SELECT * FROM Employees", objConn)

    objConn.Open()

    objRdr = objCmd.ExecuteReader()
    ddlEmployees.DataSource = objRdr
    ddlEmployees.DataValueField = "EmployeeID"
    ddlEmployees.DataTextField = "Name"
    ddlEmployees.DataBind()
    objRdr.Close()

    objRdr = objCmd.ExecuteReader()
    lbEmployees.DataSource = objRdr
    lbEmployees.DataValueField = "EmployeeID"
    lbEmployees.DataTextField = "Name"
    lbEmployees.DataBind()
    objRdr.Close()

    objConn.Close()
  End If
End Sub
```

```
C#                                              File: admintools.aspx (excerpt)

void Page_Load() {
  if (!IsPostBack) {
    objCmd = new OleDbCommand("SELECT * FROM Employees", objConn);

    objConn.Open();

    objRdr = objCmd.ExecuteReader();
    ddlEmployees.DataSource = objRdr;
    ddlEmployees.DataValueField = "EmployeeID";
    ddlEmployees.DataTextField = "Name";
    ddlEmployees.DataBind();
    objRdr.Close();

    objRdr = objCmd.ExecuteReader();
    lbEmployees.DataSource = objRdr;
    lbEmployees.DataValueField = "EmployeeID";
```

```
    lbEmployees.DataTextField = "Name";
    lbEmployees.DataBind();
    objRdr.Close();

    objConn.Close();
  }
}
```

As you can see in Figure 8.12, when the page loads for the first time, both the DropDownList control and ListBox control are populated with the employees' names.

Figure 8.12. Both the DropDownList and ListBox controls are populated with employees' names.

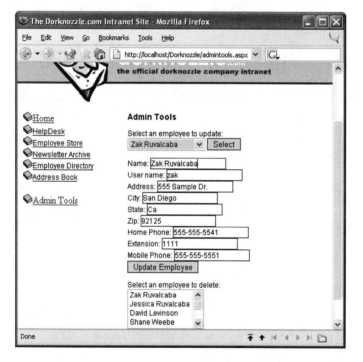

Next, let's add the Button control to handle the delete interaction as follows:

File: **admintools.aspx** (excerpt)

```
<asp:Button id="btnDelete" CssClass="Button"
    Text="Delete Employee" OnClick="DeleteEmployee"
    runat="server" />
```

As you can see, we set the `OnClick` attribute to call a new method named `DeleteEmployee()`. To handle the `Button Click` event, we'll add this new method as follows:

VB.NET   File: **admintools.aspx (excerpt)**

```
Sub DeleteEmployee(s As Object, e As EventArgs)

End Sub
```

C#   File: **admintools.aspx (excerpt)**

```
void DeleteEmployee(Object s, EventArgs e) {

}
```

Finally, we can add the code to handle the deletion as follows:

VB.NET   File: **admintools.aspx (excerpt)**

```
Sub DeleteEmployee(s As Object, e As EventArgs)
  objCmd = New OleDbCommand( _
    "DELETE FROM Employees " & _
    "WHERE EmployeeID=@EmployeeID", objConn)
  objCmd.Parameters.Add("@EmployeeID",
    lbEmployees.SelectedItem.Value)
  objConn.Open()
  objCmd.ExecuteNonQuery()
  objConn.Close()
End Sub
```

C#   File: **admintools.aspx (excerpt)**

```
void DeleteEmployee(Object s, EventArgs e) {
  objCmd = new OleDbCommand(
    "DELETE FROM Employees " +
    "WHERE EmployeeID=@EmployeeID", objConn);
  objCmd.Parameters.Add("@EmployeeID",
    lbEmployees.SelectedItem.Value);
  objConn.Open();
  objCmd.ExecuteNonQuery();
  objConn.Close();
}
```

Save your work and test it within the browser. Select an employee within the `ListBox` and click the Delete button. Figure 8.13 shows the record was indeed removed from the database table.

Figure 8.13. The selected record was deleted from the database table.

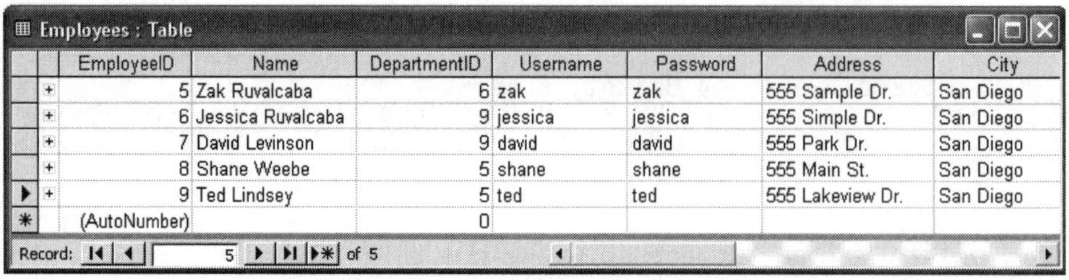

	EmployeeID	Name	DepartmentID	Username	Password	Address	City
+	5	Zak Ruvalcaba	6	zak	zak	555 Sample Dr.	San Diego
+	6	Jessica Ruvalcaba	9	jessica	jessica	555 Simple Dr.	San Diego
+	7	David Levinson	9	david	david	555 Park Dr.	San Diego
+	8	Shane Weebe	5	shane	shane	555 Main St.	San Diego
▶ +	9	Ted Lindsey	5	ted	ted	555 Lakeview Dr.	San Diego
*	(AutoNumber)		0				

Record: ◄◄ ◄ 5 ► ►◄ ►* of 5

Although the functionality is working, there's still something of usability issue here. When you update or delete a record from within the application, you're not immediately sure if the update or deletion actually occurred because the record isn't immediately removed (if deleted) or changed (if updated) in the `DropDownList` and `ListBox` controls. Let's look at how to take care of that with postback.

Handling Updates with Postback

One of the problems with the admin tools page is that the employee's name within the `DropDownList` and `ListBox` controls does not update when the user's information is updated. I've also pointed out that an employee, when deleted from the database, will still appear in the `DropDownList` and `ListBox` controls. This is by no means a failure of the ASP.NET controls, but rather, depends on how we've arranged the code.

If you remember, the code that binds the employee name list to the `DropDownList` control appears within the `Page_Load()` event handler. In the code we have to this point, I was careful to only load the employee records when each user first loads the page, by checking for postback:

VB.NET   File: **admintools.aspx (excerpt)**
```
Sub Page_Load()
  If Not IsPostBack Then
    ...load database records...
  End If
End Sub
```

If we reloaded the database records on postback, it would solve our problem of the drop-down and menu not being updated, but any selections the user had made in the controls would be lost, which would keep our interface from working as intended. What we need to do is modify our code to update the lists at the appropriate times.

As you know, we currently have four methods within the code declaration block:

Page_Load()   Binds all employee names within DropDownList and ListBox controls *only* when the page is first loaded by the browser—not on postback.

SelectEmployee()   Binds the selected employee's information to the TextBox controls when the Select Button control is clicked.

UpdateEmployee()   Updates selected employee with necessary changes from the TextBox controls.

DeleteEmployee()   Deletes from the database table the employee whose name was selected in the ListBox control.

We need to change the logic so that our page reloads the database data for the DropDownList and ListBox controls whenever it makes changes to the Employees table. To make it easier to refresh the lists on cue, let's first move our data binding code into a separate method that we'll call BindData(). We'll then call this method from PageLoad(), and also whenever records are changed or deleted.

The new Page_Load() method is now simply:

VB.NET   File: **admintools.aspx (excerpt)**
```
Sub Page_Load()
  If Not IsPostBack Then
    BindData()
  End If
End Sub
```

C#   File: **admintools.aspx (excerpt)**
```
void Page_Load() {
  if (!IsPostBack) {
    BindData();
  }
}
```

As I said, the BindData() method will contain the data binding code that used to be inside PageLoad(). Here's what it should look like:

VB.NET   File: **admintools.aspx (excerpt)**

```vbnet
Sub BindData()
  objCmd = New OleDbCommand("SELECT * FROM Employees", objConn)

  objConn.Open()

  objRdr = objCmd.ExecuteReader()
    ddlEmployees.DataSource = objRdr
    ddlEmployees.DataValueField = "EmployeeID"
    ddlEmployees.DataTextField = "Name"
    ddlEmployees.DataBind()
  objRdr.Close()

  objRdr = objCmd.ExecuteReader()
    lbEmployees.DataSource = objRdr
    lbEmployees.DataValueField = "EmployeeID"
    lbEmployees.DataTextField = "Name"
    lbEmployees.DataBind()
  objRdr.Close()

  objConn.Close()
End Sub
```

C#   File: **admintools.aspx (excerpt)**

```csharp
void BindData() {
  objCmd = new OleDbCommand("SELECT * FROM Employees", objConn);

  objConn.Open();

  objRdr = objCmd.ExecuteReader();
    ddlEmployees.DataSource = objRdr;
    ddlEmployees.DataValueField = "EmployeeID";
    ddlEmployees.DataTextField = "Name";
    ddlEmployees.DataBind();
  objRdr.Close();

  objRdr = objCmd.ExecuteReader();
    lbEmployees.DataSource = objRdr;
    lbEmployees.DataValueField = "EmployeeID";
    lbEmployees.DataTextField = "Name";
    lbEmployees.DataBind();
  objRdr.Close();

  objConn.Close();
}
```

Finally, just add the line `BindData()` right at the end of both the `UpdateEmployee()` and `DeleteEmployee()` methods (if you have any doubts, check the finished version of `admintools.aspx` in the code archive). The reason for this is simple: since we've performed either an update or a delete, we want the page to refresh the user listings from the database, effectively resetting the `DropDownList` and `ListBox` controls to their default states. Once complete, the application should function as expected. Figure 8.14 shows that Zak Ruvalcaba is removed from the `ListBox` control when I delete my name from the list.

Figure 8.14. The name is removed from the list.

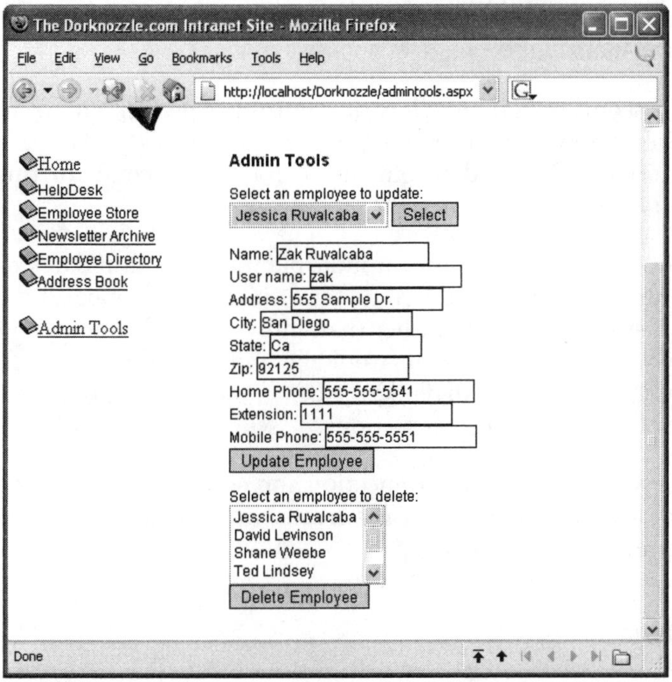

Working with Transactions

The database modifications we've seen thus far have been cut and dried: users decide that they want to insert new records, they fill out the appropriate forms, click Insert, and the new records are inserted into the database table. Users may also update information within a database table; they change the necessary fields on the appropriate ASP.NET page, click Update, and the corresponding fields within the database table are updated. For every one page that a user fills out or makes modifications to, one record within the database is affected. However, inserts and updates don't have to be so simple, and you can perform multiple insertions or updates into multiple tables at the same time.

When handling inserts and updates in real world applications, the problem of data loss comes into play. Say, for instance, I were transferring money from my savings account to my checking account using online banking. It might first execute the following statement, to subtract $500 from my checking account:

```
UPDATE Checking SET Balance = Balance - 500 WHERE Customer='zak'
```

The next statement would add $500 to my savings account:

```
UPDATE Savings SET Balance = Balance + 500 WHERE Customer='zak'
```

Everything to this point seems fine, right? However, nothing's perfect, and from time to time servers do go down. Imagine what would happen if the database server crashed right after the first update but just before the second. In this scenario, I would be very upset!

ADO.NET **transactions** allow you to perform multiple inserts and updates to database tables as a whole, meaning that a given set of inserts and updates are performed together in a single operation, rather than individually. If one should fail, any changes made by previous statements would be undone, or **rolled back**. This ultimately reduces the risk of overall data loss. Let's take a look at the same online transfer scenario this time using transactions.

As before, we declare new instances of the connection and command classes, but now we also need a transaction object. We can also create two new string instances so that we may store our SQL statements:

VB.NET
```
Dim objConn As OleDbConnection
Dim objTran As OleDbTransaction
Dim cmdSavings, cmdChecking As OleDbCommand
Dim strSavings, strChecking As String
```

Next, we can create the SQL statements and initialize the connection and command objects:

VB.NET
```
objConn = New OleDbConnection( _
    "Provider=Microsoft.Jet.OleDb.4.0;" & _
    "Data Source=C:\Inetpub\wwwroot\SampleDatabase\bank.mdb")
```

```
strChecking = "UPDATE Checking SET Balance = Balance - 500 " & _
  "WHERE Customer='zak'"
strSavings = "UPDATE Savings SET Balance = Balance + 500 " & _
  "WHERE Customer='zak'"

cmdChecking = New OleDbCommand(strChecking, objConn)
cmdSavings = New OleDbCommand(strSavings, objConn)
```

Now, we open the connection:

VB.NET

```
objConn.Open()
```

Then, we begin a transaction using the connection object:

VB.NET

```
objTran = objConn.BeginTransaction()
```

Next, we assign the transaction to the commands:

VB.NET

```
cmdChecking.Transaction = objTran
cmdSavings.Transaction = objTran
```

Next, we can use a `Try-Catch-Finally` statement to **try** the two updates and then **commit** the transaction, **catch** any errors and rollback the transaction if either of the updates fail, and **finally**, close the connection. We'll be discussing `Try-Catch` blocks in greater detail in Chapter 13.

VB.NET

```
Try
  cmdChecking.ExecuteNonQuery()
  cmdSavings.ExecuteNonQuery()
  objTran.Commit()
Catch
  objTran.RollBack()
Finally
  objConn.Close()
End Try
```

Here's the equivalent code in C#:

C#

```
OleDbConnection objConn;
OleDbTransaction objTran;
OleDbCommand cmdSavings;
```

```
OleDbCommand cmdChecking;
String strSavings;
String strChecking;

objConn = new OleDbConnection(
  "Provider=Microsoft.Jet.OleDb.4.0;" +
  "Data Source=C:\\Inetpub\\wwwroot\\SampleDatabase\\bank.mdb");

strChecking = "UPDATE Checking SET Balance = Balance - 500 " +
  "WHERE Customer='zak'";
strSavings = "UPDATE Savings SET Balance = Balance + 500 " +
  "WHERE Customer='zak'";

cmdChecking = new OleDbCommand(strChecking, objConn);
cmdSavings = new OleDbCommand(strSavings, objConn);

objConn.Open();

objTran = objConn.BeginTransaction();

cmdChecking.Transaction = objTran;
cmdSavings.Transaction = objTran;

try {
   cmdChecking.ExecuteNonQuery();
   cmdSavings.ExecuteNonQuery();
   objTran.Commit();
} catch {
   objTran.RollBack();
} finally {
   objConn.Close();
}
```

Improving Performance with Stored Procedures

So far, you've learned how to query, insert, update, and delete information in the database through your ASP.NET pages. You've learned how to create a connection passing in a connection string for your database, and a command passing in an SQL statement. You've learned how to open and close connections, populate a DataReader, and how to bind the DataReader to controls within your page.

Every part of the process of interacting with the database incurs overhead on the server and decreases the performance of your Web application. Everything from opening a connection, to binding controls to a `DataReader` object, involves some level of system resources and ultimately impacts on performance. One of the most inefficient processes in terms of computer resources is that of calling an SQL statement. Every time an SQL command is executed within an ASP.NET page, it must be parsed, compiled, and optimized.

Enter: **stored procedures**. Stored procedures are bits of code that are packaged as "functions" within the framework of an SQL Server/MSDE database. Be aware, however, that stored procedures are not supported in Access. Stored procedures, unlike commands that are created within the scope of an ASP.NET page, are not parsed, compiled, and optimized every time they are executed; rather, they are parsed, compiled, and optimized only once. Even better, you can create multiple commands within a stored procedure and execute them all as a group rather than individually, as is the case within an ASP.NET page. Another benefit to using stored procedures is that, if you change the structure of your particular database table, you potentially only need to make changes to the relevant stored procedures, rather than every ASP.NET page that uses data from that table.

There are many more benefits to using stored procedures, not the least of which is the increase in overall performance of your Web applications. Let's take a look at a simple stored procedure that we'll use to insert a new helpdesk request ticket into our MSDE database. Obviously, we've already created the code that inserts the helpdesk request into the `HelpDesk` table within Access, but, as Access does not support stored procedures, let's look at inserting records into MSDE through the use of a stored procedure instead. Start by following the steps outlined below:

1. Open your copy of Web Data Administrator at http://localhost/SqlWebAdmin.

2. Type your user name, server name, and login.

3. Select the `Dorknozzle` database.

4. Select Stored Procedures from the navigation menu on the left.

5. Select Create new stored procedure.

6. Type the name of the stored procedure as **InsertHelpDesk** and click Create as shown in Figure 8.15.

Figure 8.15. Type the name of the new stored procedure.

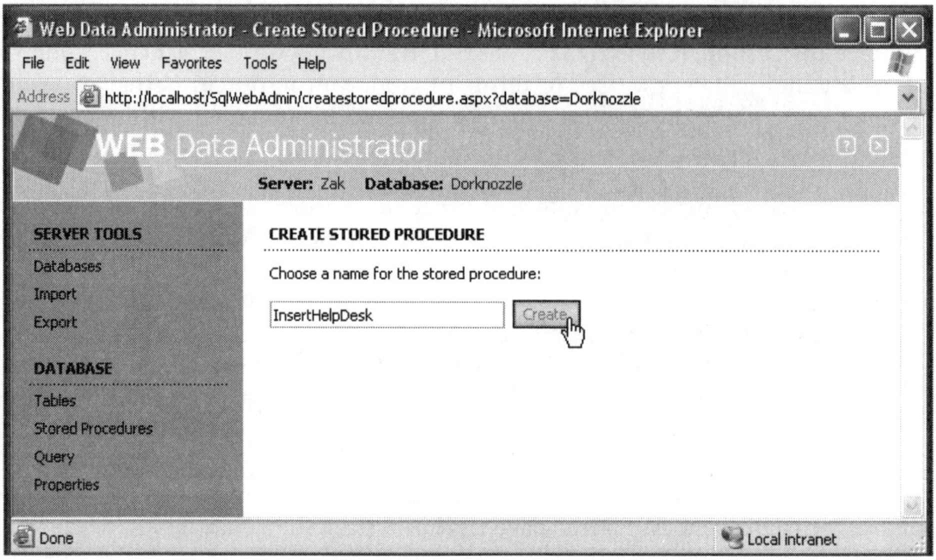

7. Provide the code for the procedure. For example, a stored procedure that performs a simple INSERT statement would be specified in the following format:

```
CREATE PROCEDURE ProcedureName
(
  @Value1 DataType,
  @Value2 DataType,
  …
)
AS
INSERT INTO TableName (Field1, Field2, …)
VALUES (@Value1, @Value2, …)
```

What we have here are the SQL keywords CREATE PROCEDURE, followed by the name that we'll use to call the procedure from our code, then a list of parameter names along with the type required for each, and finally the SQL statement that the stored procedure will perform. Note that a stored procedure can run any type of SQL statement—not just INSERT—and also, that we can use the specified parameters in the statement by preceding them with the @ character.

For our example, delete the code that Web Administrator has added by default, and create the stored procedure with the following code:

```
CREATE PROCEDURE InsertHelpDesk
(
  @EmployeeID Int,
  @StationNumber Int,
  @CategoryID Int,
  @SubjectID Int,
  @Description NText,
  @StatusID Int
)
AS
INSERT INTO HelpDesk
(EmployeeID, StationNumber, CategoryID, SubjectID,
  Description, StatusID)
VALUES
(@EmployeeID, @StationNumber, @CategoryID, @SubjectID,
  @Description, @StatusID)
```

When finished, click Save.

The new stored procedure will now appear within the User Stored Procedures list.

Next, you can modify the code within your helpdesk page to use the stored procedure. If you've been using Access, you'll also have to change it to import the `System.Data.SqlClient` namespace, and then do a search and replace to change occurrences of `OleDb` to `Sql` to swap over all the class names. Finally, you'll need to change the connection string as described in the early pages of this chapter. If you remember, the method for inserting the helpdesk request resembled the following:

VB.NET   File: **helpdesk.aspx (excerpt)**
```
Sub SubmitHelpDesk(s As Object, e As EventArgs)
  objCmd = New OleDbCommand( _
    "INSERT INTO HelpDesk (EmployeeID, StationNumber, " & _
    "CategoryID, SubjectID, Description, StatusID) " & _
    "VALUES (@EmployeeID, @StationNumber, @CategoryID, " & _
    "@SubjectID, @Description, @StatusID)", objConn)
  objCmd.Parameters.Add("@EmployeeID", 5)
  objCmd.Parameters.Add("@StationNumber", txtStationNum.Text)
  objCmd.Parameters.Add("@CategoryID", _
    ddlCategory.SelectedItem.Value)
  objCmd.Parameters.Add("@SubjectID", _
    ddlSubject.SelectedItem.Value)
```

```
    objCmd.Parameters.Add("@Description", txtDescription.Text)
    objCmd.Parameters.Add("@StatusID", 1)
    objConn.Open()
    objCmd.ExecuteNonQuery()
    objConn.Close()
End Sub
```

C#   File: **helpdesk.aspx (excerpt)**

```csharp
void SubmitHelpDesk(Object s, EventArgs e) {
    objCmd = new OleDbCommand(
        "INSERT INTO HelpDesk (EmployeeID, StationNumber, " +
        "CategoryID, SubjectID, Description, StatusID) " +
        "VALUES (@EmployeeID, @StationNumber, @CategoryID, " +
        "@SubjectID, @Description, @StatusID)", objConn);
    objCmd.Parameters.Add("@EmployeeID", 5);
    objCmd.Parameters.Add("@StationNumber", txtStationNum.Text);
    objCmd.Parameters.Add("@CategoryID",
        ddlCategory.SelectedItem.Value);
    objCmd.Parameters.Add("@SubjectID",
        ddlSubject.SelectedItem.Value);
    objCmd.Parameters.Add("@Description", txtDescription.Text);
    objCmd.Parameters.Add("@StatusID", 1);
    objConn.Open();
    objCmd.ExecuteNonQuery();
    objConn.Close();
}
```

We can modify this code slightly to use the stored procedure instead. To do so, we simply need to remove the SQL statement, and pass in the name of the stored procedure, as follows:

VB.NET   File: **helpdesk.aspx (excerpt)**

```
objCmd = new OleDbCommand("InsertHelpDesk", objConn)
```

Next, we set the command type property of the command object to the stored procedure, as follows:

VB.NET   File: **helpdesk.aspx (excerpt)**

```
objCmd.CommandType = CommandType.StoredProcedure
```

Since the CommandType class we use here is in the System.Data namespace, you'll need to add another Import directive at the top of the page:

```
<%@ Import Namespace="System.Data.SqlClient" %>
<%@ Import Namespace="System.Data" %>
```

The completed code using the new stored procedure will resemble the following:

VB.NET   File: **helpdesk.aspx (excerpt)**

```
Sub SubmitHelpDesk(s As Object, e As EventArgs)
  objCmd = new SqlCommand("InsertHelpDesk", objConn)
  objCmd.CommandType = CommandType.StoredProcedure
  objCmd.Parameters.Add("@EmployeeID", 5)
  objCmd.Parameters.Add("@StationNumber", txtStationNum.Text)
  objCmd.Parameters.Add("@CategoryID", _
    ddlCategory.SelectedItem.Value)
  objCmd.Parameters.Add("@SubjectID", _
    ddlSubject.SelectedItem.Value)
  objCmd.Parameters.Add("@Description", txtDescription.Text)
  objCmd.Parameters.Add("@StatusID", 1)
  objConn.Open()
  objCmd.ExecuteNonQuery()
  objConn.Close()
End Sub
```

C#   File: **helpdesk.aspx (excerpt)**

```
void SubmitHelpDesk(Object s, EventArgs e) {
  objCmd = new SqlCommand("InsertHelpDesk", objConn);
  objCmd.CommandType = CommandType.StoredProcedure;
  objCmd.Parameters.Add("@EmployeeID", 5);
  objCmd.Parameters.Add("@StationNumber", txtStationNum.Text);
  objCmd.Parameters.Add("@CategoryID",
    ddlCategory.SelectedItem.Value);
  objCmd.Parameters.Add("@SubjectID",
    ddlSubject.SelectedItem.Value);
  objCmd.Parameters.Add("@Description", txtDescription.Text);
  objCmd.Parameters.Add("@StatusID", 1);
  objConn.Open();
  objCmd.ExecuteNonQuery();
  objConn.Close();
}
```

Summary

In this chapter, you learned how to create simple Web applications that interact with databases. First, you learned about the various classes included with

ADO.NET, such as `Connection`, `Command`, and `DataReader`. You learned how to use these classes to create simple applications that query the database, insert records into a database, update records within a database, and delete records from a database. You also learned important topics for querying database data, including using parameters and control binding. Later in the chapter, you learned about transactions and how to improve application performance through the use of stored procedures.

The next chapter will expand on what we learned here and introduce the rest of the data controls: the `DataGrid` and `DataList`.

The **DataGrid** and **DataList** Controls

In the previous chapter, you learned some important concepts for data access and presentation. You learned that when connecting to a database, we have to establish a connection using either the `OleDbConnection` class or the `SqlConnection` class. You also learned that in order to retrieve data from the database table, we must write an SQL statement within a command using either the `OleDbCommand` class or the `SqlCommand` class. You discovered that in order to fill the database records into a virtual container of some sort, we have to create a `DataReader` using either the `OleDbDataReader` class or the `SqlDataReader` class. Finally, you learned that presenting the data within the `DataReader` was simply a matter of binding the `DataReader` to a data control such as the `Repeater` control.

The `Repeater` control offers flexibility in the sense that its templates can be easily customized with inline HTML, in conjunction with code render blocks, to display the `DataReader`'s contents in a clean and neatly formatted manner. So far, the `Repeater` control has been great! It certainly has its place, and I'm not about to discourage its use. However, the control does have certain limitations and reminds ASP developers too much of the bad old days when we had to write our HTML table and table row tags in a `While` loop. Within those table row tags we would also have to add code render blocks to show the contents of the `Recordset`. If the contents of the table needed any formatting, inline CSS or HTML style information had to be used. The `Repeater` control, as you've probably noticed, isn't much different. HTML table row tags still have to be added within the `<HeaderTemplate>`, `<ItemTemplate>`, and `<FooterTemplate>` tags, code render blocks must still be used within the table data cells, and formatting still has to be accomplished through the use of inline CSS or HTML styles.

Although the `Repeater` control saves us time because our code implementation is a bit cleaner and easier to write, there is something substantially better! Enter: `DataGrid` and `DataList`. These controls, part of ASP.NET's set of data controls, give developers much more power and flexibility over presentation than does the `Repeater` control, as you'll see in the next few sections. How information within a table is presented, formatted, and edited has been completely revamped with `DataGrids` and `DataLists`. Excited to see the new controls? Good! This chapter will change the way you'll choose to display your database content—guaranteed!

Working with `DataGrids`

`DataGrids` solve a problem that has plagued developers for years: data presentation. Because `DataGrids` act like typical HTML tables, information within a `DataGrid` is presented in a familiar, cleanly formatted, tabular structure. Similar to the `Repeater` control, the `DataGrid` can also automatically repeat all the content contained in a `DataReader` onto a page, based on styles we set within its templates. Unlike the `Repeater` control, however, the `DataGrid` offers several more advanced features, such as headers for field names that allow for sorting. `DataGrids` have paging capabilities (i.e. splitting a large result set into pages) built in, and enables users to modify data the pages contain. To sum up, `DataGrids` provide the following functionality:

❑ Database table-like presentation

❑ Table headers and footers

❑ Paging

❑ Sorting

❑ Style modification through templates

❑ Customizable columns for advanced editing

Before we begin to talk about the points mentioned above, let's take a quick look at a `DataGrid` example. Because `DataGrids` are controls, they are added to the page just as any other control would be:

```
<asp:DataGrid id="myDataGrid" runat="server"></asp:DataGrid>
```

Once the `DataGrid` is added to the page, you can bind a `DataReader` to it as follows:

VB.NET

```
myDataGrid.DataSource = myDataReader
myDataGrid.DataBind()
```

So far, the `DataGrid` doesn't seem to look or function very differently than the `Repeater` control, right? Think again! The `Repeater` control didn't work unless we specified content within the required `<ItemTemplate>` tag. The `DataGrid`, however, takes the structure of the database table and presents the data to the user in a cleanly-formatted HTML view.

Let's take a look at a `DataGrid` in use by building up the address book page. You can start by creating a new file called addressbook.aspx[1] from the template.aspx page contained within the `Template` folder, and adding to it a `DataGrid` and the usual `Import` directive, as highlighted below.

File: **SimpleDataGrid.aspx**

```
<%@ Import Namespace="System.Data.OleDb" %>
<html>
<head>
<title>The Dorknozzle.com Intranet Site</title>
<link href="styles.css" rel="stylesheet" />
</head>
<body>
<form runat="server">
<table width="100%" border="0" cellspacing="0" cellpadding="0"
    background="Images/header_bg.gif">
  <tr>
    <td><img src="Images/header_top.gif" width="450" height="142"
        alt="the official dorknozzle company intranet" /></td>
  </tr>
</table>

<table width="100%" border="0" cellspacing="0" cellpadding="0">
  <tr>
    <td width="157"><img src="Images/header_bottom.gif"
        width="157" height="37" alt="" /></td>
```

---

[1]The examples in this chapter will show different file names as we progress towards the finished addressbook.aspx file, to match the files that you'll find in the code archive, but you'll probably want to use addressbook.aspx if you're typing along.

```
      <td></td>
    </tr>
</table>

<table width="100%" border="0" cellspacing="0" cellpadding="10">
  <tr>
    <td valign="top" width="160">
      <!-- HyperLink Controls for navigation -->
      ...
      <!-- End HyperLink Controls -->
    </td>
    <td valign="top">
      <h1>Address Book</h1>
      <asp:DataGrid id="dgAddressBook" runat="server">
      </asp:DataGrid>
    </td>
  </tr>
</table>
</form>
</body>
</html>
```

Next, add code to the <head> tag to create a database connection, Command object, DataReader, and binding functionality, as follows:

VB.NET   File: **SimpleDataGrid.aspx (excerpt)**

```
<script runat="server" language="VB">
Dim objConn As New OleDbConnection( _
  "Provider=Microsoft.Jet.OleDb.4.0;" & _
  "Data Source=C:\Inetpub\wwwroot\Dorknozzle\Database\" & _
  "Dorknozzle.mdb")
Dim objCmd As OleDbCommand
Dim objRdr As OleDbDataReader
Dim strCmd As String

Sub Page_Load()
  If Not IsPostBack Then
    BindData()
  End If
End Sub

Sub BindData()
  objCmd = New OleDbCommand("SELECT * FROM Employees", objConn)
  objConn.Open()
  objRdr = objCmd.ExecuteReader()
  dgAddressBook.DataSource = objRdr
```

```
  dgAddressBook.DataBind()
  objRdr.Close()
  objConn.Close()
End Sub
</script>
```

C#   File: **SimpleDataGrid.aspx (excerpt)**

```
<script runat="server" language="C#">
OleDbConnection objConn = new OleDbConnection(
  "Provider=Microsoft.Jet.OleDb.4.0;" +
  "Data Source=C:\\Inetpub\\wwwroot\\Dorknozzle\\Database\\" +
  "Dorknozzle.mdb");
OleDbCommand objCmd;
OleDbDataReader objRdr;
String strCmd;

void Page_Load() {
  if (!IsPostBack) {
    BindData();
  }
}

void BindData() {
  objCmd = new OleDbCommand("SELECT * FROM Employees", objConn);
  objConn.Open();
  objRdr = objCmd.ExecuteReader();
  dgAddressBook.DataSource = objRdr;
  dgAddressBook.DataBind();
  objRdr.Close();
  objConn.Close();
}
</script>
```

What's going on? Similar to the examples in the previous chapter, here, we've added steps to retrieve the information from the database table:

1. We've created a new connection object by passing in the connection string.

2. We've created a new command object, passing in the SQL statement and connection object. The SQL statement in this case selects all employees within the Employees table.

3. We've opened the connection.

4. We've called the `ExecuteReader()` method of the command object to return a populated `DataReader`.

5. Finally, we've bound the `DataReader` to the `DataGrid`, closed the `DataReader`, and closed the connection.

Once you've added the HTML, `DataGrid`, and code, save your work and open the page within the browser. Figure 9.1 shows how the `DataGrid` presents all of the data within the `Employees` table in a cleanly formatted structure.

Figure 9.1. The `DataGrid` presents database data in a cleanly formatted structure.

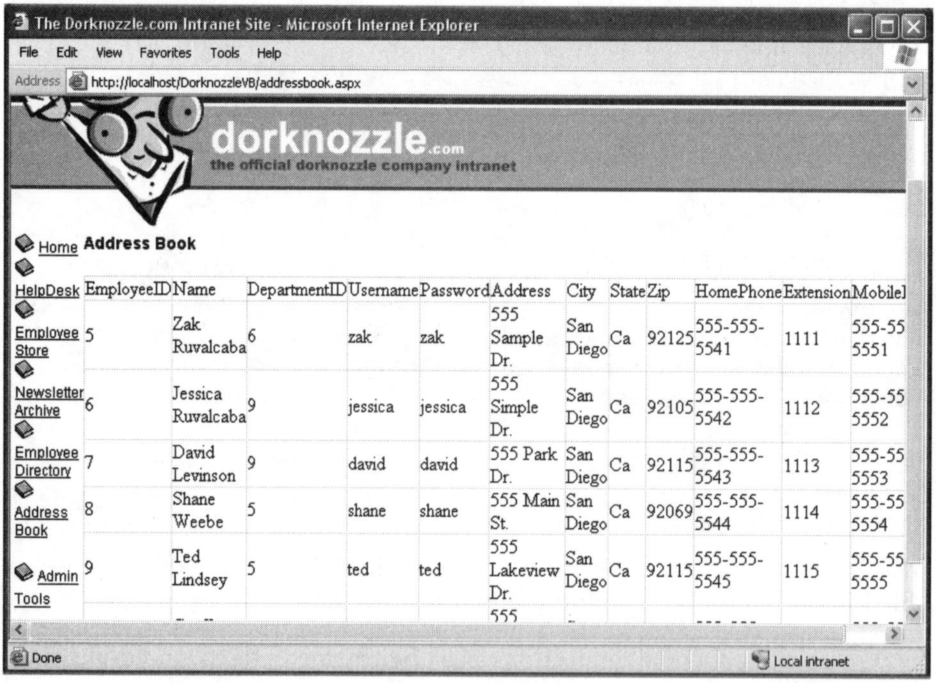

Well, okay, perhaps it doesn't look all that clean right now! However, that will change as we check out the `DataGrid`'s powerful yet intuitive formatting capabilities. You'll notice that the `DataGrid` closely resembles the structure of the `Employees` database table as it would appear in the Datasheet view in Access (or in the Web Administrator if you're using MSDE). All the column names in the database table show as headers within the `DataGrid`, and all rows contained within the database table are repeated down the page.

There's no doubt that the `DataGrid`'s automatic presentational features are impressive, but you will, no doubt, have noticed that *all* of the `Employees` information is shown within the `DataGrid`, and that the `DataGrid` looks fairly ugly from a design standpoint. The next few sections will teach you how to customize the `DataGrid` so that you can decide which columns within the database table to show. You'll then learn about creating and working with styles to modify the overall appearance of the `DataGrid`.

Customizing DataGrids

So our `DataGrid`, although impressive in its simplicity, doesn't look all that nice, and *all* employee information is shown within it. Assuming that this were a real address book, why would we want to show user name and password information? Is it really necessary to display each employee's ID? And what would you do if you wanted to use different names for the column headers? As we shall see, all of these questions and more can be answered through the use of styles and column customization.

Customizing DataGrid Columns

If you wish to restrict the information that appears within your `DataGrid`, you can pick the columns you want to display by making a few simple modifications. When you bind a `DataReader` to the `DataGrid` you are, by default, presented with a quick and simple representation of your database table. Headers for the `DataGrid` columns are produced on the basis of the database table's column names, and the rows are automatically generated based on the content that the database table contains. The key words here are "automatically generated." One of the properties a `DataGrid` has is `AutoGenerateColumns`. By default, this value is set to `True`. If you want to construct the columns that your `DataGrid` contains manually, you must set this property to `False`, as follows:

File: **BoundColumns.aspx (excerpt)**

```
<asp:DataGrid id="dgAddressBook" runat="server"
    AutoGenerateColumns="false">
</asp:DataGrid>
```

If you save your work at this point and test it within the browser, however, nothing shows up. The reason for this is simple: because you've set the `DataGrid`'s `AutoGenerateColumns` property to `False`, you must now manually construct all the columns for the `DataGrid` using the `<Columns>` tag:

File: **BoundColumns.aspx (excerpt)**

```
<asp:DataGrid id="dgAddressBook" runat="server"
    AutoGenerateColumns="false">
  <Columns>
  </Columns>
</asp:DataGrid>
```

Inside this tag, you must define all columns that are to be bound within the DataGrid using the BoundColumn control. The BoundColumn control contains a DataField property that specifies the name of the database table's column, and a HeaderText property that sets the name of the column as you want it displayed to the user. Try the following code:

File: **BoundColumns.aspx (excerpt)**

```
<asp:DataGrid id="dgAddressBook" runat="server"
    AutoGenerateColumns="false">
  <Columns>
    <asp:BoundColumn DataField="Name" HeaderText="Name" />
    <asp:BoundColumn DataField="Address" HeaderText="Address" />
    <asp:BoundColumn DataField="City" HeaderText="City" />
    <asp:BoundColumn DataField="State" HeaderText="State" />
    <asp:BoundColumn DataField="Zip" HeaderText="Zip" />
    <asp:BoundColumn DataField="HomePhone"
        HeaderText="Home Phone" />
    <asp:BoundColumn DataField="MobilePhone"
        HeaderText="Mobile Phone" />
  </Columns>
</asp:DataGrid>
```

Now, save your work and try it in the browser again. This time, only the columns that you specified to be bound are displayed within the DataGrid. The results will be as shown in Figure 9.2.

Figure 9.2. The `DataGrid` presents only the columns that you specify as bound columns.

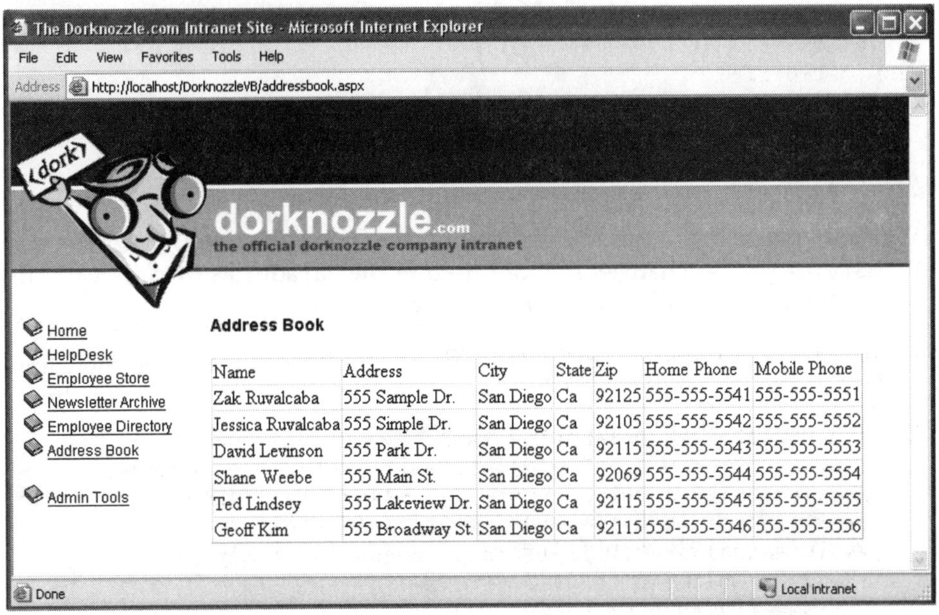

Note that if you leave off the `HeaderText` property for any of the bound columns, that column will not have a header. We've now solved the problem of displaying our own information, but the `DataGrid` still looks plain. In the next section, we'll use styles to customize the look of our `DataGrid`.

Modifying the Appearance of `DataGrids` with Styles

Similar to the `Repeater` control, the `DataGrid` contains four parts, all of which can be customized using built-in style tags. For instance, if we wanted to modify the look of the rows within the `DataGrid`, we would simply add an `<ItemStyle>` tag to the `DataGrid`, as follows:

File: **DataGridWithStyles.aspx (excerpt)**

```
<asp:DataGrid id="dgAddressBook" runat="server"
   AutoGenerateColumns="false">
 <ItemStyle Font-Name="Arial" Font-Size="10pt"
     ForeColor="#000000" />
 <Columns>
   <asp:BoundColumn DataField="Name" HeaderText="Name" />
```

```
    <asp:BoundColumn DataField="Address" HeaderText="Address" />
    <asp:BoundColumn DataField="City" HeaderText="City" />
    <asp:BoundColumn DataField="State" HeaderText="State" />
    <asp:BoundColumn DataField="Zip" HeaderText="Zip" />
    <asp:BoundColumn DataField="HomePhone"
        HeaderText="Home Phone" />
    <asp:BoundColumn DataField="MobilePhone"
        HeaderText="Mobile Phone" />
  </Columns>
</asp:DataGrid>
```

Save your work and view the results in the browser. You'll see that the
<ItemStyle> tag has changed the font used in the DataGrid's rows (but not its
headers) from the default, Times New Roman, to Arial.

As you can see, the items in the DataGrid can be styled by altering their font
type, color, and size. You can also style the column headers and apply an alternating item style to alternate rows in the table:

File: **DataGridWithStyles.aspx (excerpt)**

```
<asp:DataGrid id="dgAddressBook" runat="server"
    AutoGenerateColumns="false">
  <ItemStyle Font-Name="Arial" Font-Size="10pt"
      ForeColor="#000000" />
  <HeaderStyle Font-Name="Arial" Font-Size="10pt" Font-Bold="true"
      BackColor="#003366" ForeColor="#FFFFFF" />
  <AlternatingItemStyle Font-Name="Arial" Font-Size="10pt"
      BackColor="#CCCCCC" />
  <Columns>
    <asp:BoundColumn DataField="Name" HeaderText="Name" />
    <asp:BoundColumn DataField="Address" HeaderText="Address" />
    <asp:BoundColumn DataField="City" HeaderText="City" />
    <asp:BoundColumn DataField="State" HeaderText="State" />
    <asp:BoundColumn DataField="Zip" HeaderText="Zip" />
    <asp:BoundColumn DataField="HomePhone"
        HeaderText="Home Phone" />
    <asp:BoundColumn DataField="MobilePhone"
        HeaderText="Mobile Phone" />
  </Columns>
</asp:DataGrid>
```

Save your work again, and view your results within the browser window. The
results should be as shown in Figure 9.3; the column headings are styled, and
different styles are applied to alternate rows in the DataGrid.

Figure 9.3. Modifying the alternating item and header styles allows you to customize the DataGrid further.

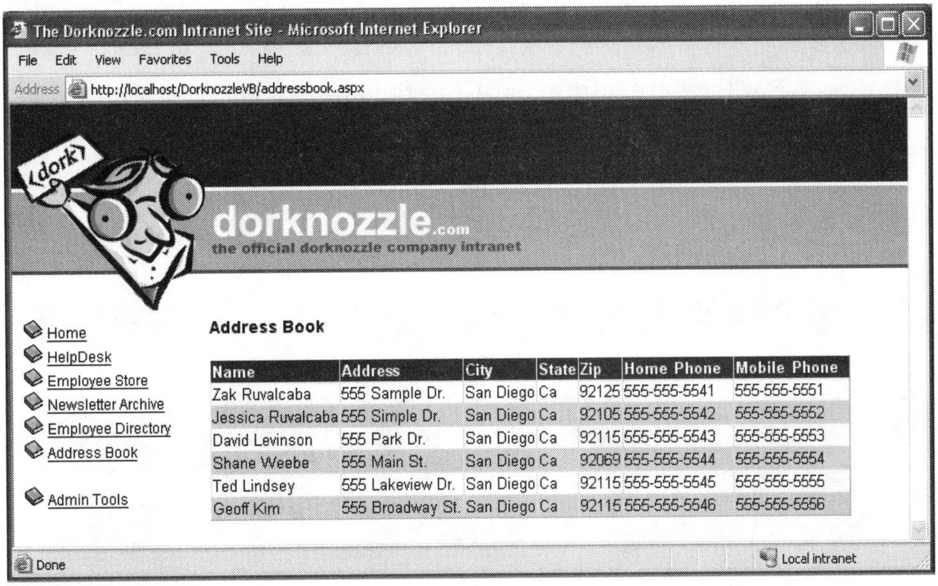

Once you're happy with the way the header, items, and alternating items within your DataGrid look, you can focus your attention on the customization of the DataGrid itself. This next listing shows how we can choose to turn the grid lines off and add a bit of cell padding for breathing room:

File: **DataGridWithStyles.aspx (excerpt)**

```
<asp:DataGrid id="dgAddressBook" runat="server"
    AutoGenerateColumns="false" CellPadding="4" GridLines="None">
  <ItemStyle Font-Name="Arial" Font-Size="10pt"
      ForeColor="#000000" />
  <HeaderStyle Font-Name="Arial" Font-Size="10pt" Font-Bold="true"
      BackColor="#003366" ForeColor="#FFFFFF" />
  <AlternatingItemStyle Font-Name="Arial" Font-Size="10pt"
      BackColor="#CCCCCC" />
  <Columns>
    <asp:BoundColumn DataField="Name" HeaderText="Name" />
    <asp:BoundColumn DataField="Address" HeaderText="Address" />
    <asp:BoundColumn DataField="City" HeaderText="City" />
    <asp:BoundColumn DataField="State" HeaderText="State" />
    <asp:BoundColumn DataField="Zip" HeaderText="Zip" />
    <asp:BoundColumn DataField="HomePhone"
```

```
        HeaderText="Home Phone" />
    <asp:BoundColumn DataField="MobilePhone"
        HeaderText="Mobile Phone" />
  </Columns>
</asp:DataGrid>
```

This time, when the DataGrid is viewed in the browser, we have a little more room between cells, and the lines surrounding the DataGrid are gone. Your results should be similar to Figure 9.4.

Figure 9.4. Modify the DataGrid itself to customize properties for the entire DataGrid.

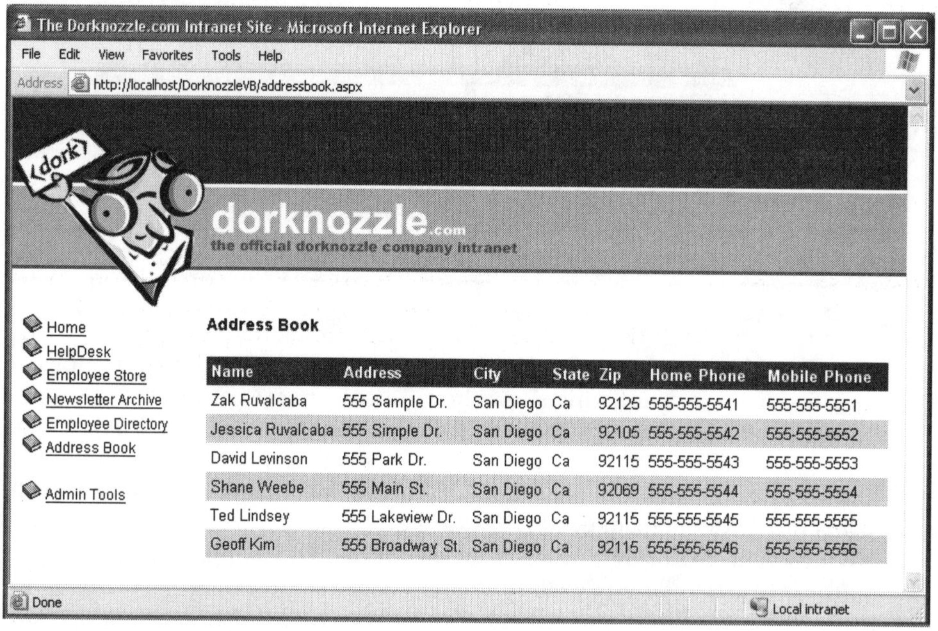

Creating a Master/Detail Form with the HyperLinkColumn

We've already done quite a lot to our DataGrid, and the best thing about these changes is that they've hardly required any coding—just the scripts to bind the DataGrid to the DataReader object. In many cases, however, you'll want to allow users to interact with the DataGrid by letting them click on certain columns.

You won't be surprised to discover that we can do exactly that—providing columns that, when clicked, raise events and call methods just as ordinary buttons would. There are several types of column that we can create in a `DataGrid`, in addition to the `BoundColumn` control you've already seen, that allow you to perform various tasks. For instance, we could create a column containing a button or a link that, when clicked, presented expanded information about the item in that row. The complete set of controls and their descriptions are listed below:

BoundColumn
As you've seen, the `BoundColumn` provides flexibility in presentation by allowing you to specify the columns that will appear within the `DataGrid`.

HyperLinkColumn
Use the `HyperLinkColumn` to display a clickable link within the `DataGrid`. We'll be looking at this feature throughout this section.

EditCommandColumn
This control displays commands that allows the user to edit, update, and cancel editing of data within the `DataGrid`. We'll be looking at this functionality in the next section.

TemplateColumn
Use the `TemplateColumn` in conjunction with `EditCommandColumns` to display customized, editable data within the `DataGrid` using templates.

ButtonColumn
Use the `ButtonColumn` to display a clickable button within the `DataGrid`.

A common application of the `HyperLinkColumn` control is in creating a **master/detail page**. Master/detail pages are pages that initially show very little information, but, when an item within the initial page is clicked, display details pertaining to that item. This kind of functionality is often seen on ecommerce sites. For instance, you might initially present users with very little information about all available products, to reduce download time and make the information more readable. Users could then click a `HyperLinkColumn` control to see a more detailed view of a particular product. Let's see how this works. We'll start by changing the `DataGrid`'s `BoundColumns` to show only the employee names and phone extensions, as follows:

File: **MasterDetail.aspx (excerpt)**

```
<asp:DataGrid id="dgAddressBook" runat="server"
    AutoGenerateColumns="false" CellPadding="4" GridLines="None">
  <ItemStyle Font-Name="Arial" Font-Size="10pt">
```

```
          ForeColor="#000000" />
  <HeaderStyle Font-Name="Arial" Font-Size="10pt" Font-Bold="true"
      BackColor="#003366" ForeColor="#FFFFFF" />
  <AlternatingItemStyle Font-Name="Arial" Font-Size="10pt"
      BackColor="#CCCCCC" />
  <Columns>
    <asp:BoundColumn DataField="Name" HeaderText="Name" />
    <asp:BoundColumn DataField="Extension" HeaderText="Extension"
        />
  </Columns>
</asp:DataGrid>
```

Figure 9.5 shows the new slimmed-down version of the `DataGrid`.

Figure 9.5. Modify the `DataGrid` to show only names and phone extensions.

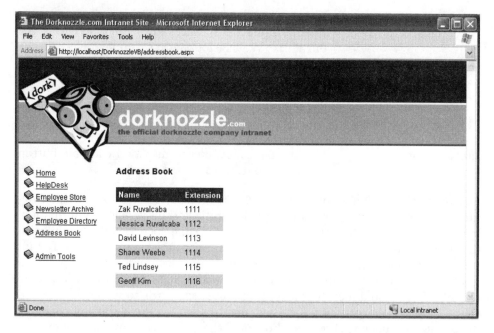

We'll create the page so that, if users decide that they want to see all the information on a particular employee, they need only click a corresponding hyperlink within the `DataGrid`. Once the hyperlink is clicked, we'll pass the employee's ID to the code, so that a new `DataReader` can be created for the selected employee. Once the new `DataReader` is created with the new information, it is bound to a new `DataGrid` that displays all the information, rather than just names and phone extensions.

You can add a `HyperLinkColumn` within the `DataGrid` by replacing the `<asp:BoundColumn>` tag for the Name column with a new `<asp:HyperLinkColumn>`, as follows:

File: **MasterDetail.aspx (excerpt)**

```
<asp:DataGrid id="dgAddressBook" runat="server"
    AutoGenerateColumns="false" CellPadding="4" GridLines="None">
  <ItemStyle Font-Name="Arial" Font-Size="10pt"
      ForeColor="#000000" />
  <HeaderStyle Font-Name="Arial" Font-Size="10pt" Font-Bold="true"
      BackColor="#003366" ForeColor="#FFFFFF" />
  <AlternatingItemStyle Font-Name="Arial" Font-Size="10pt"
      BackColor="#CCCCCC" />
  <Columns>
    <asp:HyperLinkColumn DataTextField="Name"
        DataNavigateUrlField="EmployeeID"
        DataNavigateUrlFormatString="addressbook.aspx?id={0}"
        HeaderText="Name" />
    <asp:BoundColumn DataField="Extension" HeaderText="Extension"
        />
  </Columns>
</asp:DataGrid>
```

We've created the `HyperLinkColumn` with a variety of properties that you have not yet seen. The first, `DataTextField`, accepts the name of the database table column to use as the linked text. The next two, `DataNavigateUrlField` and `DataNavigateUrlFormatString`, are used together to provide the URL of the page to which we want to redirect users when they click. Notice the {0} that appears in the value of the format string property—this will be replaced with the value of the column specified in the URL field property, which, in this case, is `EmployeeID`.

You can see that we're actually redirecting to the `addressbook.aspx` page itself. However, we're creating a query string that contains the unique employee ID that we can then use within the `WHERE` clause of an SQL query to retrieve the correct details.

Finally, we set the `HeaderText` to `Name`. When you view the page in the browser window now, the `DataGrid` displays with linked employee names, similar to Figure 9.6.

Figure 9.6. The `HyperLinkColumn` allows you to define a link within a column in the `DataGrid`.

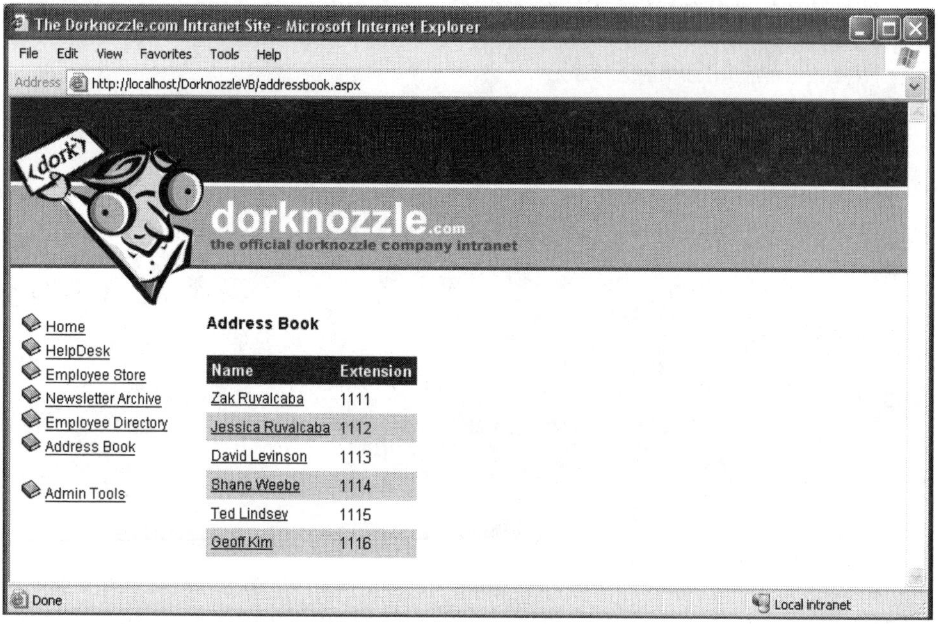

Try rolling over one of the links within the `DataGrid`. Rolling over a link displays the dynamically generated link in the browser's status bar, using `EmployeeID` as the `id` value. Now, click a name within the `DataGrid`. Because we specified `DataNavigateUrlFormatString` as `addressbook.aspx`, the page should link to itself. The difference, however, is that the unique identifier (`EmployeeID`) is passed along in the query string as a variable named `id`. Now, we need to change the code in `addressbook.aspx` to check for this ID, and display details of the appropriate employee. We can do this simply by modifying the `BindData()` method as follows:

VB.NET   File: **MasterDetail.aspx (excerpt)**

```
Sub BindData()
  objConn.Open()
  If (Request.QueryString("id") <> "") Then
    objCmd = New OleDbCommand( _
      "SELECT * FROM Employees WHERE EmployeeID=" & _
      Request.QueryString("id"), objConn)
    objRdr = objCmd.ExecuteReader()
    dgAddressBookDetails.DataSource = objRdr
```

```
      dgAddressBookDetails.DataBind()
  Else
    objCmd = New OleDbCommand("SELECT * FROM Employees", objConn)
    objRdr = objCmd.ExecuteReader()
    dgAddressBook.DataSource = objRdr
    dgAddressBook.DataBind()
  End If
  objRdr.Close()
  objConn.Close()
End Sub
```

C# requires slightly different syntax for the `QueryString` collection:

File: **MasterDetail.aspx (excerpt)**

```csharp
void BindData() {
  objConn.Open();
  if (Request.QueryString["id"] != null) {
    objCmd = new OleDbCommand(
      "SELECT * FROM Employees WHERE EmployeeID=" +
      Request.QueryString["id"], objConn);
    objRdr = objCmd.ExecuteReader();
    dgAddressBookDetails.DataSource = objRdr;
    dgAddressBookDetails.DataBind();
  } else {
    objCmd = new OleDbCommand("SELECT * FROM Employees", objConn);
    objRdr = objCmd.ExecuteReader();
    dgAddressBook.DataSource = objRdr;
    dgAddressBook.DataBind();
  }
  objRdr.Close();
  objConn.Close();
}
```

As you can see, the modified `BindData()` method checks for the `id` variable in the URL string using the `QueryString` property of the built-in `Request` object. The `QueryString` property is a collection that lets you obtain a query string variable's value given its name. In the above code, we use an `If` statement to check the value of the variable and make sure it's not empty. If it's not, the SQL statement is modified to query the `Employees` table where the `EmployeeID` is equal to the value contained within the `id` variable. Once the `DataReader` is returned, we bind it to a new `DataGrid`, called `dgAddressBookDetails`, which we'll create in a minute. If the query string is in fact empty, this means that the page is loading for the first time; as such, we load all the basic employee information into the master `DataGrid` as before.

We're almost done! The final task is to add the details `DataGrid`:

File: **MasterDetail.aspx (excerpt)**

```
<asp:DataGrid id="dgAddressBookDetails" runat="server"
    AutoGenerateColumns="false">
  <ItemStyle Font-Name="Arial" Font-Size="10pt"
      ForeColor="#000000" />
  <HeaderStyle Font-Name="Arial" Font-Size="10pt" Font-Bold="true"
      BackColor="#003366" ForeColor="#FFFFFF" />
  <AlternatingItemStyle Font-Name="Arial" Font-Size="10pt"
      BackColor="#CCCCCC" />
  <Columns>
    <asp:BoundColumn DataField="Name" HeaderText="Name" />
    <asp:BoundColumn DataField="Address" HeaderText="Address" />
    <asp:BoundColumn DataField="City" HeaderText="City" />
    <asp:BoundColumn DataField="State" HeaderText="State" />
    <asp:BoundColumn DataField="Zip" HeaderText="Zip" />
    <asp:BoundColumn DataField="HomePhone" HeaderText="Phone" />
    <asp:BoundColumn DataField="Extension" HeaderText="Extension"
        />
    <asp:BoundColumn DataField="MobilePhone" HeaderText="Mobile"
        />
  </Columns>
</asp:DataGrid>
```

Save your work and test the results in the browser. Figure 9.7 shows the results of the new `DataGrid` when a name within the master grid is selected.

Figure 9.7. The user selects an employee's name and all of that person's data is shown within the details DataGrid.

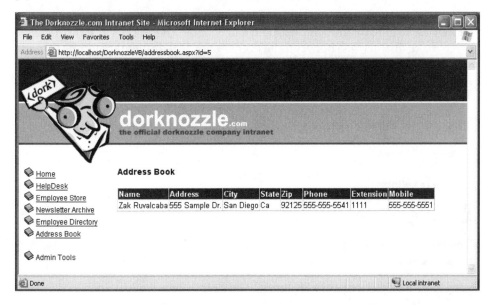

Notice the browser address bar in the image. As you can see, the query string is formatted according to the `DataNavigateUrlField` and the `DataNavigateUrlFormatString` properties. The number that's attached at the end of the URL string is the employee's ID. Query strings represent an interesting way of transferring pertinent information—usually IDs, search strings, etc.—from one page to the next. Query strings were the method of choice in traditional ASP, but, because of ASP.NET's unique single page-based coding structure, you'll find they're needed less and less.

As with all examples in this book, you can obtain the completed code for this section in the code archive.

Event Bubbling

The next few sections deal with user interaction as it relates to the `DataGrid` and `DataList` controls. Interaction within these controls is possible because of **event bubbling**. Event bubbling describes the process by which a child control passes an event to a containing (or parent) control that can handle the event. The `Repeater`, the `DataList`, and, in this case, the `DataGrid` control allow you to capture events within their child controls. When an event is raised within a

DataGrid's child controls (`Button`, `HyperLink`, etc.), the event "bubbles up" to the containing control (`DataGrid`), which can then call the necessary method to handle the event.

The `DataGrid` control and, as you'll see a little later, the `DataList` control, allow you to make distinctions between the events raised by different columns through the use of the following five attributes:

- ☐ `OnItemCommand`

- ☐ `OnUpdateCommand`

- ☐ `OnEditCommand`

- ☐ `OnDeleteCommand`

- ☐ `OnCancelCommand`

These attributes are defined on the containing control, in this case, the `DataGrid`, and let us assign a handler for that particular event, as follows:

```
<asp:DataGrid id="dgAddressBook" runat="server"
    OnUpdateCommand="dg_Update">
...
</asp:DataGrid>
```

You'd then use the `CommandName` property within the specific child control to trigger the appropriate event. For instance, if we had a `LinkButton` control within the `<Columns>` tag of the `DataGrid` that the user could click to update changed information, we would want that link button to fire the `UpdateCommand` event, like so:

```
<asp:LinkButton id="myLink" runat="server" CommandName="Update" />
```

In this case, when the user selects the `LinkButton` control, the event bubbles up to the `DataGrid`. Because we've set the `OnUpdateCommand` attribute of the `DataGrid`, it will catch that event, and call the handler method specified in that property, namely `dg_Update()` in this example.

To see just what role these events play in a typical `DataGrid`, let's look at a new column type—`EditCommandColumn`—which can single-handedly generate three of these five events.

Working with the `EditCommandColumn`

You can use the `EditCommandColumn` control to create editable rows within your `DataGrid`. For instance, you could allow employees to search within the address book for their names, click an "Edit" hyperlink within the `DataGrid`, make necessary changes to their information within a `TextBox` control, and finally click an "Update" hyperlink to have their information within the database updated. Figure 9.8 shows what I have in mind.

Figure 9.8. The "Edit" hyperlink appears within each `DataGrid` row.

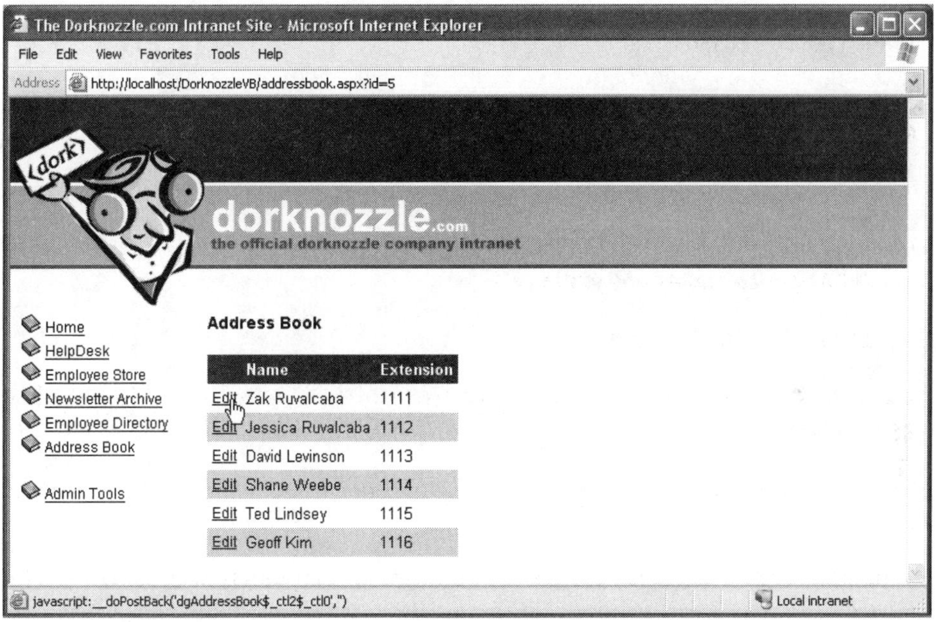

You can add this functionality to your address book page, first by adding the following code to the `DataGrid`. As is the case with all column tags, the `EditCommandColumn` must be placed within the `<Columns>` tag in the `DataGrid`:

File: **EditUpdateCancel.aspx (excerpt)**

```
<asp:EditCommandColumn EditText="Edit" CancelText="Cancel"
    UpdateText="Update" />
```

The only significant properties that the EditCommandColumn control accepts are the text labels to be displayed for the clickable links that appear within the DataGrid. The EditCommandColumn control is unusual in that the CommandName property is not needed. It is implied that when users select the "Edit", "Update" and "Cancel" hyperlinks, they'll be raising the EditCommand, UpdateCommand and CancelCommand events, respectively. Knowing this, you can finish the DataGrid by adding the necessary event handlers. Also, change the name column back to a regular bound column, as follows:

File: **EditUpdateCancel.aspx (excerpt)**

```
<asp:DataGrid id="dgAddressBook" runat="server"
    AutoGenerateColumns="false" CellPadding="4" GridLines="None"
    OnEditCommand="dg_Edit" OnCancelCommand="dg_Cancel"
    OnUpdateCommand="dg_Update">
  <ItemStyle Font-Name="Arial" Font-Size="10pt"
      ForeColor="#000000" />
  <HeaderStyle Font-Name="Arial" Font-Size="10pt" Font-Bold="true"
      BackColor="#003366" ForeColor="#FFFFFF" />
  <AlternatingItemStyle Font-Name="Arial" Font-Size="10pt"
      BackColor="#CCCCCC" />
  <Columns>
    <asp:EditCommandColumn EditText="Edit" CancelText="Cancel"
        UpdateText="Update" />
    <asp:BoundColumn DataField="Name" HeaderText="Name" />
    <asp:BoundColumn DataField="Extension" HeaderText="Extension"
        />
  </Columns>
</asp:DataGrid>
```

Save your work, but don't run the page in the browser just yet. Notice that we specified various method names within the OnEditCommand, OnCancelCommand, and OnUpdateCommand attributes. We still need to write the code to handle those events. Begin by creating three empty methods within your code, as follows:

VB.NET   File: **EditUpdateCancel.aspx (excerpt)**

```
Sub dg_Edit(s As Object, e As DataGridCommandEventArgs)

End Sub

Sub dg_Cancel(s As Object, e As DataGridCommandEventArgs)

End Sub

Sub dg_Update(s As Object, e As DataGridCommandEventArgs)
```

```
End Sub
```

```
C#                                          File: EditUpdateCancel.aspx (excerpt)
void dg_Edit(Object s, DataGridCommandEventArgs e) {

}

void dg_Cancel(Object s, DataGridCommandEventArgs e) {

}

void dg_Update(Object s, DataGridCommandEventArgs e) {

}
```

You'll notice that the parameters passed into these methods are different than normal. The DataGrid has its own special set of events; we know that now. To handle those events, we must pass in DataGridCommandEventArgs instead of the standard EventArgs. With the event handlers defined, we can now create the required functionality.

Let's start with the easiest method, and work our way down. Within dg_Edit(), write the following code:

```
VB.NET                                      File: EditUpdateCancel.aspx (excerpt)
Sub dg_Edit(s As Object, e As DataGridCommandEventArgs)
  dgAddressBook.EditItemIndex = e.Item.ItemIndex
  BindData()
End Sub
```

```
C#                                          File: EditUpdateCancel.aspx (excerpt)
void dg_Edit(Object s, DataGridCommandEventArgs e) {
  dgAddressBook.EditItemIndex = e.Item.ItemIndex;
  BindData();
}
```

As you can deduce from the above code, e has a property named Item. What's e? e is the object of class DataGridCommandEventArgs that is passed to the event handler with information about the event and the DataGrid item (i.e. the row) that triggered it. e.Item gives us that item. In order to allow the user to edit it, we need to know its index—the number of the row in which it appears. This we can get as e.Item.ItemIndex.

The `DataGrid` control is unique in that it will display a row of `TextBox` controls to allow editing on cue. In order to trigger that functionality, we must set the `DataGrid`'s `EditItemIndex` property to the index of the row we wish to edit (`e.Item.ItemIndex`). That's what the above code does. The second line simply calls the `BindData()` method to bind the database data to the `TextBox` controls that will appear within the `DataGrid` once they show.

Try saving your work at this stage and testing the results in your browser. Selecting the "Edit" hyperlink should create populated `TextBox` controls. You'll also notice that the "Edit" hyperlink changes to "Update" and "Cancel" hyperlinks similar to Figure 9.9.

Figure 9.9. Populated `TextBox` controls appear once the user selects the "Edit" hyperlink.

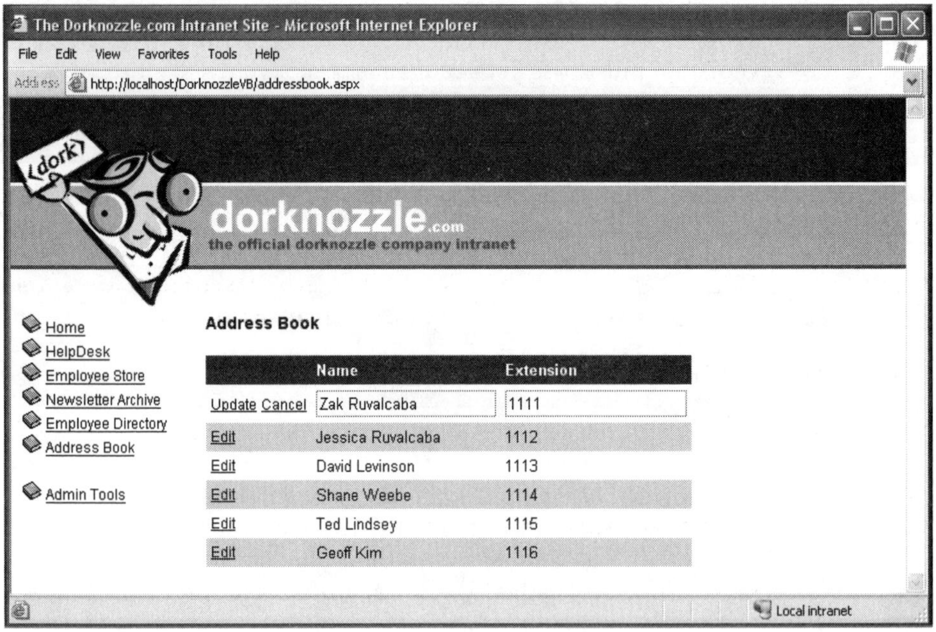

The "Cancel" event handler is also easy to write. The `EditItemIndex` property can either be set to the index of a row to be edited (as we did above), or `-1`. Setting the `EditItemIndex` property to `-1` switches the "Edit" functionality back off. With this in mind, you can write the following code to complete the "Cancel" functionality:

```
VB.NET                                          File: EditUpdateCancel.aspx (excerpt)
Sub dg_Cancel(s As Object, e As DataGridCommandEventArgs)
  dgAddressBook.EditItemIndex = -1
  BindData()
End Sub
```

```
C#                                              File: EditUpdateCancel.aspx (excerpt)
void dg_Cancel(Object s, DataGridCommandEventArgs e) {
  dgAddressBook.EditItemIndex = -1;
  BindData();
}
```

Try saving your work and testing the page again in a browser. This time, you should be able to click the "Edit" and "Cancel" hyperlinks to switch the DataGrid between editing a row and its original state. When you click the "Cancel" hyperlink, the "Update" and "Cancel" hyperlinks change back to an "Edit" hyperlink.

The "Update" functionality will be a little more challenging, so, rather than presenting you with the complete code, we'll take it line by line. Let's begin. When a user triggers the EditCommand event by clicking an "Edit" link, TextBox controls are automatically drawn within the selected row of the DataGrid. Unfortunately, because we didn't manually add the TextBox controls to the interface, we can't access them by their IDs. Instead, we must access them through the **controls collection** common to the DataGrid and DataList controls. As its name implies, this collection stores all the controls contained within our DataGrid, including those elusive TextBoxes. We'll come back to this shortly.

We can start by declaring an integer variable that will hold the selected employee's ID, and two string variables to hold the values entered into the DataGrid TextBoxes:

```
VB.NET                                          File: EditUpdateCancel.aspx (excerpt)
Sub dg_Update(s As Object, e As DataGridCommandEventArgs)
  Dim intEmployeeID As Integer
  Dim strName, strExtension As String
```

```
C#                                              File: EditUpdateCancel.aspx (excerpt)
void dg_Update(Object s, DataGridCommandEventArgs e) {
  int intEmployeeID;
  String strName, strExtension;
```

Remember, updating records within a database is usually done on a single record identified by the WHERE clause of an UPDATE statement. In our case, we need to update a specific employee. In order to update that employee's information, we'll need his or her employee ID. To get the employee ID, we can set within the `DataGrid` a unique key that's equal to the employee's ID. To do this, you can set a property within the `DataGrid` called `DataKeyField`, as follows:

```
<asp:DataGrid id="dgAddressBook" runat="server"
    AutoGenerateColumns="false" CellPadding="3" GridLines="None"
    OnEditCommand="dg_Edit" OnCancelCommand="dg_Cancel"
    OnUpdateCommand="dg_Update" DataKeyField="EmployeeID">
```

Now, when the `DataGrid` is loaded, each row will contain a unique key. That unique key, which is hidden from view, can be used within code to establish the unique identifier for the `WHERE` clause of the SQL statement. You can obtain the `DataKeyField` value for the selected item with the next line of code:

VB.NET   File: **EditUpdateCancel.aspx (excerpt)**
```
intEmployeeID = dgAddressBook.DataKeys(e.Item.ItemIndex)
```

C#   File: **EditUpdateCancel.aspx (excerpt)**
```
intEmployeeID = (int)dgAddressBook.DataKeys[e.Item.ItemIndex];
```

Remember that we talked about `e.Item.ItemIndex` earlier—its the numerical index of the selected row of the `DataGrid`. In this case, we can use it to get the key (the employee ID) of the selected row by grabbing the value of the corresponding element of the `DataKeys` property of the `DataGrid` object, which is a collection (or array).

Next, we'll need to find the values in the `TextBox` controls that appear within the `DataGrid` and save them as variables. This is where we need to use that controls collection I mentioned earlier:

VB.NET   File: **EditUpdateCancel.aspx (excerpt)**
```
strName = CType(e.Item.Cells(1).Controls(0), TextBox).Text
strExtension = CType(e.Item.Cells(2).Controls(0), TextBox).Text
```

C#   File: **EditUpdateCancel.aspx (excerpt)**
```
strName = ((TextBox)e.Item.Cells[1].Controls[0]).Text;
strExtension = ((TextBox)e.Item.Cells[2].Controls[0]).Text;
```

We can obtain a particular control from this collection by specifying the cell that contains the control (`Cells(n)` or `Cells[n]`), then specifying the particular control within that cell (`Controls(n)` or `Controls[n]`). In both cases, $n=0$ for the first cell or control, $n=1$ for the second, and so on. Since the first cell of each row contains the command hyperlinks, `Cells(1)` or `Cells[1]` will give us the cell with the `TextBox` for the employee's name, while `Cells(2)` or `Cells[2]` will give the cell containing the `TextBox` with the employee's extension. Because we have only one control in each of these cells, we can get the `TextBox` within each cell with `Controls(0)` or `Controls[0]`.

Now, ASP.NET doesn't automatically know what type of controls it's pulling out of these cells, but *we* know they're `TextBoxes`. To *treat* them as `TextBoxes`, not just generic controls (e.g. to pull the text out of them), we must first convert (or **cast**) them to `TextBox` objects (with `CType(…, TextBox)` in VB.NET or `(TextBox)` in C#). We can then find the value it contains using the `Text` property of the object.

You might be confused at first that we've pulled out the control, cast it to a `TextBox`, and then grabbed its `Text` property all in one line, but once you're used to the language this is a much neater way of doing it. Here's the more verbose alternative if you want to compare:

VB.NET
```
Dim nameControl As Control = e.Item.Cells(1).Controls(0)
Dim nameTextBox As TextBox = CType(nameControl, TextBox)
strName = nameTextBox.Text

Dim extControl As Control = e.Item.Cells(2).Controls(0)
Dim extTextBox As TextBox = CType(extControl, TextBox)
strExtension = extTextBox.Text
```

C#
```
Control nameControl = e.Item.Cells[1].Controls[0];
TextBox nameTextBox = (TextBox)nameControl;
strName = nameTextBox.Text;

Control extControl = e.Item.Cells[2].Controls[0];
TextBox extTextBox = (TextBox)extControl;
strExtension = extTextBox.Text;
```

Though more readable, this code involves creating two extra variables for each `TextBox`. For greater efficiency and tighter code, we'll stick with the one-liners.

Next, we'll update the database with the following code:

VB.NET   File: **EditUpdateCancel.aspx (excerpt)**
```
strCmd = "UPDATE Employees SET Name=@Name, " & _
   "Extension=@Extension " & _
   "WHERE EmployeeID=@EmployeeID"
objCmd = New OleDbCommand(strCmd, objConn)
objCmd.Parameters.Add("@Name", strName)
```

```
objCmd.Parameters.Add("@Extension", strExtension)
objCmd.Parameters.Add("@EmployeeID", intEmployeeID)
objConn.Open()
objCmd.ExecuteNonQuery()
objConn.Close()
```

C#   File: **EditUpdateCancel.aspx (excerpt)**

```
strCmd = "UPDATE Employees SET Name=@Name, " +
  "Extension=@Extension " +
  "WHERE EmployeeID=@EmployeeID";
objCmd = new OleDbCommand(strCmd, objConn);
objCmd.Parameters.Add("@Name", strName);
objCmd.Parameters.Add("@Extension", strExtension);
objCmd.Parameters.Add("@EmployeeID", intEmployeeID);
objConn.Open();
objCmd.ExecuteNonQuery();
objConn.Close();
```

Once the update has occurred, we'll cancel out of the update view, return back
to the original **DataGrid** state, and rebind the new data from the database table
with the following code:

VB.NET   File: **EditUpdateCancel.aspx (excerpt)**

```
dgAddressBook.EditItemIndex = -1
  BindData()
End Sub
```

C#   File: **EditUpdateCancel.aspx (excerpt)**

```
dgAddressBook.EditItemIndex = -1;
  BindData();
}
```

Save your work and test the results in the browser. You can click the "Edit" hyperlink to display information for a specific employee, similar to Figure 9.10.

Figure 9.10. Click the Edit hyperlink to edit information for a specific employee.

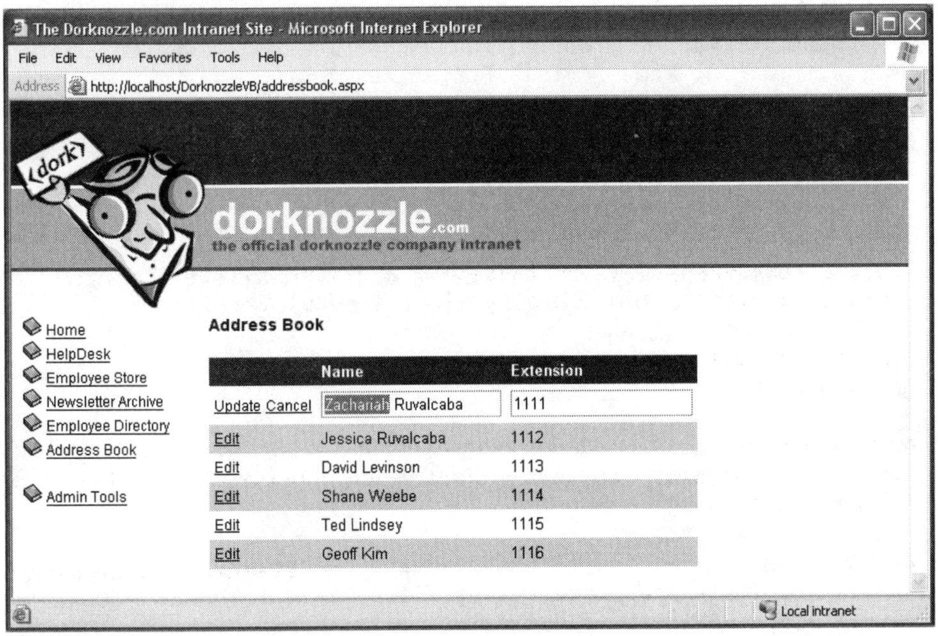

This time, when you make changes and click the "Update" hyperlink, the `DataGrid` rebinds and presents to you the updated database information.

The complete code for this example is of course included in the code archive for this book.

Using Templates

As nice as the `EditCommandColumn` is, there are still drawbacks to its use. For instance, when you click the "Edit" hyperlink, all cells within that row of the `DataGrid` become editable. What if you didn't want a user to be able to modify the phone number extension? And what about validation? A user could leave the name field blank and update the database without any problems. Fortunately, you can use templates to add validation controls, and identify particular cells as editable, using `TextBox` controls. The following code is a simple modification of the original:

VB.NET   File: **DataGridTemplates.aspx (excerpt)**

```
<asp:DataGrid id="dgAddressBook" runat="server"
    AutoGenerateColumns="false" CellPadding="4" GridLines="None"
    OnEditCommand="dg_Edit" OnCancelCommand="dg_Cancel"
    OnUpdateCommand="dg_Update" DataKeyField="EmployeeID">
  <ItemStyle Font-Name="Arial" Font-Size="10pt"
      ForeColor="#000000" />
  <HeaderStyle Font-Name="Arial" Font-Size="10pt" Font-Bold="true"
      BackColor="#003366" ForeColor="#FFFFFF" />
  <AlternatingItemStyle Font-Name="Arial" Font-Size="10pt"
      BackColor="#CCCCCC" />
  <Columns>
    <asp:EditCommandColumn EditText="Edit" CancelText="Cancel"
        UpdateText="Update" />
    <asp:TemplateColumn>
      <HeaderTemplate>
        Name
      </HeaderTemplate>
      <ItemTemplate>
        <%# Container.DataItem("Name") %>
      </ItemTemplate>
      <EditItemTemplate>
        <asp:TextBox id="txtName" runat="server"
            Text='<%# Container.DataItem("Name") %>' />
        <asp:RequiredFieldValidator id="rfvName" Display="Dynamic"
            ErrorMessage="Name is required!"
            ControlToValidate="txtName" runat="server" />
      </EditItemTemplate>
    </asp:TemplateColumn>
    <asp:BoundColumn DataField="Extension" HeaderText="Extension"
        ReadOnly="true" />
  </Columns>
</asp:DataGrid>
```

If you're using C#, you'll need to replace the two occurrences of `Container.DataItem("Name")` in this code with `DataBinder.Eval(Container.DataItem, "Name")`.

Notice that, instead of using a `BoundColumn` for the employee names, we've used a `TemplateColumn`, with an `<ItemTemplate>` tag containing a code render block. To display the `TextBox` control to edit the name, we use an `<EditItemTemplate>` tag containing a `TextBox` control with ID `txtName`. We can also add a `RequiredFieldValidator` to validate the `TextBox` control. Lastly, because the name is the only column we want to be editable, we set the extension column's `ReadOnly` property to `true`, to prevent users from editing that field.

As we're hard-coding the name of the TextBox control as txtName, we don't need to reference it by the Cell and Control arrays. In order to locate the control within the DataGrid, we now use the FindControl() method of the e.Item object instead. You'll need to modify the dg_Update() event handler accordingly:

VB.NET   File: **DataGridTemplates.aspx (excerpt)**

```vbnet
Sub dg_Update(s As Object, e As DataGridCommandEventArgs)
  Dim intEmployeeID As Integer
  Dim strName As String

  intEmployeeID = dgAddressBook.DataKeys(e.Item.ItemIndex)
  strName = CType(e.Item.FindControl("txtName"), TextBox).Text

  strCmd = "UPDATE Employees SET Name=@Name " & _
      "WHERE EmployeeID=@EmployeeID"
  objCmd = New OleDbCommand(strCmd, objConn)
  objCmd.Parameters.Add("@Name", strName)
  objCmd.Parameters.Add("@EmployeeID", intEmployeeID)
  objConn.Open()
  objCmd.ExecuteNonQuery()
  objConn.Close()

  dgAddressBook.EditItemIndex = -1
  BindData()
End Sub
```

C#   File: **DataGridTemplates.aspx (excerpt)**

```csharp
void dg_Update(Object s, DataGridCommandEventArgs e) {
  int intEmployeeID;
  String strName;

  intEmployeeID = (int)dgAddressBook.DataKeys[e.Item.ItemIndex];
  strName = ((TextBox)e.Item.FindControl("txtName")).Text;

  strCmd = "UPDATE Employees SET Name=@Name " +
      "WHERE EmployeeID=@EmployeeID";
  objCmd = new OleDbCommand(strCmd, objConn);
  objCmd.Parameters.Add("@Name", strName);
  objCmd.Parameters.Add("@EmployeeID", intEmployeeID);
  objConn.Open();
  objCmd.ExecuteNonQuery();
  objConn.Close();

  dgAddressBook.EditItemIndex = -1;
```

```
  BindData();
}
```

You're probably wondering where the code for the extension field went? Remember, we're not updating extensions any more, so that code had to be removed. Save your work and test the results within the browser window. You can click the "Edit" hyperlink, but, this time, only the "Name" cell is returned with a populated TextBox control.

If I leave the TextBox control blank and click "Update", an error message will appear.

Adding ButtonColumns to Delete Rows within a DataGrid

Just as you were able to edit and update information within the database directly from the DataGrid, you can also delete records from the database directly from your DataGrid by using the ButtonColumn. The ButtonColumn is similar to the HyperLinkColumn, but allows you to specify a CommandName and ButtonType to use. For instance, the following code can be added within our DataGrid's <Columns> tag to produce a "Delete" hyperlink similar to the one shown in Figure 9.11.

File: **DataGridDelete.aspx (excerpt)**

```
<asp:ButtonColumn ButtonType="LinkButton" Text="Delete"
    CommandName="Delete" />
```

Figure 9.11. The `ButtonColumn` allows you to create either a clickable `Button` control or `LinkButton` control within the `DataGrid`.

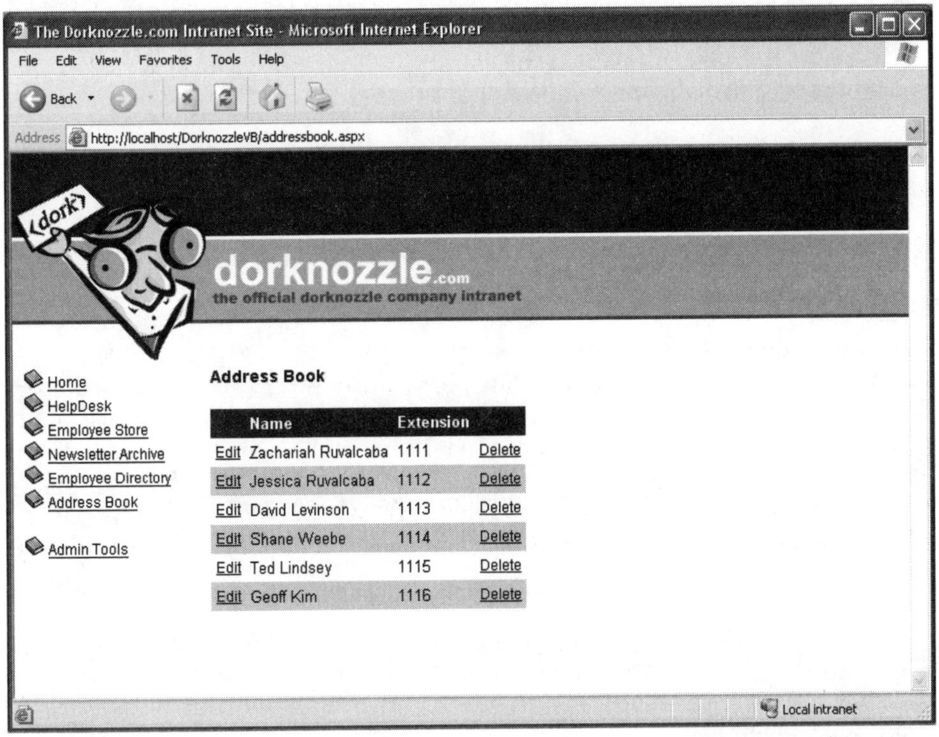

The two important properties here are `ButtonType` and `CommandName`. `ButtonType` specifies the type of button control to use. Possible values are `LinkButton` and `PushButton`. The `CommandName`, as you've seen, raises the event specified. As we've added a `Delete` command, we'll need to handle that by adding the `OnDeleteCommand` attribute within the parent `DataGrid` tag:

File: **DataGridDelete.aspx (excerpt)**

```
<asp:DataGrid id="dgAddressBook" runat="server"
    AutoGenerateColumns="false" CellPadding="4" GridLines="None"
    OnEditCommand="dg_Edit" OnCancelCommand="dg_Cancel"
    OnUpdateCommand="dg_Update" OnDeleteCommand="dg_Delete"
    DataKeyField="EmployeeID">
```

Lastly, we'll add to the code the event handler that performs the actual delete within the database table, as follows:

VB.NET   File: **DataGridDelete.aspx** (excerpt)

```
Sub dg_Delete(s As Object, e As DataGridCommandEventArgs)
  Dim intEmployeeID As Integer

  intEmployeeID = dgAddressBook.DataKeys(e.Item.ItemIndex)

  strCmd = "DELETE FROM Employees WHERE EmployeeID=@EmployeeID"
  objCmd = New OleDbCommand(strCmd, objConn)
  objCmd.Parameters.Add("@EmployeeID", intEmployeeID)
  objConn.Open()
  objCmd.ExecuteNonQuery()
  objConn.Close()

  dgAddressBook.EditItemIndex = -1
  BindData()
End Sub
```

C#   File: **DataGridDelete.aspx** (excerpt)

```
void dg_Delete(Object s, DataGridCommandEventArgs e) {
  int intEmployeeID;

  intEmployeeID = (int)dgAddressBook.DataKeys[e.Item.ItemIndex];

  strCmd = "DELETE FROM Employees WHERE EmployeeID=@EmployeeID";
  objCmd = new OleDbCommand(strCmd, objConn);
  objCmd.Parameters.Add("@EmployeeID", intEmployeeID);
  objConn.Open();
  objCmd.ExecuteNonQuery();
  objConn.Close();

  dgAddressBook.EditItemIndex = -1;
  BindData();
}
```

Similar to the update event handler, the delete event handler obtains the unique identifier (EmployeeID) from the DataGrid's selected row, and appends it to the end of the SQL statement's WHERE clause. Next, the code issues the command by passing in the SQL statement and connection objects, opens the connection, executes the command, and closes the connection. Finally, the DataGrid is reset back to normal (in case the "Delete" link was clicked in and is rebound. Figure 9.11 showed how the DataGrid looked before the delete hyperlink was selected for employee "Zak Ruvalcaba." Figure 9.12 shows how the DataGrid looks after the delete hyperlink is selected for employee "Zak Ruvalcaba."

Figure 9.12. The selected employee is deleted from the database.

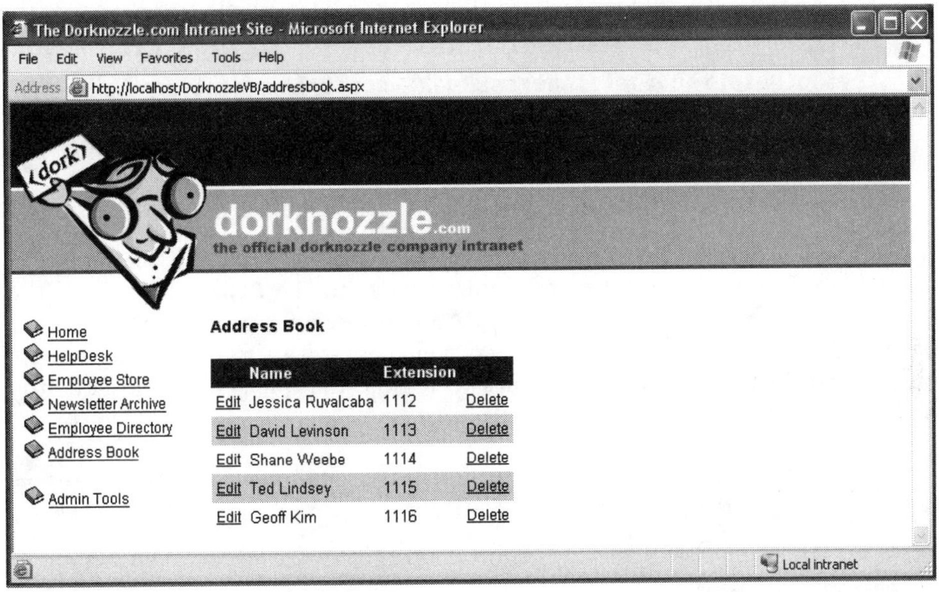

Zak's been fired!

Using the DataList Control

Similar to the DataGrid control, the DataList allows you to bind and customize the presentation of database data. There are significant differences with the DataList control, however. For instance, the DataList control is cell-based, whereas the DataGrid control is row-based. When you trigger the EditCommand event on a DataGrid, by default, the entire row shows with populated TextBox controls. A DataList control, however, requires the use of templates to control the presentation and editing features within it. DataGrids allow for quick binding and presentation. You simply add a DataGrid to the page, bind a DataReader to it, and when you run it in a browser, your data appears. A DataList, on the other hand, must use code render blocks within templates in order for the data to work within the browser window.

Because a DataList is cell-based, rather than row-based, you control presentation and editing features for individual cells, rather than an array of cells. Let's take a look at an example of how the DataList is presented within the page once a DataReader is bound to it. Let's begin with a blank Dorknozzle template. First, I'll create a new DataList within the page:

VB.NET File: **SimpleDataList.aspx (excerpt)**

```
<asp:DataList id="dlAddressBook" runat="server">
  <ItemTemplate>
    <%# Container.DataItem("Name") %><br />
  </ItemTemplate>
</asp:DataList>
```

In C#, you'll have to use DataBinder.Eval(Container.DataItem, "Name") again here. Initially, the DataList seems similar to the Repeater, and to the DataGrid when we used ItemTemplates. And, for the most part, it *is* very similar. Next, I'll add a script block in the <head> element with the same code that we created within the DataGrid examples to handle the query, and subsequently bind to the DataList:

VB.NET File: **SimpleDataList.aspx (excerpt)**

```
Dim objConn As New OleDbConnection( _
  "Provider=Microsoft.Jet.OleDb.4.0;" & _
  "Data Source=C:\Inetpub\wwwroot\Dorknozzle\Database\" & _
  "Dorknozzle.mdb")
Dim objCmd As OleDbCommand
Dim objRdr As OleDbDataReader
Dim strCmd As String

Sub Page_Load()
  If Not IsPostBack Then
    BindData()
  End If
End Sub

Sub BindData()
  objConn.Open()
  objCmd = New OleDbCommand("SELECT * FROM Employees", objConn)
  objRdr = objCmd.ExecuteReader()
  dlAddressBook.DataSource = objRdr
  dlAddressBook.DataBind()
  objRdr.Close()
  objConn.Close()
End Sub
```

C#   File: **SimpleDataList.aspx (excerpt)**

```csharp
OleDbConnection objConn = new OleDbConnection(
  "Provider=Microsoft.Jet.OleDb.4.0;" +
  "Data Source=C:\\Inetpub\\wwwroot\\Dorknozzle\\Database\\" +
  "Dorknozzle.mdb");
OleDbCommand objCmd;
OleDbDataReader objRdr;
String strCmd;

void Page_Load() {
  if (!IsPostBack) {
    BindData();
  }
}

void BindData() {
  objConn.Open();
  objCmd = new OleDbCommand("SELECT * FROM Employees", objConn);
  objRdr = objCmd.ExecuteReader();
  dlAddressBook.DataSource = objRdr;
  dlAddressBook.DataBind();
  objRdr.Close();
  objConn.Close();
}
```

As before, we've created a method called BindData() to handle the actual query. Because we'll eventually call this method from many other methods, it's helpful to pull that logic out of the Page_Load() method and into its own. Also, because we'll use the Connection, Command, and DataReader objects within multiple locations, we place those at the top of the page, creating global variables that can be reused in all our methods.

Save your work and test it in a browser. The employees' information should appear one after the next, similar to Figure 9.13.

Figure 9.13. The employees' information is listed within the page.

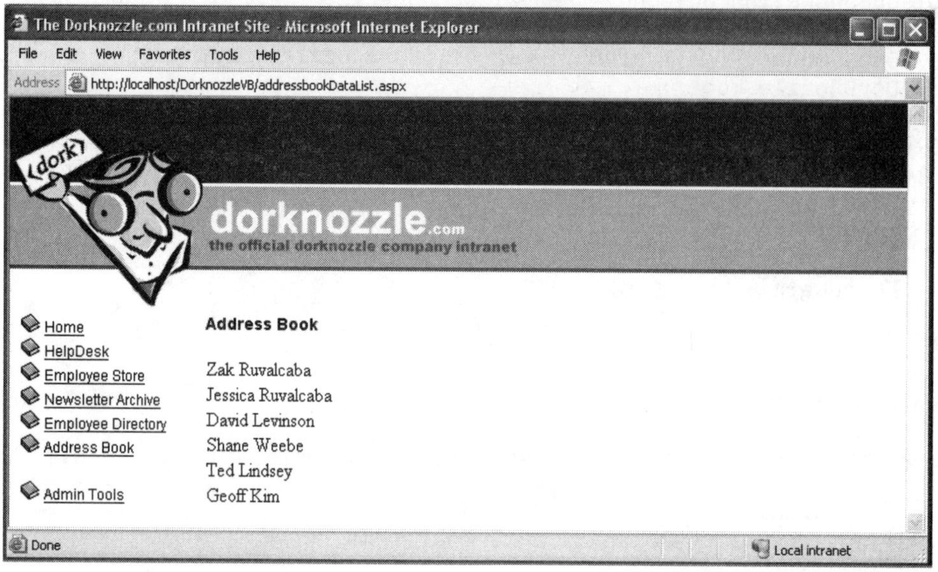

To prove the point that the DataList is cell-based, let's go ahead and add a separator, using a `<SeparatorTemplate>` tag as follows:

VB.NET   File: **SimpleDataList.aspx (excerpt)**

```
<asp:DataList id="dlAddressBook" runat="server">
  <ItemTemplate>
    <%# Container.DataItem("Name") %><br />
  </ItemTemplate>
  <SeparatorTemplate><hr noshade="noshade" size="1" />
  </SeparatorTemplate>
</asp:DataList>
```

DataList's `<SeparatorTemplate>` tag works similarly to that of the Repeater control. Figure 9.14 shows how a horizontal line is placed just after each name.

Figure 9.14. A horizontal line is added after each employee.

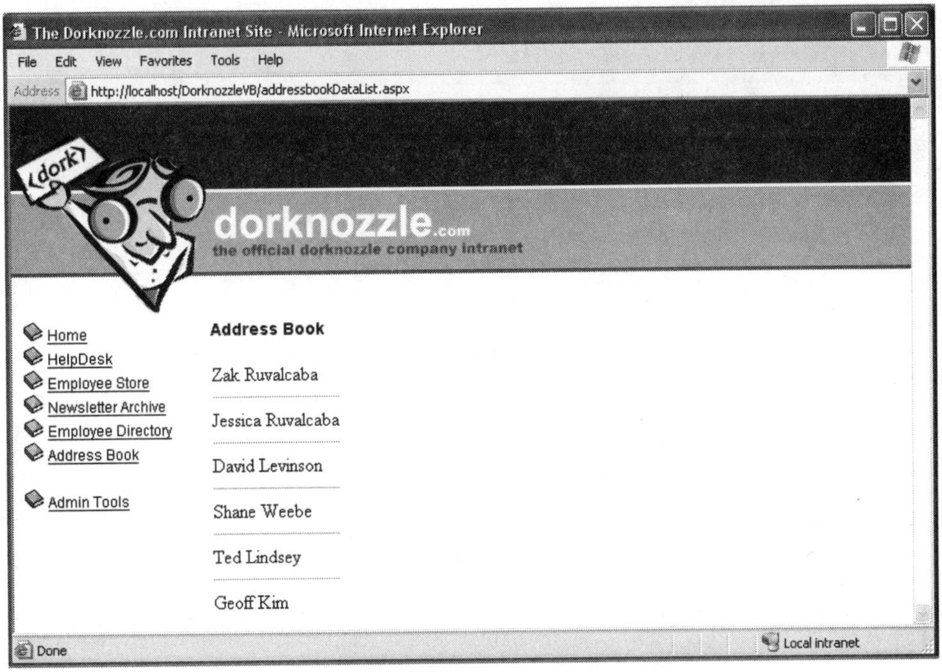

You can add more database fields to the `<ItemTemplate>` tag simply by adding a new code render block. The following code adds each employee's phone extension below his or her name:

VB.NET   File: `SimpleDataList.aspx (excerpt)`

```
<asp:DataList id="dlAddressBook" runat="server">
  <ItemTemplate>
    <%# Container.DataItem("Name") %><br />
    <%# Container.DataItem("Extension") %>
  </ItemTemplate>
  <SeparatorTemplate><hr noshade="noshade" size="1" />
  </SeparatorTemplate>
</asp:DataList>
```

Again, if you're using C#, you'll need to use `<%# DataBinder.Eval(Container.DataItem, "Extension") %>` rather than `<%# Container.DataItem("Extension") %>`. When we display the results in the browser window, the employee's name, followed by an extension, appears, similar to Figure 9.15.

Figure 9.15. Each employee's name and extension is displayed within the browser.

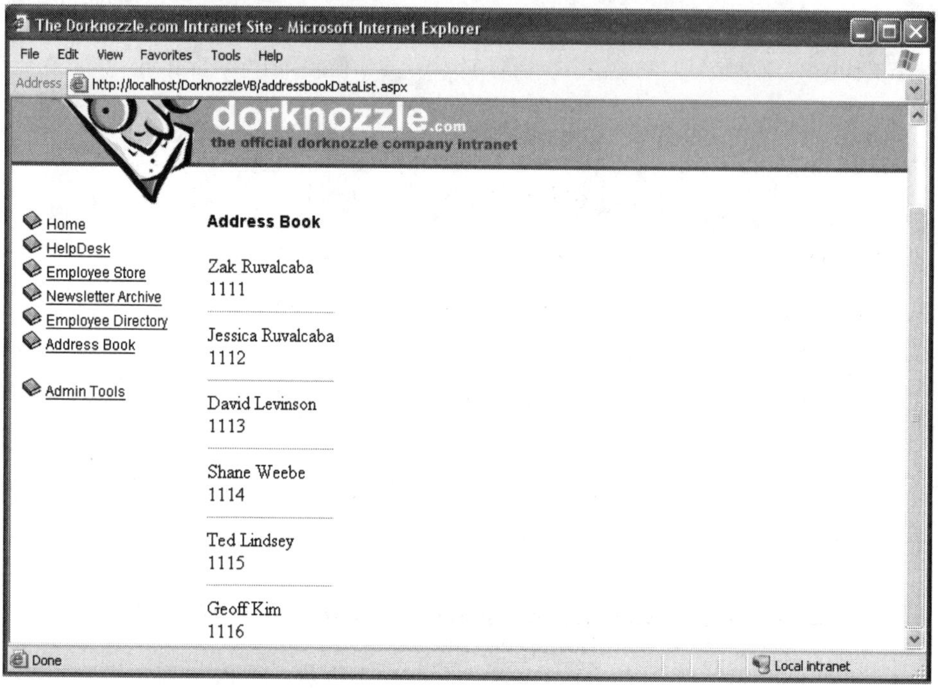

As you can see, the `DataList` is easy to use, and closely resembles both the humble `Repeater` and the `DataGrid` when templates are used. As a rule of thumb, you'll want to use the `DataGrid` when working with rows of data that are similar to the structure of a database table. You'll want to use the `DataList` when working with lists of data that need to be presented and formatted within a cell.

At this stage, you may be wondering what the difference between a `Repeater` and a `DataList` is, exactly. In the next few sections, you'll learn how to customize the `DataList` with styles, create editable cells within the `DataList`, and use styles and templates together within a `DataList` to create a fully dynamic navigation menu.

Customizing `DataLists` Using Styles

As was the case with the `DataGrid`, items within the `DataList` can be customized with the use of certain styles. `DataGrid` headers, footers, separators, items, etc., can all be customized to suit your needs. The `DataList` supports customization through the use of the following styles:

HeaderStyle

Customizes the appearance of the `DataList`'s heading.

ItemStyle

Customizes the appearance of each item displayed within the `DataList`.

AlternatingItemStyle

Customizes the appearance of every other item displayed within the `DataList`.

FooterStyle

Customizes the appearance of the `DataList`'s footer.

SelectedItemStyle

Customizes the appearance of a selected item within the `DataList`.

EditItemStyle

Customizes the appearance of the `DataList` when in edit mode.

The following code includes style modifications for `DataList` items and alternating items:

VB.NET   File: **DataListWithStyles.aspx (excerpt)**

```
<asp:DataList id="dlAddressBook" runat="server"
    DataKeyField="EmployeeID">
  <ItemStyle Font-Name="Arial" Font-Size="10pt"
      ForeColor="#000000" />
  <AlternatingItemStyle BackColor="#CCCCCC" />
  <ItemTemplate>
    <%# Container.DataItem("Name") %><br/>
    <%# Container.DataItem("Extension") %>
  </ItemTemplate>
  <SeparatorTemplate><hr noshade="noshade" size="1" />
  </SeparatorTemplate>
</asp:DataList>
```

This time, when you run your page within the browser, all items appear as Arial, ten point, and black, as opposed to the default font (Times New Roman, size three, black). Your results will appear similar to Figure 9.16.

Figure 9.16. Modify styles within your DataList to customize the font face, size, and color properties

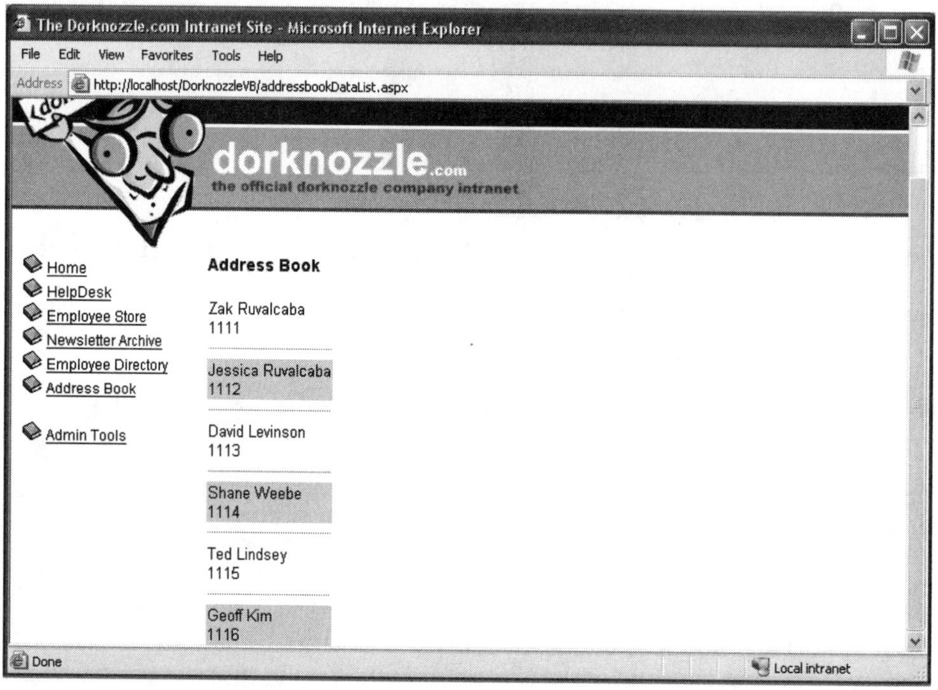

Editing Items within a DataList

You can create editable cells within the DataList similarly to the way you created editable rows within the DataGrid. However, the DataList works differently than the DataGrid. For instance, the DataGrid contained a special column—the EditButtonColumn; the DataList has no such feature. Instead, we have to create LinkButton controls within the <ItemTemplate> tag, complete with CommandName properties. When the LinkButton is selected, the event "bubbles up" and raises the specified event within the DataList. The following example, for instance, shows a LinkButton control that has a link reading "Edit" within the <ItemTemplate> tag, and the EditCommand event calling the dl_Edit() method:

VB.NET   File: **EditDataList.aspx (excerpt)**

```
    <asp:DataList id="dlAddressBook" runat="server"
        OnEditCommand="dl_Edit">
      <ItemStyle Font-Name="Arial" Font-Size="10pt"
```

```
        ForeColor="#000000" />
    <AlternatingItemStyle BackColor="#CCCCCC" />
    <ItemTemplate>
      <%# Container.DataItem("Name") %><br />
      <%# Container.DataItem("Extension") %><br />
      <asp:LinkButton id="lbEdit" runat="server" Text="Edit"
        CommandName="Edit" />
    </ItemTemplate>
    <SeparatorTemplate><hr noshade="noshade" size="1" />
    </SeparatorTemplate>
  </asp:DataList>
```

Next, we'll add the necessary method to handle the `EditCommand` event:

VB.NET   File: **EditDataList.aspx (excerpt)**

```
Sub dl_Edit(s As Object, e As DataListCommandEventArgs)
  dlAddressBook.EditItemIndex = e.Item.ItemIndex
  BindData()
End Sub
```

C#   File: **EditDataList.aspx (excerpt)**

```
void dl_Edit(Object s, DataListCommandEventArgs e) {
  dlAddressBook.EditItemIndex = e.Item.ItemIndex;
  BindData();
}
```

Again, the code for editing the `DataList` differs very little from that we'd use with the `DataGrid`. Next, we'll add the `<EditItemTemplate>` tag to the `DataList`. Remember, this allows us to define the editable parts of the cell with `TextBox` controls:

VB.NET   File: **EditDataList.aspx (excerpt)**

```
<asp:DataList id="dlAddressBook" runat="server"
    OnEditCommand="dl_Edit" OnCancelCommand="dl_Cancel">
  <ItemStyle Font-Name="Arial" Font-Size="10pt"
      ForeColor="#000000" />
  <AlternatingItemStyle BackColor="#CCCCCC" />
  <ItemTemplate>
    <%# Container.DataItem("Name") %><br />
    <%# Container.DataItem("Extension") %><br />
    <asp:LinkButton id="lbEdit" runat="server" Text="Edit"
        CommandName="Edit" />
  </ItemTemplate>
  <EditItemTemplate>
    <asp:TextBox id="txtName" runat="server"
```

```
        Text='<%# Container.DataItem("Name") %>' /><br />
    <asp:TextBox id="txtExtension" runat="server"
        Text='<%# Container.DataItem("Extension") %>' /><br />
    <asp:LinkButton id="lbCancel" runat="server" Text="Cancel"
        CommandName="Cancel" />
</EditItemTemplate>
<SeparatorTemplate><hr noshade="noshade" size="1" />
</SeparatorTemplate>
</asp:DataList>
```

As you've probably noticed, another `LinkButton` has also been added to provide "Cancel" button functionality. Next, you can add the method for the `CancelCommand` event, as follows:

VB.NET   File: **EditDataList.aspx (excerpt)**

```
Sub dl_Cancel(s As Object, e As DataListCommandEventArgs)
  dlAddressBook.EditItemIndex = -1
  BindData()
End Sub
```

C#   File: **EditDataList.aspx (excerpt)**

```
void dl_Cancel(Object s, DataListCommandEventArgs e) {
  dlAddressBook.EditItemIndex = -1;
  BindData();
}
```

Again, the cancel functionality differs very little from that of the `DataGrid`'s. An "Edit" `LinkButton` control appears for every cell within the `DataGrid`. When we click the "Edit" `LinkButton` control for a cell, a pair of populated `TextBox` controls appears, and the "Edit" `LinkButton` control changes to a "Cancel" `LinkButton` control, similar to Figure 9.17.

Figure 9.17. Populated TextBox controls and the "Cancel" LinkButton control appear once I select the "Edit" LinkButton control.

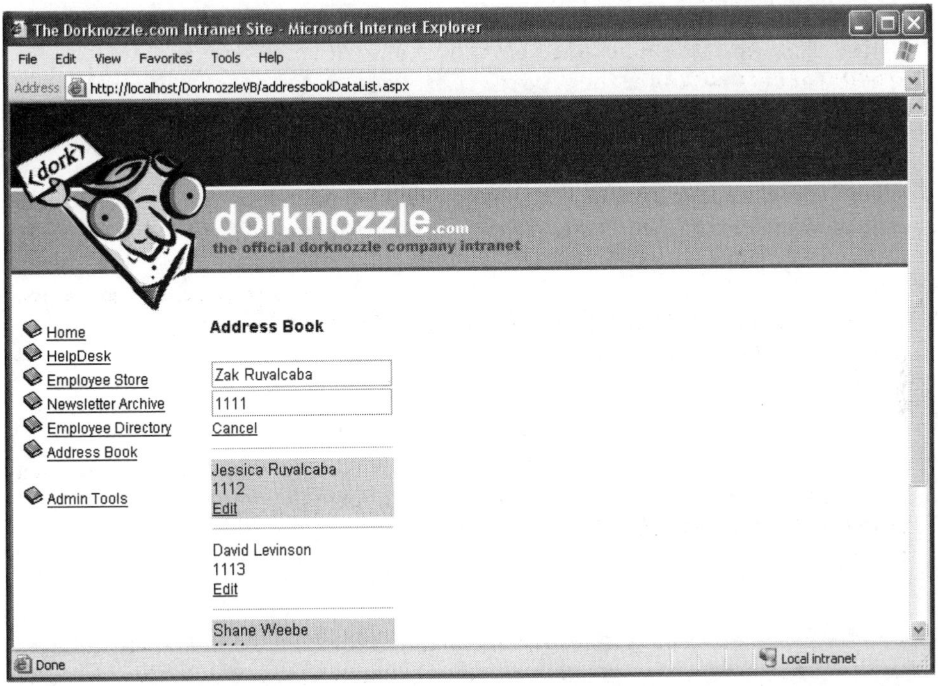

Now, we can add the update functionality. First, we'll add a new LinkButton control next to the "Cancel" LinkButton control. We'll also want to handle the UpdateCommand event by adding the OnUpdateCommand attribute that calls the appropriate method (dl_Update()). Finally, we'll need to specify the unique identifier to be used within the SQL statement—we can add the DataKeyField property to the DataList to handle this. The completed code will resemble the following:

VB.NET   File: **EditDataList.aspx (excerpt)**

```
<asp:DataList id="dlAddressBook" runat="server"
    OnEditCommand="dl_Edit" OnCancelCommand="dl_Cancel"
    OnUpdateCommand="dl_Update" DataKeyField="EmployeeID">
  <ItemStyle Font-Name="Arial" Font-Size="10pt"
      ForeColor="#000000" />
  <AlternatingItemStyle BackColor="#CCCCCC" />
  <ItemTemplate>
```

```
     <%# Container.DataItem("Name") %><br />
     <%# Container.DataItem("Extension") %><br />
     <asp:LinkButton id="lbEdit" runat="server" Text="Edit"
         CommandName="Edit" />
  </ItemTemplate>
  <EditItemTemplate>
     <asp:TextBox id="txtName" runat="server"
         Text='<%# Container.DataItem("Name") %>' /><br />
     <asp:TextBox id="txtExtension" runat="server"
         Text='<%# Container.DataItem("Extension") %>' /><br />
     <asp:LinkButton id="lbCancel" runat="server" Text="Cancel"
         CommandName="Cancel" /> |
     <asp:LinkButton id="lbUpdate" runat="server" Text="Update"
         CommandName="Update" />
  </EditItemTemplate>
  <SeparatorTemplate><hr noshade="noshade" size="1" />
  </SeparatorTemplate>
</asp:DataList>
```

Lastly, we add the code for the dl_Update() method, as follows:

VB.NET   File: **EditDataList.aspx (excerpt)**

```
Sub dl_Update(s As Object, e As DataListCommandEventArgs)
  Dim intEmployeeID As Integer
  Dim strName, strExtension As String

  intEmployeeID = dlAddressBook.DataKeys(e.Item.ItemIndex)
  strName = CType(e.Item.FindControl("txtName"), TextBox).Text
  strExtension = CType(e.Item.FindControl("txtExtension"),
      TextBox).Text

  strCmd = "UPDATE Employees SET Name=@Name, " & _
      "Extension=@Extension " & _
      "WHERE EmployeeID=@EmployeeID"
  objCmd = New OleDbCommand(strCmd, objConn)
  objCmd.Parameters.Add("@Name", strName)
  objCmd.Parameters.Add("@Extension", strExtension)
  objCmd.Parameters.Add("@EmployeeID", intEmployeeID)
  objConn.Open()
  objCmd.ExecuteNonQuery()
  objConn.Close()

  dlAddressBook.EditItemIndex = -1
  BindData()
End Sub
```

C#   File: **EditDataList.aspx (excerpt)**

```csharp
void dl_Update(Object s, DataListCommandEventArgs e) {
  int intEmployeeID;
  String strName, strExtension;

  intEmployeeID = (int)dlAddressBook.DataKeys[e.Item.ItemIndex];
  strName = ((TextBox)e.Item.FindControl("txtName")).Text;
  strExtension =
      ((TextBox)e.Item.FindControl("txtExtension")).Text;

  strCmd = "UPDATE Employees SET Name=@Name, " +
    "Extension=@Extension " +
    "WHERE EmployeeID=@EmployeeID";
  objCmd = new OleDbCommand(strCmd, objConn);
  objCmd.Parameters.Add("@Name", strName);
  objCmd.Parameters.Add("@Extension", strExtension);
  objCmd.Parameters.Add("@EmployeeID", intEmployeeID);
  objConn.Open();
  objCmd.ExecuteNonQuery();
  objConn.Close();

  dlAddressBook.EditItemIndex = -1;
  BindData();
}
```

Figure 9.18 shows how we can edit content within the TextBox control of an editable DataList.

Figure 9.18. Selecting the "Edit" `LinkButton` control allows us to edit text boxes within the `DataList`.

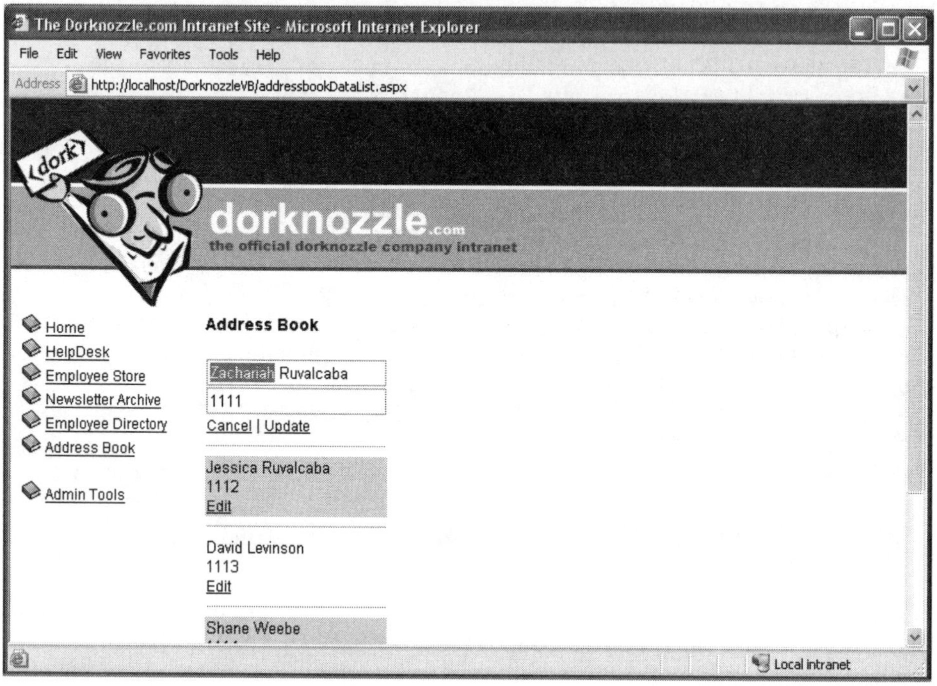

When we click the "Update" `LinkButton` control, the specific record within the database table is updated.

Items can be deletedfrom the database table using the `DataList` just as easily as they are selected and updated. To add this functionality, we insert a new `LinkButton` control into the `DataList`, and add the `OnDeleteCommand` attribute to handle the call from the `LinkButton` control's `CommandName` property:

VB.NET   File: **EditDataList.aspx (excerpt)**

```
<asp:DataList id="dlAddressBook" runat="server"
    OnEditCommand="dl_Edit" OnCancelCommand="dl_Cancel"
    OnUpdateCommand="dl_Update" OnDeleteCommand="dl_Delete"
    DataKeyField="EmployeeID">
  <ItemStyle Font-Name="Arial" Font-Size="10pt"
      ForeColor="#000000" />
  <AlternatingItemStyle BackColor="#CCCCCC" />
  <ItemTemplate>
```

```
    <%# Container.DataItem("Name") %><br />
    <%# Container.DataItem("Extension") %><br />
    <asp:LinkButton id="lbEdit" runat="server" Text="Edit"
        CommandName="Edit" /> |
    <asp:LinkButton id="lbDelete" runat="server" Text="Delete"
        CommandName="Delete" />
  </ItemTemplate>
  <EditItemTemplate>
    <asp:TextBox id="txtName" runat="server"
        Text='<%# Container.DataItem("Name") %>' /><br />
    <asp:TextBox id="txtExtension" runat="server"
        Text='<%# Container.DataItem("Extension") %>' /><br />
    <asp:LinkButton id="lbCancel" runat="server" Text="Cancel"
        CommandName="Cancel" /> |
    <asp:LinkButton id="lbUpdate" runat="server" Text="Update"
        CommandName="Update" />
  </EditItemTemplate>
  <SeparatorTemplate><hr noshade="noshade" size="1" />
  </SeparatorTemplate>
</asp:DataList>
```

Next, let's create the dl_Delete() method to process the deletion of specific data from the database table:

VB.NET   File: **EditDataList.aspx (excerpt)**

```
Sub dl_Delete(s As Object, e As DataListCommandEventArgs)
  Dim intEmployeeID As Integer

  intEmployeeID = dlAddressBook.DataKeys(e.Item.ItemIndex)

  strCmd = "DELETE FROM Employees WHERE EmployeeID=@EmployeeID"
  objCmd = New OleDbCommand(strCmd, objConn)
  objCmd.Parameters.Add("@EmployeeID", intEmployeeID)
  objConn.Open()
  objCmd.ExecuteNonQuery()
  objConn.Close()

  dlAddressBook.EditItemIndex = -1
  BindData()
End Sub
```

C#   File: **EditDataList.aspx (excerpt)**

```
void dl_Delete(Object s, DataListCommandEventArgs e) {
  int intEmployeeID;

  intEmployeeID = (int)dlAddressBook.DataKeys[e.Item.ItemIndex];
```

```
strCmd = "DELETE FROM Employees WHERE EmployeeID=@EmployeeID";
objCmd = new OleDbCommand(strCmd, objConn);
objCmd.Parameters.Add("@EmployeeID", intEmployeeID);
objConn.Open();
objCmd.ExecuteNonQuery();
objConn.Close();

dlAddressBook.EditItemIndex = -1;
BindData();
}
```

When we test the page within the browser now, the "Delete" hyperlink appears next to the "Edit" hyperlink.

Creating a Navigation Menu using `DataLists`

I've found that one of the best uses for a `DataList` is to create a dynamic, database-driven navigation menu. Have you ever built a 400–500 page Website? If you have, you know what a hassle it can be when navigational items or links need to be changed throughout the site. You can eliminate this hassle in one of two ways: you could create a separate `.aspx` file containing just the navigation menu, and insert that `.aspx` file automatically (as a server-side include) into every page within the site, or you could create your navigation menu in a database table, and bind that database table to a `DataList` within every page in the site.

Both solutions would work, but if you know or remember anything about traditional ASP, you might recall that server-side includes were used to death, and sometimes caused more trouble than good. The latter solution would serve us better in this case. Let's create a dynamic navigation menu using an Access database table and a `DataList` (if you're using MSDE, you can import the SQL script file from the archive to create the necessary table).

Open the database and immediately create a new table. Within the new table, create three new columns: `NavigationID` (AutoNumber, Primary Key), `Item` (Text), and `Link` (Text). The result will look similar to Figure 9.19.

Figure 9.19. Create three new fields within the new database table.

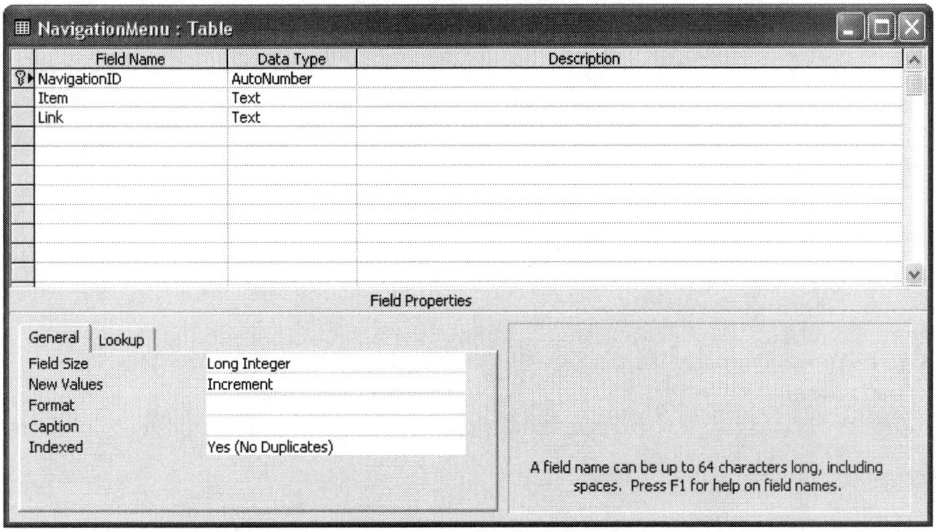

Now let's add the navigation items and corresponding links to the Navigation-Menu table, as in Figure 9.20, with the Datasheet View.

Figure 9.20. Add all the navigation menu items and their corresponding links.

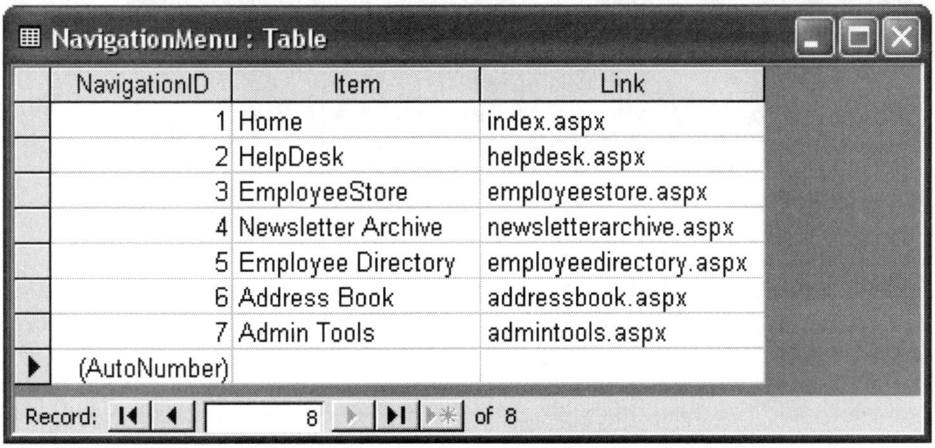

Save your new table as `NavigationMenu` and close Access.

Now, create a new `.aspx` file called `nav.aspx` within your project's directory, and add the following code:

File: nav.aspx (excerpt)

```
<%@ Import Namespace="System.Data.OleDb" %>
<html>
<head>
<title>The Dorknozzle.com Intranet Site</title>
<link href="styles.css" rel="stylesheet" />
</head>
<body>
<form runat="server">
<asp:DataList id="dlNavMenu" runat="server" CellSpacing="2"
    CellPadding="2">
</asp:DataList>
</form>
</body>
</html>
```

For now, all we're really doing is creating a standard HTML framework, along with the `DataList` that will serve as the navigation menu.

To create the clickable links within the `DataList`, add a new `HyperLink` control within an `<ItemTemplate>` tag, as follows:

VB.NET File: nav.aspx (excerpt)

```
<asp:DataList id="dlNavMenu" runat="server" CellSpacing="2"
    CellPadding="2">
  <ItemTemplate>
    <asp:HyperLink id="hlMenuItem"
        NavigateUrl='<%# Container.DataItem("Link") %>'
        Text='<%# Container.DataItem("Item") %>' runat="server" />
  </ItemTemplate>
</asp:DataList>
```

C# users must remember to use the `DataBinder.Eval(…)` syntax here. You'll notice that the `HyperLink` control contains two important properties: `NavigateUrl` will accept the "Link" database table field name; `Text` will accept the "Item" database table field name.

Now, let's add the code that will query the database, return a `DataReader`, and bind that `DataReader` to our `DataList`:

```vb
<script runat="server" language="VB">
Dim objConn As New OleDbConnection( _
  "Provider=Microsoft.Jet.OleDb.4.0;" & _
  "Data Source=C:\Inetpub\wwwroot\Dorknozzle\Database\" & _
  "Dorknozzle.mdb")
Dim objCmd As OleDbCommand
Dim objRdr As OleDbDataReader

Sub Page_Load()
  If Not IsPostBack Then
    BindData()
  End If
End Sub

Sub BindData()
  objConn.Open()
  objCmd = New OleDbCommand("SELECT * FROM NavigationMenu",
      objConn)
  objRdr = objCmd.ExecuteReader()
  dlNavMenu.DataSource = objRdr
  dlNavMenu.DataBind()
  objRdr.Close()
  objConn.Close()
End Sub
</script>
```

```csharp
<script runat="server" language="C#">
OleDbConnection objConn = new OleDbConnection(
  "Provider=Microsoft.Jet.OleDb.4.0;" +
  "Data Source=C:\\Inetpub\\wwwroot\\Dorknozzle\\Database\\" +
  "Dorknozzle.mdb");
OleDbCommand objCmd;
OleDbDataReader objRdr;

void Page_Load() {
  if (!IsPostBack) {
    BindData();
  }
}

void BindData() {
  objConn.Open();
  objCmd = new OleDbCommand("SELECT * FROM NavigationMenu",
      objConn);
```

```
  objRdr = objCmd.ExecuteReader();
  dlNavMenu.DataSource = objRdr;
  dlNavMenu.DataBind();
  objRdr.Close();
  objConn.Close();
}
</script>
```

Save your work and test the results within the browser. When the page loads, the list of items within the database table is presented vertically down the page as a list of hyperlinks similar to Figure 9.21.

Figure 9.21. The items within the database table are presented as links within the browser.

Try clicking a link. Assuming that the file is saved in the same directory as all your other files, you should be sent to the page whose link you clicked.

Now, let's make this navigation menu look like a real navigation menu, rather that a simple list of links. We can start by adding the book image just before the HyperLink control, as follows:

VB.NET   File: **nav.aspx (excerpt)**

```
<asp:DataList id="dlNavMenu" runat="server" CellSpacing="2"
   CellPadding="2">
 <ItemTemplate>
   <img src="Images/Book_Closed.gif" />
   <asp:HyperLink id="hlMenuItem"
       NavigateUrl='<%# Container.DataItem("Link") %>'
       Text='<%# Container.DataItem("Item") %>' runat="server" />
 </ItemTemplate>
</asp:DataList>
```

When the page loads in the browser this time, the small book appears just before each link, similar to Figure 9.22.

Figure 9.22. Add the book image to the DataList to make the image appear just before every link.

To finish off the DataList navigation menu, we'll give the items some style as follows:

```
<asp:DataList id="dlNavMenu" runat="server" CellSpacing="2"
   CellPadding="2">
 <ItemStyle BackColor="#CCCCCC" BorderStyle="Solid"
```

```
      BorderWidth="1pt" BorderColor="#000000" />
  <ItemTemplate>
    <img src="Images/Book_Closed.gif" />
    <asp:HyperLink id="hlMenuItem"
        NavigateUrl='<%# Container.DataItem("Link") %>'
        Text='<%# Container.DataItem("Item") %>' runat="server" />
  </ItemTemplate>
</asp:DataList>
```

As you can see in Figure 9.23, this makes the links appear as if they were buttons.

Figure 9.23. Add an item style to your `DataList` to make all links appear as if they were buttons.

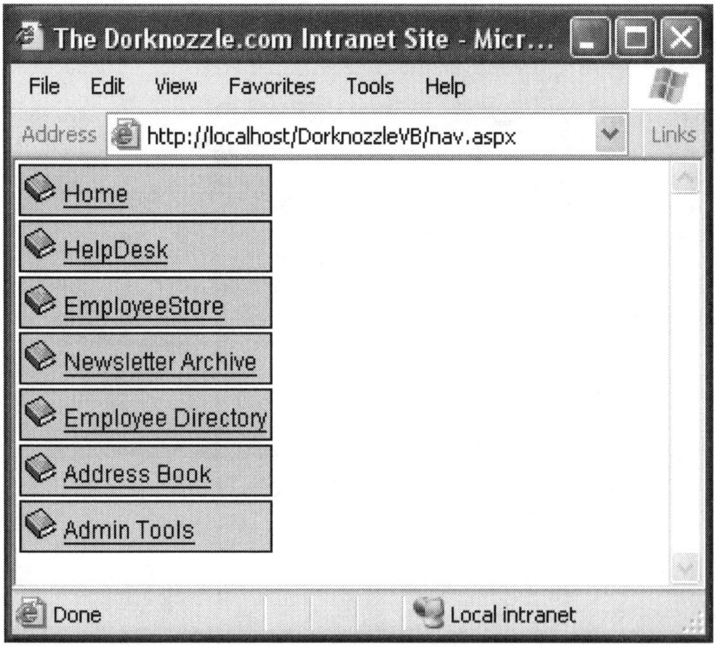

Now it truly looks like a navigation menu! Hang on to this file, because we'll be using it again in Chapter 16, where you'll see how user controls can streamline the way dynamic files are created and inserted into multiple pages throughout the site.

Summary

As you've seen, `DataGrids` and `DataLists` provide enormous flexibility and power in terms of presenting database data dynamically within the browser. First, you learned how to create both of these data controls and bind your data to them. Second, you learned about customizing the appearance of elements using templates and styles. Next, you saw how various commands allow you to create edit, update, and delete functionality within your `DataGrids` and `DataLists`. Lastly, you looked at creating a fully dynamic navigation menu using a `DataList`, a database table, and a few lines of code.

The next chapter will begin to introduce you to advanced programming topics in `DataSets`. As you will learn, `DataSets` open up a whole new world in terms of presenting and working with Microsoft's vision of "disconnected" data.

10

DataSets

In the last two chapters, you learned some important concepts of data access and presentation. In Chapter 8, you learned how to use the `Connection` class to establish a connection to the database, you learned how to use the `Command` class to execute a query on a database table, and you learned how to return the results of the command into a `DataReader` for use within the application. In Chapter 9, you learned about data presentation within `DataGrids` and `DataLists`. You learned that once a `DataReader` is returned from the database, that `DataReader` can be easily bound to `DataGrids` and `DataLists` for the quick, easy, customizable presentation of your data within an application. Although `DataGrids` and `DataLists` can have their appearance customized using templates and styles, they are limited in terms of the ways in which they can present data from a `DataReader`.

In this chapter, you'll learn about an alternative to using a `DataReader`: `DataSets`. `DataSets` are virtual databases—purely memory-resident representations of the actual data stored within the database. As you will see, comparable to the `Recordset` in traditional ASP, `DataReaders` don't allow you to work with data in any really useful way. Once you populate a `DataReader` with the contents from the database table, you can't navigate from the end of the `DataReader` to the beginning. You must bind the `DataReader` to a control in order to display its contents to the user. What's worse is that you can't sort, filter, or even page through a populated `DataReader` without a lot of trickery and code wizardry in the background. DataSets represent the new Microsoft model for "disconnected" data, allowing you to page, sort, and even filter through data simply and easily.

Understanding DataSets

By now, you should have a basic understanding of ADO.NET. You've learned about the Connection, Command and DataReader classes. But ADO.NET isn't that simple. If ADO.NET contained only the three classes we've discussed so far, its difference from traditional ADO would be minimal. In fact, ADO.NET represents a radical change in development. For instance, with ADO.NET, Microsoft added the new DataSet class, along with a whole host of complementary classes that are used when working with DataSets, all of which we will discuss in the next section. For now, be aware that DataSets are Microsoft's new model for presenting "disconnected" data. Disconnected data (that which resides in memory and is completely independent of the data source) represents a whole new way of developing not only desktop and Web applications, but mobile applications as well. Just saying that magic word—"mobile"—should begin to open some eyes. Microsoft understands that current development trends are going mobile. People want to take their PDAs, cell phones, laptops, and Tablet PCs wherever they go, so applications on the desktop or the Web must accommodate this need. How will DataSets help? Let's take a look.

In Chapter 8, we used the analogy of a bridge to describe the role DataReaders play in relation to your applications and your database data. When you need to access data from a database, you create a connection and command. The command is returned into a new DataReader object, then you use that DataReader within your application by binding it to a data control for presentational purposes. Figure 10.1 shows an illustration of the process.

Figure 10.1. The `DataReader` acts as a bridge between your application and your data.

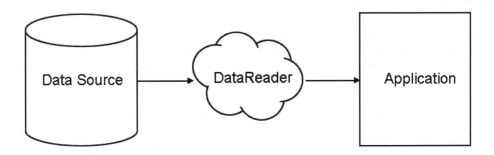

So, what's the problem? Well, `DataReader`s can't be used to work with the data as a whole—you can't sort, filter, or page through the data. As the arrows in the illustration show, `DataReader`s present a forward-only stream of data to the application. You can't go back to a previous record, or reuse that `DataReader` somewhere else within code without closing the `DataReader`, repopulating it, and rebinding to a different control. Moreover, once a `DataReader` has been created, it remains tied to the database. What this means is that you can't make multiple requests to a database or even navigate to a new page without having to recreate the `DataReader` from scratch.

`DataSet`s, on the other hand, are much more flexible. Imagine a virtual database within code and you have a `DataSet`. As we'll see in the next section, `DataSet`s have all the bells and whistles that databases offer, including tables, columns, rows, relationships, and even queries (views)! `DataSet`s are memory-resident representations of database data, so, once a `DataSet` has been created, it can be stored in memory and its ties to the database can be broken. When you need to work with the data, you don't need to re-query the database—you simply present the data from the `DataSet` again and again. Figure 10.2 illustrates this point.

Figure 10.2. Once a `DataSet` has been created, its ties to the data source can be broken.

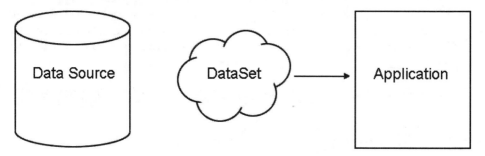

An even greater advantage is that `DataSets` can be shared along multiple requests, illustrated in Figure 10.3.

Figure 10.3. Multiple pages can make multiple requests from the same `DataSet`.

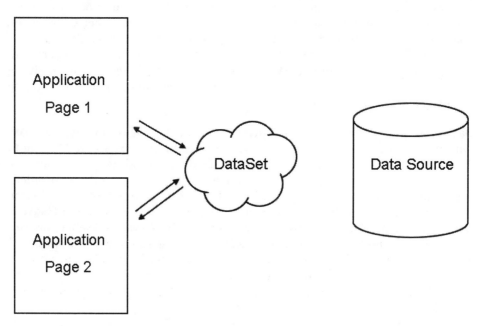

What this means is that you simply need to create the `DataSet` once. Once the `DataSet` has been created, it can be used by many different pages, all making multiple and even different requests to the `DataSet`. However, `DataSets` require much more memory and resources than does the `DataReader`. For the most part, if you simply need to extract records from the database and present them to your users within a single page, as in the previous chapter's examples, `DataReaders` would be the way to go. If, however, you plan to work with the same query over multiple requests and different documents, then `DataSets` would be the best solution.

This chapter will teach you everything you need to know to begin working with `DataSets`.

DataSet Elements

As I mentioned briefly above, `DataSets` are comprised of many parts, all of which are required for its usage. The following classes will be introduced and discussed throughout this chapter:

☐ `DataSet`

☐ `DataAdapter`

☐ `DataTable`

☐ `DataColumn`

☐ `DataRow`

☐ `DataRelation`

☐ `DataView`

Most of these elements are required for us to work with `DataSets`. For instance, the `DataAdapter` class acts as the communication point between the `DataSet` and the database. A `DataSet` will always contain at least one `DataTable`, but can contain many. `DataTables` within a `DataSet` contain `DataColumns` and `DataRows`. If you need to establish a relationship between multiple `DataTables` within a `DataSet`, you would use `DataRelations`. Finally, you would create `DataViews` for working with various queries within a `DataSet`, including filtering and sorting data.

As you may guess, a `DataSet` mirrors the structure of a modern relational database, as illustrated in Figure 10.4.

Figure 10.4. The structure of a DataSet closely resembles that of a database.

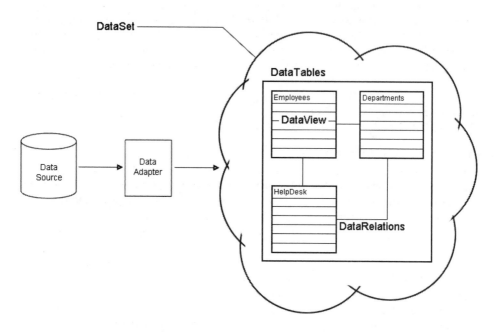

As you can see, the structure of the DataSet closely resembles that of a database. A database contains tables; here, the DataSet contains DataTables. Tables in a database have columns and rows; our DataTables have DataColumns and DataRows. When working in a database, we establish relationships between tables; here, we would create DataRelations. In either Access or MSDE, you could create and save queries and views, which would return data based on filtering criteria from the database. In the DataSet, we would set up DataViews. The only major difference between a DataSet and a database is that DataSets are virtual databases and are purely memory-resident duplicates of the actual data stored within the database.

Let's look at how to create a DataSet within code.

Binding DataSets to Controls

Now that you have some understanding of the structure of a typical DataSet, let's look at the process involved in creating and binding a DataSet from within code. To illustrate this example, we'll recreate the address book page we looked at in the previous chapter, this time using a `DataGrid` with a `DataSet` instead of a `DataReader`.

Create the new page from `template.aspx` as usual. As we go through, I'll highlight only those parts of the code that are different from those we're used to with the `DataReader`. You can find the complete code in the code archive. First, I'll import the necessary namespaces using the `Import` directive, as follows:

File: **addressbookDS.aspx (excerpt)**

```
<%@ Import Namespace="System.Data" %>
<%@ Import Namespace="System.Data.OleDb" %>
```

We need to import the `System.Data` namespace as it includes the classes needed for working with `DataSets`. We still use `System.Data.OleDb` to work with data connection classes such as `OleDbConnection` (remember, we're sticking with Access for these examples; if you plan on using MSDE, simply import the `System.Data.SqlClient` namespace and make the other changes to the code described previously). Next, we'll instantiate the necessary classes, like this:

VB.NET File: **addressbookDS.aspx (excerpt)**

```
<script runat="server" language="VB">
Dim objConn As New OleDbConnection( _
  "Provider=Microsoft.Jet.OleDb.4.0;" & _
  "Data Source=C:\Inetpub\wwwroot\Dorknozzle\Database\" & _
  "Dorknozzle.mdb")
Dim objDA As OleDbDataAdapter
Dim objDS As New DataSet()
```

C# File: **addressbookDS.aspx (excerpt)**

```
<script runat="server" language="C#">
OleDbConnection objConn = new OleDbConnection(
  "Provider=Microsoft.Jet.OleDb.4.0;" +
  "Data Source=C:\\Inetpub\\wwwroot\\Dorknozzle\\Database\\" +
  "Dorknozzle.mdb");
OleDbDataAdapter objDA;
DataSet objDS = new DataSet();
```

We're not using the `OleDbCommand` and `OleDbDataReader` any more, nor do we need a separate `strCmd` variable for the SQL command. Instead, we've created a new instance of the `OleDbDataAdapter` class, which will handle the necessary SQL query for us. The next line creates a new `DataSet` object. As before, in `Page_Load()` we check for postback and call the `BindData()` method:

```
VB.NET                                         File: addressbookDS.aspx (excerpt)
Sub Page_Load()
  If Not IsPostBack Then
    BindData()
  End If
End Sub
```

```
C#                                             File: addressbookDS.aspx (excerpt)
void Page_Load() {
  if (!IsPostBack) {
    BindData();
  }
}
```

We can now create the new `BindData()` method. For the most part, the code will be very similar to that which creates a `DataReader`:

```
VB.NET                                         File: addressbookDS.aspx (excerpt)
Sub BindData()
  objDA = New OleDbDataAdapter("SELECT * FROM Employees", objConn)
  objDA.Fill(objDS, "Employees")
  dgAddressBook.DataSource = objDS
  dgAddressBook.DataBind()
End Sub
</script>
```

```
C#                                             File: addressbookDS.aspx (excerpt)
void BindData() {
  objDA = new OleDbDataAdapter("SELECT * FROM Employees",
      objConn);
  objDA.Fill(objDS, "Employees");
  dgAddressBook.DataSource = objDS;
  dgAddressBook.DataBind();
}
</script>
```

As you can see, the `DataAdapter` object is created much the same way as the `Command` object. We pass in the SQL statement and `Connection` object as parameters. The second line, however, does all the work. The `Fill()` method of the `DataAdapter` fills the our `DataSet` with the data obtained from the SQL query. The `Fill()` method accepts two parameters: the first is the `DataSet` object that needs to be filled, the second is the name of the table that we want to create within the `DataSet`. The last two lines bind the `DataSet` to the `DataGrid`. Finally, we can create the `DataGrid` just as before:

File: **addressbookDS.aspx (excerpt)**

```
<h1>Address Book</h1>
<p><asp:DataGrid id="dgAddressBook" runat="server"
    AutoGenerateColumns="false" CellPadding="4" GridLines="None"
    DataKeyField="EmployeeID">
  <ItemStyle Font-Name="Arial" Font-Size="10pt"
      ForeColor="#000000" />
  <HeaderStyle Font-Name="Arial" Font-Size="10pt" Font-Bold="true"
      BackColor="#003366" ForeColor="#FFFFFF" />
  <AlternatingItemStyle Font-Name="Arial" Font-Size="10pt"
      BackColor="#CCCCCC" />
  <Columns>
    <asp:BoundColumn DataField="Name" HeaderText="Name" />
    <asp:BoundColumn DataField="Extension" HeaderText="Extension"
        />
  </Columns>
</asp:DataGrid></p>
```

Save your work and test the page within the browser. The results should look similar to Figure 10.5.

Figure 10.5. The new **DataSet** is bound to the **DataGrid**, presenting the user with all employees.

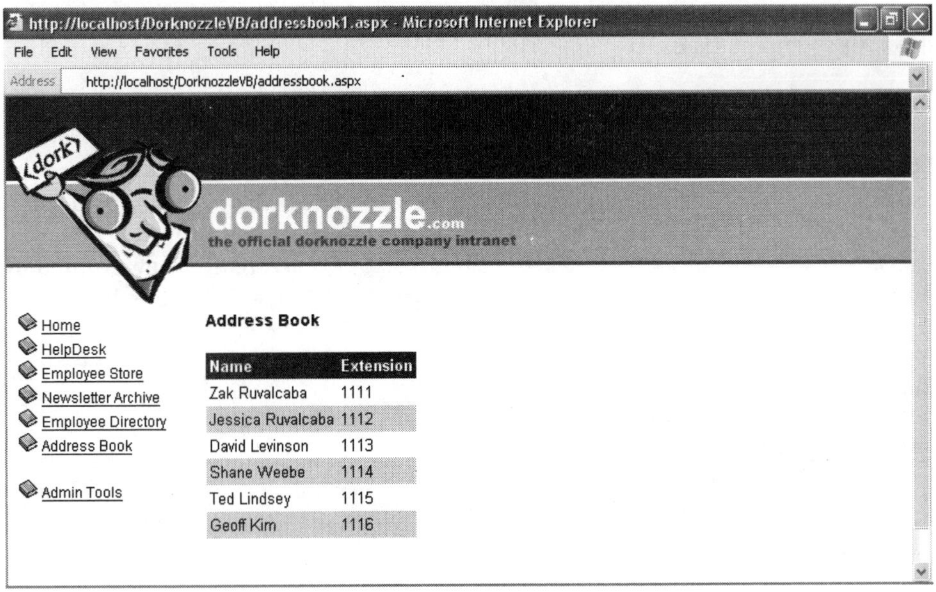

369

The data that you can see within the page is the `DataSet` data bound to the `DataGrid`. If you recall, we used the following lines to bind the `DataSet` to the actual `DataGrid`:

VB.NET   File: **addressbookDS.aspx (excerpt)**
```
dgAddressBook.DataSource = objDS
dgAddressBook.DataBind()
```

As a side note, you can't *technically* bind a `DataSet` to a control; you can only bind a `DataView` to a control. As we'll see later, a `DataView` represents a particular view of some or all of the data stored in a `DataSet`. The above code is actually shorthand for the following:

VB.NET
```
dgAddressBook.DataSource = objDS.Tables("Employees").DefaultView
dgAddressBook.DataBind()
```

You'll notice that we're binding the `DefaultView` of the `Employees` `DataTable` to the `DataSource` property of the `DataGrid`. Because our `DataSet` only contains one table, it's implied that we mean the first and only table within the `DataSet`. The above code could also be written as follows:

VB.NET
```
dgAddressBook.DataSource = objDS
dgAddressBook.DataMember = "Employees"
dgAddressBook.DataBind()
```

This time, the `DataMember` property of the `DataGrid` is used to specify the table within the `DataSet` to which you want to bind. It's only when you have multiple `DataTables` within a `DataSet` that you either need to use the `DataMember` property, or access the `Tables` collection's default view. Moving on, let's look at how you can create multiple `DataTables` within one `DataSet`. The following code uses the `SelectCommand` property of the `DataAdapter` object to create a new command on the fly, and fill the same `DataSet` with a new `DataTable` called `Departments`:

VB.NET   File: **addressbookDS.aspx (excerpt)**
```
Sub BindData()
  objDA = New OleDbDataAdapter("SELECT * FROM Employees", objConn)
  objDA.Fill(objDS, "Employees")
  objDA.SelectCommand = New OleDbCommand( _
      "SELECT * FROM Departments", objConn)
  objDA.Fill(objDS, "Departments")
  dgAddressBook.DataSource = objDS
  dgAddressBook.DataBind()
```

```
End Sub
</script>
```

C#   File: **addressbookDS.aspx (excerpt)**

```
void BindData() {
  objDA = new OleDbDataAdapter("SELECT * FROM Employees",
      objConn);
  objDA.Fill(objDS, "Employees");
  objDA.SelectCommand = new OleDbCommand(
      "SELECT * FROM Departments", objConn);
  objDA.Fill(objDS, "Departments");
  dgAddressBook.DataSource = objDS;
  dgAddressBook.DataBind();
}
</script>
```

Now, we have two DataTables within our DataSet, one for Employees, and one for Departments. How can we tell? Let's create a new DataGrid for Departments below the existing one, as follows:

File: **addressbookDS.aspx (excerpt)**

```
<p><asp:DataGrid id="dgDepartments" runat="server" CellPadding="4"
    GridLines="None">
  <ItemStyle Font-Name="Arial" Font-Size="10pt"
      ForeColor="#000000" />
  <HeaderStyle Font-Name="Arial" Font-Size="10pt" Font-Bold="true"
      BackColor="#003366" ForeColor="#FFFFFF" />
  <AlternatingItemStyle Font-Name="Arial" Font-Size="10pt"
      BackColor="#CCCCCC" />
</asp:DataGrid></p>
```

Next, we'll modify the code to use the DataMember property of both DataGrids to show the appropriate table name, as follows:

VB.NET   File: **addressbookDS.aspx (excerpt)**

```
Sub BindData()
  objDA = New OleDbDataAdapter("SELECT * FROM Employees", objConn)
  objDA.Fill(objDS, "Employees")
  objDA.SelectCommand = New OleDbCommand( _
      "SELECT * FROM Departments", objConn)
  objDA.Fill(objDS, "Departments")
  dgAddressBook.DataSource = objDS
  dgAddressBook.DataMember = "Employees"
  dgAddressBook.DataBind()
  dgDepartments.DataSource = objDS
```

```
    dgDepartments.DataMember = "Departments"
    dgDepartments.DataBind()
End Sub
```

C#   File: **addressbookDS.aspx (excerpt)**

```
void BindData() {
  objDA = new OleDbDataAdapter("SELECT * FROM Employees",
      objConn);
  objDA.Fill(objDS, "Employees");
  objDA.SelectCommand = new OleDbCommand(
      "SELECT * FROM Departments", objConn);
  objDA.Fill(objDS, "Departments");
  dgAddressBook.DataSource = objDS;
  dgAddressBook.DataMember = "Employees";
  dgAddressBook.DataBind();
  dgDepartments.DataSource = objDS;
  dgDepartments.DataMember = "Departments";
  dgDepartments.DataBind();
}
```

As you can see, both DataGrids use the same DataSet as the DataSource. However, they don't use the same table. We need to bind different DataTables to each DataGrid, so we set the appropriate table name for the DataMember property for each DataGrid. Save your work, and view it in the browser. The result is shown in Figure 10.6.

Figure 10.6. Each **DataGrid** shows its own table from the **DataSet**. This is possible because of the **DataMember** property.

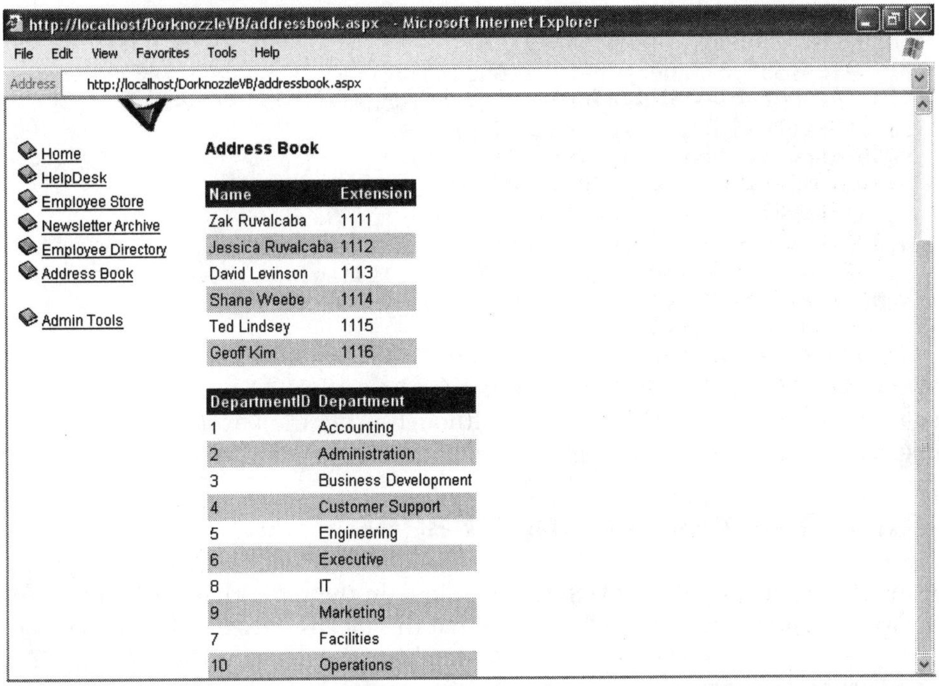

Incidentally, we're still using shorthand of a sort. The previous code could be written more verbosely as follows:

VB.NET
```
Sub BindData()
  objDA = New OleDbDataAdapter("SELECT * FROM Employees", objConn)
  objDA.Fill(objDS, "Employees")
  objDA.SelectCommand = New OleDbCommand( _
      "SELECT * FROM Departments", objConn)
  objDA.Fill(objDS, "Departments")
  dgAddressBook.DataSource = objDS.Tables("Employees").DefaultView
  dgAddressBook.DataBind()
  dgDepartments.DataSource = _
      objDS.Tables("Departments").DefaultView
  dgDepartments.DataBind()
End Sub
```

C#

```
void BindData() {
  objDA = new OleDbDataAdapter("SELECT * FROM Employees",
      objConn);
  objDA.Fill(objDS, "Employees");
  objDA.SelectCommand = new OleDbCommand(
      "SELECT * FROM Departments", objConn);
  objDA.Fill(objDS, "Departments");
  dgAddressBook.DataSource =
      objDS.Tables["Employees"].DefaultView;
  dgAddressBook.DataBind();
  dgDepartments.DataSource =
      objDS.Tables["Departments"].DefaultView;
  dgDepartments.DataBind();
}
```

We'll come back to this more verbose syntax later in the chapter. For now, just be aware that either method is valid, although using the `DataMember` property might be easier to remember right now.

Creating a `DataGrid` that Pages

As previously mentioned, `DataSets` are unique in the sense that they allow you to navigate anywhere within a data set. What this means is that, rather than being presented with a forward-only stream of database records, as is the case with the `DataReader`, the `DataSet` can be bound to data controls, for instance, a `DataGrid`, and can be paged through using the `DataGrid`'s paging properties and methods. Paging—always a monumental task in traditional ASP—now becomes simple, thanks to the `DataGrid` and its easily modifiable properties that allow you to customize presentation so that a `DataGrid`'s records can be paged through. Imagine having within the address book page an employee list that was one thousand employees long. Rather than creating a giant list of employees, it would be a simple matter to customize the `DataGrid` so that it pages every three or four records. Figure 10.7 shows the newly created `Employees DataGrid` within the address book page. Notice that only three records are shown and the user is presented options for paging to the next set of records.

Figure 10.7. The `DataGrid`, in conjunction with a `DataSet`, supports the ability to page through sets of records.

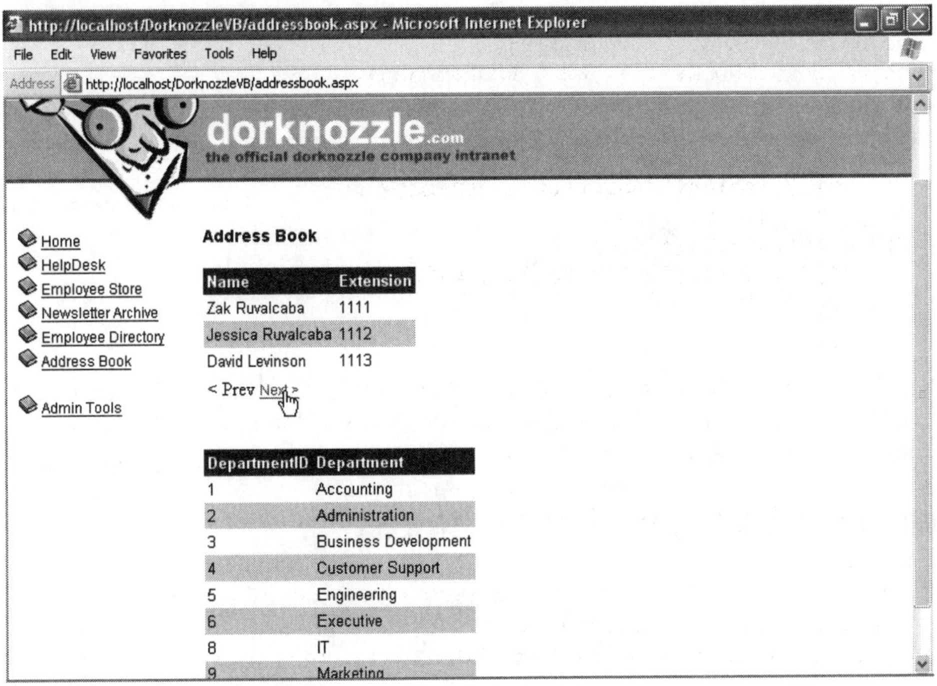

Paging a `DataGrid` involves modifying a few properties. These properties include:

`AllowPaging`   When `True`, enables paging for a `DataGrid`.

`PageSize`   Specifies the amount of records to show per page within the `DataGrid`.

`PagerStyle-Mode`   Specifies the type of paging to use. Possible values are `NextPrev` and `NumericPages`. When `NextPrev` is set, custom paging links can be presented using `PagerStyle-NextPageText` and `PagerStyle-PrevPageText`.

`PagerStyle-NextPageText`   Specifies the custom text to use for the next page hyperlink.

PagerStyle-PrevPageText	Specifies the custom text to use for the previous page hyperlink.
PagerStyle-Position	Specifies the position within the footer of the DataGrid.

You can add paging functionality to your `Employees` `DataGrid`, first by adding the necessary properties within the `DataGrid`, as shown here:

File: **DataGridPaging.aspx (excerpt)**

```
<asp:DataGrid id="dgAddressBook" runat="server"
    AutoGenerateColumns="false" CellPadding="4" GridLines="None"
    AllowPaging="True" PageSize="3" PagerStyle-Mode="NextPrev"
    PagerStyle-NextPageText="Next &gt;"
    PagerStyle-PrevPageText="&lt; Prev"
    OnPageIndexChanged="dg_Page" DataKeyField="EmployeeID">
  <ItemStyle Font-Name="Arial" Font-Size="10pt"
      ForeColor="#000000" />
  <HeaderStyle Font-Name="Arial" Font-Size="10pt" Font-Bold="true"
      BackColor="#003366" ForeColor="#FFFFFF" />
  <AlternatingItemStyle Font-Name="Arial" Font-Size="10pt"
      BackColor="#CCCCCC" />
  <Columns>
    <asp:BoundColumn DataField="Name" HeaderText="Name" />
    <asp:BoundColumn DataField="Extension" HeaderText="Extension"
        />
  </Columns>
</asp:DataGrid>
```

As you can see, we use the `AllowPaging` property to enable paging for the `DataGrid`. Next, we set the `PageSize` property to 3, effectively setting the number of records to show within the `DataGrid` at a time. Then, we set the `PagerStyle-Mode` to show next and previous links, using the `NextPrev` value. We also supply custom text for our next and previous hyperlinks, using the `PagerStyle-NextPageText` and `PagerStyle-PrevPageText` properties, which we set to `Next >` and `< Prev`, respectively. Finally, we must specify within the `OnPageIndexChanged` attribute the method that will handle the paging functionality.

We now need to add the `PageIndexChanged` event handler to our code, as follows:

VB.NET
File: **DataGridPaging.aspx (excerpt)**

```
Sub dg_Page(s As Object, e As DataGridPageChangedEventArgs)
  dgAddressBook.CurrentPageIndex = e.NewPageIndex
```

```
  BindData()
End Sub
```

```
void dg_Page(Object s, DataGridPageChangedEventArgs e) {
  dgAddressBook.CurrentPageIndex = e.NewPageIndex;
  BindData();
}
```

You will notice that in this event handler we pass in an instance of `DataGridPageChangedEventArgs`. As is the case with `DataGridCommandEventArgs`, which we saw in Chapter 9, `DataGridPageChangedEventArgs` exposes functionality for handling the paging of `DataGrid`s. Next, we set the `CurrentPageIndex` property of the `DataGrid` equal to the new page index of the `DataGrid`. This property stores the zero-based index of the page currently being displayed, and we get the new page index from the appropriately named property of the `e` object that's passed in.

Save your work and test the page in the browser.

Understanding `DataTables`

As you've learned thus far, `DataTables` are the elements that hold data within a `DataSet`. Like tables within a database, `DataTables` are automatically constructed with columns, properties for those columns, and rows within the `DataSet`. Until now, you've had no control over how the `DataTables`, `DataColumns`, or `DataRows` are constructed within the `DataSet`, because everything has been done automatically for you through the use of the `DataAdapter`. However, we can also use the `DataAdapter` to construct `DataTables` without building them from a database table. This would enable us, for instance, to construct a purely memory-resident shopping cart system.

By manually constructing `DataTables` and `DataColumns` (for the shopping cart), and adding `DataRows` (items) to those `DataTables`, employees could very easily interact with a memory-resident shopping cart system—built entirely using `DataTables`, `DataColumns`, and `DataRows`! In the next few sections, we'll see how we can create our own `DataSets` using the `DataTable`, `DataColumn`, and `DataRow` classes.

Creating `DataTables` Programmatically

As you have seen, `DataTables`, `DataColumns`, and `DataRows` are automatically constructed within a `DataSet` when you fill the `DataSet` with the `DataAdapter`. For instance, in the previous examples, we create a new instance of the `DataAdapter` class as follows:

VB.NET
```
objDA = New OleDbDataAdapter("SELECT * FROM Employees", objConn)
```

When we're ready to create the `DataSet`, complete with the new `Employees` `DataTables`, we simply call the `Fill()` method of the `DataAdapter` object, passing in the `DataSet` object along with a `DataTable` name of our choice, as follows:

VB.NET
```
objDA.Fill(objDS, "Employees")
```

For the most part, the process we saw above involved just these two lines of code, and was fairly automatic. But when creating your own `DataTables`, you no longer use the `DataAdapter` class. Instead, `DataTables` are constructed simply through the creation of new instances of the `DataTable` class. We provide a name for the `DataTable`, then add the newly created `DataTable` to a `DataSet` object, as follows:

VB.NET   File: **CreatingDataTablesProgrammatically.aspx**
```
<%@ Import Namespace="System.Data" %>
<html>
<head>
<title>Creating DataTables using VB.NET</title>
<script language="VB" runat="server">
Sub Page_Load()
  Dim objDS As New DataSet
  Dim objDT1 As DataTable = New DataTable("Employees")

  objDS.Tables.Add(objDT1)

  lblMessage.Text = "You have " & objDS.Tables.Count & _
    " DataTable(s) in your DataSet.<br />The names are: " & _
    objDS.Tables(0).ToString()
End Sub
</script>
</head>
<body>
<form runat="server">
  <asp:Label id="lblMessage" runat="server"/>
```

```
</form>
</body>
</html>
```

C#   File: **CreatingDataTablesProgrammatically.aspx**

```
<%@ Import Namespace="System.Data" %>
<html>
<head>
<title>Creating DataTables using C#</title>
<script language="C#" runat="server">
void Page_Load() {
  DataSet objDS = new DataSet();
  DataTable objDT1 = new DataTable("Employees");

  objDS.Tables.Add(objDT1);

  lblMessage.Text = "You have " +
    Convert.ToString(objDS.Tables.Count) +
    " DataTable(s) in your DataSet. <br />The names are: " +
    Convert.ToString(objDS.Tables[0]);
}
</script>
</head>
<body>
<form runat="server">
  <asp:Label id="lblMessage" runat="server"/>
</form>
</body>
</html>
```

Let's break down the code to make it more understandable. Initially, we simply write the necessary HTML, the Import directive to work with DataSets, and the <script> tag as follows:

VB.NET   File: **CreatingDataTablesProgrammatically.aspx** (excerpt)

```
<%@ Import Namespace="System.Data" %>
<html>
<head>
<title>Creating DataTables using VB.NET</title>
<script language="VB" runat="server">
```

C#   File: **CreatingDataTablesProgrammatically.aspx** (excerpt)

```
<%@ Import Namespace="System.Data" %>
<html>
<head>
```

```
<title>Creating DataTables using C#</title>
<script language="C#" runat="server">
```

Next, we define the `Page_Load()` event handler:

VB.NET   File: **CreatingDataTablesProgrammatically.aspx (excerpt)**

```
Sub Page_Load()
```

C#   File: **CreatingDataTablesProgrammatically.aspx (excerpt)**

```
void Page_Load() {
```

The handler code starts by creating new `DataSet` and `DataTable` object variables, as follows:

VB.NET   File: **CreatingDataTablesProgrammatically.aspx (excerpt)**

```
Dim objDS As New DataSet
Dim objDT1 As DataTable = New DataTable("Employees")
```

C#   File: **CreatingDataTablesProgrammatically.aspx (excerpt)**

```
DataSet objDS = new DataSet();
DataTable objDT1 = new DataTable("Employees");
```

You'll notice that we provide a name for the `DataTable` simply by passing the name as a parameter to the `DataTable` class. Next, we'll add the newly constructed `DataTable` to our `DataSet` like so:

VB.NET   File: **CreatingDataTablesProgrammatically.aspx (excerpt)**

```
objDS.Tables.Add(objDT1)
```

C#   File: **CreatingDataTablesProgrammatically.aspx (excerpt)**

```
objDS.Tables.Add(objDT1);
```

Remember, the `DataSet` has a collection of tables. We can add to this collection by calling the `Add()` method of the `Tables` collection and passing in the name of the `DataTable` object variable. Now, let's write out the total number of `DataTables` and the name within a `Label` control, close the event handler, and close the `<script>` tag, as shown below:

VB.NET   File: **CreatingDataTablesProgrammatically.aspx (excerpt)**

```
lblMessage.Text = "You have " & objDS.Tables.Count & _
    " DataTable(s) in your DataSet.<br />The names are: " & _
    objDS.Tables(0).ToString()
End Sub
</script>
```

File: CreatingDataTablesProgrammatically.aspx (excerpt)

```csharp
    lblMessage.Text = "You have " +
      Convert.ToString(objDS.Tables.Count) +
      " DataTable(s) in your DataSet.<br />The names are: " +
      Convert.ToString(objDS.Tables[0]);
}
</script>
```

There are two items that are being written to the `Label` control here. The first is the total number of `DataTables` in the `DataSet`, which is accessed using the `Count` property of the `Tables` collection. The second is the `DataTable`'s name, which is returned by accessing the index of the `DataTable` within the `DataSet`.

Finally, we'll write the rest of the HTML code as follows:

```html
</head>
<body>
<form runat="server">
  <asp:Label id="lblMessage" runat="server"/>
</form>
</body>
</html>
```

Save your work and test the results in the browser. When the page loads, a new `DataSet` and `DataTable` is created, the `DataTable` is added to the `DataSet`, and the total number of `DataTables`, as well as the `DataTable` name, are written into a `Label` control.

Now that you've seen how the `DataTables` are created, try creating a new `DataTable` called `Departments`, and add that to the `DataSet` as well. Your code should resemble the following:

VB.NET **File: CreatingDataTablesProgrammatically.aspx (excerpt)**

```vbnet
Sub Page_Load()
  Dim objDS As New DataSet
  Dim objDT1 As DataTable = New DataTable("Employees")
  Dim objDT2 As DataTable = New DataTable("Departments")

  objDS.Tables.Add(objDT1)
  objDS.Tables.Add(objDT2)

  lblMessage.Text = "You have " & objDS.Tables.Count & _
    " DataTable(s) in your DataSet.<br />The names are: " & _
    objDS.Tables(0).toString() & ", " & _
```

```
      objDS.Tables(1).toString()
End Sub
```

```
C#                          File: CreatingDataTablesProgrammatically.aspx (excerpt)
void Page_Load() {
  DataSet objDS = new DataSet();
  DataTable objDT1 = new DataTable("Employees");
  DataTable objDT2 = new DataTable("Departments");

  objDS.Tables.Add(objDT1);
  objDS.Tables.Add(objDT2);

  lblMessage.Text = "You have " +
    Convert.ToString(objDS.Tables.Count) +
    " DataTable(s) in your DataSet.<br />The names are: " +
    Convert.ToString(objDS.Tables[0]) + ", " +
    Convert.ToString(objDS.Tables[1]);
}
```

In this case, another DataTable, similar to the first, called Departments was created. The new DataTable is then added to the DataSet immediately after the addition of the first. Finally, we access the name of the second DataTable within the DataSet by its index (1) in the Tables collection. By testing the result in your browser, you should get a similar result to Figure 10.8.

Figure 10.8. The DataTables are manually created and added to the DataSet. The total number of DataTables and their names are written within a Label control.

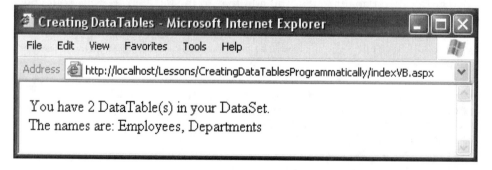

Creating DataColumns Programmatically

In the previous section, we created DataTables programmatically. We wrote the total number of DataTables and the names of each within a Label control. Although everything seemed to function well, there are two things missing. First, the DataTables have no structure. DataTables, just like database tables, require columns with specific data types. Second, the DataTables don't contain any information. In this section, we'll explore how to use DataColumns to create structure within our DataTables. In the next section, we'll learn how to populate the DataTable with rows of information, using the DataRow class. Let's get started!

To create DataColumns within your DataTable, simply modify your code to insert new DataColumns as follows:

VB.NET   File: **CreatingDataColumnsProgrammatically.aspx (excerpt)**

```
Sub Page_Load()
  Dim objDS As New DataSet
  Dim objDT As DataTable = New DataTable("Employees")
  Dim objDC As DataColumn

  objDC = New DataColumn("EmployeeID", GetType(String))
  objDT.Columns.Add(objDC)
  objDC = New DataColumn("Name", GetType(String))
  objDT.Columns.Add(objDC)
  objDC = New DataColumn("Extension", GetType(String))
  objDT.Columns.Add(objDC)

  objDS.Tables.Add(objDT)

  dg.DataSource = objDS
  dg.DataBind()
End Sub
```

C#   File: **CreatingDataColumnsProgrammatically.aspx (excerpt)**

```
void Page_Load() {
  DataSet objDS = new DataSet();
  DataTable objDT = new DataTable("Employees");
  DataColumn objDC;

  objDC = new DataColumn("EmployeeID",
      Type.GetType("System.String"));
  objDT.Columns.Add(objDC);
  objDC = new DataColumn("Name", Type.GetType("System.String"));
  objDT.Columns.Add(objDC);
```

```
objDC = new DataColumn("Extension",
    Type.GetType("System.String"));
objDT.Columns.Add(objDC);

objDS.Tables.Add(objDT);

dg.DataSource = objDS;
dg.DataBind();
}
```

In this case, we create a new instance of the `DataColumn` class. Next, we create a new `DataColumn` object and pass in the name and data type of the column. Then, we add the new column to the `DataTable`'s `Column` collection, using the `Add()` method, and pass in the name of the `DataColumn` object. Repeat this process as many times as you need to in order to construct columns within your `DataTable`.

You may have noticed those last two lines in which we bind our `DataSet` to an object called `dg`. As you may guess, this is a `DataGrid`. Replace the `Label` with an empty `DataGrid` control, like this:

File: **CreatingDataColumnsProgrammatically.aspx (excerpt)**

```
<asp:DataGrid id="dg" runat="server" />
```

Save your work and test the results in the browser. This time, the `DataGrid` is bound to the `DataSet`, similar to Figure 10.9.

Figure 10.9. The `DataGrid` is bound to the `DataSet` without failure because the `DataTable` contains column structure.

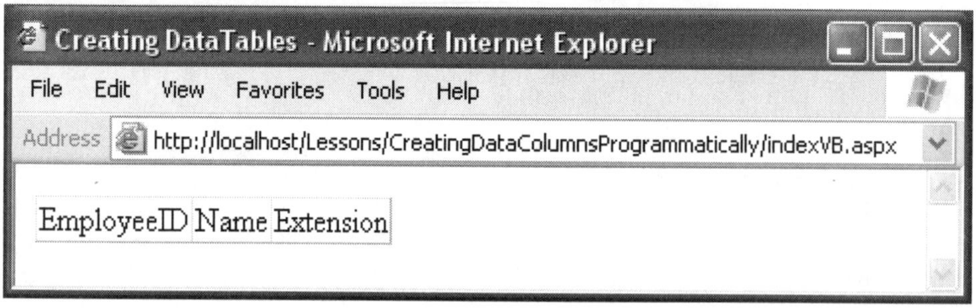

Our programmatically generated `DataSet` is beginning to take shape! Let's press on, and see exactly how rows of data can be added using the `DataRow` class.

Creating DataRows Programmatically

Now that you've seen how DataTables are constructed and added to a DataSet, and how DataColumns are created and added to the DataTables collection, it's time to add the content that the DataTables will contain. The following code modification adds two new DataRows to the Employees DataTable:

VB.NET   File: **CreatingDataRowsProgrammatically.aspx** (excerpt)

```vb
Sub Page_Load()
  Dim objDS As New DataSet
  Dim objDT As DataTable = New DataTable("Employees")
  Dim objDC As DataColumn
  Dim objDR As DataRow

  objDC = New DataColumn("EmployeeID", GetType(String))
  objDT.Columns.Add(objDC)
  objDC = New DataColumn("Name", GetType(String))
  objDT.Columns.Add(objDC)
  objDC = New DataColumn("Extension", GetType(String))
  objDT.Columns.Add(objDC)

  objDR = objDT.NewRow()
  objDR("EmployeeID") = 1
  objDR("Name") = "Zak Ruvalcaba"
  objDR("Extension") = 1111
  objDT.Rows.Add(objDR)

  objDR = objDT.NewRow()
  objDR("EmployeeID") = 2
  objDR("Name") = "Jessica Ruvalcaba"
  objDR("Extension") = 1112
  objDT.Rows.Add(objDR)

  objDS.Tables.Add(objDT)

  dg.DataSource = objDS
  dg.DataBind()
End Sub
```

C#   File: **CreatingDataRowsProgrammatically.aspx** (excerpt)

```csharp
void Page_Load() {
  DataSet objDS = new DataSet();
  DataTable objDT = new DataTable("Employees");
  DataColumn objDC;
  DataRow objDR;
```

```
objDC = new DataColumn("EmployeeID",
    Type.GetType("System.String"));
objDT.Columns.Add(objDC);
objDC = new DataColumn("Name", Type.GetType("System.String"));
objDT.Columns.Add(objDC);
objDC = new DataColumn("Extension",
    Type.GetType("System.String"));
objDT.Columns.Add(objDC);

objDR = objDT.NewRow();
objDR["EmployeeID"] = 1;
objDR["Name"] = "Zak Ruvalcaba";
objDR["Extension"] = 1111;
objDT.Rows.Add(objDR);

objDR = objDT.NewRow();
objDR["EmployeeID"] = 2;
objDR["Name"] = "Jessica Ruvalcaba";
objDR["Extension"] = 1112;
objDT.Rows.Add(objDR);

objDS.Tables.Add(objDT);

dg.DataSource = objDS;
dg.DataBind();
}
```

Save the page and view it within the browser. As Figure 10.10 shows, two new employees are displayed within the DataGrid.

Figure 10.10. Two new employees are added to the `DataTable`. The `DataTable` is then bound to the `DataGrid` displaying the data to the user.

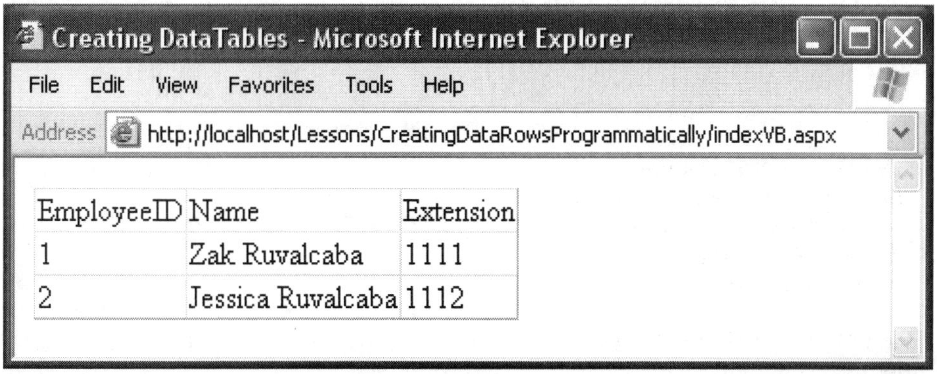

Let's break down the code and make it a bit more understandable. First, we create a variable to hold the `DataRows` we are about to create:

VB.NET   File: **CreatingDataRowsProgrammatically.aspx (excerpt)**
```
Dim objDR As DataRow
```

C#   File: **CreatingDataRowsProgrammatically.aspx (excerpt)**
```
DataRow objDR;
```

Next, we call the `DataTable`'s `NewRow()` method to return a new row complete with the column information for the specific `DataTable`, as follows:

VB.NET   File: **CreatingDataRowsProgrammatically.aspx (excerpt)**
```
objDR = objDT.NewRow()
```

C#   File: **CreatingDataRowsProgrammatically.aspx (excerpt)**
```
objDR = objDT.NewRow();
```

We then assign the values to the specific cells in the `DataTable`. We can do this by referencing the column names like so:

VB.NET   File: **CreatingDataRowsProgrammatically.aspx (excerpt)**
```
objDR("EmployeeID") = 1
objDR("Name") = "Zak Ruvalcaba"
objDR("Extension") = 1111
```

```
C#                                        File: CreatingDataRowsProgrammatically.aspx (excerpt)
objDR["EmployeeID"] = 1;
objDR["Name"] = "Zak Ruvalcaba";
objDR["Extension"] = 1111;
```

Finally, we add the new row to the DataTable's Rows collection using the Add() method:

```
VB.NET                                    File: CreatingDataRowsProgrammatically.aspx (excerpt)
objDT.Rows.Add(objDR)
```

```
C#                                        File: CreatingDataRowsProgrammatically.aspx (excerpt)
objDT.Rows.Add(objDR);
```

See how easy that was? Yet, as nice as this functionality seems, who really wants to add new rows to the DataTable manually? In the next chapter, you'll learn how to add new rows to the DataTable on the fly according to user selections from a menu of items within the employee store. Before we get to that, however, let's first have a look at setting the properties of our DataTables programmatically—for example, to set a particular column as a primary key.

Setting DataTable Properties Programmatically

At times, working with DataTables will require that certain properties be set. We can define the following properties for a DataTable:

CaseSensitive
When searching, filtering, or sorting DataTables, use the CaseSensitive property to determine whether or not to search, filter, or sort in case sensitive fashion. By default, this is False.

MinimumCapacity
Specifies the number of rows that the DataTable is initially prepared to accept. If you insert more than this number of rows, the DataTable will expand to accomodate them, but such expansions take time to perform, so it's good to allow enough space for the number of records you expect up front. Be careful how high you set this number—the higher you make it, the more memory is consumed by the empty DataSet. Default is 25.

| **PrimaryKey** | Specifies an array of columns to use as the primary key for the DataTable. |
| **TableName** | Assigns a unique name to the DataTable. |

You can work with the properties in code by following the steps outlined below. First, create new instances of the DataSet, DataTable, DataColumn, and DataRow classes:

VB.NET   File: **DataTablePropertiesProgrammatically.aspx (excerpt)**

```
Sub Page_Load()
  Dim objDS As New DataSet()
  Dim objDT As New DataTable("Employees")
  Dim objDC As DataColumn
  Dim PKColumn(1) As DataColumn
  Dim objDR As DataRow
```

C#   File: **DataTablePropertiesProgrammatically.aspx (excerpt)**

```
void Page_Load() {
  DataSet objDS = new DataSet();
  DataTable objDT = new DataTable("Employees");
  DataColumn objDC;
  DataColumn[] PKColumn = new DataColumn[1];
  DataRow objDR;
```

Notice that all we're doing differently here is declaring an array of DataColumns, called PKColumn. This array contains a single element—we'll explain why in a moment. It will be used to set the PrimaryKey property of the DataTable. First, we'll set the MinimumCapacity property to 100 and the CaseSensitive property to True for the DataTable:

VB.NET   File: **DataTablePropertiesProgrammatically.aspx (excerpt)**

```
  objDT.MinimumCapacity = 100
  objDT.CaseSensitive = True
```

C#   File: **DataTablePropertiesProgrammatically.aspx (excerpt)**

```
  objDT.MinimumCapacity = 100;
  objDT.CaseSensitive = true;
```

Now, as we create the three new DataColumns within the DataTable, we want to set the primary key of the DataTable to the first column (EmployeeID); we do this using the DataTable's PrimaryKey property. This property takes an array of DataColumns, which is why we created that array earlier. We have to set the one item of our array to contain the `EmployeeID` `DataColumn`; then we can set the property:

```
VB.NET                              File: DataTablePropertiesProgrammatically.aspx (excerpt)
objDC = New DataColumn("EmployeeID", GetType(String))
objDT.Columns.Add(objDC)
PKColumn(0) = objDC
objDT.PrimaryKey = PKColumn
objDC = New DataColumn("Name", GetType(String))
objDT.Columns.Add(objDC)
objDC = New DataColumn("Extension", GetType(String))
objDT.Columns.Add(objDC)
```

```
C#                                  File: DataTablePropertiesProgrammatically.aspx (excerpt)
objDC = new DataColumn("EmployeeID",
    Type.GetType("System.String"));
objDT.Columns.Add(objDC);
PKColumn[0] = objDC;
objDT.PrimaryKey = PKColumn;
objDC = new DataColumn("Name", Type.GetType("System.String"));
objDT.Columns.Add(objDC);
objDC = new DataColumn("Extension",
    Type.GetType("System.String"));
objDT.Columns.Add(objDC);
```

Why does the `PrimaryKey` property need an array of `DataColumns`? Wouldn't it be simpler just to allow it to take a single `DataColumn`? Well, cast your mind back to Chapter 6, in which we discussed primary keys. We said that, in some cases, a primary key might comprise two or more columns, and in that event, we would need to construct our `PKColumn` array to contain more than one `DataColumn`.

Next, we add the same two rows to our `DataTable` as before, add the `DataTable` to the `DataSet`, and bind the `DataSet` to the `DataGrid`. That's all there is to it. If you save your work and test the results within the browser, you won't actually see any difference. However, the employee ID is now designated as the `DataTable`'s primary key, which means it must be unique, and may not be null (empty).

If you like, you can test this by changing the code to set Jessica's employee ID to 1 (the same as Zak's ID), and saving the changes. If you then reload the page, you'll see an error message stating that we've tried to set the column's value to one that already exists, as in Figure 10.11.

Figure 10.11. Running the code with a non-unique employee ID results in an error.

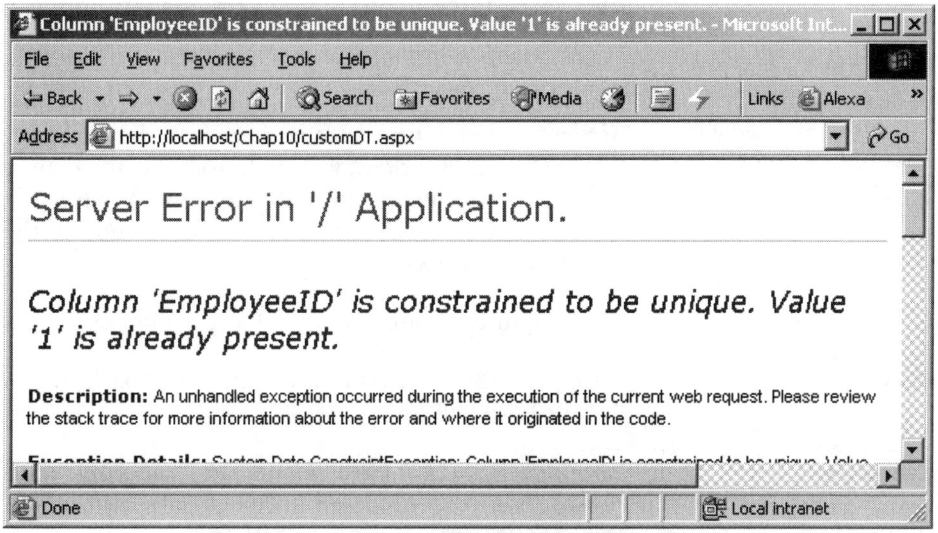

Setting **DataColumn** Properties Programmatically

Just as with DataTables, DataColumns have many properties that you can set programmatically. The properties should look very similar to column properties within a database:

AllowDBNull   Specifies whether or not a DataColumn can accept null values. The default value is True, but is automatically set to False for columns designated as primary keys.

AutoIncrement   Creates a DataColumn that increments its values automatically.

AutoIncrementSeed   Represents the initial value to use when AutoIncrement is True.

AutoIncrementStep   Represents the increment value to use when AutoIncrement is True.

ColumnName   Specifies the name of the DataColumn.

DataType	Specifies the data type of the `DataColumn`. The following data types are supported: Boolean, Byte, Char, DateTime, Decimal, Double, Int16, Int32, Int64, SByte, Single, String, TimeSpan, UInt16, UInt32, and UInt64.
DefaultValue	Specifies the default value of a column. This will come in handy when a user adds an item into the shopping cart. When a user does, we can automatically assume that he or she wants to add one item. Within the `DataGrid`, we can then allow the user to modify the quantity if they wish.
Expression	Allows you to create columns that calculate.
MaxLength	Specifies the maximum length of text that a `DataColumn` will accept.
ReadOnly	Specifies a `DataColumn` should be read-only. This means that your code can only read the contents of the `DataColumn`—it cannot write to it.
Unique	Specifies a `DataColumn` as unique. Default is `False`. If you're working with a `DataColumn` that automatically increments, then it's a safe bet you'll want to make it unique as well. This property is automatically set to `True` for columns designated as primary keys.

The next couple of sections will introduce you to these properties within code.

Assigning Default Values to `DataColumns`

As was mentioned in the previous section, you can assign default values within `DataColumns` using the `DefaultValue` property for the specific `DataColumn`. An example of a situation when you might like to use the `DefaultValue` property might be a shopping cart. Rather than requiring your users to pick a quantity initially, you could set a default value of one that's used every time a user adds an item. Later, you could allow the user to modify the quantity from within whichever control you're using to present the cart on screen.

To demonstrate this point, make a copy of the file we've been using in our examples so far (or grab a copy of `DataTablePropertiesProgrammatically.aspx` from the code archive), and replace the `Page_Load()` code with the following:

```vb.net
Sub Page_Load()
  Dim objDS As New DataSet()
  Dim objDT As New DataTable("Cart")
  Dim objDC As DataColumn
  Dim objDR As DataRow

  objDC = New DataColumn("ItemID", GetType(String))
  objDT.Columns.Add(objDC)
  objDC = New DataColumn("Item", GetType(String))
  objDT.Columns.Add(objDC)
  objDC = New DataColumn("Quantity", GetType(String))
  objDC.DefaultValue = 1
  objDT.Columns.Add(objDC)

  objDR = objDT.NewRow()
  objDR("ItemID") = 1
  objDR("Item") = "Widget 1"
  objDT.Rows.Add(objDR)

  objDR = objDT.NewRow()
  objDR("ItemID") = 2
  objDR("Item") = "Widget 2"
  objDT.Rows.Add(objDR)

  objDS.Tables.Add(objDT)

  dg.DataSource = objDS
  dg.DataMember = "Cart"
  dg.DataBind()
End Sub
```

```csharp
void Page_Load() {
  DataSet objDS = new DataSet();
  DataTable objDT = new DataTable("Cart");
  DataColumn objDC;
  DataRow objDR;

  objDC = new DataColumn("ItemID", Type.GetType("System.String"));
  objDT.Columns.Add(objDC);
  objDC = new DataColumn("Item", Type.GetType("System.String"));
  objDT.Columns.Add(objDC);
  objDC = new DataColumn("Quantity",
      Type.GetType("System.String"));
  objDC.DefaultValue = 1;
```

```
    objDT.Columns.Add(objDC);

    objDR = objDT.NewRow();
    objDR["ItemID"] = 1;
    objDR["Item"] = "Widget 1";
    objDT.Rows.Add(objDR);

    objDR = objDT.NewRow();
    objDR["ItemID"] = 2;
    objDR["Item"] = "Widget 2";
    objDT.Rows.Add(objDR);

    objDS.Tables.Add(objDT);

    dg.DataSource = objDS;
    dg.DataMember = "Cart";
    dg.DataBind();
}
```

As you can see in the lines I've highlighted, the `DefaultValue` property was assigned the value 1 for the `Quantity` `DataColumn`. Since we're assigning this default value, we don't have to set that `DataColumn` within each row. Try saving your work and view the results within the browser. Figure 10.12 illustrates that the default value 1 shows within the `Quantity` column in the `DataGrid`.

Figure 10.12. A default value of 1 shows within the `Quantity` column in the `DataGrid`.

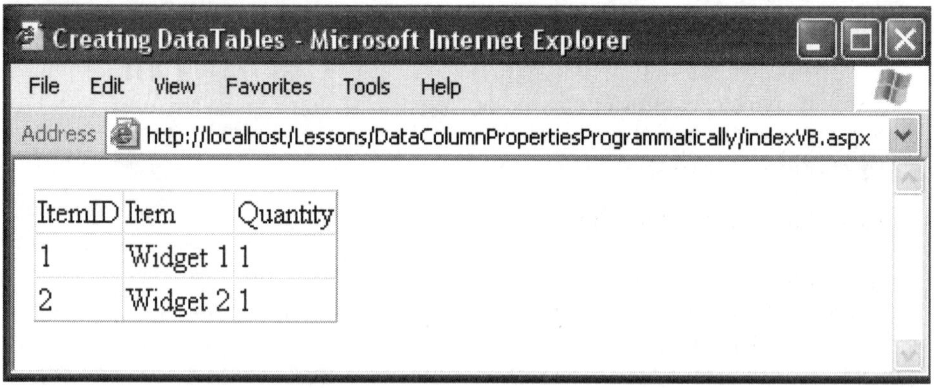

Auto Incrementing and Making `DataColumns` Unique

You can create `DataColumns` that auto increment and have a unique constraint applied, using the `AutoIncrement`, `AutoIncrementSeed`, `AutoIncrementStep`, and `Unique` properties of the `DataColumn`. The following code defines the `ItemID` `DataColumn` as unique, and allows it to auto increment:

VB.NET   File: **DataColumnPropertiesProgrammatically.aspx (excerpt)**

```
Sub Page_Load()
  Dim objDS As New DataSet()
  Dim objDT As New DataTable("Cart")
  Dim objDC As DataColumn
  Dim objDR As DataRow

  objDC = New DataColumn("ItemID", GetType(String))
  objDC.AutoIncrement = True
  objDC.AutoIncrementSeed = 1
  objDC.AutoIncrementStep = 1
  objDC.Unique = True
  objDT.Columns.Add(objDC)

  objDC = New DataColumn("Item", GetType(String))
  objDT.Columns.Add(objDC)
  objDC = New DataColumn("Quantity", GetType(String))
  objDC.DefaultValue = 1
  objDT.Columns.Add(objDC)

  objDR = objDT.NewRow()
  objDR("Item") = "Widget 1"
  objDT.Rows.Add(objDR)

  objDR = objDT.NewRow()
  objDR("Item") = "Widget 2"
  objDT.Rows.Add(objDR)

  objDS.Tables.Add(objDT)

  dg.DataSource = objDS
  dg.DataMember = "Cart"
  dg.DataBind()
End Sub
```

C#   File: **DataColumnPropertiesProgrammatically.aspx (excerpt)**

```
void Page_Load() {
  DataSet objDS = new DataSet();
```

```
DataTable objDT = new DataTable("Cart");
DataColumn objDC;
DataRow objDR;

objDC = new DataColumn("ItemID", Type.GetType("System.String"));
objDC.AutoIncrement = true;
objDC.AutoIncrementSeed = 1;
objDC.AutoIncrementStep = 1;
objDC.Unique = true;
objDT.Columns.Add(objDC);
objDC = new DataColumn("Item", Type.GetType("System.String"));
objDT.Columns.Add(objDC);
objDC = new DataColumn("Quantity",
    Type.GetType("System.String"));
objDC.DefaultValue = 1;
objDT.Columns.Add(objDC);

objDR = objDT.NewRow();
objDR["Item"] = "Widget 1";
objDT.Rows.Add(objDR);

objDR = objDT.NewRow();
objDR["Item"] = "Widget 2";
objDT.Rows.Add(objDR);

objDS.Tables.Add(objDT);

dg.DataSource = objDS;
dg.DataMember = "Cart";
dg.DataBind();
}
```

As you can see, in this example we set the AutoIncrement, AutoIncrementSeed, AutoIncrementStep, and Unique properties for the ItemID DataColumn. Again, we don't need to create this row manually. The results should be the same as we saw in Figure 10.12.

Adding DataColumn Values

One of the more important aspects of programmatically creating DataTables and DataColumns is being able to use columns in calculations. For instance, if you were creating a shopping cart, you could very well have a column for cost. Within the Cost column, you would enter the price for a specific item that a user has added into the cart. As the user adds items into the cart, you may want to keep a running total of the items within the cart, and present that total to the user within a `Label` control toward the bottom of the page. You can add this functionality to your `DataTables` using the `Compute()` method of the `DataTable` class. For instance, the following code uses the `Compute()` method to add all rows within the `Cost` column of the `DataTable`:

VB.NET
```
objDT.Compute("SUM(Cost)", Nothing)
```

The `Compute()` method accepts two parameters. The first is the calculation that you want to perform. This parameter accepts an **aggregate function**. As I explained in Chapter 7, an aggregate function is a function that performs a computation on a set of values, rather than on a single value. For example, finding the sum of a collection of rows within a `DataColumn` is an aggregate function. There are numerous aggregate functions you can use within the `Compute()` method, including `AVG`, `COUNT`, `MAX`, `MIN`, `STDEV` (standard deviation of values), `SUM`, and `VAR` (variance of values in a column). In our case, we've used the `SUM` function to return the sum of all rows within the `Cost DataColumn`.

The second parameter is used for row filtering. Think of it as the equivalent of a `WHERE` clause. For instance, if you wanted to return the sum for just the first row, you would change your statement as follows:

VB.NET
```
objDT.Compute("SUM(Cost)", "ItemID=1")
```

Since we want no restrictions (we want the sum of all rows), we'll stick with `Nothing` (VB.NET) or `null` (C#) for the second parameter, which basically means select all rows. To demonstrate this usage, we'll modify our code slightly, as follows:

VB.NET   File: **AddingDataColumnValues.aspx (excerpt)**
```
Sub Page_Load()
  Dim objDS As New DataSet()
  Dim objDT As New DataTable("Cart")
  Dim objDC As DataColumn
  Dim objDR As DataRow

  objDC = New DataColumn("ItemID", GetType(String))
  objDC.AutoIncrement = True
  objDC.AutoIncrementSeed = 1
  objDC.AutoIncrementStep = 1
  objDC.Unique = True
```

```
    objDT.Columns.Add(objDC)
    objDC = New DataColumn("Item", GetType(String))
    objDT.Columns.Add(objDC)
    objDC = New DataColumn("Quantity", GetType(String))
    objDC.DefaultValue = 1
    objDT.Columns.Add(objDC)
    objDC = New DataColumn("Cost", GetType(Decimal))
    objDT.Columns.Add(objDC)

    objDR = objDT.NewRow()
    objDR("Item") = "Widget 1"
    objDR("Cost") = "13.00"
    objDT.Rows.Add(objDR)

    objDR = objDT.NewRow()
    objDR("Item") = "Widget 2"
    objDR("Cost") = "15.00"
    objDT.Rows.Add(objDR)

    objDS.Tables.Add(objDT)

    Dim intSumTotal As Integer
    intSumTotal = objDT.Compute("SUM(Cost)", Nothing)
    lblTotal.Text = "Your current total is: " & _
        intSumTotal.ToString("c")

    dg.DataSource = objDS
    dg.DataMember = "Cart"
    dg.DataBind()
End Sub
```

C#   File: **AddingDataColumnValues.aspx (excerpt)**

```
void Page_Load() {
    DataSet objDS = new DataSet();
    DataTable objDT = new DataTable("Cart");
    DataColumn objDC;
    DataRow objDR;

    objDC = new DataColumn("ItemID", Type.GetType("System.String"));
    objDC.AutoIncrement = true;
    objDC.AutoIncrementSeed = 1;
    objDC.AutoIncrementStep = 1;
    objDC.Unique = true;

    objDT.Columns.Add(objDC);
    objDC = new DataColumn("Item", Type.GetType("System.String"));
```

```
objDT.Columns.Add(objDC);
objDC = new DataColumn("Quantity",
    Type.GetType("System.String"));
objDC.DefaultValue = 1;
objDT.Columns.Add(objDC);
objDC = new DataColumn("Cost", Type.GetType("System.Decimal"));
objDT.Columns.Add(objDC);

objDR = objDT.NewRow();
objDR["Item"] = "Widget 1";
objDR["Cost"] = "13.00";
objDT.Rows.Add(objDR);

objDR = objDT.NewRow();
objDR["Item"] = "Widget 2";
objDR["Cost"] = "15.00";
objDT.Rows.Add(objDR);

objDS.Tables.Add(objDT);

int intSumTotal;
intSumTotal = Convert.ToInt32(objDT.Compute("SUM(Cost)", null));
lblTotal.Text = "Your current total is: " +
    intSumTotal.ToString("c");

dg.DataSource = objDS;
dg.DataMember = "Cart";
dg.DataBind();
}
```

As the bolded code shows, first we create a new DataColumn for Cost. Second, we add some values into the Rows collection of the DataTable. Finally, we set a Label control equal to the sum of the values of the rows within the Cost DataColumn. This last step is done over three lines. The first creates an integer[1] variable called intSumTotal. The second line uses the Compute() method, as we discussed, to calculate the sum of the costs in the table and store the result in intSumTotal (note that in C# we must explicitly convert our result to an integer before we can store it). Finally, the last line sets the Label text to display the value we stored in intSumTotal. In order to display the number as a currency value (i.e. with two decimal places), we convert it to this format with a special

---

[1] In this simplistic example, we'll assume that all prices are whole dollar amounts—integers. In a practical application, you may want to use integers as well, as they are more accurate than floating point data types like double, but store the price in cents instead of dollars.

form of the `ToString()` method: `intSumTotal.ToString("c")`, where `"c"` stands for 'currency'.

Of course, we need to add the `Label` control below our `DataGrid`, like so:

File: **AddingDataColumnValues.aspx (excerpt)**

```
<asp:DataGrid id="dg" runat="server" /><br />
<asp:Label id="lblTotal" runat="server" />
```

The result will look similar to Figure 10.13.

Figure 10.13. The `Label` control returns the sum of all rows within the `Cost` `DataColumn`.

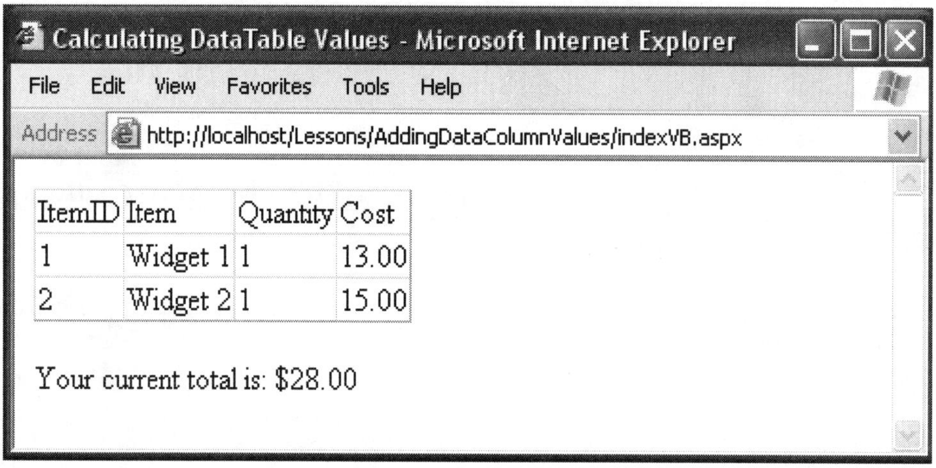

Defining `DataRelations` Between `DataTables`

You can define relationships between your `DataTables` just as you would define relationships between tables in a database. To define a relation between two `DataTables` programmatically, you would use the `DataRelation` class, like so:

VB.NET

```
objRelation = New DataRelation("EmployeesDepartments", _
    objDS.Tables("Departments").Columns("DepartmentID"), _
    objDS.Tables("Employees").Columns("DepartmentID"))
```

Databases require that relationships be established between tables that have a parent-child link (in other words, a one-to-many relationship). `DataSets` require them as well. For this reason, the constructor for the `DataRelation` class accepts three parameters. This first is the name of the relationship, the second is the parent table's primary key column, and the third is the child table's foreign key column.

In the example above, a new `DataRelation` object is created. The `DataRelation` accepts the three parameters: the name of the relationship (`EmployeesDepart-ments`), the second is the primary key column within the `Departments` DataTable, and the third is the foreign key column within the `Employees` DataTable.

Using our intranet example database, we could present a list of departments and all employees that belong to each department, as follows:

VB.NET   File: **DataRelations.aspx (excerpt)**

```
Sub Page_Load()
  Dim objConn As New OleDbConnection( _
    "Provider=Microsoft.Jet.OLEDB.4.0;" & _
    "Data Source=C:\Inetpub\wwwroot\Dorknozzle\Database\" & _
    "dorknozzle.mdb")
  Dim objDA As OleDbDataAdapter
  Dim objDS As New DataSet()
  Dim objDRParent, objDRChild As DataRow
  Dim objRelation As DataRelation

  objDA = New OleDbDataAdapter("SELECT * FROM Employees", objConn)
  objDA.Fill(objDS, "Employees")
  objDA.SelectCommand = New OleDbCommand( _
      "SELECT * FROM Departments", objConn)
  objDA.Fill(objDS, "Departments")

  objRelation = New DataRelation("EmployeesDepartments",
    objDS.Tables("Departments").Columns("DepartmentID"),
    objDS.Tables("Employees").Columns("DepartmentID"))
  objDS.Relations.Add(objRelation)

  For Each objDRParent In objDS.Tables("Departments").Rows
    lblRelations.Text &= "<h3>" & objDRParent("Department") & _
      "</h3>"
    lblRelations.Text &= "<ul>"
    For Each objDRChild In _
        objDRParent.GetChildRows("EmployeesDepartments")
      lblRelations.Text &= "<li>" & objDRChild("Name") & "</li>"
    Next
    lblRelations.Text &= "</ul>"
```

```
    Next
End Sub
```

C#   File: `DataRelations.aspx (excerpt)`

```
void Page_Load() {
  OleDbConnection objConn = new OleDbConnection(
    "Provider=Microsoft.Jet.OLEDB.4.0;" +
    "Data Source=C:\\Inetpub\\wwwroot\\Dorknozzle\\Database\\" +
    "dorknozzle.mdb");
  OleDbDataAdapter objDA;
  DataSet objDS = new DataSet();
  DataRelation objRelation;

  objDA = new OleDbDataAdapter("SELECT * FROM Employees",
      objConn);
  objDA.Fill(objDS, "Employees");
  objDA.SelectCommand = new OleDbCommand( _
      "SELECT * FROM Departments", objConn);
  objDA.Fill(objDS, "Departments");

  objRelation = new DataRelation("EmployeesDepartments",
    objDS.Tables["Departments"].Columns["DepartmentID"],
    objDS.Tables["Employees"].Columns["DepartmentID"]);
  objDS.Relations.Add(objRelation);

  foreach (DataRow objDRParent in
      objDS.Tables["Departments"].Rows) {
    lblRelations.Text += "<h3>" + objDRParent["Department"] +
      "</h3>";
    lblRelations.Text += "<ul>";
    foreach (DataRow objDRChild in
      objDRParent.GetChildRows("EmployeesDepartments")) {
      lblRelations.Text += "<li>" + objDRChild["Name"] + "</li>";
    }
    lblRelations.Text += "</ul>";
  }
}
```

Half the code above should look relatively familiar—it builds on the code we've already seen in the first part of this chapter. We're simply establishing a connection, creating a DataSet and a DataAdapter to fill it, filling the DataSet with our Employees DataTable, and then filling the same DataSet with our Departments DataTable.

The real work begins when the `objRelation` variable is set to a new instance of the `DataRelation`. We've called the `DataRelation` `EmployeesDepartments`, simply because it's a relationship between those two `DataTables`. As we saw before, the second and third parameters used to create the relation are the primary and foreign key columns, respectively. Next, we add the `DataRelation` to the `DataSet` as follows:

VB.NET   File: **DataRelations.aspx (excerpt)**
```
objDS.Relations.Add(objRelation)
```

C#   File: **DataRelations.aspx (excerpt)**
```
objDS.Relations.Add(objRelation);
```

Now, we can simply loop through the rows of the parent table (`Departments`) and write the contents within a `Label` control, as follows:

VB.NET   File: **DataRelations.aspx (excerpt)**
```
For Each objDRParent In objDS.Tables("Departments").Rows
  lblRelations.Text &= "<h3>" & objDRParent("Department") & _
    "</h3>"
Next
```

C#   File: **DataRelations.aspx (excerpt)**
```
foreach (DataRow objDRParent in _
    objDS.Tables["Departments"].Rows) {
  lblRelations.Text += "<h3>" + objDRParent["Department"] +
    "</h3>";
}
```

Within the above `For Each` loop, we create a second, nested `For Each` loop to iterate through the rows of the parent table and write those results within the `Label` control, like so:

VB.NET   File: **DataRelations.aspx (excerpt)**
```
    lblRelations.Text &= "<ul>"
    For Each objDRChild In _
        objDRParent.GetChildRows("EmployeesDepartments")
      lblRelations.Text &= "<li>" & objDRChild("Name") & "</li>"
    Next
    lblRelations.Text &= "</ul>"
```

C#   File: **DataRelations.aspx (excerpt)**
```
    lblRelations.Text += "<ul>";
    foreach (DataRow objDRChild in
```

```
      objDRParent.GetChildRows("EmployeesDepartments")) {
    lblRelations.Text += "<li>" + objDRChild["Name"] + "</li>";
  }
  lblRelations.Text += "</ul>";
```

You'll notice that we're not looping through the Employees DataTable specifically. Doing so would simply write out a list of all employees in one spot. Instead, we loop through the *child* rows of the parent table using the GetChildRows() method, and passing in the name of the DataRelation object.

All that's left is to make sure we have a Label control with ID lblRelations to display all this data:

File: **DataRelations.aspx (excerpt)**

```
<asp:Label id="lblRelations" runat="server"/>
```

This gives us our list of employees for each department, similar to Figure 10.14.

Figure 10.14. All employees for each department are displayed within a list.

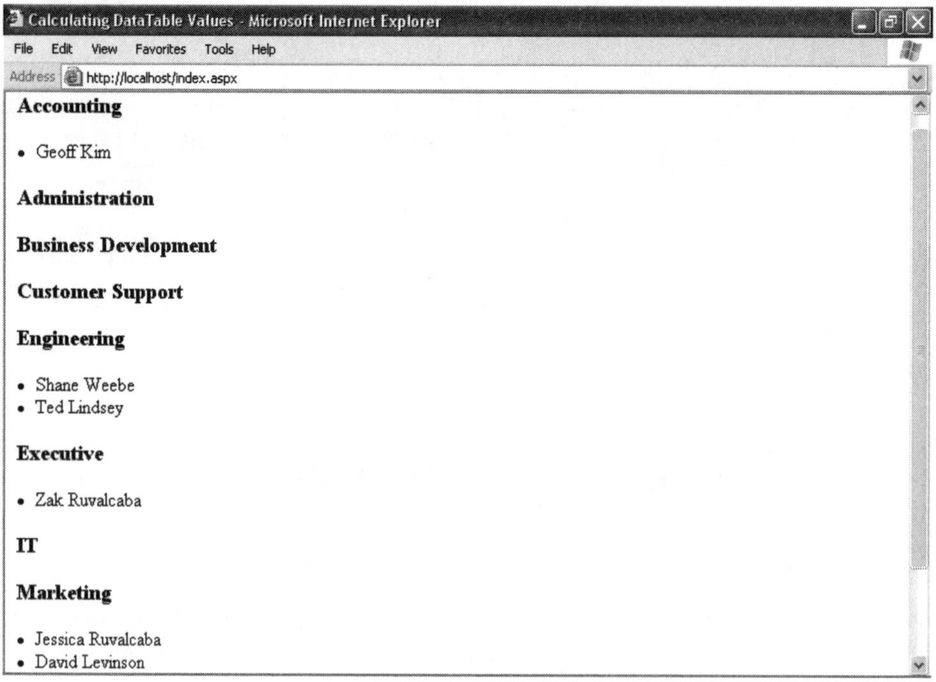

404

If you create `DataRelations.aspx` yourself, don't forget to import the `System.Data.OleDb` namespace. You can, of course, use MSDE if you prefer, by making the usual adjustments to the code. As usual, the completed file is available in the code archive.

Understanding `DataViews`

`DataViews` are arguably one of the most important aspects of the `DataSet` class. As I mentioned in the first few sections of this chapter, you can bind a `DataSet` to a `DataGrid` using the following code:

```
dg.DataSource = objDS
dg.DataBind()
```

I also mentioned that this was shorthand for writing the following:

```
dg.DataSource = objDS.Tables("Table Name").DefaultView
dg.DataBind()
```

Technically, you can't bind an entire `DataSet` to a data control, or even an entire `DataTable`; instead, you must bind a `DataView`. `DataViews` represent a customized view of a `DataTable` for sorting, filtering, searching, editing, and navigation. For instance, the following code creates a new instance of the `DataView` class, sets the `objDV` variable equal to the `DefaultView` of the `Employees DataTable`, filters out all but one employee using the `RowFilter` property of the `DataView`, and, thus, only binds `Zak Ruvalcaba` to the `DataGrid`:

VB.NET
```
Dim objDV As DataView
objDV = objDS.Tables("Employees").DefaultView
objDV.RowFilter = "Name = 'Zak Ruvalcaba'"
dg.DataSource = objDV
dg.DataBind()
```

C#
```
DataView objDV;
objDV = objDS.Tables["Employees"].DefaultView;
objDV.RowFilter = "Name = 'Zak Ruvalcaba'";
dg.DataSource = objDV;
dg.DataBind();
```

The question is: why would you ever want to return one result to a `DataView`? This question and others will be answered in the next couple of sections, through which you'll learn more about filtering records and sorting records within DataViews.

Filtering DataViews

As I suggested in the previous section, you can filter the records held within a DataTable for presentation using DataViews. The DataView has a property named RowFilter that allows you to specify an expression similar to that of an SQL statement's WHERE clause. For instance, the following filter selects all employees with names that contain Ruvalcaba:

VB.NET   File: **DataViewsFiltering.aspx (excerpt)**

```
Sub Page_Load()
  Dim objConn As New OleDbConnection( _
    "Provider=Microsoft.Jet.OLEDB.4.0;" & _
    "Data Source=C:\Inetpub\wwwroot\Dorknozzle\Database\" & _
    "dorknozzle.mdb")
  Dim objDA As OleDbDataAdapter
  Dim objDS As New DataSet()
  Dim objDV As DataView

  objDA = New OleDbDataAdapter("SELECT * FROM Employees", objConn)
  objDA.Fill(objDS, "Employees")

  objDV = objDS.Tables("Employees").DefaultView
  objDV.RowFilter = "Name LIKE '%Ruvalcaba%'"
  ddlEmployees.DataSource = objDV
  ddlEmployees.DataValueField = "EmployeeID"
  ddlEmployees.DataTextField = "Name"
  ddlEmployees.DataBind()
End Sub
```

C#   File: **DataViewsFiltering.aspx (excerpt)**

```
void Page_Load() {
  OleDbConnection objConn = new OleDbConnection(
    "Provider=Microsoft.Jet.OLEDB.4.0;" +
    "Data Source=C:\\Inetpub\\wwwroot\\Dorknozzle\\Database\\" +
    "dorknozzle.mdb");
  OleDbDataAdapter objDA;
  DataSet objDS = new DataSet();
  DataView objDV;

  objDA = new OleDbDataAdapter("SELECT * FROM Employees",
      objConn);
```

```
objDA.Fill(objDS, "Employees");

objDV = objDS.Tables["Employees"].DefaultView;
objDV.RowFilter = "Name LIKE '%Ruvalcaba%'";
ddlEmployees.DataSource = objDV;
ddlEmployees.DataValueField = "EmployeeID";
ddlEmployees.DataTextField = "Name";
ddlEmployees.DataBind();
}
```

You can try this yourself, by using this Page_Load() code along with the following DropDownList control to display the results:

File: **DataViewsFiltering.aspx (excerpt)**

```
<asp:DropDownList id="ddlEmployees" runat="server" />
```

Open the new page in your browser, and you should get something like Figure 10.15.

Figure 10.15. The RowFilter property of the DataView allows you to specify an expression for filtering records within a DataTable.

Following the code, we get the default view of the DataTable and store it in a variable. Next, we select only the records that we want to present, using the RowFilter property, and, finally, we bind the view to the DropDownList control. Similarly, we could add the NOT keyword before the LIKE keyword to filter out all employees with the name Ruvalcaba, as follows:

VB.NET   File: **DataViewsFiltering.aspx (excerpt)**

```
objDV.RowFilter = "Name NOT LIKE '%Ruvalcaba%'"
```

In this case, all other employees are returned and used to populate the DropDownList control, similar to Figure 10.16.

Figure 10.16. All employees that do not contain the name Ruvalcaba are returned to the DropDownList control.

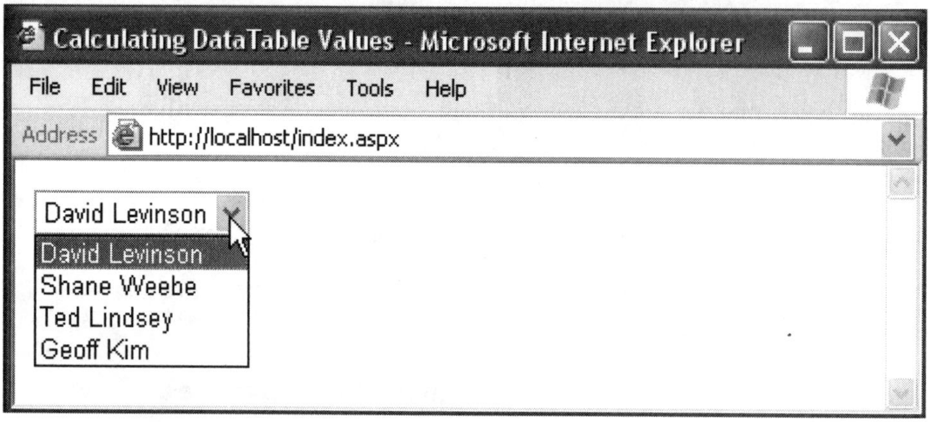

Sorting Columns in a **DataGrid**

Another great feature of the DataGrid control is that it offers the ability to sort columns. Figure 10.17 shows how we can click a linked header within our DataGrid to sort alphabetically through columns.

Figure 10.17. You can sort through the columns in a `DataGrid` alphabetically.

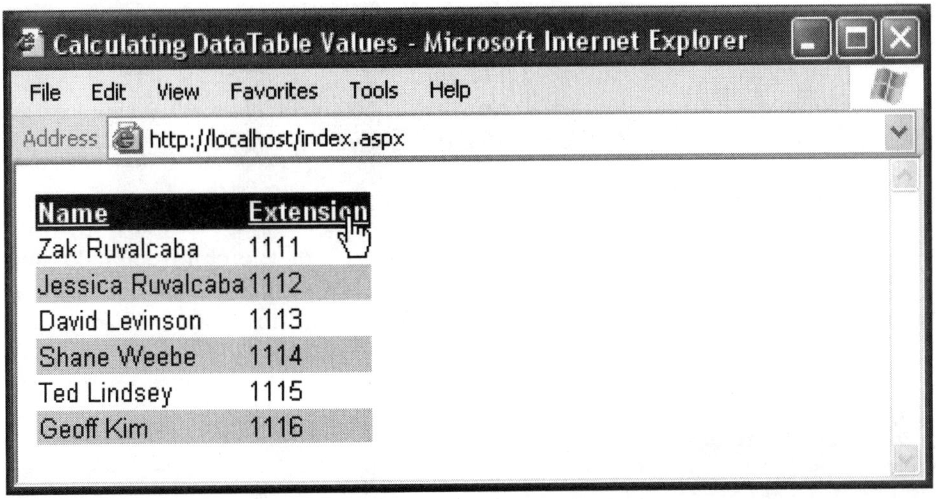

The `DataGrid`, in conjunction with the `Sort` property of the `DataView`, can allow your users easily and intuitively to sort through columns in the `DataGrid`. Let's build a new page to try this. Start with the `<form>` tag shown below, which contains a run-of-the-mill `DataGrid`:

File: **DataViewsSorting.aspx** (excerpt)

```
<form runat="server">
<asp:DataGrid id="dgEmployees" runat="server"
    AutoGenerateColumns="false" GridLines="None">
  <ItemStyle Font-Name="Arial" Font-Size="10pt"
      ForeColor="#000000" />
  <HeaderStyle Font-Name="Arial" Font-Size="10pt" Font-Bold="true"
      BackColor="#003366" ForeColor="#FFFFFF" />
  <AlternatingItemStyle Font-Name="Arial" Font-Size="10pt"
      BackColor="#CCCCCC" />
  <Columns>
    <asp:BoundColumn DataField="Name" HeaderText="Name" />
    <asp:BoundColumn DataField="Extension" HeaderText="Extension"
        />
  </Columns>
</asp:DataGrid>
</form>
```

Next, enable sorting within the `DataGrid` by setting the `AllowSorting` property to `True`. We'll also want an `OnSortCommand` attribute that gives a suitable name for the event handler. When a user clicks a column header, the event "bubbles up" to the parent control, the `SortCommand` event is raised, and the named method will be called:

File: **DataViewsSorting.aspx (excerpt)**

```
<asp:DataGrid id="dgEmployees" runat="server"
    AutoGenerateColumns="false" GridLines="None"
    AllowSorting="true" OnSortCommand="dgEmployees_Sort">
```

Next, we need to assign a sort expression for each of the child `BoundColumn` controls of the `DataGrid`. For our purposes, the sort expression should be the same as the column within the `DataTable` that's bound to the `DataGrid`:

File: **DataViewsSorting.aspx (excerpt)**

```
<asp:BoundColumn DataField="Name" HeaderText="Name"
    SortExpression="Name" />
<asp:BoundColumn DataField="Extension" HeaderText="Extension"
    SortExpression="Extension" />
```

As we'll see in a moment, the sort expression is passed to the `dgEmployees_Sort()` method as an argument.

The complete `DataGrids` now looks like this:

File: **DataViewsSorting.aspx (excerpt)**

```
<form runat="server">
<asp:DataGrid id="dgEmployees" runat="server"
    AutoGenerateColumns="false" GridLines="None"
    OnSortCommand="dgEmployees_Sort" AllowSorting="true">
  <ItemStyle Font-Name="Arial" Font-Size="10pt"
      ForeColor="#000000" />
  <HeaderStyle Font-Name="Arial" Font-Size="10pt" Font-Bold="true"
      BackColor="#003366" ForeColor="#FFFFFF" />
  <AlternatingItemStyle Font-Name="Arial" Font-Size="10pt"
      BackColor="#CCCCCC" />
  <Columns>
    <asp:BoundColumn DataField="Name" HeaderText="Name"
        SortExpression="Name" />
    <asp:BoundColumn DataField="Extension" HeaderText="Extension"
        SortExpression="Extension" />
  </Columns>
</asp:DataGrid>
</form>
```

Next, we add the Page_Load() event handler within our code declaration block:

```
VB.NET                                    File: DataViewsSorting.aspx (excerpt)
Dim objDV As DataView

Sub Page_Load()
  Dim objConn As New OleDbConnection( _
    "Provider=Microsoft.Jet.OLEDB.4.0;" & _
    "Data Source=C:\Inetpub\wwwroot\Dorknozzle\Database\" & _
    "dorknozzle.mdb")
  Dim objDA As OleDbDataAdapter
  Dim objDS As New DataSet()

  objDA = New OleDbDataAdapter("SELECT * FROM Employees", objConn)
  objDA.Fill(objDS, "Employees")

  objDV = objDS.Tables("Employees").DefaultView

  dgEmployees.DataSource = objDV
  dgEmployees.DataBind()
End Sub
```

```
C#                                        File: DataViewsSorting.aspx (excerpt)
DataView objDV;

void Page_Load() {
  OleDbConnection objConn = new OleDbConnection(
    "Provider=Microsoft.Jet.OLEDB.4.0;" +
    "Data Source=C:\\Inetpub\\wwwroot\\Dorknozzle\\Database\\" +
    "dorknozzle.mdb");
  OleDbDataAdapter objDA;
  DataSet objDS = new DataSet();

  objDA = new OleDbDataAdapter("SELECT * FROM Employees",
      objConn);
  objDA.Fill(objDS, "Employees");

  objDV = objDS.Tables["Employees"].DefaultView;

  dgEmployees.DataSource = objDV;
  dgEmployees.DataBind();
}
```

This code will begin to look similar to that created in previous examples. We're simply creating a new Connection, DataAdapter, and DataSet, filling the

DataTable within the DataSet with the data returned from the database, and putting the default view of the DataTable into a variable, objDV. Finally, we bind the DataView to the DataGrid. Next, you can add the dgEmployees_Sort() event handler as follows:

VB.NET   File: **DataViewsSorting.aspx (excerpt)**

```
Sub dgEmployees_Sort(s As Object, _
    e As DataGridSortCommandEventArgs)
  objDV.Sort = e.SortExpression
  dgEmployees.DataSource = objDV
  dgEmployees.DataBind()
End Sub
```

C#   File: **DataViewsSorting.aspx (excerpt)**

```
void dgEmployees_Sort(Object s, DataGridSortCommandEventArgs e) {
  objDV.Sort = e.SortExpression;
  dgEmployees.DataSource = objDV;
  dgEmployees.DataBind();
}
```

As you can see, the method accepts a DataGridSortCommandEventArgs argument. This parameter allows us to work with the SortExpression passed in from a child control (BoundColumn) of the DataGrid. Next, we use the Sort property of the DataView and set it equal to the SortExpression property of e, the DataGridSortCommandEventArgs object. Finally, we bind the new DataView to the DataGrid to produce the results. Open the new page in your browser and try to click on the Name or Extension column to sort through the records either alphabetically or numerically.

Updating a Database from a Modified DataSet

So far, we've used the DataSet exclusively for retrieving and binding database data to a data control such as a DataGrid. The opposite operation, updating data within a database from a DataSet, is also possible using the Update() method of the DataAdapter.

The DataAdapter has the following four properties, which represent the main database commands:

☐ SelectCommand

❏ InsertCommand

❏ UpdateCommand

❏ DeleteCommand

You've already seen the SelectCommand and its usage. When you want to insert multiple tables into the same DataSet, you can simply set the SelectCommand of the DataAdapter equal to a new OleDbCommand object before calling Fill(). The other three properties are quite similar, except that you must call the Update() method instead. If you want to insert records into a database, simply add the records to your DataSet and call the Update() method of the DataAdapter—the InsertCommand is called automatically to perform the insert. Similarly, when you want to update existing records within a database, simply modify the DataSet accordingly and call the Update() method of the DataAdapter—the UpdateCommand is called automatically. Likewise, if you remove one item and then insert two new items into a DataSet and then call the Update() method of the DataAdapter, a DeleteCommand and two UpdateCommands are executed.

The next example selects all departments from the Departments table, and binds them to a DataGrid. Next, it performs the following insert, update, and delete operations:

❏ Adds a new department called IS

❏ Modifies the Business Development department

❏ Deletes the Administration department

Once the insert, update, and delete occur, the modified results are bound to a second DataGrid.

Let's take a look at how we'll accomplish this, beginning with the Page_Load() method. First, we create variables for all the objects we need, including: Connection, DataAdapter, DataSet, DataTable, DataRow, and a CommandBuilder—which we'll discuss in a moment.

VB.NET   File: **UpdatingDatabaseUsingDataSet.aspx (excerpt)**

```
Sub Page_Load()
  Dim objConn As New OleDbConnection( _
    "Provider=Microsoft.Jet.OLEDB.4.0;" & _
    "Data Source=C:\Inetpub\wwwroot\Dorknozzle\Database\" & _
```

```
      "dorknozzle.mdb")
    Dim objDA As OleDbDataAdapter
    Dim objDS As New DataSet()
    Dim objDT As DataTable
    Dim objDR As DataRow
    Dim objCB As OleDbCommandBuilder
```

C#   File: **UpdatingDatabaseUsingDataSet.aspx** (excerpt)

```csharp
void Page_Load() {
  OleDbConnection objConn = new OleDbConnection(
    "Provider=Microsoft.Jet.OLEDB.4.0;" +
    "Data Source=C:\\Inetpub\\wwwroot\\Dorknozzle\\Database\\" +
    "dorknozzle.mdb");
  OleDbDataAdapter objDA;
  DataSet objDS = new DataSet();
  DataTable objDT;
  DataRow objDR;
  OleDbCommandBuilder objCB;
```

Next, we create a new DataAdapter object that queries the Departments table. We fill our empty DataSet with the department data, and then store the resulting DataTable in objDT, for easy access:

VB.NET   File: **UpdatingDatabaseUsingDataSet.aspx** (excerpt)

```vbnet
objDA = New OleDbDataAdapter("SELECT * FROM Departments", _
    objConn)
objDA.Fill(objDS, "Departments")
objDT = objDS.Tables("Departments")
```

C#   File: **UpdatingDatabaseUsingDataSet.aspx** (excerpt)

```csharp
objDA = new OleDbDataAdapter("SELECT * FROM Departments",
    objConn);
objDA.Fill(objDS, "Departments");
objDT = objDS.Tables["Departments"];
```

Next, we'll bind the data to the DataGrid:

VB.NET   File: **UpdatingDatabaseUsingDataSet.aspx** (excerpt)

```vbnet
dgDepartments.DataSource = objDS
dgDepartments.DataBind()
```

C#   File: **UpdatingDatabaseUsingDataSet.aspx** (excerpt)

```csharp
dgDepartments.DataSource = objDS;
dgDepartments.DataBind();
```

Now, let's add a new row to the `DataTable` by calling the `NewRow()` method of the `DataTable`. Next, we'll add a value to the `Department` column and add the row into the `DataTable`:

VB.NET   File: **UpdatingDatabaseUsingDataSet.aspx (excerpt)**

```
objDR = objDT.NewRow()
objDR("Department") = "IS"
objDT.Rows.Add(objDR)
```

C#   File: **UpdatingDatabaseUsingDataSet.aspx (excerpt)**

```
objDR = objDT.NewRow();
objDR["Department"] = "IS";
objDT.Rows.Add(objDR);
```

Next, we'll update the third row in the `DataTable` (`Business Development`) by accessing the `Rows` collection of the `DataTable`. Next, we set the new value of the `Department` column for that row:

VB.NET   File: **UpdatingDatabaseUsingDataSet.aspx (excerpt)**

```
objDR = objDT.Rows(2)
objDR("Department") = "BusDev"
```

C#   File: **UpdatingDatabaseUsingDataSet.aspx (excerpt)**

```
objDR = objDT.Rows[2];
objDR["Department"] = "BusDev";
```

Finally, we can delete the second row within the `DataTable` (`Administration`) by calling the `Delete()` method for that row:

VB.NET   File: **UpdatingDatabaseUsingDataSet.aspx (excerpt)**

```
objDT.Rows(1).Delete()
```

C#   File: **UpdatingDatabaseUsingDataSet.aspx (excerpt)**

```
objDT.Rows[1].Delete();
```

Now the *real* work begins. We create an `OleDbCommandBuilder` object, passing in our `DataAdapter`. The `CommandBuilder` object is responsible for detecting modifications to the `DataTable` and deciding what needs to be inserted, updated, or deleted to apply those changes to the database. Having done this, it generates the necessary SQL commands and stores them in the `DataAdapter` for the `Update()` method to use. It should be no surprise, then, that our next action is to call the `Update()` method of the `DataAdapter` object, passing in the `DataSet` and the name of the `DataTable` that needs updating:

VB.NET   File: **UpdatingDatabaseUsingDataSet.aspx (excerpt)**

```
objCB = New OleDbCommandBuilder(objDA)
objDA.Update(objDS, "Departments")
```

C#   File: **UpdatingDatabaseUsingDataSet.aspx (excerpt)**

```
objCB = new OleDbCommandBuilder(objDA);
objDA.Update(objDS, "Departments");
```

Finally, we bind the updated `DataSet` to a second `DataGrid`:

VB.NET   File: **UpdatingDatabaseUsingDataSet.aspx (excerpt)**

```
dgDepartmentsModified.DataSource = objDS
dgDepartmentsModified.DataBind()
End Sub
```

C#   File: **UpdatingDatabaseUsingDataSet.aspx (excerpt)**

```
dgDepartmentsModified.DataSource = objDS;
dgDepartmentsModified.DataBind();
}
```

The last thing we need to do is create the controls we're using in the `<form>` tag:

File: **UpdatingDatabaseUsingDataSet.aspx (excerpt)**

```
<form runat="server">
<h1>Original Table</h1>
<asp:DataGrid id="dgDepartments" runat="server" />
<h1>Modified Table</h1>
<asp:DataGrid id="dgDepartmentsModified" runat="server" />
</form>
```

That's all there is to it! Save your work and run the page within the browser. Figure 10.18 shows the original `DataGrid` on top and the modified `DataGrid` on the bottom.

Figure 10.18. The first `DataGrid` shows the original data. The second `DataGrid` shows the modified data.

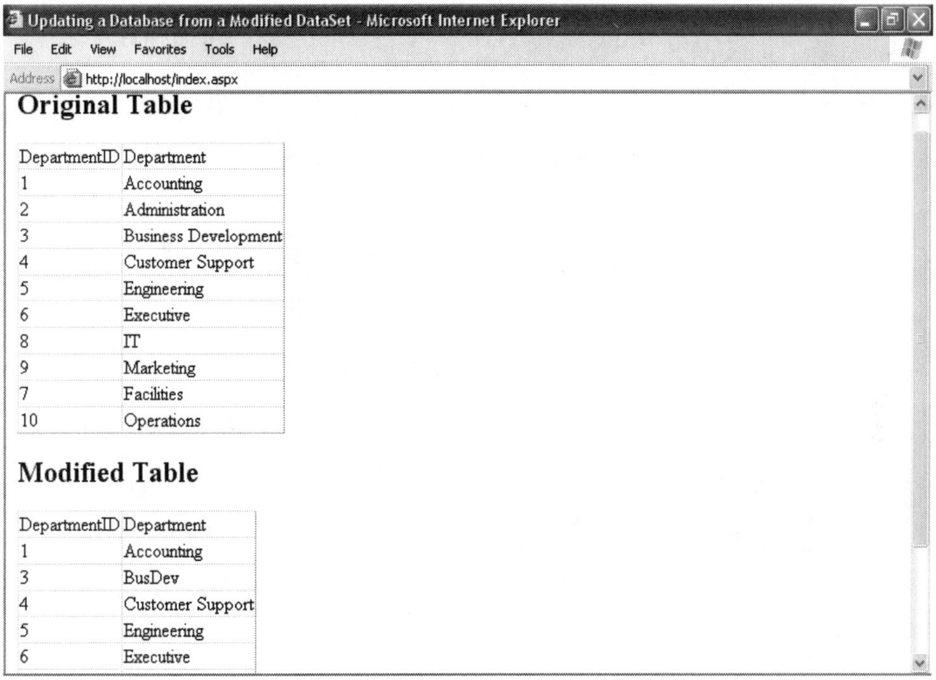

Figure 10.19 shows how the database was also modified.

Figure 10.19. The database is also updated with the new row, modified department, and deleted department.

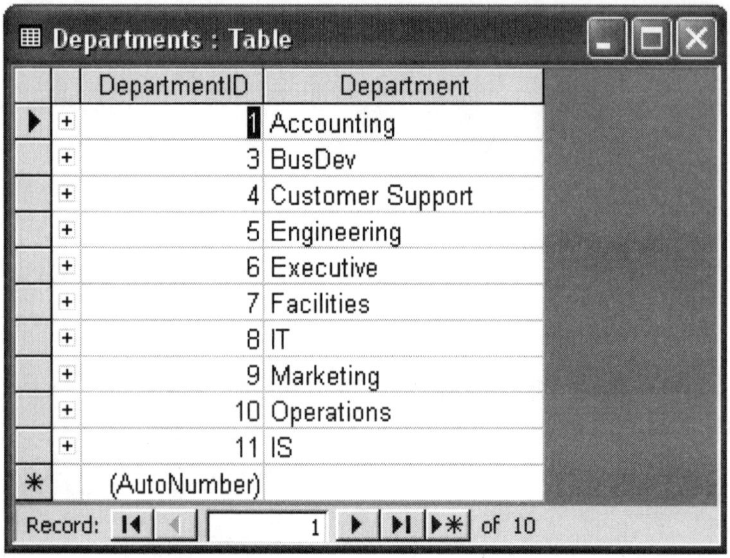

Summary

This chapter, the most advanced we've seen so far, has taught you some important concepts about ADO.NET, specifically, about DataSets. You learned that ADO.NET includes many new enhancements, including the new DataSet object. First, you learned about the DataSet and how to use it in our intranet Web application. You then moved on to learn about the constructs of DataSets, including DataTables, DataAdapters, DataRelations, and DataViews. Then, you learned about the elements within a DataTable, including DataColumns and DataRows. Later, you learned about creating DataTables, DataColumns, and DataRows programmatically, and even learned about the properties that each class has. Finally, you looked at sorting and filtering using DataViews and saw how to update a data source from a modified DataSet using the CommandBuilder and the Update() method of the DataAdapter object.

11

Web Applications

Although I've referred to "ASP.NET Web applications" many times in this book, as yet, we haven't really discussed their defining characteristics, nor even set up a true ASP.NET Web application. Granted, we have created the Dorknozzle Intranet Application, but so far, we've simply housed it in a regular subfolder of our wwwroot folder. In this chapter, we'll be looking closer at what ASP.NET Web applications are, what they have to do with IIS Virtual Directories, and the benefits of creating and defining ASP.NET applications within IIS.

Once you have a solid understanding of applications within IIS, we'll then talk about application state and discuss how we can work with application-level variables. During our discussion of application state, we'll dive into the Global.asax file and look at how to handle application Start, Init, and BeginRequest events.

Next, we'll cover important application configuration topics with the Web.config file, discuss each of the configuration sections within it, and explore how you can customize its sections to meet your development needs. We'll then get into important ASP.NET caching techniques and see how you can utilize ASP.NET's built-in caching properties to increase application performance. We'll finish the chapter with a quick overview of user sessions. We'll talk about the ways in which you can use session variables to store for each user data that can be used for the duration of that user's visit.

It's an action-packed chapter—let's get cracking!

Overview of ASP.NET Applications

Microsoft defines a **Web Application** as the collection of all files, pages, handlers, modules, and executable code that can be invoked or run within a given directory on a Web server. You can create an application from an existing Website subfolder off the wwwroot folder by performing the following steps:

1. Access the Internet Services Manager by selecting Start, Programs, Administrative Tools, Internet Information Services[1]. Windows 2000 Professional users can find the Internet Information Services icon in the Administrative Tools section of the Control Panel.

2. Expand the node for your computer in the left-hand pane, then expand in turn the Web Sites and Default Web Site nodes that appear. All the folders that exist within the wwwroot directory will be listed.

3. Right-click on the directory that you want to turn into a Web application (e.g. the directory that contains the Dorknozzle Intranet Application files), and select Properties.

4. Click the Create button located within the lower Application Settings panel of the Directory tab.

5. The Web application is created using the same name as the folder you selected by default, although you can change it if you wish. Click OK.

By defining the directory as an IIS application, you've essentially isolated all that directory's pages and subdirectories into what is called an **application domain**. Separating your Websites into these application domains has numerous benefits:

Code Isolation   Code that executes within one application cannot access code located within a different application. The benefit here is that you can host many different types of applications on the same Web server without worrying about cross-referencing code or resources from a different application. So, even if we built an intranet

---

[1]If the Administrative Tools folder is not visible in your Windows XP Start Menu, adjust your Taskbar and Start Menu Properties (right-click on the Taskbar and choose Properties) to make this item visible. On the Start Menu tab, click Customize…, then on the Advanced tab under Start menu items set the System Administrative Tools item to be visible on the All Programs menu.

Web application and a generic Web application for external users within the same Web server, code would never cross reference or conflict between those two applications.

Application Stabilization

Because each application is isolated from all others, if one application crashes or stops running, it has no effect on other applications within the same Web server.

Application Level Security Policies

You can set different permissions for different applications. What this means is that the credentials used for logging into one application can be totally different from those used to access a second application. This will be discussed with greater detail in Chapter 14.

Configure Settings per Application

There are numerous other configuration settings you can affect for each application through Internet Services Manager, and by utilizing two files, `Global.asax` and `Web.config`, both of which are found in the root directory of the application.

The `Global.asax` file handles application-wide events and defines objects declared with application scope, while the `Web.config` file specifies configuration settings that apply to the application as a whole. We'll talk more about the `Global.asax` file and the `Web.config` file a little later.

In addition to these two special files, every ASP.NET application defined within Internet Services Manager may contain an additional special directory, called `bin` (which takes its name from "binary files," rather than having anything to do with a dustbin). This directory is used to store custom **Assemblies**. Discussed in greater detail in Chapter 17, assemblies are precompiled files, usually with the `.dll` filename extension, that contain code that you wish to reuse within your applications. But, that's not all! Assemblies don't have to be stored and used with only one application. Utilizing the **Global Assembly Cache (GAC)**, a given assembly may be shared across multiple applications. The GAC is a special folder called `assembly`, and is located within the `Windows` or `WINNT` directory of the server.

Using Application State

You can save variables and objects you want to use throughout an entire application by storing them within **application state**—this allows you to share these items between all pages in a particular ASP.NET application very easily. Application state is related to another Web application concept, called **session state**. The key difference between the two is that sessions store variables and objects for one particular user for the duration of their current visit, or **browser session**, whereas application state stores objects and variables that are shared between all users of an application at the same time. Thus, application state is ideal for storing data that is constantly being reused by multiple users of the same application. In ASP.NET, session and application state are both implemented as collections, with which you should be fairly familiar by now. For example, we could store a `DataSet` within application state like so:

VB.NET
```
Application("DataSet") = objDS
```

C#, of course, uses square brackets for collections:

C#
```
Application["DataSet"] = objDS;
```

Any pages in that application can then retrieve and bind this `DataSet` directly to a `DataGrid`, simply by binding the `DataGrid` to the application variable as follows:

VB.NET
```
dgMyDataGrid.DataSource = Application("DataSet")
dgMyDataGrid.DataBind()
```

C#
```
dgMyDataGrid.DataSource = Application["DataSet"];
dgMyDataGrid.DataBind();
```

In traditional ASP, developers used application state to cache data. Although there's nothing to prevent you from doing so here, ASP.NET provides a new object, `Cache`, specifically for that purpose. We'll discuss the `Cache` object in greater detail later in this chapter. You can remove an object from application state using the `Remove()` method, as follows:

VB.NET
```
Application.Remove("DataSet")
```

If you find you have multiple objects and application variables lingering about in application state, you can remove them all at once using the `RemoveAll()` method, as follows:

•

VB.NET

```
Application.RemoveAll()
```

It's important to be cautious when using application variables. Objects remain in application state until the application is shut down in IIS, or you remove them using either the `Remove()` or `RemoveAll()` methods. Inappropriate use of application state can therefore waste server resources, and dramatically decrease performance within your applications.

Let's take a look at a classic example of an application variable in use. The following example uses an application variable to create a page hit counter:

VB.NET   File: **ApplicationState/ApplicationState.aspx**

```
<html>
<head>
<title>Application State (Page Counter)</title>
<script language="VB" runat="server">
Sub Page_Load()
  Application("PageCounter") += 1
  lblCounter.Text = Application("PageCounter")
End Sub
</script>
</head>
<body>
The page has been requested:
<asp:Label id="lblCounter" runat="server" /> times!
</body>
</html>
```

C#   File: **ApplicationState/ApplicationState.aspx**

```
<html>
<head>
<title>Application State (Page Counter)</title>
<script language="C#" runat="server">
void Page_Load() {
  if (Application["PageCounter"] == null) {
    Application["PageCounter"] = 0;
  }
  Application["PageCounter"] =
      (int)Application["PageCounter"] + 1;
  lblCounter.Text = Convert.ToString(Application["PageCounter"]);
}
</script>
</head>
<body>
```

```
<asp:Label id="lblCounter" runat="server" /> times!
</body>
</html>
```

As you can see, the above code increments the `PageCounter` application variable every time the page is loaded. Notice that because the `Application` collection stores everything as a generic `Object` type, the C# code has to do a bit more work to set up the application variable when it doesn't exist (when it equals null), and convert the application variable to the type it expects (an integer); VB.NET handles such conversions automatically. Next, a `Label` control's `Text` property is set to the value of the variable. Try saving your work and testing the results within the browser. In Figure 11.1, the page tells us that it has been requested once.

Figure 11.1. The first time the page loads, the `Label` control will tell you that it has been requested once.

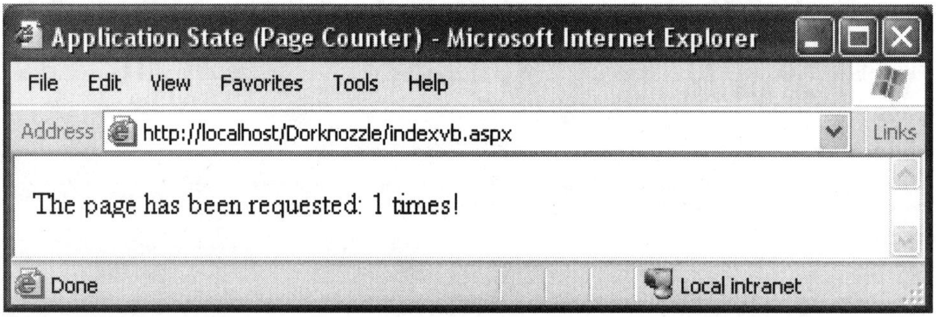

Try refreshing the page. This time it should increment to two. Now, close the browser window altogether, and reopen it. Because we're storing the value within application state, the page count remembers its previous value. Figure 11.2 shows how we now have had three requests.

Figure 11.2. Close the browser, reopen it, launch the hit counter page. This time, the request count indicates three.

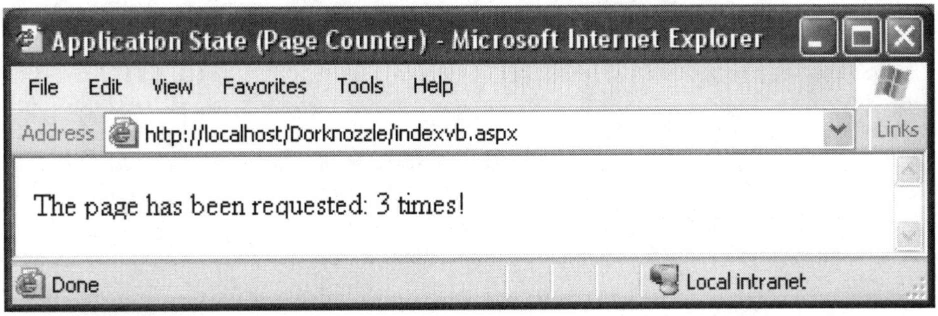

Yet, there's one small problem with our code. If two people were to open the page at the same time, the value could increment only by one, rather than two. The reason for this has to do with this line:

VB.NET   File: **ApplicationState/ApplicationState.aspx (excerpt)**
```
Application("PageCounter") += 1
```

This line is actually shorthand for the following:

VB.NET
```
Application("PageCounter") = Application("PageCounter") + 1
```

The expression to the right of the = operator is evaluated first. To do this, the server must read the value of the **PageCounter** variable stored in the application. It then adds one to this value before storing it back into the **PageCounter** variable.

Now, if two users are visiting this page at the same time, the copy of this code running for the first visitor might read the **PageCounter** variable and obtain a value of, say, **3**, to which it would add **1** to obtain **4**. But before it had a chance to store this new value into the **PageCounter** variable, the copy of the code running for the second user might read it and *also* obtain the value **3**. Both copies of the page will have read the same value, and both will store an updated value of **4**!

Instead, we want to lock the variable for each user, increment the variable (reading its current value and then storing the new value), and then unlock it so that other users are able to do the same thing in turn. We can modify our code slightly to achieve this:

```
VB.NET                                    File: ApplicationState/ApplicationState.aspx (excerpt)
Sub Page_Load()
  Application.Lock()
  Application("PageCounter") += 1
  lblCounter.Text = Application("PageCounter")
  Application.UnLock()
End Sub
```

```
C#                                        File: ApplicationState/ApplicationState.aspx (excerpt)
void Page_Load() {
  Application.Lock();
  if (Application["PageCounter"] == null) {
    Application["PageCounter"] = 0;
  }
  Application["PageCounter"] =
      (int)Application["PageCounter"] + 1;
  lblCounter.Text = Convert.ToString(Application["PageCounter"]);
  Application.UnLock();
}
```

In this case, the Lock() method guarantees that only one user can work with the application variable at any one time. Next, we call the UnLock() method to unlock the application variable for the next request. Our use of Lock() and UnLock() in this scenario guarantees that the application variable is incremented by one for each visit to the page.

Working With the Global.asax File

As I mentioned earlier, the Global.asax file is a special file that can be added to the root of an application. The Global.asax file defines handlers for application-wide events, and these handlers can be used to declare application-wide objects. For instance, the Application_Start() handler is executed the first time the application runs after we've restarted the server. We could define the Application_Start() event handler to load a DataSet within an application variable for use throughout the life of the application. All users could then make use of the application variable (containing the DataSet) within the code at any time. Another handler is Application_Error(), into which we can place code that is to be performed whenever an unhandled error occurs within a page. The following is a list of handlers that you'll use most often within the Global.asax file:

Application_AuthenticateRequest()
Raised before authenticating a user

`Application_AuthorizeRequest()`
Raised before authorizing a user

`Application_BeginRequest()`
Raised by every request to the server

`Application_End()`
Raised immediately before the end of all application instances

`Application_EndRequest()`
Raised at the end of every request to the server

`Application_Error()`
Raised by an unhandled error in the application

`Application_PreSendRequestContent()`
Raised before sending content to the browser

`Application_PreSendRequestHeaders()`
Raised before sending headers to the browser

`Application_Start()`
Raised immediately after the application is created; this event occurs once only

`Dispose()`
Raised immediately before the end of an application instance

`Init()`
Raised immediately after each application instance is created; this event can occur more than once

The `Global.asax` file is created very easily. Simply open a new page in your favorite text editor, add the event handler to the page, insert the code you want handled when the event is raised, and finally, save your work as `Global.asax`. A typical event handler within a `Global.asax` file resembles the following:

VB.NET
```
Sub Application_EventName(sender As Object, e As EventArgs)
    ...
End Sub
```

```
C#
void Application_EventName(Object sender, EventArgs e) {
  ...
}
```

Changes to Global.asax

Be cautious when you add and modify code within the `Global.asax` file.
Any additions or modifications you make within this file will cause the application to restart, losing any data stored in application state.

To demonstrate the use of the `Global.asax` file, let's look at the
`Application_Start()` event handler. You can use this event to initialize variables
or objects for an application only once, and keep them active for the lifetime of
the application. Imagine that we've just launched our intranet Web application
for the first time, and we want to store all the items contained within the `Employ-`
`eeStore` database table in a `DataSet` within application state. Doing this would
improve performance because the `Connection`, `Command`, and `DataSet` objects
are created just once, not every time a user requests items from the `EmployeeStore`
table. If a different user accesses the employee store, the `DataSet` will again be
taken from the application state. All the items remain in application state until
an item is added to, modified within, or removed from the database—when this
occurs, the application must recognize the change and resynchronize the data.
Let's take a look at the `Global.asax` file:

VB.NET   File: **UsingGlobalASAX/Global.asax**
```vbnet
<%@ Import Namespace="System.Data.OleDb" %>
<%@ Import Namespace="System.Data" %>

<script runat="server" language="VB">
Sub Application_Start(sender As Object, e As EventArgs)
  Dim objConn As New OleDbConnection( _
    "Provider=Microsoft.Jet.OleDb.4.0;" & _
    "Data Source=C:\Inetpub\wwwroot\Samples\Database\" & _
    "Dorknozzle.mdb")
  Dim objDA As OleDbDataAdapter
  Dim objDS As New DataSet()

  objDA = New OleDbDataAdapter("SELECT * FROM EmployeeStore", _
      objConn)
  objDA.Fill(objDS, "EmployeeStore")

  Application("EmployeeStoreItems") = objDS
```

```
End Sub
</script>
```

C#   File: **UsingGlobalASAX/Global.aspx**

```
<%@ Import Namespace="System.Data.OleDb" %>
<%@ Import Namespace="System.Data" %>

<script runat="server" language="C#">
void Application_Start(Object sender, EventArgs e) {
  OleDbConnection objConn = new OleDbConnection(
    "Provider=Microsoft.Jet.OleDb.4.0;" +
    "Data Source=C:\\Inetpub\\wwwroot\\Samples\\Database\\" +
    "Dorknozzle.mdb");
  OleDbDataAdapter objDA;
  DataSet objDS = new DataSet();

  objDA = new OleDbDataAdapter("SELECT * FROM EmployeeStore",
      objConn);
  objDA.Fill(objDS, "EmployeeStore");

  Application["EmployeeStoreItems"] = objDS;
}
</script>
```

As you can see, the Global.asax file doesn't look too different from a typical ASP.NET page. We defined the Application_Start() event handler and added to it code that will extract all items from the EmployeeStore database table, fill a new DataSet called objDS, and then store that DataSet within an application variable for use within application state. It's important to realize, however, that the Global.asax file, though very closely resembling a typical ASP.NET page, doesn't function like one; viewing the Global.asax file within the browser results in an error. To use the newly created DataSet that is stored within application state, we need to create a new ASP.NET page within the same directory in which the Global.asax file resides (or any of its subdirectories, as a Global.asax file applies to the entire ASP.NET application), and add the following code:

VB.NET   File: **UsingGlobalASAX/index.aspx (excerpt)**

```
<html>
<head>
<title>Application_Start Event</title>
<script language="VB" runat="server">
Sub Page_Load()
  dgEmployeeStoreItems.DataSource = _
      Application("EmployeeStoreItems")
  dgEmployeeStoreItems.DataBind()
```

```
End Sub
</script>
</head>
<body>
<asp:DataGrid id="dgEmployeeStoreItems" runat="server" />
</body>
</html>
```

C#   File: **UsingGlobalASAX**/index.aspx **(excerpt)**

```
<html>
<head>
<title>Application_Start Event</title>
<script language="C#" runat="server">
void Page_Load() {
  dgEmployeeStoreItems.DataSource =
      Application["EmployeeStoreItems"];
  dgEmployeeStoreItems.DataBind();
}
</script>
</head>
<body>
<asp:DataGrid id="dgEmployeeStoreItems" runat="server" />
</body>
</html>
```

As you can see, we're simply binding the DataGrid to the application variable—it's as easy as that! Figure 11.3 shows the result within the browser.

Figure 11.3. The `DataSet` contained within application state is bound to the `DataGrid`.

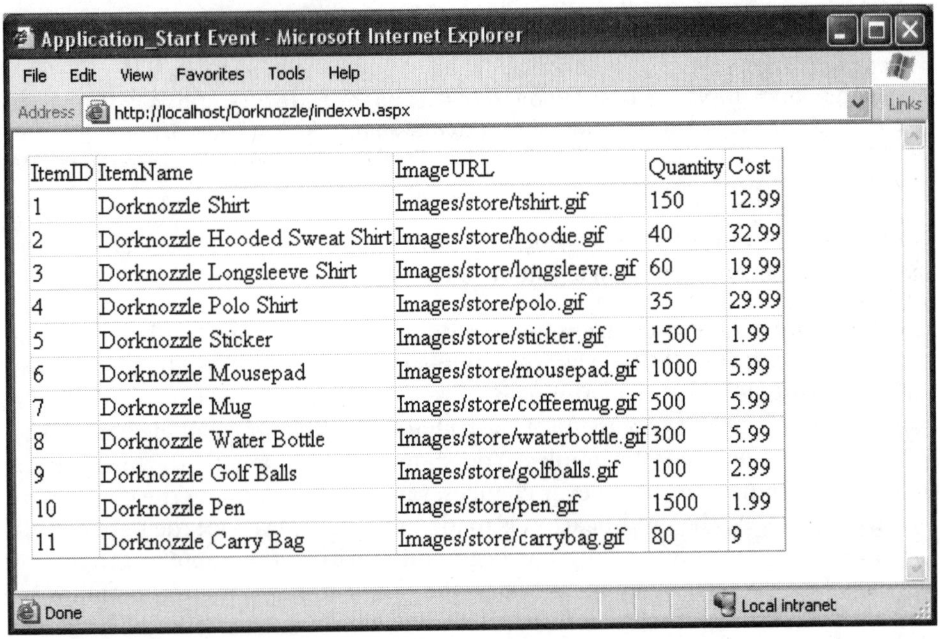

ItemID	ItemName	ImageURL	Quantity	Cost
1	Dorknozzle Shirt	Images/store/tshirt.gif	150	12.99
2	Dorknozzle Hooded Sweat Shirt	Images/store/hoodie.gif	40	32.99
3	Dorknozzle Longsleeve Shirt	Images/store/longsleeve.gif	60	19.99
4	Dorknozzle Polo Shirt	Images/store/polo.gif	35	29.99
5	Dorknozzle Sticker	Images/store/sticker.gif	1500	1.99
6	Dorknozzle Mousepad	Images/store/mousepad.gif	1000	5.99
7	Dorknozzle Mug	Images/store/coffeemug.gif	500	5.99
8	Dorknozzle Water Bottle	Images/store/waterbottle.gif	300	5.99
9	Dorknozzle Golf Balls	Images/store/golfballs.gif	100	2.99
10	Dorknozzle Pen	Images/store/pen.gif	1500	1.99
11	Dorknozzle Carry Bag	Images/store/carrybag.gif	80	9

The great part about storing the `DataSet` within application state is that it guarantees a performance increase. If the items within the database don't change, why should every user have to make the same request to the database over and over again?

Using the `Web.config` File

By default, ASP.NET applications are configured by the `Machine.config` file, which resides in the following directory on the computer:

```
C:\Windows\Microsoft.NET\Framework\Version\CONFIG
```

For the most part, you won't want to make any modifications to this file. You can, however, override certain settings of the `Machine.config` file by adding a `Web.config` file to the root directory of your application. The `Web.config` file is an XML configuration management file that can hold global configuration settings for the application in which the file resides. We'll cover XML in detail later in the book, but, as an example, imagine you had an application that used the same connection string across ten different pages to access a database (the Dorknozzle Intranet Application isn't far from this, actually). It might be beneficial to store the connection string in the `Web.config` file like this:

```
<configuration>
  <appSettings>
    <add key="DSN" value="Provider=Microsoft.Jet.OleDb.4.0;Data So
urce=C:\Inetpub\wwwroot\Samples\Database\Dorknozzle.mdb" />
  </appSettings>
</configuration>
```

Note that the `value` attribute, which we have wrapped here for page size limitations, should appear on a single line in the code.

Go ahead and create in your application directory a `Web.config` file containing just the code shown above. Use the connection string you've already used in previous examples, but, if you're using C#, note that, as this isn't actually C# code, you won't need to escape backslash characters (just use a single backslash). We'll use this file in later examples. You should see the benefit to this immediately. If the connection string ever changes, rather than changing the connection string on all pages, the modification is made in a single location: the `Web.config` file. Once the connection string has been added within the `<appSettings>` tag as a new key, you can make reference to that key within your code as follows:

VB.NET

```
Dim objConn As OleDbConnection
objConn = New OleDbConnection(
    ConfigurationSettings.AppSettings("DSN"))
```

C#

```
OleDbConnection objConn;
objConn = new OleDbConnection(
    ConfigurationSettings.AppSettings["DSN"]);
```

As you can see, the connection string defined within the key of the `Web.config` file can be used within any page; we must simply pass the key name to the `AppSettings` collection of the built-in `ConfigurationSettings` object. We'll continue to use this method of specifying our database connection for the remainder of this book.

The `Web.config` file's root element is always a `<configuration>` tag. The `<configuration>` tag may contain three different types of elements:

Configuration section handler declarations

ASP.NET's configuration file system is so flexible that it allows you define new *types* of settings—called **configuration sections**. For our purposes, the built-in configuration sections will do nicely, but if we wanted to include some custom configuration sections, we would need to tell ASP.NET how to handle them. This is done by declaring a configuration section handler for each custom configuration section you want to allow for. This is pretty advanced stuff that we won't worry about in this book.

Configuration section groups

Because there is a lot about ASP.NET and the rest of the .NET Framework that can be configured, configuration files would get a bit jumbled without a way to break the files up into groups of related settings, called configuration section groups. A number of predefined **section grouping tags** let you do just that. For example, settings specific to ASP.NET must be placed inside a `<system.web>` section grouping tag, while settings to do with .NET's networking classes belong in a `<system.net>` tag.

General settings like the `<appSettings>` tag we saw above should stand on their own, outside the section grouping tags. In this book, though, our configuration files will also contain a number of ASP.NET-specific settings, which we'll put inside a `<system.web>` tag.

Configuration sections

These are the actual setting tags in our configuration file. Because a single tag can contain a number of settings (e.g. the `<appSettings>` tag we saw earlier could provide a number of different strings for the application to use, instead of just a single database connection string), Microsoft calls each of these tags a **configuration section**. ASP.NET provides a wide range of built-in configuration sections to control the various aspects of your Web applications.

The following list outlines some of the commonly used ASP.NET configuration sections, all of which must appear within a `<system.web>` section grouping tag:

`<authentication>`	This section outlines configuration settings for user authentication, and is covered in detail in Chapter 14.
`<authorization>`	This section specifies users and roles for access to specific files within an application, and is discussed in detail in Chapter 14.
`<compilation>`	This section contains information for compiling pages. You can specify the default language used for compiling pages as C#, VB.NET, or J#.
`<customErrors>`	Use this section to customize the way errors should be displayed.
`<globalization>`	Use this section to customize character encoding for requests and responses.
`<identity>`	This section configures user account impersonation.
`<machineKey>`	This section is used for sharing a standard encryption key across groups of related servers (Web farms)..
`<pages>`	This section outlines configuration information for specific ASP.NET pages. For instance, you could disable session state, buffering, or even view state within this section.
`<sessionState>`	This section contains configuration information for modifying session state (i.e. variables associated with a particular user's visit to your site). You can use this section to enable in-process, out-of-process, or cookieless sessions.
`<trace>`	This section contains information for page and application tracing, as is discussed in more detail in the next chapter.

Now that you have an idea of the different sections of a `Web.config` file, let's take a look at a "cookie cutter" `Web.config` file from one of my personal applications:

```
<configuration>

  <appSettings>
```

```
      <add key="DSN" value="Data Source=…"/>
   </appSettings>

   <system.web>
      <compilation defaultLanguage="vb" debug="true" />
      <customErrors mode="Off" />
      <authentication mode="Windows" />
      <authorization>
         <allow users="*" />
      </authorization>
      <trace enabled="false" requestLimit="10" pageOutput="false"
         traceMode="SortByTime" localOnly="true" />
      <globalization requestEncoding="utf-8"
         responseEncoding="utf-8" />
   </system.web>

</configuration>
```

The file has the familiar `<appSettings>` configuration section, as well as a number of ASP.NET-specific tags grouped inside the mandatory `<system.web>` tag. I've used `<compilation>` to set the default language for page compilation as VB.NET. I've switched `<customErrors>` off. I've also used `<authentication>` in conjunction with `<authorization>` to set security rights within the application (which we'll discuss in Chapter 14). Then, I've used `<trace>` to disable the printing of application and page level variables, and objects within the page, when an error occurs (discussed in Chapter 13). Finally, I've used `<globalization>` to set the encoding properties of the page.

Although we've only briefly glanced over the `Web.config` file, we'll cover it in much greater detail, starting with Chapter 14.

Caching ASP.NET Applications

As you build larger-scale applications, performance will be a key aspect that you'll want to take into consideration during the development process. It's one thing to build a simple application for yourself, but developing an application on which the life of your company depends is a whole different ball game. If your business's lifeblood is selling products to customers, your performance will be measured on how fast your Web application presents those products to customers. No one wants to wait aeons for data to load onto the page after an item has been selected from a list or menu.

As we've seen in previous sections, we can use the `Global.asax` file, in conjunction with application variables, to store data in application state. Doing this ultimately increases performance because the data is loaded once—when the application starts—and remains in application state until the application is restarted, or an addition or modification has been made to the items within the database. Individual client requests never have to make trips to the database, which would consume resources and slow the performance of your Web applications. It's all good! ...Or is it?

The problem with application state is that it lasts for as long as the application runs. For things that rarely change, like your database connection string, that's fine. But what if you wanted to make the employee directory page more efficient? Your company may not hire and fire employees every day, but when it *does* happen you'd like the list to be updated within a reasonable amount of time. If you were to use application state, you'd have to write extra code that would periodically update the employee list from the database.

In this section, we'll examine **caching**. Caching, as you will see, is a method for storing and holding onto data for a specific period of time. Similar to the way in which images and data are cached by your browser when you visit Websites, ASP.NET caching has the ability to cache pages (page output caching), parts of pages (page fragment caching), or objects within pages (page data caching). Like application state, cached data can be used across multiple user requests, thereby eliminating the need to make continuous calls to the database. But unlike application state, cached data will automatically expire after a specified period, after which it will be refreshed from the database server.

Using Page Output Caching

In Chapter 9, we built a number of pages using ASP.NET data controls to display lists of employees pulled from a database. When these pages loaded within the browser, all the entries in the `Employees` database table were displayed within the page using a `DataList` control. For each request to one of these pages, the application had to open a connection to the database, extract the database contents into a `DataSet`, and eventually present the data back to the user, though this data will almost certainly be identical to that which was obtained in response to previous requests. This scenario might be fine if you have one user, but what happens if you're writing an Intranet application for a huge, multinational company? That one user suddenly becomes hundreds of users—even thousands. Continuous requests to the server and database would result in a severe performance hit.

Obviously, making repeated trips to the server is entirely unnecessary in this case. To avoid this unnecessary strain on your server, we can implement page output caching. Page output caching allows you to store the state of the page in cache for a specified period; once this time is up, another trip must be made to the server. You can add page output caching to your page by inserting the following directive at the top of your page:

```
<%@ OutputCache Duration="300" VaryByParam="None" %>
```

In this case, we use the `OutputCache` directive, set the `Duration` to 300 seconds (five minutes), and set the `VaryByParams` attribute to `None`. You can use the `VaryByParams` attribute to cache a page only until the specified parameter is found. Let's look at a simple example of page output caching in action:

VB.NET   File: **PageOutputCaching/CachedTime.aspx**

```
<%@ OutputCache Duration="10" VaryByParam="None" %>
<html>
<head>
<title>Page Output Caching</title>
</head>
<body>
<p>This time will refresh in 10 seconds: <%= Now() %></p>
</body>
</html>
```

C#   File: **PageOutputCaching/CachedTime.aspx**

```
<%@ OutputCache Duration="10" VaryByParam="None" %>
<html>
<head>
<title>Page Output Caching</title>
</head>
<body>
<p>This time will refresh in 10 seconds: <%= DateTime.Now %></p>
</body>
</html>
```

Save the page and view the results in your browser. Try refreshing the page continuously. The time will only refresh after ten seconds have passed, because the `Duration` attribute of the `OutputCache` directive is set to 10 seconds.

Let's look at a more useful example of how we would use page output caching within the scope of an application. The following example caches a page containing a `DataGrid` for ten seconds:

```
VB.NET                                    File: PageOutputCaching/CachedGrid.aspx
<%@ OutputCache Duration="10" VaryByParam="None" %>
<%@ Import Namespace="System.Data.OleDb" %>
<%@ Import Namespace="System.Data" %>
<html>
<head>
<title>Cached DataGrid</title>
<script runat="server" language="VB">
Dim objConn As New OleDbConnection(
    ConfigurationSettings.AppSettings("DSN"))
Dim objDA As OleDbDataAdapter
Dim objDS As New DataSet()

Sub Page_Load()
  objDA = New OleDbDataAdapter("SELECT * FROM Employees", objConn)
  objDA.Fill(objDS, "Employees")
  dgEmployees.DataSource = objDS
  dgEmployees.DataBind()
End Sub
</script>
</head>
<body>
<asp:DataGrid id="dgEmployees" runat="server" />
<p>The data will be refreshed 10 seconds from now: <%= Now() %>
</p>
</body>
</html>
```

```
C#                              File: PageOutputCaching/CachedGrid.aspx (excerpt)
<%@ OutputCache Duration="10" VaryByParam="None" %>
<%@ Import Namespace="System.Data.OleDb" %>
<%@ Import Namespace="System.Data" %>
<html>
<head>
<title>Cached DataGrid</title>
<script runat="server" language="C#">
OleDbConnection objConn = new
    OleDbConnection(ConfigurationSettings.AppSettings["DSN"]);
OleDbDataAdapter objDA;
DataSet objDS = new DataSet();

void Page_Load() {
  objDA = new OleDbDataAdapter("SELECT * FROM Employees",
      objConn);
  objDA.Fill(objDS, "Employees");
  dgEmployees.DataSource = objDS;
```

```
  dgEmployees.DataBind();
}
</script>
</head>
<body>
<asp:DataGrid id="dgEmployees" runat="server" />
<p>The data will be refreshed 10 seconds from now:
<%= DateTime.Now %></p>
</body>
</html>
```

Here, we use the `AppSettings` collection to get the `Web.config` key that holds the database connection string. We created this key a few pages back—you'll need to make sure you created a `Web.config` file as instructed earlier. Try saving your work, and view the results in your browser. Figure 11.4 shows the populated `DataGrid`, complete with all the employees' data.

Figure 11.4. The cached data is presented to the user within a `DataGrid` control.

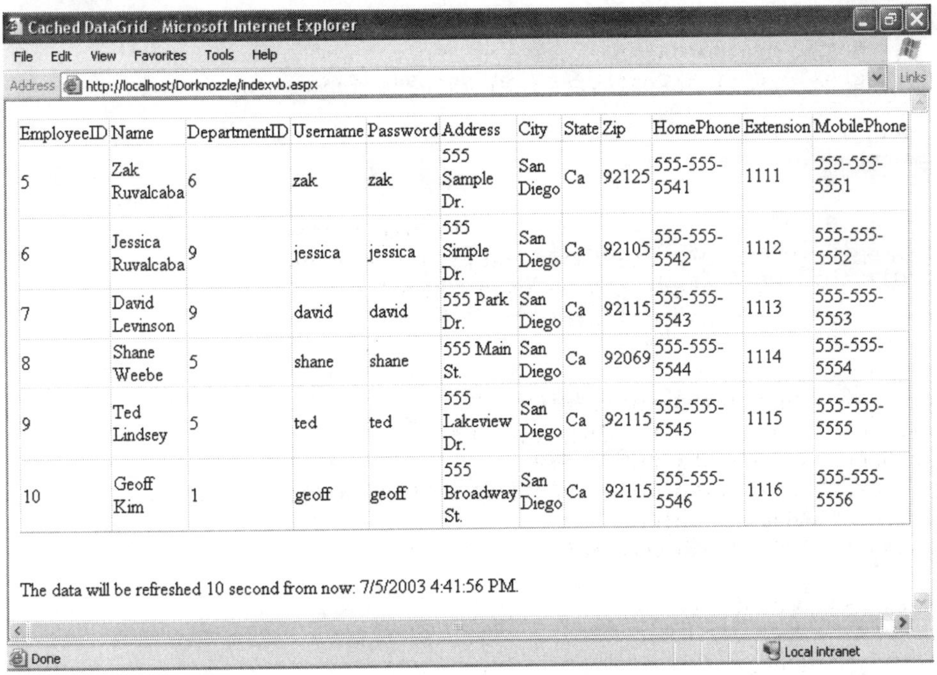

EmployeeID	Name	DepartmentID	Username	Password	Address	City	State	Zip	HomePhone	Extension	MobilePhone
5	Zak Ruvalcaba	6	zak	zak	555 Sample Dr.	San Diego	Ca	92125	555-555-5541	1111	555-555-5551
6	Jessica Ruvalcaba	9	jessica	jessica	555 Simple Dr.	San Diego	Ca	92105	555-555-5542	1112	555-555-5552
7	David Levinson	9	david	david	555 Park Dr.	San Diego	Ca	92115	555-555-5543	1113	555-555-5553
8	Shane Weebe	5	shane	shane	555 Main St.	San Diego	Ca	92069	555-555-5544	1114	555-555-5554
9	Ted Lindsey	5	ted	ted	555 Lakeview Dr.	San Diego	Ca	92115	555-555-5545	1115	555-555-5555
10	Geoff Kim	1	geoff	geoff	555 Broadway St.	San Diego	Ca	92115	555-555-5546	1116	555-555-5556

The data will be refreshed 10 second from now: 7/5/2003 4:41:56 PM.

Try repeatedly refreshing the page. The page refreshes and displays the content within the cache. Every ten seconds, the page makes a trip to the server to grab the latest data.

Using Page Data Caching

In the previous section, you looked at how ASP.NET pages can be cached in an effort to increase performance. In many instances, however, it may make more sense to cache only the data on the page, rather than the entire page itself.

For example, we could very easily create a DataGrid that displayed all the employees within our database. An HR manager using the application might want to sort the records on specific columns within the DataGrid. We could accomplish this by placing the following code block in an ASP.NET page:

VB.NET   File: **PageDataCaching/CachedGrid.aspx (excerpt)**

```vbnet
<script language="VB" runat="server">
Dim objDV As DataView

Sub Page_Load()
  If Not IsPostBack Then
    dgEmployees.DataSource = GetEmployees()
    dgEmployees.DataBind()
  End If
End Sub

Function GetEmployees() As DataView
  Dim objDS As New DataSet()
  Dim objConn As New OleDbConnection( _
      ConfigurationSettings.AppSettings("DSN"))
  Dim objDA As OleDbDataAdapter

  objDA = New OleDbDataAdapter("SELECT * FROM Employees", _
      objConn)
  objDA.Fill(objDS, "Employees")
  objDV = objDS.Tables("Employees").DefaultView()

  Return objDV
End Function

Sub dgEmployees_Sort(s As Object, _
    e As DataGridSortCommandEventArgs)
  objDV = GetEmployees()
  objDV.Sort = e.SortExpression
```

```
    dgEmployees.DataSource = objDV
    dgEmployees.DataBind()
End Sub
</script>
```

C# File: **PageDataCaching/CachedGrid.aspx (excerpt)**

```csharp
<script language="C#" runat="server">
DataView objDV;

void Page_Load() {
  if (!IsPostBack) {
    dgEmployees.DataSource = GetEmployees();
    dgEmployees.DataBind();
  }
}

DataView GetEmployees() {
  DataSet objDS = new DataSet();
  OleDbConnection objConn = new
    OleDbConnection(ConfigurationSettings.AppSettings["DSN"]);
  OleDbDataAdapter objDA;

  objDA = new OleDbDataAdapter("SELECT * FROM Employees",
      objConn);
  objDA.Fill(objDS, "Employees");
  objDV = objDS.Tables["Employees"].DefaultView;

  return objDV;
}

void dgEmployees_Sort(Object s, DataGridSortCommandEventArgs e) {
  objDV = GetEmployees();
  objDV.Sort = e.SortExpression;

  dgEmployees.DataSource = objDV;
  dgEmployees.DataBind();
}
</script>
```

The DataGrid itself is then created in a server-side `<form>` tag as usual:

File: **PageDataCaching/CachedGrid.aspx (excerpt)**

```
<form runat="server">
<asp:DataGrid id="dgEmployees" runat="server" AllowSorting="true"
    DataKeyField="EmployeeID" AutoGenerateColumns="false"
```

```
   OnSortCommand="dgEmployees_Sort" GridLines="None">
  <Columns>
    <asp:BoundColumn DataField="Name" HeaderText="Name"
        SortExpression="Name" />
    <asp:BoundColumn DataField="Extension" HeaderText="Extension"
        SortExpression="Extension" />
  </Columns>
</asp:DataGrid>
</form>
```

As you can see, we've created a new method called GetEmployees(), which has a DataView return type. Both the Page_Load() and dgEmployees_Sort() methods use this function to retrieve a filled DataView.

The problem with this example is that it is inefficient. Every time the user clicks on a header to sort that specific column, a trip is made to the database, and the DataView is repopulated with new records. To make things more efficient, we could store the DataView within ASP.NET's built-in cache. We must simply add the DataView to the Cache collection, as follows:

VB.NET
```
Cache("Employees") = objDV
```

Later within the code, we could use the cached object as follows:

VB.NET
```
dg.DataSource = Cache("Employees")
dg.DataBind()
```

As usual, C# uses square brackets to read and write values in the Cache collection. The object stays within the cache until we force its expiration, or server resources become too low, in which case items are removed from the cache oldest-first. The GetEmployees() method in the previous example could be rewritten to utilize the ASP.NET cache as follows:

VB.NET   File: **PageDataCaching/CachedGrid.aspx (excerpt)**
```
Function GetEmployees() As DataView
  Dim objDS As New DataSet()
  Dim objConn As New OleDbConnection( _
    ConfigurationSettings.AppSettings("DSN"))
  Dim objDA As OleDbDataAdapter

  objDV = Cache("Employees")
  If objDV Is Nothing Then
    objDA = New OleDbDataAdapter("SELECT * FROM Employees", objConn)
```

```
    objDA.Fill(objDS, "Employees")
    objDV = objDS.Tables("Employees").DefaultView
    Cache("Employees") = objDV
  End If

  Return objDV
End Function
```

C#   File: **PageDataCaching/CachedGrid.aspx (excerpt)**

```csharp
DataView GetEmployees() {
  DataSet objDS = new DataSet();
  OleDbConnection objConn = new
    OleDbConnection(ConfigurationSettings.AppSettings["DSN"]);
  OleDbDataAdapter objDA;

  objDV = (DataView)Cache["Employees"];
  if (objDV == null) {
    objDA = new OleDbDataAdapter("SELECT * FROM Employees",
        objConn);
    objDA.Fill(objDS, "Employees");
    objDV = objDS.Tables["Employees"].DefaultView;
    Cache["Employees"] = objDV;
  }

  return objDV;
}
```

As the bolded text shows, we start by copying the cache data into the objDV DataView. Next, we check to make sure the DataView is not empty. If it is empty, it means we've not yet accessed this page before, or the cache has been emptied since we last accessed the page. Thus, we populate objDV from the database as before, remembering to store the retrieved DataView into the cache. As such, the trip to the database server is only made if the cache is empty or not present. Save your work and test the results in the browser. Figure 11.5 shows all the employees bound to the DataGrid.

Figure 11.5. Cached employees are shown within the `DataGrid`

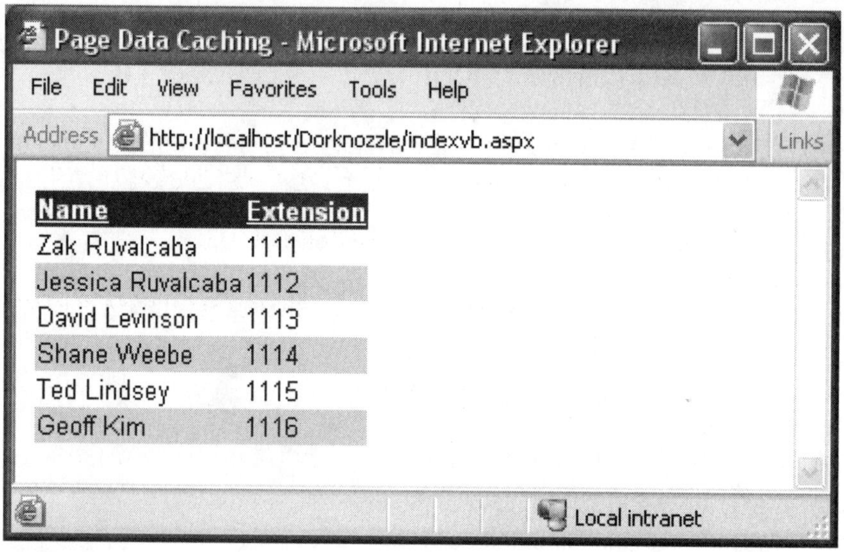

Try sorting the headings as quickly as possible. You should experience virtually no lag time. This is due to the fact that you're sorting information that's held within the cache, rather than having to extract it from the database and resort it on the `DataView`. It has to be said that you probably wouldn't experience a lag time anyway in this example—even without the cache object—because we don't have very many employees within the database, and you've probably stored your database on the same machine as ASP.NET itself. If, however, you had thousands of employees within your organization, and a more distributed set up, caching would definitely be a good idea.

Working with User Sessions

Like application variables and the cache, **session variables** are an important way to store temporary information across multiple page requests. While a variable defined within code is typically only available within the same code block on the page, session variables can be created and reused across multiple pages and requests. Unlike application variables and cached values, which are accessible to all users, each session variable is associated with a particular user's visit to your site. Stored on the server, session variables allocate each user free memory on that server for the temporary storage of strings, integers, objects, etc.

For example, in the page hit counter example that we created earlier in this chapter, we stored the hit count in the application state, which created a single hit count shared by all users of the site. By using a session variable as the hit counter, we can instead have independent hit counters for every user who visits the site.

Session variables are easy to write, and are declared using the same process we applied in our discussions of application and cache variables. To illustrate their usage, let's go ahead and modify our page counter example to use a session variable and thus produce a separate hit count for each user on the site:

VB.NET   File: `SessionState/SessionState.aspx`

```
<html>
<head>
<title>Session State (Page Counter)</title>
<script language="VB" runat="server">
Sub Page_Load()
  Session("PageCounter") += 1
  lblCounter.Text = Session("PageCounter")
End Sub
</script>
</head>
<body>
You have requested this page:
<asp:Label id="lblCounter" runat="server" /> times!
</body>
</html>
```

C#   File: `SessionState/SessionState.aspx`

```
<html>
<head>
<title>Session State (Page Counter)</title>
<script language="C#" runat="server">
void Page_Load() {
  if (Session["PageCounter"] == null) {
    Session["PageCounter"] = 0;
  }
  Session["PageCounter"] = (int)Session["PageCounter"] + 1;
  lblCounter.Text = Convert.ToString(Session["PageCounter"]);
}
</script>
</head>
<body>
You have requested this page:
<asp:Label id="lblCounter" runat="server" /> times!
```

```
</body>
</html>
```

Save this on your server and open it in your browser. Refresh it a few times and observe how the counter increments. Then open a separate copy of your browser (by launching it a second time—not by creating a new window from the existing window) and navigate to the page from there as well. Refresh each window a few times and observe how a separate hit count is maintained for each.

Like application variables, session variables linger on the server even after the user leaves the page that created them. This will become especially important in Chapter 12 when we use a session variable to store the contents of each user's shopping cart. We don't want our users to lose the items they have selected to purchase just because they make a side trip to another page of your site prior to confirming their purchase!

Unlike application variables, however, session variables will disappear after a certain period of inactivity on the user's part. Since Web browsers don't notify Web servers when a user leaves a Web site, ASP.NET can only assume that a user has left your site after a period of receiving no page requests from that user. By default, a user's session will expire after twenty minutes of inactivity. This period of time can be increased or decreased simply by changing the `Timeout` property of the `Session` object, as follows:

VB.NET
```
Session.Timeout = 60
```

C#
```
Session.Timeout = 60;
```

You can do this anywhere in your code, but the most common place to set the `Timeout` property is in the `Global.asax` file. In addition to the application event handlers we saw earlier in this chapter, `Global.asax` can also contain event handlers that will run each time a user session begins and ends:

Session_Start()   Run prior to processing the first request of each user's visit to your site. Gives you the opportunity to initialize their session variables.

Session_End()   Run each time a user's session is terminated, usually due to a period of inactivity. Gives you the opportunity to perform cleanup operations in response to a user leaving your site.

Here's what a `Global.asax` file that sets the `Timeout` property to 60 minutes should look like:

VB.NET   File: **SessionState/Global.asax**

```
<script runat="server" language="VB">
Sub Session_Start(sender As Object, e As EventArgs)
  Session.Timeout = 60
End Sub
</script>
```

C#   File: **SessionState/Global.asax**

```
<script runat="server" language="C#">
void Session_Start(Object sender, EventArgs e) {
  Session.Timeout = 60;
}
</script>
```

Summary

In this chapter, we discussed Web applications. You learned how to control and store content for the lifetime of an application using application state. Next, you learned how to modify configuration properties for an application using the `Global.asax` file and the `Web.config` file. Then, we looked at improving performance within Web applications by caching the whole ASP.NET page, and only part of the page, using the cache object. Finally, you learned about sessions and, more importantly, how to store data within session variables so that they can be used across multiple requests.

In Chapter 12, we will pause to consolidate many of the bits and pieces we've discussed over the past few chapters as we turn our attention back to the Dorknozzle Intranet Application and tackle the employee store, paying particular attention to the shopping cart.

Building an ASP.NET Shopping Cart

Virtual shopping cart capability is something for which Website owners are willing to pay good money. Companies such as VeriSign, WebAssist, and Link-Point charge to provide tools that let developers add shopping cart functionality to their Websites. But why pay three or four hundred dollars for a solution that someone else built, when you can develop one just as easily yourself using ASP.NET? This chapter will show you how easy it is to develop and implement your own shopping cart for your Website. Initially, you'll learn about the structure of a common shopping cart and how you can build one using ASP.NET, along with `DataTables`, `DataColumns`, and `DataRows`. Next, you'll learn more on updating `DataGrids` that have been created on the fly, and, finally, we'll introduce PayPal, so that you can put everything together and begin making money with your customized shopping cart solution.

What Is a Shopping Cart?

The term "shopping cart" has been thrown around in the context of Web applications for a few years now. But what exactly *is* a shopping cart? We know a shopping cart to be the basket on wheels that you push around at a grocery store. Think about why you use the grocery store shopping cart. You go to your local grocery store, push around the cart, and add items from the shelves. When you've decided that you're finished shopping, you push your shopping cart all the way to the front of the store, where the checkout counters are located. At the checkout counter, you provide your debit card, cash, or check to the cashier, finish the transaction, and off you go.

A store on the Web is no different; rather than a physical shopping cart, though, you're provided with a virtual shopping cart, which is little more than a cookie, user session (which we'll be covering in the next chapter), or temporary array. The premise is entirely the same: users add as many items to their carts as they see fit. The cart—a virtual table of some sort—takes the requested item from the database and stores it into a temporary location (cookie, session, or array) until the users are ready to check out. If users decide they want another item or more of the same item, they keep adding to the cart. Similar to the grocery store checkout counters, virtual checkouts enable users to enter credit card information to complete the purchase. However, rather than physically walking away with the items, users have them conveniently mailed to their doorsteps.

Indeed, in many Web applications, the products ordered may not even need to be delivered. Shareware sales sites such as share*it![1] and stock photo sites such as Photodisc[2] and Corbis[3] use the shopping cart concept, but, rather than having the purchased items mailed to you, you simply download them. Nevertheless, the underlying shopping cart metaphor and its implementation is the same.

In the next few sections, you'll learn about the many aspects that must be considered when you're building a shopping cart using ASP.NET. You'll learn about storage using public shared properties, creating a cart using `DataTables`, adding to the cart using a `Button` control, and modifying the items within the cart using the `EditCommandColumn` of the `DataGrid`. Towards the end of the chapter, you'll learn about PayPal and how you can hook your shopping cart into the free PayPal collection service so that you start to make money with your new shopping cart immediately. Let's get started—we have a lot to go over!

The Intranet Shopping Cart

Shopping carts provide users with the ability to quickly add items, view them, and purchase when they're ready. The `employeestore.aspx` page within our Intranet application will offer this same functionality. Initially, all the items located within the `EmployeeStore` database table will be repeated down the page using a `DataList` control, shown in Figure 12.1.

---

[1] http://www.shareit.com/
[2] http://www.photodisc.com/
[3] http://www.corbis.com/

Figure 12.1. All the items within the `EmployeeStore` database table are listed on the page.

Users need only click an *Add to Cart* Button control within the `DataList` to add that specific item to the cart. The `DataList` containing all the items is then hidden, and a `DataGrid` bound to the shopping cart presents users with the most recent addition, similar to Figure 12.2.

Figure 12.2. Users select the "Add To Cart" button, and are redirected to a DataGrid that represents the addition.

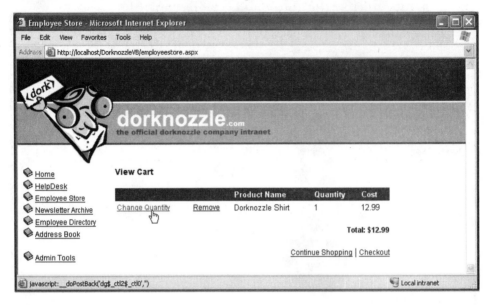

The initial quantity of any item added to the cart will always be one, but users can modify the quantity of each item they purchase by selecting the Change Quantity hyperlink within the DataGrid. Once users select the Change Quantity hyperlink, they'll be given the ability to change the quantity figure for a selected item, as shown in Figure 12.3.

Figure 12.3. Users are able to change the number of items within the cart by selecting the Change Quantity hyperlink, and altering the quantity within the Quantity TextBox control.

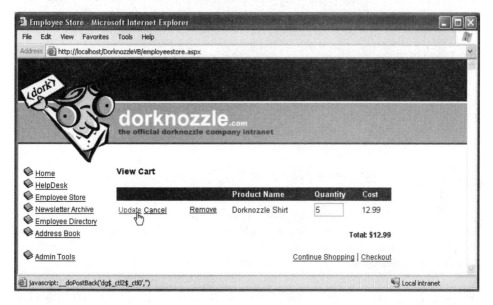

Once users make the modification to the number of items within the cart, the quantity and cost columns are multiplied and presented as a total within a Label control. Users are also able to remove items from their cart by selecting the Remove hyperlink. They can then click Continue Shopping or Checkout.

Theoretically, you know how the shopping cart will work. You can see how it will be presented to users; how users will interact with items they may want to purchase, and how items will be added to, modified, and deleted from the cart. What we haven't yet defined are the inner workings of the ASP.NET implementation. The next few sections will introduce you to the components that we'll use for the shopping cart implementation, including the structure of the database table, the shopping cart interface, and the functionality that the user will use to add to, modify, and remove from the cart.

Defining the Cart Framework

Now that you have a basic idea as to how the cart will work, let's start putting the pieces together. You know that users will have an opportunity to affect (add, modify, and remove) the items in the cart—that's obvious. What we have not yet defined, however, is how and where the items that will be presented to the user will be stored. We have also yet to define the components and the architecture that we'll use within the shopping cart application.

We can begin to define the shopping cart application by looking at its core aspects:

❏ The database

❏ The interface

❏ The methods

Let's define each.

The Database

The backbone of the employee store application is the database. Initially, the user will interact with one database table, `EmployeeStore`. You'll recall that this table contains the details of all of the products offered for sale through the intranet site. Figure 12.4 shows the database table that you built in Chapter 6.

Figure 12.4. The `EmployeeStore` database table contains all the components with which users will interact.

ItemID	ItemName	ImageURL	Quantity	Cost
1	Dorknozzle Shirt	Images/store/tshirt.gif	150	$12.99
2	Dorknozzle Hooded Sweat Shirt	Images/store/hoodie.gif	40	$32.99
3	Dorknozzle Longsleeve Shirt	Images/store/longsleeve.gif	60	$19.99
4	Dorknozzle Polo Shirt	Images/store/polo.gif	35	$29.99
5	Dorknozzle Sticker	Images/store/sticker.gif	1500	$1.99
6	Dorknozzle Mousepad	Images/store/mousepad.gif	1000	$5.99
7	Dorknozzle Mug	Images/store/coffeemug.gif	500	$5.99
8	Dorknozzle Water Bottle	Images/store/waterbottle.gif	300	$5.99
9	Dorknozzle Golf Balls	Images/store/golfballs.gif	100	$2.99
10	Dorknozzle Pen	Images/store/pen.gif	1500	$1.99
11	Dorknozzle Carry Bag	Images/store/carrybag.gif	80	$9.00
(AutoNumber)			0	$0.00

As you can see, our store will sell t-shirts, hooded sweatshirts, mouse pads, pens, etc., all bearing the company logo. Within the database table, you'll notice the unique `ItemID` (Primary Key), which will be used to make reference to specific items that users select; `ItemName`, which will be used to present the titles of items to users; `Quantity`, which is the number of items currently in stock; `Cost`, which displays the cost of the item; and `ImageURL`, which represents the URL of the item's image, and is unique in that it will be constructed dynamically within a code render block. Rather than hard coding the image file paths, we can instead store image paths within the database. This allows us to reference the file directly within a code render block inside an `<img>` HTML tag. All the GIF images are stored within a `Store` folder inside the `Images` folder.

As we'll place the `employeestore.aspx` file within the root directory, we can add the image file paths into the database table. This allows us to move the `Images` folder anywhere within the Web application's directory, as we only have to make changes within the database table, rather than altering each `<img>` tag's `src` attribute.

The Interface

Now that you've seen where all the data will be stored, let's take a look at the presentational elements within the application. The interface can be divided up into the following controls:

DataList	All items within the `EmployeeStore` database table will be bound to the `dlItems` DataList. Within the `DataList`, we'll place an `<img>` tag to hold the item's image. As I mentioned earlier, that image will use a code render block within the `src` attribute of the tag to set dynamically the item's image URL. Within the same DataList, we'll also display the item's name and cost.
Button	Each `DataList` item will contain a `Button` control. This `Button` control will be used to add specific items to users' carts.
DataGrid	Once users add an item to their cart, they'll be presented with a `DataGrid` view of the items within it. The `DataGrid` will support the `OnEditCommand`, `OnUpdateCommand`, `OnDeleteCommand`, and `OnCancel-Command` event handlers, and will raise their respective events. We'll be using templates within the `DataGrid` to allow users to modify only the `Quantity` column, and also, to perform validation on the `TextBox` control within the cell.

LinkButton	We'll use `LinkButton` controls for the Continue Shopping and Checkout links.
Panel	`Panel` controls will be used to hide the `DataList` when the "View Cart" `DataGrid` needs to be shown, and vice versa. As you saw in Chapter 4, `Panel` controls are a great way of hiding and making visible large amounts of information within a single page.

Getting excited about building the application? Great! There are only a few items left to define.

The Methods

The final piece of the employee store application is the application logic. The following list outlines the methods that we will use throughout the application:

Page_Load()	When the page loads for the first time (i.e. not on postback), the items within the `EmployeeStore` database table will be bound to the `DataList`. The cart `DataTable` and `DataColumn` structure will also be created here.
AddToCart()	When users click the Add to Cart `Button` control within the `DataList`, the unique ID from the specific row in the `DataList` will be captured and passed into the `findItem()` method. Results will be returned within a `DataSet`, and, finally, they'll be added as a new row within the cart `DataTable`.
FindItem()	This finds all the information from the `EmployeeStore` database table, based on a unique ID (`ItemID`) that's passed in from the `AddToCart()` method.
GetItemTotal()	Keeps a running total of the cost of the items within the cart. The grand total is presented within a `Label` control.
dgCart_Edit()	This allows users to edit the quantity freely within the cart `DataGrid`.
dgCart_Cancel()	Users can cancel out from making edits within the cart `DataGrid`, with the help of this method.

dgCart_Update()	Commits the modified quantity to the cart `DataGrid`. Updates are made to the cart `DataTable`.
dgCart_Delete()	This removes an item from the cart `DataTable`.
ContinueShopping()	This method allows users to switch from "View Cart" mode back to the complete list of employee store items.
CheckOut()	As you'll see in the final section, we'll use the `CheckOut()` method to process the user's order using PayPal.

I know it seems like there's a lot to do, but rest assured that each method will be covered concisely. Once we're done, we'll have a fully-functional shopping cart that can be used with any project. Let's get started!

Building the Employee Store Interface

Initially, the interface for the employee store application will look no different than the rest of the Dorknozzle pages that we've been working with to this point. In fact, you can start by taking a copy of the `template.aspx` page out of the `Template` folder and renaming it `employeestore.aspx`. Here's the HTML, complete with the required `Import` directives:

File: **employeestore.aspx (excerpt)**

```
<%@ Import Namespace="System.Data.OleDb" %>
<%@ Import Namespace="System.Data" %>
<html>
<head>
<title>Employee Store</title>
<link href="styles.css" rel="stylesheet" />
</head>
<body>
<form runat="server">

<table width="100%" border="0" cellspacing="0" cellpadding="0"
    background="Images/header_bg.gif">
  <tr>
    <td><img src="Images/header_top.gif" width="450" height="142"
        alt="the dorknozzle company intranet"/></td>
  </tr>
</table>
```

```
<table width="100%" border="0" cellspacing="0" cellpadding="0">
  <tr>
    <td width="157"><img src="Images/header_bottom.gif"
        width="157" height="37" alt="" /></td>
    <td></td>
  </tr>
</table>

<table width="100%" border="0" cellspacing="0" cellpadding="10">
  <tr>
    <td valign="top" width="160">
      <!-- HyperLink Controls for navigation -->
      <img src="Images/book_closed.gif" width="16" height="16"
          alt="+" /><asp:HyperLink NavigateUrl="index.aspx"
          runat="server" Text="Home" /><br />
      <img src="Images/book_closed.gif" width="16" height="16"
          alt="+" /><asp:HyperLink NavigateUrl="helpdesk.aspx"
          runat="server" Text="HelpDesk" /><br />
      <img src="Images/book_closed.gif" width="16" height="16"
          alt="+" /><asp:HyperLink
          NavigateUrl="employeestore.aspx" runat="server"
          Text="Employee Store" /><br />
      <img src="Images/book_closed.gif" width="16" height="16"
          alt="+" /><asp:HyperLink
          NavigateUrl="newsletterarchive.aspx"
          runat="server" Text="Newsletter Archive" /><br />
      <img src="Images/book_closed.gif" width="16" height="16"
          alt="+" /><asp:HyperLink
          NavigateUrl="employeedirectory.aspx" runat="server"
          Text="Employee Directory" /><br />
      <img src="Images/book_closed.gif" width="16" height="16"
          alt="+" /><asp:HyperLink NavigateUrl="addressbook.aspx"
          runat="server" Text="Address Book" /><br /><br />
      <img src="Images/book_closed.gif" width="16" height="16"
          alt="+" /><asp:HyperLink NavigateUrl="admintools.aspx"
          runat="server" Text="Admin Tools" />
      <!-- End HyperLink Controls -->
  </td>
  <td valign="top">
      <!-- Add Heading Here -->
  </td>
  </tr>
</table>

</form>
```

```
</body>
</html>
```

The store will have the same basic content and structure as all the other Dorknozzle pages, providing our site with the consistent look and feel that we want. As far as the interactive elements are concerned, however, there are two controls that we'll add right away in place of the bolded Add Heading Here comment. The first, the DataList control, will be used to present all items from the EmployeeStore database table to the user. Add this control as shown below:

VB.NET   File: **employeestore.aspx (excerpt)**

```
<asp:Panel id="pnlShowItems" runat="server">
  <h1>Employee Store</h1>
  <asp:DataList id="dlItems" runat="server" DataKeyField="ItemID"
      OnEditCommand="AddToCart">
    <ItemTemplate>
      <table width="400" border="0" cellspacing="0"
          cellpadding="0">
        <tr>
          <td width="200" valign="top" align="center">
            <img src="<%# Container.DataItem("ImageURL") %>" />
          </td>
          <td width="200">
            <strong><%# Container.DataItem("ItemName") %></strong>
            <br />
            Cost: $<%# Container.DataItem("Cost") %><br /><br />
            <asp:Button id="btnAddToCart" runat="server"
                Text="Add To Cart" CommandName="Edit"/>
          </td>
        </tr>
        <tr>
          <td colspan="2" width="400"><hr noshade height="1" />
          </td>
        </tr>
      </table>
    </ItemTemplate>
  </asp:DataList>
</asp:Panel>
```

As you can see, the DataList is nested within a Panel control. Notice the Add to Cart Button control we've created inside the DataList. When this is pressed, the new row will be added to the cart, this Panel control will be hidden from view, and the cart DataGrid within a second Panel control (which we've not yet added) will become visible. You can see that our DataList defines for each item a template containing a table. In that table, we place code render blocks for the binding that will occur between the `EmployeeStore` database table and the items in the `DataList`. The first code render block handles the binding of the image file path:

VB.NET   File: **employeestore.aspx (excerpt)**

```
<img src="<%# Container.DataItem("ImageURL") %>" />
```

As we mentioned earlier in the chapter, the file path for each image will be taken from the `ImageURL` column of the `EmployeeStore` database table and dynamically constructed for each table's cell. As we have seen in the past, outputting a database value in a code render block requires slightly different syntax in C#:

C#   File: **employeestore.aspx (excerpt)**

```
<img src="<%# DataBinder.Eval(Container.DataItem, "ImageURL") %>"
    />
```

The second and third render blocks list each item's name and cost:

VB.NET   File: **employeestore.aspx (excerpt)**

```
<strong><%# Container.DataItem("ItemName") %></strong><br />
Cost: $<%# Container.DataItem("Cost") %><br /><br />
```

C#   File: **employeestore.aspx (excerpt)**

```
<strong><%# DataBinder.Eval(Container.DataItem, "ItemName")
    %></strong><br />
Cost: $<%# DataBinder.Eval(Container.DataItem, "Cost") %><br />
<br />
```

Next, we come to the `Button` control in the `DataList`, just underneath the Cost code render block. This handles the "add to cart" functionality, which we'll cover in the next section:

File: **employeestore.aspx (excerpt)**

```
<asp:Button id="btnAddToCart" runat="server" Text="Add To Cart"
    CommandName="Edit" />
```

As you can see, the `Button` control contains the `CommandName` property. When the button is clicked, the command bubbles up to the `DataList`. The `DataList` then raises the `EditCommand` event, and calls the `AddToCart()` method as defined by its `OnEditCommand` attribute.

The second control that we'll add is the `DataGrid` control. The `DataGrid` control will be bound to the cart `DataTable`:

```
<asp:Panel id="pnlShowCart" runat="server">
  <h1>View Cart</h1>
  <asp:DataGrid id="dgCart" runat="server"
      AutoGenerateColumns="false" GridLines="None" CellPadding="3"
      Width="100%" DataKeyField="ItemID"
      OnEditCommand="dgCart_Edit"
      OnCancelCommand="dgCart_Cancel"
      OnUpdateCommand="dgCart_Update"
      OnDeleteCommand="dgCart_Delete">
    <HeaderStyle Font-Name="arial" BackColor="#003366"
        ForeColor="#FFFFFF" Font-Bold="true" Font-Size="10" />
    <ItemStyle Font-Name="arial" Font-Size="10" />
    <Columns>
      <asp:EditCommandColumn EditText="Edit" CancelText="Cancel"
          UpdateText="Update" />
      <asp:BoundColumn DataField="Item" HeaderText="Product Name"
          ReadOnly="true" />
      <asp:TemplateColumn HeaderText="Quantity">
        <ItemTemplate>
          <%# Container.DataItem("Quantity") %>
        </ItemTemplate>
        <EditItemTemplate>
          <asp:TextBox id="txtQuantity" runat="server" Width="50"
              Text='<%# Container.DataItem("Quantity") %>' />
        </EditItemTemplate>
      </asp:TemplateColumn>
      <asp:BoundColumn DataField="Cost" HeaderText="Cost"
          ReadOnly="true" />
    </Columns>
  </asp:DataGrid>
  <p align="right"><strong>Total: <asp:Label id="lblTotal"
      runat="server" /></strong></p>
  <p align="right"><asp:LinkButton id="lbContinue"
      Text="Continue Shopping" runat="server"
      OnClick="ContinueShopping" /> |
      <asp:LinkButton id="lbCheckOut" Text="Checkout"
      runat="server" OnClick="CheckOut" /></p>
</asp:Panel>
```

Again, the DataGrid is nested within a Panel control, which allows us to switch easily between the DataList and DataGrid controls. When the user is in "View Cart" mode, this Panel control will be visible, and the DataList Panel control will be hidden. When the user is in "Shopping" mode, the DataGrid Panel control will be hidden, and the DataList Panel control will be visible.

The `DataGrid` control contains some important aspects that are worth mentioning here. First, we set some commands that will be used to raise events triggered by the `DataGrid` child controls; the `DataGrid` will call the appropriate method in response to each event:

File: **employeestore.aspx (excerpt)**

```
Width="100%" DataKeyField="ItemID"
OnEditCommand="dgCart_Edit"
OnCancelCommand="dgCart_Cancel"
OnUpdateCommand="dgCart_Update"
OnDeleteCommand="dgCart_Delete">
```

Next appear the actual columns within the `DataGrid`:

VB.NET   File: **employeestore.aspx (excerpt)**

```
<Columns>
  <asp:EditCommandColumn EditText="Edit" CancelText="Cancel"
     UpdateText="Update" />
  <asp:BoundColumn DataField="Item" HeaderText="Product Name"
     ReadOnly="true" />
  <asp:TemplateColumn HeaderText="Quantity">
    <ItemTemplate>
      <%# Container.DataItem("Quantity") %>
    </ItemTemplate>
    <EditItemTemplate>
      <asp:TextBox id="txtQuantity"
          Text='<%# Container.DataItem("Quantity") %>'
          runat="server" Width="50" />
    </EditItemTemplate>
  </asp:TemplateColumn>
  <asp:BoundColumn DataField="Cost" HeaderText="Cost"
     ReadOnly="true" />
</Columns>
```

As always, the code render blocks differ slightly in the C# version:

C#   File: **employeestore.aspx (excerpt)**

```
<Columns>
  <asp:EditCommandColumn EditText="Edit" CancelText="Cancel"
     UpdateText="Update" />
  <asp:BoundColumn DataField="Item" HeaderText="Product Name"
     ReadOnly="true" />
  <asp:TemplateColumn HeaderText="Quantity">
    <ItemTemplate>
      <%# DataBinder.Eval(Container.DataItem, "Quantity") %>
```

```
    </ItemTemplate>
    <EditItemTemplate>
      <asp:TextBox id="txtQuantity"
          Text='<%# DataBinder.Eval(Container.DataItem,
              "Quantity") %>'
          runat="server" Width="50" />
    </EditItemTemplate>
  </asp:TemplateColumn>
  <asp:BoundColumn DataField="Cost" HeaderText="Cost"
      ReadOnly="true" />
</Columns>
```

The first is the EditCommandColumn, which will be used for the edit, update, and cancel functionality. The second and fourth columns are BoundColumns, which are used for presenting particular information within the cart DataTable. We don't want to allow our users to alter this information, so we set the ReadOnly property for both columns to true. We *do* want the user to be able to modify the Quantity column, however, so this has been created as a TemplateColumn containing an <EditItemTemplate> tag.

Finally, in addition to a simple Label for the total cost, the panel contains a couple of LinkButton controls to handle the Continue Shopping and Checkout functionality:

File: **employeestore.aspx (excerpt)**

```
<p align="right"><strong>Total: <asp:Label id="lblTotal"
    runat="server" /></strong></p>
<p align="right"><asp:LinkButton id="lbContinue"
    Text="Continue Shopping" runat="server"
    OnClick="ContinueShopping" /> |
  <asp:LinkButton id="lbCheckOut" Text="Checkout"
    runat="server" OnClick="CheckOut" /></p>
```

For now, that's all there is to the interface.

Showing Items and Creating the Cart Structure

Now that you have developed the presentational items within the page, let's begin writing the code that we'll use to build the cart structure, and write out the items within the page. You can begin by creating empty methods for all those that we'll eventually use:

```vbnet
<script runat="server" language="VB">
Sub Page_Load(s As Object, e As EventArgs)

End Sub

Sub AddToCart(s As Object, e As DataListCommandEventArgs)

End Sub

Function FindItem(ItemID As Integer) As DataSet

End Function

Function GetItemTotal() As Decimal

End Function

Sub dgCart_Edit(s As Object, e As DataGridCommandEventArgs)

End Sub

Sub dgCart_Cancel(s As Object, e As DataGridCommandEventArgs)

End Sub

Sub dgCart_Update(s As Object, e As DataGridCommandEventArgs)

End Sub

Sub dgCart_Delete(s As Object, e As DataGridCommandEventArgs)

End Sub

Sub ContinueShopping(s As Object, e As EventArgs)

End Sub

Sub CheckOut(s As Object, e As EventArgs)

End Sub
</script>
```

```csharp
<script runat="server" language="C#">
void Page_Load() {
```

```
}

void AddToCart(Object s, DataListCommandEventArgs e) {

}

DataSet FindItem(int ItemID) {

}

Decimal GetItemTotal() {

}

void dgCart_Edit(Object s, DataGridCommandEventArgs e) {

}

void dgCart_Cancel(Object s, DataGridCommandEventArgs e) {

}

void dgCart_Update(Object s, DataGridCommandEventArgs e) {

}

void dgCart_Delete(Object s, DataGridCommandEventArgs e) {

}

void ContinueShopping(Object s, EventArgs e) {

}

void CheckOut(Object s, EventArgs e) {

}
</script>
```

We create all these empty methods first, as there are attributes within the DataList and DataGrid that make reference to them. The mere existence of an empty method with the required name will prevent an error from occurring when we test the functionality as we develop it.

Next, we'll create all of the variables that we'll use within the page, including the `Connection`, `DataAdapter`, `DataSet`, and `DataRow`, as follows:

VB.NET   File: **employeestore.aspx (excerpt)**

```vb
<script runat="server" language="VB">
Dim objConn As New OleDbConnection( _
    ConfigurationSettings.AppSettings("DSN"))
Dim objDA As OleDbDataAdapter
Dim objDS As New DataSet()
Dim objDR As DataRow
Dim objCartDT As DataTable

Sub Page_Load()
  ...
```

C#   File: **employeestore.aspx (excerpt)**

```csharp
<script runat="server" language="C#">
OleDbConnection objConn = new OleDbConnection(
    ConfigurationSettings.AppSettings["DSN"]);
OleDbDataAdapter objDA;
DataSet objDS = new DataSet();
DataRow objDR;
DataTable objCartDT;

void Page_Load() {
  ...
```

Within the `Page_Load()` event handler, we'll create the code that binds the items within the `EmployeeStore` table to the `DataList`, displaying the list of items for sale in the store.

VB.NET   File: **employeestore.aspx (excerpt)**

```vb
Sub Page_Load()
  If Not IsPostBack Then
    objDA = New OleDbDataAdapter("SELECT * FROM EmployeeStore", _
        objConn)
    objDA.Fill(objDS, "Store")
    dlItems.DataSource = objDS
    dlItems.DataBind()

    pnlShowCart.Visible = False
  End If
```

C#   File: **employeestore.aspx (excerpt)**

```
void Page_Load() {
  if (!IsPostBack) {
    objDA = new OleDbDataAdapter("SELECT * FROM EmployeeStore",
        objConn);
    objDA.Fill(objDS, "Store");
    dlItems.DataSource = objDS;
    dlItems.DataBind();

    pnlShowCart.Visible = false;
  }
```

Remember, we only want to bind to the DataList when the user first navigates to the store; the DataList will automatically retain its contents as the user interacts with the page, making additional requests. For this reason, we do a postback check. We also hide the DataGrid, by setting pnlShowCart.Visible to false, so that, initially, only the DataList appears.

Also in Page_Load(), we'll load the user's shopping cart from the Session collection. As we saw in Chapter 11, values stored in Session become associated with the one user's visit to the site, are preserved throughout their visit, and are accessible on any page in the site. It's no coincidence that these are the exact features we need for our shopping cart! Of course, when the user first visits the employee store we need to create an empty shopping cart for them, as none will yet exist. The code below will detect this condition, create a new DataTable to act as the cart, define its DataColumn structure, and then store it in Session.

VB.NET   File: **employeestore.aspx (excerpt)**

```
  objCartDT = Session("Cart")
  If objCartDT Is Nothing Then
    objCartDT = New DataTable("Cart")
    objCartDT.Columns.Add("CartID", GetType(Integer))
    objCartDT.Columns("CartID").AutoIncrement = True
    objCartDT.Columns("CartID").AutoIncrementSeed = 1
    objCartDT.Columns.Add("ItemID", GetType(Integer))
    objCartDT.Columns.Add("Quantity", GetType(Integer))
    objCartDT.Columns.Add("Item", GetType(String))
    objCartDT.Columns.Add("Cost", GetType(Decimal))
    Session("Cart") = objCartDT
  End If
End Sub
```

```
C#                                                        File: employeestore.aspx (excerpt)
  objCartDT = (DataTable)Session["Cart"];
  if (objCartDT == null) {
    objCartDT = new DataTable("Cart");
    objCartDT.Columns.Add("CartID", typeof(Int32));
    objCartDT.Columns["CartID"].AutoIncrement = true;
    objCartDT.Columns["CartID"].AutoIncrementSeed = 1;
    objCartDT.Columns.Add("ItemID", typeof(Int32));
    objCartDT.Columns.Add("Quantity", typeof(Int32));
    objCartDT.Columns.Add("Item", typeof(string));
    objCartDT.Columns.Add("Cost", typeof(Decimal));
    Session["Cart"] = objCartDT;
  }
}
```

Unlike controls like our DataList, page variables like objCartDT don't automatically preserve their values; that's why we load the cart regardless of the outcome of our postback check.

As you can see from the code above, our objCartDT DataTable will contain five columns. The first, CartID, is an auto incremented column that serves only one purpose: to keep the items within the DataTable unique. The second, ItemID, represents the ID from the EmployeeStore database table. The Quantity, Item, and Cost columns represent the remainder of the item specific information contained within the EmployeeStore database table.

Once you've added the necessary code, save your work and trial the page within the browser. It should resemble the display we saw in Figure 12.1.

Try clicking the Add to Cart Button control. Nothing happens, right? That's because we haven't written the code to handle this interaction yet—the AddToCart() method is empty. In the next section, we'll implement this functionality, which will add a new row to our cart DataTable and bind the results to the DataGrid control.

Adding to the Cart

The next section of the functionality that we'll address is the ability for the user to add an item to the shopping cart. Remember, the structure of the cart DataTable has already been built (and stored in the user's session) within the Page_Load() method. All we have to do now is add the item as a DataRow within the cart DataTable. To do this, we'll fill out the AddToCart() method as follows:

VB.NET   File: **employeestore.aspx (excerpt)**

```vbnet
Sub AddToCart(s As Object, e As DataListCommandEventArgs)
  pnlShowItems.Visible = False
  pnlShowCart.Visible = True

  Dim ItemID As Integer = dlItems.DataKeys(e.Item.ItemIndex)
  Dim objItemInfo As DataSet = FindItem(ItemID)

  objDR = objCartDT.NewRow()
  objDR("ItemID") = ItemID
  objDR("Item") = _
      objItemInfo.Tables("ItemInfo").Rows(0).Item("ItemName")
  objDR("Quantity") = 1
  objDR("Cost") = _
      objItemInfo.Tables("ItemInfo").Rows(0).Item("Cost")
  objCartDT.Rows.Add(objDR)

  dgCart.DataSource = objCartDT
  dgCart.DataBind()
End Sub
```

C#   File: **employeestore.aspx (excerpt)**

```csharp
void AddToCart(Object s, DataListCommandEventArgs e) {
  pnlShowItems.Visible = false;
  pnlShowCart.Visible = true;

  int ItemID = Convert.ToInt32(
      dlItems.DataKeys[e.Item.ItemIndex]);
  DataSet objItemInfo = FindItem(ItemID);

  objDR = objCartDT.NewRow();
  objDR["ItemID"] = ItemID;
  objDR["Item"] =
      objItemInfo.Tables["ItemInfo"].Rows[0]["ItemName"];
  objDR["Quantity"] = 1;
  objDR["Cost"] = objItemInfo.Tables["ItemInfo"].Rows[0]["Cost"];
  objCartDT.Rows.Add(objDR);

  dgCart.DataSource = objCartDT;
  dgCart.DataBind();
}
```

Let's break down the code. Once a user adds an item to the cart, we'll immediately want to shift the focus to the DataGrid and hide the DataList. That's what our first two lines will do:

VB.NET   File: **employeestore.aspx (excerpt)**

```
pnlShowItems.Visible = False
pnlShowCart.Visible = True
```

C#   File: **employeestore.aspx (excerpt)**

```
pnlShowItems.Visible = false;
pnlShowCart.Visible = true;
```

Once the user selects an item to add to the cart, the `DataList` will be hidden, and the `DataGrid` will be made visible. Next, we call the `FindItem()` function and pass in the unique item ID directly from the `DataList`'s `DataKeyField` property:

VB.NET   File: **employeestore.aspx (excerpt)**

```
Dim ItemID As Integer = dlItems.DataKeys(e.Item.ItemIndex)
Dim objItemInfo As DataSet = FindItem(ItemID)
```

C#   File: **employeestore.aspx (excerpt)**

```
int ItemID = Convert.ToInt32(
    dlItems.DataKeys[e.Item.ItemIndex]);
DataSet objItemInfo = FindItem(ItemID);
```

The `FindItem()` method, which we'll define in a minute, returns a populated `DataSet` complete with all of the item information specific to the item ID that was passed in as a parameter. That filled `DataSet` is then used to populate a new row for the item in our cart `DataTable`:

VB.NET   File: **employeestore.aspx (excerpt)**

```
objDR = objCartDT.NewRow()
objDR("ItemID") = ItemID
objDR("Item") = _
    objItemInfo.Tables("ItemInfo").Rows(0).Item("ItemName")
objDR("Quantity") = 1
objDR("Cost") = _
    objItemInfo.Tables("ItemInfo").Rows(0).Item("Cost")
objCartDT.Rows.Add(objDR)
```

C#   File: **employeestore.aspx (excerpt)**

```
objDR = objCartDT.NewRow();
objDR["ItemID"] = ItemID;
objDR["Item"] =
    objItemInfo.Tables["ItemInfo"].Rows[0]["ItemName"];
objDR["Quantity"] = 1;
```

```
objDR["Cost"] = objItemInfo.Tables["ItemInfo"].Rows[0]["Cost"];
objCartDT.Rows.Add(objDR);
```

As you can see, we create a new row, `objDR`, by calling the `NewRow()` method of the `DataTable` object. Once we have created the new row, we fill each column with the item ID, name, quantity (initially set to 1), and cost, pulling the values from the first row of the `ItemInfo` table in `objItemInfo`. Finally, we add the new row to the `Rows` collection of the `DataTable`.

Next, we bind the cart `DataTable` to the `DataGrid`:

VB.NET   File: **employeestore.aspx (excerpt)**
```
dgCart.DataSource = objCartDT
dgCart.DataBind()
```

C#   File: **employeestore.aspx (excerpt)**
```
dgCart.DataSource = objCartDT;
dgCart.DataBind();
```

The `FindItem()` method is written as follows:

VB.NET   File: **employeestore.aspx (excerpt)**
```
Function FindItem(ItemID As Integer) As DataSet
  Dim objItemInfo As New DataSet()

  objDA = New OleDbDataAdapter( _
    "SELECT * FROM EmployeeStore WHERE ItemID=" & ItemID, objConn)
  objDA.Fill(objItemInfo, "ItemInfo")

  Return objItemInfo
End Function
```

C#   File: **employeestore.aspx (excerpt)**
```
DataSet FindItem(int ItemID) {
  DataSet objItemInfo = new DataSet();

  objDA = new OleDbDataAdapter(
    "SELECT * FROM EmployeeStore WHERE ItemID=" + ItemID,
    objConn);
  objDA.Fill(objItemInfo, "ItemInfo");

  return objItemInfo;
}
```

As you can see, the function is relatively straightforward. All we're doing is passing in the unique `ItemID`, and using that as the filter criteria within the `WHERE` clause of the SQL statement. Next, we fill the `DataSet` and return it.

With that code complete, save your work and test the results in the browser. Figure 12.5 shows how you can add an item to your cart.

Figure 12.5. The item is added to the cart.

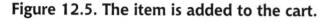

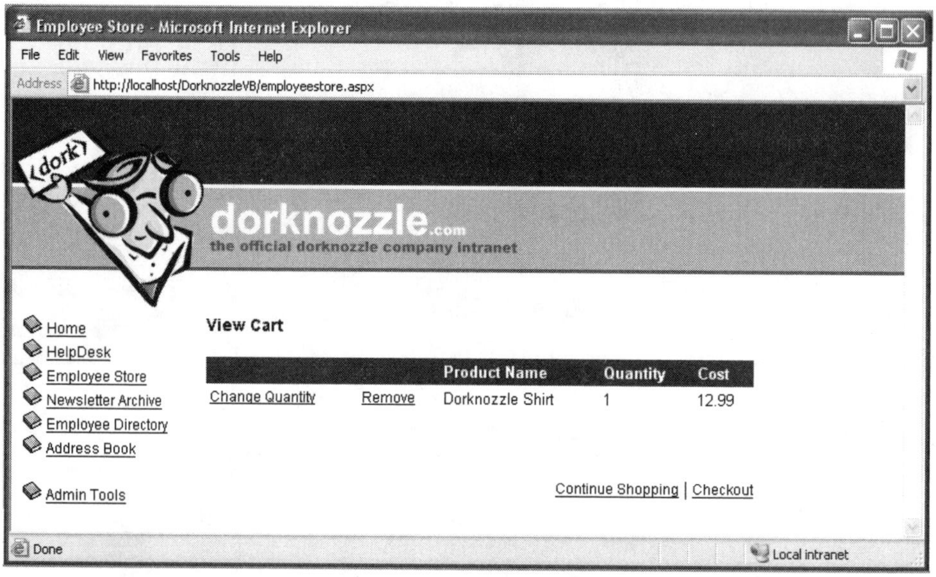

Hit your browser's Back button and add the same item to your cart again. You'll notice that the system adds the same item to the `DataTable` in a separate row, rather than simply recalculating the quantity and incrementing the number. You can improve on this by changing the `AddToCart()` method. Add the code below immediately after the call to `FindItem()`, and just before the `NewRow()` method of the `DataTable`:

VB.NET   File: **employeestore.aspx (excerpt)**

```
Dim blnMatch As Boolean = False
For Each objDR In objCartDT.Rows
   If objDR("ItemID") = ItemID Then
      objDR("Quantity") += 1
      blnMatch = True
      Exit For
```

```
    End If
Next
```

C#   File: employeestore.aspx (excerpt)

```
bool blnMatch = false;
foreach (DataRow objDR in objCartDT.Rows) {
  if (Convert.ToInt32(objDR["ItemID"]) == ItemID) {
    int Quantity = Convert.ToInt32(objDR["Quantity"]);
    Quantity += 1;
    objDR["Quantity"] = Quantity;
    blnMatch = true;
    break;
  }
}
```

In this case, we create a new Boolean variable called blnMatch, and set it to False. We then loop through each DataRow within the DataTable and check to see if the ItemID exists. If it does, we increment the Quantity by one, set the Boolean variable to True, and exit/break out of the loop.

We now have to check the Boolean variable before we add the new row, because we don't want to increment an existing row *and* add a new one:

VB.NET   File: employeestore.aspx (excerpt)

```
If Not blnMatch Then
  objDR = objCartDT.NewRow
  objDR("ItemID") = ItemID
  objDR("Item") = _
      objItemInfo.Tables("ItemInfo").Rows(0).Item("ItemName")
  objDR("Quantity") = 1
  objDR("Cost") = _
      objItemInfo.Tables("ItemInfo").Rows(0).Item("Cost")
  objCartDT.Rows.Add(objDR)
End If
```

C#   File: employeestore.aspx (excerpt)

```
if (!blnMatch) {
  objDR = objCartDT.NewRow();
  objDR["ItemID"] = ItemID;
  objDR["Item"] =
      objItemInfo.Tables["ItemInfo"].Rows[0]["ItemName"];
  objDR["Quantity"] = 1;
  objDR["Cost"] =
      objItemInfo.Tables["ItemInfo"].Rows[0]["Cost"];
```

```
      objCartDT.Rows.Add(objDR);
  }
```

If the blnMatch variable is False, it means that the item was not found in the cart, in which case we'll go ahead and create a new row for it. If, on the other hand, it is True, then we know that we've already found the item and incremented the quantity in the loop above. Now, save your work and run the page within the browser again. This time you can add an item to the cart, hit the back button, and add the same item again; the quantity will be increased to two.

The "add to cart" functionality should be working fairly well now. This is a big project, so if you get stuck along the way, feel free to grab the finished code from the code archive. Next, let's talk about retrieving the total cost of items within the cart.

Keeping the Order Total

The next order of business is to write a function that returns a value for the total cost of items within the cart. If you recall, the method we'll use is called GetItemTotal(), and can be written as follows:

VB.NET   File: **employeestore.aspx (excerpt)**

```
Function GetItemTotal() As Decimal
  Dim decRunningTotal As Decimal = 0

  For Each objDR In objCartDT.Rows
    decRunningTotal += _
        Decimal.Round(objDR("Cost") * objDR("Quantity"), 2)
  Next

  Return decRunningTotal
End Function
```

C#   File: **employeestore.aspx (excerpt)**

```
Decimal GetItemTotal() {
  decimal decRunningTotal = 0;

  foreach (DataRow objDR in objCartDT.Rows) {
    decRunningTotal +=
        Decimal.Round(Convert.ToDecimal(objDR["Cost"]) *
            Convert.ToInt32(objDR["Quantity"]), 2);
  }
```

```
    return decRunningTotal;
}
```

We start by creating a variable, decRunningTotal, a decimal variable in which we'll calculate the total cost of items in the cart. This will be the value that we'll return and eventually bind to the Label control below the DataGrid.

Next, we loop through the Rows collection within the DataTable, from each, we extract the cost and quantity of the item and multiply them to obtain the price, which we add to our running total. Note that we're using Decimal.Round() method to make sure the cost is calculated to two decimal places.

Finally, we close the loop, return the value, and close the function.

Don't try to view the result within the browser just yet. We still have to set the returned value of the function to a Label control within the AddToCart() method. You can do this by adding the bold line below as the very last line of the method:

VB.NET   File: **employeestore.aspx (excerpt)**

```
  dgCart.DataSource = objCartDT
  dgCart.DataBind()

  lblTotal.Text = "$" & GetItemTotal()
End Sub
```

C#   File: **employeestore.aspx (excerpt)**

```
  dgCart.DataSource = objCartDT;
  dgCart.DataBind();

  lblTotal.Text = "$" + GetItemTotal();
}
```

As you can see, we're simply returning the result of the function and setting that result to a Label control's Text property. Now, save your work and test the page within the browser. Figure 12.6 shows how the total is incremented within the Label control each time you add an item to the cart.

Figure 12.6. The total cost of items within your cart is shown within a Label control underneath the `DataGrid`.

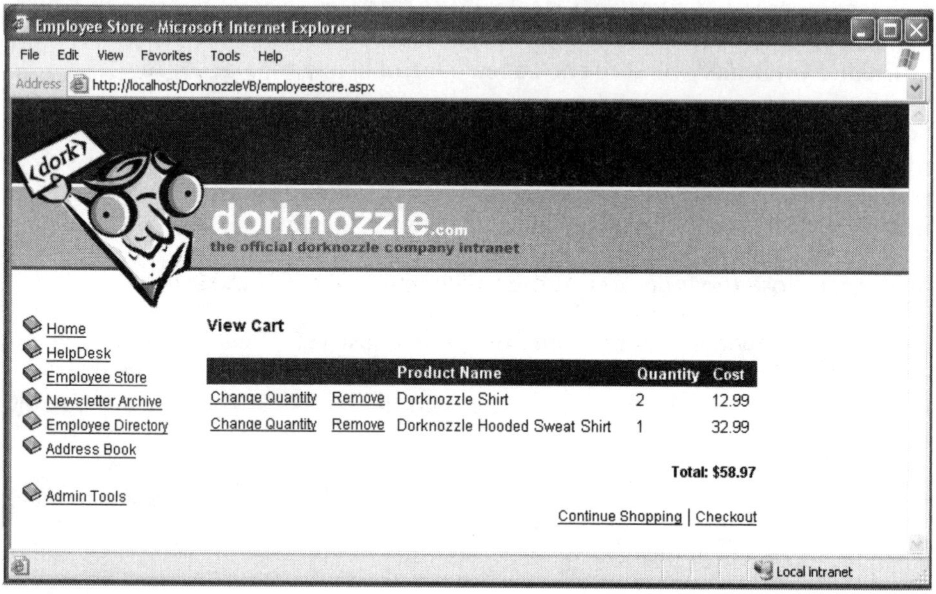

The cart is starting to take shape! Next, we'll outline how we can make the quantities within the `DataGrid` modifiable.

Modifying Cart Quantities

As you've probably already realized, we'll be modifying items within the cart by using the `EditCommandColumn` within the `DataGrid`. On the `DataGrid` tag itself, you should have already declared the four methods to handle the `EditCommand`, `CancelCommand`, `UpdateCommand` and `DeleteCommand` events, like so:

File: **employeestore.aspx** (excerpt)

```
...
Width="100%" DataKeyField="CartID"
OnEditCommand="dgCart_Edit"
OnCancelCommand="dgCart_Cancel"
OnUpdateCommand="dgCart_Update"
OnDeleteCommand="dgCart_Delete">
```

You'll also have noticed that the `DataKeyField` value, in this case, is the unique identifier that we created within the `Page_Load()` method for the cart. This value, if you can recall, was set to auto increment, which will also mean it is unique. As this is the case, we can use its value to retrieve specific row information from the `DataGrid`. You'll also remember that the `DataGrid` contains one editable column, the quantity column:

C#   File: **employeestore.aspx (excerpt)**

```
<asp:TemplateColumn HeaderText="Quantity">
  <ItemTemplate>
    <%# DataBinder.Eval(Container.DataItem, "Quantity") %>
  </ItemTemplate>
  <EditItemTemplate>
    <asp:TextBox id="txtQuantity"
        Text='<%# DataBinder.Eval(Container.DataItem,
            "Quantity") %>'
        runat="server" Width="50" />
  </EditItemTemplate>
</asp:TemplateColumn>
```

Using `<TemplateColumn>` for just the quantity column means that when the `EditItemIndex` property of the `DataGrid` is set to something other than -1, only that column will be editable. With that in mind, let's write the `dgCart_Edit()` method:

VB.NET   File: **employeestore.aspx (excerpt)**

```
Sub dgCart_Edit(s As Object, e As DataGridCommandEventArgs)
  dgCart.EditItemIndex = e.Item.ItemIndex

  dgCart.DataSource = objCartDT
  dgCart.DataBind()
End Sub
```

C#   File: **employeestore.aspx (excerpt)**

```
void dgCart_Edit(Object s, DataGridCommandEventArgs e) {
  dgCart.EditItemIndex = e.Item.ItemIndex;

  dgCart.DataSource = objCartDT;
  dgCart.DataBind();
}
```

As you can see, we set the `EditItemIndex` property of the `DataGrid` equal to the row that the user has selected. This activates any `<EditItemTemplate>` tags for that row active. Therefore, for the quantity column, there will be a `TextBox` control bound to the number of items currently in the cart. Finally, we simply rebind the cart `DataTable` to the `DataGrid`.

Now, let's add the `dgCart_Cancel()` method so that the user may cancel out of edit mode. As you might remember from Chapter 9, this method, like `dgCart_Edit()`, is pretty simple, and can be written as follows:

```
VB.NET                                    File: employeestore.aspx (excerpt)
Sub dgCart_Cancel(s As Object, e As DataGridCommandEventArgs)
  dgCart.EditItemIndex = -1

  dgCart.DataSource = objCartDT
  dgCart.DataBind()
End Sub
```

```
C#                                        File: employeestore.aspx (excerpt)
void dgCart_Cancel(Object s, DataGridCommandEventArgs e) {
  dgCart.EditItemIndex = -1;

  dgCart.DataSource = objCartDT;
  dgCart.DataBind();
}
```

This method is pretty much the reverse of `dgCart_Edit()`, setting the `EditItemIndex` property of the `DataGrid` to -1, canceling out of edit mode. We finish by rebinding the cart `DataTable` to the `DataGrid`.

Now, let's look at the `dgCart_Update()` method. From what you learned in Chapter 9, you should expect this method to be the most complex of the three. We'll add the following code:

```
VB.NET                                    File: employeestore.aspx (excerpt)
Sub dgCart_Update(s As Object, e As DataGridCommandEventArgs)
  Dim txtQuantity As TextBox
  Dim intCartID As Integer

  intCartID = dgCart.DataKeys(e.Item.ItemIndex)
  txtQuantity = e.Item.FindControl("txtQuantity")

  For Each objDR In objCartDT.Rows
    If objDR("CartID") = intCartID Then
      objDR("Quantity") = Int32.Parse(txtQuantity.Text)
      Exit For
    End If
  Next

  lblTotal.Text = "$" & GetItemTotal()
  dgCart.EditItemIndex = -1
```

```
  dgCart.DataSource = objCartDT
  dgCart.DataBind()
End Sub
```

C#   File: **employeestore.aspx (excerpt)**

```csharp
void dgCart_Update(Object s, DataGridCommandEventArgs e) {
  TextBox txtQuantity;
  int intCartID;

  intCartID = Convert.ToInt32(dgCart.DataKeys[e.Item.ItemIndex]);
  txtQuantity = (TextBox)e.Item.FindControl("txtQuantity");

  foreach (DataRow objDR in objCartDT.Rows) {
    if (intCartID == (int)objDR["CartID"]) {
      objDR["Quantity"] = Convert.ToInt32(txtQuantity.Text);
      break;
    }
  }

  lblTotal.Text = "$" + GetItemTotal();
  dgCart.EditItemIndex = -1;

  dgCart.DataSource = objCartDT;
  dgCart.DataBind();
}
```

Let's walk through this code. Initially, we create two variables:

VB.NET   File: **employeestore.aspx (excerpt)**

```
  Dim txtQuantity As Textbox
  Dim intCartID As Integer
```

C#   File: **employeestore.aspx (excerpt)**

```csharp
  TextBox txtQuantity;
  int intCartID;
```

First, we create a `TextBox` variable, which is used to keep a reference for the `TextBox` control within the `DataGrid`. The second is an integer, and will be used to store the value of the `DataKeyField` for the `DataGrid` row being updated. Next, we find that value by taking it from the `DataKeys` collection of the `DataGrid`, and passing in the `ItemIndex` from the selected row:

VB.NET   File: **employeestore.aspx (excerpt)**

```
  intCartID = dgCart.DataKeys(e.Item.ItemIndex)
```

C#   File: **employeestore.aspx (excerpt)**

```csharp
intCartID = Convert.ToInt32(dgCart.DataKeys[e.Item.ItemIndex]);
```

Next, we find the control within the `DataGrid` called `txtQuantity` using the `FindControl()` method of the selected row. We assign that value to our newly created `TextBox` variable, `txtQuantity`:

VB.NET   File: **employeestore.aspx (excerpt)**

```vb
txtQuantity = e.Item.FindControl("txtQuantity")
```

C#   File: **employeestore.aspx (excerpt)**

```csharp
txtQuantity = (TextBox)e.Item.FindControl("txtQuantity");
```

We then use a `For Each` loop to iterate through the `Rows` collection of the cart `DataTable`. Inside this loop, we use an `If` statement to check whether the data key we stored in `intCartID` matches the `CartID` field within the cart `DataTable`. If it does, we know we've found the row of our cart that needs to be updated, and we'll adjust the `Quantity` field to match the value the user entered into the `TextBox` control. We also exit/break out of the loop, to avoid needlessly iterating through the remaining rows:

VB.NET   File: **employeestore.aspx (excerpt)**

```vb
For Each objDR In objCartDT.Rows
  If objDR("CartID") = intCartID Then
    objDR("Quantity") = Int32.Parse(txtQuantity.Text)
    Exit For
  End If
Next
```

C#   File: **employeestore.aspx (excerpt)**

```csharp
foreach (DataRow objDR in objCartDT.Rows) {
  if (intCartID == (int)objDR["CartID"]) {
    objDR["Quantity"] = Convert.ToInt32(txtQuantity.Text);
    break;
  }
}
```

We'll update the displayed total of the cart's contents by calling the `GetItemTotal()` method and assigning the returned value to the `Label`. Finally, we cancel out of edit mode for the `DataGrid` by setting the `EditItemIndex` property to `-1`, and rebind the `DataGrid` to the cart `DataTable`:

VB.NET   File: **employeestore.aspx (excerpt)**

```
lblTotal.Text = "$" & GetItemTotal()
dgCart.EditItemIndex = -1

dgCart.DataSource = objCartDT
dgCart.DataBind()
```

C#   File: **employeestore.aspx (excerpt)**

```
lblTotal.Text = "$" + GetItemTotal();
dgCart.EditItemIndex = -1;

dgCart.DataSource = objCartDT;
dgCart.DataBind();
```

Save your work and test the results in the browser. Figure 12.7 shows how you can add an item to the cart and select the Change Quantity hyperlink to display the TextBox control within the selected row in the DataGrid.

Figure 12.7. Add an item to your cart and select the edit hyperlink to modify the quantity of an item within your cart.

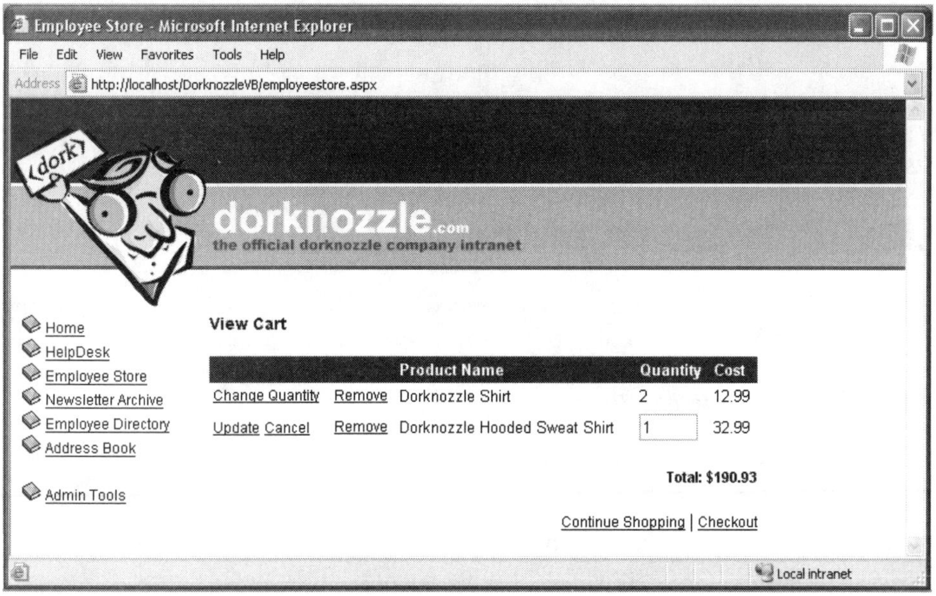

Now, select the Update hyperlink. The quantity and grand total should change.

Now would be a great time to add the "continue shopping" functionality. Although this link looks like a regular hyperlink, it doesn't function like one. Instead, we've set the `OnClick` attribute of the `LinkButton` control to call the `ContinueShopping()` method, as follows:

File: **employeestore.aspx (excerpt)**

```
<asp:LinkButton id="lbContinue" Text="Continue Shopping"
    runat="server" OnClick="ContinueShopping" />
```

Now, let's add the `ContinueShopping()` method:

VB.NET
File: **employeestore.aspx (excerpt)**

```
Sub ContinueShopping(s As Object, e As EventArgs)
  pnlShowCart.Visible = False
  pnlShowItems.Visible = True
End Sub
```

C#
File: **employeestore.aspx (excerpt)**

```
void ContinueShopping(Object s, EventArgs e) {
  pnlShowCart.Visible = false;
  pnlShowItems.Visible = true;
}
```

As you can see, this is a very simple method—all it has to do is switch `Panel`s. First, we hide the cart `Panel` control that contains the `DataGrid` by setting its `Visible` property to `False`. We then reveal the `DataList Panel` control by setting its `Visible` property to `True`.

Removing Items from the Cart

Now that users can add and modify items within the cart, you're probably going to want to provide the ability for them to remove items from the cart as well. We'll need to add a suitable `ButtonColumn` as the second element within the `<Columns>` tag of the `DataGrid`, like so:

```
<asp:ButtonColumn ButtonType="LinkButton" Text="Remove"
    CommandName="Delete" />
```

Next, we specify the name of the method that will handle this command, by setting the `OnDeleteCommand` attribute on the `DataGrid` tag:

```
<asp:DataGrid id="dgCart" runat="server"
    AutoGenerateColumns="false" GridLines="None" CellPadding="3"
    Width="100%" DataKeyField="CartID"
```

```
      OnEditCommand="dgCart_Edit" OnCancelCommand="dgCart_Cancel"
      OnUpdateCommand="dgCart_Update"
      OnDeleteCommand="dgCart_Delete">
```

Finally, we can add the method that handles the actual deletion:

VB.NET   File: **employeestore.aspx (excerpt)**

```vbnet
Sub dgCart_Delete(s As Object, e As DataGridCommandEventArgs)
  objCartDT.Rows(e.Item.ItemIndex).Delete()

  dgCart.DataSource = objCartDT
  dgCart.DataBind()

  lblTotal.Text = "$" & GetItemTotal()
End Sub
```

C#   File: **employeestore.aspx (excerpt)**

```csharp
void dgCart_Delete(Object s, DataGridCommandEventArgs e) {
  objCartDT.Rows[e.Item.ItemIndex].Delete();

  dgCart.DataSource = objCartDT;
  dgCart.DataBind();

  lblTotal.Text = "$" + GetItemTotal();
}
```

Let's step through the code. Initially, we call the `Delete()` method of the `DataRow` that corresponds to the item to be deleted in the cart. We get the `DataRow` from the cart `DataTable`'s `Rows` collection:

VB.NET   File: **employeestore.aspx (excerpt)**

```vbnet
  objCartDT.Rows(e.Item.ItemIndex).Delete()
```

C#   File: **employeestore.aspx (excerpt)**

```csharp
  objCartDT.Rows[e.Item.ItemIndex].Delete();
```

Next, we rebind the cart `DataTable` with the `DataGrid`:

VB.NET   File: **employeestore.aspx (excerpt)**

```vbnet
  dgCart.DataSource = objCartDT
  dgCart.DataBind()
```

C#   File: **employeestore.aspx (excerpt)**

```csharp
  dgCart.DataSource = objCartDT;
  dgCart.DataBind();
```

Finally, we update the cart total by calling the `GetItemTotal()` function, and assigning the returned value to the `Label` control's `Text` property:

VB.NET   File: **employeestore.aspx (excerpt)**

```
lblTotal.Text = "$" & GetItemTotal()
```

C#   File: **employeestore.aspx (excerpt)**

```
lblTotal.Text = "$" + GetItemTotal();
```

Save your work and open the page in the browser. Check that you can now remove any items you add to the cart by clicking the Remove hyperlink.

This is a pretty simple cart, and there's certainly a lot of functionality that we could add. Perhaps the most important would be to integrate our shopping cart with some sort of payment system. In the next section, we'll explore how to do just that using PayPal.

Processing Orders Using PayPal

Now the shopping cart is built and functioning smoothly. But what good does it do you if you can't start collecting and processing orders somehow? Our next step is to add a means to process the orders that people make. For instance, we'll want to allow users to enter credit card information, their shipping address, and a shipping method. Doing all this ourselves is far beyond the scope of this book. Instead, let's use a third-party company to handle the processing of our orders for us. Although there are many third-party companies that you can integrate with your shopping cart, we'll have a look at PayPal.

PayPal is free to set up. You are charged a small fee only when the transaction is processed, the system offers great tools to use for order management, and the company has great technical support. Perhaps most importantly, PayPal is a well-known company that people are prepared to trust with their sensitive details.

In this section, we'll explore how you can integrate the shopping cart you just created with a free PayPal business account.

Creating a PayPal Account

I love using eBay[4]... in fact, I'm a self proclaimed eBay junkie. I started using eBay in 1997, but only occasionally, to search for and buy items that I wasn't

[4] http://www.ebay.com/

able to find at a store in my town. A few years back, I discovered PayPal, and my online purchasing habits jumped from once a month to an item a week—sometimes more!

The great part about PayPal is that it's not just a useful tool from a buyer's perspective; it's also a great service if you're a seller. They've taken the pain out of integrating your online store with costly processing software, and have made it a simple process. Initially, we create a business account on PayPal's site for free. Then, we modify our code a little, to send the order information to PayPal so that they can process the request. PayPal charges us a small percentage of the cost of each item that we sell. It's as simple as that.

Now that you have an idea as to what PayPal is and what it does, let's begin the integration. As I mentioned above, our first step is to create a PayPal account. You can begin the process by following the steps outlined below:

1. Visit https://www.paypal.com/signup.

2. Select Business Account, choose your country, and click Continue.

3. Enter your business information.

4. Enter your personal information.

5. When you're done, you'll be sent a confirmation email.

6. Follow the steps outlined in the email to complete your new account setup.

That's it! You've effectively completed the steps necessary for Dorknozzle to start making money by selling items from our online store. Next, we'll look at the functionality that needs to be added within our code so that we can send our orders over to our PayPal account.

Integrating the Shopping Cart with your PayPal Account

In order to get our orders from point A (Dorknozzle Website) to point B (PayPal), we'll simply configure a few variables that PayPal requires. These variables are easy to configure, and are fairly intuitive when you see them in use. Before we get ahead of ourselves, however, let's define how the user will actually initiate the transfer of data from Dorknozzle to PayPal. If you remember, you created a `LinkButton` control called `lbCheckOut`:

```
<asp:LinkButton id="lbCheckOut" Text="Checkout" runat="server" />
```

When the user clicks this LinkButton, something needs to happen. That some-thing is the transfer of information from Dorknozzle to PayPal. But how does PayPal know what's in our cart? The answer is simple, and was mentioned in the opening paragraph: custom variables that you define and attach as parameters to the link. Here's a partial list of configurable variables and their values:

cmd

An internal variable that alerts PayPal that information is coming from a prebuilt shopping cart.

Value   _cart

Required   Yes

upload

Another internal variable that alerts PayPal as to how the information is being sent.

Value   1

Required   Yes

business

This indicates the PayPal account to which the payment should be made. Use the email address you provided when you signed up with PayPal.

Value   E.g. sales@dorknozzle.com

Required   Yes

item_name_*n*

This indicates the name of the *n*th item in the shopping cart.

Value   E.g. Dorknozzle Shirt

Required   Yes

item_number_*n*

This indicates the quantity of the *n*th item in the shopping cart.

Value   E.g. 4

Required   No

amount_n

This provides the total cost of the *n*th item in the shopping cart (Cost ×
Quantity).

Value   E.g. 32.99

Required   Yes

While you need specify each of the first three variables only once, the last three
need to appear once for each item in the user's shopping cart, where *n* is the
number of the row of the cart in which it appears (beginning with 1).

Now that you have an idea as to the variables you'll be required to submit, let's
begin to add the necessary code. Initially, we'll add the OnClick attribute to our
LinkButton control:

```
<asp:LinkButton id="lbCheckOut" Text="Checkout" runat="server"
    OnClick="CheckOut" />
```

When the user clicks the LinkButton control, the Click event will be raised, and
the CheckOut() method will be called. Let's define the CheckOut() method next:

VB.NET   File: **employeestore.aspx (excerpt)**

```
Sub CheckOut(s As Object, e As EventArgs)
  Dim cartBusiness As String = "sales@dorknozzle.com"
  Dim cartProduct As String
  Dim cartQuantity As Integer
  Dim cartCost As Decimal
  Dim itemNumber As Integer = 1

  cartBusiness = Server.UrlEncode(cartBusiness)

  Dim strPayPal As String = _
      "https://www.paypal.com/cgi-bin/webscr" & _
      "?cmd=_cart&upload=1&business=" & cartBusiness

  For Each objDR In objCartDT.Rows
    cartProduct = Server.UrlEncode(objDR("Item"))
    cartQuantity = objDR("Quantity")
    cartCost = objDR("Cost")

    strPayPal &= "&item_name_" & itemNumber & "=" & cartProduct
    strPayPal &= "&item_number_" & itemNumber & "=" & cartQuantity
```

```
      strPayPal &= "&amount_" & itemNumber & "=" & _
         Decimal.Round(cartQuantity * cartCost, 2)

      itemNumber = itemNumber + 1
   Next

   Response.Redirect(strPayPal)
End Sub
```

C#   File: **employeestore.aspx (excerpt)**

```
void CheckOut(Object s, EventArgs e) {
   String cartBusiness = "sales@dorknozzle.com";
   String cartProduct;
   int cartQuantity;
   Decimal cartCost;
   int itemNumber = 1;

   cartBusiness = Server.UrlEncode(cartBusiness);

   String strPayPal = "https://www.paypal.com/cgi-bin/webscr" +
      "?cmd=_cart&upload=1&business=" + cartBusiness;

   foreach (DataRow objDR in objCartDT.Rows) {
      cartProduct = Server.UrlEncode((String)objDR["Item"]);
      cartQuantity = (int)objDR["Quantity"];
      cartCost = (Decimal)objDR["Cost"];

      strPayPal += "&item_name_" + itemNumber + "=" + cartProduct;
      strPayPal += "&item_number_" + itemNumber + "=" +
         cartQuantity;
      strPayPal += "&amount_" + itemNumber + "=" +
         Decimal.Round(cartQuantity * cartCost, 2);

      itemNumber++;
   }

   Response.Redirect(strPayPal);
}
```

Let's break down this code. We begin by creating variables that will hold your PayPal account email address, a product, its quantity and its price, and a number indicating which row of the cart we are processing.

VB.NET   File: **employeestore.aspx (excerpt)**

```
Dim cartBusiness As String = "sales@dorknozzle.com"
Dim cartProduct As String
```

```
Dim cartQuantity As Integer
Dim cartCost As Decimal
Dim itemNumber As Integer = 1
```

C#   File: **employeestore.aspx (excerpt)**

```
String cartBusiness = "sales@dorknozzle.com";
String cartProduct;
int cartQuantity;
Decimal cartCost;
int itemNumber = 1;
```

Next, since we will be passing all of these values in a URL, we must ensure that any special characters (such as spaces or certain symbol characters) in these values are replaced with URL-safe codes that represent these characters. We haven't yet gotten around to populating most of our variables, but right away we can see that `cartBusiness` contains an email address, which contains a potentially problematic @ character. Here's how to **URL encode** this value using the `UrlEncode()` method of the built-in `Server` object:

VB.NET   File: **employeestore.aspx (excerpt)**

```
cartBusiness = Server.UrlEncode(cartBusiness)
```

C#   File: **employeestore.aspx (excerpt)**

```
cartBusiness = Server.UrlEncode(cartBusiness);
```

Next, we'll start to generate the URL that will be used to send the order details to PayPal:

VB.NET   File: **employeestore.aspx (excerpt)**

```
Dim strPayPal As String = _
    "https://www.paypal.com/cgi-bin/webscr" & _
    "?cmd=_cart&upload=1&business=" & cartBusiness
```

C#   File: **employeestore.aspx (excerpt)**

```
String strPayPal = "https://www.paypal.com/cgi-bin/webscr?" +
    "cmd=_cart&upload=1&business=" + cartBusiness;
```

As you can see, the string variable is set to PayPal's order submission URL (https://www.paypal.com/cgi-bin/webscr), to which is appended a query string containing the first three variables and their values. Now, for each item in the user's cart, we need to add three variables to this query string: the item's name, quantity, and total price. For this, we'll use a `For Each` loop, as we did in the `GetItemTotal()` method previously:

489

VB.NET   File: **employeestore.aspx (excerpt)**

```
For Each objDR In objCartDT.Rows
```

C#   File: **employeestore.aspx (excerpt)**

```
foreach (DataRow objDR in objCartDT.Rows) {
```

Each time through the loop, we store the item name, quantity, and individual item cost into our three variables. We then URL encode the product name, as it may contain spaces and other troublesome characters that are not allowed in a URL query string.

VB.NET   File: **employeestore.aspx (excerpt)**

```
cartProduct = objDR("Item")
cartQuantity = objDR("Quantity")
cartCost = objDR("Cost")

cartProduct = Server.UrlEncode(cartProduct)
```

C#   File: **employeestore.aspx (excerpt)**

```
cartProduct = (String)objDR["Item"];
cartQuantity = (int)objDR["Quantity"];
cartCost = (Decimal)objDR["Cost"];

cartProduct = Server.UrlEncode(cartProduct);
```

We then use these variables to add the item_name_*n*, item_number_*n*, and amount_*n* values to the query string, where *n* is given by the itemNumber variable we initialized earlier. Note that the amount_*n* variable contains the total price when more than one of a given item is purchased, so we must calculate this with the cartQuantity and cartCost variables:

VB.NET   File: **employeestore.aspx (excerpt)**

```
strPayPal &= "&item_name_" & itemNumber & "=" & cartProduct
strPayPal &= "&item_number_" & itemNumber & "=" & cartQuantity
strPayPal &= "&amount_" & itemNumber & "=" & _
    Decimal.Round(cartQuantity * cartCost, 2)
```

C#   File: **employeestore.aspx (excerpt)**

```
strPayPal += "&item_name_" + itemNumber + "=" + cartProduct;
strPayPal += "&item_number_" + itemNumber + "=" +
    cartQuantity;
strPayPal += "&amount_" + itemNumber + "=" +
    Decimal.Round(cartQuantity * cartCost, 2);
```

Finally, we increment `itemNumber` in preparation for the next run through the loop:

VB.NET   File: **employeestore.aspx (excerpt)**

```
    itemNumber = itemNumber + 1
  Next
```

C#   File: **employeestore.aspx (excerpt)**

```
    itemNumber++;
  }
```

With our URL complete, all that's left is to send the browser to the URL with the `Redirect()` method of the `Response` object.

VB.NET   File: **employeestore.aspx (excerpt)**

```
  Response.Redirect(strPayPal)
End Sub
```

C#   File: **employeestore.aspx (excerpt)**

```
  Response.Redirect(strPayPal);
}
```

That's it! Let's test the functionality and see how it works. First, navigate to the employee store page and add an item to your cart. Now, click the Checkout `LinkButton`. You'll immediately be transferred to a business-specific, customized page displaying the amount you owe, similar to Figure 12.8.

Figure 12.8. The user is redirected to a co-branded business payment page.

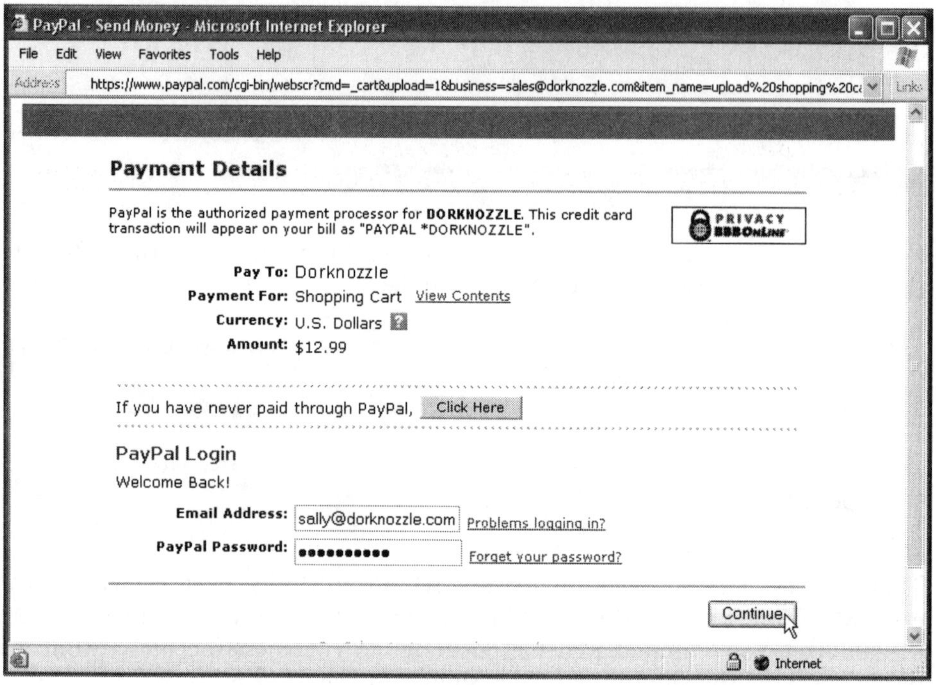

As a user, I simply enter my login credentials and click Continue. I'm instantly redirected to a page that allows me to click Pay.

As a PayPal user, I can authorize the transaction on my credit card, or have the funds deducted from my PayPal account balance. I also have the option of providing my shipping address.

If users don't have a PayPal account[1], they simply click the Click Here button, and they'll be directed to a sign up page, complete with credit card information. You can even click the View Contents link to display the product and cost that was transferred over from the Dorknozzle account, similar to Figure 12.9.

---

[1] As this book goes to press, PayPal have added the option for users to make credit card payments without logging into or even creating a PayPal account.

Figure 12.9. The View Contents link directs you to a table that contains the items you wish to purchase.

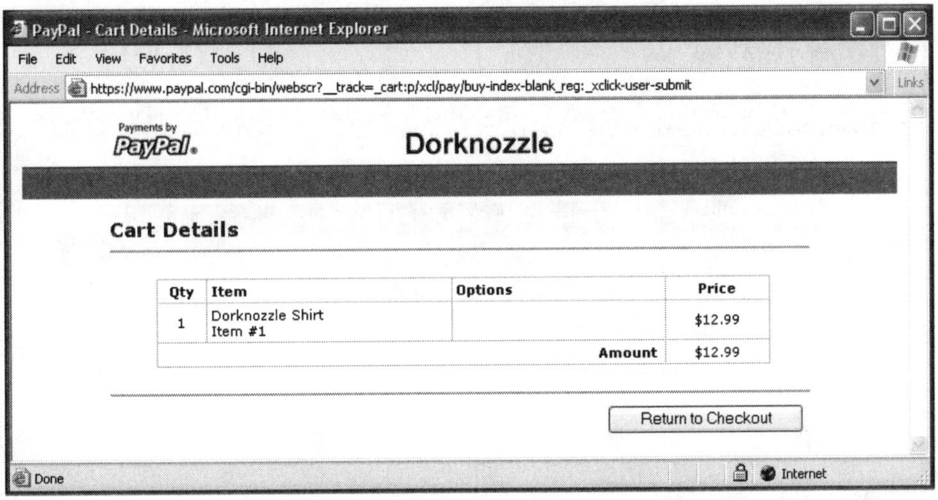

From a development standpoint, there's a lot of functionality that we can add to this. For instance, PayPal has a feature called Instant Payment Notification (IPN), which essentially returns the result of the purchase back to the seller. We could use this feature to capture the completed transaction, store it in a PendingShipping table within our database, or have it directly emailed to our fictitious shipping and receiving department. If you don't want to get that fancy, you can also log into your business account and view a summary of completed orders. This view is shown in Figure 12.10.

Figure 12.10. PayPal's Account Profile page displays a list of completed orders.

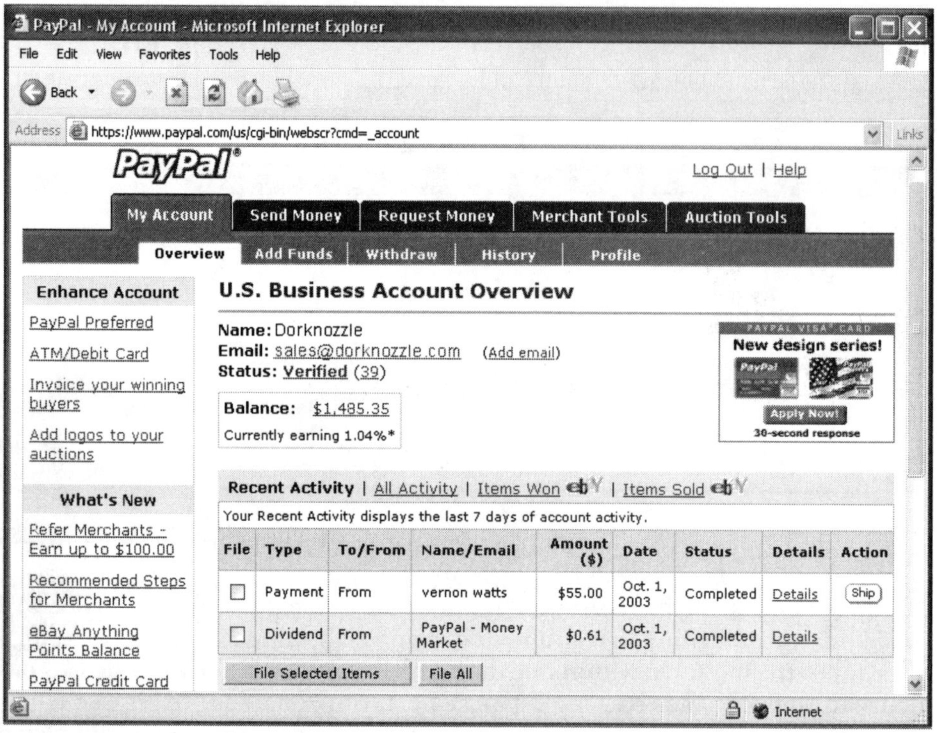

Summary

As you've seen, using `DataTables` to create a shopping cart is cheaper and easier than buying some company's proprietary solution and then spending days trying to figure out how to use it. In this chapter, we covered all the basics necessary for creating a shopping cart application, including creating the interface, cart structure, add to cart, update cart quantities, and remove from cart functionality. Towards the end of the chapter, you even saw how to integrate the cart with a payment processing solution like PayPal.

13 Error Handling

ASP.NET has some outstanding built-in functionality for identifying and correcting problems with your ASP.NET applications either before or after they occur. This chapter will introduce you to this functionality, a process known as **error handling**. You'll see how it lets us identify, correct, and prevent errors from happening within ASP.NET applications before users have a chance to see them.

As you progress through this chapter, you'll learn about the various types of errors an ASP.NET page can produce. Then, you'll learn how to use code to prevent such errors from interrupting the user experience. Finally, you'll learn about the .NET debugger, which will aid you in identifying and correcting hard-to-find errors within an ASP.NET page.

Introduction to Error Handling

We've all been there: we're so entrenched in an application that we tend to lose focus on the overall goal. We work so hard to meet deadlines, and concentrate so closely on functionality in order to get the job done, that we can overlook the effects of code additions that may cause errors down the road. Other errors we simply can't predict. For instance, the connection to a remote database may be down. This has nothing to do with errors in our code, but we still need to identify such eventualities and handle them gracefully, so the user doesn't end up seeing an ugly error message. It's for these reasons that most companies employ quality assurance professionals whose job it is to test our applications. They find our errors, we fix them, and the cycle continues relentlessly until all issues are resolved, and the product can go live. Sometimes, the process can take weeks—or even months.

Fortunately, ASP.NET has some very powerful capabilities for handling errors gracefully. In this section, we'll look at the different types of errors that you may encounter as a developer. We'll also talk about how to view error information so that you can troubleshoot problematic areas. Finally, we'll talk about a few methods you can use to handle errors before your users experience them.

Types of Errors

Knowing the types of errors that exist will help you troubleshoot and correct problems later. There are four main types of errors that can occur within an ASP.NET application, and they are:

Configuration errors Caused by problems in the `Web.config` file

Parser errors Caused by incorrect syntax within an ASP.NET page

Compilation errors Raised by either the Visual Basic or C# compiler

Runtime errors Detected when the page is executed

Configuration errors are the easiest to detect, and, arguably, the easiest to fix, as they're caused by a problem within the `Web.config` file. Because the `Web.config` file is XML-based, a configuration error usually means one of three things: you have inconsistencies in your tags' casings, you completely misspelled a tag or property name, or you simply forgot to close a tag. See if you can spot the errors in the following simple `Web.config` file:

```
<configuration>
<appSettings>
<add key="DSN" value="my connection string></add>
</appsettings>
</configuration>
```

There are two problems with this `Web.config` file. First, the closing quote is missing from the end of the `value` attribute; second, the closing `</appSettings>` tag needs a capital S. XML is case-sensitive, so `<appsettings>` and `<appSettings>` would be viewed as two different tags. The above `Web.config` file would produce a configuration error similar to Figure 13.1.

Figure 13.1. Configuration errors are usually caused by poorly written `Web.config` files.

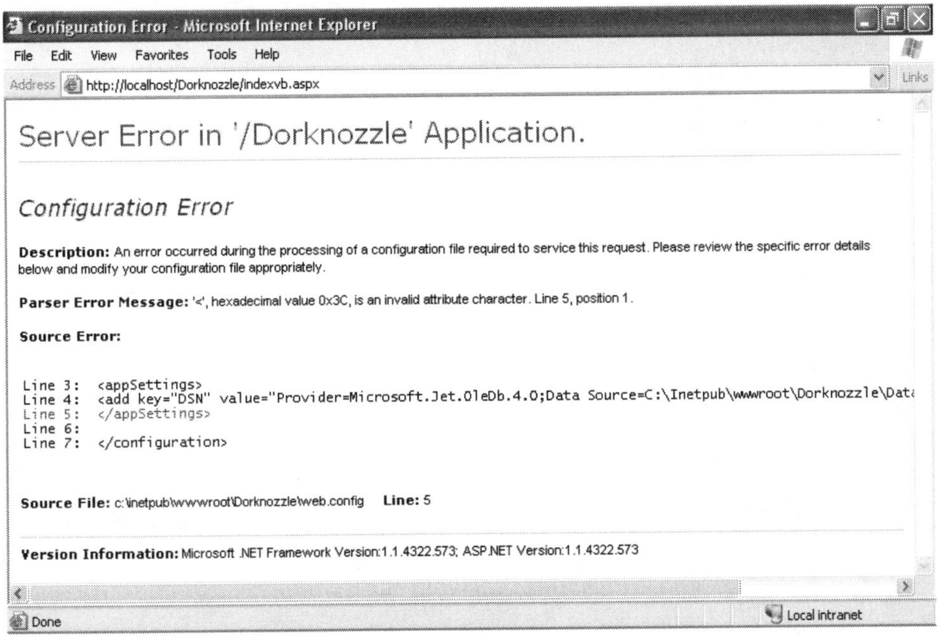

Parser errors are more difficult to spot than configuration errors, yet they aren't as difficult to figure out as compilation errors. Parser errors are usually caused by poorly written controls. Can you spot the error in the following `DataGrid`'s markup?

```
<asp:DataGrid id="dgEmployees" AutoGenerateColumns="false"
    runat="server">
  <Columns>
    <asp:BoundColumn DataField="Name" HeaderText="Name"/>
    <asp:BoundColumn DataField="Extension" HeaderText="Extension"
        />
  </Column>
</asp:DataGrid>
```

In this code snippet, the closing `</Columns>` tag is missing an s. Trying to include this code within an ASP.NET page would result in a parser error similar to Figure 13.2.

Figure 13.2. Parser errors are usually caused by poorly written controls.

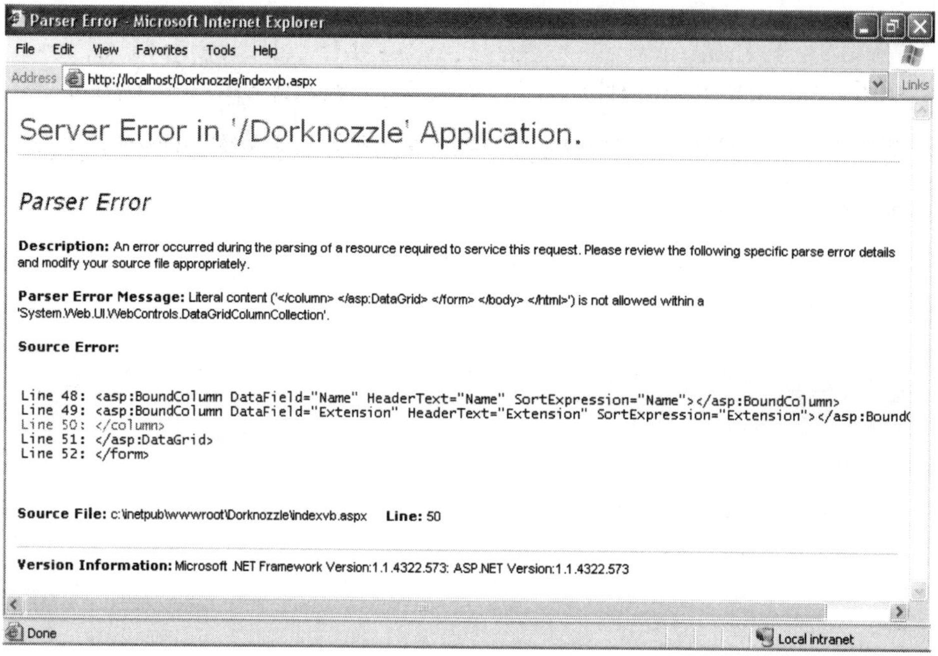

Compilation errors are usually more difficult to remedy than the errors we've already seen; sometimes, they can require hours of investigation. Compilation errors are generally caused by poorly or incorrectly written application logic. See if you can spot the error in the following code:

VB.NET

```vbnet
Sub Page_Load()
  If Not IsPostBack Then
    dgEmployees.DataSource = GetEmployees()
    dgEmployees.DataBind()
End Sub
```

C#

```csharp
void Page_Load() {
  if (!IsPostBack) {
    dgEmployees.DataSource = GetEmployees();
    dgEmployees.DataBind();
}
```

In this case, I forgot to add the closing End If in the VB.NET example, and the closing brace (}) in the C# example. Trying to run this code within an ASP.NET page would result in a compilation error similar to Figure 13.3.

Figure 13.3. Compilation errors can be difficult to spot and are usually caused by poorly written or incorrectly written code.

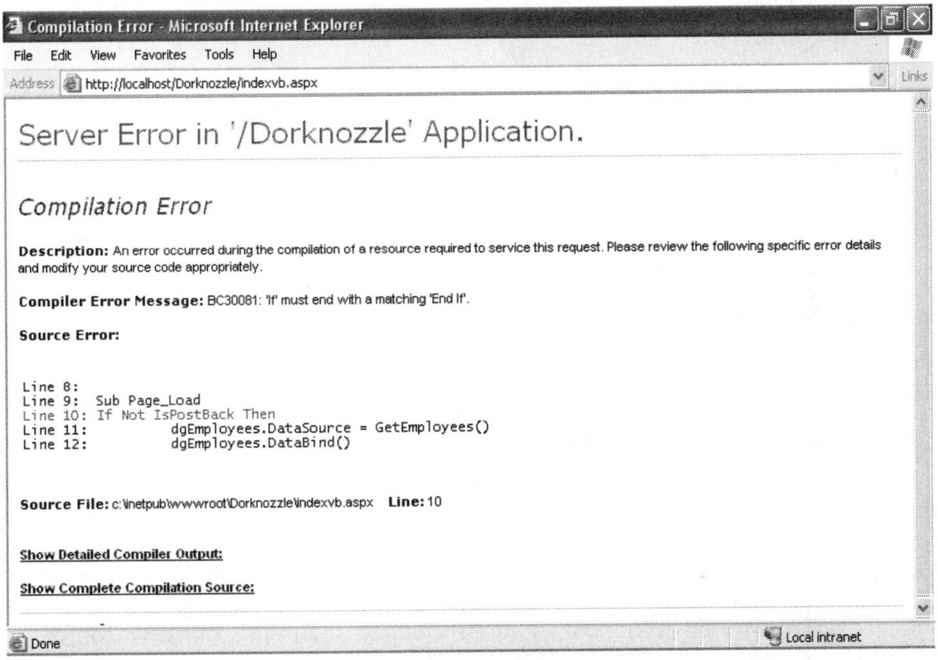

The last type of error that can occur within an ASP.NET page is a **runtime error**. Runtime errors are generated after the page is executed. If your page initially loads correctly, but then results in errors after you raise a particular event, you probably have a runtime error. Can you spot the error in the following code?

VB.NET
```
<html>
<head>
<title>Runtime Error</title>
<script language="VB" runat="server">
Sub ButtonClick(s As Object, e As EventArgs)
  Dim lblLabel As Label
  lblLabel.Text = "Hello World"
End Sub
```

```
</script>
</head>
<body>
<form runat="server">
<asp:Button id="btnSubmit" runat="server" OnClick="ButtonClick"
    Text="Click" />
</form>
</body>
</html>
```

C#

```
<html>
<head>
<title>Runtime Error</title>
<script language="C#" runat="server">
void ButtonClick(Object s, EventArgs e) {
  Label lblLabel;
  lblLabel.Text = "Hello World";
}
</script>
</head>
<body>
<form runat="server">
<asp:Button id="btnSubmit" runat="server" OnClick="ButtonClick"
    Text="Click" />
</form>
</body>
</html>
```

In this example, we created a Label variable called lblLabel, but then forgot to fill it with an actual object before attempting to set its Text property. Since we can't set properties on empty variables, when the button is clicked, this code results in a runtime error similar to Figure 13.4.

Figure 13.4. Runtime errors are caused after the page is executed.

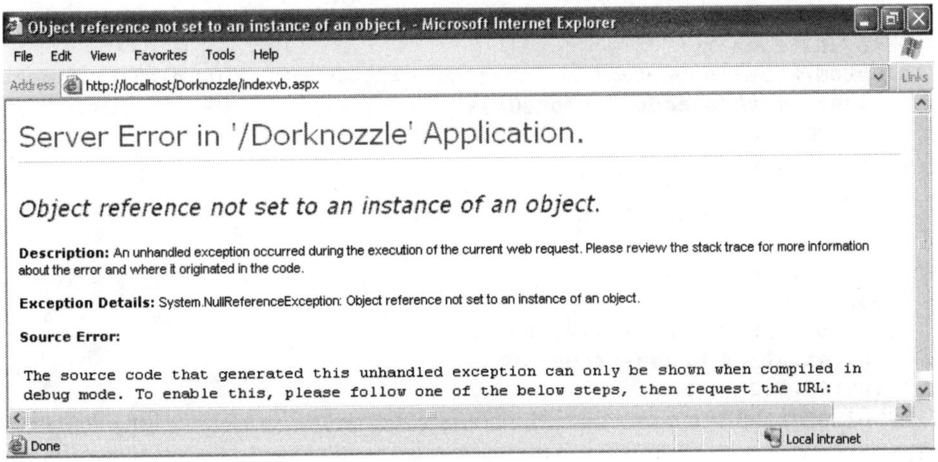

Viewing Error Information

For the most part, error information is displayed to you when the page is run within the browser. At times, however, the error information that's displayed is vague and, in rare cases, useless. ASP.NET provides two configuration settings in the Web.config file that can make error information a bit more useful:

Custom errors mode When custom errors are enabled, ASP.NET's detailed error messages are hidden from view. This setting has three possible values:

1. Off: ASP.NET uses its default error page for both local and remote users.

2. On: ASP.NET uses user-defined custom error pages, instead of its default error page, for both local and remote users.

3. RemoteOnly: The ASP.NET error page is shown only to local users.

Debug mode Enabling debug mode provides you with additional and, I like to think, more intuitive error information for runtime errors.

You can enable custom errors within the `Web.config` file's `<system.web>` configuration section group, as follows:

```
<configuration>
  <system.web>
    <customErrors mode="RemoteOnly" />
  </system.web>
</configuration>
```

Similarly, you can enable debug mode as follows:

```
<configuration>
  <system.web>
    <customErrors mode="RemoteOnly" />
    <compilation debug="true" />
  </system.web>
</configuration>
```

Now, when you run the "empty `Label` variable" example above within the browser, you are presented with a little more detail as to what caused the error, as shown in Figure 13.5.

Figure 13.5. Setting `customErrors` mode to `RemoteOnly` and setting `compilation` debug to true results in more intuitive error information.

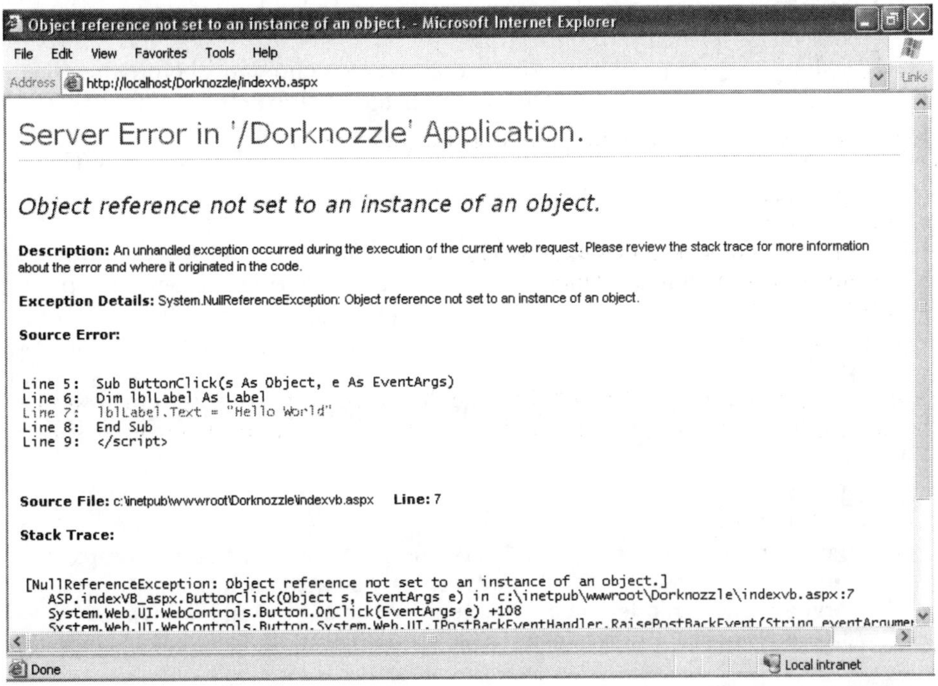

As you can see from the screenshot, ASP.NET separates the error description into a number of distinct parts:

General Description   This provides a brief description of the error. This is the italicized, maroon text that you see near the top. In our case, because we didn't create an instance of the `Label` control, the error description alerts us that our variable (or object reference) does not contain an object.

Description   A description of why the application failed is also presented. In our case, an unhandled exception occurred. **Exceptions** are errors that unexpectedly occur. They're discussed a little later in this chapter.

Exception Details   Detailed information about the exception is provided.

Source Error	This section identifies the line of code within the application that generated the exception.
Source File	The name of the file within the application that generated the exception is included here.
Stack Trace	The methods that were executed just before the exception occurred are listed at this point.
Version Information	This item details the version of the .NET Framework that's processing the request.

The `<customErrors>` tag can be used for more than simply setting the error display mode. You can use this tag to your benefit by creating custom error pages. This means that when errors occur, the user will be redirected to a "friendly" error page that you create. Simply create one or more custom error pages as new ASP.NET pages, complete with your company's logo, navigation, and any other useful components, and change the `<customErrors>` configuration handler to reference your error pages like so:

```
<configuration>
  <system.web>
    <customErrors mode="On" defaultRedirect="genericError.aspx">
      <error statusCode="404" redirect="pagenotfound.aspx" />
      <error statusCode="500" redirect="applicationerror.aspx" />
    </customErrors>
    <compilation debug="true" />
  </system.web>
</configuration>
```

As you can see, this modification redirects our users to `genericError.aspx` if our page generates errors that are not handled more specifically by a child `<error>` tag. In this case, we have a couple of these `<error>` tags. The first redirects users to `pagenotfound.aspx` if a file they request is not found, which is indicated by the infamous HTTP 404 error. If an application error occurs, as indicated by HTTP 500, users are redirected to `applicationerror.aspx`.

Handling Errors

As we've said, error handling can be thought of as the process of anticipating errors that are likely to occur within your code, and dealing with them gracefully so that your users never know they've even occurred. Error handling is an important part of programming applications, and it's safe to say that all applications should carry it out to some extent.

To demonstrate the process of error handling, let's first look at code that works, then purposely break it, and, finally, handle the errors that will inevitably be produced. You can start by creating a page containing the following code, which essentially queries the `Employees` table and returns the results within a `DataGrid` in the page:

VB.NET   File: **TryCatch.aspx**

```
<%@ Import Namespace="System.Data.OleDb" %>
<html>
<head>
<title>Handling Errors</title>
<script language="VB" runat="server">
Sub Page_Load()
  Dim objConn As New OleDbConnection( _
      ConfigurationSettings.AppSettings("DSN"))
  Dim objCmd As OleDbCommand

  objConn.Open()
  objCmd = New OleDbCommand("SELECT * FROM Employees", objConn)
  dgAddressBook.DataSource = objCmd.ExecuteReader()
  dgAddressBook.DataBind()
  objConn.Close()
End Sub
</script>
</head>
<body>
<form runat="server">
<asp:DataGrid id="dgAddressBook" runat="server"/>
</form>
</body>
</html>
```

C#   File: **TryCatch.aspx**

```
<%@ Import Namespace="System.Data.OleDb" %>
<html>
<head>
<title>Handling Errors</title>
<script language="C#" runat="server">
void Page_Load() {
  OleDbConnection objConn = new OleDbConnection(
      ConfigurationSettings.AppSettings["DSN"]);
  OleDbCommand objCmd;
```

```
  objConn.Open();
  objCmd = new OleDbCommand("SELECT * FROM Employees", objConn);
  dgAddressBook.DataSource = objCmd.ExecuteReader();
  dgAddressBook.DataBind();
  objConn.Close();
}
</script>
</head>
<body>
<form runat="server">
<asp:DataGrid id="dgAddressBook" runat="server"/>
</form>
</body>
</html>
```

Note that this requires the use of the `Web.config` file we created in Chapter 11, as we're using the `DSN` connection string.

Figure 13.6 shows how all of the employees within the `Employees` database table are bound to the `DataGrid`.

Figure 13.6. All employees are bound to the `DataGrid`.

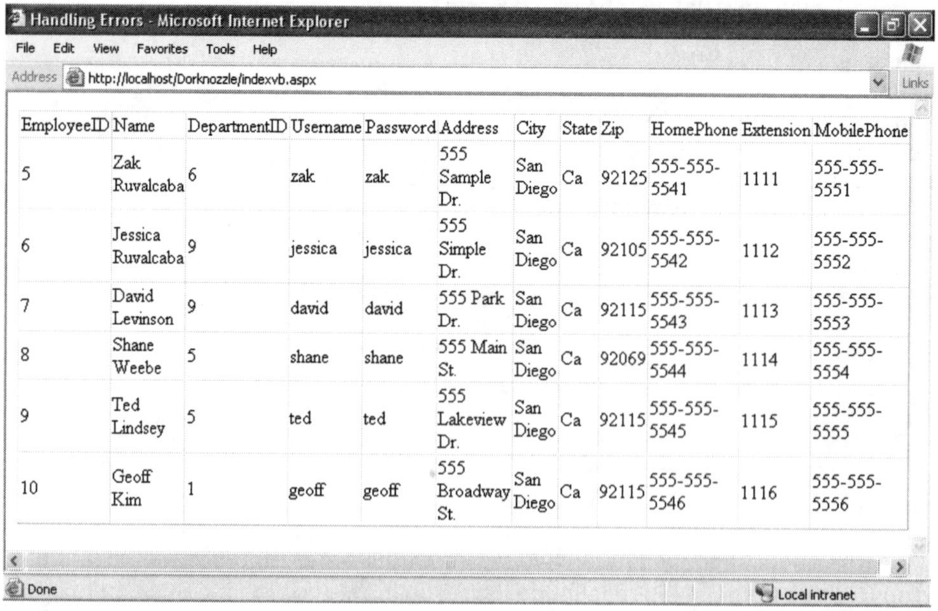

EmployeeID	Name	DepartmentID	Username	Password	Address	City	State	Zip	HomePhone	Extension	MobilePhone
5	Zak Ruvalcaba	6	zak	zak	555 Sample Dr.	San Diego	Ca	92125	555-555-5541	1111	555-555-5551
6	Jessica Ruvalcaba	9	jessica	jessica	555 Simple Dr.	San Diego	Ca	92105	555-555-5542	1112	555-555-5552
7	David Levinson	9	david	david	555 Park Dr.	San Diego	Ca	92115	555-555-5543	1113	555-555-5553
8	Shane Weebe	5	shane	shane	555 Main St.	San Diego	Ca	92069	555-555-5544	1114	555-555-5554
9	Ted Lindsey	5	ted	ted	555 Lakeview Dr.	San Diego	Ca	92115	555-555-5545	1115	555-555-5555
10	Geoff Kim	1	geoff	geoff	555 Broadway St.	San Diego	Ca	92115	555-555-5546	1116	555-555-5556

We assume that the code above works because we see the results bound to the DataGrid. But, what if it doesn't work? What happens if the database server is down, for instance? If this were the case, users would receive an error, and they probably wouldn't know what to do next. If you're running an online business and this were to happen, it could cost you both customers and money. The next sections will show you how to catch these errors and handle them appropriately.

Catching Errors with Try...Catch

We can simulate an error with the database server by changing the Web.config file as follows:

File: **Web.config (excerpt)**

```
<add key="DSN" value="Provider=Microsoft.Jet.OleDb.4.0;Data Source
=C:\Inetpub\wwwroot\Samples\Database\Dooknozzle.mdb" />
```

In this case, our database name is spelled incorrectly. If you try to view this page in the browser now, it will display an error.

To catch and handle errors like these, we can use a Try...Catch block. Try...Catch blocks allow you to try some code that you think is likely to cause an error, catch any error that does occur, and respond accordingly. The previous code could be modified with a Try...Catch block as follows:

VB.NET   File: **TryCatch.aspx (excerpt)**

```
Sub Page_Load()
  Try
    Dim objConn As New OleDbConnection( _
        ConfigurationSettings.AppSettings("DSN"))
    Dim objCmd As OleDbCommand

    objConn.Open()
    objCmd = New OleDbCommand("SELECT * FROM Employees", objConn)
    dgAddressBook.DataSource = objCmd.ExecuteReader()
    dgAddressBook.DataBind()
    objConn.Close()
  Catch
    Response.Write("We are experiencing problems with our " & _
        "database at the moment.<br /> Please try again later.")
  End Try
End Sub
```

```
C#                                              File: TryCatch.aspx (excerpt)
void Page_Load() {
  try {
    OleDbConnection objConn = new OleDbConnection(
        ConfigurationSettings.AppSettings["DSN"]);
    OleDbCommand objCmd;

    objConn.Open();
    objCmd = new OleDbCommand("SELECT * FROM Employees", objConn);
    dgAddressBook.DataSource = objCmd.ExecuteReader();
    dgAddressBook.DataBind();
    objConn.Close();
  } catch {
    Response.Write("We are experiencing problems with our " +
        "database at the moment.<br /> Please try again later.");
  }
}
```

This time, because we're using a Try...Catch block, the page tries the code, catches the error, and displays a nicely written message to the user, similar to Figure 13.7.

Figure 13.7. Try...Catch blocks allow you gracefully to handle and present error messages to your users.

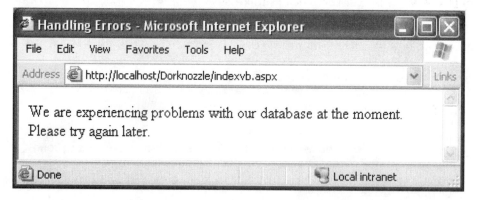

As a user, the message reads well—I'd see the error and simply revisit the site at a later date. From our perspective as developers, however, that error is useless, as it doesn't tell us much at all about the cause of the error. The solution is to use the Exception class to produce more detailed descriptions of the errors that are produced. The next section will show you how!

Catching and Handling Exceptions

As you saw in the last section, we gracefully handled a connection problem using a **Try...Catch** block. Unfortunately, as developers, we don't know much about the cause of the error. This is where exception handling comes in. By definition, an exception is a problem or change in conditions that is so drastic that the computer is unable to continue; such situations require the computer to stop what it's doing and handle the problem in a separate routine. Ever hear the term "fatal exception?" A fatal exception occurs when the application running your program is forced to terminate.

The .NET Framework provides an **Exception** class for working with these unforeseen circumstances. The **Exception** class contains the following properties:

Message	Returns a string representing the error message
Source	Returns a string representing the object that caused the error
StackTrace	Returns a string representing the methods that were called just before the error occurred
TargetSite	Returns a **MethodBase** object representing the methods that caused the error

Expanding on our previous example, you could catch the exception and display the values of the above properties within the page:

VB.NET   File: **CatchingExceptions.aspx**

```
<%@ Import Namespace="System.Data.OleDb" %>
<html>
<head>
<title>Handling Errors</title>
<script language="VB" runat="server">
Sub Page_Load()
  Try
    Dim objConn As New OleDbConnection( _
        ConfigurationSettings.AppSettings("DSN"))
    Dim objCmd As OleDbCommand

    objConn.Open()
    objCmd = New OleDbCommand("SELECT * FROM Employees", objConn)
    dgAddressBook.DataSource = objCmd.ExecuteReader()
    dgAddressBook.DataBind()
```

```
      objConn.Close()
    Catch objException As Exception
      Response.Write("<ul>")
      Response.Write("<li><b>Message:</b> " & _
          objException.Message & "</li>")
      Response.Write("<li><b>Source:</b> " & objException.Source & _
          "</li>")
      Response.Write("<li><b>StackTrace:</b> " & _
          objException.StackTrace & "</li>")
      Response.Write("<li><b>TargetSite:</b> " & _
          objException.TargetSite.Name & "</li>")
      Response.Write("</ul>")
    End Try
End Sub
</script>
</head>
<body>
<form runat="server">
<asp:DataGrid id="dgAddressBook" runat="server"/>
</form>
</body>
</html>
```

C#   File: **CatchingExceptions.aspx (excerpt)**

```
<%@ Import Namespace="System.Data.OleDb" %>
<html>
<head>
<title>Handling Errors</title>
<script language="C#" runat="server">
void Page_Load() {
  try {
    OleDbConnection objConn = new OleDbConnection(
        ConfigurationSettings.AppSettings["DSN"]);
    OleDbCommand objCmd;

    objConn.Open();
    objCmd = new OleDbCommand("SELECT * FROM Employees", objConn);
    dgAddressBook.DataSource = objCmd.ExecuteReader();
    dgAddressBook.DataBind();
    objConn.Close();
  } catch (Exception objException) {
    Response.Write("<ul>");
    Response.Write("<li><b>Message:</b> " + objException.Message +
        "</li>");
    Response.Write("<li><b>Source:</b> " + objException.Source +
        "</li>");
```

```
    Response.Write("<li><b>StackTrace:</b> " +
        objException.StackTrace + "</li>");
    Response.Write("<li><b>TargetSite:</b> " +
        objException.TargetSite.Name + "</li>");
    Response.Write("</ul>");
  }
}
</script>
</head>
<body>
<form runat="server">
<asp:DataGrid id="dgAddressBook" runat="server"/>
</form>
</body>
</html>
```

In this case, the error message, source, stack trace, and target site, are all displayed on the screen, similar to Figure 13.8.

Figure 13.8. The exception's properties including message, source, stack trace, and target site are all printed within the page.

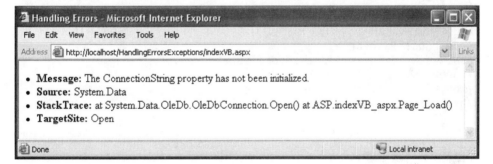

The `Exception` class represents a generic exception. To access more detailed information about a specific exception, you could catch one of the more specialized exception classes that the .NET Framework has to offer. For instance, if you wanted to specifically catch database errors, you could modify your `Catch` line to catch exceptions of class `OleDbException`, rather than the generic `Exception` class, as follows:

VB.NET   File: **SpecificExceptions.aspx**

```
<%@ Import Namespace="System.Data.OleDb" %>
<html>
<head>
```

```
<title>Handling Errors</title>
<script language="VB" runat="server">
Sub Page_Load()
  Try
    Dim objConn As New OleDbConnection( _
        ConfigurationSettings.AppSettings("DSN"))
    Dim objCmd As OleDbCommand

    objConn.Open()
    objCmd = New OleDbCommand("SELECT * FROM Employees", objConn)
    dgAddressBook.DataSource = objCmd.ExecuteReader()
    dgAddressBook.DataBind()
    objConn.Close()
  Catch objOleDbException As OleDbException
    Dim objError As OleDbError
    Response.Write("<ul>")
    For Each objError In objOleDbException.Errors
      Response.Write("<li>" & objError.Message & "</li>")
    Next
    Response.Write("</ul>")
  End Try
End Sub
</script>
</head>
<body>
<form runat="server">
<asp:DataGrid id="dgAddressBook" runat="server" />
</form>
</body>
</html>
```

C#   File: **SpecificExceptions.aspx**

```
<%@ Import Namespace="System.Data.OleDb" %>
<html>
<head>
<title>Handling Errors</title>
<script language="C#" runat="server">
void Page_Load() {
  try {
    OleDbConnection objConn = new OleDbConnection(
        ConfigurationSettings.AppSettings["DSN"]);
    OleDbCommand objCmd;

    objConn.Open();
    objCmd = new OleDbCommand("SELECT * FROM Employees", objConn);
    dgAddressBook.DataSource = objCmd.ExecuteReader();
```

```
      dgAddressBook.DataBind();
      objConn.Close();
  } catch (OleDbException objOleDbException) {
    Response.Write("<ul>");
    foreach (OleDbError objError in objOleDbException.Errors) {
      Response.Write("<li>" + objError.Message + "</li>");
    }
    Response.Write("</ul>");
  }
}
</script>
</head>
<body>
<form runat="server">
<asp:DataGrid id="dgAddressBook" runat="server" />
</form>
</body>
</html>
```

Because a number of database errors can combine to cause a single .NET exception, the OleDbException class includes a collection of error messages (OleDbError objects) in its Errors property. In the above code, we use a For Each loop to iterate through these error messages and display them in a list. Try viewing the result in the browser.

If you prefer to use an SQL Server database, you can use the SqlException and SqlError classes instead of OleDbException and OleDbError, respectively.

Although the result is similar to the previous example, we're now using a specific Exception subclass, which gives us access to information specific to the type of exception that has occurred. Programming using specific Exception classes, rather than the generic Exception class, will help you better understand and respond to errors.

Logging Errors to the Event Log

In most cases, you won't always be monitoring your applications as closely as you have within the scope of these examples. You'll usually want to create your applications and let them run while you build other applications. But if errors *do* occur, you'll want to know about them. Fortunately, the .NET Framework includes a handy tool, the EventLog class, which you can use to write error messages to the server's event log. You can then periodically check the event log to see if any errors have occurred and, if so, fix them as soon as possible.

You can view the event log using the Event Viewer, which you can find in the Administrative Tools subfolder of your Windows Control Panel. As shown in Figure 13.9, the event log monitors application, security, and system errors.

Figure 13.9. The event log allows you to monitor application, security, and system errors.

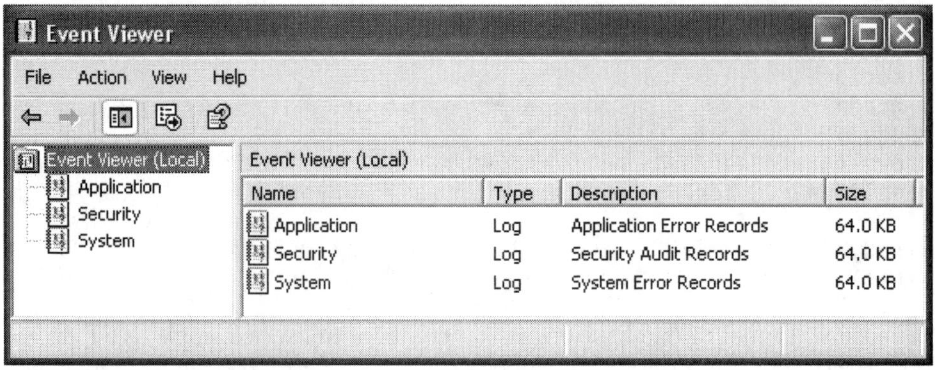

You can monitor Windows application, security, or system errors by viewing the particular event log you require. Try selecting the Application log. The right hand pane shows warnings, errors, and generic comments that were written by other applications running within Windows. You, too, can take advantage of the event log for your Web applications. Begin by creating a new ASP.NET page, and adding the following code:

File: **HandlingErrorsEventLog.aspx**

```
<%@ Import Namespace="System.Diagnostics" %>
<html>
<head>
<title>Logging Errors</title>
</head>
<body>
<form runat="server">
<p><asp:Button id="btnError" runat="server"
    OnClick="writeError" Text="Add a New Error" />
<asp:Button id="btnInformation" runat="server"
    OnClick="writeInformation" Text="Add New Information" />
<asp:Button id="btnAlert" runat="server"
    OnClick="writeWarning" Text="Add a New Warning" /></p>
</form>
</body>
</html>
```

You'll notice the addition of the `System.Diagnostics` namespace. This namespace contains handy classes for working with the event log, including `EventLog` itself. You should also notice that we've specified a different method for the `OnClick` event handler of each of the three buttons we're creating. It is these methods that will do the actual writing to the log. Let's create them now:

VB.NET   File: **HandlingErrorsEventLog.aspx (excerpt)**

```vb
<script language="VB" runat="server">
Dim objLog As New EventLog()

Sub writeError(s As Object, e As EventArgs)
  objLog.Source = "Dorknozzle"
  objLog.WriteEntry("There was an error", EventLogEntryType.Error)
End Sub

Sub writeInformation(s As Object, e As EventArgs)
  objLog.Source = "Dorknozzle"
  objLog.WriteEntry("This is some information", _
      EventLogEntryType.Information)
End Sub

Sub writeWarning(s As Object, e As EventArgs)
  objLog.Source = "Dorknozzle"
  objLog.WriteEntry("This is a new Warning", _
      EventLogEntryType.Warning)
End Sub
</script>
```

C#   File: **HandlingErrorsEventLog.aspx (excerpt)**

```csharp
<script language="C#" runat="server">
EventLog objLog = new EventLog();

void writeError(Object s, EventArgs e) {
  objLog.Source = "Dorknozzle";
  objLog.WriteEntry("There was an error",
      EventLogEntryType.Error);
}

void writeInformation(Object s, EventArgs e) {
  objLog.Source = "Dorknozzle";
  objLog.WriteEntry("This is some information", _
      EventLogEntryType.Information);
}

void writeWarning(Object s, EventArgs e) {
```

```
  objLog.Source = "Dorknozzle";
  objLog.WriteEntry("This is a new Warning", _
    EventLogEntryType.Warning);
}
</script>
```

Initially, we simply create a new instance of the `EventLog` class. Next, within each `Button` control's event handler, we set the source of our particular error to "Dorknozzle" so that it's easy to identify in the event log. Finally, we call the `WriteEntry()` method and pass in two parameters. The first is the text that we want to write to the event log, while the second is the type of event we want to display. Before you test the results in the browser, clear out the event log by right clicking on the Application log, and selecting Clear All Events. Now, save your work and test the result within the browser. Click all three buttons, switch to the event log, then refresh the Application log.

Dealing with SecurityException: Requested registry access is not allowed.

The first time you run this example, the .NET Framework will attempt to register "Dorknozzle" as a source of events for the Application log. Unfortunately, the special user account that all ASP.NET applications run as by default does not have the privileges required to do this, which will normally result in an ugly Security Exception.

To solve this, you need to register the source yourself. Here's how:

1. Click Start, Run…, then type **regedit** in the Open field and click OK. The Windows Registry Editor will open.

2. By expanding tree nodes, navigate through HKEY_LOCAL_MACHINE, SYSTEM, CurrentControlSet, Services, Eventlog and Application.

3. Right-click on the Application folder in the tree and choose New, Key. Type **Dorknozzle** for the name of the new key, then press Enter.

4. Select the newly-created Dorknozzle key.

5. Right-click in the background of the right-hand pane; choose New, String Value.

6. Type **EventMessageFile** as the name of the new value, then press Enter.

7. Double-click the new EventMessageFile value. In the Value data field, type `C:\WINDOWS\Microsoft.NET\Framework\ver\EventLogMessages.dll`, where *ver* is the most recent version of the .NET Framework installed on your computer. You'll probably want to browse to the directory in Explorer to confirm the name of this folder. Then click OK and close the Registry Editor.

Once you've registered the source in this way, you should be able to run the example without any difficulty.

Back in the Event Viewer, click the Refresh button and the three new errors will appear in the Application log, similar to Figure 13.10.

Figure 13.10. New events appear within the Application log.

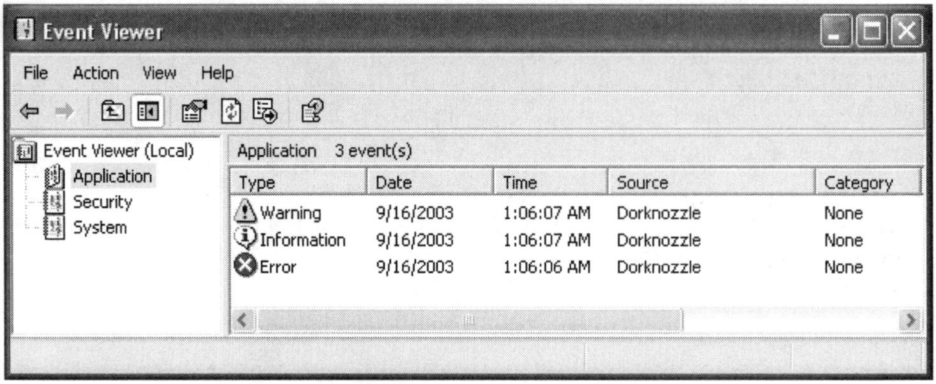

Event Viewer
File Action View Help
Event Viewer (Local)
Application
Security
System
Application 3 event(s)
Type Date Time Source Category
Warning 9/16/2003 1:06:07 AM Dorknozzle None
Information 9/16/2003 1:06:07 AM Dorknozzle None
Error 9/16/2003 1:06:06 AM Dorknozzle None

Tip

Create a custom error log

If you don't like having messages from your ASP.NET application mixed in with the other messages in the Application log, you can use the `CreateEventSource()` method of the `EventLog` class to create a custom event log to receive the messages. Refer to the .NET Framework SDK Documentation[1] for details and examples of this method in use.

You can also create a simple and quick application to read from the Application log, first by adding the following `DataGrid`, and a `Button` control to refresh it:

File: **HandlingErrorsEventLog.aspx (excerpt)**

```
<form runat="server">
<p><asp:Button id="btnError" runat="server"
  OnClick="writeError" Text="Add a New Error" />
<asp:Button id="btnInformation" runat="server"
  OnClick="writeInformation" Text="Add New Information" />
<asp:Button id="btnAlert" runat="server"
  OnClick="writeWarning" Text="Add a New Warning" /></p>
<p><asp:Button id="btnRefresh" runat="server"
  OnClick="refreshLog" Text="Refresh Log" /></p>
<asp:DataGrid id="dgLog" runat="server" />
</form>
```

Next, we can create the `refreshLog()` method that was specified as the `OnClick` handler of the new button, like this:

[1] http://msdn.microsoft.com/library/en-us/cpref/html/frlrfSystemDiagnosticsEventLogClassCreateEventSourceTopic.asp

```
VB.NET                              File: HandlingErrorsEventLog.aspx (excerpt)
Sub refreshLog(s As Object, e As EventArgs)
  objLog.Log = "Application"
  dgLog.DataSource = objLog.Entries
  dgLog.DataBind()
End Sub
```

```
C#                                  File: HandlingErrorsEventLog.aspx (excerpt)
void refreshLog(Object s, EventArgs e) {
  objLog.Log = "Application";
  dgLog.DataSource = objLog.Entries;
  dgLog.DataBind();
}
```

In this case, we set the Log property of the event log to Application, which tells it we want to read from the Application log. Next, we bind the DataGrid to the log entries, which are automatically loaded into the Entries property of the event log object. Save your work and test the results within the browser. Click the Refresh Log Button control. The result will appear similar to Figure 13.11.

Figure 13.11. Bind the contents of the event log to a DataGrid for a quick view.

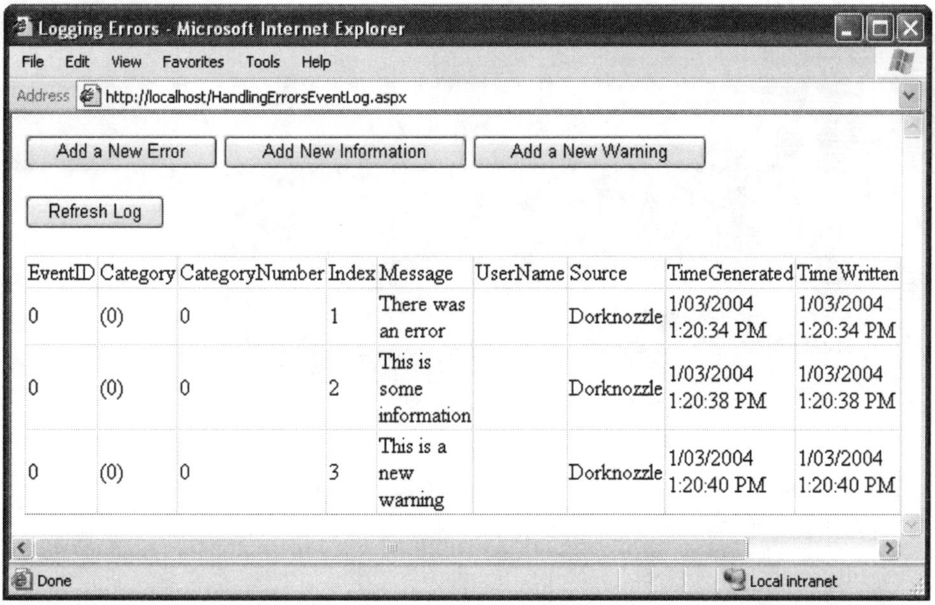

Using the .NET Debugger

In many instances, your ASP.NET pages will be so large that fixing errors, and even coding mistakes, becomes a very arduous a task. There will be other times when the error messages are so vague and incomprehensible that they leave you frustrated, and no closer to finding a resolution to the problem. Fortunately, the .NET Framework SDK comes packaged with a development tool called the Debugger. The Debugger is a visual tool that allows you manually to step through each line of an executing page. With the Debugger, you can closely monitor the execution of statements (called "stepping" through the code, meaning you can watch the code execute line by line), create breakpoints so that the execution of the code stops at a specific location, and view values of variables as they are set and changed. The following sections will teach you how to use the Debugger to aid the error handling process.

Launch the Debugger by double-clicking the `DbgCLR.exe` icon in the `C:\Program Files\Microsoft.NET\SDK\v1.1\GuiDebug` folder. You can create a shortcut to this file in your Start Menu if you expect to use the Debugger often. Figure 13.12 shows the Debugger interface that you'll see.

Figure 13.12. The Debugger is available as a free development tool with the .NET Framework SDK.

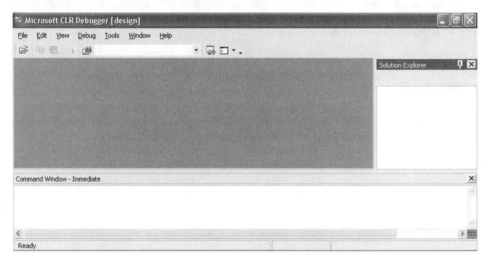

Attaching a Process to the Debugger

Before you can begin using the Debugger, your application needs to be configured to run in debug mode. You can do this by adding the `<compilation>` tag to the `<system.web>` section of your application's `Web.config` file as follows:

```
<system.web>
  <compilation debug="true" />
</system.web>
```

Next, you'll want to attach the debugger to the ASP.NET **process**. Windows runs applications as processes. Everything from Microsoft Word to your favorite game consumes computer resources and, thus, must be managed as a process by the operating system—ASP.NET is no exception. If you open the Windows Task Manager by pressing Ctrl-Alt-Delete (and clicking the Task Manager button in Windows 2000), you will be able to find the `aspnet_wp.exe` process listed in the Processes tab. This is the so-called **ASP.NET worker process**, and is responsible for performing all the processing required by any ASP.NET pages requested from your machine. What we need to do is attach the Debugger to that process. This will allow us to step through each line of code while the process is executing, and identify errors line by line.

To attach the Debugger to the `aspnet_wp.exe` process for a particular page, follow the steps outlined below:

1. In the Debugger window, select Open File from the File menu, and navigate to the page you want to debug. In this case, we'll look at `helpdesk.aspx` from Chapter 8. When you've found it, click Open, and the code will appear within the Debugger's code window, similar to Figure 13.13.

Figure 13.13. Open the page to be debugged within the Debugger.

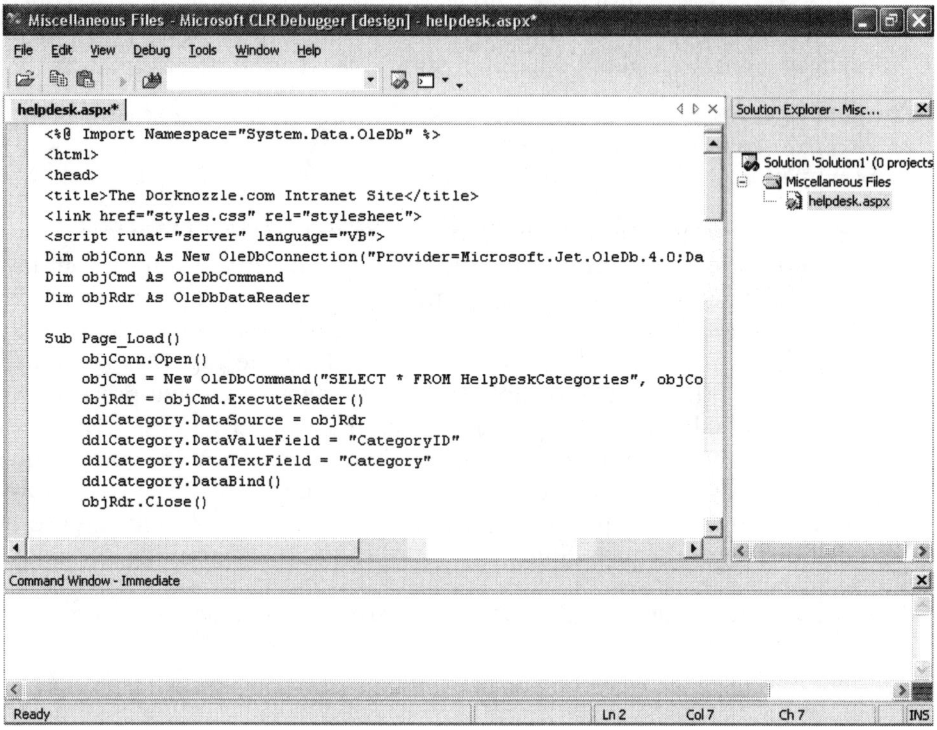

2. Select Processes from the Debug menu to open the Processes dialog box, as shown in Figure 13.14.

Figure 13.14. Open the Processes dialog box from the Debug menu.

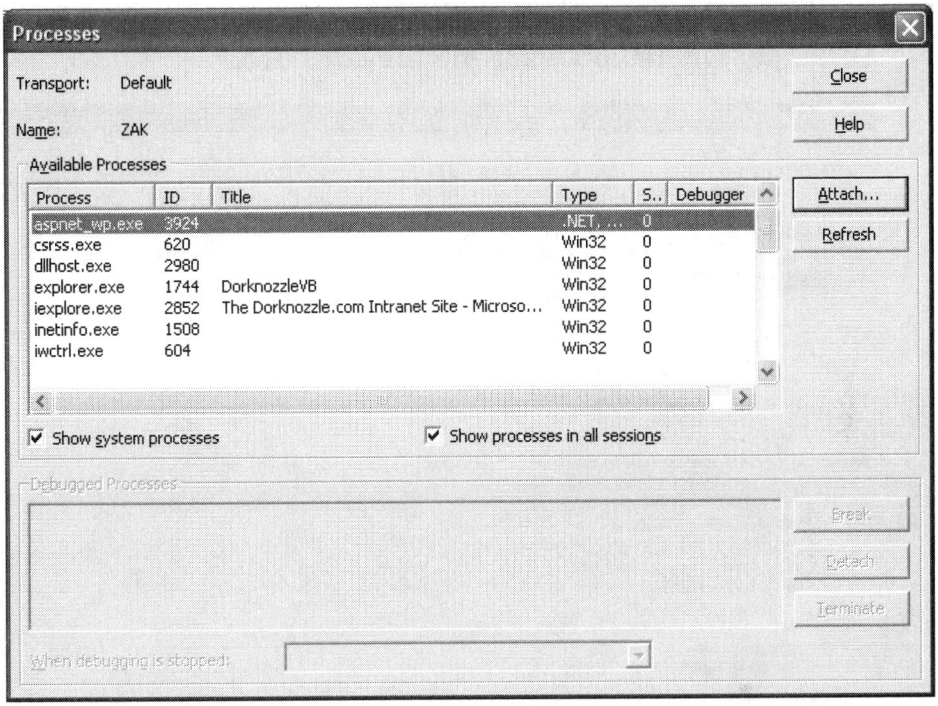

3. Select `aspnet_wp.exe` and click Attach.

4. Close the Process dialog box.

The Debugger will remain attached to the process until you either detach it, or close the Debugger.

Creating Breakpoints and Stepping Through Code

In order to step through the code and view the values of variables as they are being set, you must create **breakpoints**. When an executing page reaches a breakpoint, the application switches to break mode, allowing you to step through the remaining code line by line. You can add a breakpoint to your code by clicking in the margin of the line for which you'd like to enter a breakpoint. Figure 13.15 shows how I've added a breakpoint at the first line of code in

Page_Load(). If you're following along, add a second breakpoint on the first line in SubmitHelpDesk() as well.

Figure 13.15. Add two breakpoints within the margin of the Debugger where you want the break to occur.

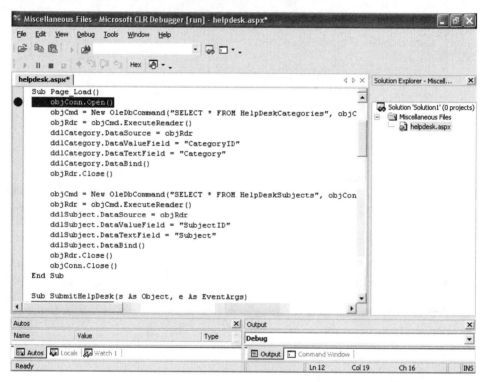

As you can see, the entire line that has the breakpoint is highlighted in red. At this stage, you may find your Debugger only shows a red circle with a question mark. This will change to become a red line, like the one shown here, once you open the page in your browser. Now, try refreshing the page within the browser. Immediately, the browser loses focus, the Debugger gains window focus, and the first breakpoint is highlighted in yellow, similar to Figure 13.16.

Figure 13.16. The Debugger gains focus, while execution has stopped at the first breakpoint.

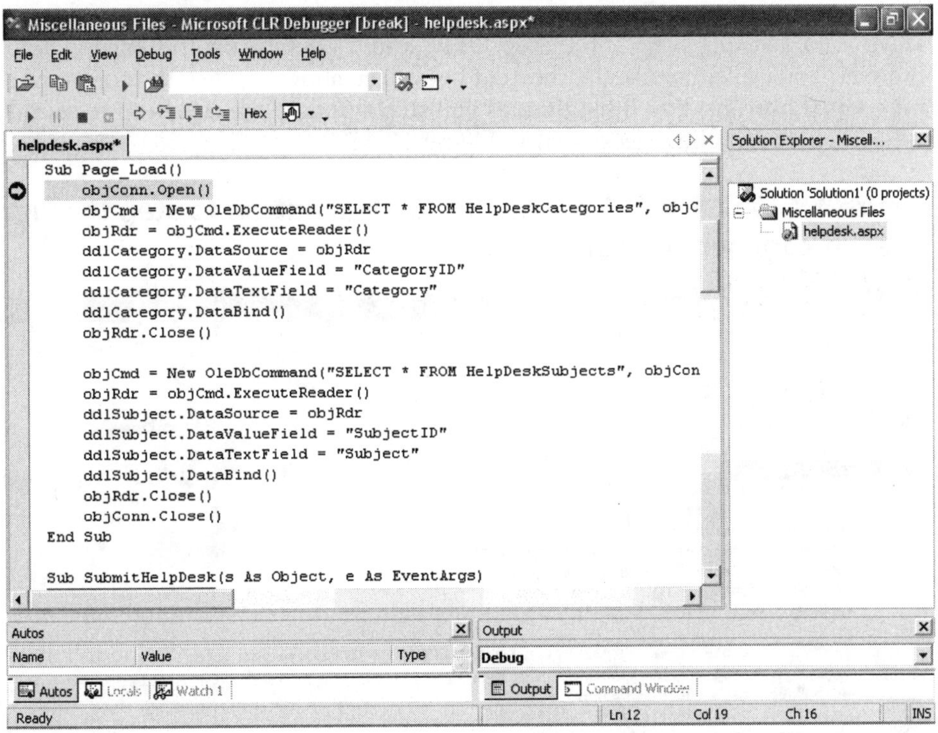

You can step through each line of code while the page is executing using the following commands:

Step Into (F11)   Steps into the current line of code. If the line calls a method and the Debugger has access to the code for that method, it will step inside the method and allow you to step through it line by line.

Step Over (F12)   Steps immediately to the next line, without stepping through any method calls in the current line. You can use this when you know that any methods that may be called are working properly and don't need testing.

Step Out (Shift-F11)   Executes the remainder of the current method, stop-
ping again on the line following the original call to the
method.

Have a go at using Step Into, Step Over, and Step Out on the page in your
browser. You can either use the shortcut keys given above, or click the corresponding toolbar buttons. You'll see that, as you step through, the current line of code
is highlighted in yellow, as shown in Figure 13.17.

Figure 13.17. Click F11 or use the Step Into button to step through lines of code within a statement.

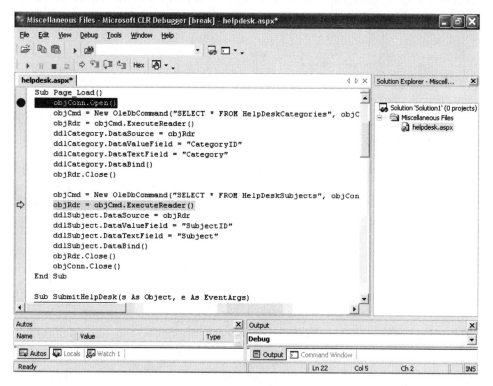

Stepping through code line by line like this can be invaluable in tracking down
and resolving errors that aren't immediately obvious from the message they produce.

Creating Watches

Once you've added breakpoints to your code within the Debugger, you can view the values of variables used in that code in one of three ways. First, you can hover the mouse over a variable name to view its contents, as is shown for the variable named objCmd in Figure 13.18. As you can see, objCmd contains an instance of the OleDbCommand class.

Figure 13.18. Roll over a variable to see its contents.

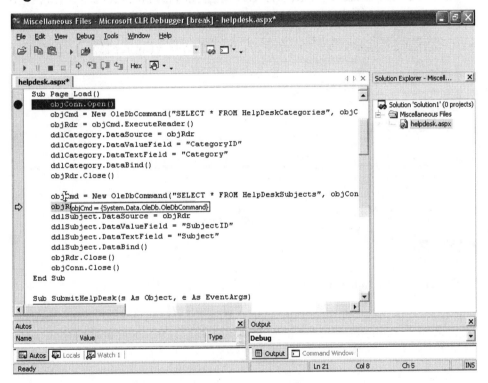

You can also use the QuickWatch window to view the values of variables. To use the QuickWatch window, right-click the name of the variable, and choose QuickWatch. Figure 13.19 shows what happens when you open QuickWatch for the objCmd variable. The window displays all the properties of the OleDbCommand class, along with their values at the moment.

Figure 13.19. Use the QuickWatch window to view values of variables.

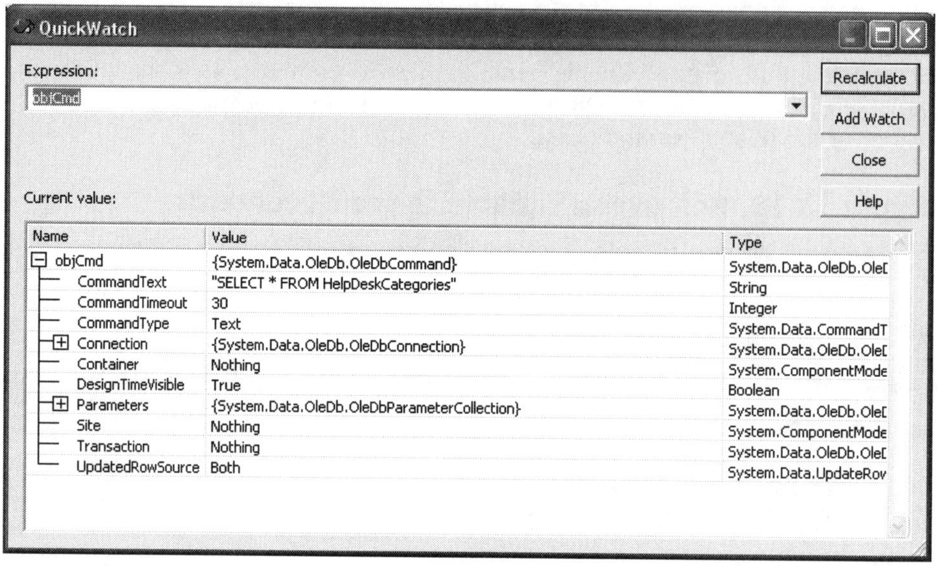

Alternatively, you can choose Add Watch, which causes the status of the variable to be continuously monitored in the Watch panel of the main Debugger window.

Summary

In this chapter, you learned about the various types of errors that an ASP.NET page can produce. You learned how to identify the four main types of errors, and how to handle those errors within code so that your users don't have to. Toward the end of the chapter, you learned about the .NET Debugger and how to use it to identify errors within an ASP.NET page.

14

Security and User Authentication

The issue of security is important for many facets of information technology, and is especially so for Web development. While you'll want to make sure that your Website users are able to go where they need to go and see what they're allowed to see, you also want to prevent unauthorized and malicious users from getting into the system. One common approach is to make sure that visitors to your site log in before they can view certain pages, and also, that restricted pages cannot be accessed simply by typing in the appropriate URLs, unless the user has been specifically allowed to view those pages. Although different solutions exist for the various applications you may create—for instance, IIS could provide certain pages to users who have been authenticated by Windows user groups within an intranet environment—this chapter focuses on the more straightforward form/script-based authentication.

Using ASP.NET, in combination with some simple coding techniques, you'll see just how easy it is to secure your Web applications.

Securing ASP.NET Applications

The ASP.NET server model offers several robust options when it comes to storing user information. With previous versions of ASP, user names and passwords were either hard-coded into the ASP file, or stored in an external data store such as a database. Although these options are still available in ASP.NET, there are also three new user authentication methods:

Windows Authentication
Windows authentication uses IIS in conjunction with the users' operating system user accounts to allow or deny access to certain parts of your Web application.

Forms Authentication
Offering the most flexibility, forms authentication provides the most control and customization to the developer. Using forms authentication, you now have a choice between traditional methods of validation (XML file, database, and hard-coded) as well as new methods (`Web.config`, cookies), or even a combination of both.

Passport Authentication
By far the newest addition to user validation methods, Passport authentication is the centralized authentication service provided through the .NET initiative by Microsoft. Because users rely on their Microsoft Passport accounts, which are associated with their email addresses, developers need never worry about storing credential information on their own servers. When users log in to a site that has Passport authentication enabled, they are redirected to the Passport Website, where they enter their passport and password information. After users' information is validated, they are automatically redirected back to the original site. The downside to this method is that it requires all users to have a Passport account in order to be authenticated on your site.

Although these are three great authentication methods, we cannot cover them all within the scope of this book. Instead, we'll focus on the simplest and most practical—namely, forms authentication.

Working with Forms Authentication

Forms authentication is by far the most popular authentication method because of its flexibility in terms of the user. An advantage of forms authentication lies in the fact that with it, you are able to store user names and passwords in virtually any data store, such as the `Web.config` file, an XML file, a database, or a combination of the three.

Forms authentication is cookie-based, meaning that each user's login is maintained with a cookie, which is just a temporary file stored on the user's computer. After forms authentication is enabled, protected pages are unable to be accessed without the proper **authentication ticket**, which is stored in users' cookies once they've successfully logged in. They contain the name of the user, cookie expiration dates, and more. Without the proper ticket, a user can be redirected automatically to the original page and required to log in again.

The three classes within the `System.Web.Security` namespace that you'll use most often in your work with user authentication are:

`FormsAuthentication`	Contains several methods for working with forms authentication.
`FormsAuthenticationTicket`	Represents the authentication ticket that's stored in the user's cookie.
`FormsIdentity`	Represents the authenticated user's identity.

Let's walk through an example that looks at how a basic login page is constructed. There are three steps that we need to take:

1. Configure the authentication mode for the application within the `Web.config` file.

2. Configure the authorization section to allow or deny certain users within the `Web.config` file.

3. Create the login page that your users will use.

The first step is to configure the authentication mode for the application. To do this, open the `Web.config` file and add the `<authentication>` tag shown here:

File: **SimpleLogin/Web.config**

```
<configuration>
  <system.web>
    <authentication mode="Forms" />
  </system.web>
</configuration>
```

There are four possibilities for the `mode` attribute: `Forms`, `Windows`, `Passport`, and `None`. Since we are working with forms authentication, we set the `mode` to `Forms`.

Next, set up the authorization scheme by adding the `<authorization>` tag:

File: **SimpleLogin/Web.config**

```
<configuration>
  <system.web>
    <authentication mode="Forms" />
    <authorization>
      <deny users="?" />
    </authorization>
  </system.web>
</configuration>
```

As you'll see in more detail in the next few sections, the question mark (**?**) symbol represents all anonymous users—that is, users who have not logged in. Essentially, this configuration reads: "Deny all non-logged-in users." If users try to access a page controlled by this **Web.config** file and do not have the appropriate authentication ticket, they will be redirected to the login page. Now, all we need do is create that login page.

You can create a simple login page by adding the necessary HTML, two **TextBox** controls, and a **Button** control, as follows:

File: **SimpleLogin/login.aspx**

```
<html>
<head>
  <title>Login</title>
</head>
<body>
<form runat="server">
<p>User name:<br /><asp:TextBox id="username" runat="server" />
</p>
<p>Password:<br /><asp:TextBox id="password" runat="server"
      TextMode="Password" /></p>
<p><asp:Button id="btnSubmit" runat="server" Text="Login"
      OnClick="LoginUser" /></p>
</form>
</body>
</html>
```

As you can see, the page contains two **TextBox** controls, one of which has the **TextMode** set to **Password**, which means that asterisks will show when a user types anything into this field. The other is a **Button** control, the **OnClick** attribute for which calls the **LoginUser()** method. Next, we'll add the server-side script for this method; this will validate the login credentials as follows:

```
VB.NET                                    File: SimpleLogin/login.aspx (excerpt)
<script runat="server" language="VB">
Sub LoginUser(s As Object, e As EventArgs)
  If (username.Text = "zak" And password.Text = "password") Then
    FormsAuthentication.RedirectFromLoginPage(username.Text, True)
  End If
End Sub
</script>
```

```
C#                                        File: SimpleLogin/login.aspx (excerpt)
<script runat="server" language="C#">
void LoginUser(Object s, EventArgs e) {
  if (username.Text == "zak" && password.Text == "password") {
    FormsAuthentication.RedirectFromLoginPage(username.Text,
        true);
  }
}
</script>
```

In the preceding code, two lines make everything happen. First, the If statement used to check if the user typed in the right user name and password:

```
VB.NET                                    File: SimpleLogin/login.aspx (excerpt)
If (username.Text = "zak" And password.Text = "password") Then
```

```
C#                                        File: SimpleLogin/login.aspx (excerpt)
if (username.Text == "zak" && password.Text == "password") {
```

If the user name and password entered are zak and password respective, the next line processed will be this one:

```
VB.NET                                    File: SimpleLogin/login.aspx (excerpt)
FormsAuthentication.RedirectFromLoginPage(username.Text, True)
```

```
C#                                        File: SimpleLogin/login.aspx (excerpt)
FormsAuthentication.RedirectFromLoginPage(username.Text, true);
```

This line calls the RedirectFromLoginPage() method, passing in two parameters. The first parameter is the user name to be stored in the user's authentication ticket. We'll simply use the user name entered into the form for this example. The second parameter is a Boolean value that indicates whether a persistent cookie should be created. By setting this value to True, you are essentially allowing your users to close their browser windows, open them again, navigate back to your site, and still be logged in. Setting this value to False allows users to be logged in only as long as their browser windows remain open. If they close their browsers, reopen them, and navigate to your site, they'll have to log in again.

Save your page as `login.aspx`. By default, if a cookie representing the authentication ticket does not exist on the user's machine, the application will redirect to `login.aspx`, which is why this page must be called `login.aspx`, rather than `Default.aspx` or `index.aspx`. Before you can test your work, however, you'll have to create a second page named `Default.aspx`. By default, with forms authentication, a successful login will redirect to a page named `Default.aspx`, so this has to exist. Make a `Default.aspx` page like this:

File: **SimpleLogin/Default.aspx (excerpt)**

```
<html>
<head>
<title>Successful login</title>
</head>
<body>
<p>Successful login!</p>
</body>
</html>
```

Next, make sure that you have created an application within IIS for the folder from which you are working. Because authentication within ASP.NET is application-based by default, it will not work if an application has not been created for the directory to be protected. You can reset your directory to an application by following the steps outlined below:

1. Open the Internet Information Services manager and select the Default Web Site in the tree.

2. Find the folder you're working in, right-click it, and select Properties.

3. While in the Directory tab, click the Create button to create an application.

4. Click OK to commit the changes.

Now, try logging into `login.aspx`. This time you will be redirected to the `Default.aspx` page, as shown in Figure 14.1.

Figure 14.1. Entering the correct credentials results in a redirection to `Default.aspx`.

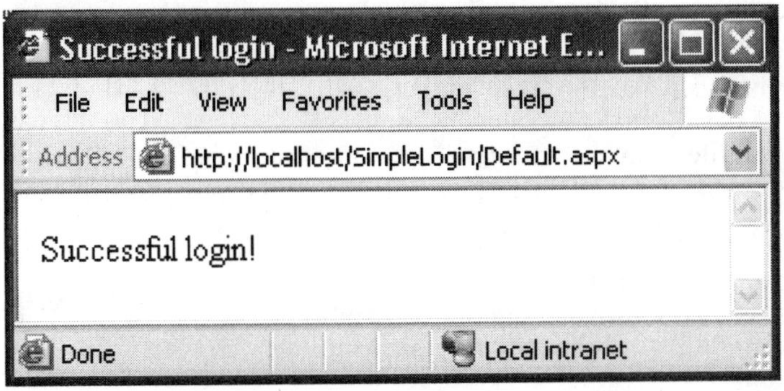

The login page you have just built is the simplest form you can possibly implement. The next sections will enable you to further customize the form and develop a better means of storing valid login credentials than hard-coding them.

Configuring Forms Authentication

In the previous section, you learned how to create a basic login page. You also learned how to modify the `Web.config` file to enable the forms authentication mode. In this section, we'll explore the forms authentication section within the `Web.config` file in greater detail.

Aside from the basic authentication mode, the `<authentication>` tag within the `Web.config` file may contain a `<forms>` element. The `<forms>` element accepts the following attributes:

`loginUrl`	The page that the user is redirected to when authentication is necessary. By default, this page is called `login.aspx`. Using this attribute, you can modify the file name to anything you like.
`name`	The name of the cookie to be stored on the user's machine. By default, the name is set to `.ASPXAUTH`.
`timeout`	The amount of time in minutes before the cookie expires. By default, this value is set to thirty minutes.

path	The path to the location at which the cookie is stored. By default, this value is set to /.
protection	The way(s) the cookie data is protected. Values include All, None, Encryption, and Validation. The default value is All.

An example Web.config file with the <forms> element could look like this:

```
<configuration>
  <system.web>
    <authentication mode="Forms">
      <forms name=".LoginCookie" loginUrl="index.aspx"
          protection="All" timeout="40" path="/" />
    </authentication>
    <authorization>
      …
    </authorization>
  </system.web>
</configuration>
```

Configuring Forms Authorization

As is the case with the <authentication> section of the Web.config file, the <authorization> tag can be modified to accept or deny certain users within your application. You can make extremely specific decisions regarding who will and who will not be accepted into your application—for instance, the following code allows all non-anonymous users except for zruvalcaba.

```
<configuration>
  <system.web>
    <authentication …>
      …
    </authentication>
    <authorization>
      <deny users="?" />
      <deny users="zruvalcaba" />
    </authorization>
  </system.web>
</configuration>
```

Here, we're again using the question mark (?) to force users to log in, thus denying access to anonymous users. We've also added another <deny> tag, for the user `zruvalcaba`. In a nutshell, the two `<deny>` lines will allow everyone except `zruvalcaba` to log in.

In addition to `<deny>` tags, the `<authorization>` tag may contain `<allow>` tags. We'll see an example of this in a moment. For each user who attempts to access the application, ASP.NET will read through the tags in `<authorization>` and find the first tag that matches that user. If that turns out to be a `<deny>` tag, they are denied access to the application; if it's an `<allow>` tag, or if no matching tag is found, they are granted access.

The `users` attribute of the `<allow>` and `<deny>` tags doesn't only accept the question mark (?) symbol, however—you can use any one of the following values:

?	Use this value to allow or deny all anonymous users. This is the most common value used with forms authentication.
*	Use this value to allow or deny all users. This includes users who are logged in.
user(s)	As we did with `zruvalcaba` above, you can deny access to a specific user. You can list several users by separating their names by a comma.

We could modify the code a bit further in an effort to allow only specific users:

```
<configuration>
  <system.web>
    <authentication …>
      …
    </authentication>
    <authorization>
      <allow users="jruvalcaba,zruvalcaba" />
      <deny users="*" />
    </authorization>
  </system.web>
</configuration>
```

In this case, the users with the login names of `jruvalcaba` and `zruvalcaba` are allowed access to the application, but all other users (whether logged in or not) will be denied access.

Now that you have a basic understanding as to how user access is configured within the `Web.config` file, let's see how we can use `Web.config` to store a list of users for our application.

Web.config File Authentication

The great thing about the Web.config file is that it is secure enough to allow you to store user names and passwords within it. The <credentials> tag shown here, appearing within the <forms> element of the Web.config file, defines login credentials for two users:

File: **WebConfigAuthentication/Web.config**

```
<configuration>
  <system.web>
    <authentication mode="Forms">
      <forms>
        <credentials passwordFormat="Clear" >
          <user name="zak" password="ruvalcaba" />
          <user name="jessica" password="ruvalcaba" />
        </credentials>
      </forms>
    </authentication>
    <authorization>
      <deny users="?" />
    </authorization>
  </system.web>
</configuration>
```

As we want to prevent users from browsing our site unless they've logged in, we use the appropriate <deny> tag in our <authorization> tag. The names and passwords of the users we will permit can then simply be specified in the <credentials> tag. Change your Web.config file to match the one shown above, and we'll try an example.

You can now modify the code that lies within the <head> tag of the login.aspx page to validate the user names and passwords based on the Web.config file. Here's what this change looks like:

VB.NET   File: **WebConfigAuthentication/login.aspx**

```
<html>
<head>
<title>Login</title>
<script runat="Server" language="VB">
Sub LoginUser(s As Object, e As EventArgs)
  If FormsAuthentication.Authenticate(username.Text, _
      password.Text) Then
    FormsAuthentication.RedirectFromLoginPage(username.Text, True)
  End If
```

```
End Sub
</script>
</head>
<body>
<form runat="server">
<p>User name:<br /><asp:TextBox id="username" runat="server" />
</p>
<p>Password:<br /><asp:TextBox id="password" runat="server"
     TextMode="Password" /></p>
<p><asp:Button id="btnSubmit" runat="server" Text="Login"
     OnClick="LoginUser" /></p>
</form>
</body>
</html>
```

C#   File: **WebConfigAuthentication/login.aspx**

```
<html>
<head>
<title>Login</title>
<script runat="server" language="C#">
void LoginUser(Object s, EventArgs e) {
  if (FormsAuthentication.Authenticate(username.Text,
     password.Text)) {
    FormsAuthentication.RedirectFromLoginPage(username.Text,
       true);
  }
}
</script>
</head>
<body>
<form runat="server">
<p>User name:<br /><asp:TextBox id="username" runat="server" />
</p>
<p>Password:<br /><asp:TextBox id="password" runat="server"
     TextMode="Password" /></p>
<p><asp:Button id="btnSubmit" runat="server" Text="Login"
     OnClick="LoginUser" /></p>
</form>
</body>
</html>
```

In this case, we use the Authenticate() method of the FormsAuthentication class, which checks a user name and password against the users defined within the <credentials> tag in the Web.config file. Save your work and test the results within the browser. Again, when you enter credentials matching those within the Web.config file, you're redirected to Default.aspx.

Database Authentication

Arguably, the best method of storing user names and passwords is in a database table. This approach brings certain advantages, the first of which is that user names and passwords can be added, modified, and removed by an administrator or a user from a custom built administration page. Second, no administrative privileges are required for modification (as is the case with the `Web.config` file).

This section shows you how to use the `Employees` database table to validate employee credentials for our Intranet application. Before you begin, make sure the root directory of your intranet application contains a `Web.config` file with the following `<appSettings>` and `<system.web>` sections:

File: **Web.config**

```
<configuration>
  <appSettings>
    <add key="DSN" value="Provider=Microsoft.Jet.OLEDB.4.0;Data So
urce=C:\Inetpub\wwwroot\Dorknozzle\Database\dorknozzle.mdb"/>
  </appSettings>

  <system.web>
    <authentication mode="Forms" />
    <authorization>
      <deny users="?" />
    </authorization>
  </system.web>
</configuration>
```

Next, turn the Dorknozzle Intranet project into an IIS application (if you haven't already) by opening the IIS control panel, locating the site within the Web Sites subtree, right-clicking on the folder that contains your Dorknozzle application files, selecting Properties, and clicking the Create button within the Directory tab to create the application.

Click OK and close the IIS control panel. Next, create the interface for a login page by opening the `template.aspx` page and adding the required `TextBox` controls and a Button:

File: **login.aspx (excerpt)**

```
<h1>Login</h1>
<p>Username: <br /><asp:TextBox id="username" runat="server" />
</p>
<p>Password: <br /><asp:TextBox id="password" runat="server"
```

```
        TextMode="Password" /></p>
<p><asp:Button id="btnSubmit" runat="server" Text="Login"
        OnClick="LoginUser" /></p>
```

Because this is a login page, you'll also want to remove the navigation menu, as we don't want lead users to believe they can access other pages before they log in. Were they left in, the links would simply redirect them back to the login page. You can remove the navigation menu simply by deleting the block of hyperlinks. This is indicated in the version in the code archive as follows:

File: **login.aspx (excerpt)**

```
<td valign="top" width="160">
  <!-- HyperLink Controls removed from login page -->
</td>
```

Save your work as `login.aspx` and test the results in the browser. Rather than navigating to `login.aspx`, simply type the URL of the Web application folder (e.g. http://localhost/Dorknozzle/). Because the project is an ASP.NET Web application and the `Web.config` file is set to forms authentication, ASP.NET intercepts the request, and automatically redirects the user to `login.aspx`, as shown in Figure 14.2.

Figure 14.2. The user is automatically redirected to `login.aspx`.

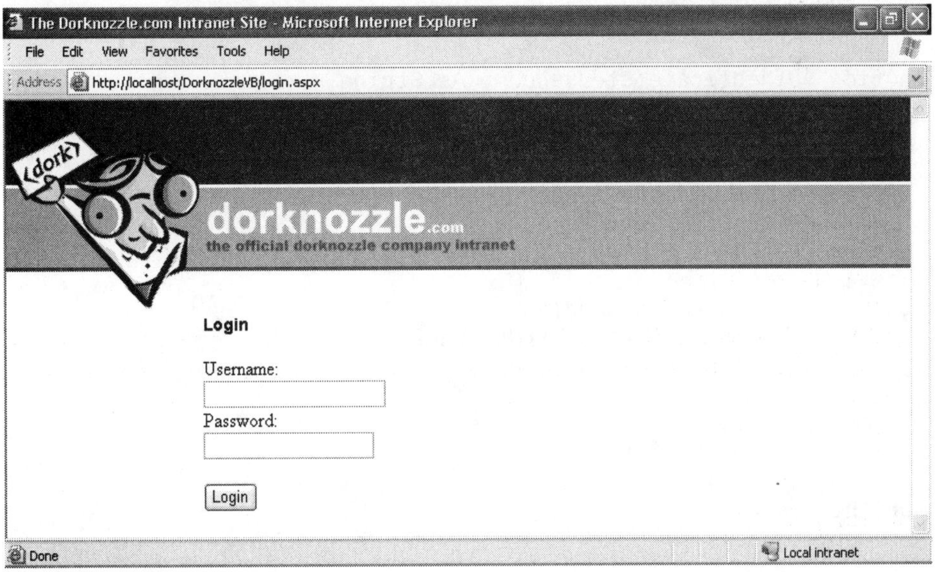

The next step is to retrieve, and validate the user-entered data against the user details that are stored within the `Employees` table of the database. Because we're working with a database, you'll need to import the appropriate namespace. Assuming you're working with Access, you would import the `System.Data.OleDb` namespace as follows:

```
<%@ Import Namespace="System.Data.OleDb" %>
```

Next, add the `OnClick` property to the Button control like this:

```
<asp:Button ID="btnSubmit" runat="server" Text="Login"
    OnClick="LoginUser" />
```

Now, add the following code within the `<head>` tag of your `login.aspx` file to attempt authentication for the specified user:

VB.NET   File: **login.aspx (excerpt)**

```vb
<script runat="server" language="VB">
Sub LoginUser(s As Object, e As EventArgs)
  Dim blnAuthenticate As Boolean = Authenticate(username.Text, _
      password.Text)
  If blnAuthenticate Then
    FormsAuthentication.RedirectFromLoginPage(username.Text, _
        False)
  End If
End Sub

Function Authenticate(strUsername As String, _
    strPassword As String) As Boolean
  Dim objConn As New OleDbConnection( _
      ConfigurationSettings.AppSettings("DSN"))
  Dim objCmd As OleDbCommand
  Dim objDR As OleDbDataReader
  Dim userFound As Boolean

  objCmd = New OleDbCommand("SELECT * FROM Employees " & _
      "WHERE Username='" & strUsername & _
      "' AND Password='" & strPassword & "'", objConn)

  objConn.Open()
  objDR = objCmd.ExecuteReader()
  userFound = objDR.Read()
  objDR.Close()
  objConn.Close()

  Return userFound
```

```
End Function
</script>
```

C#   File: login.aspx (excerpt)

```
<script runat="server" language="C#">
void LoginUser(Object s, EventArgs e) {
  bool blnAuthenticate = Authenticate(username.Text,
      password.Text);
  if (blnAuthenticate) {
    FormsAuthentication.RedirectFromLoginPage(username.Text,
        false);
  }
}

bool Authenticate(string strUsername, string strPassword) {
  OleDbConnection objConn = new OleDbConnection(
      ConfigurationSettings.AppSettings["DSN"]);
  OleDbCommand objCmd;
  OleDbDataReader objDR;
  bool userFound;

  objCmd = new OleDbCommand("SELECT * FROM Employees " +
      "WHERE Username='" + strUsername +
      "' AND Password='" + strPassword + "'", objConn);

  objConn.Open();
  objDR = objCmd.ExecuteReader();
  userFound = objDR.Read();
  objDR.Close();
  objConn.Close();

  return userFound;
}
</script>
```

Let's pick apart the code to help you better understand how the user is validated. We start out within the LoginUser() event handler that the Button control's Click event calls:

VB.NET   File: login.aspx (excerpt)

```
Sub LoginUser(s As Object, e As EventArgs)
  Dim blnAuthenticate As Boolean = Authenticate(username.Text, _
      password.Text)
  If blnAuthenticate Then
    FormsAuthentication.RedirectFromLoginPage(username.Text, _
        False)
```

```
    End If
End Sub
```

C#   File: **login.aspx (excerpt)**

```csharp
void LoginUser(Object s, EventArgs e) {
  bool blnAuthenticate = Authenticate(username.Text,
      password.Text);
  if (blnAuthenticate) {
    FormsAuthentication.RedirectFromLoginPage(username.Text,
        false);
  }
}
```

In this case, we use a new variable called blnAuthenticate to store the return value of the Authenticate() method, which we'll talk about in a moment. Just like the built-in FormsAuthentication.Authenticate() method that we used before, this Authenticate() method (which we will write ourselves) takes the name and password to check as its two parameters. In this case, we pass in the value of the username TextBox control, and the value of the password TextBox control. The return value is then checked. If the it's true, the RedirectFromLoginPage() method of the FormsAuthentication class is called, which grants the user access to the page they originally requested.

Our Authenticate() method is what performs most of the work. The method, which has a Boolean return type, accepts two string parameters, strUsername and strPassword, which come from the two TextBox control values:

VB.NET   File: **login.aspx (excerpt)**

```vbnet
Function Authenticate(strUsername As String, _
    strPassword As String) As Boolean
```

C#   File: **login.aspx (excerpt)**

```csharp
bool Authenticate(string strUsername, string strPassword) {
```

The next lines of code create the variables we'll be using within the method:

VB.NET   File: **login.aspx (excerpt)**

```vbnet
Dim objConn As New OleDbConnection( _
    ConfigurationSettings.AppSettings("DSN"))
Dim objCmd As OleDbCommand
Dim objDR As OleDbDataReader
Dim userFound As Boolean
```

C#

```
OleDbConnection objConn = new OleDbConnection(
    ConfigurationSettings.AppSettings["DSN"]);
OleDbCommand objCmd;
OleDbDataReader objDR;
bool userFound;
```

As you can see, we'll be using the OleDbConnection, OleDbCommand, and OleDbDataReader classes to access our database, so change these to their SQL Server variants if you're using MSDE. Next, we create a new instance of the OleDbCommand class, passing in the query and the connection object, to return a new command object:

VB.NET

```
objCmd = New OleDbCommand("SELECT * FROM Employees " & _
    "WHERE Username='" & strUsername & _
    "' AND Password='" & strPassword & "'", objConn)
```

C#

```
objCmd = new OleDbCommand("SELECT * FROM Employees " +
    "WHERE Username='" + strUsername +
    "' AND Password='" + strPassword + "'", objConn);
```

Now we execute the command, but rather than looping through the results or binding them to a control, we simply call the Read() method of the OleDbDataReader, noting the return value. If a record matching the user name and password is found in the database, Read() will find a record in the result set to read, and it will therefore return true. If not, it will return false. We store this return value in a variable named userFound.

VB.NET

```
objConn.Open()
objDR = objCmd.ExecuteReader()
userFound = objDR.Read()
objDR.Close()
objConn.Close()
```

C#

```
objConn.Open();
objDR = objCmd.ExecuteReader();
userFound = objDR.Read();
objDR.Close();
objConn.Close();
```

Having closed the `OleDbDataReader` and connection objects, we can simply return the stored `userFound` value—true if the login details are valid, false if not.

Save your work and test the results in the browser. Try opening the `index.aspx` page (e.g. http://localhost/Dorknozzle/index.aspx). You should immediately be redirected to the login page. Try logging in with fake credentials. The page should simply refresh. You'll notice, however, that the address bar changes with the addition of the `ReturnURL` parameter, which we'll discuss in more detail in the next section.

Now, try entering a user name and password that does appear in the `Employees` table (e.g. **zak** and **zak**). If all goes well, you will be redirected to `index.aspx`. In the next section, you'll learn how to add error messages so that your users aren't left wondering why they can't log in.

Custom Error Messages

As you saw in the previous section, if users enter the wrong credentials, the page simply refreshes—it doesn't alert users that their credentials were invalid. Rather than leaving users wondering what happened, you can create a custom error message to tell them what went wrong during login, and that they may need to reenter their credentials. Creating custom error messages within your ASP.NET pages is simple, and can usually be accomplished with a `Label` control in your HTML and a conditional statement within the code.

Let's start by adding a `Label` control after the login `Button` control. You'll also want to change the `ForeColor` property to `Red` as a further hint to the user that an error has occurred. Your control may resemble the following:

```
<asp:Label ID="lblError" ForeColor="Red" Runat="Server" />
```

Now, change the `LoginUser()` method so that it resembles the one below:

VB.NET   File: `login.aspx (excerpt)`

```
Sub LoginUser(s As Object, e As EventArgs)
  Dim blnAuthenticate As Boolean = Authenticate(username.Text, _
      password.Text)
  If blnAuthenticate Then
    FormsAuthentication.RedirectFromLoginPage(Username.Text, _
        False)
  Else
    lblError.Text = "Your login was invalid. Please try again."
```

```
  End If
End Sub
```

C# File: **login.aspx (excerpt)**

```
void LoginUser(Object s, EventArgs e) {
  bool blnAuthenticate = Authenticate(username.Text, _
      password.Text);
  if (blnAuthenticate) {
    FormsAuthentication.RedirectFromLoginPage(username.Text, _
        false);
  } else {
    lblError.Text = "Your login was invalid. Please try again.";
  }
}
```

This time, when a user enters the wrong credentials, rather than the page simply reloading, the user will receive an error message similar to Figure 14.3.

Figure 14.3. Entering the wrong credentials results in an error message being displayed.

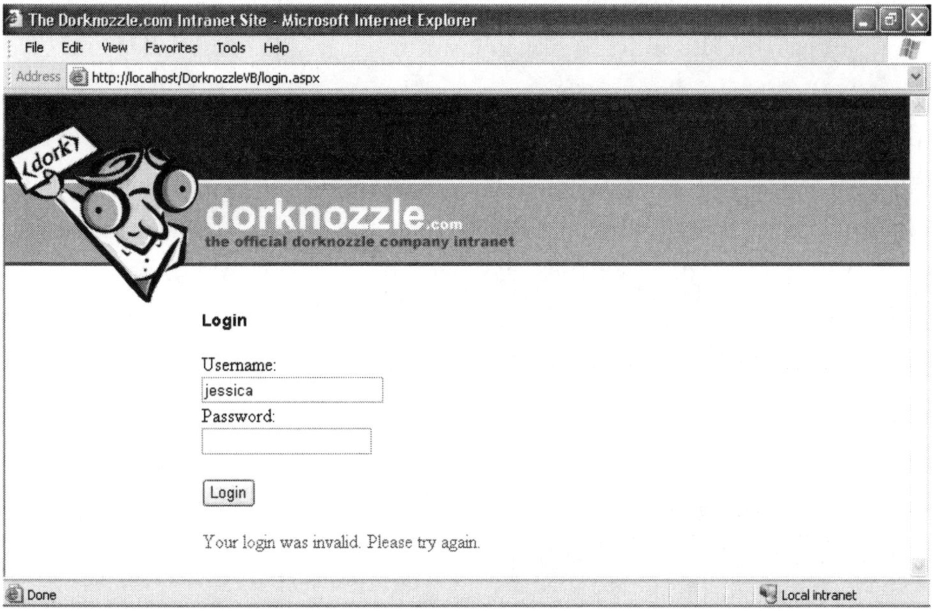

Logging Users Out

When your users have finished browsing your site, you'll normally want to provide them the ability to log out. People gain security from the knowledge that they have successfully logged out, and rightly so, as it's possible for a hacker to take over (or **spoof**) an existing login while it remains active. The first thing to do in order to create log out functionality within your application, is to insert a suitable control that users can click on when they're finished browsing. For instance, we could have a LinkButton control somewhere within index.aspx... perhaps below the header image?

File: **index.aspx (excerpt)**

```
<table width="100%" border="0" cellspacing="0" cellpadding="0">
  <tr>
    <td width="157"><img src="Images/header_bottom.gif"
        width="157" height="37" alt="" /></td>
    <td align="right"><asp:LinkButton id="lbLogOut" Text="Log Out"
        OnClick="Logout" runat="server" /></td>
  </tr>
</table>
```

Don't forget that this must be placed inside a server-side <form> element.

Next, you'll want to add a code declaration block within the <head> tag of the page, complete with a new method called Logout() to handle the LinkButton's Click event:

VB.NET   File: **index.aspx (excerpt)**

```
<script runat="server" language="VB">
Sub Logout(s As Object, e As EventArgs)
  FormsAuthentication.SignOut()
  Response.Redirect("login.aspx")
End Sub
</script>
```

C#   File: **index.aspx (excerpt)**

```
<script runat="server" language="C#">
void Logout(Object s, EventArgs e) {
  FormsAuthentication.SignOut();
  Response.Redirect("login.aspx");
}
</script>
```

As you can see, the `SignOut()` method of the `FormsAuthentication` class is used to clear the authentication cookie. The next line simply redirects the user to the login page.

Building Your Own Authentication Ticket

In the previous sections, you saw how forms authentication can streamline the way you create and work with security in your Web applications. You learned that when you work with forms authentication, an authentication ticket is automatically stored on the user's computer in the form of a cookie. For the most part, the authentication ticket that's automatically created contains all the information you'll need. There may be instances, however, in which you'll want to construct your own authentication ticket manually.

The authentication ticket that's automatically generated contains details that pertain to its expiration date, persistence information, and a custom property for storing any kind of information, called `UserData`. We can change all these variables. The authentication ticket is represented by the `FormsAuthenticationTicket` class. Its constructor accepts the following parameters:

version	The version of the authentication ticket; typically this value will be one
name	The user name associated with the authentication ticket
issueDate	The date that the authentication ticket was issued
expiration	The date that the authentication ticket should expire
isPersistent	A Boolean value indicating whether to allow the ticket to persist after the user closes the browser
userData	A string value of any data that you would like to store. For example, I like to store email addresses and department roles within this property.

Let's create a page to demonstrate how you can build your own custom authentication ticket. We'll start with the following HTML:

File: **CustomAuthenticationTicket/login.aspx**

```html
<html>
<head>
<title>Login</title>
</head>
<body>
<form runat="server">
<p><b>Username:</b><br />
<asp:TextBox id="txtUsername" runat="server" /></p>
<p><b>Password:</b><br />
<asp:TextBox id="txtPassword" TextMode="Password" runat="server"
    /></p>
<asp:Button id="btnLogin" Text="Create Ticket" OnClick="Login"
    runat="server" />
</form>
</body>
</html>
```

Next, add the following code declaration block within the <head> tag of the page:

VB.NET   File: **CustomAuthenticationTicket/login.aspx** (excerpt)

```vbnet
<script runat="server" language="VB">
Sub Login(s As Object, e As EventArgs)
  If (txtUsername.Text = "zak" And txtPassword.Text = "zak") Then
    Dim objTicket As FormsAuthenticationTicket
    Dim objCookie As HttpCookie

    objTicket = New FormsAuthenticationTicket(1, _
        txtUsername.Text, Now, Now.AddMinutes(60), True, _
        "zak@modulemedia.com")
    objCookie = New HttpCookie(".ASPXAUTH")
    objCookie.Value = FormsAuthentication.Encrypt(objTicket)
    Response.Cookies.Add(objCookie)

    Response.Redirect("Default.aspx")
  End If
End Sub
</script>
```

C#   File: **CustomAuthenticationTicket/login.aspx** (excerpt)

```csharp
<script runat="server" language="C#">
void Login(Object s, EventArgs e) {
  if (txtUsername.Text == "zak" && txtPassword.Text == "zak") {
    FormsAuthenticationTicket objTicket;
    HttpCookie objCookie;
```

```
    objTicket = new FormsAuthenticationTicket(1, txtUsername.Text,
        DateTime.Now, DateTime.Now.AddMinutes(60), true,
        "zak@modulemedia.com");
    objCookie = new HttpCookie(".ASPXAUTH");
    objCookie.Value = FormsAuthentication.Encrypt(objTicket);
    Response.Cookies.Add(objCookie);

    Response.Redirect("Default.aspx");
  }
}
</script>
```

Let's break down the code. First, we check to make sure that the credentials entered are valid, using a simple If statement:

VB.NET   File: **CustomAuthenticationTicket/login.aspx (excerpt)**
```
If (txtUsername.Text = "zak" And txtPassword.Text = "zak") Then
```

C#   File: **CustomAuthenticationTicket/login.aspx (excerpt)**
```
if (txtUsername.Text == "zak" && txtPassword.Text == "zak") {
```

As you can see, for this example, we've simply hard-coded the user details, although it wouldn't be difficult to change this to check validity based on the data in the Employees table. In fact, you might find it a useful exercise to do just that. Next, we create variables to contain FormsAuthenticationTicket and HttpCookie objects:

VB.NET   File: **CustomAuthenticationTicket/login.aspx (excerpt)**
```
Dim objTicket As FormsAuthenticationTicket
Dim objCookie As HttpCookie
```

C#   File: **CustomAuthenticationTicket/login.aspx (excerpt)**
```
FormsAuthenticationTicket objTicket;
HttpCookie objCookie;
```

Now, we'll create a new authentication ticket object, passing in the six parameters I described above into the FormsAuthenticationTicket constructor as follows:

VB.NET   File: **CustomAuthenticationTicket/login.aspx (excerpt)**
```
objTicket = New FormsAuthenticationTicket(1, _
    txtUsername.Text, Now, Now.AddMinutes(60), True,
    "zak@modulemedia.com")
```

```
C#                              File: CustomAuthenticationTicket/login.aspx (excerpt)
    objTicket = new FormsAuthenticationTicket(1, txtUsername.Text,
        DateTime.Now, DateTime.Now.AddMinutes(60), true,
        "zak@modulemedia.com");
```

You'll notice that the parameters accepted correspond to the version, name, issue date, expiration date, persistent Boolean value, and user data as described above. For the user data, we'll store an email address. In a practical application, this would be pulled from the record for the user that is logging in.

Now, we write the code that creates the new cookie, sets the value of the cookie equal to an encrypted version of the authentication ticket, adds the cookie to the Cookies collection, then redirects the user to the default.aspx page:

```
VB.NET                          File: CustomAuthenticationTicket/login.aspx (excerpt)
    objCookie = New HttpCookie(".ASPXAUTH")
    objCookie.Value = FormsAuthentication.Encrypt(objTicket)
    Response.Cookies.Add(objCookie)

    Response.Redirect("Default.aspx")
```

```
C#                              File: CustomAuthenticationTicket/login.aspx (excerpt)
    objCookie = new HttpCookie(".ASPXAUTH");
    objCookie.Value = FormsAuthentication.Encrypt(objTicket);
    Response.Cookies.Add(objCookie);

    Response.Redirect("Default.aspx");
```

Next create the Default.aspx page like so:

```
VB.NET                          File: CustomAuthenticationTicket/Default.aspx (excerpt)
<%@ Import Namespace="System.Web.Security" %>
<html>
<head>
<title>Default</title>
<script runat="server" language="VB">
Sub Page_Load()
  Dim objTicket As FormsIdentity

  objTicket = User.Identity
  lblName.Text = objTicket.Ticket.Name
  lblIssueDate.Text = objTicket.Ticket.IssueDate
  lblExpiration.Text = objTicket.Ticket.Expiration
  lblIsPersistent.Text = objTicket.Ticket.IsPersistent
  lblVersion.Text = objTicket.Ticket.Version
```

```
  lblUserData.Text = objTicket.Ticket.UserData
End Sub
</script>
</head>
<body>
<h2>Here is your authentication ticket info:</h2>
<p>User: <asp:Label id="lblName" runat="server" /><br />
Issue Date: <asp:Label id="lblIssueDate" runat="server" /><br />
Expiration Date: <asp:Label id="lblExpiration" runat="server" />
<br />
Is the cookie persistent? <asp:Label id="lblIsPersistent"
    runat="server" /><br />
Version: <asp:Label id="lblVersion" runat="server" /><br />
User data: <asp:Label id="lblUserData" runat="server" /></p>
</body>
</html>
```

C#   File: **CustomAuthenticationTicket/Default.aspx (excerpt)**

```
<%@ Import Namespace="System.Web.Security" %>
<html>
<head>
<title>Default</title>
<script runat="server" language="C#">
void Page_Load() {
  FormsIdentity objTicket;

  objTicket = (FormsIdentity)User.Identity;
  lblName.Text = objTicket.Ticket.Name;
  lblIssueDate.Text = objTicket.Ticket.IssueDate.ToString();
  lblExpiration.Text = objTicket.Ticket.Expiration.ToString();
  lblIsPersistent.Text = objTicket.Ticket.IsPersistent.ToString();
  lblVersion.Text = objTicket.Ticket.Version.ToString();
  lblUserData.Text = objTicket.Ticket.UserData;
}
</script>
</head>
<body>
<h2>Here is your authentication ticket info:</h2>
<p>User: <asp:Label id="lblName" runat="server" /><br />
Issue Date: <asp:Label id="lblIssueDate" runat="server" /><br />
Expiration Date: <asp:Label id="lblExpiration" runat="server" />
<br />
Is the cookie persistent? <asp:Label id="lblIsPersistent"
    runat="server" /><br />
Version: <asp:Label id="lblVersion" runat="server" /><br />
User data: <asp:Label id="lblUserData" runat="server" /></p>
```

```
</body>
</html>
```

As you can see, `Default.aspx` imports the `System.Web.Security` namespace. This allows us to work with the `FormsIdentity` class, which contains properties and methods for working with the user's authentication ticket. Next, we grab the user's `FormsIdentity` object from the `Identity` property of the `User` object, and store it in the `objTicket` variable. We can then access all the information within the authentication ticket and write it out to `Label` controls.

Save your work and test the results within the browser. Make sure you have defined within IIS an application for the directory within which you're working, so that the `Web.config` file will take effect. Figure 14.4 shows the login page you'll see.

Figure 14.4. Log in to create a custom authentication ticket and to be redirected to the `Default.aspx` page.

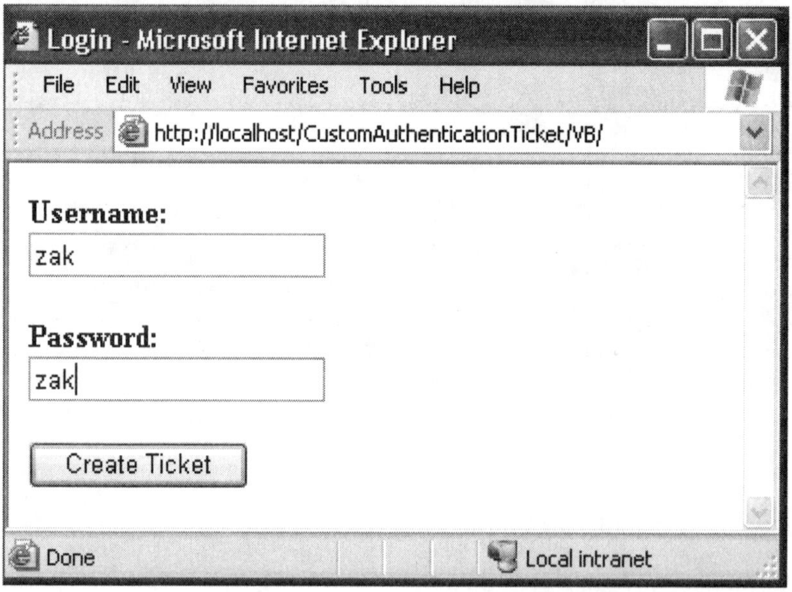

Entering the correct credentials creates a new authentication ticket within a user cookie. The information within the authentication ticket is written within `Label` controls in the `Default.aspx` page, as shown in Figure 14.5.

Figure 14.5. The information contained within the authentication ticket is written within `Label` controls in the `Default.aspx` page.

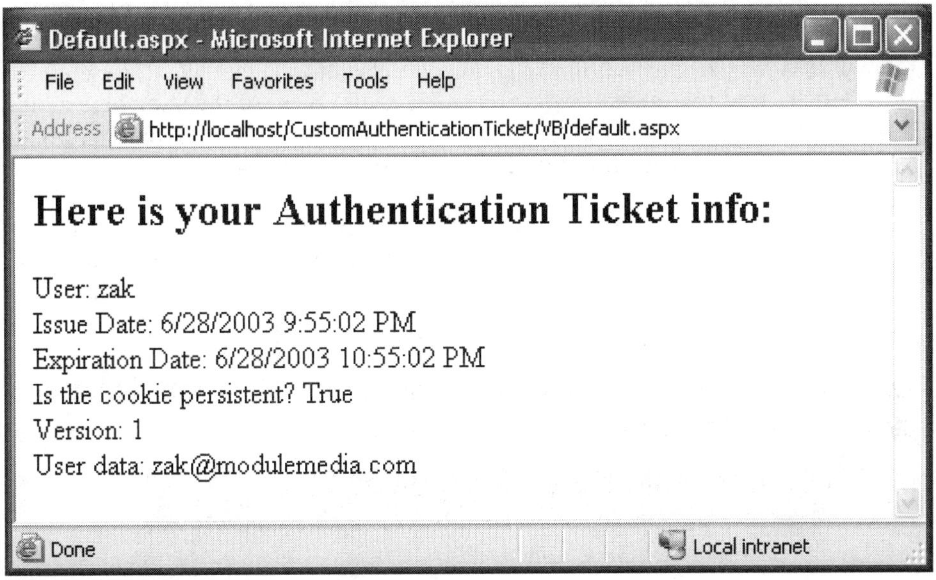

Summary

In this chapter, you examined ways of securing your ASP.NET applications. You learned how to create a simple login page, configure the `Web.config` file to handle authentication and authorization, and you learned how to check for user names and passwords using a database. The next chapter will introduce you to working with files and directories using ASP.NET.

15

Working with Files and Email

The .NET Framework exposes a set of classes for working with text files, drives, and directories, through the `System.IO` namespace. This namespace exposes functionality that allows you to read from, write to, and update content within directories and text files. There are many occasions where you would want to read from and write to a text file. Text files almost always use a format based on the ASCII standard, which is perhaps the most widely accepted cross-platform file format, and has been around since the sixties. This makes it a very useful way of exchanging information between programs, even when they are running on different platforms and operating systems.

As you'll see through the following sections, you can use the set of classes exposed by the `System.IO` namespace to complete the following tasks:

Write to text files   The sales department within our fictitious company may want to write sales and forecast information to a text file.

Read from text files   As a member of the Web development team, you may want to use the data within a text file to create dynamic graphs and charts to display sales and revenue forecasts on the Web.

Upload files from the client to the server	You may want to create for the human resources department an interface that allows staff to upload company documentation for reference by employees.
Access directories and directory information	While uploading files to the server, you may want to give the human resources department a choice of drive to which it may upload files. For instance, you may have one drive dedicated to spreadsheets, and another just for Word documents.

Once you have a firm grasp on working with text files and directory information, you'll learn how to send email in ASP.NET using the `System.Web.Mail` namespace. Finally, we'll finish the chapter with a quick introduction to serialization.

Writing to Text Files

The `System.IO` namespace enables ASP.NET to read from and write to a text file directly from an ASP.NET page, through the use of file **streams**. I'll explain the concept of a stream with the analogy of a simple water hose. While a water hose seems fairly useless by itself, it becomes extremely handy when you screw it into a water spigot. If I need to fill a bucket, I simply place the hose in the bucket, turn the water on, and the bucket is filled with water. The stream of water that flows through the hose is comparable to a file stream. The spigot would be your data source, the bucket would be the text file, and the hose would represent the file stream. And that's not all—the `System.IO` namespace also exposes classes for working with directories. There are three different groups of classes that are exposed by the `System.IO` namespace, namely:

1. Classes for working with files.

2. Classes for working with streams.

3. Classes for working with directories.

As we progress through this chapter, you'll learn about all the classes for each group. In this and the next section, however, we will discuss writing to and reading from text files with the aid of the classes from the groups that work with files and streams, specifically:

File	Contains methods for working with files

FileStream	Represents a stream for reading and writing to files
StreamReader	Reads characters from a text file
StreamWriter	Writes characters to a text file
Path	Contains methods for manipulating a file or directory

For the most part, you read from and write to text files by first using the `File` class to return a stream. If you want to write to a text file, you use the `StreamWriter` class; conversely, to read from a text file you use the `StreamReader` class.

To begin the examples in this section, start by creating a new directory within `wwwroot` with the name `Samples`. You'll want to make sure that write permission is enabled for that directory, as it's disabled by default:

1. In a standard Windows folder window (*not* in the IIS control panel), right-click on the new directory and select Properties.

2. Select the Security tab[1].

3. Add either `ASPNET` (the ASP.NET Machine Account) or `Users` group to the directory (`Users` will probably already be there), and enable write permissions by selecting the user or group and checking the Allow checkbox next to Write in the permissions list.

4. Click OK.

For our first example, let's make a Web page that creates a simple text file containing some text supplied by the user. Open your favorite text editor and create in the Samples directory a new ASP.NET page that contains the following code:

File: **TextFileReadWrite/index.aspx**

```
<%@ Import Namespace="System.IO" %>
<html>
<head>
<title>Writing to Text Files</title>
```

---

[1] In Windows XP, simple file sharing is enabled by default. This feature prevents you from granting write access to Web applications in a directory. To disable simple file sharing, select Tools, Folder Options in any folder window, then on the View tab uncheck Use simple file sharing (Recommended).

```
</head>
<body>
<form runat="server">
<p>Write the following text within a text file:<br />
  <asp:TextBox id="txtMyText" runat="server" />
  <asp:Button id="btnWrite" Text="Write" runat="server"
      OnClick="WriteText" /></p>
</form>
</body>
</html>
```

As you can see, we import the System.IO namespace first, so that our page can work with text files. Next, we add a TextBox control to handle collection of the user's text, and a Button control to send the information to the server for processing. Next, in the head tag, we'll create the WriteText() method specified in the OnClick attribute of the Button. This method will write the contents of the TextBox to the text file:

VB.NET   File: **TextFileReadWrite/index.aspx (excerpt)**
```
<script language="VB" runat="server">
Sub WriteText(s As Object, e As EventArgs)
  Dim objStreamWriter As StreamWriter
  objStreamWriter = File.CreateText( _
      "C:\Inetpub\wwwroot\Samples\myText.txt")
  objStreamWriter.WriteLine(txtMyText.Text)
  objStreamWriter.Close()
End Sub
</script>
```

C#   File: **TextFileReadWrite/index.aspx (excerpt)**
```
<script language="C#" runat="server">
void WriteText(Object  s, EventArgs e) {
  StreamWriter objStreamWriter;
  objStreamWriter = File.CreateText(
      "C:\\Inetpub\\wwwroot\\Samples\\myText.txt");
  objStreamWriter.WriteLine(txtMyText.Text);
  objStreamWriter.Close();
}
</script>
```

As you can see, the method consists of only four lines, and is pretty straightforward. The first line creates a StreamWriter variable, called objStreamWriter. Next, we call the CreateText() method of the File class, passing in the location of the text file, which returns a new StreamWriter:

VB.NET   File: **TextFileReadWrite/index.aspx (excerpt)**

```
objStreamWriter = File.CreateText( _
    "C:\Inetpub\wwwroot\Samples\myText.txt")
```

C#   File: **TextFileReadWrite/index.aspx (excerpt)**

```
objStreamWriter = File.CreateText(
    "C:\\Inetpub\\wwwroot\\Samples\\myText.txt");
```

Don't forget that C# needs to escape backslashes when they're used in strings, so the path to our file must use \\ to separate folder names.

There's another thing I'd like to point out here. Normally, when we call a method of a particular class, we call that method on a particular instance of the class, usually on a variable of that type. However, some classes define what VB.NET calls **shared methods**, and what are known in C# as **static methods**. Shared or static methods can be called without the need for an actual instance of the class. In the above code, `CreateText()` is a shared/static method, because we can call it directly from the `File` class, without having to create an instance of that class.

Compare this with the way we call the `WriteLine()` method on the `StreamWriter` class in the next line:

VB.NET   File: **TextFileReadWrite/index.aspx (excerpt)**

```
objStreamWriter.WriteLine(txtMyText.Text)
```

C#   File: **TextFileReadWrite/index.aspx (excerpt)**

```
objStreamWriter.WriteLine(txtMyText.Text);
```

The `WriteLine()` method, along with most of the methods that we've worked with thus far, are known as **instance methods**. Instance methods require an instance of the class—`objStreamWriter` in this case—to be obtained before we can call them.

The `WriteLine()` method is passed a string, which it then writes to the stream on which it is called. Here, we pass in the text from the `TextBox` control.

Once we've finished working with a particular file, we need to close its associated `StreamWriter` so the file can be used by another program. We do this with the last line of the method.

Test the results in the browser. Initially, all you see is the interface similar to Figure 15.1.

Figure 15.1. The interface contains a TextBox control to collect the data and a Button control to submit it to the server for processing.

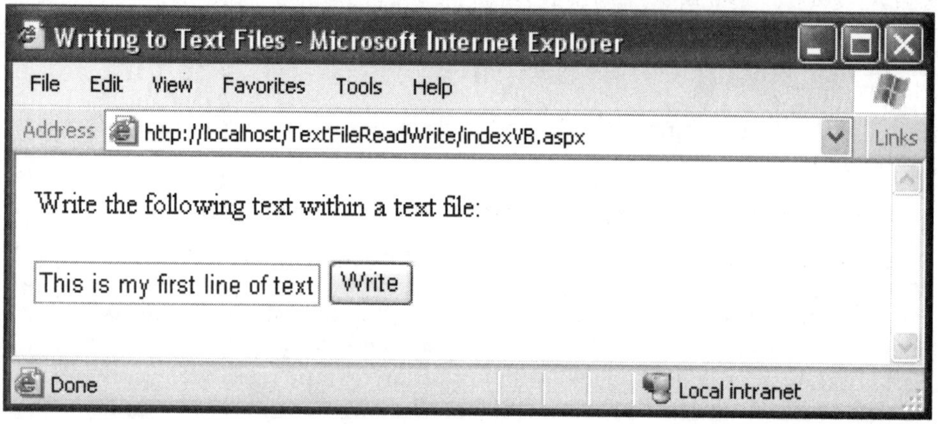

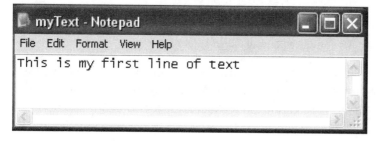

Type some text into the TextBox control, and click the Write Button to submit it for processing. As Figure 15.2 indicates, opening the text file reveals the newly created text.

Figure 15.2. The text appears within the text file.

If you try to enter a different value into the TextBox control and click the Write Button, the existing text is overwritten with the new content. To prevent this from happening, you can replace the CreateText() method of the File class with the AppendText() method. As Figure 15.3 shows, the AppendText() method simply adds to existing text rather than replacing it.

Figure 15.3. Use the `AppendText()` method to add to text files rather than replacing existing content altogether.

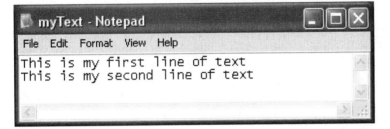

Also note that, rather than specifying the full path of the text file, you can use the `MapPath()` method to generate the full path to the text file automatically given a path relative to the current directory, as follows:

VB.NET   File: **TextFileReadWrite/index.aspx (excerpt)**

```
objStreamWriter = File.AppendText(MapPath("Samples\myText.txt"))
```

C#   File: **TextFileReadWrite/index.aspx (excerpt)**

```
objStreamWriter = File.AppendText(MapPath(
    "Samples\\myText.txt"));
```

The `MapPath()` method returns the full path to the file that you pass in as a parameter, and can make for cleaner code that's easier to read.

Reading from Text Files

Just as you used the `CreateText()` and `AppendText()` methods of the `File` class to return a new `StreamWriter` object, you use the `OpenText()` method of the `File` class to return a new `StreamReader`. Once the `StreamReader` has been established, you can loop through the text file using a `While` loop, in conjunction with the `ReadLine()` method of the `StreamReader`, to examine the contents of the text file. Begin the process of reading from text files first, by adding the following tags to your current page:

```
<form runat="server">
<p>Write the following text within a text file:<br />
  <asp:TextBox id="txtMyText" runat="server" />
  <asp:Button id="btnWrite" Text="Write" runat="server"
    OnClick="WriteText" /></p>
<p><asp:Button id="btnRead" Text="Read" runat="server"
```

```
      OnClick="ReadText" /></p>
<p><asp:Label id="lblResult" runat="server"/></p>
</form>
```

As you can see, we're simply adding new `Button` and `Label` controls. When the user clicks the `Button`, the `Click` event will be raised and the `ReadText()` method will be called. Let's add this method next. It will read the text from the text file and write it out to the `Label` control:

VB.NET   File: **TextFileReadWrite/index.aspx (excerpt)**

```vbnet
Sub ReadText(s As Object, e As EventArgs)
  Dim objStreamReader As StreamReader
  Dim strInput As String

  lblResult.Text = ""
  objStreamReader = File.OpenText(MapPath("Samples\myText.txt"))
  strInput = objStreamReader.ReadLine()
  While (strInput <> Nothing)
    lblResult.Text &= strInput & "<br />"
    strInput = objStreamReader.ReadLine()
  End While
  objStreamReader.Close()
End Sub
```

C#   File: **TextFileReadWrite/index.aspx (excerpt)**

```csharp
void ReadText(Object s, EventArgs e) {
  StreamReader objStreamReader;
  string strInput;

  lblResult.Text = "";
  objStreamReader = File.OpenText(MapPath("Samples\\myText.txt"));
  strInput = objStreamReader.ReadLine();
  while (strInput != null) {
    lblResult.Text += strInput + "<br />";
    strInput = objStreamReader.ReadLine();
  }
  objStreamReader.Close();
}
```

Similarly to the way the `StreamWriter` was used, a new instance of the `StreamReader` is created. We also declare a new `String` variable, called `strInput`, to hold the lines we'll read from the text file. Next, we set the text value of the `Label` control to an empty string. We do this in case the user presses the Read `Button` when the `Label` already contains text from a previous click. The next thing our method has to do is call the `OpenText()` method of the `File` class to return a new `StreamReader` object, again passing in the full path to the text file:

VB.NET   File: **TextFileReadWrite/index.aspx (excerpt)**

```
objStreamReader = File.OpenText(MapPath("Samples\myText.txt"))
```

C#   File: **TextFileReadWrite/index.aspx (excerpt)**

```
objStreamReader = File.OpenText(MapPath("Samples\\myText.txt"));
```

Next, we call the `ReadLine()` method of the `StreamReader` object to get the first line of the file:

VB.NET   File: **TextFileReadWrite/index.aspx (excerpt)**

```
strInput = objStreamReader.ReadLine()
```

C#   File: **TextFileReadWrite/index.aspx (excerpt)**

```
strInput = objStreamReader.ReadLine();
```

Now, we loop through, reading the remaining lines of the file and adding each one to the end of the `Label` text:

VB.NET   File: **TextFileReadWrite/index.aspx (excerpt)**

```
While (strInput <> Nothing)
  lblResult.Text &= strInput & "<br />"
  strInput = objStreamReader.ReadLine()
End While
```

C#   File: **TextFileReadWrite/index.aspx (excerpt)**

```
while (strInput != null) {
  lblResult.Text += strInput + "<br />";
  strInput = objStreamReader.ReadLine();
}
```

Remember, `While` loops are used when you want to repeat the loop while a condition remains true. In our case, we want to loop through, reading in lines from the file until the `ReadLine()` method returns the value `Nothing` (`null` in C#), which indicates that we've reached the end of the file. Within the loop, we simply append the value of the string variable to the `Label` control's `Text` property using the `&=` operator (`+=` in C#). The last line in the loop simply reads the next line within the `StreamReader` object, and places it into the `strInput` variable.

Finally, we close the `StreamReader` using the `Close()` method. Remember, the `StreamReader`, like the `Connection` class in ADO.NET establishes and opens a connection to a data source. Rather than connecting to a database, we are connecting to a text file. That connection, or, in our case, the StreamReader, should be closed as soon as it's no longer needed to conserve server resources.

Save your work and test the results in the browser. Figure 15.4 shows that you can add another line of text within the TextBox control and then click the Read Button control to display the contents of the text file.

Figure 15.4. Use the StreamReader to examine and write out the contents of a text file.

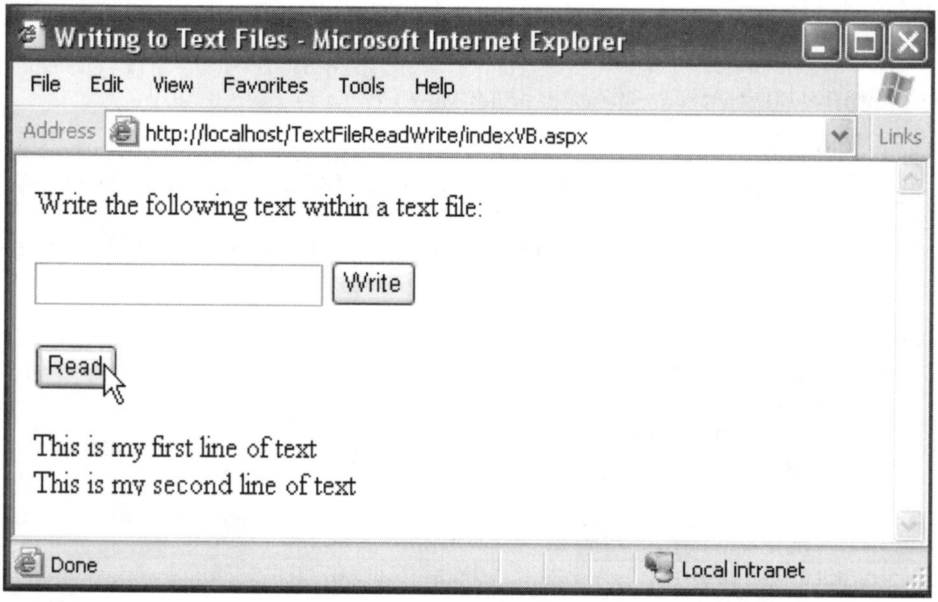

Accessing Directories and Directory Information

Now that you have some understanding of writing to and reading from text files, let's take a look at how you can access the directories in which those files are located. The classes in the System.IO namespace for working with directories and directory information are:

Directory Contains shared/static methods for creating, moving, and retrieving the contents of directories

DirectoryInfo
Contains instance methods for creating, moving, and retrieving the contents of directories

Just like the File class, the Directory class contains shared/static methods, which means that you're not required to instantiate the class. The DirectoryInfo class, on the other hand, requires instantiation as it contains instance methods. The Directory class contains the following useful methods:

GetDirectories()
Returns a string array of directory names

GetFiles()
Returns a string array of filenames from a specific drive or directory

GetFileSystemEntries()
Returns a string array of directory and filenames

Let's build an example page, on which users can use a DropDownList control to display either the directories, files, or directories *and* files within the server's C: drive. Our page needs to contain the following HTML:

File: **AccessingDirectoryInfo/index.aspx**

```
<%@ Import Namespace="System.IO" %>
<html>
<head>
<title>Directory Info</title>
</head>
<body>
<form runat="server">
<p>What do you want to view:<br />
  <asp:DropDownList id="ddlDirectories" runat="server"
      OnSelectedIndexChanged="ViewDriveInfo" AutoPostBack="true">
    <asp:ListItem Text="Directories" />
    <asp:ListItem Text="Files" />
    <asp:ListItem Text="Directories/Files" />
  </asp:DropDownList></p>
<asp:DataGrid id="dg" runat="server"/>
</form>
</body>
</html>
```

As you can see, our interface consists of a DropDownList control containing the three choices from which the user can select (Directories, Files, or Directories/Files). When a user selects an item from the DropDownList control, the SelectedIndexChanged event is raised, and ViewDriveInfo() is called. Now, let's write the `ViewDriveInfo()` method, which will write the specified information to a `DataGrid` control:

VB.NET   File: **AccessingDirectoryInfo/index.aspx (excerpt)**

```vb
<script language="VB" runat="server">
Sub ViewDriveInfo(s As Object, e As EventArgs)
  Select Case ddlDirectories.SelectedItem.Text
  Case "Directories"
    dg.DataSource = Directory.GetDirectories("C:\")
  Case "Files"
    dg.DataSource = Directory.GetFiles("C:\")
  Case "Directories/Files"
    dg.DataSource = Directory.GetFileSystemEntries("C:\")
  End Select
  dg.DataBind()
End Sub
</script>
```

C#   File: **AccessingDirectoryInfo/index.aspx (excerpt)**

```csharp
<script language="C#" runat="server">
void ViewDriveInfo(Object s, EventArgs e) {
  switch (ddlDirectories.SelectedItem.Text) {
  case "Directories":
    dg.DataSource = Directory.GetDirectories("C:\\");
    break;
  case "Files":
    dg.DataSource = Directory.GetFiles("C:\\");
    break;
  case "Directories/Files":
    dg.DataSource = Directory.GetFileSystemEntries("C:\\");
    break;
  }
  dg.DataBind();
}
</script>
```

You might remember from Chapter 3 that we use `Select Case` (VB.NET) / `switch` (C#) statements to check for multiple possible values of an object, rather than just one. The `Select Case` / `switch` specifies the value that is to be checked (in this case, the `Text` property of the selected list item):

VB.NET   File: **AccessingDirectoryInfo/index.aspx (excerpt)**

```vb
Select Case ddlDirectories.SelectedItem.Text
```

C#   File: **AccessingDirectoryInfo/index.aspx (excerpt)**

```
switch (ddlDirectories.SelectedItem.Text) {
```

Next, we use **Case** to specify the action to be performed for each significant value:

VB.NET   File: **AccessingDirectoryInfo/index.aspx (excerpt)**

```
Case "Directories"
  dg.DataSource = Directory.GetDirectories("C:\")
Case "Files"
  dg.DataSource = Directory.GetFiles("C:\")
Case "Directories/Files"
  dg.DataSource = Directory.GetFileSystemEntries("C:\")
End Select
```

```
case "Directories":
  dg.DataSource = Directory.GetDirectories("C:\\");
  break;
case "Files":
  dg.DataSource = Directory.GetFiles("C:\\");
  break;
case "Directories/Files":
  dg.DataSource = Directory.GetFileSystemEntries("C:\\");
  break;
}
```

Save your work and test the results in the browser. Figure 15.5 shows the result of selecting an item from the **DropDownList** control within a **DataGrid** control.

Figure 15.5. Use the `Directory` class to view specific files, directories, or both from a specific drive.

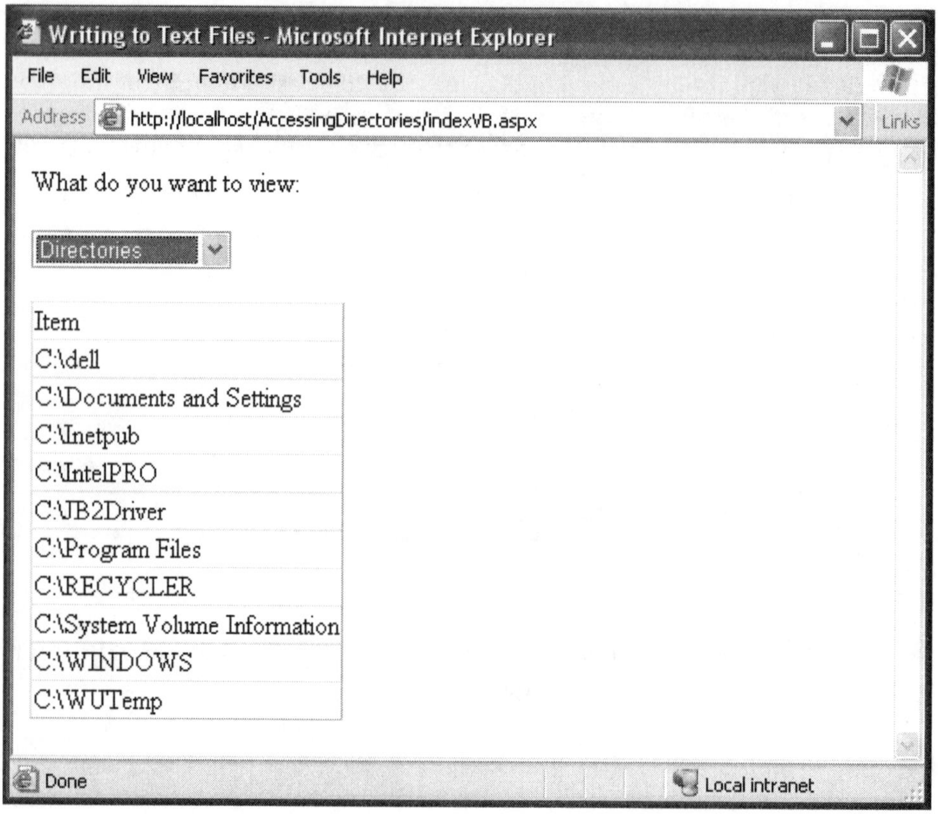

The `GetDirectories()`, `GetFiles()`, and `GetFileSystemEntries()` accept more than simply the drive or directory from which the user wants to view information. For instance, if you only wanted to view text files, you could write the following:

VB.NET

```
Directory.GetFiles("C:\", "*.txt")
```

In this example, the `GetFiles()` method would retrieve from the root of the `C:` drive all files that have the `.txt` extension.

Working with Directory and File Paths

The System.IO namespace also includes a utility class named Path that contains methods for retrieving path information from files and directories. As an example, let's build a simple application that retrieves the directory and path information for a text file. Create an empty text file called myText.txt in your Web root, then create a new ASP.NET page in the same directory, starting with the following markup:

File: **AccessingPathInfo/index.aspx**

```
<%@ Import Namespace="System.IO" %>
<html>
<head>
<title>Directory and Path Information</title>
</head>
<body>
<form runat="server">
<asp:Label id="lblResult" runat="server" />
</form>
</body>
</html>
```

The page contains just a simple Label control, which we'll use to show all the directory and path information. Next, let's add the code that actually returns the path and directory information:

VB.NET   File: **AccessingPathInfo/index.aspx (excerpt)**

```
<script language="VB" runat="server">
Sub Page_Load(s As Object, e As EventArgs)
  Dim strPath As String
  strPath = MapPath("myText.txt")
  lblResult.Text &= "File Path: " & strPath & "<br />"
  lblResult.Text &= "File name: " & Path.GetFileName(strPath) & _
    "<br />"
  lblResult.Text &= "Directory: " & _
    Path.GetDirectoryName(strPath) & "<br />"
  lblResult.Text &= "Extension: " & Path.GetExtension(strPath) & _
    "<br />"
  lblResult.Text &= "Name w/out Extension: " & _
      Path.GetFileNameWithoutExtension(strPath)
End Sub
</script>
```

```
C#                                    File: AccessingPathInfo/index.aspx (excerpt)
<script language="C#" runat="server">
void Page_Load(Object s, EventArgs e) {
  string strPath;
  strPath = MapPath("myText.txt");
  lblResult.Text += "File Path: " + strPath + "<br />";
  lblResult.Text += "File name: " + Path.GetFileName(strPath) +
      "<br />";
  lblResult.Text += "Directory: " +
      Path.GetDirectoryName(strPath) + "<br />";
  lblResult.Text += "Extension: " + Path.GetExtension(strPath) +
      "<br />";
  lblResult.Text += "Name w/out Extension: " +
      Path.GetFileNameWithoutExtension(strPath);
}
</script>
```

Initially, we create a new string variable and set it equal to the full path of the text file:

```
VB.NET                                File: AccessingPathInfo/index.aspx (excerpt)
Dim strPath As String
strPath = MapPath("myText.txt")
```

```
C#                                    File: AccessingPathInfo/index.aspx (excerpt)
string strPath;
strPath = MapPath("myText.txt");
```

Next, we write into the Label control the complete file path, file name, directory, extension, and name without extension:

```
VB.NET                                File: AccessingPathInfo/index.aspx (excerpt)
lblResult.Text = "File Path: " & strPath & "<br />"
lblResult.Text &= "File name: " & Path.GetFileName(strPath) & _
    "<br />"
lblResult.Text &= "Directory: " & _
    Path.GetDirectoryName(strPath) & "<br />"
lblResult.Text &= "Extension: " & Path.GetExtension(strPath) & _
    "<br />"
lblResult.Text &= "Name w/out Extension: " &
    Path.GetFileNameWithoutExtension(strPath)
```

```
C#                                    File: AccessingPathInfo/index.aspx (excerpt)
lblResult.Text = "File Path: " + strPath + "<br />";
lblResult.Text += "File name: " + Path.GetFileName(strPath) +
```

```
    "<br />";
lblResult.Text += "Directory: " +
    Path.GetDirectoryName(strPath) + "<br />";
lblResult.Text += "Extension: " + Path.GetExtension(strPath) +
    "<br />";
lblResult.Text += "Name w/out Extension: " +
    Path.GetFileNameWithoutExtension(strPath);
```

Save your work and test the results in your browser. Figure 15.6 shows how all the information for the text file is displayed.

Figure 15.6. Retrieve the file name, path, file extension, and file name without an extension from the text file.

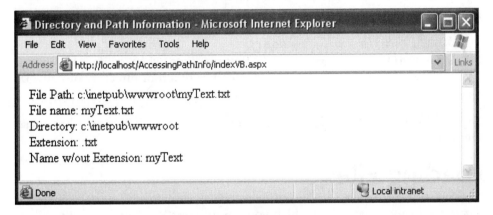

This example demonstrates the use of the `GetFileName()`, `GetDirectoryName()`, `GetExtension()`, and `GetFileNameWithoutExtension()` methods. But those aren't the only methods to which the `Path` class gives us access. The following list outlines all of the methods you can use:

ChangeExtension()	Enables you to modify a file extension
Combine()	Enables you to join two file paths
GetDirectoryName()	Returns the directory part of a complete file path
GetExtension()	Returns the file extension from a file path
GetFileName()	Returns the file name from a file path

`GetFileNameWithoutExtension()`	Returns the filename without the file extension from a file path
`GetFullPath()`	Expands the supplied file path with a fully qualified file path
`GetPathRoot()`	Gets the root of the current path
`GetTempFileName()`	Creates a uniquely named file and returns the name of the new file
`GetTempPath()`	Returns the path to the server's `temp` directory
`HasExtension()`	Returns True when a file path contains a file extension
`IsPathRooted()`	Returns True when a file path makes reference to a root directory or network share.

See the .NET Framework SDK Documentation for full details on all of these methods.

Uploading Files

There are many situations in which you'll want your Web application to allow users to upload files to the server. For example, you could create a photo album site on which users upload images for others to view. ASP.NET offers the `HTMLInputFile` control for file uploading, which provides a text box and Browse button to allow users to select a file from their own computer and transfer it to the server with ease. The `HTMLInputFile` control has the following properties:

| `Accept` | Specifies a comma delimited list of MIME types to accept for upload. For instance, use `image/gif` for GIF files. Visit the following link for a complete list of MIME types: http://hostutopia.com/support/s058.html |
| `MaxLength` | Specifies the maximum number of characters, including the dot and extension, which can be entered for the filename and path in the upload box |

PostedFile   Returns the file uploaded by the user

Size   Indicates the character size of the upload text box

Let's build on our intranet site by creating a centralized location for all Human Resources forms, where HR representatives can upload important documents to share with other colleagues in the company. First, save a copy of the provided `template.aspx` page under the name `hrupload.aspx`. Next, import the `System.IO` namespace at the top of the page:

File: **hrupload.aspx (excerpt)**

```
<%@ Import Namespace="System.IO" %>
```

Now, add the `enctype` attribute to the `<form>` tag as follows:

File: **hrupload.aspx (excerpt)**

```
<form enctype="multipart/form-data" runat="server">
```

Because we're dealing with files and path information, the `enctype` attribute must be added to the `<form>` tag. This specifies the content type used to encode the form data set for submission to the server. Next, to create the interface, add the following code to the main content area of the page:

File: **hrupload.aspx (excerpt)**

```
<h1>HR File Upload:</h1>
<p><input id="txtUpload" type="file" runat="server" /></p>
<p><input id="btnUpload" type="button" value="Upload"
      OnServerClick="Upload" runat="server" /></p>
<p><asp:Label id="lblMessage" runat="server" /></p>
```

The first `<input>` tag we're adding here creates the `HTMLInputFile` control. We also need an HTML button control that users can press when they've chosen the file and wish to upload it. We set its `OnServerClick` attribute, naming a method that will be called, when the button is clicked, to perform the actual file upload. Lastly, we have a `Label` control, which will display the result of the upload. Now, we can write the code for the method that process the uploaded file as follows:

VB.NET   File: **hrupload.aspx (excerpt)**

```
<script language="VB" runat="server">
Sub Upload(s As Object, e As EventArgs)
  If Not (txtUpload.PostedFile Is Nothing) Then
    Dim postedFile As HttpPostedFile = txtUpload.PostedFile
    Dim filename As String = Path.GetFileName(postedFile.FileName)
```

```
      postedFile.SaveAs("C:\" & filename)
      lblMessage.Text = "File has been uploaded"
    End If
  End Sub
</script>
```

C#   File: **hrupload.aspx (excerpt)**

```
<script language="C#" runat="server">
void Upload(Object s, EventArgs e) {
  if (txtUpload.PostedFile != null) {
    HttpPostedFile postedFile = txtUpload.PostedFile;
    string filename = Path.GetFileName(postedFile.FileName);

    postedFile.SaveAs("C:\\" + filename);
    lblMessage.Text = "File has been uploaded";
  }
}
</script>
```

Let's break down that code. Initially, we use an If statement to avoid processing the file upload if the user did not choose to upload a file:

VB.NET   File: **hrupload.aspx (excerpt)**

```
If Not (txtUpload.PostedFile Is Nothing) Then
```

C#   File: **hrupload.aspx (excerpt)**

```
if (txtUpload.PostedFile != null) {
```

Next, we retrieve the uploaded file by accessing the PostedFile property of the control to return a new instance of the HttpPostedFile class. The HttpPostedFile class contains all the necessary properties and methods for working with uploaded files:

VB.NET   File: **hrupload.aspx (excerpt)**

```
Dim postedFile As HttpPostedFile = txtUpload.PostedFile
```

C#   File: **hrupload.aspx (excerpt)**

```
HttpPostedFile postedFile = txtUpload.PostedFile;
```

Next, we store the FileName of the posted file into a new string variable:

VB.NET   File: **hrupload.aspx (excerpt)**

```
Dim filename As String = Path.GetFileName(postedFile.FileName)
```

C#   File: **hrupload.aspx (excerpt)**
```
string filename = Path.GetFileName(postedFile.FileName);
```

Finally, we access the `SaveAs()` method of the `HttpPostedFile` object, pass in the directory[2] and name of the file, and change the `Label` control to display a "File has been uploaded" message. The `SaveAs()` method effectively saves the file onto the server.

Save your work and test the results in a browser. Initially, you're able to select the Browse button to select a file. Next, click the Upload button to send the file from the client to the server. The message "File has been uploaded" will appear in the browser if the upload was successful. Now, look within the root of `C:` to see the newly uploaded file. Before you finish up, be sure to add a link to this newly created `hrupload.aspx` page from the `admintools.aspx` page to allow users to visit the page without any problems.

Sending Email in ASP.NET

Suppose for a moment that you're the Webmaster for an online store, and you want to send an email confirmation to your customers regarding an order that they had just placed. Rather than manually firing off an email to every customer regarding his or her order, you could automate the process using ASP.NET. The .NET Framework contains two classes for working with email:

MailMessage   Contains properties and methods for creating email messages

SmtpMail   Contains methods and properties for working with SMTP Virtual Mail services within IIS

Most email programs, such as Outlook, Outlook Express, Eudora, Hotmail, etc., have a core set of features in common. For instance, they all allow you to send an email to someone by typing the recipient's email address in a "To" field. They allow you to specify who the email is from, the subject of the email, and even the body of the email. All these properties—and more—are available through the `MailMessage` class of the `System.Web.Mail` namespace. A partial list of the properties that the `MailMessage` class supports appears below:

---

[2]For the purposes of this example, we've chosen to save uploaded files to the root of `C:`. You'd definitely want to change this in a practical application, as cluttering your root directory with application-specific files is messy to say the least. Whatever directory you choose, make sure it's outside of your Web server's document root unless you want users to be able to download the files directly.

`Attachments`	A collection of items or files attached to the email message
`Bcc`	Specifies the blind carbon copy field of the email message
`Body`	Defines the body of the email message
`BodyFormat`	Specifies whether to send the email as text or HTML
`Cc`	Specifies the carbon copy field of the email message
`From`	Specifies the address that the email message is to be sent from. The format of this field must be an email address.
`Priority`	Specifies a value from the `MailPriority` enumeration to use when sending the email message. Possible values are `Low`, `Normal`, and `High`.
`Subject`	Specifies the subject of the email message
`To`	Specifies the address that the email message is to be sent to. The format of this field must be an email address.

The `SmtpMail` class contains just one property and one method as follows:

`SmtpServer`	Defines the email server to use
`Send()`	Sends the email; accepts a `MailMessage` object as a parameter

In the next few sections, you'll see how to use the `MailMessage` and `SmtpMail` classes to generate a company newsletter page for our intranet site. You'll also learn how to use some of the various properties and methods available for both these classes. Before you do anything, however, you must first configure IIS to send email.

Configuring IIS to Send Email

IIS uses the standard email protocol, called the **Simple Mail Transfer Protocol (SMTP)**. For working with SMTP mail, Windows provides the SMTP service, which is included with the installation of IIS. When you use ASP.NET to send an email, the message is relayed through the SMTP service and onto its final destination, as illustrated in Figure 15.7.

Figure 15.7. The client makes a request to the server. The server processes the request, relays it through IIS, and a response in the form of an email message is sent to the client's email program.

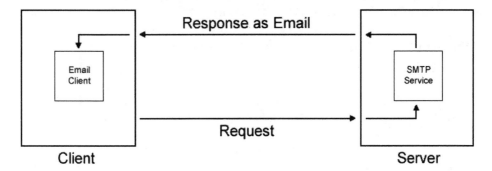

In order for email to be relayed correctly, the following configuration steps need to be performed so that your server has permissions to send email:

1. Open the IIS control panel.

2. Right-click Default SMTP Virtual Server and choose Properties.

3. Select the Access tab.

4. Select Relay.

5. Click the Add button.

6. Add the localhost IP address: 127.0.0.1

7. Uncheck the Allow all computers checkbox. The dialog should now look similar to Figure 15.8.

Figure 15.8. Configure IIS to allow the email to be sent through the localhost.

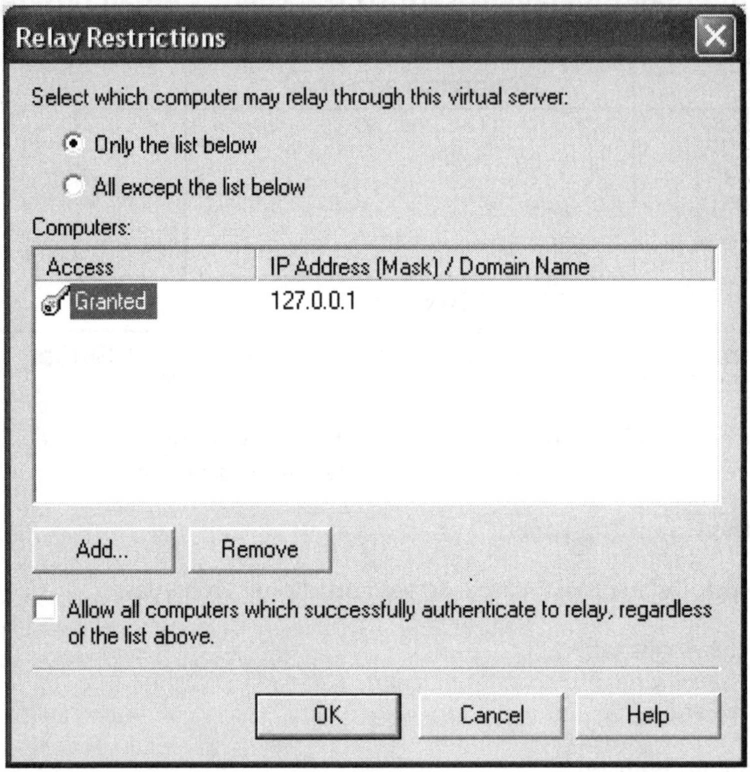

8. Select OK and close IIS.

Now you're ready to create the interface. Let's do that next.

Creating the Company Newsletter Page

The last page within the navigation bar of our Dorknozzle project that hasn't yet been built is the newsletter page. This page will allow HR representatives to send email to everyone in the company. You can begin by creating a new page, called newsletterarchive.aspx, from the template file, and adding the following controls to define the interface in the usual place:

File: **newsletterarchive.aspx (excerpt)**

```
<h1>Create Newsletter</h1>
<p>To:<br />
  <asp:TextBox id="txtTo" runat="server" /></p>
<p>Subject:<br />
  <asp:TextBox id="txtSubject" runat="server" /></p>
<p>Introduction:<br />
  <asp:TextBox id="txtIntroduction" runat="server"
     TextMode="MultiLine" Width="300" Height="100" /></p>
<p>Employee Of The Month:<br />
  <asp:TextBox id="txtEmployee" runat="server" /></p>
<p>Featured Event:<br />
  <asp:TextBox id="txtEvent" runat="server" /></p>
<p>Featured Store Item:<br />
  <asp:TextBox id="txtStoreItem" runat="server" /></p>
<p><asp:Button id="btnSend" runat="server" Text="Send Newsletter"
    OnClick="SendNewsletter" /></p>
<p><asp:Label id="lblResult" runat="server" /></p>
```

As you can see, the interface comprises six TextBoxcontrols, plus a button and label. The boxes will allow the user to specify who the email is to be sent to, what the subject is, a simple introduction as the body, the employee of the month, a featured company event, and a featured store item. The Button control is used to submit the form, while the Label control will display a confirmation message once the email has been sent. You won't be able to view the page until the button's click handler has been created, but Figure 15.9 shows the layout we're creating.

Figure 15.9. Create the interface that will allow HR representatives to send email to everyone within the company.

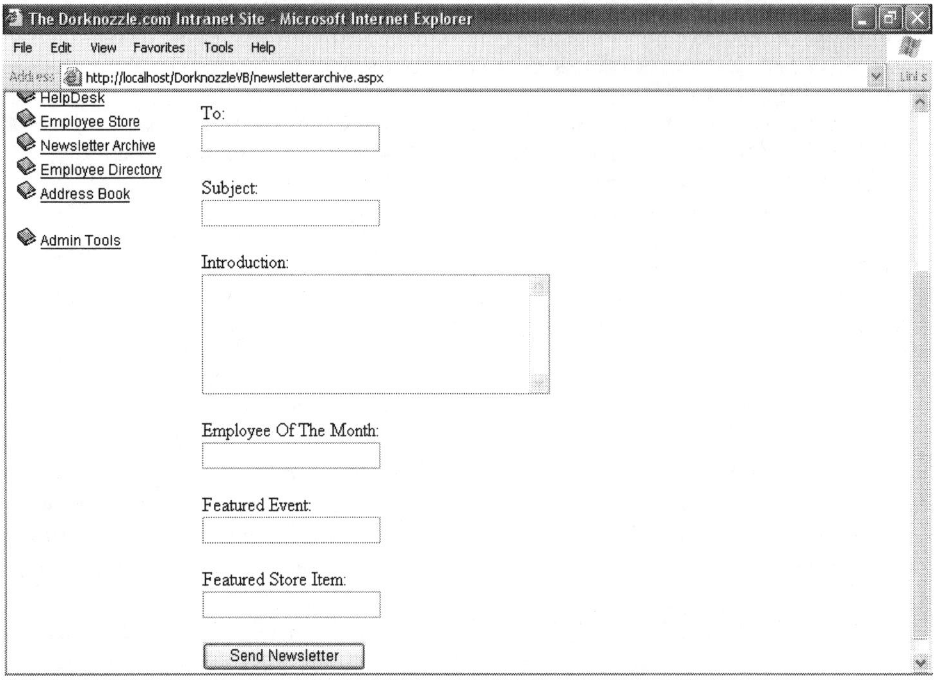

Next, we'll import the mail namespace at the top of the page, as follows:

File: **newsletterarchive.aspx** (excerpt)

```
<%@ Import Namespace="System.Web.Mail" %>
```

Now, add the method that will format the email and send it out:

VB.NET   File: **newsletterarchive.aspx** (excerpt)

```
<script runat="server" language="VB">
Sub SendNewsletter(s As Object, e As EventArgs)
  Dim objMail As New MailMessage()
  objMail.From = "hr@dorknozzle.com"
  objMail.To = txtTo.Text
  objMail.Subject = txtSubject.Text
  objMail.BodyFormat = MailFormat.Html
  objMail.Body = "<html><head><title>" & _
      HttpUtility.HtmlEncode(txtSubject.Text) & _
      "</title></head><body>"
```

```
    objMail.Body &= "<img src=""http://www.dorknozzle.com" & _
        "/images/newsletter_header.gif"" />"
    objMail.Body &= "<p>" & _
        HttpUtility.HtmlEncode(txtIntroduction.Text) & "</p>"
    objMail.Body &= "<p>Employee of the month: " & _
        HttpUtility.HtmlEncode(txtEmployee.Text) & "</p>"
    objMail.Body &= "<p>This months featured event: " & _
        HttpUtility.HtmlEncode(txtEvent.Text) & "</p>"
    objMail.Body &= "<p>This months featured store item: " & _
        HttpUtility.HtmlEncode(txtStoreItem.Text) & "</p>"
    objMail.Body &= "</body></html>"
    SmtpMail.SmtpServer = "localhost"
    SmtpMail.Send(objMail)
    lblResult.Text = "The newsletter has been sent!"
End Sub
</script>
```

C#   File: **newsletterarchive.aspx (excerpt)**

```
<script runat="server" language="C#">
void SendNewsletter(Object s, EventArgs e) {
  MailMessage objMail = new MailMessage();
  objMail.From = "hr@dorknozzle.com";
  objMail.To = txtTo.Text;
  objMail.Subject = txtSubject.Text;
  objMail.BodyFormat = MailFormat.Html;
  objMail.Body = "<html><head><title>" +
      HttpUtility.HtmlEncode(txtSubject.Text) +
      "</title></head><body>";
  objMail.Body += "<img src=\"http://www.dorknozzle.com/images/" +
      "newsletter_header.gif\" />";
  objMail.Body += "<p>" +
      HttpUtility.HtmlEncode(txtIntroduction.Text) + "</p>";
  objMail.Body += "<p>Employee of the month: " +
      HttpUtility.HtmlEncode(txtEmployee.Text) + "</p>";
  objMail.Body += "<p>This months featured event: " +
      HttpUtility.HtmlEncode(txtEvent.Text) + "</p>";
  objMail.Body += "<p>This months featured store item: " +
      HttpUtility.HtmlEncode(txtStoreItem.Text) + "</p>";
  objMail.Body += "</body></html>";
  SmtpMail.SmtpServer = "localhost";
  SmtpMail.Send(objMail);
  lblResult.Text = "The newsletter has been sent!";
}
</script>
```

Let's go through the code to make it more understandable. Initially, we create a new instance of the `MailMessage` class, called `objMail`:

VB.NET   File: **newsletterarchive.aspx (excerpt)**

```
Dim objMail As New MailMessage()
```

C#   File: **newsletterarchive.aspx (excerpt)**

```
MailMessage objMail = new MailMessage();
```

Next, we begin to define the email message by setting some of the properties that the `MailMessage` class exposes:

VB.NET   File: **newsletterarchive.aspx (excerpt)**

```
objMail.From = "hr@dorknozzle.com"
objMail.To = txtTo.Text
objMail.Subject = txtSubject.Text
objMail.BodyFormat = MailFormat.Html
```

C#   File: **newsletterarchive.aspx (excerpt)**

```
objMail.From = "hr@dorknozzle.com";
objMail.To = txtTo.Text;
objMail.Subject = txtSubject.Text;
objMail.BodyFormat = MailFormat.Html;
```

You'll notice we've set the `BodyFormat` property to indicate that this will be an HTML email message. By default, this property is set to `MailFormat.Text`.

Next, we need to create the body of the email, which will essentially be an HTML document:

VB.NET   File: **newsletterarchive.aspx (excerpt)**

```
objMail.Body = "<html><head><title>" & _
    HttpUtility.HtmlEncode(txtSubject.Text) & _
    "</title></head><body>"
objMail.Body &= "<img src=""http://www.dorknozzle.com" & _
    "/images/newsletter_header.gif"" />"
objMail.Body &= "<p>" & _
    HttpUtility.HtmlEncode(txtIntroduction.Text) & "</p>"
objMail.Body &= "<p>Employee of the month: " & _
    HttpUtility.HtmlEncode(txtEmployee.Text) & "</p>"
objMail.Body &= "<p>This months featured event: " & _
    HttpUtility.HtmlEncode(txtEvent.Text) & "</p>"
objMail.Body &= "<p>This months featured store item: " & _
    HttpUtility.HtmlEncode(txtStoreItem.Text) & "</p>"
objMail.Body &= "</body></html>"
```

File: **newsletterarchive.aspx (excerpt)**

```csharp
objMail.Body = "<html><head><title>" +
    HttpUtility.HtmlEncode(txtSubject.Text) +
    "</title></head><body>";
objMail.Body += "<img src=\"http://www.dorknozzle.com/images/" +
    newsletter_header.gif\" />";
objMail.Body += "<p>" +
    HttpUtility.HtmlEncode(txtIntroduction.Text) + "</p>";
objMail.Body += "<p>Employee of the month: " +
    HttpUtility.HtmlEncode(txtEmployee.Text) + "</p>";
objMail.Body += "<p>This months featured event: " +
    HttpUtility.HtmlEncode(txtEvent.Text) + "</p>";
objMail.Body += "<p>This months featured store item: " +
    HttpUtility.HtmlEncode(txtStoreItem.Text) + "</p>";
objMail.Body += "</body></html>";
```

Because we are building an HTML document, we need to be careful to convert special characters (like <, >, &) into their character entity equivalents (<, >, &). The HtmlEncode() method of the HttpUtility class does this for us. Also note that the image we'll use in the email has to be hosted on a site somewhere. In this case, we've used an example URL. To get this example to work properly, you'll need to host an image on your Website and use the appropriate URL in the code.

We set the SmtpServer property of the SmtpMail class to localhost, indicating that the same computer that is acting as our ASP.NET server should also act as our outgoing mail server. Finally, we call the Send() method of the SmtpMail class, pass in the mail object, and display the confirmation to the user within the Label control:

VB.NET File: **newsletterarchive.aspx (excerpt)**

```vbnet
SmtpMail.SmtpServer = "localhost"
SmtpMail.Send(objMail)
lblResult.Text = "The newsletter has been sent!"
```

C# File: **newsletterarchive.aspx (excerpt)**

```csharp
SmtpMail.SmtpServer = "localhost";
SmtpMail.Send(objMail);
lblResult.Text = "The newsletter has been sent!";
```

Save your work and run the page in the browser. Enter all the necessary information into the newsletter page and click Send Newsletter. You should receive the "Newsletter has been sent!" message once the email is sent. Check your email account for the new email message. Figure 15.10 shows the email message that was sent to me from this example.

Figure 15.10. A new email from hr@dorknozzle.com confirms that the functionality works.

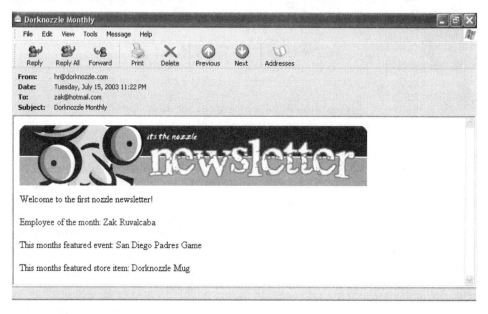

Serialization

Serialization is the process of converting objects, such as arrays, controls, etc., into a stream of bytes for storage. Why would you want to do this? To answer this question, think about your email program. Outlook, for instance, saves calendar information, emails, contacts, and other details onto your computer. You open Outlook, and all this information appears. But where is all that information kept? Outlook uses a file on your computer for storage. But it doesn't write all of that information the way we have seen, using the `StreamWriter`. Instead, Outlook uses more complex file access methods to read and write all this binary information to a file in a custom binary format.

Web applications rarely need such a complex data storage solution, especially since it is common practice to store such information on a database server so that it can be shared and reused by related applications. That said, you may occasionally face the need to store to disk .NET objects that don't translate easily to text files. In such cases, you can ask the .NET Framework to **serialize** those objects into a format suitable for file storage. Later, your application can read that data from the file and ask the .NET Framework to **deserialize** the data to get your objects again.

The .NET Framework includes the following classes for serializing and deserializing objects:

BinaryFormatter   Enables you to serialize and deserialize objects to a binary format. This is the class that we'll be using in these examples.

SoapFormatter   Enables you to serialize and deserialize objects to a SOAP format (SOAP is covered with more detail in Chapter 17)

XMLSerializer   Enables you to serialize and deserialize objects to an XML format

For most operations, including the example in this section, the BinaryFormatter class will suffice. To demonstrate the usage of the BinaryFormatter, first create a new page and import the following namespaces:

File: **Serialization/serialize.aspx (excerpt)**

```
<%@ Import Namespace="System.IO" %>
<%@ Import
    Namespace="System.Runtime.Serialization.Formatters.Binary" %>
```

Next, add the following code:

VB.NET   File: **Serialization/serialize.aspx (excerpt)**

```
<html>
<head>
<script runat="server" language="VB">
Sub Page_Load()
  Dim arrList As ArrayList
  Dim objFileStream As FileStream
  Dim objBinaryFormatter As BinaryFormatter

  arrList = New ArrayList()
  arrList.Add("Milk")
  arrList.Add("Water")
  arrList.Add("Juice")
```

```
   objFileStream = New FileStream(MapPath("myFile.data"),
       FileMode.Create)
   objBinaryFormatter = New BinaryFormatter()
   objBinaryFormatter.Serialize(objFileStream, arrList)
   objFileStream.Close()
End Sub
</script>
</head>
<body>
<p>Array has been serialized!</p>
</body>
</html>
```

C#   File: **Serialization/serialize.aspx (excerpt)**

```
<html>
<head>
<script runat="server" language="C#">
void Page_Load() {
  ArrayList arrList;
  FileStream objFileStream;
  BinaryFormatter objBinaryFormatter;

  arrList = new ArrayList();
  arrList.Add("Milk");
  arrList.Add("Water");
  arrList.Add("Juice");

  objFileStream = new FileStream(MapPath("myFile.data"),
      FileMode.Create);
  objBinaryFormatter = new BinaryFormatter();
  objBinaryFormatter.Serialize(objFileStream, arrList);
  objFileStream.Close();
}
</script>
</head>
<body>
<p>Array has been serialized!</p>
</body>
</html>
```

Let's have a closer look at that code. When the page loads, we create `ArrayList`, `FileStream`, and `BinaryFormatter` variables:

```vb.net
Dim arrList As ArrayList
Dim objFileStream As FileStream
Dim objBinaryFormatter As BinaryFormatter
```

```csharp
ArrayList arrList;
FileStream objFileStream;
BinaryFormatter objBinaryFormatter;
```

Next, we create a new array, and add items to it:

```vb.net
arrList = New ArrayList()
arrList.Add("Milk")
arrList.Add("Water")
arrList.Add("Juice")
```

```csharp
arrList = new ArrayList();
arrList.Add("Milk");
arrList.Add("Water");
arrList.Add("Juice");
```

Then, we create a new instance of the `FileStream` class, passing in the name of a file to create (`myFile.data`):

```vb.net
objFileStream = New FileStream(MapPath("myArrayList.data"),
    FileMode.Create)
```

```csharp
objFileStream = new FileStream(MapPath("myArrayList.data"),
    FileMode.Create);
```

Now, we create a new instance of the `BinaryFormatter` and call the `Serialize()` method, passing in as parameters the `FileStream` and the object to serialize:

```vb.net
objBinaryFormatter = New BinaryFormatter
objBinaryFormatter.Serialize(objFileStream, arrList)
```

```
C#                                      File: Serialization/serialize.aspx (excerpt)
objBinaryFormatter = new BinaryFormatter();
objBinaryFormatter.Serialize(objFileStream, arrList);
```

Lastly, we close the `FileStream` using the `Close()` method. Save your work under a suitable name, such as `serialize.aspx`, and open the page in your browser. All you should see is a message that alerts you that the file has been serialized. Now, try opening `myFile.data` within a text editor. Because the file contains serialized data, you should see a string of garbled information.

To use the data in the file, you'll have to deserialize it. You can deserialize the file by creating a new page called `deserialize.aspx` that contains the following code:

```
VB.NET                                      File: Serialization/deserialize.aspx
<%@ Import Namespace="System.IO" %>
<%@ Import
    Namespace="System.Runtime.Serialization.Formatters.Binary" %>

<html>
<head>
<script runat="server" language="VB">
Sub Page_Load()
Dim arrList As ArrayList
  Dim objFileStream As FileStream
  Dim objBinaryFormatter As BinaryFormatter
  Dim strItem As String

  objFileStream = New FileStream(MapPath("myFile.data"),
      FileMode.Open)
  objBinaryFormatter = New BinaryFormatter()
  arrList = CType(objBinaryFormatter.Deserialize(objFileStream),
      ArrayList)
  objFileStream.Close()

  lblShowFile.Text &= "<ul>"
  For Each strItem In arrList
    lblShowFile.Text &= "<li>" & strItem & "</li>"
  Next
  lblShowFile.Text &= "</ul>"
End Sub
</script>
</head>
<body>
<form runat="server">
```

```
  <p><asp:Label id="lblShowFile" runat="server" /></p>
</form>
</body>
</html>
```

C#   File: **Serialization/deserialize.aspx (excerpt)**

```
<%@ Import Namespace="System.IO" %>
<%@ Import
    Namespace="System.Runtime.Serialization.Formatters.Binary" %>

<html>
<head>
<script runat="server" language="C#">
void Page_Load() {
  ArrayList arrList;
  FileStream objFileStream;
  BinaryFormatter objBinaryFormatter;

  objFileStream = new FileStream(MapPath("myFile.data"),
    FileMode.Open);
  objBinaryFormatter = new BinaryFormatter();
  arrList = (ArrayList)objBinaryFormatter.Deserialize(
      objFileStream);
  objFileStream.Close();

  lblShowFile.Text += "<ul>";
  foreach (string strItem in arrList) {
    lblShowFile.Text += "<li>" + strItem + "</li>";
  }
  lblShowFile.Text += "</ul>";
}
</script>
</head>
<body>
<form runat="server">
  <p><asp:Label id="lblShowFile" runat="server" /></p>
</form>
</body>
</html>
```

Let's break down the code. Initially, we simply instantiate the three classes that we'll use: ArrayList, FileStream, and BinaryFormatter:

VB.NET   File: **Serialization/deserialize.aspx (excerpt)**

```
Dim arrList As ArrayList
Dim objFileStream As FileStream
```

```
Dim objBinaryFormatter As BinaryFormatter
Dim strItem As String
```

C#   File: **Serialization/deserialize.aspx (excerpt)**

```
ArrayList arrList;
FileStream objFileStream;
BinaryFormatter objBinaryFormatter;
```

Next, we create a new instance of the `FileStream` class, passing in the full path of the serialized file (using `MapPath()`) and `FileMode.Open` to return a new `FileStream` object:

VB.NET   File: **Serialization/deserialize.aspx (excerpt)**

```
objFileStream = New FileStream(MapPath("myFile.data"),
    FileMode.Open)
```

C#   File: **Serialization/deserialize.aspx (excerpt)**

```
objFileStream = new FileStream(MapPath("myFile.data"),
    FileMode.Open);
```

Then, we create a new instance of the `BinaryFormatter` class, call its `Deserialize()` method, convert the deserialized object into an `ArrayList` using the `CType` function in VB.NET (or cast in C#), and close the `FileStream` object:

VB.NET   File: **Serialization/deserialize.aspx (excerpt)**

```
objBinaryFormatter = New BinaryFormatter
arrList = CType(objBinaryFormatter.Deserialize(objFileStream),
    ArrayList)
objFileStream.Close()
```

C#   File: **Serialization/deserialize.aspx (excerpt)**

```
objBinaryFormatter = new BinaryFormatter();
arrList = (ArrayList)objBinaryFormatter.Deserialize(
    objFileStream);
objFileStream.Close();
```

Finally, we use a `For Each` loop to iterate through each item within the `ArrayList`, writing it out to our `Label` control:

VB.NET   File: **Serialization/deserialize.aspx (excerpt)**

```
lblShowFile.Text &= "<ul>"
For Each strItem In arrList
  lblShowFile.Text &= "<li>" & strItem & "</li>"
Next
lblShowFile.Text &= "</ul>"
```

```
C#                                        File: Serialization/deserialize.aspx (excerpt)
lblShowFile.Text += "<ul>";
foreach (string strItem in arrList) {
  lblShowFile.Text += "<li>" + strItem + "</li>";
}
lblShowFile.Text += "</ul>";
```

Save your work and check the result in your browser. As we see in Figure 15.11, our data appears within a bulleted list.

Figure 15.11. The deserialized file displays within a bulleted list.

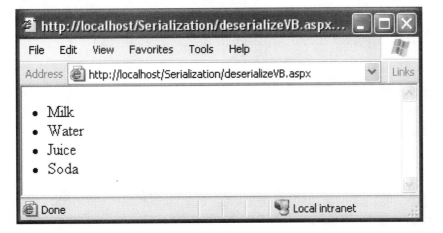

Summary

This chapter introduced you to some important topics, specifically the ability to read and write to files, access directory information, upload files from the client to the server, and send emails in ASP.NET. The topics you covered in this chapter will prove invaluable as you develop applications with ASP.NET. Whether you are reading from, or writing to, text-based log files, retrieving path information for files on your computer, creating functionality so that users can upload files to your server, or sending customer newsletters through an email blaster, this chapter covered everything you need to know to get started!

16

Rich Controls and User Controls

In the first part of this chapter, you'll learn about a powerful set of controls included with the .NET Framework, called rich controls. As we progress, you will learn about the three controls that make up the rich controls grouping, including the `Xml` control, the `AdRotator` control, and the `Calendar` control. You'll learn how to present XML documents in the browser using XSLT. Next, you'll examine the `AdRotator` control and learn how to create randomized banner advertisements. Finally, we'll conclude the first part of the chapter with an overview of the `Calendar` control, which you will use to build an interactive meeting scheduler.

The second part of this chapter will introduce you to custom control development with user controls. As you'll see, user controls provide great flexibility in that they expose events, properties, and methods within ASP.NET pages. But, rather than choosing from a prebuilt library of controls, user controls are built and customized by you.

Introduction to Rich Controls

We've already learned about three core sets of controls within the .NET Framework: HTML controls, Web controls and validation controls. Ninety percent of the functionality you need on your pages can be achieved with these controls. You will, however, come across instances where Web controls and validation controls are simply not enough. Situations may arise in which you'll want to include banner advertisements on your page, work with dates within a calendar, or even format XML documents so that they're legible to a user. If this is the case, then you'll need to work with **rich controls**. The controls that make up this category include:

`Xml` control	This control allows you to combine XML and XSLT files together for presentation to the client.
`AdRotator` control	Using an XML file, this control allows you to randomize banner advertisements within a Web page.
`Calendar` control	This control displays an interactive calendar allowing the user to select months and days. Using built-in methods, you can capture the user's selections for programmatic use within an application.

We'll begin our introduction to rich controls with a discussion of the XML control. Before we begin, however, you need to get up to speed on XML and XSLT.

An Introduction to XML and XSLT

HTML, as you know, is short for Hypertext Markup Language. "Markup" refers to the library of tags that describe how data should be presented within a page. The browser uses the information in those tags to present the page to site visitors in a friendly and legible fashion. The big disadvantage of HTML, at least traditionally, is that it mixes the data with presentation details.

In essence, XML is simply a text-based format for the transfer or storage of data; it contains no details on how that data should be presented. However, XML has much in common with HTML, in that both are largely comprised of tags inside angle brackets (< and >), and any tag may contain attributes specific to that tag. The biggest difference between the two is that, rather than providing a fixed set of tags as HTML does, XML allows us to create our own tags to describe the data we wish to represent.

Like HTML, XML's purpose is to describe the content of a document. Unlike HTML, however, XML does not describe how that content should be displayed. Instead, it describes what that content is. Using XML, the Web author can mark up the contents of a document, describing that content in terms of its relevance as data. Take a look at the following HTML element:

```
<p>Star Wars Episode I: The Phantom Menace</p>
```

This example describes the contents within the tags as a paragraph. This is fine if all we are concerned with is displaying the words "Star Wars Episode I: The Phantom Menace" within a Web page. But what if we want to access those words as data? Using XML, we can mark up the words "Star Wars Episode I: The Phantom Menace" in a way that better reflects their significance as data:

```
<film>
  <title>Star Wars Episode I: The Phantom Menace</title>
</film>
```

Here, XML tag names have been chosen that best describe the contents of the element. We also define our own attribute names as necessary. For instance, in the preceding example, you may need to differentiate between the VHS version and the DVD version. This can be achieved by using an attribute to describe the type. Let's call our attribute `format`:

```
<film format="DVD">
  <title>Star Wars Episode I: The Phantom Menace</title>
</film>
```

The following document describes the contents of a personal video library:

```
<h1>The Library of Zak Ruvalcaba</h1>
<table>
  <tr>
    <td>Star Wars Episode I: The Phantom Menace</td>
    <td>Star Wars Episode I: The Phantom Menace</td>
    <td>Star Wars: The Return of the Jedi</td>
  </tr>
</table>
```

This document provides us with information, but that information is not too clear. Does Zak own two copies of the same film? Does he own a DVD version and a VHS version? An equivalent XML document might be more descriptive:

```
<library>
  <owner>Zak Ruvalcaba</owner>
  <films>
    <film format="DVD">
      <title>Star Wars Episode I: The Phantom Menace</title>
    </film>
    <film format="VHS">
      <title>Star Wars Episode I: The Phantom Menace</title>
    </film>
    <film format="VHS">
      <title>Star Wars: The Return of the Jedi</title>
```

```
   </film>
  </films>
</library>
```

But, if XML does not describe how data should be presented, what good is that to us as Web developers who are normally concerned with presenting data? If you tried to view this XML document in a browser, you would get little more than a simple collapsible menu, as shown in Figure 16.1.

Figure 16.1. Viewing an XML document in a browser displays a collapsible XML tree.

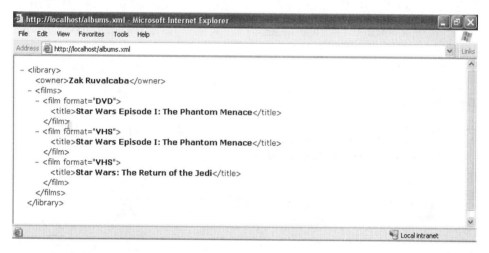

In fact, the only reason XML is formatted in different colors with collapsible nodes is because Internet Explorer does a little extra work for us. What it actually does is apply the default style sheet (not a standard style sheet, but Microsoft's own) that renders our XML documents in that format. The use of style sheets is key to presenting XML data in a useful and attractive form in the browser, and to do this, we use **Extensible Stylesheet Language Transformations (XSLT)**. As its name implies, XSLT allows you to transform an XML file into some other type of document, including HTML. It does this by specifying rules that are applied to the XML tags to transform them into a different type of tag (such as an HTML tag).

Consider the following XML data, which represents information about a particular CD within a music catalog:

```xml
<?xml-stylesheet type="text/xsl" href="titlesTransform.xsl"?>
<catalog>
  <cd>
    <title>No Control</title>
    <artist>Bad Religion</artist>
    <country>USA</country>
    <company>Epitaph</company>
    <price>10.99</price>
    <year>1989</year>
  </cd>
</catalog>
```

You could potentially have hundreds—perhaps even thousands—of CDs within the catalog. Imagine you need a way to present that data in a browser-friendly format.

The first line of the above code is the key, here. The `<?xml-stylesheet ?>` **processing instruction** tells the browser to use the specified XSLT style sheet to display the XML data. Here's what the style sheet might look like:

```xsl
<xsl:stylesheet version="1.0"
    xmlns:xsl="http://www.w3.org/1999/XSL/Transform">
  <xsl:template match="catalog">
    <html>
      <head>
        <title>My CD Collection</title>
      </head>
      <body>
        <h2>My CD Collection</h2>
        <table border="1">
          <tr bgcolor="silver">
            <th align="left">Title</th>
            <th align="left">Artist</th>
          </tr>
          <xsl:apply-templates/>
        </table>
      </body>
    </html>
  </xsl:template>

  <xsl:template match="catalog/cd">
    <tr>
      <td><xsl:value-of select="title"/></td>
      <td><xsl:value-of select="artist"/></td>
    </tr>
```

```
   </xsl:template>
</xsl:stylesheet>
```

This stylesheet contains two **templates**, each of which will match a portion of the XML document and transform it accordingly. The first template matches the `<catalog>` tag, and outputs the skeleton of an HTML document. The `<apply–templates>` tag sends the stylesheet looking for templates matching tags within the `<catalog>` tag. It's at this stage that the second template, which matches `<cd>` tags occurring within a `<catalog>` tag, comes into play. It outputs a table row for each `<cd>` element that it matches, outputting the values of the `<title>` and `<artist>` child tags with `<value-of>` tags.

As Figure 16.2 shows, attaching this style sheet to our XML document produces a HTML table view of the album titles and artists.

Figure 16.2. XSLT provides HTML-like formatting features for XML documents.

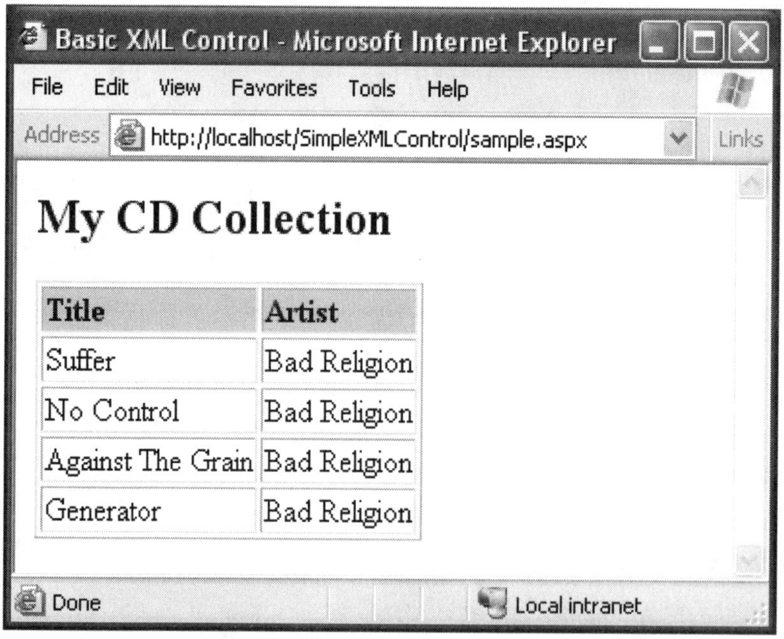

This would work just as well whether our XML document contained information on hundreds of CD elements, or just this one.

Unfortunately, we can't get into a detailed discussion of XML and XSLT here, but if you want to know more, check out the following articles on the SitePoint Website:

❏ *Introduction to XML*: http://www.sitepoint.com/article/930

 This article contains everything you need to know about the basics of XML.

❏ *Get XSL To Do Your Dirty Work*: http://www.sitepoint.com/article/595

 Kevin Yank introduces XSL Transformations and shows how they can be used to transform XML into HTML in this handy guide.

Simplifying it All with the `Xml` Control

Hopefully, this very brief introduction has demonstrated some of the benefits of XML and XSLT. You can define your data using XML, and present it within a browser using XSLT. Since not all browsers yet support XSLT natively, however, we cannot depend on the transformation happening on the client side.

ASP.NET lets us programmatically display XML files with a particular style sheet, using the `Xml` control. Not only does the `Xml` control load style sheets programmatically, but it makes the process of joining your XML files with their corresponding XSLT file a lot easier. The `Xml` control contains the following important properties:

`DocumentSource`	The path to the XML file
`TransformSource`	The path to the XSLT file
`Document`	A preloaded XML document
`Transform`	A preloaded XSLT document

To demonstrate the use of the `Xml` control, let's take a look at a simple XML file, called `titles.xml`, which contains the contents of my CD collection. Note that we no longer need the `<?xml-stylesheet?>` processing instruction, as we'll be linking this file to the style sheet from ASP.NET:

File: **SimpleXMLControl/titles.xml**

```
<catalog>
  <cd>
    <title>Suffer</title>
```

```
      <artist>Bad Religion</artist>
      <country>USA</country>
      <company>Epitaph</company>
      <price>10.99</price>
      <year>1987</year>
    </cd>
    <cd>
      <title>No Control</title>
      <artist>Bad Religion</artist>
      <country>USA</country>
      <company>Epitaph</company>
      <price>10.99</price>
      <year>1989</year>
    </cd>
    <cd>
      <title>Against The Grain</title>
      <artist>Bad Religion</artist>
      <country>USA</country>
      <company>Epitaph</company>
      <price>10.99</price>
      <year>1990</year>
    </cd>
    <cd>
      <title>Generator</title>
      <artist>Bad Religion</artist>
      <country>USA</country>
      <company>Epitaph</company>
      <price>10.99</price>
      <year>1992</year>
    </cd>
</catalog>
```

You've already seen the style sheet file, called `titlesTransform.xsl`, which we use to style the XML file as HTML:

File: **SimpleXMLControl/titlesTransform.xsl**

```
<xsl:stylesheet version="1.0"
    xmlns:xsl="http://www.w3.org/1999/XSL/Transform">
  <xsl:template match="catalog">
    <html>
      <head>
        <title>My CD Collection</title>
      </head>
      <body>
        <h2>My CD Collection</h2>
        <table border="1">
```

```
        <tr bgcolor="silver">
          <th align="left">Title</th>
          <th align="left">Artist</th>
        </tr>
        <xsl:apply-templates/>
      </table>
    </body>
  </html>
</xsl:template>

<xsl:template match="catalog/cd">
  <tr>
    <td><xsl:value-of select="title"/></td>
    <td><xsl:value-of select="artist"/></td>
  </tr>
</xsl:template>
</xsl:stylesheet>
```

The ASP.NET Xml control uses the DocumentSource property to specify the XML document, and the TransformSource property to link it to the XSLT style sheet:

File: **SimpleXMLControl/sample.aspx (excerpt)**

```
<asp:Xml id="titles" DocumentSource="titles.xml"
    TransformSource="titlesTranform.xsl" runat="server" />
```

As you can see, the Xml control resembles most other controls that you might work with on a typical ASP.NET page. Place the above tag in a server-side form inside a new .aspx page, and view it within a browser. Figure 16.3 shows how the Xml control formats the XML document with the XSLT file to produce the HTML for the browser.

Figure 16.3. The Xml control formats the XML document using the XML and XSLT files.

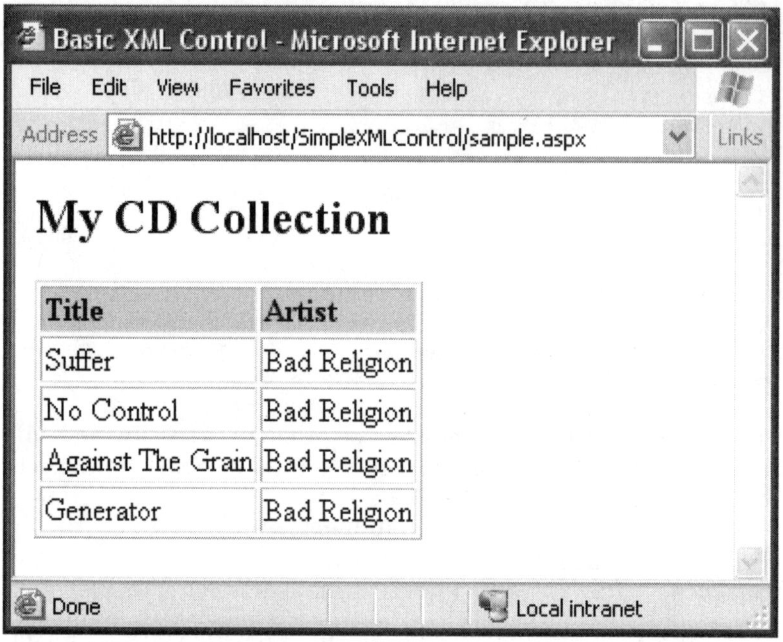

So far, the Xml control does little more than format an XML document according to a fixed set of rules. The next example demonstrates how you can use a CheckBox control to allow the user to determine the presentation of data within the page by selecting which style sheet to use. To demonstrate this, we'll create a second XSLT file called titlesTranformAll.xsl that renders all the data from the XML file as HTML:

File: **AdvancedXMLControl/titlesTransformAll.xsl**

```
<xsl:stylesheet version="1.0"
    xmlns:xsl="http://www.w3.org/1999/XSL/Transform">
  <xsl:template match="catalog">
    <html>
      <head>
        <title>My CD Collection</title>
      </head>
      <body>
        <h2>My CD Collection</h2>
        <table border="1">
          <tr bgcolor="silver">
```

```
            <th align="left">Title</th>
            <th align="left">Artist</th>
            <th align="left">Country</th>
            <th align="left">Company</th>
            <th align="left">Price</th>
            <th align="left">Year</th>
          </tr>
          <xsl:apply-templates/>
        </table>
      </body>
    </html>
  </xsl:template>

  <xsl:template match="catalog/cd">
    <tr>
      <td><xsl:value-of select="title"/></td>
      <td><xsl:value-of select="artist"/></td>
      <td><xsl:value-of select="country"/></td>
      <td><xsl:value-of select="company"/></td>
      <td><xsl:value-of select="price"/></td>
      <td><xsl:value-of select="year"/></td>
    </tr>
  </xsl:template>
</xsl:stylesheet>
```

This style sheet transforms all the data associated with each album (not just the title and artist) into an HTML table. The next step involves adding some conditional code to our ASP.NET page. If the user selects a checkbox to view all headers, you will want the XML control to load `titlesTransformAll.xsl` rather than `titlesTransform.xsl`. You can include this functionality by adding the `CheckBox` control:

File: **AdvancedXMLControl/sample.aspx (excerpt)**

```
<asp:CheckBox id="chkTitles" AutoPostBack="true" runat="server"
    OnCheckedChanged="TitlesTransform" Text="Show all information"
    />
```

Now add the following code declaration block to the `<head>` element of your page:

VB.NET   File: **AdvancedXMLControl/sample.aspx (excerpt)**

```
<script runat="server" language="VB">
Sub TitlesTransform(s As Object, e As EventArgs)
  If (chkTitles.Checked) Then
    titles.TransformSource = "titlesTranformAll.xsl"
```

```
  Else
    titles.TransformSource = "titlesTranform.xsl"
  End If
End Sub
</script>
```

C#	File: **AdvancedXMLControl/sample.aspx (excerpt)**

```
<script runat="server" language="C#">
void TitlesTransform(Object s, EventArgs e) {
  if (chkTitles.Checked) {
    titles.TransformSource = "titlesTranformAll.xsl";
  } else {
    titles.TransformSource = "titlesTranform.xsl";
  }
}
</script>
```

As soon as the user selects the checkbox to show all information, the CheckBoxChanged event is raised and the TitlesTransform() method is called. Within the TitlesTransform() method, we use an If statement to confirm whether the checkbox was selected. If it was, the Xml control's TransformSource property is set to use titlesTransformAll.xsl; otherwise, it will use titlesTransform.xsl.

Save your work and test the results in the browser. Figure 16.4 shows how all the information in the document is displayed when I select the checkbox. When the checkbox is unselected, only the title and artist are shown.

Figure 16.4. Selecting the CheckBox control displays all information within the XML document.

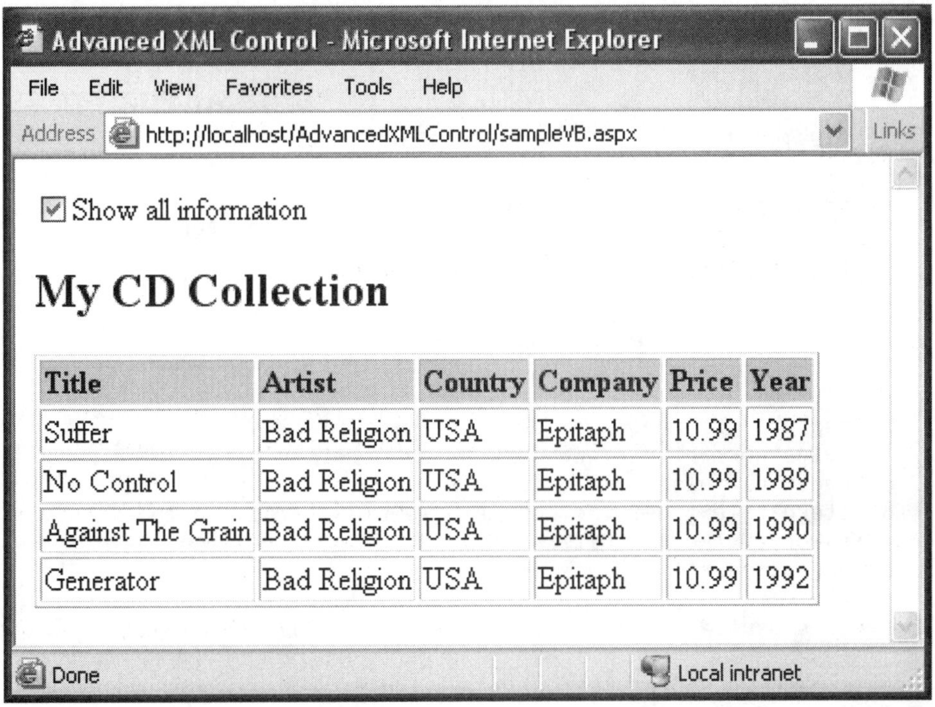

The AdRotator Control

Let's now discuss another important rich control: the AdRotator control. The AdRotator control allows you randomly to display a list of banner advertisements within your Web application. But it's more than a mere substitute to creating a randomization script from scratch.

The AdRotator control displays its content feed from an XML file, essentially making the administration and updating of banner advertisement files and their properties a snap. Also, the XML file allows you to control the banner's image, link, link target, and frequency of appearance in relation to other banner ads. The benefits to using this control don't stop there, however. Because most of the AdRotator control's properties reside within an XML file, if you wished, you could share that XML file on the Web, essentially allowing value added resellers (VARS), or possibly your companies' partners, to use your banner advertisements on *their* Websites. For a complete list of properties, methods, and events supported by the AdRotator control, turn to Appendix B.

As I mentioned above, the banner advertisements that the AdRotator control displays are fed in via an advertisement file, an XML file like the one shown below:

File: **AdRotatorControl/ads.xml**

```
<Advertisements>
  <Ad>
    <ImageUrl>workatdorknozzle.gif</ImageUrl>
    <NavigateUrl>http://www.dorknozzle.com</NavigateUrl>
    <TargetUrl>_blank</TargetUrl>
    <AlternateText>Work at Dorknozzle.com!</AlternateText>
    <Keyword>HR Sites</Keyword>
    <Impressions>2</Impressions>
  </Ad>
  <Ad>
    <ImageUrl>getthenewsletter.gif</ImageUrl>
    <NavigateUrl>http://www.dorknozzle.com</NavigateUrl>
    <TargetUrl>_blank</TargetUrl>
    <AlternateText>Get the Nozzle Newsletter!</AlternateText>
    <Keyword>Marketing Sites</Keyword>
    <Impressions>1</Impressions>
  </Ad>
</Advertisements>
```

As you can see, the <Advertisements> tag is the root tag, and in accordance with the XML specification appears once. For each individual advertisement, we simply add an <Ad> child tag. For instance, the above advertisement file contains details for two banner advertisements.

As you've probably noticed by now, the file enables you to specify properties for each banner advertisement using child tags. These tags include:

<ImageUrl>	The URL of the image to display for the banner ad
<NavigateUrl>	The Web page that your users will navigate to when they click the banner ad
<AlternateText>	The alternative text to display for browsers that do not support images
<Keyword>	The keyword to use for categorizing your banner ad; if you use the KeywordFilter property of the

AdRotator control, you can specify the categories of banner ads to display.

<Impressions> The relative frequency that a particular banner ad should be shown in relation to other banner advertisements. The higher the number, the more frequent that specific banner shows on the browser. The number can be as low as one, but cannot exceed 2,048,000,000, or the page throws an exception.

All these properties are optional, except for <ImageURL>. Also, if you specify a banner ad without defining the <NavigateURL> property, the banner ad will display without a hyperlink.

To create a banner advertisement using the AdRotator control, first create an XML file called ads.xml with the XML content defined above. You can create your own banners, or use the ones provided in the code archive for this book. Now, create a new ASP.NET page, called AdRotator.aspx, with the following code:

File: **AdRotatorControl/AdRotator.aspx**

```
<html>
<head>
<title>AdRotator Control</title>
</head>
<body>
<form runat="server">
<asp:AdRotator AdvertisementFile="ads.xml" id="adRotator"
    runat="server" />
</form>
</body>
</html>
```

Save your work and test it in the browser. Refresh the page a few times. You will notice that the first banner appears more often than the second banner. This is because the <Impression> for the first tag is set to show twice as often as the second banner.

The Calendar Control

You can use the Calendar control to display an interactive calendar on a page. Initially, the Calendar control requires very little customization, but allows the user to select days, weeks, or months from an intuitive visual interface. A `Calendar` control can be created within a page like this:

```
<asp:Calendar id="myCalendar" runat="server"/>
```

Figure 16.5 shows the `Calendar` control.

Figure 16.5. The `Calendar` control at its most basic.

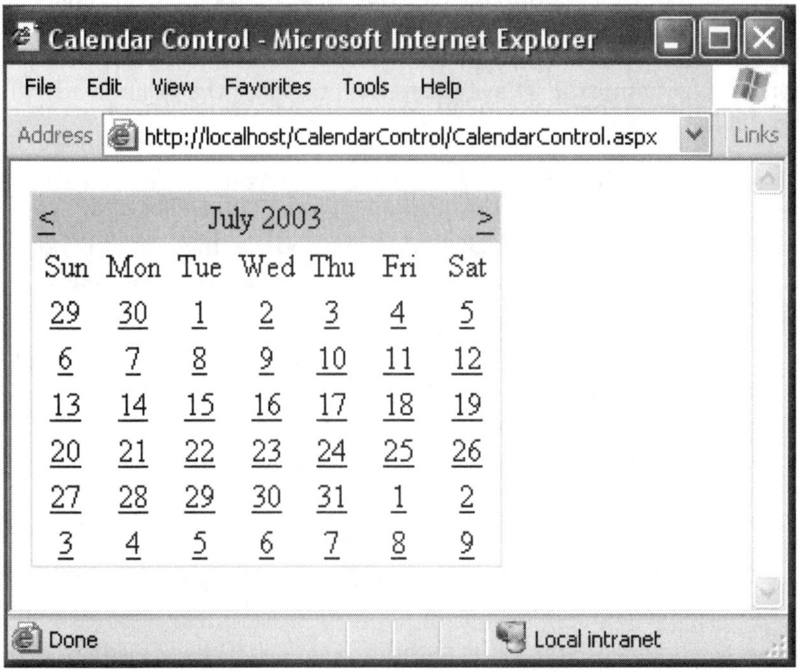

The `Calendar` control contains a healthy number of properties, methods, and events. Each of these is outlined in greater detail within Appendix B. However, some of the basic properties we'll be discussing in our examples are listed in Table 16.1.

Table 16.1. Some of the `Calendar` Control's Properties

Property	Description
DayNameFormat	Sets the format of the day names. Possible values are `FirstLetter`, `FirstTwoLetters`, `Full`, and `Short`. Default is `Short`, which displays the three letter abbreviation.
FirstDayOfWeek	Sets the day of the week that begins each week in the calendar. By default, this is determined by your server's region settings, but you can set this to `Sunday` or `Monday` if you want to control it.
NextPrevFormat	Set to `CustomText` by default, this property can be set to `ShortMonth` or `FullMonth` to control the format of the next/previous month links.
SelectedDate	Contains a `DateTime` value that specifies the highlighted day. When programming in code, you'll use this property a lot to determine which day that user has selected.
SelectionMode	Determines whether days, weeks, or months can be selected. Possible values are `Day`, `DayWeek`, `DayWeekMonth`, and `None`. Default is `Day`. When `Day` is selected, a user can only select a day. When `DayWeek` is selected, a user can also select an entire week, for example.
SelectMonthText	Controls the text of the link that is displayed to allow users to select an entire month from the calendar.
SelectWeekText	Controls the text of the link that is displayed to allow users to select an entire week from the calendar.
ShowDayHeader	If `True`, displays the names of the days of the week. Default is `True`.
ShowGridLines	If `True`, renders the calendar with grid lines. Default is `True`.
ShowNextPrevMonth	If `True`, displays next/previous month links. Default is `True`.
ShowTitle	If `True`, displays the calendar's title. Default is `False`.
TitleFormat	Determines how the month name appears in the title bar. Possible values are `Month` and `MonthYear`. Default is `MonthYear`.
TodaysDate	A `DateTime` value that sets the calendar's current date. By default, this value is not highlighted within the `Calendar` control.

Property	Description
VisibleDate	A DateTime value that controls which month is displayed.

Let's take a look at an example that uses some of these properties, events, and methods to create a Calendar control that allows users to select days, weeks, and months. You can start by creating a new ASP.NET page and adding the Calendar control, as follows:

File: **CalendarControl/CalendarControl.aspx**

```
<html>
<head>
<title>Calendar Control</title>
</head>
<body>
<form runat="server">
<asp:Calendar id="myCalendar" runat="server"
    DayNameFormat="Short" FirstDayOfWeek="Sunday"
    NextPrevFormat="FullMonth" SelectionMode="DayWeekMonth"
    SelectWeekText="Select Week" SelectMonthText="Select Month"
    TitleFormat="Month"
    OnSelectionChanged="Calendar_SelectionChanged"/>
<p><asp:Label id="lblSelected" runat="server"/></p>
</form>
</body>
</html>
```

We've set several properties of the Calendar control, all of which are described in Table 16.1. Additionally, we've added a OnSelectionChanged attribute, which specifies the event handler to be called when the user makes a selection.

We've also added a Label control to display the day, week, or month that the user selects. Now, let's add the code that will react to the user's selection:

VB.NET   File: **CalendarControl/CalendarControl.aspx (excerpt)**

```
<script runat="server" language="VB">
Sub Calendar_SelectionChanged(s As Object, e As EventArgs)
  Dim dtmDate As DateTime
  lblSelected.Text = _
      "<h2>You've selected the following dates:</h2>"
  lblSelected.Text &= "<ul>"
  For Each dtmDate In myCalendar.SelectedDates
    lblSelected.Text &= "<li>" & dtmDate.ToString("D") & "</li>"
  Next
  lblSelected.Text &= "</ul>"
```

```
End Sub
</script>
```

C#   File: **CalendarControl/CalendarControl.aspx (excerpt)**

```
<script runat="server" language="C#">
void Calendar_SelectionChanged(Object s, EventArgs e) {
  lblSelected.Text =
      "<h2>You've selected the following dates:</h2>";
  lblSelected.Text += "<ul>";
  foreach (DateTime dtmDate in myCalendar.SelectedDates) {
    lblSelected.Text += "<li>" + dtmDate.ToString("D") + "</li>";
  }
  lblSelected.Text += "</ul>";
}
</script>
```

Save your work and test it within a browser. Try selecting a day, week, or month. The selection will be highlighted, similar to Figure 16.6.

Figure 16.6. The selected day, week, or month becomes highlighted.

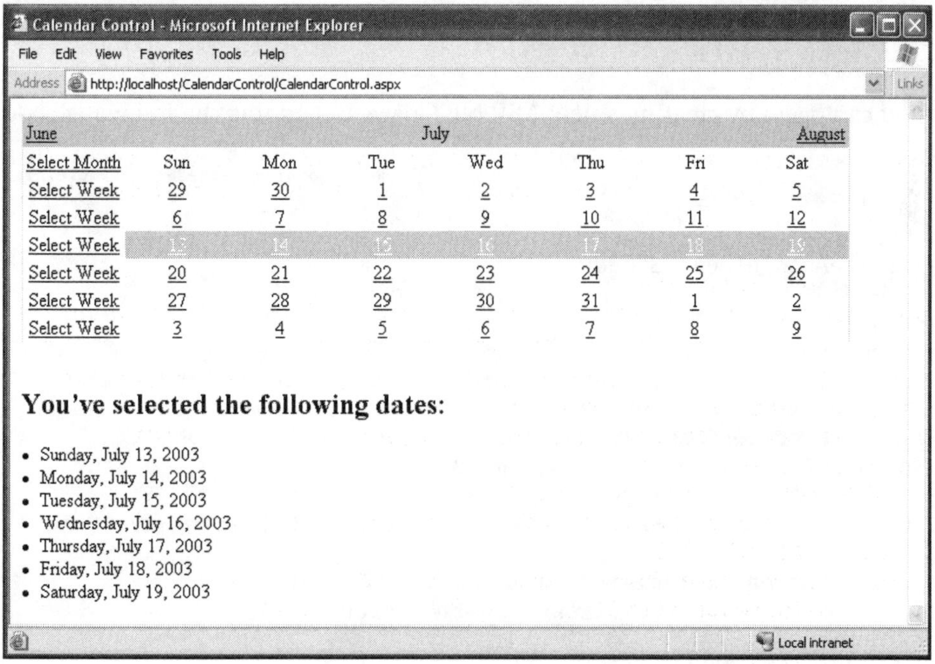

By now, you should be able to follow the code of the event handler. After adding some default text to the Label control, we loop through each date that the user has selected, and append it to an HTML list.

In the next section, we'll take the Calendar control one step further and see how we can use it to build an appointment scheduler for our intranet project.

Building the Interactive Appointment Scheduler

There are many programs that will allow you to save appointment information by time and date. Outlook, Outlook Express, and Eudora, for instance, allow you to manage contact, email, and appointment information simply and easily. But what if you wanted to create a schedule application that was similar to Outlook, but made for the Web? Fortunately for you, the Calendar control is flexible enough to provide functionality as powerful as that of Outlook or Eudora. In this section, you'll build an interactive appointment scheduler using the Calendar control and some programming concepts that you've already learned, including:

❑ Caching

❑ Serialization

❑ Writing to text files

You can begin by creating a new ASP.NET page and adding the following code:

File: **AppointmentScheduler/sample.aspx**

```
<html>
<head>
<title>Appointment Scheduler</title>
</head>
<body>
<form runat="server">
<asp:Calendar id="myCalendar" Width="100%" ShowGridLines="true"
    runat="server" OnDayRender="Calendar_RenderDay"
    OnSelectionChanged="Get_Appt" />
<p><asp:TextBox id="myNotes" TextMode="MultiLine" Columns="50"
    Rows="10" runat="server" /></p>
<p><asp:Button id="Save" Text="Save Changes" OnClick="Save_Click"
    runat="server" />
  <asp:Button id="Delete" Text="Delete Changes"
      OnClick="Delete_Click" runat="server" /></p>
</form>
```

```
</body>
</html>
```

As you can see, the `Calendar` control will raise the `DayRender` event and call a method we've named `Calendar_RenderDay()`. The `DayRender` event is raised each time the `Calendar` control is loaded, and our method will eventually highlight those days on which an appointment exists. We also set the `OnSelectionChanged` attribute; we'll see why shortly.

As well as the calendar, we create a text box in which users can enter appointment details for a given day, and buttons to allow them to save changes to an appointment, or delete it entirely. Now, let's import the three namespaces that we'll use:

File: **AppointmentScheduler/sample.aspx** (excerpt)

```
<%@ Import Namespace="System.IO" %>
<%@ Import
    Namespace="System.Runtime.Serialization.Formatters.Binary" %>
<%@ Import Namespace="System.Drawing" %>
```

As we're going to be writing to a text file, we'll need the `System.IO` namespace. To serialize the properties for the `Calendar` control, we'll need the `System.Runtime.Serialization.Formatters.Binary` namespace, which exposes the `BinaryFormatter` class. Lastly, as we want to highlight selected days, we'll require the `System.Drawing` namespace, which contains all the classes for working with colors, bitmaps, fonts, icons, shapes, etc., programmatically in your ASP.NET pages. We'll use the `Color` classes exposed by this namespace to highlight the day of the month the user selects.

The appointment scheduler will contain the following methods:

`Page_Load()`	Creates an array of dates that will be stored in the cache. If the cache already exists, it binds the array with the `Calendar` control.
`Save_Click()`	Adds information from the `TextBox` control into the array, then serializes it into a text file.
`Calendar_RenderDay()`	While our selected day will use one color, we'll create this separate method to handle colors for the other days with which appointments are associated
`Get_Appt()`	When the user selects a particular day, we'll need to check to see whether that day already has any appoint-

ments scheduled. If it does, we will display them in the TextBox.

Delete_Click()	Removes an appointment for a selected day.

The first thing we need to do is add a code declaration block to the `<head>` tag of the ASP.NET page. This block defines a new **multidimensional string array** that will represent the twelve months of the year, and the thirty-one possible days within a month:

VB.NET   File: **AppointmentScheduler/sample.aspx (excerpt)**

```vbnet
<script runat="server" language="VB">
Dim arrCalendar(12, 31) As String
Dim fmtrBinaryFormatter As New BinaryFormatter()
Dim strmFileStream As FileStream
Dim dtmDate As DateTime
</script>
```

C#   File: **AppointmentScheduler/sample.aspx (excerpt)**

```csharp
<script runat="server" language="C#">
String[,] arrCalendar = new String[12, 31];
BinaryFormatter fmtrBinaryFormatter = new BinaryFormatter();
FileStream strmFileStream;
DateTime dtmDate;
</script>
```

You'll also notice that we've created a new instance of the `BinaryFormatter` class, and we've instantiated new `FileStream` and `DateTime` objects. Now, let's build the `Page_Load()` event handler by adding the following code to the same script block:

VB.NET   File: **AppointmentScheduler/sample.aspx (excerpt)**

```vbnet
Sub Page_Load()
  If Cache("arrCalendar") Is Nothing Then
    If File.Exists("C:\schedule.bin") Then
      strmFileStream = New FileStream("C:\schedule.bin", _
        FileMode.Open)
      arrCalendar = CType( _
        fmtrBinaryFormatter.Deserialize(strmFileStream), Array)
      strmFileStream.Close()
      Cache("arrCalendar") = arrCalendar
    End If
  Else
    arrCalendar = Cache("arrCalendar")
```

```
   End If
End Sub
```

C#   File: **AppointmentScheduler/sample.aspx (excerpt)**

```csharp
void Page_Load() {
  if (Cache["arrCalendar"] == null) {
    if (File.Exists("C:\\schedule.bin")) {
      strmFileStream = new FileStream("C:\\schedule.bin",
        FileMode.Open);
      arrCalendar = (String[,])
        fmtrBinaryFormatter.Deserialize(strmFileStream);
      strmFileStream.Close();
      Cache["arrCalendar"] = arrCalendar;
    }
  } else {
    arrCalendar = (String[,])Cache["arrCalendar"];
  }
}
```

Let's break down the `Page_Load()` method to make it a bit more understandable. Initially, we perform a check to see whether the cache contains a copy of the schedule:

VB.NET   File: **AppointmentScheduler/sample.aspx (excerpt)**

```
If Cache("arrCalendar") Is Nothing Then
```

C#   File: **AppointmentScheduler/sample.aspx (excerpt)**

```csharp
if (Cache["arrCalendar"] == null) {
```

If there is no cached schedule, then we want to perform another check to see if our `schedule.bin` data file exists[1]:

VB.NET   File: **AppointmentScheduler/sample.aspx (excerpt)**

```
If File.Exists("C:\Schedule.bin") Then
```

C#   File: **AppointmentScheduler/sample.aspx (excerpt)**

```csharp
if (File.Exists("C:\\Schedule.bin")) {
```

If it does exist, we need to read it and deserialize the stored array to the `Cache` object. We'll first create a new instance of the `FileStream` class, passing in the name of the `schedule.bin` file and `FileMode.Open` to indicate we want to read the file. Next we deserialize the first (and, we expect, only) object in the file into

---

[1]Once again, we're using the root of `C:` to store our data file in this example. In a practical application, you would want to choose a more appropriate place for this file.

an array and place it into the `arrCalendar` variable. Finally, we close the `FileStream` object and place the array into the cache:

```
VB.NET                                    File: AppointmentScheduler/sample.aspx (excerpt)
strmFileStream = New FileStream("C:\schedule.bin", FileMode.Open)
arrCalendar = CType( _
    fmtrBinaryFormatter.Deserialize(strmFileStream), Array)
strmFileStream.Close()
Cache("arrCalendar") = arrCalendar
```

```
C#                                        File: AppointmentScheduler/sample.aspx (excerpt)
strmFileStream = new FileStream("C:\\schedule.bin",
    FileMode.Open);
arrCalendar = (String[,])
    fmtrBinaryFormatter.Deserialize(strmFileStream);
strmFileStream.Close();
Cache["arrCalendar"] = arrCalendar;
```

Now that the `Page_Load()` method is built, let's build the `Save_Click()` method by adding the following code:

```
VB.NET                                    File: AppointmentScheduler/sample.aspx (excerpt)
Sub Save_Click(s As Object, e As EventArgs)
  dtmDate = myCalendar.SelectedDate
  arrCalendar(dtmDate.Month - 1, dtmDate.Day - 1) = myNotes.Text
  strmFileStream = New FileStream("C:\schedule.bin", _
      FileMode.Create)
  fmtrBinaryFormatter.Serialize(strmFileStream, arrCalendar)
  strmFileStream.Close()
  Cache("arrCalendar") = arrCalendar
End Sub
```

```
C#                                        File: AppointmentScheduler/sample.aspx (excerpt)
void Save_Click(Object s, EventArgs e) {
  dtmDate = myCalendar.SelectedDate;
  arrCalendar[dtmDate.Month - 1, dtmDate.Day - 1] = myNotes.Text;
  strmFileStream = new FileStream("C:\\schedule.bin",
      FileMode.Create);
  fmtrBinaryFormatter.Serialize(strmFileStream, arrCalendar);
  strmFileStream.Close();
  Cache["arrCalendar"] = arrCalendar;
}
```

Let's break down this method to make it more understandable. Initially, we take the selected date, and place it into the `dtmDate` object variable by accessing the `SelectedDate` property of the `Calendar` control:

VB.NET   File: **AppointmentScheduler/sample.aspx (excerpt)**

```
dtmDate = myCalendar.SelectedDate
```

C#   File: **AppointmentScheduler/sample.aspx (excerpt)**

```
dtmDate = myCalendar.SelectedDate;
```

Next, we place the value of the `TextBox` control into the `arrCalendar` array, at a location specified by the selected month and day:

VB.NET   File: **AppointmentScheduler/sample.aspx (excerpt)**

```
arrCalendar(dtmDate.Month - 1, dtmDate.Day - 1) = myNotes.Text
```

C#   File: **AppointmentScheduler/sample.aspx (excerpt)**

```
arrCalendar[dtmDate.Month - 1, dtmDate.Day - 1] = myNotes.Text;
```

We then create open a stream to write a new `schedule.bin` file containing this updated information:

VB.NET   File: **AppointmentScheduler/sample.aspx (excerpt)**

```
strmFileStream = New FileStream("C:\schedule.bin",
    FileMode.Create)
```

C#   File: **AppointmentScheduler/sample.aspx (excerpt)**

```
strmFileStream = new FileStream("C:\\schedule.bin",
    FileMode.Create);
```

Finally, we call the `Serialize()` method of the `BinaryFormatter` object, passing in the `FileStream` object and `Array` object. Lastly, we close the `FileStream`, and save the updated array back into the cache:

VB.NET   File: **AppointmentScheduler/sample.aspx (excerpt)**

```
fmtrBinaryFormatter.Serialize(strmFileStream, arrCalendar)
strmFileStream.Close()
Cache("arrCalendar") = arrCalendar
```

C#   File: **AppointmentScheduler/sample.aspx (excerpt)**

```
fmtrBinaryFormatter.Serialize(strmFileStream, arrCalendar);
strmFileStream.Close();
Cache["arrCalendar"] = arrCalendar;
```

Now, let's build the `Calendar_RenderDay()` method by adding the following code:

```
VB.NET                          File: AppointmentScheduler/sample.aspx (excerpt)
Sub Calendar_RenderDay(s As Object, e As DayRenderEventArgs)
  Dim dtmDate As DateTime = e.Day.Date
  Dim ctlCell As TableCell = e.Cell

  If arrCalendar(dtmDate.Month - 1, dtmDate.Day - 1) <> "" Then
    ctlCell.BackColor = Color.FromName("Red")
  End If
End Sub
```

```
C#                              File: AppointmentScheduler/sample.aspx (excerpt)
void Calendar_RenderDay(Object s, DayRenderEventArgs e) {
  DateTime dtmDate = e.Day.Date;
  TableCell ctlCell = e.Cell;

  if (arrCalendar[dtmDate.Month - 1, dtmDate.Day - 1] != null) {
    ctlCell.BackColor = Color.FromName("Red");
  }
}
```

As I already mentioned, this code is responsible for coloring the cells that have appointments associated with them. This event handler will be called just before ASP.NET renders each of the day cells in the `Calendar` control, so it's up to us to detect when the day in question has an appointment and adjust the cell color accordingly. We can get both the day in question (`e.Day.Date`) and the cell to be rendered (`e.Cell`) from the `DayRenderEventArgs` object passed to the handler.

To begin with, we take the day and place it into a new `DateTime` variable. Then, we take the current cell and place that into a new `TableCell` object variable:

```
VB.NET                          File: AppointmentScheduler/sample.aspx (excerpt)
Dim dtmDate As DateTime = e.Day.Date
Dim ctlCell As TableCell = e.Cell
```

```
C#                              File: AppointmentScheduler/sample.aspx (excerpt)
DateTime dtmDate = e.Day.Date;
TableCell ctlCell = e.Cell;
```

Next, we check to see if the array element for the current day contains an appointment. If it does, we change the background color of the selected cell by setting the `BackColor` property to the color `Red`. This color is accessible by calling the `FromName()` method of the `Color` class (from the `System.Drawing` namespace):

VB.NET   File: **AppointmentScheduler/sample.aspx (excerpt)**

```
If arrCalendar(dtmDate.Month - 1, dtmDate.Day - 1) <> "" Then
  ctlCell.BackColor = Color.FromName("Red")
End If
```

C#   File: **AppointmentScheduler/sample.aspx (excerpt)**

```
if (arrCalendar[dtmDate.Month - 1, dtmDate.Day - 1] != null) {
  ctlCell.BackColor = Color.FromName("Red");
}
```

The next method to implement is `Get_Appt()`, which is called through the `OnSelectionChanged` attribute of the `Calendar` control when the user selects a new date. This is actually a very simple method:

VB.NET   File: **AppointmentScheduler/sample.aspx (excerpt)**

```
Sub Get_Appt(s As Object, e As EventArgs)
  dtmDate = myCalendar.SelectedDate
  myNotes.Text = arrCalendar(dtmDate.Month - 1, dtmDate.Day - 1)
End Sub
```

C#   File: **AppointmentScheduler/sample.aspx (excerpt)**

```
void Get_Appt(Object s, EventArgs e) {
  dtmDate = myCalendar.SelectedDate;
  myNotes.Text = arrCalendar[dtmDate.Month - 1, dtmDate.Day - 1];
}
```

All this does is set the `Text` property of the `TextBox` to the value stored in the array for the newly selected date. If no appointment is scheduled, this will simply be an empty string, so the effect will be to clear the text box. If, however, there is an appointment scheduled for that day, the effect will be to display its descriptive text.

All that's left now is to create the "delete appointment" functionality by adding the following method:

VB.NET   File: **AppointmentScheduler/sample.aspx (excerpt)**

```
Sub Delete_Click(s As Object, e As EventArgs)
  dtmDate = myCalendar.SelectedDate
  arrCalendar(dtmDate.Month - 1, dtmDate.Day - 1) = ""
  strmFileStream = New FileStream("C:\schedule.bin", _
      FileMode.Create)
```

```
   fmtrBinaryFormatter.Serialize(strmFileStream, arrCalendar)
   strmFileStream.Close()
   Cache("arrCalendar") = arrCalendar
End Sub
```

C#   File: **AppointmentScheduler/sample.aspx (excerpt)**
```
void Delete_Click(Object s, EventArgs e) {
  dtmDate = myCalendar.SelectedDate;
  arrCalendar[dtmDate.Month - 1, dtmDate.Day - 1] = null;
  strmFileStream = new FileStream("C:\\schedule.bin",
      FileMode.Create);
  fmtrBinaryFormatter.Serialize(strmFileStream, arrCalendar);
  strmFileStream.Close();
  Cache["arrCalendar"] = arrCalendar;
}
```

You may have noticed that the code looks similar to that of the `Save_Click()` method. The only difference between this block of code and the code contained within the `Save_Click()` method is the following line[2]:

VB.NET   File: **AppointmentScheduler/sample.aspx (excerpt)**
```
arrCalendar(dtmDate.Month - 1, dtmDate.Day - 1) = ""
```

C#   File: **AppointmentScheduler/sample.aspx (excerpt)**
```
arrCalendar[dtmDate.Month - 1, dtmDate.Day - 1] = null;
```

In this case, rather than adding the content the user enters in the `TextBox` control into the array, we simply place an empty value into the array. Save your work and run it within a browser. Notice that when you enter information into the `TextBox` control and save it, the day of the appointment becomes a different color. Now, select a different date and come back to the original date. The information that was added should stay bound to that day. This will also work if you close the browser and reopen it. The result will look similar to Figure 16.7.

---

[2]As an exercise, you might try writing another method that these two methods could each call. This method could contain the code for storing the updated array, instead of having to repeat the same code in two places.

Figure 16.7. You can enter appointment information for a certain day. No matter where you navigate to, the information remains for that specific day.

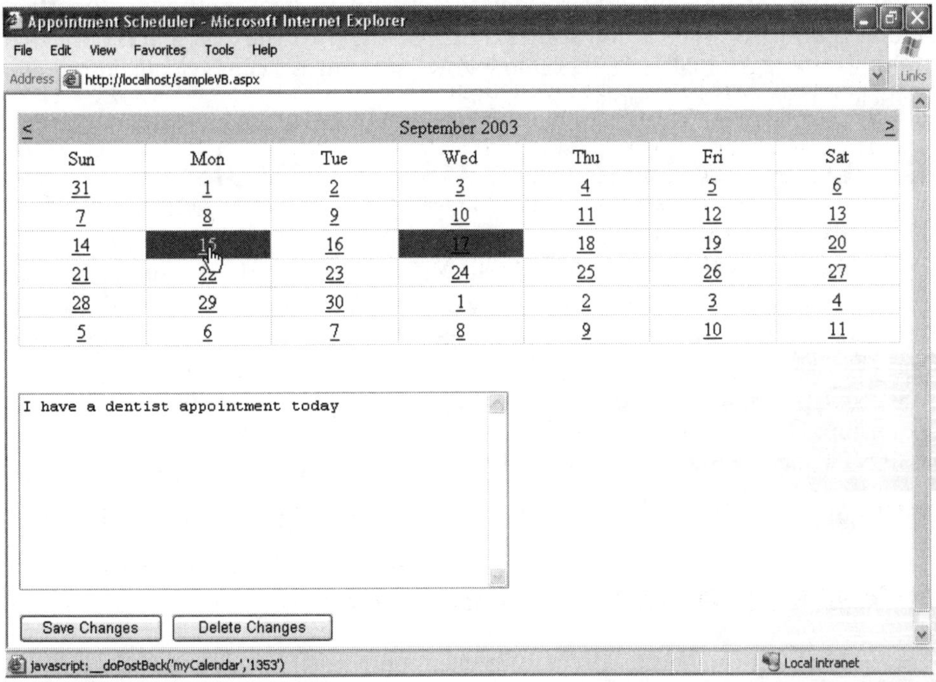

Now, look at the root directory of `C:` drive. The new `schedule.bin` should reside there. It will remain there, storing your appointment schedule even when you reboot the server.

Introduction to User Controls

In this section, we'll look at an interesting functionality that's uniquely supported in the .NET Framework, known as user controls. **User controls** are controls that you construct out of existing ASP.NET pages. For example, our current navigation menu is a set of hyperlinks within a table that's manually inserted into every page. If you ever needed to insert a new hyperlink or change an existing one, the same change must be made in every page that uses the navigation menu, which is pretty inefficient, right? In this section, we'll take the navigation menu we created in Chapter 9, turn it into a user control, and use that control within every page that requires a navigation menu. In this case, if a global change needs to be made, it's made once within the user control, and, instantly, all files that use the control are updated.

Later in this section, you'll learn how to define your own methods, properties, and events within a user control, and expose them to the ASP.NET page that uses that control. Finally, we'll examine how user controls can be loaded programmatically through your application logic.

Globalizing Content with User Controls

As I've just mentioned, user controls are simply ASP.NET pages that can be included within any number of other ASP.NET pages. But that's not all: because they're treated as ASP.NET controls, we can build functionality within them, add them to an ASP.NET page, and then work with the properties, methods, and events exposed by the control. Although ASP.NET controls are essentially ASP.NET pages, we don't use the `.aspx` file extension; instead, we use the `.ascx` extension. Once the user control has been created, it can be referenced from any ASP.NET page using the `Register` directive, as follows:

```
<%@ Register TagPrefix="dorknozzle" TagName="Nav" Src="nav.ascx" %>
```

The `Register` directive requires three attributes:

TagPrefix   The prefix for the user control, which allows you to group together related controls, and avoid tag naming conflicts

TagName   The control's tag name, which will be used when adding the control to the ASP.NET page

Src   The path to the `.ascx` file that describes the user control

Having added the above directive, you can then use the user control within the page with the following tag:

```
<dorknozzle:Nav id="navigation" runat="server"/>
```

We use the `TagPrefix` (dorknozzle), followed by a colon, and then the `TagName` (Nav) to reference that particular user control, as defined in the directive above. As is the case with all controls, the user control requires a unique `id` and the `runat="server"` attribute.

We can demonstrate the use of user controls through an example within our intranet project. In Chapter 9, we created the navigation menu using a `DataList` within a separate ASP.NET page. This page connected to the database, extracted the contents of the `Navigation` table, and presented the list within a formatted `DataList`. We can turn that `nav.aspx` page into a user control by changing the name to `nav.ascx`. The only other change we need to make to this file is to remove the `<form runat="server">` tag, along with the other supporting HTML tags (`<html>`, `<head>`, `<body>`, etc.). We do this because, as we're now using the file as a control in its own right, its code will reside within the tags of the page that uses the control.

For your reference, here's the updated code of `nav.ascx`. In addition to the changes described above, I've also changed it to use the database connection string from the `Web.config` file:

VB.NET   File: **nav.ascx**

```vbnet
<%@ Import Namespace="System.Data.OleDb" %>

<script runat="server" language="VB">
Dim objConn As New OleDbConnection( _
    ConfigurationSettings.AppSettings("DSN"))
Dim objCmd As OleDbCommand
Dim objRdr As OleDbDataReader

Sub Page_Load()
  If Not IsPostBack Then
    BindData()
  End If
End Sub

Sub BindData()
  objConn.Open()
  objCmd = New OleDbCommand("SELECT * FROM NavigationMenu", _
      objConn)
  objRdr = objCmd.ExecuteReader()
  dlNavMenu.DataSource = objRdr
  dlNavMenu.DataBind()
  objRdr.Close()
  objConn.Close()
End Sub
</script>
<asp:DataList id="dlNavMenu" runat="server" CellSpacing="2"
    CellPadding="2">
  <ItemStyle BackColor="#CCCCCC" BorderStyle="Solid"
      BorderWidth="1pt" BorderColor="#000000" />
```

```
  <ItemTemplate>
    <img src="Images/Book_Closed.gif" />
    <asp:HyperLink id="hlMenuItem"
        NavigateUrl='<%# Container.DataItem("Link") %>'
        Text='<%# Container.DataItem("Item") %>'
        runat="server" />
  </ItemTemplate>
</asp:DataList>
```

C#   File: **nav.ascx**

```
<%@ Import Namespace="System.Data.OleDb" %>

<script runat="server" language="C#">
OleDbConnection objConn = new OleDbConnection(
    ConfigurationSettings.AppSettings["DSN"]);
OleDbCommand objCmd;
OleDbDataReader objRdr;

void Page_Load() {
  if (!IsPostBack) {
    BindData();
  }
}

void BindData() {
  objConn.Open();
  objCmd = new OleDbCommand("SELECT * FROM NavigationMenu",
      objConn);
  objRdr = objCmd.ExecuteReader();
  dlNavMenu.DataSource = objRdr;
  dlNavMenu.DataBind();
  objRdr.Close();
  objConn.Close();
}
</script>
<asp:DataList id="dlNavMenu" runat="server" CellSpacing="2"
    CellPadding="2">
  <ItemStyle BackColor="#CCCCCC" BorderStyle="Solid"
      BorderWidth="1pt" BorderColor="#000000" />
  <ItemTemplate>
    <img src="Images/Book_Closed.gif" />
    <asp:HyperLink id="hlMenuItem"
        NavigateUrl='<%# DataBinder.Eval(Container.DataItem,
            "Link") %>'
        Text='<%# DataBinder.Eval(Container.DataItem,
            "Item") %>'
```

```
        runat="server" />
    <asp:HyperLink id="hlMenuItem"
        NavigateUrl='<%# Container.DataItem["Link"] %>'
        Text='<%# Container.DataItem["Item"] %>'
        runat="server" />
  </ItemTemplate>
</asp:DataList>
```

Next, open `index.aspx` and add the `Register` directive as the first line of code of the page:

```
<%@ Register TagPrefix="dorknozzle" TagName="Nav" Src="nav.ascx"
%>
```

Now, locate the existing navigation menu, a knot of images and hyperlinks that consumes a lot of space in the code. You can now replace that code with our new user control, as follows:

```
<dorknozzle:Nav id="navigation" runat="server" />
```

Save your work and test the results within the browser. Figure 16.8 shows how the new navigation bar replaces what was there previously.

Figure 16.8. The new user control navigation menu replaces the old navigation menu.

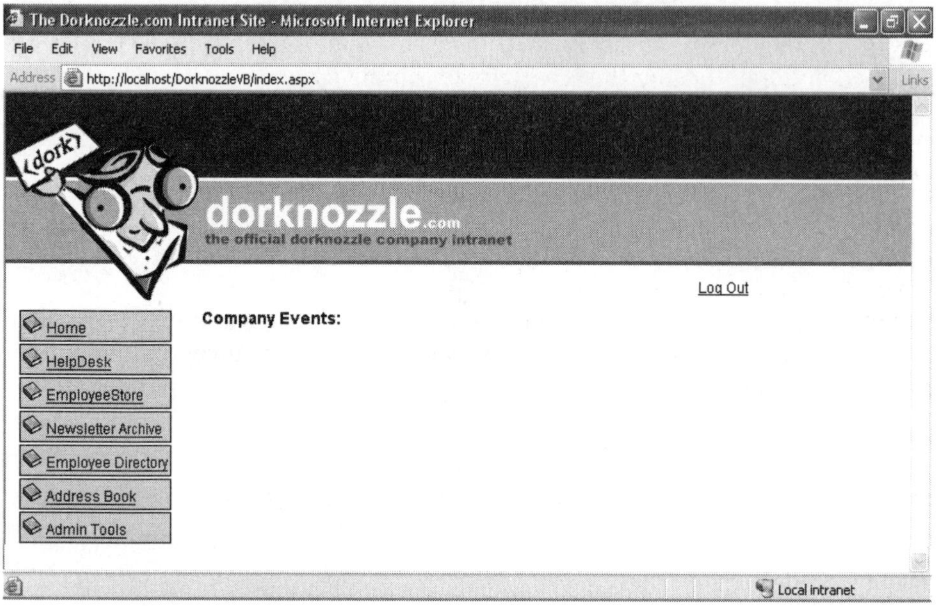

Now, open the remaining pages of your project, add the `Register` directive, and replace the remaining navigation menus with the new navigation user control. If this sounds overly tedious, just grab the updated files from the code archive for this book. When you're done, every page within your project will use the user control as the navigation menu. Now, if you ever need to make changes or additions to the navigation menu, you simply make them once within the `.ascx` file, save it, and, instantly, all your files that use the control will change.

Exposing Properties and Methods in User Controls

In the previous example, you created a static navigation user control and applied that control to every page of your project. The benefit to this approach is that you now have a single chunk of code that might appear on every single page, yet can be modified in a single location. Ironically, the drawback of this approach is the same as the advantage—every page of the project will end up using the same navigation bar. What would you do if the navigation bar within the `admin-tools.aspx` page had to be different? What if, when the user entered the `admin-tools.aspx` page, more hyperlinks that represented all of the different tasks that an administrator could perform needed to be displayed along with the other links? Our current approach wouldn't allow for either of these scenarios.

User controls don't have to be static files, as was traditionally the case with server side includes. Instead, they can contain properties and methods that are accessed and modified by the control's containing pages.

As a simple example of a user control exposing properties to its containing page, take a look at the following code:

VB.NET   File: **UserControlsProperties/datetime.ascx**

```
<script runat="server" language="VB">
  Public DateTime As String
</script>

The time and date is: <%= DateTime %>
```

C#   File: **UserControlsProperties/datetime.ascx**

```
<script runat="server" language="C#">
  public string DateTime;
</script>

The time and date is: <%= DateTime %>
```

In this example, the user control simply exposes a public string variable called `DateTime`. Because the variable is declared as `Public`, the variable is exposed as a property of the user control.

Next, you'll notice that we use a code render block to write out the value of `DateTime`. You're probably wondering where the value of `DateTime` will be coming from. We'll create a second page that consumes the user control and dynamically sets the `DateTime` property at the click of a button:

VB.NET   File: **UserControlsProperties/sample.aspx**

```
<%@ Register TagPrefix="dorknozzle" TagName="DateTime"
    Src="datetime.ascx" %>
<script runat="server" language="VB">
Sub MyClick(s As Object, e As EventArgs)
  ctlDateTime.DateTime = Now.ToString()
End Sub
</script>
<html>
<head>
<title>User Controls (Properties)</title>
```

```
</head>
<body>
<form runat="server">
  <p><dorknozzle:DateTime id="ctlDateTime"
      DateTime="July 18th, 2003" runat="server" /></p>
  <asp:Button id="myButton" runat="server"
      Text="Click to set the control's property"
      OnClick="MyClick" />
</form>
</body>
</html>
```

C#   File: **UserControlsProperties/sample.aspx**

```
<%@ Register TagPrefix="dorknozzle" TagName="DateTime"
    Src="datetime.ascx" %>
<script runat="server" language="C#">
void MyClick(Object s, EventArgs e) {
  ctlDateTime.DateTime = DateTime.Now.ToString();
}
</script>
<html>
<head>
<title>User Controls (Properties)</title>
</head>
<body>
<form runat="server">
  <p><dorknozzle:DateTime id="ctlDateTime"
      DateTime="July 18th, 2003" runat="server" /></p>
  <asp:Button id="myButton" runat="server"
      Text="Click to set the control's property"
      OnClick="MyClick" />
</form>
</body>
</html>
```

Just as with previous examples, the `Register` directive is inserted into the page, and the `Src` property is set to the `datetime.ascx` user control. Take a look at the way the user control is inserted into the page. Because the `DateTime` variable is exposed as a property of the user control, we can set it when inserting the control within the page:

File: **UserControlsProperties/sample.aspx (excerpt)**

```
<dorknozzle:DateTime id="ctlDateTime" DateTime="July 18th, 2003"
    runat="server" />
```

Next, we add a `Button` control, the `OnClick` attribute of which is set to call the `MyClick()` method. The `MyClick()` method sets the exposed `DateTime` property of the user control equal to the current system date and time:

VB.NET   File: **UserControlsProperties/sample.aspx (excerpt)**

```
Sub MyClick(s As Object, e As EventArgs)
  ctlDateTime.DateTime = Now.ToString()
End Sub
```

C#   File: **UserControlsProperties/sample.aspx (excerpt)**

```
void MyClick(Object s, EventArgs e) {
  ctlDateTime.DateTime = DateTime.Now.ToString();
}
```

When the page loads, the default value that's set within the `DateTime` attribute is displayed on the page through the code render block in the user control. When the user clicks the `Button` control, the `Click` event is raised, `MyClick()` method is called, and the `DateTime` property is set to the current system date and time, similar to Figure 16.9.

Figure 16.9. The user control's property is set dynamically when the user clicks the `Button` control.

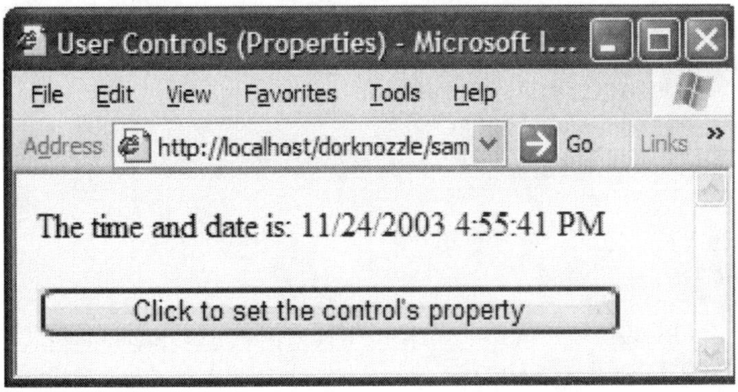

In the previous example, you saw how to read and set properties exposed by the user control within the ASP.NET page. Similar to the way properties are read and set, user controls also allow you to define methods that the containing ASP.NET page can execute, passing in any required parameters. The following user control demonstrates this:

VB.NET   File: **UserControlsMethods/DisplayName.ascx**

```
<script runat="server" language="VB">
Public Sub DisplayName(Name As String)
  Response.Write("Welcome: " & Name)
End Sub
</script>
```

C#   File: **UserControlsMethods/DisplayName.ascx**

```
<script runat="server" language="C#">
public void DisplayName(string Name) {
  Response.Write("Welcome: " + Name);
}
</script>
```

As you can see, the method is created as a `Public` method so that it's available to the containing page. It accepts a string value, and writes that value using the `Write()` method of the `Response` object. Next, we'll create the containing page as follows:

VB.NET   File: **UserControlsMethods/CollectName.aspx**

```
<%@ Register TagPrefix="dorknozzle" TagName="DisplayName"
    Src="DisplayName.ascx" %>
<html>
<head>
<title>User Controls (Methods)</title>
<script runat="server" language="VB">
Sub CollectName(s As Object, e As EventArgs)
  ctlDisplayName.DisplayName(txtName.Text)
End Sub
</script>
</head>
<body>
<form runat="server">
<p><asp:TextBox id="txtName" runat="server" />
  <asp:Button id="btnSubmit" runat="server" Text="Print Name"
      OnClick="CollectName" /></p>
<p><dorknozzle:DisplayName id="ctlDisplayName" runat="server"
    /></p>
</form>
</body>
</html>
```

C#   File: **UserControlsMethods/CollectName.aspx**

```
<%@ Register TagPrefix="dorknozzle" TagName="DisplayName"
    Src="DisplayName.ascx" %>
```

```
<html>
<head>
<title>User Controls (Methods)</title>
<script runat="server" language="C#">
void CollectName(Object s, EventArgs e) {
  ctlDisplayName.DisplayName(txtName.Text);
}
</script>
</head>
<body>
<form runat="server">
<p><asp:TextBox id="txtName" runat="server" />
  <asp:Button id="btnSubmit" runat="server" Text="Print Name"
      OnClick="CollectName" /></p>
<p><dorknozzle:DisplayName id="ctlDisplayName" runat="server"
    /></p>
</form>
</body>
</html>
```

In this case, a `TextBox` and `Button` control are added to the page. When the user clicks the `Button` control, the `Click` event is raised and the `CollectName()` method is called. The `CollectName()` method calls the `DisplayName()` method of the user control, passing in the `Text` value of the `TextBox` control. Notice that to call this method, we use the ID of our user control, followed by the dot operator (`.`), then the method name, along with any parameters required.

The user control collects the value and displays the result as in Figure 16.10.

Figure 16.10. The user control exposes a public method that can be executed within the ASP.NET page.

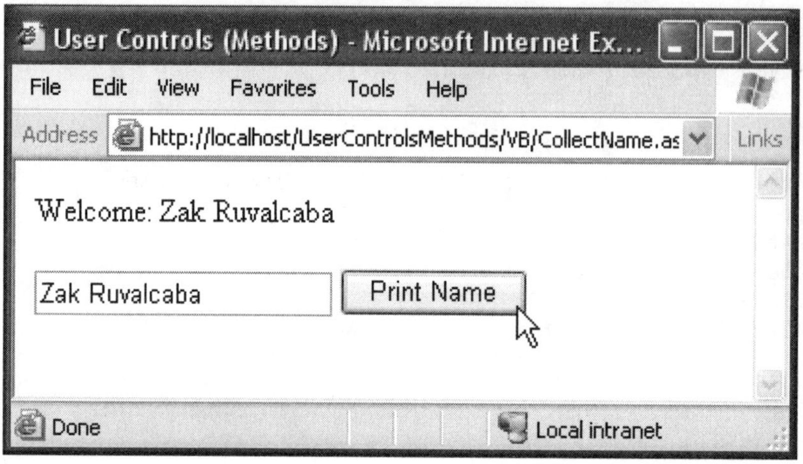

Loading User Controls Programmatically

On occasion, you may want to work with multiple controls within one ASP.NET page. For example, take the Admin Tools section of our intranet application. Obviously, we wouldn't want normal employees to access this section—only administrators should have access. To facilitate this, we can create two separate user controls: one that loads all items from the Navigation table in the database, and another that loads all items *except* for Admin Tools. Once both user controls are created, we can load the appropriate control in accordance with the login credentials.

The code for the adminstrators' menu is very similar to the navigation menu we created earlier in this chapter, except that we'll load the menu items into a DataSet using OleDbDataAdapter (see Chapter 10), instead of simply binding an OleDbDataReader to the DataList:

VB.NET   File: **UserControlsLoadingProgrammatically/navadmin.ascx**

```
<%@ Import Namespace="System.Data" %>
<%@ Import Namespace="System.Data.OleDb" %>
<script runat="server" language="VB">
Dim objConn As New OleDbConnection( _
    ConfigurationSettings.AppSettings("DSN"))
Dim objDA As OleDbDataAdapter
```

```
Dim objDS As New DataSet()

Sub Page_Load()
  If Not IsPostBack Then
    BindData()
  End If
End Sub

Sub BindData()
  objDA = New OleDbDataAdapter("SELECT * FROM NavigationMenu", _
    objConn)
  objDA.Fill(objDS, "NavMenu")

  dlNavMenu.DataSource = objDS
  dlNavMenu.DataBind()
End Sub
</script>
<asp:DataList id="dlNavMenu" runat="server" CellSpacing="2"
    CellPadding="2">
  <ItemStyle BackColor="#CCCCCC" BorderStyle="Solid"
      BorderWidth="1pt" BorderColor="#000000" />
  <ItemTemplate>
    <img src="Images/Book_Closed.gif" />
    <asp:HyperLink id="hlMenuItem"
        NavigateUrl='<%# Container.DataItem("Link") %>'
        Text='<%# Container.DataItem("Item") %>'
        runat="server" />
  </ItemTemplate>
</asp:DataList>
```

C#   File: **UserControlsLoadingProgrammatically/navadmin.ascx**

```
<%@ Import Namespace="System.Data" %>
<%@ Import Namespace="System.Data.OleDb" %>
<script runat="server" language="C#">
OleDbConnection objConn = new OleDbConnection(
    ConfigurationSettings.AppSettings["DSN"]);
OleDbDataAdapter objDA;
DataSet objDS = new DataSet();

void Page_Load() {
 if (!IsPostBack) {
  BindData();
 }
}

void BindData() {
```

```
  objDA = new OleDbDataAdapter("SELECT * FROM NavigationMenu",
    objConn);
  objDA.Fill(objDS, "NavMenu");

  dlNavMenu.DataSource = objDS;
  dlNavMenu.DataBind();
}
</script>
<asp:DataList id="dlNavMenu" runat="server" CellSpacing="2"
    CellPadding="2">
  <ItemStyle BackColor="#CCCCCC" BorderStyle="Solid"
      BorderWidth="1pt" BorderColor="#000000" />
  <ItemTemplate>
    <img src="Images/Book_Closed.gif" />
    <asp:HyperLink id="hlMenuItem"
        NavigateUrl='<%# DataBinder.Eval(Container.DataItem,
            "Link") %>'
        Text='<%# DataBinder.Eval(Container.DataItem,
            "Item") %>'
        runat="server" />
    <asp:HyperLink id="hlMenuItem"
        NavigateUrl='<%# Container.DataItem["Link"] %>'
        Text='<%# Container.DataItem["Item"] %>'
        runat="server" />
  </ItemTemplate>
</asp:DataList>
```

For the normal users' menu, we'll want to filter out the Admin Tools option. To accomplish this, we'll use the same code as above, though this time, we'll change the code to add a new DataView. We'll set the RowFilter property of that DataView to select all items except Admin Tools from the Navigation database table. Here's what the code declaration block looks like in this case:

VB.NET   File: **UserControlsLoadingProgrammatically/nav.ascx (excerpt)**

```
<script runat="server" language="VB">
Dim objConn As New OleDbConnection( _
    ConfigurationSettings.AppSettings("DSN"))
Dim objDA As OleDbDataAdapter
Dim objDS As New DataSet()
Dim objDV As DataView

Sub Page_Load()
  If Not IsPostBack Then
    BindData()
  End If
End Sub
```

```
Sub BindData()
  objDA = New OleDbDataAdapter("SELECT * FROM NavigationMenu", _
      objConn)
  objDA.Fill(objDS, "NavMenu")

  objDV = New DataView(objDS.Tables("NavMenu"))
  objDV.RowFilter = "Item <> 'Admin Tools'"

  dlNavMenu.DataSource = objDV
  dlNavMenu.DataBind()
End Sub
</script>
```

| C# | File: UserControlsLoadingProgrammatically/nav.ascx (excerpt) |

```
<script runat="server" language="C#">
OleDbConnection objConn = new OleDbConnection(
    ConfigurationSettings.AppSettings["DSN"]);
OleDbDataAdapter objDA;
DataSet objDS = new DataSet();
DataView objDV;

void Page_Load() {
  if (!IsPostBack) {
    BindData();
  }
}

void BindData() {
  objDA = new OleDbDataAdapter("SELECT * FROM NavigationMenu",
      objConn);
  objDA.Fill(objDS, "NavMenu");

  objDV = new DataView(objDS.Tables["NavMenu"]);
  objDV.RowFilter = "Item <> 'Admin Tools'";

  dlNavMenu.DataSource = objDV;
  dlNavMenu.DataBind();
}
</script>
```

Next, we'll create an ASP.NET page to demonstrate how to select and display one of the two controls programmatically. Here's the HTML interface code:

File: **UserControlsLoadingProgrammatically/sample.aspx**

```
<html>
<head>
<title>Navigation Control</title>
</head>
<body>
<asp:PlaceHolder id="plhNav" runat="server" />
</body>
</html>
```

We've used a PlaceHolder control here. If you're unsure about what this does, I don't blame you—we covered it way back in Chapter 4. In short, this control doesn't actually display anything on the page, but serves as a spot into which we can place one or more controls with our code.

The code that selects which control to load into the PlaceHolder can be added within a code declaration block inside the <head> element. Here it is:

VB.NET   File: **UserControlsLoadingProgrammatically/sample.aspx (excerpt)**

```
<script runat="Server" language="VB">
Sub Page_Load()
  Dim ctlControl As Control

  If (Request.QueryString("Login") = "Admin") Then
    ctlControl = LoadControl("navadmin.ascx")
  Else
    ctlControl = LoadControl("nav.ascx")
  End If

  plhNav.Controls.Add(ctlControl)
End Sub
</script>
```

C#   File: **UserControlsLoadingProgrammatically/sample.aspx (excerpt)**

```
<script runat="Server" language="C#">
void Page_Load() {
  Control ctlControl;

  if (Request.QueryString["Login"] == "Admin") {
    ctlControl = LoadControl("navadmin.ascx");
  } else {
    ctlControl = LoadControl("nav.ascx");
  }

  plhNav.Controls.Add(ctlControl);
```

```
}
</script>
```

When the page loads, we declare a variable that will hold an object of class `Control`, or any child class thereof (i.e. any ASP.NET control, including user controls):

VB.NET   File: **UserControlsLoadingProgrammatically/sample.aspx (excerpt)**

```
Dim ctlControl As Control
```

C#   File: **UserControlsLoadingProgrammatically/sample.aspx (excerpt)**

```
Control ctlControl;
```

Then, we use an `If` statement to check whether the admin links should be displayed. Now, in a practical application, we would check if the logged-in user is an administrator or not. This is the kind of information that we can store in a custom authentication ticket (see Chapter 14), and I encourage you to implement such a system as an exercise. For the purposes of this simple example however, we'll check for a variable called `Login` in the query string with a value of `Admin`.

If we determine that the administrator menu should be displayed, we call the `LoadControl()` method to load `navadmin.ascx`, and save it in our `ctlControl` variable:

VB.NET   File: **UserControlsLoadingProgrammatically/sample.aspx (excerpt)**

```
If (Request.QueryString("Login") = "Admin") Then
  ctlControl = LoadControl("navadmin.ascx")
```

C#   File: **UserControlsLoadingProgrammatically/sample.aspx (excerpt)**

```
if (Request.QueryString["Login"] == "Admin") {
  ctlControl = LoadControl("navadmin.ascx");
```

If the query string parameter doesn't exist, we call the `LoadControl()` method to load `nav.ascx`:

VB.NET   File: **UserControlsLoadingProgrammatically/sample.aspx (excerpt)**

```
Else
  ctlControl = LoadControl("nav.ascx")
End If
```

C#   File: **UserControlsLoadingProgrammatically/sample.aspx (excerpt)**

```
} else {
  ctlControl = LoadControl("nav.ascx");
}
```

Finally, we call the Add() method of the Controls collection for the PlaceHolder control, passing in our newly-loaded control:

VB.NET   File: **UserControlsLoadingProgrammatically/sample.aspx (excerpt)**

```
plhNav.Controls.Add(ctlControl)
```

C#   File: **UserControlsLoadingProgrammatically/sample.aspx (excerpt)**

```
plhNav.Controls.Add(ctlControl);
```

Save your work and test the results in the browser. Figure 16.11 shows how the page loads with the navigation menu without the Admin Tools link.

Figure 16.11. The Admin Tools link does not appear by default.

When we add ?Login=Admin to the query string, however, the Admin Tools link appears as shown in Figure 16.12.

Figure 16.12. The Admin Tools link appears with the variable in the query string.

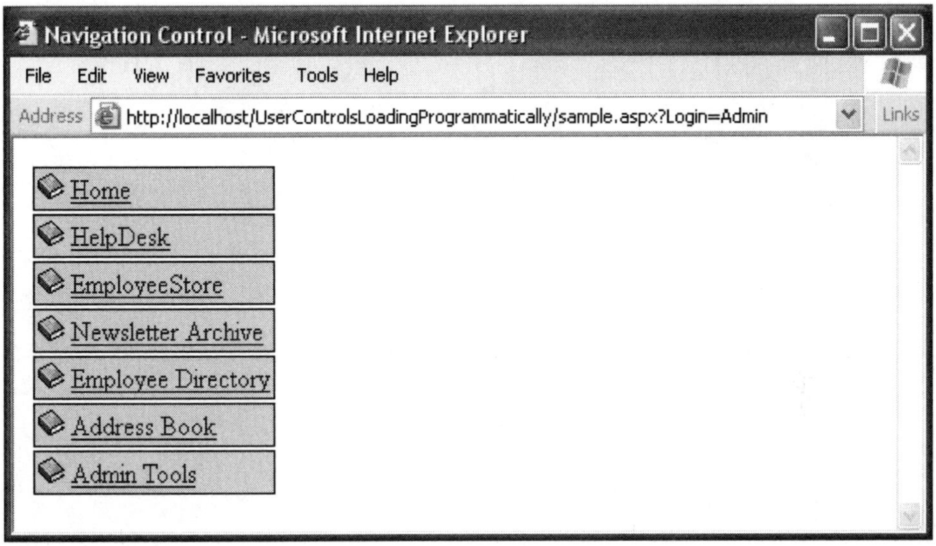

Summary

This chapter introduced you to important functionality in ASP.NET: rich controls and user controls. You learned how to use XML and XSLT with the Xml control, you learned how to add randomized banner advertisements using the AdRotator control, and you learned how to use the Calendar control to create an interactive appointment scheduler. The second part of the chapter introduced you to user controls. You learned how to create your own Web controls by adding properties and methods to a user control, then adding and using that control within an ASP.NET page.

17 XML Web Services

Looking back over the past few years, it's hard to imagine networked computers without the Internet. The Internet allows for communication between millions of computers running on hundreds of different networks. All those computers use different operating systems or different versions of operating systems; some use the Internet as an advertising medium, others use it as a sales vehicle; others, still, use the Internet as a platform for the distribution and/or integration of the services provided by various computers on these networks. Prior to the advent of Web Services, interoperability (the ability of software and hardware on different machines from different vendors to share data) and integration was cumbersome and restricted by the differences between different platforms.

Web Services are a new technology that solves the problem that has plagued distributed computing for years: interoperability. In a nutshell, Web Services provide a solution that is language independent, platform agnostic, and not tied to any particular company. Basically, all you need is a network that allows you to transmit HTTP requests—which is almost all of them—and you're good to go. Throughout this chapter, you'll be introduced to a library of new terms, including CORBA, DCOM, SOAP, XML, HTTP, UDDI, and WSDL, each of which plays its own part in the world of Web Services. And, while we cannot begin to cover all there is to know on the subject, we can gain an understanding of how Web Services aim to solve the dilemma that is information exchange on the Internet. Let's get started!

Introduction to XML Web Services

Web Services are a new type of Web application. They are self-contained, modular programs that can be published, found, and invoked via the Web. Each Web Service serves a specific function, which might range from validating a credit card to updating hotel reservations. After a Web Service is deployed, users, applications, and other Web Services can invoke the methods that are exposed by that Web Service. Web Services are currently being used in Microsoft's My Services and Passport initiatives. The Passport authentication service[1], for example, is a self-contained Web Service that exposes an authentication scheme allowing other developers and applications to validate a user's credentials from one location. What this means is that, if every developer used the Passport authentication service, you'd never have to program your own login page again. I know—it seems like *that* eventuality is a long way off! Nevertheless, although the Passport initiative has yet to gain the momentum that Microsoft hoped it would achieve, companies such as eBay have already adopted Passport as one of their authentication methods.

Microsoft has a database full of Passport accounts, typically in the form of Hotmail or MSN accounts. When you sign on to eBay using your Passport account, your details are validated against a database of users through the Passport Web Service. Once those details have been validated, eBay assumes that you are who you say you are, and grants you access to the site. That said, Web Services don't have to be as simple as validating a user.

Web Services are currently in place in the travel and financial industries, as well as government, education, and other sectors. Wherever there's a need for direct communication between applications in an interoperable way, there is a need for Web Services. In fact, as you'll see later in this chapter, Google even provides a Web Service that you can use within your applications. Using the Google Search Service, you can create within your Web application a search page that will utilize the Google search engine.

Before we get ahead of ourselves, however, let's go over one more example that's a bit closer to home. Most experienced Internet users have heard of PayPal[2]—in fact, we used PayPal in Chapter 12. Well, imagine a Web Service made available by PayPal to allow online shopping sites to notify them of purchases made by users (this is technically known as **consuming** a Web Service). In order to shop

[1] http://www.passport.net/
[2] http://www.paypal.com/

at any one of these sites, I would only need to enter my credit card information, personal details, and shipping preferences once. PayPal's Web Service would collect the items I added to my shopping cart, no matter what online store I happened to be visiting.

In a nutshell, as the user, I could add items from all those stores to my cart, and, when I was ready to check out, I'd go to PayPal and click Pay. I would never have to enter credit card information, a shipping method, or even my delivery address, because PayPal would already have saved that information. The various online stores will get paid according to the products I placed into my cart. Even better, they never had to deal with shopping carts, credit card authorizations, or other merchant headaches. Take a look at Figure 17.1, which shows clearly the model outlined above.

Figure 17.1. PayPal exposes a Web Service that is consumed by its business partners.

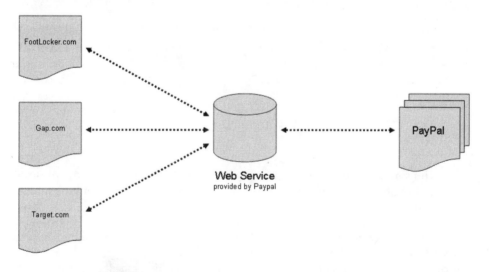

How cool is that? From PayPal's standpoint, this is a definite sell! The business partners never have to create a shopping cart, they never have to authorize credit cards, they don't even have to worry about asking users how they want the items shipped. The Web Service handles all this information for them. Basically, all Gap.com, Target.com, and FootLocker.com ever have to do is ship the product.

There is a lingering problem, though: the user still has to register and log into every site. Imagine all three online stores also use the Passport service to allow their users to login. The user visits the online store, the user logs in through Passport, and is validated. If the user–entered credentials match those stored in the Passport database, the customer can begin shopping. Figure 17.2 illustrates this point.

Figure 17.2. Gap.com, Target.com, and FootLocker.com could use the PayPal Web Service and the Passport Web Service as a validation mechanism.

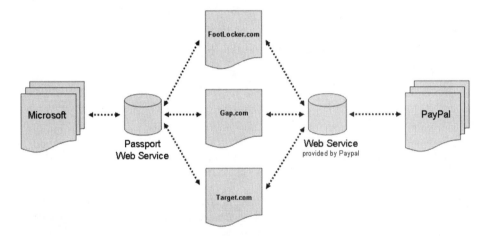

That's the simplicity that Web Services can bring, Web Services allow pieces of functionality offered by different companies to work together, exchanging inform- ation seamlessly.

OK, enough discussion… I have a feeling that, by now, you have a pretty good idea as to what Web Services are, and the potential they offer. In the next few sections, we'll actually begin building a Web Service, but first, let's get under the hood and discuss the inner workings of Web Services, including a brief history of distributed computing.

Understanding Web Service Standards

Web Services let business applications communicate with other business applications. It all sounds great, right? In fact, the concept has been around for quite some time, in a number of forms. Here are just a few:

❑ RPC (Remote Procedure Call) is a client/server infrastructure that increases the interoperability, portability, and flexibility of a large-scale enterprise application by allowing it to be spread, or distributed, over multiple servers. This is essentially what Web Services aim to do; however, what lets RPC down is that there is no single standard for implementation, and different features may be offered by individual RPC implementations. This hurdle is compounded by the complexity of RPC and the proprietary and unique nature of RPC implementations, which make training essential even for the experienced programmer.

❑ CORBA (Common Object Request Broker Architecture) is an architecture and specification for creating, distributing, and managing distributed program objects in a network, and has been available for quite some time. It allows programs at different locations that have been developed by different organizations to communicate in a network through an "interface broker." Typically, CORBA works only in UNIX environments.

❑ DCOM (Distributed Component Object Model), which is similar to CORBA, is a set of Microsoft concepts and program interfaces through which client program objects can request services from server program objects on other computers in the network. DCOM is based on COM, which provides a set of interfaces that allow clients and servers to communicate within the same computer. While there are many similarities between CORBA and DCOM, there are significant differences between them, which makes it difficult for them to interoperate. CORBA and DCOM are great for closely monitored networks, but not ideal when applications must span networks or even platforms. Also, CORBA and DCOM are meant for applications running on the same network; they are not designed for the Internet.

Web Services represent the next level in Internet scalability. They pick up where CORBA and DCOM failed. How? Well, Web Services are platform independent and language agnostic. While CORBA is UNIX-based, and DCOM is Windows-based, Web Services rely on open standards for communication—standards with which you may already be familiar, such as HTTP, XML, SOAP, WSDL, and UDDI:

XML   XML is the key to Web Services. As you'll see throughout this chapter, SOAP, WSDL, and UDDI are all based on XML. While CORBA and DCOM are based on complex data and request formats, Web Services are based on XML and XML Schema specifications. XML is simple, flexible, readable, and has been widely adopted by many organizations already.

HTTP   The Hypertext Transfer Protocol, or HTTP, is the mechanism allowing us to access information on the Web.

SOAP   The Simple Object Access Protocol is a standard protocol used to transmit XML data over a network. XML messages are wrapped within a SOAP envelope and transmitted via HTTP in the form of SOAP requests and SOAP responses.

As you can see in Figure 17.3, a consumer communicates with the Web Service provider. The formatted XML messages are wrapped within SOAP envelopes and transmitted via HTTP.

Figure 17.3. XML messages are wrapped within SOAP envelopes and transmitted via HTTP.

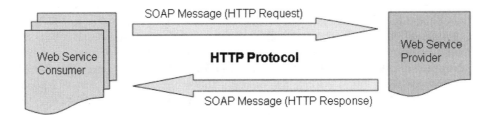

OK, everything so far sounds great, but what does a Web Service do for us that is so useful? Any Web Service will provide one or more **Web Methods** that our programs can call. Just as normal methods in programming code provide functionality to perform useful tasks, Web Methods provide the means to access the functionality exposed by Web Services. But how do we know what Web Methods are provided by another company's Web Services? Clearly, I could phone them up and ask them, but there is a better way.

WSDL (Web Services Definition Language) provides an automated means for Web Service providers to describe how and what their Web Services do, where they reside, and how others may invoke them. When you create a Web Service using ASP.NET (which we'll do in the next section) a WSDL document is automatically generated for you, so that those who want to use your Web service can get the information they need. To better understand WSDL, and how it fits in to the model illustrated in Figure 17.3, take a look at the illustration in Figure 17.4.

Figure 17.4. WSDL describes what the Web Service can do, where it resides, and how it can be invoked.

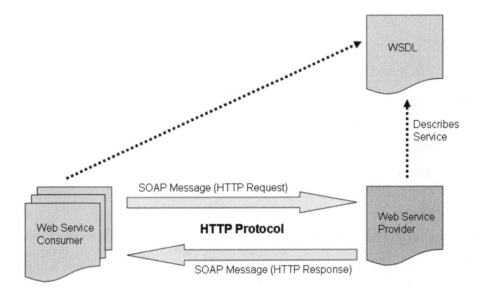

Now you know about some of the open standards that make up Web Services, how Web Services are consumed (at least conceptually), and how they are described. But once we know that Web Services are what we need, how do we find specific services that perform the functions we require? The answer again is simple, and can be found in UDDI (Universal Description, Discovery, and Integration). UDDI can be thought of as a telephone directory for Web Services, providing a mechanism for developers to find the Web Services they need, and even for programs to find required Web Services on the fly! Figure 17.5 adds to our previous illustration and completes the "ideal" model for Web Service discovery, description, and integration.

Figure 17.5. UDDI provides an interface through which an application can locate and use other Web Services.

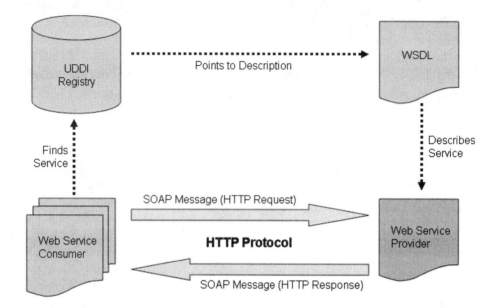

As the illustration above shows, the Web Service is used by a "consumer" (user or application). The consumer can search for a particular Web Service through a UDDI registry. Once the Web Service has been found, the consumer accesses its WSDL document, or contract, which defines the makeup of the Web Service, including all its Web Methods. Finally, the consumer interacts with the Web Service by making HTTP requests to it. Again, the above illustration is the ideal model for Web Services. It's important to note that UDDI, although an important part of the Web Service model, has not been widely adopted as of yet.

Take a look at Table 17.1, which compares the characteristics of CORBA, DCOM, and Web Services:

Table 17.1. Web Service use of Existing Open Standards

Characteristic	CORBA	DCOM	Web Services
Method Calling	Internet InterORB Protocol	Distributed Computing Environment RPC	HTTP
Encoding	Common Data Representation	Network Data Representation	XML
Interface Description	Interface Definition Language	Interface Definition Language	WSDL
Discovery	Naming and Trading Service	System Registry	UDDI
Firewall Friendly	No	No	Yes
Cross Platform	Partly	No	Yes

As you can see from the table above, Web Services virtually eliminate old and convoluted standards. Unfortunately, we cannot begin to cover all the information contained in the above table—such as encoding, interface description, and discovery—however, you can definitely begin to see a distinct pattern. Web Services rely on open standards and existing protocols like HTTP and XML.

Although the process seems relatively complex, in reality, it's not. In fact, from the developer's standpoint it's fairly straightforward and involves little interaction with the above concepts. To prove the point, let's walk through the process of building a simple Web Service together.

A Simple Calculator Web Service

By the end of this section you should understand that Web Services are not all that complex, and, in fact, can be rather fun to develop and use. As you have some familiarity with what Web Services do and how they are composed, let's build a simple Web Service that adds two numbers together and returns the result to the user. First, create a new folder within C:\Inetpub\wwwroot called Calculate. Next, turn that folder into an application within IIS. Create a new file called calculate.asmx within the directory (.asmx is the extension given to ASP.NET Web Service pages). Next, add the following code:

```
VB.NET                                              File: Calculate/calculate.asmx
<%@ WebService language="VB" class="CalcService" %>
Imports System.Web.Services
Public Class CalcService
  <WebMethod()> _
  Public Function Calculate(x As Integer, y As Integer) As Integer
    Return x + y
  End Function
End Class
```

```
C#                                                  File: Calculate/calculate.asmx
<%@ WebService language="C#" class="CalcService" %>
using System.Web.Services;
public class CalcService {
  [WebMethod]
  public int Calculate(int x, int y) {
    return x + y;
  }
}
```

Let's break down the code. Initially, we add the WebService directive to the top of the page:

```
VB.NET                                      File: Calculate/calculate.asmx (excerpt)
<%@ WebService language="VB" class="CalcService" %>
```

```
C#                                          File: Calculate/calculate.asmx (excerpt)
<%@ WebService language="C#" class="CalcService" %>
```

You'll notice that we set the class attribute equal to the class we are about to create. Next, we import the System.Web.Services namespace:

```
VB.NET                                      File: Calculate/calculate.asmx (excerpt)
Imports System.Web.Services
```

```
C#                                          File: Calculate/calculate.asmx (excerpt)
using System.Web.Services;
```

Now, we define a new public class, and give it a descriptive name such as CalcService:

VB.NET   File: **Calculate/calculate.asmx (excerpt)**

```
Public Class CalcService

  ...
End Class
```

C#   File: **Calculate/calculate.asmx (excerpt)**

```
public class CalcService {

  ...
}
```

This class is the heart of the Web Service. We create a new method inside it called Calculate(), tagging it as a Web Method with the special <WebMethod()>/[WebMethod] attribute:

VB.NET   File: **Calculate/calculate.asmx (excerpt)**

```
<WebMethod()> _
Public Function Calculate(x As Integer, y As Integer) As Integer
  Return x + y
End Function
```

C#   File: **Calculate/calculate.asmx (excerpt)**

```
[WebMethod]
public int Calculate(int x, int y) {
  return x + y;
}
```

The method accepts two integer arguments (x and y), performs a simple addition, and returns the result as an integer to the consumer.

With the Web Service now created, let's test the result. In your browser, navigate to http://localhost/Calculate/calculate.asmx. The service screen shows you a list of all available Web Methods, similar to Figure 17.6.

Figure 17.6. The service contains the `Calculate()` method.

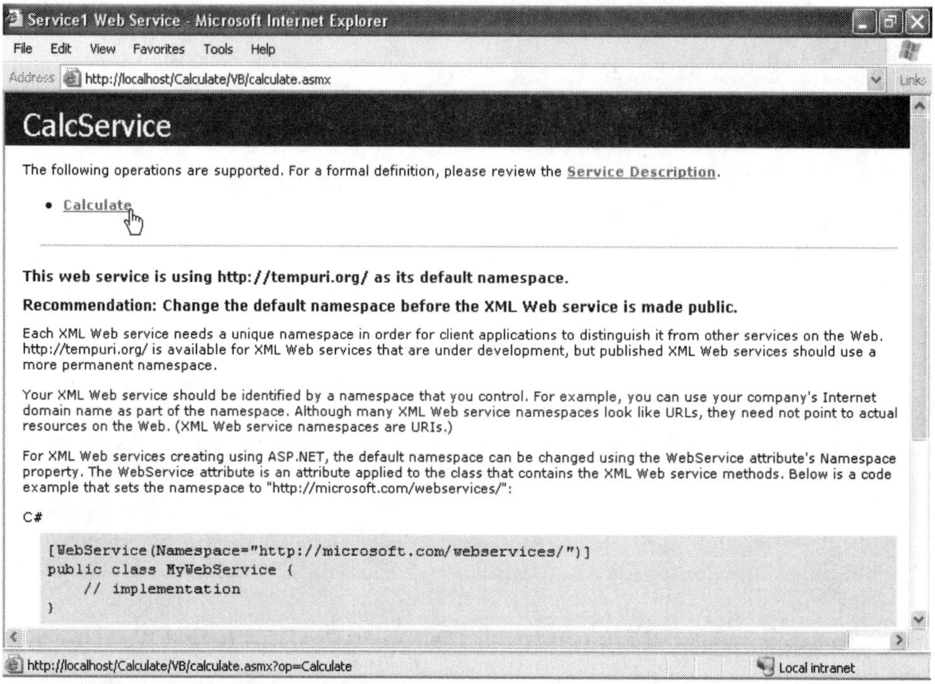

Because we've only created one Web Method, the Web Service browser tool (the page that is displayed) simply displays Calculate. Obviously you didn't create most of the page that you're seeing—it's generated by ASP.NET so that we (and our customers) can test our Web Services easily. Now, select the Calculate link. You will be redirected to a new screen that will allow you to input the x and y arguments that the Web Method requires. Once you've entered the necessary values, click the Invoke button, as shown in Figure 17.7.

Figure 17.7. Click the Invoke button to invoke the function.

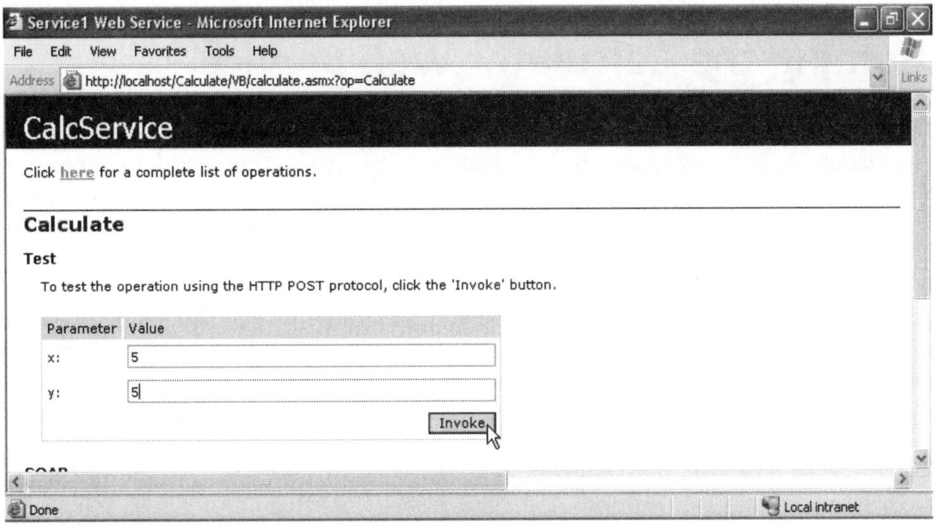

The result of the calculation is returned in XML format, similar to Figure 17.8.

Figure 17.8. The result of the calculation is shown in XML format.

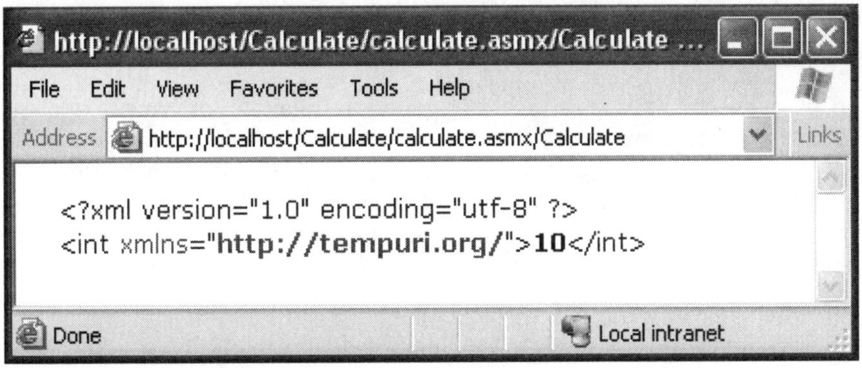

Requests and responses are generated as SOAP request and response messages. Since SOAP is an XML document format, the result of the Web Service request will always be an XML document. With the help of the automatically generated request page, we've made a request to the Web Service. We passed in two values, and clicked the Invoke button. As a result, the request page made a SOAP request to the Web Service on our behalf. The Web Service then performed the necessary calculation, and returned the response in XML format.

Consuming the Calculator Web Service

As cool as the Web Service browser tool is, we wouldn't want to present that to our users. Web Services are designed for use by applications, so let's create an application that uses the service in some meaningful way. The process involved is slightly more complex, but it's nothing you can't handle.

We have to start out by generating what's called a **proxy class**. The proxy class sits in between our application and the Web Service we want to consume. It offers the same methods as the Web Service, automatically translating any call to one of those methods into a SOAP request, sending that request to the Web Service, and then translating the XML response back into a simple return value.

Once the proxy class file has been created, we must compile it to an **assembly** in order to use it in one or more ASP.NET pages. But what exactly is an assembly?

.NET assemblies are simply compiled code files, which bear a `.dll` filename extension. Once we have compiled our code into a `.dll` assembly, we must put it in a folder called `Bin` within the application's main directory. Any and all ASP.NET pages in the application will then be able to use the classes contained within the assembly. Let's demonstrate this process by walking through steps involved in creating an assembly.

We start by using the `wsdl.exe` utility to generate the code for our proxy class. The `wsdl.exe` utility comes with the .NET Framework SDK, and is located in the `C:\Program Files\Microsoft.NET\SDK\version\Bin` directory. Next, we compile the proxy into an assembly, using either the VB.NET or C# compiler (`vbc.exe` or `csc.exe`), both of which are located within `Microsoft.NET\Framework\version` subdirectory of your Windows directory (usually `C:\WINDOWS` or `C:\WINNT`).

As we have to use both of these utilities from the command line, it'll be easier if you adjust the `Path` environment variable for your computer so that you don't have manually to switch back and forth between these directories. To modify the Path for your computer in Windows 2000 or later, right-click the My Computer icon on your desktop or on the Start menu and select Properties, choose the Advanced tab, and click the Environment Variables button. Within the System Variables pane, scroll down until you find `Path`, select it, and click Edit. The Edit System Variable dialog will appear. Now, add the path to `wsdl.exe` on your computer to the end of the current variable value as follows, where *version* is likely to be v1.1 as of this writing:

```
C:\Program Files\Microsoft.NET\SDK\version\Bin;
```

Next, add the path to the compilers to the variable value:

```
;C:\WINDOWS\Microsoft.NET\Framework\version;
```

Note that your Windows directory may be called WINNT, and the *version* in this second path is likely to differ from the first (v1.1.4322 is current as of this writing). Make sure to verify the path on your machine in Explorer first.

Once you're finished, click OK to close the Edit System Variable dialog. Click OK to close the Environment Variables window, and click OK once more, to close the System Properties window.

You can now begin the process of generating the proxy class! Follow these steps:

1. Select Start, Run..., type **cmd** and click OK. The Command Prompt window will open[1].

2. Before you do anything, move to the root directory of C: by typing this command (only type the part shown in bold):

```
cd \
```

3. Now, use the wsdl.exe program to generate the code for your proxy class. If you want to generate VB.NET code, type this command:

```
wsdl /l:vb http://localhost/Calculate/calculate.asmx?WSDL
```

To create the C# version of the code, use this command instead:

```
wsdl /l:cs http://localhost/Calculate/calculate.asmx?WSDL
```

As you can see, we type wsdl to execute the utility, and follow it with the language switch (/l) and the location of the Web Service's WSDL description. In our case, we simply add ?WSDL to the end of our Web Service's URL to have ASP.NET create the WSDL for us. When this is complete, the

---

[1] If you have difficulty understanding how to use the Command Prompt, you can find a more complete description in the SitePoint article entitled *Kev's Command Prompt Cheat Sheet* at http://www.sitepoint.com/article/command-prompt-cheat-sheet.

command window will display the result, alerting you that the proxy was written to the current directory (C:\).

4. We're not done yet! Next, we'll compile the proxy into an assembly that our application can use by typing the following command for the VB.NET version:

```
vbc /t:library /r:System.dll,System.Web.Services.dll,System.Xml.dll CalcService.vb
```

For the C# version, you need to use the C# compiler instead:

```
csc /t:library /r:System.dll,System.Web.Services.dll,System.Xml.dll CalcService.cs
```

When you're finished, CalcService.dll will reside in the current directory, C:\. Before we move forward, let's review exactly what's happening here. Initially, we generated the source code file for our proxy class using the wsdl.exe utility. Next, we compiled that code file into a usable assembly using either the VB or C# compiler. Remember, we must compile classes into assemblies before our ASP.NET applications can use them. The .vb or .cs code file does us little good alone, but, when it's in the form of a .dll, our application can use it.

Next, create a new folder called bin in your Web application directory (C:\Inetpub\wwwroot\Calculate), and move the compiled assembly (CalcService.dll) into that folder. Also, move the proxy source code into the root of the application directory just in case you need it later.

Now that you have created the assembly, and you've placed it within your application's bin folder, you're ready to create an ASP.NET page that will access the service. Start by adding the following code into a new ASP.NET page:

File: **Calculate/calculate.aspx**

```
<html>
<head>
<title>Calculate Web Service</title>
</head>
<body>
<form runat="server">
<p><asp:TextBox id="txtX" runat="server" /><br />
  <asp:TextBox id="txtY" runat="server" /></p>
<p><asp:Button id="btnSubmit" runat="server" Text="Calculate"
    OnClick="Calculate" /></p>
<p><asp:Label id="lblResult" runat="server" /></p>
</form>
```

```
</body>
</html>
```

As you can see, the interface is fairly simple. It uses two `TextBox` controls that allow the user to input the x and y values. Second, we add a `Button` control to call the method that handles the interaction with the Web Service. Finally, we add a `Label` control, so that we have somewhere to display the result of the calculation.

Now, we'll need to create the code that uses the Web Service to perform the calculation when the `Button` is clicked:

VB.NET   File: `Calculate/calculate.aspx (excerpt)`

```
<script runat="server" language="VB">
Sub Calculate(s As Object, e As EventArgs)
  Dim objService As New CalcService()
  lblResult.Text = objService.Calculate(txtX.Text, txtY.Text)
End Sub
</script>
```

C#   File: `Calculate/calculate.aspx (excerpt)`

```
<script runat="server" language="C#">
void Calculate(Object s, EventArgs e) {
  CalcService objService = new CalcService();
  lblResult.Text = Convert.ToString(objService.Calculate(
      Convert.ToInt32(txtX.Text), Convert.ToInt32(txtY.Text)));
}
</script>
```

This code is relatively straightforward. We first create a new instance of the `CalcService` proxy class, which is provided by the assembly we compiled above. Next, we set the `Text` property of the `Label` control equal to the value returned by the `Calculate()` method, when we call it with the numbers entered into the two text fields. Save your work and test the result in the browser. Type a value for x and a value for y, and click the Calculate `Button` control. The result is shown in Figure 17.9.

Figure 17.9. Set values for x and y and invoke the method by pressing the Calculate button.

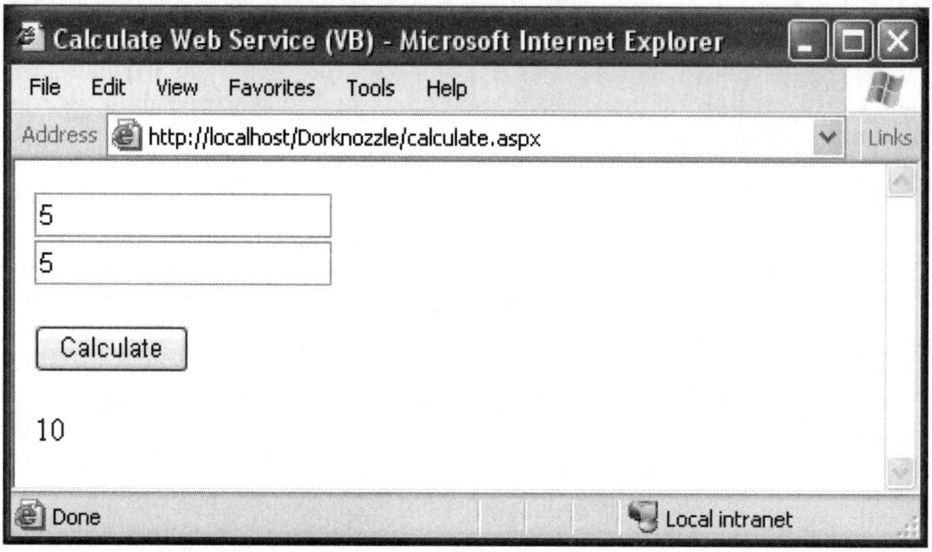

Notice that the application functions similarly to that which we used to test the .asmx file earlier in the chapter, though now we've created our own interface to consume the service.

Now, although both the ASP.NET page and the Web Service are running on the same server at this point, there is nothing about the system that requires that to be the case. You could host the calculate.asmx file on another server, generate a proxy class using its new URL, and then run the ASP.NET page that uses it on your own server. That's the magic of Web Services—the functionality provided by the service can be accessed transparently by an application running on a completely different machine.

Imagine how complex this can get—you could create Web Services to handle all sorts of functions. In fact, already available are hundreds of Web Services that allow you to perform tasks such as checking the weather, viewing stock tickers, and so on. In the next example, you'll learn a little more about WSDL, and how you can use third party Web Services to create applications—specifically, a Google Search application.

Using WSDL to Consume Third-Party Web Services

As you can see, building a simple Web Service is not complicated. The toughest part is generating the proxy class and the assembly at the command prompt. In this section, we'll explore further the process of programming with Web Service components using WSDL.

You've seen how you can create your own Web Service to expose whatever type of method you may need over the Internet, but how exactly would you use someone else's Web Services? The answer lies in WSDL, the XML-based description language for Web Services. A WSDL contract for a Web Service contains the technical information that applications need in order to communicate with the Web Service using SOAP, such as its location (as a URI) and the methods it exposes. As we've seen, ASP.NET generates the WSDL file for a Web Service automatically, and we can access it simply by appending ?WSDL to the end of the .asmx URL.

To demonstrate this, reopen the Calculate service within the built-in service explorer, by typing its URL (http://localhost/calculate/calculate.asmx) in the browser window. You'll notice a link just above the function that allows you to view the service description. This link redirects you to the WSDL contract associated with that particular Web Service, as shown in Figure 17.10.

Figure 17.10. WSDL describes the methods and properties exposed by the Web Service.

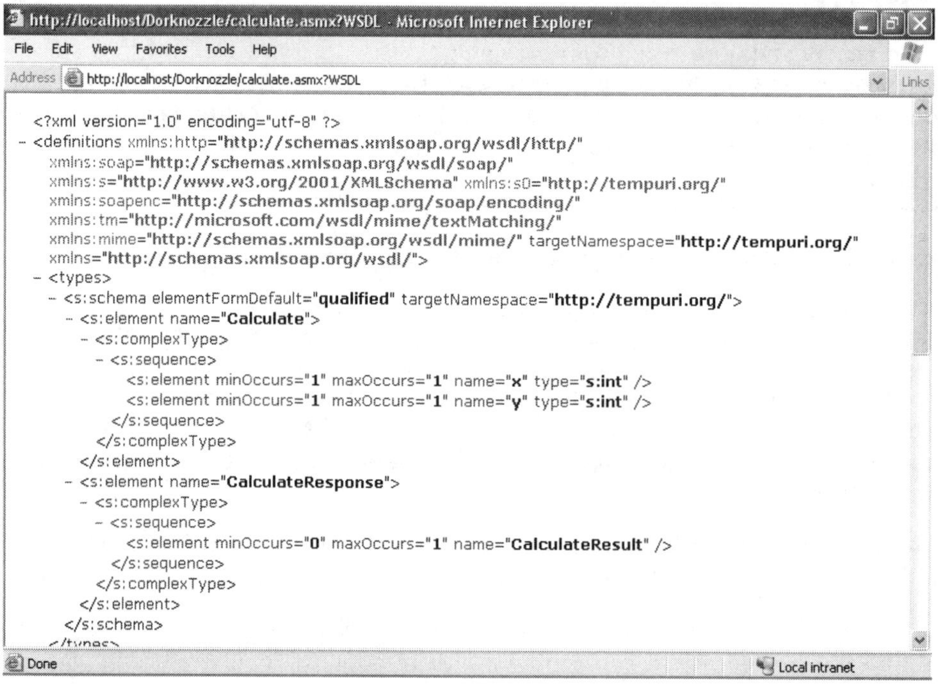

```
http://localhost/Dorknozzle/calculate.asmx?WSDL - Microsoft Internet Explorer

File   Edit   View   Favorites   Tools   Help

Address    http://localhost/Dorknozzle/calculate.asmx?WSDL                               Links

    <?xml version="1.0" encoding="utf-8" ?>
  - <definitions xmlns:http="http://schemas.xmlsoap.org/wsdl/http/"
      xmlns:soap="http://schemas.xmlsoap.org/wsdl/soap/"
      xmlns:s="http://www.w3.org/2001/XMLSchema" xmlns:s0="http://tempuri.org/"
      xmlns:soapenc="http://schemas.xmlsoap.org/soap/encoding/"
      xmlns:tm="http://microsoft.com/wsdl/mime/textMatching/"
      xmlns:mime="http://schemas.xmlsoap.org/wsdl/mime/" targetNamespace="http://tempuri.org/"
      xmlns="http://schemas.xmlsoap.org/wsdl/">
    - <types>
      - <s:schema elementFormDefault="qualified" targetNamespace="http://tempuri.org/">
        - <s:element name="Calculate">
          - <s:complexType>
            - <s:sequence>
                <s:element minOccurs="1" maxOccurs="1" name="x" type="s:int" />
                <s:element minOccurs="1" maxOccurs="1" name="y" type="s:int" />
              </s:sequence>
            </s:complexType>
          </s:element>
        - <s:element name="CalculateResponse">
          - <s:complexType>
            - <s:sequence>
                <s:element minOccurs="0" maxOccurs="1" name="CalculateResult" />
              </s:sequence>
            </s:complexType>
          </s:element>
        </s:schema>
      </types>

Done                                                              Local intranet
```

But in practical applications you may not always have the luxury of working with a Web Service that you have written yourself. Indeed, the true power of Web Services is best demonstrated by using someone *else's* Service. Thanks to all the work that has gone into standardizing Web Services, however, the process is not all that different.

Finding the Service and Creating the Assembly

The Google Search Service is a Web Service that's exposed by Google at no cost, in order for developers to create a customizable search application using Google's search functionality. Throughout this section, we'll look at building such an application by following the steps we discussed at the start of this chapter. First, we must search for the service through a UDDI directory, which provides you with a list of Web Services that you can use. Some directories are free; others require either a subscription or a one-time fee. There are a few well-known directories, but the one I like to use is XMethods[6]. Go to their site and click View Full List at the top of the Recent Listings section, and find the Google Search API link. Click the link, and, at the top of the page that appears, you'll see a link to the WSDL file, followed by various other information relating to the service. We need the WSDL link when we use the `wsdl.exe` utility to create a proxy class for consuming Google's Web Service. Open the command prompt and type in one of these commands to generate the code for a new proxy class (either in VB.NET or in C#):

```
wsdl /l:vb http://api.google.com/GoogleSearch.wsdl
```

```
wsdl /l:cs http://api.google.com/GoogleSearch.wsdl
```

If everything goes smoothly, the proxy class code file will be created within the current directory. You may get a couple of 'Schema Validation Warnings' during this process, but they can safely be ignored. Now, type one of these commands to compile the proxy into an assembly:

```
vbc /t:library /r:System.dll,System.Web.Services.dll,System.Xml.dl
l GoogleSearchService.vb
```

```
csc /t:library /r:System.dll,System.Web.Services.dll,System.Xml.dl
l GoogleSearchService.cs
```

When you're finished, the `GoogleSearchService.dll` assembly will appear within the current directory. Now that you've created the new assembly, create a new folder within `C:\Inetpub\wwwroot` called `GoogleSearch`. Within the `GoogleSearch` folder, create a `bin` folder and place the assembly within it. Don't forget to create an application out of the `GoogleSearch` directory within the IIS control panel, as this is required in order for the assembly located within the `bin` folder to work.

Registering to Use the Google Search Service

Now, what? The assembly has been created, but we don't have a clue as to how to use it. For starters, visit http://www.google.com/apis/. There, you will find a complete reference for the methods and properties that the Web Service exposes, and the steps you need to go through to create your own application using Google Web Services. You won't need to complete the first step—downloading the developer's kit—as you've already created the proxy class and assembly, which is

---

[6] http://www.xmethods.net/

essentially what you get with the developer's kit. The second step, however, you *will* need to complete.

Part of the application requires that you submit a key. Because this service is free, its functionality is limited to 1,000 searches per day per developer. A license key is created for each developer who's interested in using the service. Click the Create Account link, enter your email address and a password, and click the button to create your account. Within a few seconds, you should receive an email containing your license key. Keep that email handy—you'll need it in the next section.

To perform a search using the Google Search Web Service, you must create an instance of the `GoogleSearchService` proxy class, and then call its `doGoogleSearch()` method. This method takes the following arguments:

key	This is the key that you just obtained. Google uses it for authentication and logging.
q	This is the search string.
start	This refers to the zero-based index of the first desired result.
maxResults	This identifies the number of results desired per query. The maximum value per query is ten.
filter	This parameter activates or deactivates automatic results filtering, which hides very similar results and results that all come from the same Web host.
restrict	This parameter restricts the search to a subset of the Google Web index, such as a country like "Mexico," or a topic like "Microsoft."
safeSearch	This identifies a Boolean value that enables filtering of adult content in the search results.
lr	You can use Language Restrictions to restrict the search to documents within one or more languages.

The method returns the search response in the form of a `GoogleSearchResult` object, which contains the following properties:

estimatedTotalResultsCount	This is an integer value that represents the estimated total number of results that exist for the query.
resultElements	This is a collection that contains the actual list of search results.
searchQuery	This is a string value that represents the value of q in the search request.
startIndex	This indicates the index (1-based) of the first search result in resultElements.
endIndex	This indicates the index (1-based) of the last search result in resultElements.
summary	This is a string value representing the summary of the searched item.
URL	This parameter contains the URL of the search result, returned as a string, with an absolute URL path.
title	This identifies the title of the search result, returned as HTML.
cachedSize	This is a string value indicating that a cached version of the URL is available; its size is indicated in kilobytes (kB).
directoryTitle	The title that appears in Google's directory appears here as a string.

That's the nuts and bolts of it! Let's move on to building an application that uses the Google Search Web Service.

Consuming the Google Search Service

Let's build the application that will actually consume the Google Search Web Service. As you can see from Figure 17.11, our application will contain a simple TextBox control, a Button control, and a Label control to display the results of the search query.

Figure 17.11. Our application will allow users to search on a keyword of their choice.

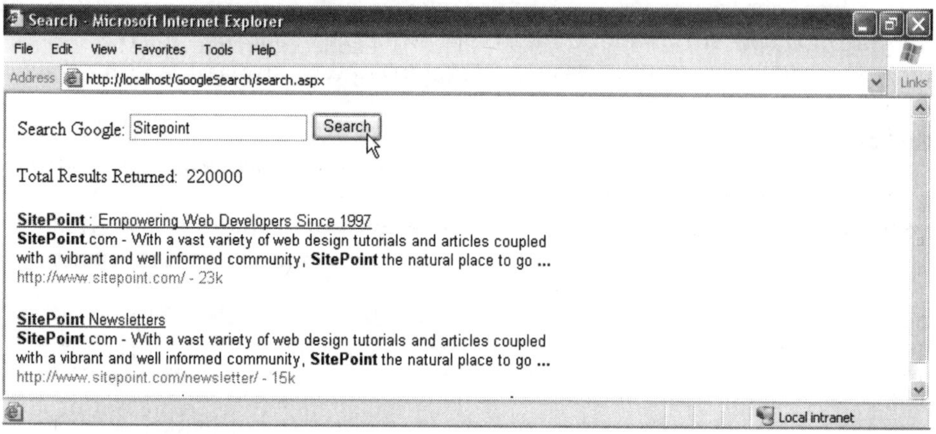

When the user enters a keyword and clicks the Search button, our application will call one of the Web Methods exposed by the Google Search Web Service, passing in the keyword, and retrieving the results in the form of an array. Before we get ahead of ourselves, let's define the interface for the application. Begin by creating a new ASP.NET page called `search.aspx`, complete with the following HTML:

File: **GoogleSearch/search.aspx**

```
<html>
<head>
<title>Google Search</title>
</head>
<body>

</body>
</html>
```

Next, we'll want to define the interface, beginning with the search form. Add all the necessary controls inside the `<body>` tag, including a `TextBox` control to allow users to enter their search queries, and a `Button` control for them to submit their queries:

File: **GoogleSearch/search.aspx (excerpt)**

```
<form runat="server">
<p>Search Google: <asp:TextBox id="searchText" runat="server" />
```

```
<asp:Button id="searchButton" runat="server" Text="Search"
    OnClick="Search" /></p>
```

Next, add a `Panel` control so that we can show or hide the results returned from our search. Within that `Panel` control, add two `Label` controls, one to display a message indicating the total results, and the second to display the result count to the user:

File: **GoogleSearch/search.aspx** (excerpt)

```
<asp:Panel id="headerPanel" runat="server">
  <p><asp:Label id="lblResults" runat="server"
      Text="Total Results Returned:" />
    <asp:Label id="lblTotalResults" runat="server" /></p>
```

Now, add the control that we'll use to display the list of results. We could use one of the data controls for this (e.g. a `DataList`), but to keep things simple we'll stick with a `Label` for now:

File: **GoogleSearch/search.aspx** (excerpt)

```
  <p><asp:Label id="resultList" runat="server" /></p>
```

Next, add two `LinkButton` controls that will represent the Previous and Next buttons for the page sets in our search results:

File: **GoogleSearch/search.aspx** (excerpt)

```
  <p><asp:LinkButton id="lbPrev" runat="server" Visible="False"
      OnClick="PrevClick">Previous</asp:LinkButton>
    <asp:LinkButton id="lbNext" runat="server" Visible="False"
      OnClick="NextClick">Next</asp:LinkButton></p>
</asp:Panel>
</form>
```

Finally, add an `Import` directive to the top of the page, and import the `System.Text` namespace as follows:

File: **GoogleSearch/search.aspx** (excerpt)

```
<%@ Import Namespace="System.Text" %>
```

This namespace is needed for the `StringBuilder` class it contains, which we'll use to format the search result.

Now, let's begin the script for the page with three variables that we'll need within the application:

VB.NET   File: **GoogleSearch/search.aspx (excerpt)**

```
<script runat="server" language="VB">
Dim key As String = "YOUR KEY GOES HERE"
Dim maxResults As Integer = 10
Dim formatString As String = _
    "<p><a href=""{1}"">{0}</a><br />{2}<br />{1} - {3}</p>"
```

C#   File: **GoogleSearch/search.aspx (excerpt)**

```
<script runat="server" language="C#">
string key = "YOUR KEY GOES HERE";
int maxResults = 10;
string formatString =
    "<p><a href=\"{1}\">{0}</a><br />{2}<br />{1} - {3}</p>";
```

As you can see, the variable key holds the license key that was given to you when you registered to use the service. The variable maxResults holds the number of records that can be viewed per page before the user must click the next/previous buttons to view the whole list. Finally, formatString contains the HTML template we will use to display each of the search results on the page.

Now, let's define the Page_Load() event handler:

VB.NET   File: **GoogleSearch/search.aspx (excerpt)**

```
Sub Page_Load(s As Object, e As EventArgs)
  If Not IsPostBack Then
    lbNext.Visible = False
    lbPrev.Visible = False
    lblResults.Visible = False
    headerPanel.Visible = False
  End If
End Sub
```

C#   File: **GoogleSearch/search.aspx (excerpt)**

```
void Page_Load(Object s, EventArgs e) {
  if (!IsPostBack) {
    lbNext.Visible = false;
    lbPrev.Visible = false;
    lblResults.Visible = false;
    headerPanel.Visible = false;
  }
}
```

Essentially, we are checking to see if the page is posting back to itself. If it's not, we set the visibility of the controls we defined above to be hidden, as there won't yet be any results to display.

Now, add the `Search()` method (the `Click` event handler for the Search button) to the page, as follows:

```
VB.NET                                    File: GoogleSearch/search.aspx (excerpt)
Sub Search(s As Object, e As EventArgs)
  resultList.Text = doQuery(searchText.Text, 0)
  Session("CurrentRecord") = 0
  headerPanel.Visible = True
End Sub
```

```
C#                                        File: GoogleSearch/search.aspx (excerpt)
void Search(Object s, EventArgs e) {
  resultList.Text = doQuery(searchText.Text, 0);
  Session["CurrentRecord"] = 0;
  headerPanel.Visible = true;
}
```

This subroutine sets the `Text` property of the `resultList` `Label` control equal to the return value of `doQuery()`, which we'll cover next. It also sets a session variable, called `CurrentRecord`, to zero. The variable will eventually be used to store the results page number that the user is currently viewing. Finally, it shows `headerPanel`, which contains the controls that display the results: `lblResults`, `lblTotalResults`, and `resultList`.

The `doQuery()` method does most of the work within this application. It instantiates the `GoogleSearchService` class, and then passes all the search criteria into the `doGoogleSearch()` method. Next, it loops through the `resultElements` array, building the HTML for the list of results as it goes.

Let's get started on this imposing method:

```
VB.NET                                    File: GoogleSearch/search.aspx (excerpt)
Function doQuery(searchText As String, record As Integer)

End Function
```

```
C#                                        File: GoogleSearch/search.aspx (excerpt)
String doQuery(string searchText, int record) {

}
```

The *searchText* parameter will be the user's search query, while the *record* parameter will represent the page of results the user wishes to view. Now, let's begin to write the code that will do all the work. First, create the variables we need for this method:

VB.NET   File: **GoogleSearch/search.aspx (excerpt)**

```
Dim totalCount As Integer
Dim displayTitle As String
Dim sb As StringBuilder = New StringBuilder()
```

C#   File: **GoogleSearch/search.aspx (excerpt)**

```
int totalCount;
String displayTitle;
StringBuilder sb = new StringBuilder();
```

As you can see, we've created an integer variable, a `String` variable, and a `StringBuilder` variable. `displayTitle` will hold the actual title of each search result; `totalCount` will identify the total number of results returned by the query; and `sb`, which contains a `StringBuilder` object, will help with formatting the results for display.

Next, let's create an instance of the `GoogleSearchService` class. With that object, we can call the `doGooogleSearch()` method, passing in the ten parameters mentioned earlier, to return a `GoogleSearchResult` object:

VB.NET   File: **GoogleSearch/search.aspx (excerpt)**

```
Dim s As GoogleSearchService = New GoogleSearchService()
Dim r As GoogleSearchResult = s.doGoogleSearch(key, _
    searchText, record, maxResults, False, "", False, "", _
    "", "")
```

C#   File: **GoogleSearch/search.aspx (excerpt)**

```
GoogleSearchService s = new GoogleSearchService();
GoogleSearchResult r = s.doGoogleSearch(key, searchText, record,
    maxResults, false, "", false, "", "", "");
```

Notice the ten parameters that are being passed into the method. These include the unique key that was given to you when you registered to use the service (`key`), the term(s) for which to search (`searchText`), the page of results to retrieve (`record`), the number of results per page (`maxResults`), and more.

Our next step is to find the total number of results returned by the search. We can identify this number by accessing the `estimatedTotalResultsCount` property of the `GoogleSearchResult` object, `r`:

VB.NET   File: **GoogleSearch/search.aspx (excerpt)**

```
totalCount = r.estimatedTotalResultsCount
```

C#   File: **GoogleSearch/search.aspx (excerpt)**

```
totalCount = r.estimatedTotalResultsCount;
```

Now we can loop through the collection of results, which is stored within the `resultElements` property, using a `For Each` loop, and combine the formatted elements into a single string of results using the `StringBuilder`:

VB.NET   File: **GoogleSearch/search.aspx (excerpt)**

```vbnet
Dim result As ResultElement
For Each result In r.resultElements
  If result.title <> "" Then
    displayTitle = result.title
  Else
    displayTitle = result.URL
  End If

  sb.Append(String.Format(formatString, displayTitle, _
      result.URL, result.snippet, result.cachedSize))
Next
```

C#   File: **GoogleSearch/search.aspx (excerpt)**

```csharp
foreach (ResultElement result in r.resultElements) {
  if (result.title != "") {
    displayTitle = result.title;
  } else {
    displayTitle = result.URL;
  }

  sb.Append(String.Format(formatString, displayTitle,
      result.URL, result.snippet, result.cachedSize));
}
```

In case you were wondering, the `ResultElement` class is yet another class provided by the proxy assembly we generated earlier. Each element within the `resultElements` collection is an object of this class. Within our loop, we use an `If` statement to check whether the element contains a title; if it doesn't, we use the element's URL as its title.

Also within the loop, we use the `Append()` method to build up a string composed of all the formatted results. Each element is formatted using the `Format()`

method of `String`, which substitutes each of the values we pass to it into the `formatString` we declared earlier.

Our next task, still in `doQuery()`, is to show or hide the Next/Previous buttons depending on the size of our result elements array. Usually the count of results that Google gives us (and which we've stored in `totalCount` at this stage) is merely an estimate, but if we're on the last (or only) page of results then the count will be exact, and the `estimateIsExact` property of the result set will be true. So when the estimate is exact, and the `endIndex` property tells us that the number of the last result on this page matches the total number of results, we know to hide the Next button. The Previous button is easier to decide on—when the query asks for the first page of results (i.e. the *record* argument is zero), the button is hidden; otherwise, we keep it visible.

VB.NET   File: **GoogleSearch/search.aspx (excerpt)**

```
If r.estimateIsExact And r.endIndex >= totalCount Then
   lbNext.Visible = False
Else
   lbNext.Visible = True
End If
If record = 0 Then
   lbPrev.Visible = False
Else
   lbPrev.Visible = True
End If
```

C#   File: **GoogleSearch/search.aspx (excerpt)**

```
if (r.estimateIsExact && r.endIndex >= totalCount) {
   lbNext.Visible = false;
} else {
   lbNext.Visible = true;
}
if (record == 0) {
   lbPrev.Visible = false;
} else {
   lbPrev.Visible = true;
}
```

As you can see, we simply change the `Visible` properties of the Next and Previous `LinkButton` controls as appropriate.

To finish off this method, we'll display the total results returned for the query within the `Label` control, show the `lblResults` `Label` that goes next to it, and finally return the HTML listing of results that we've built up in the `StringBuffer`:

File: **GoogleSearch/search.aspx (excerpt)**

```
lblTotalResults.Text = totalCount
lblResults.Visible = true
Return sb.ToString()
```

File: **GoogleSearch/search.aspx (excerpt)**

```
lblTotalResults.Text = Convert.ToString(totalCount);
lblResults.Visible = true;
return sb.ToString();
```

Let's finish off the application by adding the event handlers for the Next and Previous buttons:

File: **GoogleSearch/search.aspx (excerpt)**

```
Sub NextClick(s As Object, e As EventArgs)
  Session("CurrentRecord") += maxResults
  resultList.Text = doQuery(searchText.Text, _
     Session("CurrentRecord"))
End Sub

Sub PrevClick(s As Object, e As EventArgs)
  Session("CurrentRecord") -= maxResults
  resultList.Text = doQuery(searchText.Text, _
     Int32.Parse(Session("CurrentRecord")))
End Sub
```

File: **GoogleSearch/search.aspx (excerpt)**

```
void NextClick(Object s, EventArgs e) {
  Session["CurrentRecord"] =
     Convert.ToInt32(Session["CurrentRecord"]) + maxResults;
  resultList.Text = doQuery(searchText.Text,
     Convert.ToInt32(Session["CurrentRecord"]));
}

void PrevClick(Object s, EventArgs e) {
  Session["CurrentRecord"] =
     Convert.ToInt32(Session["CurrentRecord"]) - maxResults;
  resultList.Text = doQuery(searchText.Text,
     Convert.ToInt32(Session["CurrentRecord"]));
}
```

Again, notice the use of the session variable. The session variable contains the number of the first result to display on the current page. Since we have the number of records per page stored in the maxRecords variable, we use that to increase or decrease the value in the session variable in response to clicks of the

Next and Previous buttons, respectively. The second line of each method simply performs the search anew with the new record number, using the results thereof to update the resultList Label.

Save your work and test the results in the browser. Initially, you are presented with simple TextBox and Button controls similar to Figure 17.12.

Figure 17.12. Initially the user sees the TextBox and Button Controls.

You will notice that when you enter search criteria and click the Search button, Google-type results will appear on the page.

The great part about using this Web Service is that it's free and completely customizable. But because Google doesn't have a pricing model in place, your searches are limited to one thousand per day.

Web Service and Database Interaction

Sofar, you've learned to use Web Services to return simple calculations as strings. You've also learned to use a third party Web Service in your application. This section goes beyond these simple examples and shows you how to programmatically access data from a database through a Web Service, and expose the contents as a DataSet to the consumer.

In this section, we'll build the final part of our Dorknozzle project, the Company Events page. This page will be unusual in that we won't add the code to connect and query the database within the page; instead, we'll place all of the ADO.NET code within a Web Service. The page will be responsible for consuming the Web

Service, and binding the returned data to controls on the page. This might make sense in a practical setting if the data required were stored on a different server, which did not provide direct access to the database.

Let's start by building the Web Service. Create a new folder within the main Dorknozzle application directory called `WebService`. Next, create a new file called `selectCompanyEvents.asmx` within the new directory. To begin with, the Web Service looks similar to the others we've worked on:

VB.NET   File: **selectCompanyEvents.asmx**

```
<%@ WebService language="VB" class="selectCompanyEvents" %>
Imports System.Configuration
Imports System.Data
Imports System.Data.OleDb
Imports System.Web.Services

Public Class selectCompanyEvents
  <WebMethod()> _
  Public Function selectEvents() As DataSet
    Dim objConn As New OleDbConnection( _
        ConfigurationSettings.AppSettings("DSN"))
    Dim objDA As OleDbDataAdapter
    Dim objDS As New DataSet()

    objDA = New OleDbDataAdapter("SELECT * FROM CompanyEvents", _
        objConn)
    objDA.Fill(objDS, "Quantity")

    Return objDS
  End Function
End Class
```

C#   File: **selectCompanyEvents.asmx**

```
<%@ WebService language="C#" class="selectCompanyEvents" %>
using System.Configuration;
using System.Data;
using System.Data.OleDb;
using System.Web.Services;

public class selectCompanyEvents {
  [WebMethod]
  public DataSet selectEvents() {
    OleDbConnection objConn = new OleDbConnection(
        ConfigurationSettings.AppSettings["DSN"]);
    OleDbDataAdapter objDA;
```

```
DataSet objDS = new DataSet();

objDA = new OleDbDataAdapter("SELECT * FROM CompanyEvents",
    objConn);
objDA.Fill(objDS, "Quantity");

return objDS;
}
}
```

The difference, of course, lies in the fact that the function will return a filled DataSet. We establish a connection to the database, query the CompanyEvents table, fill a DataSet called objDS, and finally return the DataSet to the consumer. Go ahead and save the file, then open it within the browser. Clicking the Invoke button should give the result shown in Figure 17.13.

Figure 17.13. Click the Invoke button to return a DataSet of company events.

As you can see, all of the company events that reside within the `CompanyEvents` database table are written in XML format within the browser window. This isn't much use to us, so our next step will be to generate a proxy class using the `wsdl.exe` utility. Go ahead and open the command prompt, and type the one of the following commands to generate the proxy class:

```
wsdl /l:vb http://localhost/Dorknozzle/WebService/selectCompanyEve
nts.asmx?WSDL
```

```
wsdl /l:cs http://localhost/Dorknozzle/WebService/selectCompanyEve
nts.asmx?WSDL
```

Now, compile the class into an assembly by typing one of the following commands:

```
vbc /t:library /r:System.Web.dll,System.dll,System.Xml.dll,System.
Web.Services.dll,System.Data.dll selectCompanyEvents.vb
```

```
csc /t:library /r:System.Web.dll,System.dll,System.Xml.dll,System.
Web.Services.dll,System.Data.dll selectCompanyEvents.cs
```

The new assembly, `selectCompanyEvents.dll` will appear within the current directory. Next, move the assembly file into the `bin` subfolder of the main Dorknozzle application directory (create it if you need to).

Consuming the Company Events Service

Now that we've created the proxy class for the Web Service, we can use it to display the company events within the main page of the Intranet application. You can build this functionality first by adding the `DataGrid` that will handle the data presentation within the `index.aspx` page. Insert it just beneath the main heading, as follows:

File: **index.aspx** (excerpt)

```
<h1>Company Events:</h1>
<asp:DataGrid id="dgCompanyEvents" runat="server"
    AutoGenerateColumns="false" GridLines="None"
    Font-Size="10" Width="400" HeaderStyle-Font-Bold="true">
  <Columns>
    <asp:BoundColumn DataField="Event" HeaderText="Event" />
    <asp:BoundColumn DataField="Date" HeaderText="Date"
        DataFormatString="{0:d}" />
    <asp:BoundColumn DataField="Location"
        HeaderText="Location" />
```

```
        </Columns>
    </asp:DataGrid>
```

With the `DataGrid` in the page, your next step should be to insert the logic that interacts with the Web Service:

VB.NET   File: **index.aspx (excerpt)**
```
Sub Page_Load()
  Dim objWebService As New selectCompanyEvents()
  dgCompanyEvents.DataSource = objWebService.selectEvents()
  dgCompanyEvents.DataBind()
End Sub
```

C#   File: **index.aspx (excerpt)**
```
void Page_Load() {
  selectCompanyEvents objWebService = new selectCompanyEvents();
  dgCompanyEvents.DataSource = objWebService.selectEvents();
  dgCompanyEvents.DataBind();
}
```

As you can see, the code is fairly simple. We instantiate the `selectCompanyEvents` proxy class, we set the `DataSource` property of the `DataGrid` equal to the result of the `selectEvents()` method, which we know will be a `DataSet`. Finally, we call the `DataBind()` method of the `DataGrid`. Save your work and test the result in the browser. Figure 17.14 shows how the company events are displayed.

Figure 17.14. Company events are displayed within the browser.

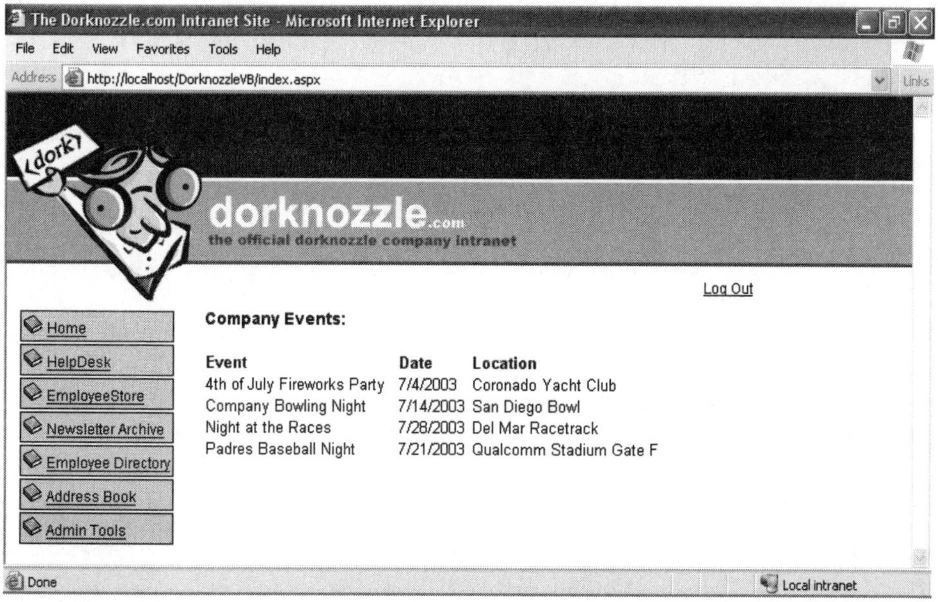

Summary

As you can see, Web Services provide a lot of programming flexibility. When used appropriately, Web Services allow you to share vital portions of your applications with the outside world. This chapter introduced you to the world of Web Services. You also learned how to work with third party Web Services, and even how to create complex Web Services that interact with databases.

I hope you enjoyed this book; now go out and use your new ASP.NET skills to change the world!

Appendix A: HTML Control Reference

When HTML tags are used in an ASP.NET page, they are ignored by the server and passed to the client browser unchanged; the browser then renders them as it would for any other HTML page. The simple addition of the `runat="server"` attribute turns an HTML tag into an HTML control, which we can then access and alter through our code by means of the identifier given in the control's `id` attribute. The following reference lists all the useful properties, methods, and events of ASP.NET's HTML controls.

HtmlAnchor Control

When an HTML anchor tag `<a>` is given a `runat="server"` attribute, it becomes accessible through code as an `HtmlAnchor` control.

Properties

Attributes	A collection of the element's attribute names and their values
Disabled	If set to `True`, the control will be disabled
Href	Contains the control's link URL
ID	Contains the control's ID
InnerHtml	Contains the content between the element's opening and closing tags
InnerText	Contains the text between the element's opening and closing tags
Name	The name of the anchor
Style	Contains the control's CSS properties
TagName	Returns the element's tag name

Target	Contains the target window or frame will be opened
Title	Contains the link's title
Visible	If set to False, the control won't be visible

Events

ServerClick	Raised when the user clicks the link

HtmlButton Control

The HtmlButton control corresponds to the <button runat="server"> HTML tag.

Properties

Attributes	A collection of the element's attribute names and their values
Disabled	If set to True, the control will be disabled
ID	Contains the control's ID
InnerHtml	Contains the content between the element's opening and closing tags
InnerText	Contains the text between the element's opening and closing tags
Style	Contains the control's CSS properties
TagName	Returns the element's tag name
Visible	If set to False, the control won't be visible

Events

ServerClick	Raised when the user clicks the button

HtmlForm Control

The HtmlForm control represents a `<form runat="server">` tag in an ASP.NET page.

Properties

Attributes	A collection of the element's attribute names and their values
Disabled	If set to True, the control will be disabled
EncType	Contains the MIME type of the form's content
ID	Contains the control's ID
InnerHtml	Contains the content between the element's opening and closing tags
InnerText	Contains the text between the element's opening and closing tags
Method	Sets how the form is posted to the server. Can be either Get or Post. The default is Post.
Name	The form's name
Style	Contains the control's CSS properties
TagName	Returns the element's tag name
Target	Sets the target frame or window to render the results of information posted to the server
Visible	If set to False, the control won't be visible

HtmlGeneric Control

The HtmlGeneric control corresponds to HTML elements that do not have their own specific HTML control, such as `<div>`, `<span>` etc.

Properties

Attributes	A collection of the element's attribute names and their values
Disabled	If set to `True`, the control will be disabled
ID	Contains the control's ID
InnerHtml	Contains the content between the element's opening and closing tags
InnerText	Contains the text between the element's opening and closing tags
Style	Contains the control's CSS properties
TagName	Returns the element's tag name.
Visible	If set to `False`, the control won't be visible

HtmlImage Control

The `HTMLImage` control corresponds to an HTML `<img>` element.

Properties

Align	Details alignment of the image with respect to other elements on the page. Can be `Top`, `Middle`, `Bottom`, `Left`, or `Right`
Alt	A caption to use if the browser doesn't support images, or the image hasn't yet downloaded
Attributes	A collection of the element's attribute names and their values
Border	Specifies the width of the border around the image
Disabled	If set to `True`, the control will be disabled
Height	Specifies the height of the image

ID	Contains the control's ID
Src	Contains the URL of the image
Style	Contains the control's CSS properties
TagName	Returns the element's tag name
Visible	If set to `False`, the control won't be visible
Width	Specifies the width of the image

HtmlInputButton Control

HtmlInputButton represents an `<input runat="server">` tag, with a `type` attribute of `button`, `submit` or `reset`.

Properties

Attributes	A collection of the element's attribute names and their values
CausesValidation	If `True`, validation is performed when the button is clicked. Default is `True`
Disabled	If set to `True`, the control will be disabled
ID	Contains the control's ID
Name	The name of the button
Style	Contains the control's CSS properties
TagName	Returns the element's tag name
Type	Contains the type of input element this is
Value	Equivalent to the `value` attribute of the HTML tag
Visible	If set to `False`, the control won't be visible

Events

`ServerClick`	Raised when the user clicks the button

HtmlInputCheckBox Control

The `HtmlInputCheckBox` control corresponds to an `<input type="checkbox" runat="server">` tag.

Properties

`Attributes`	A collection of the element's attribute names and their values
`Checked`	A Boolean value that specifies whether or not the element is to be checked. Default is `False`
`Disabled`	If set to `True`, the control will be disabled
`ID`	Contains the control's ID
`Name`	The name of the checkbox
`Style`	Contains the control's CSS properties
`TagName`	Returns the element's tag name
`Type`	Contains the type of input element this is
`Value`	Equivalent to the `value` attribute of the HTML tag
`Visible`	If set to `False`, the control won't be visible

Events

`ServerChange`	Occurs when the state of the control has changed

HtmlInputFile Control

This control corresponds to an `<input type="file" runat="server">` tag.

Properties

Accept	A comma separated list of acceptable MIME types available to the user
Attributes	A collection of the element's attribute names and their values
Disabled	If set to True, the control will be disabled
ID	Contains the control's ID
MaxLength	The maximum number of characters allowed in file path
Name	The name of the control
PostedFile	Gets access to the posted file
Size	Sets the width of the text box that will contain the file path
Style	Contains the control's CSS properties
TagName	Returns the element's tag name
Type	Contains the type of input element this is
Value	Corresponds to the value attribute of the HTML tag
Visible	If set to False, the control won't be visible

HtmlInputHidden Control

The HtmlInputHidden control corresponds to a an <input type="hidden" runat="server"> tag.

Properties

Attributes	A collection of the element's attribute names and their values
Disabled	If set to True, the control will be disabled

ID	Contains the control's ID
Name	The name of the control
Style	Contains the control's CSS properties
TagName	Returns the element's tag name
Type	Contains the type of input element this is
Value	Corresponds to the value attribute of the HTML tag
Visible	If set to False, the control won't be visible

HtmlInputImage Control

The HtmlInputImage control corresponds to an `<input type="image" runat="server">` tag.

Properties

Align	Details alignment of the image with respect to other elements on the page. Can be set to Top, Middle, Bottom, Left, or Right
Alt	A caption to use if the browser doesn't support images, or the image hasn't yet downloaded
Attributes	A collection of the element's attribute names and their values
Border	Specifies the width of the border around the image
CausesValidation	If True, validation is performed when the button is clicked. Default is True
Disabled	If set to True, the control will be disabled
ID	Contains the control's ID
Name	The name of the control
Src	Contains the URL of the image to use

Style	Contains the control's CSS properties
TagName	Returns the element's tag name
Type	Contains the type of input element this is
Value	Equivalent to the value attribute of the HTML tag
Visible	If set to False, the control won't be visible

Events

ServerClick	Raised when the user clicks the image

HtmlInputRadioButton Control

The HtmlInputRadioButton control corresponds to an <input type="radio" runat="server"> HTML tag.

Properties

Attributes	A collection of the element's attribute names and their values
Checked	A Boolean value that specifies whether or not the element is checked. Default is False
Disabled	If set to True, the control will be disabled
ID	Contains the control's ID
Name	The name of the group that this control is associated with
Style	Contains the control's CSS properties
TagName	Returns the element's tag name
Type	Contains the type of input element this is
Value	Corresponds to the value attribute of the HTML tag
Visible	If set to False, the control won't be visible

Events

ServerChange   Occurs when the state of the control has changed

HtmlInputText Control

The HtmlInputText control corresponds to an `<input runat="server">` tag with a `type` attribute of `text` or `password`.

Properties

Attributes   A collection of the element's attribute names and their values

Disabled   If set to `True`, the control will be disabled

ID   Contains the control's ID

MaxLength   Sets the maximum number of characters allowed in the text box

Name   The name of the text box

Size   The width of the text box

Style   Contains the control's CSS properties

TagName   Returns the element's tag name

Type   Contains the type of input element this is

Value   Equivalent to the `value` attribute of the HTML tag

Visible   If set to `False`, the control won't be visible

Events

ServerChange   Occurs when the text in the control has changed

HtmlSelect Control

The HtmlSelect control corresponds to an HTML <select runat="server"> tag (which creates a drop-down list).

Properties

Attributes	A collection of the element's attribute names and their values
DataMember	The set of data to bind to the control from a DataSource with multiple sets of data
DataSource	Sets the data source to use
DataTextField	The field from the DataSource to bind to the Text property of each ListItem in the control
DataValueField	The field from the DataSource to bind to the Value property of each ListItem in the control
Disabled	If set to True, the control will be disabled
ID	Contains the control's ID
InnerHtml	Contains the content between the element's opening and closing tags
InnerText	Contains the text between the element's opening and closing tags
Items	A collection that contains the items in the drop-down list
Multiple	If True, multiple items can be selected at a time. Default is False
SelectedIndex	The zero-based index currently selected item on a single selection list. In a multiple selection list, it contains the index of the first selected item. If no item is selected, this contains -1

Style	Contains the control's CSS properties
TagName	Returns the element's tag name
Value	Corresponds to the value attribute of the HTML tag
Visible	If set to False, the control won't be visible

Events

ServerChange	Occurs when the item selected has changed

HtmlTable Control

The HtmlTable control represents a `<table runat="server">` tag.

Properties

Align	Specifies the alignment of the table in relation to other elements on the page. Possible values are Left, Right and Center
Attributes	A collection of the element's attribute names and their values
BgColor	The background color of the table
Border	Sets the width of the borders around the table, in pixels
BorderColor	Specifies the table border color
CellPadding	The amount of space between the contents of a cell and the cell's border, in pixels
CellSpacing	Sets the space between adjacent cells, in pixels
Disabled	If set to True, the control will be disabled
Height	The table's height
ID	Contains the control's ID

InnerHtml	Contains the content between the element's opening and closing tags
InnerText	Contains the text between the element's opening and closing tags
Rows	An **HtmlTableRowCollection** that contains all the rows in the control, which you can use to change the rows in the table
Style	Contains the control's CSS properties
TagName	Returns the element's tag name
Visible	If set to **False**, the control won't be visible
Width	The table's width

HtmlTableCell Control

This control represents a `<td runat="server">` or `<th runat="server">` tag.

Properties

Align	Sets the horizontal alignment of the contents within the cell. Possible values are **Left**, **Right** and **Center**
Attributes	A collection of the element's attribute names and their values
BgColor	The background color of the cell
BorderColor	Specifies the color of the borders of this cell
ColSpan	Sets the number of columns this cell should occupy
Disabled	If set to **True**, the control will be disabled
Height	The height of the cell, in pixels
ID	Contains the control's ID

InnerHtml	Contains the content between the element's opening and closing tags
InnerText	Contains the text between the element's opening and closing tags
NoWrap	True if the text does not automatically wrap in the cell. The default value is False
RowSpan	The number of rows this cell should occupy
Style	Contains the control's CSS properties
TagName	Returns the element's tag name
VAlign	Sets the vertical alignment for the content of a cell. Possible values include Top, Middle and Bottom
Visible	If set to False, the control won't be visible
Width	The width of the cell, in pixels

HtmlTableRow Control

The HtmlTableRow control corresponds to a <tr runat="server"> tag.

Properties

Align	Sets the horizontal alignment of the contents within the cell. Possible values are Left, Right and Center
Attributes	A collection of the element's attribute names and their values
BgColor	The background color of the cell
BorderColor	Specifies the color of the borders of this row
Cells	A collection that represents the cells contained in the row
Disabled	If set to True, the control will be disabled

Height	The height of the row, in pixels
ID	Contains the control's ID
InnerHtml	Contains the content between the element's opening and closing tags
InnerText	Contains the text between the element's opening and closing tags
Style	Contains the control's CSS properties
TagName	Returns the element's tag name
VAlign	Sets the vertical alignment for the content of the cells in a row. Possible values include `Top`, `Middle` and `Bottom`
Visible	If set to `False`, the control won't be visible

HtmlTextArea Control

The `HtmlTextArea` control corresponds to a `<textarea runat="server">` tag.

Properties

Attributes	A collection of the element's attribute names and their values
Cols	The width of the text area, specified in characters
Disabled	If set to `True`, the control will be disabled
ID	Contains the control's ID
InnerHtml	Contains the content between the element's opening and closing tags
InnerText	Contains the text between the element's opening and closing tags
Name	The unique name for the text area

Rows	The height of the text area, in characters
Style	Contains the control's CSS properties
TagName	Returns the element's tag name
Value	The text entered in the text area
Visible	A Boolean value that indicates whether or not the control should be visible

Events

ServerChange	Raised when the contents of the text area are changed

Appendix B: Web Control Reference

The following reference includes a list of important properties, methods, and events for all Web controls. Unlike the HTML controls, the Web controls' names match those of their ASP.NET tags.

Because all the Web controls listed here are based on (or more specifically, derived from) the `WebControl` class, they inherit its properties and methods. Here are the more useful of these, which can be used with any of the Web controls.

Common Properties

`ForeColor`	The control's current foreground color
`BackColor`	The control's current background color
`Font-Bold`	Set to true to use bold text in the control
`Font-Italic`	Italicizes text
`Font-Name`	Specifies a typeface name for formatting text
`Font-Names`	Specifies a list of typeface names for formatting text
`Font-Overline`	Draws a line above the text
`Font-Size`	Changes the size of a particular font using either points or pixels
`Font-Strikeout`	Draws a line through the text
`Font-Underline`	Draws a line under the text
`CssStyle`	Indicates the style class in the current CSS style sheet which should be applied to the Web control
`Tooltip`	The text that appears in a pop-up box as the user's cursor hovers over the control

Height	The current height of the control
Width	The current width of the control
BorderStyle	Current border to draw around the web control. The default is `NotSet`, other values are `None`, `Solid`, `Double`, `Groove`, `Ridge`, `Dotted`, `Dashed`, `Inset`, and `Outset`
BorderColor	Color for the border
BorderWidth	Width of the border
Visible	Determines whether the control appears on screen in the user's browser
Enabled	Determines whether the Web control is active and able to receive user input
TabIndex	When the user presses **Tab**, controls on a page are selected in order of their `TabIndex` property, lowest first
AccessKey	Specifies a shortcut key that quickly selects a control without the user needing a mouse. The shortcut command is usually Alt plus a letter or number
Controls	A collection of all the controls contained within the Web control (its **child controls**)

Common Methods

DataBind()	Binds the Web Control to its data source
ApplyStyle()	Copies an element of a `Style` object to a control
MergeStyle()	Copies an element of a `Style` object to a control but does not overwrite existing styles

As well as these, Web Controls offer additional properties and methods specific to each control. These are listed in the following sections.

AdRotator Control

Properties

AdvertisementFile　　Specifies the path to the XML file that contains the list of banner advertisements

KeywordFilter　　Returns only advertisements that match a specific filter when the property is set

Target　　Displays the page in this window or frame. Possible values are _child, _self, _parent, and _blank

Events

AdCreated　　Raised after an advertisement is retrieved from the advertisement file and before the ad is rendered

Button Control

Properties

CommandName　　Passes a value to the Command event when the Button is clicked

CommandArgument　　Passes a value to the Command event when the Button is clicked

CausesValidation　　Allows interaction with client-side validation controls. When false, validation does not occur.

Text　　Gets or sets the text displayed by the Button

Visible　　Gets or sets the visibility of the Button

Events

Click　　Event is raised when the Button is clicked and the form is submitted to the server for processing

`Command`	Event is raised when the `Button` is clicked and the form is submitted to the server for processing. The values of the `CommandName` and `CommandArgument` properties are passed.

Calendar Control

Properties

`CellPadding`	Specifies the number of pixels between a cell and its border
`CellSpacing`	Specifies the number of pixels between cells
`DayHeaderStyle`	Specifies the style of the weekdays listed at the top of the calendar
`DayNameFormat`	Sets the format of the day names. Possible values are `FirstLetter`, `FirstTwoLetters`, `Full`, and `Short`.
`DayStyle`	Specifies the style applied to each day in the calendar
`FirstDayOfWeek`	Specifies which day of the week is displayed in the first column
`NextMonthText`	If `ShowNextPrevMonth` is `true`, specifies the text for the Next Month hyperlink
`NextPrevFormat`	Specifies the format for the Next and Previous hyperlink
`NextPrevStyle`	Specifies the style to use for next and previous month links
`OtherMonthDayStyle`	Specifies the style to use for days of a month that appear within a current month
`PrevMonthText`	If `ShowNextPrevMonth` is true, specifies the text for the Previous Month hyperlink
`SelectedDate`	Contains a date time value that specifies highlighted day

SelectedDates	Contains a collection of date time values that specify the highlighted days
SelectedDayStyle	Specifies the style to use for the currently selected day
SelectionMode	Determines whether days weeks or months can be selected. Possible values are `Day`, `DayWeek`, `DayWeek-Month`, and `None`.
SelectMonthText	Determines whether days weeks or months can be selected. Possible values are `Day`, `DayWeek`, `DayWeek-Month`, and `None`.
SelectorStyle	Specifies the style to be applied to the link for selecting week and month
SelectWeekText	Contains HTML text displayed for selecting weeks when `SelectionMode` has the value `DayWeek` or `Day-WeekMonth`
ShowDayHeader	If `true`, displays the names of the days of the week
ShowGridLines	If `true`, renders the calendar with lines around the days
ShowNextPrevMonth	If `true`, displays Next Month and Previous Month links
ShowTitle	If `true`, displays the calendar's title
TitleFormat	Determines how the month name appears in the title bar. Possible values are `Month` and `MonthYear`.
TitleStyle	Specifies the style to use for text within the title bar
TodayDayStyle	Specifies the style to use for the current day
TodaysDate	Specifies a `DateTime` value that sets the calendar's current date
VisibleDate	Specifies a `DateTime` value that sets the month to display
WeekendDayStyle	Specifies the style to use for weekend days

Events

DayRender	Raised before each day cell is rendered on the calendar
SelectionChanged	Raised when a new day, month, or week is selected
VisibleMonthChanged	Raised by clicking the Next Month or Previous Month link

CheckBox Control

Properties

AutoPostBack	When True, automatically posts the form containing the CheckBox whenever checked or unchecked
Checked	Shows the CheckBox as checked if set to True
Text	Gets or sets the text displayed next to the CheckBox
TextAlign	Determines how the text associated with the CheckBox is aligned. Possible values are Left and Right.

Events

CheckedChanged	This event is raised when the CheckBox is checked or unchecked.

CheckBoxList Control

Properties

AutoPostBack	If True, automatically posts the form containing the CheckBoxList whenever the checked or unchecked
CellPadding	Sets the number of pixels between the border and a particular check box
CellSpacing	Sets the number of pixels between individual check boxes within the CheckBoxList

DataMember	Represents the particular table within the data source
DataSource	Represents the actual data source to use when binding to a CheckBoxList
DataTextField	Represents the field within the data source to use with the CheckBoxList text label
DataTextFormatString	Gets or sets a format string that determines how the data is displayed
DataValueField	Represents the field within the data source to use with the CheckBoxList's value
Items	The collection of items within the CheckBoxList
RepeatColumns	Determines the number of columns to use when displaying the CheckBoxList
RepeatDirection	Indicates the direction in which the check boxes should repeat. Possible values are Horizontal and Vertical.
RepeatLayout	Determines how the check boxes are formatted. Possible values are Table and Flow. Default is Table.
SelectedIndex	Represents the index selected within the CheckBoxList
SelectedItem	Represents the item selected within the CheckBoxList

Events

SelectedIndexChanged	The event is raised when a check box within the CheckBoxList is selected.

DropDownList Control

Properties

AutoPostBack	Automatically posts the form containing the DropDownList whenever checked or unchecked is True
DataMember	Represents the particular table within the data source

DataSource	Represents the actual data source to use when binding to a `DropDownList`
DataTextField	Represents the field within the data source to use with the `DropDownList`'s text label
DataTextFormatString	Gets or sets a format string that determines how the `DropDownList` is displayed
DataValueField	Represents the field within the data source to use with the `DropDownList`'s value
Items	The collection of items within the `DropDownList`
SelectedIndex	Represents the index selected within the `DropDownList`
SelectedItem	Represents the item selected within the `DropDownList`

Events

SelectedIndexChanged	The event is raised when an item within the `DropDownList` is selected.

HyperLink Control

Properties

ImageURL	Specifies the location of the image to use
NavigateURL	Specifies the URL to navigate to when the hyperlink is clicked
Target	Specifies the target window or frame to display for the URL. Possible values are `_top`, `_blank`, `_self`, and `_parent`.
Text	Gets or sets the text displayed by the `HyperLink`
Visible	Gets or sets the visibility of the `HyperLink`

Image Control

Properties

AlternateText	Specifies the text to display within browsers that do not support images
ImageAlign	Specifies one of ten possible values for image alignment. Possible values include: `AbsBottom`, `AbsMiddle`, `Baseline`, `Bottom`, `Left`, `Middle`, `NotSet`, `Right`, `TextTop`, and `Top`.
ImageURL	Specifies the location of the image to use
Visible	Gets or sets the visibility of the image

ImageButton Control

Properties

AlternateText	Specifies the text to display within browsers that do not support images
CommandName	Passes a value to the `Command` event when the `ImageButton` is clicked
CommandArgument	Passes a value to the `Command` event when the `ImageButton` is clicked
CausesValidation	Allows interaction with client-side validation controls. When `False`, validation does not occur.
ImageAlign	Specifies one of ten possible values for image alignment. Possible values include: `AbsBottom`, `AbsMiddle`, `Baseline`, `Bottom`, `Left`, `Middle`, `NotSet`, `Right`, `TextTop`, and `Top`.
ImageURL	Specifies the location of the image to use
Visible	Gets or sets the visibility of the `ImageButton`

Events

`Click`	Event is raised when the `ImageButton` is clicked and the form is submitted to the server for processing
`Command`	Event is raised when the `ImageButton` is clicked and the form is submitted to the server for processing. The values of the `CommandName` and `CommandArgument` properties are provided with the event.

Label Control

Properties

`Text`	Gets or sets the text displayed by the `Label`
`Visible`	Gets or sets the visibility of the `Label`

LinkButton Control

Properties

`Text`	Gets or sets the text displayed by the `LinkButton`
`CommandName`	Passes a value to the `Command` event when the `LinkButton` is clicked
`CommandArgument`	Passes a value to the `Command` event when the `LinkButton` is clicked
`CausesValidation`	Allows interaction with client-side validation controls. When `False`, validation does not occur
`Visible`	Gets or sets the visibility of the `LinkButton`

Events

`Click`	Event is raised when the `LinkButton` is clicked and the form is submitted to the server for processing

| Command | Event is raised when the LinkButton is clicked and the form is submitted to the server for processing. The values of the CommandName and CommandArgument properties are passed. |

ListBox Control

Properties

AutoPostBack	When True, automatically posts the form containing the ListBox whenever an item is selected
DataMember	Specifies the particular table within the data source to bind to
DataSource	Represents the actual data source to use when binding
DataTextField	Represents the field within the data source to use with the ListBox's text label
DataTextFormatString	Gets or sets a format string that determines how the ListBox is displayed
DataValueField	Represents the field within the data source to use with the ListBox's value
Items	The collection of items within the ListBox
Rows	Indicates the number of rows to display within the ListBox. Default value is 4.
SelectedIndex	Represents the index selected within the ListBox
SelectedItem	Represents the item selected within the ListBox
SelectionMode	Determines whether a user can select more than one item at a time. Possible values are Multiple and Single.

Events

SelectedIndexChanged The event is raised when an item within the ListBox is selected.

Literal Control

Properties

Text Gets or sets the text displayed by the control

Panel Control

Properties

BackImageURL The URL of the background image to use within the Panel

HorizontalAlign Sets the horizontal alignment of the Panel. Possible values are Center, Justify, Left, NotSet, and Right.

Wrap Wraps the contents within the Panel when True. The default value is True.

Visible Controls the visibility of the Panel

PlaceHolder Control

Visible Controls the visibility of the PlaceHolder

RadioButton Control

AutoPostBack Automatically posts the form containing the RadioButton whenever checked or unchecked is True

Checked Shows the RadioButton as checked if set to True

GroupName Determines the name of the group that the RadioButton belongs to

Text	Gets or sets the text displayed next to the RadioButton
TextAlign	Determines how the text associated with the RadioButton is aligned. Possible values are Left and Right.

Events

CheckedChanged	The event is raised when the RadioButton is checked or unchecked.

RadioButtonList Control

AutoPostBack	Automatically posts the form containing the RadioButtonList whenever checked or unchecked is True
DataMember	Represents the particular table within the data source
DataSource	Represents the actual data source to use when binding to a RadioButtonList
DataTextField	Represents the field within the data source to use with the RadioButtonList's text label
DataTextFormatString	Gets or sets a format string that determines how the RadioButtonList is displayed
DataValueField	Represents the field within the data source to use with the RadioButtonList's value
RepeatColumns	The collection of items within the RadioButtonList
Items	Determines the number of columns to use when displaying the radio buttons
RepeatDirection	Indicates the direction that the radio buttons should repeat. Possible values are Horizontal and Vertical.
RepeatLayout	Determines how the radio buttons should be repeated. Possible values are Horizontal and Vertical.

SelectedIndex	Represents the index selected within the RadioButtonList
SelectedItem	Represents the item selected within the RadioButtonList
TextAlign	Determines how the text associated with the RadioButtonList is aligned. Possible values are Left and Right.

Events

SelectedIndexChanged	The event is raised when a radio button within the RadioButtonList is selected.

TextBox Control

Properties

AutoPostBack	Automatically posts the form containing the TextBox whenever a change is made to the contents within the TextBox
Columns	Sets the horizontal size of the TextBox in characters
MaxLength	Sets the maximum number of characters allowed to be entered
Rows	Sets the vertical size of the multiline TextBox
Text	Gets or sets the text displayed by the TextBox
TextMode	Determines whether the TextBox should render as SingleLine, Password, or MultiLine
Visible	Gets or sets the visibility of the TextBox
Wrap	Determines how a multiline TextBox wraps. If set to True, word wrapping is enabled.

Events

TextChanged   Event is raised when the contents of the **TextBox** have
                             changed.

Xml Control

Properties

Document   Specifies the **System.Xml.XmlDocument** object to dis-
                             play

DocumentContent   Specifies a string representing the XML document to
                             display

DocumentSource   Specifies the URL of a document to display

Transform   Specifies the **System.Xml.Xsl.XslTransform** object
                             used to format the XML document.

TransformArgumentList   Specifies the **XsltArgumentList** used to format the
                             XML document

TransformSource   Specifies the URL of an XSLT stylesheet used to
                             format the XML document

Appendix C: Validation Control Reference

The following reference includes a list of important properties, methods, and events for each of the validation controls. These controls all ultimately derive from the `WebControl` class, meaning that they, like the Web controls themselves, inherit its properties and methods. The more useful of these are listed at the start of Appendix B.

The `RequiredFieldValidator` Control

Properties

`ControlToValidate`	Specifies the ID of the control that you want to validate
`Display`	Shows how the error message within the validation control will be displayed. Possible values are `Static`, `Dynamic`, and `None`. Default is `Static`.
`EnableClientScript`	Enables or disables client-side validation. By default the value is set as enabled.
`Enabled`	Enables or disables client and server-side validation. By default the value is set as enabled.
`ErrorMessage`	Specifies the error message that will be displayed to the user in any associated validation summary control. If no value is set for the `Text` property, this message also appears in the control itself.
`InitialValue`	Gets or sets the initial value specified by the `ControlToValidate` property
`IsValid`	Has the value `True` when the validation check succeeds, and `False` otherwise
`Text`	Sets the error message displayed by the control when validation fails

Methods

Validate()   Performs validation and modifies the IsValid property

The CompareValidator Control

Properties

ControlToCompare   Specifies the ID of the control to use for comparing values

ControlToValidate   Specifies the ID of the control that you want to validate

Display   Shows how the error message within the validation control will be displayed. Possible values are Static, Dynamic, and None. Default is Static.

EnableClientScript   Enables or disables client-side validation. By default the value is set as Enabled.

Enabled   Enables or disables client and server-side validation. By default the value is set as Enabled.

ErrorMessage   Specifies the error message that will be displayed to the user in any associated validation summary control. If no value is set for the Text property, this message also appears in the control itself.

IsValid   Has the value True when the validation check succeeds and False otherwise

Operator   Gets or sets the operator to use when performing comparisons. Possible values are Equal, NotEqual, GreaterThan, GreaterThanEqual, LessThan, LessThanEqual, DataTypeCheck.

Text   Sets the error message displayed by the control when validation fails

Type	Gets or sets the data type to use when comparing values. Possible values are `Currency`, `Date`, `Double`, `Integer`, and `String`.
ValueToCompare	Specifies the value used when performing the comparison

Methods

`Validate()`	Performs validation and modifies the `IsValid` property

The RangeValidator Control

Properties

`ControlToValidate`	Specifies the ID of the control that you want to validate
`Display`	Shows how the error message within the validation control will be displayed. Possible values are `Static`, `Dynamic`, and `None`. Default is `Static`.
`EnableClientScript`	Enables or disables client-side validation. By default the value is set as `Enabled`.
`Enabled`	Enables or disables client and server-side validation. By default the value is set as `Enabled`.
`ErrorMessage`	Specifies the error message that will be displayed to the user in any associated validation summary control. If no value is set for the `Text` property, this message also appears in the control itself.
`IsValid`	Has the value `True` when the validation check succeeds and `False` otherwise
`MaximumValue`	Sets the maximum value in the range of permissible values
`MinimumValue`	Sets the minimum value in the range of permissible values

Text	Sets the error message displayed by the control when validation fails
Type	Gets or sets the data type to use when comparing values. Possible values are `Currency`, `Date`, `Double`, `Integer`, and `String`.

Methods

Validate()	Performs validation and modifies the `IsValid` property

The ValidationSummary Control

Properties

DisplayMode	Sets the formatting for the error messages that are displayed within the page. Possible values are `BulletList`, `List`, and `SingleParagraph`. These messages are the `ErrorMessage` properties of all validation controls for which validation has failed.
EnableClientScript	Enables or disables client-side validation. By default, the value is set as `Enabled`.
Enabled	Enables or disables client and server-side validation. By default, the value is set as `Enabled`.
HeaderText	Sets the text that is displayed to the user at the top of the summary
ShowMessageBox	When the value is set to `True`, an alert box is presented to the user with the form field's that caused errors listed within it.
ShowSummary	Enables or disables the summary of error messages

The **RegularExpressionValidator** Control

Properties

ControlToValidate	Specifies the ID of the control that you want to validate
Display	Shows how the error message within the validation control will be displayed. Possible values are Static, Dynamic, and None. Default is Static.
EnableClientScript	Enables or disables client-side validation. By default, the value is set as Enabled.
Enabled	Enables or disables client and server-side validation. By default, the value is set as Enabled.
ErrorMessage	Specifies the error message that will be displayed to the user
InitialValue	Gets or sets the initial value specified by the ControlToValidate property
IsValid	Has the value True when the validation check succeeds and False otherwise
Text	Sets the error message displayed by the control
ValidateExpression	Specifies the regular expression to use when performing validation

Methods

Validate()	Performs validation and modifies the IsValid property

The **CustomValidator** Control

ClientValidationFunction	Specifies the name of the client-side function to use for validation

`ControlToValidate`	Specifies the ID of the control that you want to validate
`Display`	Shows how the error message within the validation control will be displayed. Possible values are `Static`, `Dynamic`, and `None`. Default is `Static`.
`EnableClientScript`	Enables or disables client-side validation. By default, the value is set as `Enabled`.
`Enabled`	Enables or disables client and server-side validation. By default, the value is set as `Enabled`.
`ErrorMessage`	Specifies the error message that will be displayed to the user
`IsValid`	Has the value `True` when the validation check succeeds, and `False` otherwise
`Text`	Sets the error message displayed by the control when validation fails

Methods

`Validate()`	Performs validation and modifies the `IsValid` property

Events

`ServerValidate`	Represents the function for performing server-side validation

Index

Books for Web Developers from SitePoint

Visit http://www.sitepoint.com/books/
for sample chapters or to order!

Build Your Own

Database Driven Website

Using PHP & MySQL

By Kevin Yank

A Practical Step-by-Step Guide

sitepoint

The PHP Anthology

Object Oriented PHP Solutions
Volume I

By Harry Fuecks

Practical Solutions to Common Problems

sitepoint

The PHP Anthology

Object Oriented PHP Solutions
Volume II

By Harry Fuecks

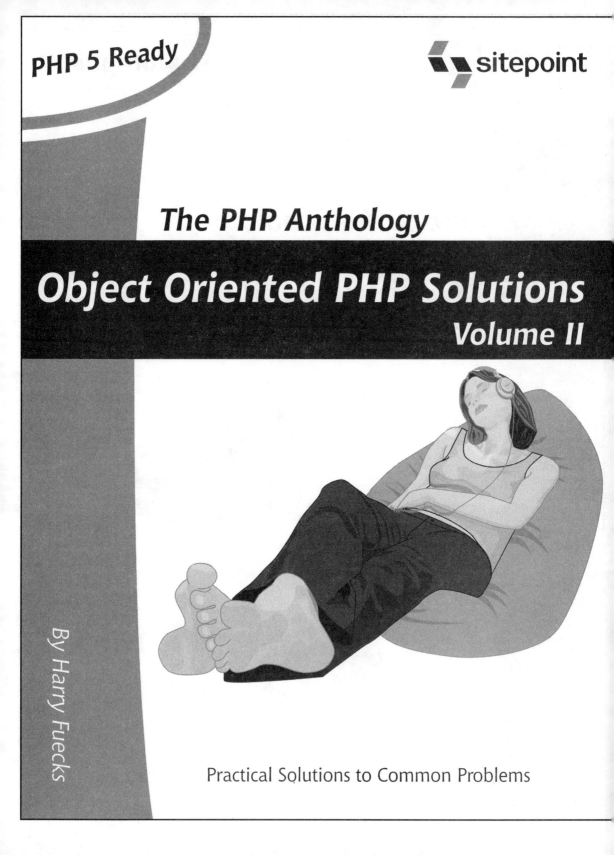

Practical Solutions to Common Problems

sitepoint

Build Your Own

ASP.NET Website

Using C# & VB.NET

By Zak Ruvalcaba

A Practical Step-by-Step Guide

HTML Utopia:
Designing Without Tables
Using CSS

By Dan Shafer

A Practical Step-by-Step Guide

The CSS Anthology

101 Essential Tips, Tricks & Hacks

By Rachel Andrew

Practical Solutions to Common Problems

DHTML Utopia:

Modern Web Design
Using JavaScript & DOM

By Stuart Langridge

A Practical Step-by-Step Guide

Flash
MX 2004

sitepoint

The Flash Anthology

Cool Effects &
Practical ActionScript

By Steven Grosvenor

Practical Solutions to Common Problems

Kits for Web Professionals from SitePoint

Available exclusively from
http://www.sitepoint.com/

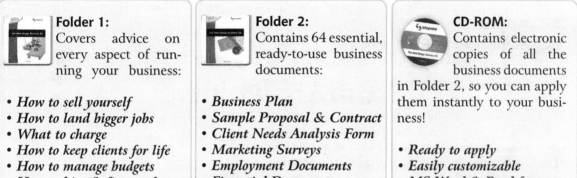